THE YEAR'S WORK
IN ENGLISH STUDIES—1975

The Year's Work
in English Studies

VOLUME 56

1975

Edited by
JAMES REDMOND

and

LAUREL BRAKE
ELIZABETH MASLEN
ROBIN ROBBINS
A. V. C. SCHMIDT
(associate editors)

Published for

THE ENGLISH ASSOCIATION
by
HUMANITIES PRESS, ATLANTIC HIGHLANDS, N.J.

Printed in Great Britain by
Redwood Burn Limited
Trowbridge and Esher
0-391-00748-3

Preface

It may help the user of this work to remember that books are sometimes published a year later in the U.S.A. than they are in the U.K. (and vice versa), that the year of publication is not always that which appears on the title-page of the book, and that the inevitable omissions of one year are made good in the next; thus the search for a notice of a book or article may have to extend to the volume after the expected one and sometimes to that which precedes it. Reports of important omissions will earn our gratitude.

Offprints of articles are always welcomed, and editors of journals that are not easily available in the U.K. are urged to join the many who already send us complete sets. These should be addressed to The Editor, *The Year's Work in English Studies,* The English Association, 1, Priory Gardens, Bedford Park, London W4 1TT. We are grateful to the authors and publishers who have made our task easier by supplying books and articles for volume 56. The editors of the *M.L.A. International Bibliography, Anglo-Saxon England, The Chaucer Review, English Language Notes, Philological Quarterly,* and *Restoration and Eighteenth Century Theatre Research* have put us deeply in their debt by providing advance proofs of their bibliographies. In drawing the reader's attention at the beginning of chapters to the main bibliographical aids, we presuppose in each case a reference to the *M.L.A. International Bibliography,* and to the *Annual Bibliography of English Language and Literature* published by the Modern Humanities Research Association.

James Redmond
Westfield College
London University

Abbreviations

ABC	American Book Collector
ABELL	Annual Bibliography of English Language and Literature
ABR	American Benedictine Review
AI	American Imago
AKML	Abhandlungen zur Kunst-, Musik-, and Literaturwissenschaft
AL	American Literature
ALASH	Acta Linguistica Academiae Scientiarum Hungaricae
AMon	Atlantic Monthly
AnL	Anthropological Linguistics
AnM	Annuale Medievale
AN&Q	American Notes and Queries
AQ	American Quarterly
AR	Antioch Review
Archiv	Archiv für das Studium der Neueren Sprachen und Literaturen
ArielE	Ariel: A Review of International English Literature
ArL	Archivum Linguisticum
ArlQ	Arlington Quarterly
ArP	Aryan Path
ArQ	Arizona Quarterly
A.R.S.	Augustan Reprint Society
AS	American Speech
ASch	American Scholar
ASE	Anglo-Saxon England
ASoc	Arts in Society
ASPR	Anglo-Saxon Poetic Records
AUMLA	Journal of Australasian Univs. Language and Literature Ass.
AUPG	American University Publishers Group Ltd.
AWR	The Anglo-Welsh Review
BA	Books Abroad
BAASB	British Association for American Studies Bulletin
BB	Bulletin of Bibliography
BBSIA	Bulletin Bibliographique de la Société Internationale Arthurienne
BC	Book Collector
BDEC	Bulletin of the Department of English (Calcutta)
BFLS	Bulletin de la Faculté des Lettres de Strasbourg
BHR	Bibliothèque d'Humanisme et Renaissance
BI	Books at Iowa
BJA	British Journal of Aesthetics
BJDC	British Journal of Disorders of Communication

ABBREVIATIONS

BJRL	*Bulletin of the John Rylands Library*
BLR	*Bodleian Library Record*
B.M.	British Museum
BMQ	*British Museum Quarterly*
BNL	*Blake Newsletter*
BNYPL	*Bulletin of the New York Public Library*
BP	*Banasthali Patrika*
BRMMLA	*Bulletin of the Rocky Mountain Modern Language Association*
BS	*Blake Studies*
BSE	*Brno Studies in English*
BSLP	*Bulletin de la Société de Linguistique de Paris*
BST	*Brontë Society Transactions*
BSUF	*Ball State University Forum*
BuR	*Bucknell Review*
Carrell	*The Carrell: Journal of the Friends of the Univ. of Miami Library*
C.B.E.L.	*Cambridge Bibliography of English Literature*
CE	*College English*
CEA	*CEA Critic*
CEAAN	*Center for Editions of American Authors Newsletter*
CentR	*The Centennial Review*
ChauR	*The Chaucer Review*
ChiR	*Chicago Review*
CHum	*Computers and the Humanities*
CJ	*Classical Journal*
CJL	*Canadian Journal of Linguistics*
CL	*Comparative Literature*
CLAJ	*College Language Association Journal*
CLC	*Columbia Library Columns*
ClioW	*Clio: An Interdisciplinary Journal*
CLJ	*Cornell Library Journal*
CLQ	*Colby Library Quarterly*
CLS	*Comparative Literature Studies*
C&M	*Classica et Medievalia*
ColF	*Columbia Forum*
CollG	*Colloquia Germanica*
ColQ	*Colorado Quarterly*
CompD	*Comparative Drama*
CompL	*Comparative Literature*
ConL	*Contemporary Literature*
ConnR	*Connecticut Review*
ContempR	*Contemporary Review*
CP	*Concerning Poetry*
CQ	*The Cambridge Quarterly*
CR	*The Critical Review*
Crit	*Critique: Studies in Modern Fiction*
Critique	*Critique* (Paris)
CritQ	*Critical Quarterly*
CSHVB	*Computer Studies in the Humanities and Verbal Bevhavior*

ABBREVIATIONS

D.A.	Dictionary of Americanisms
D.A.E.	Dictionary of American English
DHLR	The D. H. Lawrence Review
DiS	Dickens Studies
DM	The Dublin Magazine
D.N.B.	Dictionary of National Biography
DownR	Downside Review
DQR	Dutch Quarterly Review
DR	Dalhousie Review
DramS	Drama Survey (Minneapolis)
DSN	Dickens Studies Newsletter
DubR	Dublin Review
DUJ	Durham University Journal
DVLG	Deutsche Vierteljahrsschrift fur Literaturwissenschaft und Geistesgeschichte
EA	Études Anglaises
EAL	Early American Literature
E&S	Essays and Studies
ECS	Eighteenth-Century Studies
EDH	Essays by Divers Hands
E.E.T.S.	Early English Text Society
EHR	English Historical Review
EIC	Essays in Criticism
EJ	English Journal
ELangT	English Language Teaching
ELH	Journal of English Literary History
ELN	English Language Notes
ELR	English Literary Renaissance
ELT	English Literature in Transition
ELWIU	Essays in Literature (Western Illinois U.)
EM	English Miscellany
E.P.N.S.	English Place-Name Society
EPS	English Philological Studies
ES	English Studies
ESA	English Studies in Africa
ESC	English Studies In Canada
ESQ	Emerson Society Quarterly
ESRS	Emporia State Research Studies
ETJ	Educational Theatre Journal
EWN	Evelyn Waugh Newsletter
Expl	Explicator
FDS	Fountainwell Drama Series
FH	Frankfurter Hefte
FLang	Foundations of Language
FMLS	Forum of Modern Language Studies
ForumH	Forum (Houston)
GaR	Georgia Review
GRM	Germanisch-romanische Monatsschrift
HAB	Humanities Association Bulletin
HAR	Humanities Association Review

ABBREVIATIONS

HC	*The Hollins Critic*
HJ	*Hibbert Journal*
HLB	*Harvard Library Bulletin*
HLQ	*Huntington Library Quarterly*
HOPE	*History of Political Economy*
HSE	*Hungarian Studies in English*
HSL	*Hartford Studies in Literature*
HTR	*Harvard Theological Review*
HudR	*Hudson Review*
IJES	*Indian Journal of English Studies*
IndL	*Indian Literature*
IowaR	*Iowa Review*
IRAL	*International Review of Applied Linguistics*
IShav	*Independent Shavian*
IUR	*Irish University Review*
JA	*Jahrbuch für Amerikastudien*
JAAC	*Journal of Aesthetics and Art Criticism*
JAmS	*Journal of American Studies*
JBS	*Journal of British Studies*
JCSA	*Journal of the Catch Society of America*
JEGP	*Journal of English and Germanic Philology*
JFI	*Journal of the Folklore Institute*
JGE	*Journal of General Education*
JHI	*Journal of the History of Ideas*
JJQ	*James Joyce Quarterly*
JL	*Journal of Linguistics*
JML	*Journal of Modern Literature*
JMRS	*Journal of Medieval and Renaissance Studies*
JNT	*Journal of Narrative Technique*
JVLVB	*Journal of Verbal Learning and Verbal Behavior*
JWCI	*Journal of the Warburg and Courtauld Institutes*
KanQ	*Kansas Quarterly*
KN	*Kwartalnik Neofilologiczny* (Warsaw)
KR	*Kenyon Review*
KSJ	*Keats-Shelley Journal*
KSMB	*Keats-Shelley Memorial Bulletin*
L&P	*Literature and Psychology*
L&S	*Language and Speech*
Lang&S	*Language and Style*
LanM	*Les Langues Modernes*
LaS	*Louisiana Studies*
LC	*Library Chronicle*
LCP	*Library Chronical* (U. of Pennsylvania)
LCUT	*Library Chronical of the University of Texas*
LeedsSE	*Leeds Studies in English*
LHR	*Lock Haven Review*
Lib	*Library*
LMag	*London Magazine*
LWU	*Literatur in Wissenschaft und Unterricht*
MÆ	*Medium Ævum*

ABBREVIATIONS

M&H	Medievalia et Humanistica
M&L	Music and Letters
MarkhamR	Markham Review
MASJ	Midcontinent American Studies Journal
MD	Modern Drama
M.E.D.	Middle English Dictionary
MFS	Modern Fiction Studies
MHRev	Malahat Review
MichA	Michigan Academician
MiltonN	Milton Newsletter
MiltonQ	Milton Quarterly
MiltonS	Milton Studies
MinnR	Minnesota Review
MissQ	Mississippi Quarterly
MLJ	Modern Language Journal
MLN	Modern Language Notes
MLQ	Modern Language Quarterly
MLR	Modern Language Review
ModA	Modern Age
ModSp	Moderne Sprachen
MP	Modern Philology
MQ	Midwest Quarterly
MQR	Michigan Quarterly Review
MR	Massachusetts Review
MS	Mediaeval Studies
MSE	Massachusetts Studies in English
MSpr	Moderna Språk
NA	Nuova Antologia
N&Q	Notes and Queries
NCF	Nineteenth Century Fiction
NCTR	Nineteenth Century Theatre Research
NDQ	North Dakota Quarterly
NegroD	Negro Digest
NEQ	New England Quarterly
NL	Nouvelles Littéraires
NLB	Newberry Library Bulletin
NLH	New Literary History
NM	Neuphilologische Mitteilungen
NMQ	New Mexico Quarterly
NMS	Nottingham Medieval Studies
Novel	Novel: A Forum on Fiction
NRF	Nouvelle Revue Française
NS	Die Neueren Sprachen
NTM	New Theatre Magazine
NWR	Northwest Review
NYH	New York History
OB	Ord och Bild
OBSP	Oxford Bibliographical Society Proceedings
O.E.D.	Oxford English Dictionary
OEN	Old English Newsletter

ABBREVIATIONS

OL	*Orbis Litterarum*
OR	*Oxford Review*
OUR	*Ohio University Review*
PAAS	*Proceedings of the American Antiquarian Society*
PAPS	*Proceedings of the American Philosophical Society*
PBA	*Proceedings of the British Academy*
PBSA	*Papers of the Bibliographical Society of America*
PLL	*Papers on Language and Literature*
PMLA	*[Publications of the Modern Language Association of America]*
PN	*Poe Newsletter*
PP	*Philologica Pragensia*
PQ	*Philological Quarterly*
PR	*Partisan Review*
P.R.O.	Public Record Office
PULC	*Princeton University Library Chronicle*
QJS	*Quarterly Journal of Speech*
QQ	*Queen's Quarterly*
QR	*Quarterly Review*
RECTR	*Restoration and Eighteenth-Century Theatre Research*
RenD	*Renaissance Drama*
RenP	*Renaissance Papers*
RenQ	*Renaissance Quarterly*
RES	*Review of English Studies*
RHL	*Revue d'Histoire Littéraire de la France*
RLC	*Revue de Littérature Comparée*
RLMC	*Rivista di Letterature Moderne e Comparate*
RLV	*Revue des Langues Vivantes*
RMS	*Renaissance and Modern Studies*
RN	*Renaissance News*
RORD	*Research Opportunities in Renaissance Drama*
RQ	*Riverside Quarterly*
RRDS	Regents Renaissance Drama Series
RRestDS	Regents Restoration Drama Series
RS	*Research Studies*
R.S.L.	Royal Society of Literature
RUO	*Revue de l'Université d'Ottawa*
SAB	*South Atlantic Bulletin*
SAQ	*South Atlantic Quarterly*
SatR	*Saturday Review*
SB	*Studies in Bibliography*
SBC	*Studies in Browning and His Circle*
SBHT	*Studies in Burke and His Time*
SBL	*Studies in Black Literature*
SCN	*Seventeenth-Century News*
SCR	*South Carolina Review*
SDR	*South Dakota Review*
SED	*Survey of English Dialects*
SEL	*Studies in English Literature 1500–1900* (Rice University)
SELit	*Studies in English Literature* (Japan)

ABBREVIATIONS

SF&R	Scholars' Facsimiles and Reprints
SFQ	*Southern Folklore Quarterly*
SH	*Studia Hibernica* (Dublin)
ShakS	*Shakespeare Studies* (Cincinnati)
ShawR	*Shaw Review*
ShN	*Shakespeare Newsletter*
SHR	*Southern Humanities Review*
ShS	*Shakespeare Survey*
ShStud	*Shakespeare Studies* (Tokyo)
SIR	*Studies in Romanticism*
SJH	*Shakespeare-Jahrbuch* (Heidelberg)
SJW	*Shakespeare-Jahrbuch* (Weimar)
SL	*Studia Linguistica*
SLitI	*Studies in the Literary Imagination*
SLJ	*Southern Literary Journal*
SM	*Speech Monographs*
SMC	*Studies in Medieval Culture*
SN	*Studia Neophilologica*
SNL	*Satire Newsletter*
SNNTS	*Studies in the Novel* (North Texas State Univ.)
SoQ	*The Southern Quarterly*
SoR	*Southern Review* (Louisiana)
SoRA	*Southern Review* (Adelaide)
SP	*Studies in Philology*
SQ	*Shakespeare Quarterly*
SR	*Sewanee Review*
SRen	*Studies in the Renaissance*
SRO	*Shakespearean Research Opportunities*
SSF	*Studies in Short Fiction*
SSL	*Studies in Scottish Literature*
SSMP	*Stockholm Studies in Modern Philology*
S.T.C.	*Short Title Catalogue*
SWR	*Southwest Review*
TC	*The Twentieth Century*
TCBS	*Transactions of the Cambridge Bibliographical Society*
TCL	*Twentieth Century Literature*
TDR	*The Drama Review*
TEAS	Twayne's English Authors Series
ThQ	*Theatre Quarterly*
ThR	*Theatre Research*
ThS	*Theatre Survey*
THY	*The Thomas Hardy Yearbook*
TkR	*Tamkang Review*
TLS	*Times Literary Supplement*
TN	*Theatre Notebook*
TP	*Terzo Programma*
TPS	*Transactions of the Philological Society*
TQ	*Texas Quarterly*
TriQ	*Tri-Quarterly*
TSE	*Tulane Studies in English*

ABBREVIATIONS

TSL	*Tennessee Studies in Literature*
TSLL	*Texas Studies in Literature and Language*
TUSAS	Twayne's United States Authors Series
TWC	*The Wordsworth Circle*
TYDS	*Transactions of the Yorkshire Dialect Society*
UCTSE	*University of Cape Town Studies in English*
UDQ	*University of Denver Quarterly*
UES	*Unisa English Studies*
UMSE	*University of Mississippi Studies in English*
UR	*University Review* (Kansas City)
URev	*University Review* (Dublin)
UTQ	*University of Toronto Quarterly*
UWR	*University of Windsor Review*
VN	*Victorian Newsletter*
VP	*Victorian Poetry*
VPN	*Victorian Periodicals Newsletter*
VQR	*Virginia Quarterly Review*
VS	*Victorian Studies*
VWQ	*Virginia Woolf Quarterly*
WAL	*Western American Literature*
WascanaR	*Wascana Review*
WCR	*West Coast Review*
WF	*Western Folklore*
WHR	*Western Humanities Review*
WSCL	*Wisconsin Studies in Contemporary Literature*
WTW	Writers and their Work
WVUPP	*West Virginia University Bulletin: Philological Papers*
WWR	*Walt Whitman Review*
XUS	*Xavier University Studies*
YES	*Yearbook of English Studies*
YR	*Yale Review*
YULG	*Yale University Library Gazette*
YW	*The Year's Work in English Studies*
ZAA	*Zeitschrift für Anglistik und Amerikanistik*
ZCP	*Zeitschrift für Celtische Philologie*
ZDL	*Zeitschrift für Dialektologie und Linguistik*

Contents

CONTENTS

Note: Notices of books published in German, identified by the initials H.C.C., have been contributed by H. C. Castein Dr.phil. Lecturer in Modern Languages in the University of London (Goldsmiths' College)

I

Literary History and Criticism: General Works

T. S. DORSCH

1. Reference Works

Volume III of The 'Revels' History of Drama in English[1] is a work of considerable value. Covering the period 1576–1613, it recounts in some detail the development of the drama in Shakespeare's time. In 560 pages not much can be said about individual plays, except in so far as they contribute to this development or reinforce dramatic trends of the period, but the book contains a calendar of plays known to have been performed in these forty-odd most exciting years of the drama in England, a table of court performances, and a chronology of major theatrical (and literary) events. In the section entitled 'The Social and Literary Context' J. Leeds Barroll discusses the influence of the court on the evolution of the drama, and introduces the players and their audiences. Alexander Leggatt writes more fully about the companies and the actors. Richard Hosley gives descriptions of the various theatres, and with close reference to numerous plays shows how the different stage areas were employed to the best dramatic effect. In the long final section Alvin Kernan studies the most significant playwrights and plays of the age naturally Shakespeare dominates this section—and demonstrates how from unimpressive beginnings the Elizabethan drama and theatre grew to full maturity. This work must find a place in every academic literary library, whether personal or institutional.

The most recent addition to the Oxford Select Bibliographical Guides is Stanley Wells's English Drama[2] Like the previous Guides, this is made up of a series of bibliographical essays followed by lists of editions and of scholarly studies. Thus, for example, D. J. Palmer's ten pages or so of critical commentary on editions and studies of Marlowe are followed by tables of the best texts and the most significant contributions to Marlowe scholarship. To name only a few of the other participants, Samuel Schoenbaum deals with Marston, Middleton, and Massinger, Inga-Stina Ewbank with Webster, Tourneur, and Ford, K. M. Lea with the Court Masque, Allardyce Nicoll with English drama from 1900 to 1945, and John Russell Brown with drama since 1945. This volume will be found extremely helpful by all students of our drama.

---

[1] The 'Revels' History of Drama in English. Vol. III, 1576–1613, by J. Leeds Barroll, Alexander Leggatt, Richard Hosley, and Alvin Kernan. Methuen. pp. xxxiv + 526. £10.50. pb £4.50.
[2] English Drama (excluding Shakespeare). Select Bibliographical Guides. Ed. by Stanley Wells. O.U.P. pp. x + 303. pb £1.75.

S. K. Heninger's compilation, *English Prose to 1660*,[3] to give it the short title on its spine, is a useful enough work for undergraduate students of English prose of medieval and Renaissance times, but serious scholars will have to consult much fuller works, such as *New CBEL*. The book is a bibliography of major, and a certain number of minor, prose works arranged in twelve categories—all the types of fiction, as a matter of course, but also scientific and technical and polemical writings, and translations. For each primary work there is a presumed date of composition if it is earlier than 1460, or a first date of publication if it is later than 1460. It is especially in its information on secondary materials that this volume is less than satisfactory; often it records only a single work of criticism where *New CBEL* lists half a dozen, and it is similarly at fault in noting editions that are far from being the best that are available. However, it will no doubt have its uses as an outline guide to the prose of the period that it covers.

H. Swan's *Who's Who in Fiction?* was first published in 1906. Only the current American craze for reprinting almost any book that has been found interesting or useful in the past could serve as an (unsatisfactory) excuse for the present facsimile reprint,[4] for there are now other much more helpful works of the same kind, for example William Freeman's *Everyman Dictionary of Fictional Characters*, which in its revised edition of 1973 contains nearly 600 double-column pages, presenting perhaps three times as much material as the present volume. Moreover, Swan's *Who's Who?* is lavishly peppered with errors. A random check of five minutes' duration revealed the following examples of carelessness or ignorance: Hermstrong (for Hermsprong), Lizzie Hexham (for Hexam), and Teufelsdrökh (for Teufelsdröck); Old Orlick is said to have been responsible for the death of Mr. Gargery, and Feste the Fool appears as Teste, 'a clown in *Twelfth Night*'. The omissions of 'obvious' candidates for inclusion are too numerous to list. There may be libraries for which it will be thought worthwhile for some historical reason to purchase this book; probably few individual readers will wish to pay the heavy price that is asked for it.

Rhoda Thomas Tripp's *International Thesaurus of Quotations* was first published in America in 1970, and in England by Allen and Unwin in 1973. It has now been added to the Penguin Reference Books.[5] The *Thesaurus* is probably sufficiently well established not to require more than a general description here. Under head-words, with abundant cross-reference, it contains more than a thousand closely-printed pages of quotations, followed by several hundred (unpaginated) pages of indexes of head-words and authors and sources, so that it is very easy to trace the quotations that the volume contains. No such work will satisfy every reader; room can never be found for everyone's favourites. The great merit of this collection is that its compiler has, with the help of about thirty coadjutors, spread

---

[3] *English Prose, Prose Fiction, and Criticism to 1660: A Guide to Information Sources*, by S. K. Heninger, Jr. Detroit: Gale Research Co. pp. x + 255. $18.

[4] *Who's Who in Fiction? A Dictionary of Noted Names in Novels, Tales, Romances, Poetry, and Drama*, by H. Swan. London: G. Routledge & Sons, 1906. Reprinted Detroit: Gale Research Co., 1975. pp. v + 308. $14.

[5] *The International Thesaurus of Quotations*, compiled by Rhoda Thomas Tripp. Penguin Books. pp. xvi + 1067 + full indexes. £2.

her net very widely, and has included a reasonably representative gathering of European writers—not always in felicitous translations, but at any rate they are there.

Among useful reference works which have not been available as review copies, and which had not, when *YW* went to press, found their way into the generality of libraries, are new or revised editions of *Brewer's Dictionary of Phrase and Fable*;[6] *Roget's Thesaurus of English Words and Phrases*;[7] the *Princeton Encyclopedia of Poetry and Poetics*, edited by A. Preminger;[8] and *The Reader's Encyclopedia of World Drama*, edited by John Gassner and Edward Quinn.[9]

2. Collections of Essays

Essays and Studies 1975[10] is edited by Robert Ellrodt, and has an interesting and welcome international character. Most of the papers are noticed in other chapters of the present volume of *YW*, and little more than a brief survey is required here. As a contribution to the current trend to seek connections between the masque as a dramatic genre and stage-plays of the Jacobean and Caroline era, Glynne Wickham offers an interesting demonstration that *The Tempest* is 'a single unified work of art firmly held together by the successful incorporation of a masque and anti-masque within the dramatic structure of a stage-play'. Irène Simon studies the sermons of Robert South, and establishes that the conception of man and of his role in society that emerges from them is essentially one with which the Augustans were in complete agreement. Jean Perrin interestingly traces the use of 'The Actaeon Myth in Shelley's Poetry'. As A. Norman Jeffares points out, Charles Lever has been treated shabbily by most critics. Jeffares brings out Lever's mastery of comedy, tragedy, and satire in *Lord Kilgobbin*; when he wrote this novel he had 'moved from comedy through elements of tragi-comedy to a tragic view of life in the Ireland he loved'. In 'The Wandering Rocks, or the Rejection of Stephen Dedalus', Giorgio Melchiori argues that it was in the central chapter of *Ulysses*, the tenth episode known as 'The Wandering Rocks', that Joyce finally and explicitly repudiated both the aesthetic and ethical principles by which Dedalus and Bloom seem to be guided and the tainted social and religious conventions which they condemn. Dame Helen Gardner's subject is 'The Novels of Joyce Cary'. Outstanding among Cary's many gifts is his ability to 'communicate his sense of the "character" of life as capable of perpetually flowering into happiness and joy. He is a comic novelist without a trace of the satirist in his composition, and his subject is a universe freely bringing forth delight.' Writing on 'The Pursuit of Influence', Wolfgang Clemen rightly deprecates

---

[6] *Brewer's Dictionary of Phrase and Fable*. Cassell.
[7] *Roget's Thesaurus of English Words and Phrases*. New edition completely revised and modernized by Robert A. Dutch. Longmans. pp. lii + 1309.
[8] *Princeton Encyclopedia of Poetry and Poetics*, ed. by A. Preminger. Princeton U.P.
[9] *The Reader's Encyclopedia of World Drama*, ed. by John Gassner and Edward Quinn. Methuen.
[10] *Essays and Studies 1975*. N.S. Vol. XXVIII. Collected for the English Association by Robert Ellrodt. John Murray. pp. vi + 122. £2.25.

studies of influence that are undertaken for their own sake. 'They form
one of several questions which we may put when we are confronted with
issues of literary history, with single works or whole trends. But we ought
to put the question . . . It will at least sharpen our vision, make us think
about the nature of relationships and affinities, . . . and will also compel us
to find out more about the characteristic features and elements of the
work under discussion.' In 'Literature and Money' Laurence Lerner shows
how a number of writers, from Chaucer onwards, have seen the role of
money in the societies they depict, and exposes some of the fallacies in the
Marxist view of money.

   Literary Criticism: Idea and Act[11] is a collection, brought together by
W. K. Wimsatt, of some three dozen papers delivered at gatherings of the
English Institute since its foundation in 1939. This should perhaps be described as a further example of the American practice of making books for
the sake of making books, for all the papers have been published before,
and are available in the several English Institute volumes; but all have some
interest or value, and there is at least some justification for reprinting them
in a single (large) book. Many of them have been noticed in previous issues
of *YW*, and it therefore seems best, space being restricted, merely to list
them all so that readers will know what they will find in the volume. Under
the heading 'IDEA' Wimsatt has placed essays on critical theory or technique, as follows: 'The Search for English Literary Documents', by James M.
Osborn; 'Mimesis and Allegory', by W. H. Auden; 'The Parallelism between
Literature and the Arts', by René Wellek; 'The Modern Myth of the
Modern Myth', by Donald A. Stauffer; 'Imagination as a Value', by Wallace
Stevens; 'The Defense of the Illusion and the Creation of Myth: Device
and Symbol in the Plays of Shakespeare', by Leslie A. Fiedler; 'Mimesis
and Katharsis: An Archetypal Consideration', by Philip Wheelwright;
'Ramus: Rhetoric and the Pre-Newtonian Mind', by Walter J. Ong, S. J.;
'Belief and the Suspension of Disbelief', by M. H. Abrams; 'Patristic
Exegesis in the Criticism of Medieval Literature: The Opposition', by
E. Talbot Donaldson; 'The Fate of Pleasure: Wordsworth to Dostoevski',
by Lionel Trilling; 'Ghostlier Demarcations (Frye's Archetypes)', by
Geoffrey H. Hartman; 'Sign, Sense, and Roland Barthes', by Hugh M.
Davidson; and 'Whorf, Chomsky, and the Student of Literature', by
George Steiner.

   In the section headed 'ACT' Wimsatt has grouped his more 'practically'
critical papers on specific works, authors, periods, or genres. John Hollander
writes on *Musica Mundana* and *Twelfth Night*'; Stephen Booth on 'The
Value of *Hamlet*'; Daniel Seltzer on 'Shakespeare's Texts and Modern
Productions'; Harry Levin on 'The Example of Cervantes: The Novel as
Parody'; Ray L. Heffner on 'Unifying Symbols in the Comedy of Ben
Jonson'; Helen Vendler on 'The Re-invented Poem: George Herbert's
Alternatives'; C. L. Barber on 'A Mask Presented at Ludlow Castle: The
Masque as a Masque'; Louis L. Martz on 'The Rising Poet, 1645 (Milton)';
Cleanth Brooks on 'Marvell's "Horatian Ode" '; Marvin Mudrick on
'Restoration Comedy and Later'; W. K. Wimsatt on 'Imitation as Freedom,

[11] *Literary Criticism: Idea and Act*, ed. by W. K. Wimsatt. (The English Institute,
1939–1972: Selected Essays.) California U.P. 1974. pp. viii + 650.

1717-1798'; Martha W. England on 'The Satiric Blake: Apprenticeship at the Haymarket?'; Harold Bloom on 'Coleridge: The Anxiety of Influence'; Martin Price on 'The Irrelevant Detail and the Emergence of Form' (in the novel); Northrop Frye on 'Dickens and the Comedy of Humors'; Richard Ellmann on 'Two Faces of Edward' (Edwardian literature); Arthur Mizener on 'Poetic Drama and the Well-made Play'; Francis Fergusson on 'Poetry in the Theatre and the Poetry of the Theatre: Cocteau's *Infernal Machine*'; Victor Brombert on 'Sartre and the Drama of Ensnarement'; and Hugh Kenner on 'The Urban Apocalypse' (in Eliot's *Waste Land*).

Style and Text[12] is a substantial *Festschrift* presented to Nils Erik Enkvist on his fiftieth birthday. Enkvist is primarily interested in iinguistic and stylistic topics, and the thirty-odd papers in this book all deal with some aspect of style or language, and are presented under the headings 'Theory of Style', 'Style and Literary Criticism', 'Style and Linguistic Analysis', and 'Text Linguistics'. Many of them discuss from these points of view particular works of English literature, from the medieval period to today, and all are written in English. They cannot all be listed in a short notice but the names of a few of the contributors will perhaps suggest the quality of the scholarship provided: Josef Vachek, Louis T. Milic, Claes Schaar, Inna Koskenniemi, Vivian Salmon, and Jan Firbas.

C. S. Lewis has now for some decades, like his close friend J. R. R. Tolkien, been something of a cult-figure in America. The most recent evidence of this is a slim volume of papers entitled *Man's 'Natural Powers'*,[13] which is edited by Raymond P. Tripp, Jr. Those of us who were well acquainted with Lewis will know that, while he would have deplored the uncritical adulation which is often bestowed on him today, he was, with becoming modesty, thoroughly aware of his standing as one of the great literary critics, and at the same time one of the outstanding fabulists, religious allegorists, and Christian apologists of his time. He would probably not have been displeased by Tripp's collection, and he would certainly have enjoyed the opening paper, 'C. S. Lewis and Historicism', in which his old friend Owen Barfield refutes the charge, frequently brought against him, that he was out of touch with his age, but concludes that much is wanting in his 'historicism'. But what does this matter in the context of Lewis's work as a whole? Other papers deal with various aspects of the Narnia novels, with Lewis's 'scientific imagination' in his 'science fiction' religious writings, and with his 'philosophy', which was of very many kinds. The important side of Lewis that is neglected here is his high perspicacity (and perspicuity) as a literary critic, but it may be felt that that has been adequately coped with elsewhere.

The 1975 Volume of *Essays by Divers Hands*[14] was noticed in last year's issue of *YW*. *Proceedings of the British Academy*[15] for 1975 had not been published when the present volume of *YW* went to press.

[12] *Style and Text: Studies Presented to Nils Erik Enkvist*, ed by Håkan Ringbom. Stockholm: Språkförlaget Scriptor. pp. 441.
[13] *Man's 'Natural Powers': Essays for and about C. S. Lewis*, ed. by Raymond P. Tripp, Jr. Denver. Colorado: Society for New Language Study. pp. vi + 63.
[14] *Essays by Divers Hands: Being the Transactions of the Royal Society of Literature*. N.S. Vol. XXXVIII, ed. by John Guest. O.U.P. pp. viii + 158.
[15] *Proceedings of the British Academy*, vol. 51, 1975. O.U.P.

3. Forms, Genres, Themes

Were it not that it would have sounded a little clumsy, Laurence Lerner would have given his admirable *Introduction to English Poetry*[16] the longer title *An Introduction to the Study of English Poetry*, for that is what his book is. Lerner has selected fifteen poems in chronological order, from the ballad 'Clerk Saunders' down to Auden's 'City without Walls', and has subjected each to close critical analysis, and to comparison with poems of similar genres or themes. Thus, for example, he enriches our understanding of Raleigh's 'The Lie' not only by what he says about the poem itself, but also by setting beside it passages (or poems) of complaint or denunciation—excerpts from Spenser's *Colin Clout* and Tourneur's *Revenger's Tragedy*, anonymous poems from the Elizabethan anthologies, Shakespeare's 'Tired with all these . . .', and D. H. Lawrence's 'Vengeance is Mine'. Carrying out this process with the other poems of his choice—Herbert's 'Bunch of Grapes', Milton's 'On his Blindness', Crabbe's 'Peter Grimes', Browning's 'Johannes Agricola', and Hardy's 'Ruined Maid', to name a few of them—Lerner provides what is in effect an outline history of English poetry, together with much helpful discussion of the development of genres, forms, movements, and even metres; for, although he has chosen poems which are not too 'obvious' (all of them, nevertheless, very fine), his methods of comparison have involved discussion of a fairly large body of great English poetry.

J. L. Styan's latest contribution to the study of drama is entitled *Drama, Stage and Audience*.[17] 'The miracle of theatre,' says Styan, 'is that a community, an audience, has agreed to let drama happen. In the make-believe of a theatrical situation, the impossible, even the irrational, is feasible and free to take place by common consent.' In a series of chapters on 'Communication in Drama', 'Dramatic Signals' (what is seen or not seen, heard or not heard, active or still), 'Genre and Style', and 'Conditions of Performance', on acting, on illusion, and on the essential interaction between stage and audience, Styan throws much light on theatrical conventions and practice in European drama from the medieval cycles down to Brecht and Beckett, with occasional glances at the drama of ancient Greece and Rome. Much of the discussion turns on the work of 'the man whose dramatic stimuli are the richest: Shakespeare', and Styan writes interestingly about the theatrical effect of each of Shakespeare's plays. His book is a valuable contribution to dramatic theory.

The Theory of the Novel,[18] edited by J. Halperin, contains, in addition to a helpful critical introduction, a score of essays on various aspects of the novel to which justice cannot be done in a short notice. Perhaps some notion of the scope and quality of the book may be gained from the fact that in the section headed 'The Genre Today' Robert B. Martin provides 'Notes toward a Comic Fiction', Irving H. Butcher writes on 'The Aesthetics of the Supra-Novel', A. W. Friedman on 'The Modern Multivalent Novel', Max F. Schulz on 'Characters (Contra Characterization) in the Contem-

[16] *An Introduction to English Poetry*. Fifteen poems discussed by Laurence Lerner. Arnold. pp. x + 230. £1.95.
[17] *Drama, Stage and Audience*, by J. L. Styan. C.U.P. pp. viii + 256.
[18] *The Theory of the Novel*, ed. by J. Halperin. New York: O.U.P. pp. xii + 396.

porary Novel', and Frank Kermode on 'Novel and Narrative'; in the section 'The Genre Today Revisited' there are contributions from Leon Edel and Leslie A. Fiedler; and later sections have papers from, among others, Alice R. Kaminsky, Marvin Mudrick, Robert B. Heilman, Walter Allen, Richard Harter Fogle, and Dorothea Krook.

In *The Implied Reader*,[19] the original German version of which appeared in 1972, Wolfgang Iser is working towards 'a theory of literary effects and responses based on the novel', but he makes no pretensions to having come close to formulating such a theory. However, there is a theme running through the book which gives unity to his discussion of several very different types of prose fiction. Though the novel, he says, deals with social and historical norms, it does not simply reproduce contemporary values; rather it represents varying degrees of negation of these norms— 'a negation which impels the reader to seek a positive counter-balance elsewhere than in the world immediately familiar to him'. Thus the 'implied reader' of Iser's title is 'forced to take an active part in the composition of the novel's meaning, which revolves round a basic divergence from the familiar'. From this starting-point Iser proceeds to perceptive analysis of a number of fictions: *Pilgrim's Progress, Joseph Andrews* and *Tom Jones, Humphry Clinker, Waverley, Vanity Fair*, and several twentieth-century novels by, among others, William Faulkner, Ivy Compton-Burnett, Samuel Beckett, and James Joyce.

Alan Swingewood's *The Novel and Revolution*[20] aims at relating 'revolutionary movements, ideas and practices, or the threat of revolution, real or imagined', to the novel form. Swingewood is interested primarily but not solely in novels based on the Russian Revolution of 1917. In the earlier chapters he criticizes some recent 'deterministic, reductionist' theories of the novel, particularly those of Georg Lukács, Lucien Goldmann, and Ian Watt. Against these he sets what he sees as the 'more genuinely dialectical theory' of Antonio Gramsci. In the longer second section Swingewood examines, in the light of his theoretical chapters, the novels of Gissing, Conrad, Jack London, Evgeny Zamyatin, Victor Serge, Koestler, and Solzhenitsyn. This book will not be to everyone's taste, but it will no doubt be read with interest by devotees of what has come to be known as the sociology of literature.

Like her previous books, Marjorie Boulton's *The Anatomy of the Novel*[21] is intended principally for use in sixth forms and colleges, but it could be read with interest by more advanced students. She deals straightforwardly with such elements as plot and structure, characterization and setting, and various types and conventions of fiction. Her range of reference is fairly wide, but her illustrative material is drawn largely from Dickens's *Hard Times*, George Eliot's *Silas Marner*, Henry James's *The Europeans*, Arnold Bennett's *Anna of the Five Towns*, and Conrad's *The Secret Agent*.

[19] *The Implied Reader: Patterns of Communication in Prose Fiction from Bunyan to Beckett*, by Wolfgang Iser. Johns Hopkins U.P., 1974. pp. xvi + 304.
[20] *The Novel and Revolution*, by Alan Swingewood. Macmillan. pp. xii + 288. £7.95. pb £4.95.
[21] *The Anatomy of the Novel*, by Marjorie Boulton. Routledge & Kegan Paul. pp. x + 189. £3.50. pb £1.60.

Aspects of the Novel,[22] E. M. Forster's Clark Lectures of 1927, published in the same year, is a welcome addition to the Abinger Edition of Forster's works. Fifty years after its first appearance the book remains very readable. Lacking the super-subtlety of much modern criticism, it is refreshingly direct, and written in a refreshingly easy style. It has here been carefully edited, with textual notes and an annotated index, by Oliver Stallybrass. The volume includes a number of 'related writings': entries from Forster's commonplace book, some of which have clearly provided starting-points for material in *Aspects of the Novel*: a review, in Forster's most wittily ironical manner, of Clayton Hamilton's *Materials and Methods of Fiction*, together with extracts from Hamilton's book; and a broadcast talk of 1944 on 'The Art of Fiction'.

Brian Wicker's *The Story-Shaped World*[23] was not available when this chapter was being written. The bibliographical details noted below are taken from a review published elsewhere.

From Allan Rodway comes an interesting book entitled *English Comedy*.[24] In his opening chapters Rodway traces the evolution of comedy from primitive religious rituals, observing that, even before both genres became assimilated to the worship of Dionysus, the comic was associated with rites of mockery, ribaldry, and fertility, even as the tragic was associated with rites of sacrifice, solemnity, and death. Having established his terminology, drawing necessary but often very fine distinctions between such subdivisions of comedy as farce, parody, burlesque, satire, irony wit, and humour, he goes on in general terms to relate English comedy, from medieval to modern times, to the evolution of English society and English sensibility. The greater part of the book is devoted to perceptive studies of the masters of our comic writing through the past half-dozen centuries. Inevitably the main emphasis is placed on the major figures: Chaucer and Dunbar in the medieval period, the Elizabethan and the Restoration playwrights, Dryden and Pope, the eighteenth-century novelists, Jane Austen and Peacock, Byron and Shelley, and over the past century or so Butler and Shaw, Waugh and Heller, Joyce and Stoppard. This is a stimulating work, whether as a contribution to the theory of comedy or in its criticism of individual authors.

For his T. S. Eliot Memorial Lectures Frank Kermode took his cue from Eliot's paper 'What is a Classic?', and he has given to the lectures in their published form the title *The Classic*.[25] Kermode takes Virgil as his starting-point, and in his first two lectures brings out some of the ways in which Virgil's writings have influenced the development of the modern European mind and European literature, especially as these are represented by Dante, Milton, and Marvell. Making a leap forward in time, he centres the third and fourth lectures chiefly on Hawthorne's *House of the Seven Gables* and on *Wuthering Heights*. From his study of the various authors

---

[22] *Aspects of the Novel, and Related Writings*, by E. M. Forster, with an Introduction by Oliver Stallybrass. Arnold. pp. xviii + 169. £5.25.

[23] *The Story-Shaped World. Fiction and Metaphysics: Some Variations on a Theme*, by Brian Wicker. Athlone Press. pp. x + 230.

[24] *English Comedy: Its Role and Nature from Chaucer to the Present Day*, by Allan Rodway. Chatto & Windus. pp. 288.

[25] *The Classic*, by Frank Kermode. Faber. pp. 141.

whom he treats, for of course he does not restrict himself to those who have been named, Kermode concludes that the modern view of the classic 'is necessarily tolerant of change and plurality, whereas the older, regarding most forms of pluralism as heretical, holds fast to the time-transcending idea of Empire'. What in effect is happening is that the image of the 'imperial classic' is beginning to be brought down to earth.

In *The Living Principle*[26] F. R. Leavis continues his long-standing but ever increasingly necessary campaign against the 'cretinization' of our civilization (he takes the word from Stanislav Andreski's *Social Sciences as Sorcery*). In his opening sections he restates his case for the study of literature as 'a discipline of thought', and in particular reasserts the value of 'judgement and analysis' (his phrase for what is more commonly known as practical criticism) in countering the 'cretinized and cretinizing' forces by which these days we are continually beset. Leavis goes on to demonstrate ways in which his methods of judgement and analysis may enhance our understanding not only of literature, but of what literature represents— responses to life and lives. Under such headings as ' "Thought" and Emotional Quality', 'Imagery and Movement', and 'Reality and Sincerity', he compares the effects and effectiveness of several pairs of passages or works, such as Cory's 'Heraclitus' and Scott's 'Proud Maisie', Wordsworth's 'A slumber did my spirit seal' and Tennyson's 'Break, break, break', and Shakespeare's *Antony and Cleopatra* and Dryden's *All for Love*. His long final section is devoted to close analysis, and judgement, of Eliot's *Four Quartets*. Not everyone will always agree with Leavis's judgements, but there are few, surely, who will not find this book an interesting and instructive exercise in practical criticism.

Helmut Winter's *Literaturtheorie und Literaturkritik*[27] is a very sound work which, as its title indicates, falls into two parts. In the first part Winter considers a number of approaches to literary theory: among them the function of literature; the relationship between literature and truth and literature and reality; the theory of genres; stylistics; and literary values. In the second part he traces the more significant developments in English criticism from Elizabethan times to today from Sidney to Empson and Leavis. Naturally his main emphases fall on the major figures, and in his comparatively short volume he cannot discuss even those in close detail; but he has provided what will for his German readers be a useful outline history of English literary criticism.

Raymond Williams's *Keywords*[28] is an interesting attempt to trace the development into their modern meanings of about a hundred words in very common use in literary and social criticism. In a series of short 'essays', ranging in length from about a page to half a dozen pages, Williams explores the history of these 'keywords'—the ways in which they have been 'formed, altered, redefined, influenced, modified, confused, and reinforced as the historical contexts in which they were applied changed

[26] *The Living Principle: 'English' as a Discipline of Thought*, by F. R. Leavis. Chatto & Windus pp. 264.

[27] *Literaturtheorie und Literaturkritik*, by Helmut Winter. Bern & München: Francke Verlag. pp. 205. Sw. fr. 19.80.

[28] *Keywords: A Vocabulary of Culture and Society*, by Raymond Williams. Fontana/Croom Helm. pp. 286. £5.50.

to give us their current meaning and significance'. Thus, for example, with cross-references to 'doctrinaire', 'idealism', 'philosophy', and 'science', the word 'ideology' is given four pages showing what has happened to it since it was invented in 1796 by the French rationalist philosopher Destutt de Tracy with the meaning 'the science of ideas'. The pejorative modern meaning was introduced by Napoleon in an attack on the proponents of democracy, but since his time the word has been used in a variety of senses, not always pejorative, and these Williams illustrates. The same treatment is accorded to his other words—'sensibility', 'myth', 'standards', 'pragmatic', 'subjective', 'aesthetic', 'liberal', and the rest. The book provides agreeable browsing; it is also a worthwhile contribution to the study of language.

In *The Fantastic in Literature*[29] Eric S. Rabkin explores the nature of the fantastic by studying its use in fairy tales, science fiction, detective fiction, religious allegory, and other forms of literature, and relating it to psychological theory. In order that his examples may 'interilluminate', he draws them principally from what he calls 'one cultural moment'—England in the late Victorian era. However, when he is treating Gothicism, he finds it necessary to include works of the eighteenth and the twentieth centuries; for science fiction he includes American and Continental writers; and he makes other exceptions. Rabkin considers far too many works to enumerate here; among the authors whom he treats in some detail are Jorge Luis Borges, Lewis Carroll, Arthur Conan Doyle, George MacDonald, William Morris, E. A. Poe, Horace Walpole (as an early 'fantastic'), and H. G. Wells. Although he is not always persuasive, and not always easy to follow in his psychological disquisitions, he has written a book which is in the main interesting and informative.

The Don Juan legend is, in terms of the number of versions it has inspired, one of the most influential legends in western literature (and music). Stimulated by an 'outstanding' performance of Mozart's *Don Giovanni* that he attended, Otto Rank, who for some time was a close associate of Freud, and who had long been interested in the legend, made it the subject of several studies, the most substantial of which was *Die Don Juan-Gestalt*.(1924); this, in a translation by D. G. Winter, now appears under the title *The Don Juan Legend*.[30] Rank's book is a psychological analysis of the legend which begins with an 'Oedipal' interpretation of Juan, goes on to discuss the master-servant relationship between Juan and Leporello, and then turns to a detailed discussion of the role of women in the legend. It is unlikely that this work will contribute much to the understanding of English versions of the Don Juan story, but it is not without interest as an early example of the psychological (and quasi-psychoanalytical) interpretation of literature.

Denys Thompson's *What to Read in English Literature*[31] is not a pretentious work, as its title might suggest. As Thompson points out, even a one-volume history of our literature will include more than 400 authors.

[29] *The Fantastic in Literature*, by Eric S. Rabkin. Princeton U.P. pp. xii + 235. £8.70. $12.50.

[30] *The Don Juan Legend*, by Otto Rank. Transl. and ed. by D. G. Winter. Princeton U.P. pp. xii + 145.

[31] *What to Read in English Literature*, by Denys Thompson. Heinemann. pp. vi + 154.

He is writing for people who would like to read fairly seriously but have not much time—for whom 'the huge extent of the tract called English Literature can be intimidating'. He has therefore prepared 'a highly selective guide, a map . . . plotted and placed on the reading of one person, to English literature from the earliest times to about 1950', treating not much more than a hundred authors or collections. Such a guide inevitably includes the 'obvious' authors of the first rank; the choice below this level must be a personal matter, and every reviewer will probably deplore the inclusion or omission of this or that writer. However, it would be a very captious reader of *YW* who would not accept Thompson's list (and his bibliographies of background reading) as in the main judicious; it is pleasant that he has found room for a reasonable number of writers of the literary standing of, say, Thomas Deloney, Henry Mayhew, George Bourne, and Somerville and Ross.

4. Bibliographical Studies

Volume XXVIII of *Studies in Bibliography*,[32] edited like all its predecessors by Fredson Bowers, offers the usual mixed bag of bibliographical papers. In 'Joseph Johnson, an Eighteenth-Century Bookseller', Gerald P. Tyson stresses the importance of booksellers in the eighteenth century 'in introducing new authors, perhaps thus helping to establish a new vogue, or in sustaining established writers'. 'Of all the book-sellers in the second half of the century none surpasses Joseph Johnson for business acumen and literary taste.' Johnson published the first writings of Wordsworth, and all the writings of, among others, Joseph Priestley, Erasmus Darwin, Beckford, Godwin, Mary Wollstonecraft, Coleridge, Cowper, Malthus, and Maria Edgeworth. Richmond P. Bond and Marjorie N. Bond write on 'The Minute Books of the *St. James's Chronicle*', a journal which, founded in 1761, continued far into the next century, merging with several other journals on the way. In 'Further Texts of Chaucer's Minor Poems' A. I. Doyle and George B. Pace print, with commentaries, transcriptions of hitherto unpublished versions of the *A.B.C.*, of *Truth*, and of *Against Women Unconstant*, which is probably by Chaucer. Steven W. May demonstrates that the 1577 edition of *The Paradise of Dainty Devices* represents an important stage in the growth of this most popular of the Elizabethan anthologies, in that, among other innovations and corrected attributions, it introduces twelve new texts, including William Hunnis's elegy for William, First Earl of Pembroke; Hunnis was personally concerned with the make-up and printing of this edition. Compositors D and F of the Shakespeare First Folio have hitherto been somewhat shadowy figures. John O'Connor offers a careful analysis of their respective habits and contributions to the work. Following her earlier study of the second edition of *Clarissa* (*SB* XXVI), Shirley Van Marter now shows the significance of 'Richardson's Revisions of *Clarissa* in the Third and Fourth Editions'. Kenneth W. Graham outlines the history of the publication of *Vathek* both in French and in English,

---

[32] *Studies in Bibliography*, Vol. XXVIII, ed. by Fredson Bowers. Charlottesville: Virginia U.P. for the Bibliographical Society of the University of Virginia. pp. vi + 340. $17.50.

notes differences in sense and tone in passages of the two versions, and defends Samuel Henley against frequently-uttered charges of impropriety in his publication of the English *Vathek* by showing how closely Beckford collaborated with him and approved suggested alterations. In a long paper on 'Greg's Theory of Copy-Text and the Editing of American Literature' G. Thomas Tanselle justifies the adoption of W. W. Greg's 'The Rationale of Copy-Text' as the basis of the editorial principles of the Center for Editions of American authors. Hans Zeller, in 'A New Approach to the Critical Constitution of Literary Texts', discusses some of the ways in which German editorial practice is beginning to diverge from the procedures developed by Greg and Bowers.

These full-scale articles are followed by a number of shorter contributions. A. S. G. Edwards and J. Hedley show that for his edition of Chaucer in 1561 John Stow took his text of the fifteenth-century 'The Craft of Lovers' from Trinity College, Cambridge, MS R.3.19; this fact 'offers some insight into Stow's editorial practices and his unreliability as an attributor'. Ernest Sullivan establishes that manuscript corrections in John Sparrow's copies of the first and second issues of the first edition of Donne's *Bio-thanatos* are authoritative. Edward L. Saslow tries to account for the omission in the first edition of *Absalom and Achitophel* of twelve lines of the portrait of Achitophel as it appeared in the third and all subsequent editions. As a supplement to a note which he published in *SB* last year, A. B. England contributes 'Further Additions to Bond's Register of Burlesque Poems'. In 'The "Swingeing" of Cibber: The Suppression of the First Edition of. *The Refusal*' Rodney L. Hayley demonstrates that the reason why the second edition of Colley Cibber's *The Refusal* was printed earlier than the first is to be found in an attempt of Edmund Curll to discredit Cibber. Shirley Strum Kenny describes copies she possesses of extremely accomplished piracies of the 1733 editions of Farquhar's *The Beaux' Stratagem* and *The Recruiting Officer*. Pat Rogers puts forward evidence which corroborates claims that have been made that Samuel Richardson was responsible for the revisions and editorial interpolations in the second edition (1738) of Defoe's *Tour thro' the Whole Island of Great Britain*. Thomas R. Cleary, on both external and stylistic evidence, greatly strengthens 'The Case for Fielding's Authorship of *An Address to the Electors of Great Britain (1740)*'. William C. Woodson argues that the 1785 Variorum Shakespeare which George Steevens commissioned Isaac Reed to prepare as a revision of his own 1778 Variorum is more important than has been realised; it exacerbated the quarrel between Steevens and Malone, and was thus in a sense responsible for Steevens's resumption of work on the text of Shakespeare. Finally, Brian H. Finney describes 'D. H. Lawrence's Progress to Maturity' in terms of the differences that appear in certain short stories as they are to be found in holograph, in the form in which they were published in periodicals, and in their final versions in *The Prussian Officer and Other Stories* of 1914.

Although Judith Butcher's *Copy-Editing*[33] is intended primarily for use in publishing houses, it will serve also as an invaluable reference work for

[33] *Copy-Editing: The Cambridge Handbook*, by Judith Butcher, C.U.P. pp. xi + 326. £8.

anyone who is preparing typescript for printing. The book is based on the practices of the C.U.P., but the information it provides can easily be adapted to conform to the house-style of other firms. Miss Butcher explains clearly and precisely every stage in the preparation of typescript for setting, making allowance for alternative house-styles and for accepting the idiosyncrasies of authors, as long as they are consistent; and she goes through all the processes of proof-reading at the various stages, the methods of indexing, the conventions to be followed in providing references, and indeed all other matters that are the concern of the copy-editor. A large part of the book is devoted to the presentation of academic material, whether literary or scientific, whether in English or in other languages. Numerous tables, for example of proof-correction symbols, and an excellent glossary of technical terms increase the value of this admirable book.

First published in 1960, and now appearing in its fifth revised edition, the *Selective Bibliography for the Study of English and American Literature*,[34] compiled by Richard D. Altick and Andrew Wright, lists very helpful bibliographies, not of individual writers, but of reference works of whose nature and value every student of literature ought to be aware: bibliographical handbooks, literary encyclopaedias, histories of English and American literature, guides to libraries, general reference guides, bibliographies of bibliographies, public records, and the like; the works are listed, indeed, under some three dozen headings. Of the 600-odd items, seventy-one are new in this edition, and fifty-six have been modified to bring them up to date. This work will be most helpful especially to those who undertake literary research.

5. Translations, Anthologies

In the words of its General Editor, William Arrowsmith, the series The Greek Tragedy in New Translations 'is based on the conviction that poets like Æschylus, Sophocles, and Euripides can only be properly rendered by translators who are themselves poets'. Janet Lembke's translation of *The Suppliants* of Æschylus[35] is certainly more forceful and more immediate in its impact than the versions of the more academic translators tend to be. *The Suppliants* is a singularly difficult play for the modern imagination to grasp—often, too, linguistically difficult. (Even the associations of the word 'cow', a key-word or key-idea in the play, are very different for us from what they were in ancient Greece, when only rich men or aristocrats, or Homeric kings, maintained herds of cattle.) For the translator of this play, as Arrowsmith points out, 'freedom is not merely useful but absolutely necessary, . . . freedom trained and willing to take responsible imaginative risks'. A spot check suggests that Mrs. Lembke has for the most part kept pretty close to the sense of the original Greek, but she has not hesitated to change the emphases for dramatic or poetic effect. Her free verse at first seems a strange medium to use, especially in the episodic sections of the

[34] *Selective Bibliography for the Study of English and American Literature*, by Richard D. Altick and Andrew Wright. Fifth edition. Collier Macmillan. pp. xii + 168. £2.25.
[35] *Æschylus: 'Suppliants', translated by Janet Lembke. (The Greek Tragedy in New Translations.)* O.U.P. pp. xiv + 104.

drama, but the ear fairly soon becomes attuned to it. The poet who has translated *Prometheus Bound*[36] in the same series is James Scully, in collaboration with the classical scholar C. J. Herington. Here again free verse is used, and here again, after an initial shock, it is felt to be used to good effect. Scully is not always successful in conveying the richness of Æschylus's poetry in the choruses, but in its total effect his version is satisfying, and brings out most of the power of the original.

William Arrowsmith has translated many Greek tragedies. His version of the *Alcestis* of Euripides[37] for his recently inaugurated series is meant to be 'accurate, but not slavishly accurate, . . . according to the principle laid down by St. Jerome, that we should render according to the sense rather than the letter'. In the choral lyrics in particular he has been 'unashamedly interpretive [*sic*], sometimes expanding metaphors and even intruding glosses', but whenever he has departed significantly from the original he has provided an explanatory note. In the episodes as well as the lyrics he has used no identifiable metre, but has allowed the rhythms to be dictated by the sense, usually quite acceptably, although the diction is more 'familiar' than that of Euripides, presumably with the dubiously justifiable intention of making it seem more natural to modern hearers or readers (Gilbert Murray went to the opposite extreme of heightening the poetic quality of the verse). Like the other translators in the series, Arrowsmith has provided a helpful introduction and notes.

Paul Roche is also an experienced translator of Greek and Roman plays, and his versions of the *Alcestis*, the *Medea*, and *The Bacchae* of Euripides[38] will give the Greekless reader quite a good notion at least of the content of the originals He has rightly tried 'not to imitate but to recreate', and in the main his loose line of five or six stresses (but no doubt he is thinking rather in terms of rhythms than of stresses) is capable of recreating the feel of the episodes of the originals, while his lyric measures serve well enough for the choruses. There are occasional flatnesses, and not everyone will approve the colloquialisms that many translators of Greek and Latin poetry so often drop into these days; but the versions as a whole are sound and readable.

An interesting addition to the Penguin Classics is A. N. W. Saunders's translation[39] of the two pairs of speeches in which Demosthenes and Æschines, in 343 and 330 B.C., attacked each other with charges of political misconduct, and counter-attacked in defence of themselves. These are the speeches usually known in English as *On the Embassy*, in which Demosthenes arraigns the politician Æschines for malpractice on a mission to Philip of Macedon; the reply of Æschines; Æschines's speech *Against Ctesiphon*, in which Demosthenes is indirectly accused of having laid himself open to political corruption; and Demosthenes's retort, *De Corona*, a

---

[36] *Æschylus: 'Prometheus Bound'*, translated by James Scully and C. J. Herington. (The Greek Tragedy in New Translations.) O.U.P. pp. xiv + 118.

[37] *Euripides: 'Alcestis'*, translated by William Arrowsmith. (The Greek Tragedy in New Translations.) O.U.P. 1974. pp. xiv + 122.

[38] *Three Plays of Euripides: 'Alcestis', 'Medea', 'The Bacchae'*, translated by Paul Roche. New York: Norton. pp. xiv + 126.

[39] *Demosthenes and Æschines*, translated by A. N. W. Saunders. Introduction by T. T. B. Ryder. Penguin Books. pp. 336. 90p.

fascinating *apologia pro vita sua*. Saunders's translations convey the rhetorical powers of these two greatest of Greek orators without any loss of easy readability. From the greatest of the Greek to the greatest of the Roman orators. Michael Grant adds this year to the speeches of Cicero that he has translated for the Penguin Classics. His volume of Cicero's *Murder Trials*[40] contains the speeches in defence of Sextus Roscius of Ameria, of Aulus Cluentius Habitus, of Gaius Rabirius, and of King Deiotarus, together with a note on the *Pro Caelio* and the *Pro Milone*. These are accomplished translations which should appeal to readers of many kinds, and Grant has provided an interesting introduction on the prevalence of murder in the public life of Rome after the assassination in 133 B.C. of the tribune of the people Tiberius Sempronius Gracchus, and a number of appendixes which contribute helpfully to our understanding of the events with which the speeches are concerned.

Although Renaissance scholars will retain their regard for Sir John Harington's lively translation of Ariosto's *Orlando Furioso*, none of them will be so churlish as not to accept Barbara Reynolds's Penguin translation[41] as the work of a considerable scholar and a more than competent poet, as indeed she has shown herself to be in her earlier work on Dante. She has managed, with a skill obviously not as masterly as Byron's, but nevertheless extremely impressive, to make very effective use of the ottava rima stanza of an Italian original, and she has transmuted into her English version a substantial part of Ariosto's humour and irony and burlesque, as well as of his more serious writing. She has added to her translation an interesting and informative introduction on Ariosto and his works and purposes, together with helpful notes and an annotated index of the personages of the poem.

John Cairncross has produced competent and readable translations of three of Corneille's plays—*Le Cid, Cinna*, and *L'Illusion Comique*.[42] He has used blank verse very effectively to bring out both the power and the nobility of the heroic plays and the fantasy and the mock-heroics of *L'Illusion*. His volume may be recommended without reserve.

A number of the anthologies of the year ought perhaps to be noticed. *The Norton Anthology of Poetry: Revised*,[43] which since the death of Alexander W. Allison has been revised by a number of his coadjutors, is one of those vast collections which could emanate only from American academic circles. Presumably it is intended to provide American undergraduates with all that they need to know of English and American poetry. To say this is not to suggest that it is not a good anthology. It is excellent, but it will not serve the most important function of an anthology—to provide agreeable browsing in an armchair or in bed; it is very much too

---

[40] *Cicero: Murder Trials*, translated by Michael Grant. Penguin Books. pp. 368. 80p

[41] *Ludovico Ariosto: 'Orlando Furioso'*, translated, with an Introduction, by Barbara Reynolds. Penguin Books. pp. 827. £1.50.

[42] *Pierre Corneille: 'The Cid', 'Cinna', 'The Theatrical Illusion'*, translated and introduced by John Cairncross. Penguin Books. pp. 281. 75p.

[43] *The Norton Anthology of Poetry: Revised*, ed. by Alexander W. Allison *et al.* New York: Norton. pp. xlvii + 1344.

heavy for that. This collection was first published in 1970; it now appears in a revised edition. The revisers have paid special attention to recent poetry, and have represented more than thirty new twentieth-century poets, as well as (for the first time) some Canadian poets; they have increased the number of long poems, and there are now, they tell us, twice as many women poets as before. The volume covers poetry from pre-Chaucerian times to the present day, regrettably providing footnote translations of the medieval lyrics it includes and unnecessarily copious annotations for other early works. The standards by which the compilers have been guided may perhaps be gauged from the fact that Emily Dickinson is represented by forty-three lyrics, Shakespeare by thirty-four.

Douglas Gray's *Selection of Religious Lyrics*[44] is an excellent anthology of medieval religious verse. Gray has drawn his material from a large number of manuscripts, especially in the British Museum and several Oxford and Cambridge libraries, above all the Bodleian. He has arranged his ninety-odd lyrics under such headings as 'The Fall', 'The Passion of Christ', 'The Triumph of Christ', 'Mysteries of the Faith', and 'Christian Hope and Joy', and he has convincingly borne out his belief that religious lyric verse is 'one of England's most remarkable contributions to medieval literature'. His scholarly notes contribute much to the value of his collection.

The Penguin Book of English Pastoral Verse,[45] edited by John Barrell and John Bull, is an admirable gathering of 'bucolic' poetry, and is certainly one of the best of the Penguin anthologies. It opens with Barnabe Googe's pleasant third 'egloge', passages from Spenser, Sidney, and Drayton, and a number of poems from that most agreeable of Elizabethan anthologies, *Englands Helicon*, and comes down to Hopkins, Hardy, and Yeats. Presumably the editors had to have a reasonably clear *terminus post quem*, and for that reason omitted some fine pastoral verse from, for example, the medieval drama or from such poets as Henryson; and no doubt they considered, but rejected on the grounds that he is seldom freshly and sustainedly rural, Alexander Barclay, who may fairly be regarded as having introduced (if scarcely acclimatized) the classical pastoral convention into England; but it is a little disappointing to come upon an anthology of English pastoral verse which does not contain the whole of our three greatest pastoral elegies, *Lycidas*, *Adonais*, and *Thyrsis*, only the last of which is represented in an excerpt; and among the extracts from pastoral drama Allan Ramsay's *The Gentle Shepherd* ought to have found a place. However, Barrell and Bull have cast their net reasonably widely, and it is pleasant to find in their volume burlesques, like the Tuesday eclogue from Gay's *Shepherd's Week*, and a number of 'anti-pastoral' passages from such poets as Stephen Duck, Crabbe, and Clare.

The volume entitled *Later English Broadside Ballads*[46] is edited by John Holloway and Joan Black. This collection, drawn from the eighteenth

[44] *A Selection of Religious Lyrics*, ed. with an Introduction, Notes, and Glossary by Douglas Gray. O.U.P. pp. xxii + 174.
[45] *The Penguin Book of English Pastoral Verse*, ed. by John Barrell and John Bull. Allen Lane, 1974. pp. xx + 539.
[46] *Later English Broadside Ballads*, ed. by John Holloway and Joan Black. Routledge & Kegan Paul. pp. vi + 296. £6.50.

and early nineteenth centuries, contains 127 ballads which, as the blurb
reminds us, recall very entertainingly 'the bawdy, anarchic sub-culture of
England before the Industrial Revolution'.

A few titles will suggest the
kind of verse to expect: 'The Jolly Lad's Trip to Botany Bay', 'Joan's
Enquiry after a Cuckold's Cap', 'Britannia's Lamentation on the Devasta-
tion War', 'The Flying Highwayman', and 'Little Joe, the Chimney
Sweeper'. The ballads are reprinted from contemporary or near-contem-
porary broadsides in the Madden Collection in Cambridge, and the often
very expressive head and tail blocks of the originals accompany the reprints.
The editors provide a helpful historical and critical introduction and a
select bibliography. This is one of four projected volumes of English
traditional verse which will admirably supplement two volumes noticed in
past issues of *YW*, and both edited by James Reeves, *The Idiom of the
People* (1958) and *The Everlasting Circle* (1960).

The Martial Muse,[47] edited by Alan Bold, is an intelligently compiled
anthology about war and the background of war. Opening with a passage
from John Barbour's *Brus*, it comes down to a number of poets who wrote
about their experiences in or their feelings about the second world war—
Henry Reed, Dylan Thomas, Keith Douglas, Sidney Keyes, Thom Gunn,
and several of their contemporaries. In between come dozens of our poets
who have lived in stirring times: Chaucer, Shakespeare, Donne, Milton,
Wordsworth, Tennyson, Yeats and Wilfred Owen, to name only a few.
Bold's long introduction is an interesting critical survey of this genre of
writing in English literature.

Faber continue their admirable practice of bringing *The Faber Book of
Twentieth-Century Verse*[48] up to date every few years. In the third
edition, which like its predecessor is compiled by John Heath-Stubbs and
David Wright, the selection of 1965 has been revised to some degree, and
about a score of new poets have been given a place. These include a
number of poets who have in the last ten or twelve years established their
right to inclusion, such as Seamus Heaney, Richard Murphy, Tony Harrison, Tom Pickard, Geoffrey Hill, and Gavin Bantock.

The most delightful anthology of the year is James Sutherland's *Oxford
Book of Literary Anecdotes*.[49] In 350-odd pages, Sutherland has brought
together about 500 anecdotes, both grave and gay, about English writers
from Caedmon and Bede down to P. G. Wodehouse, T. S. Eliot, and Dylan
Thomas. It would be difficult to think of many 'obvious' authors who are
not represented, although Sir Thomas More, and perhaps Thomas Fuller,
are among the more surprising omissions; however Sutherland has included,
and justly included, many who would not immediately spring to mind as
potential subjects of lively anecdotes: William Tyndale, Eustace Budgell,
Joseph Ritson, George Croley, Martin Farquhar Tupper, and F. S. Boas, to
name a few. Probably every reader will miss some of his favourite literary
anecdotes, and, like the present reader, tax his memory in an attempt to

[47] *The Martial Muse: Seven Centuries of War Poetry*, selected and introduced by
Alan Bold. Wheaton & Co. (Pergamon Press). pp. 227. £1.35.
[48] *The Faber Book of Twentieth-Century Verse*. Third edition. Ed. by John
Heath-Stubbs and David Wright. Faber. pp. 347. £5.50. pb £1.50.
[49] *The Oxford Book of Literary Anecdotes*, ed. by James Sutherland. O.U.P.
pp. xii + 382. £4.25.

recall something like the words of the original. Perhaps Thomas Ellwood the Quaker's words to Milton when he had just read the manuscript of *Paradise Lost*, 'Friend, thou has said much here of Paradise lost. What hast thou to say of Paradise found?' Whereupon, Ellwood tells us, the poet fell into a profound reverie. Or Margaret Gillies's story of how, when she had completed the charming miniature of Wordsworth which now hangs in Rydal Mount and was at the door, where the chaise was waiting for her, she heard the poet at the top of the stairs say to his wife in his booming voice, 'Do you think, my dear, that it would be considered indecorous or profligate in me to offer Miss Gillies a kiss at parting?' Or, from Sir Charles Tennyson, the only words that his grandfather the poet spoke to the young woman who had with difficulty secured the place next to him at dinner to delight in his conversation: 'Mutton should be cut in wedges.' But whatever omissions he may regret, every reader will find hours of agreeable browsing in this collection.

Addendum

Since this chapter was sent to press, the new edition of *Roget's Thesaurus* (see footnote 7) has come to hand. This is essentially Robert A. Dutch's thoroughly revised and augmented edition of 1962, but the present impression contains a good many corrections and additions in the provision of which Dutch has been assisted by Norman Davis and Margaret Masterman.

II

English Language

BARBARA M. H. STRANG and JOHN PELLOWE

This chapter is divided into two sections. The first, by Barbara Strang, deals broadly speaking, with historical studies, including the history of linguistics, but it covers all lexicographical material, whether historical or not, as well as linguistic studies bearing upon the literary use of English. The second, by John Pellowe, deals broadly speaking with descriptive studies, but includes all general bibliographical material and all publications in cognate fields of enquiry relevant to the English scholar.

Section I

(a) *Introductory*
I am not yet able to break with the custom of reflecting unhappily both upon the state of historical linguistic studies and on the difficulties of getting hold of what is published in the field (cf. *YW* 55, p. 34). I am able to mention about a hundred and thirty items, but of some it has to be said that I have not been able to see them, though they are too important to omit. These items cluster in a peculiar way: the history of linguistics provides nearly a third of the material; vocabulary studies come a close second; stylistics, grammar (morphology and syntax), orthography and phonology all together furnish another third, and there are only a handful of items under other heads. It is true that the counting of items does not tell the whole story, since items are of differing weight and there are major long-term enterprises which do not necessarily yield even a light crop in a single year; but the subject is at heart not flourishing. An indication is given by three Research in Progress lists. Alan K. Brown ('Old English Research in Progress 1974-5', *NM*) in a six-page listing can muster only a dozen items which, on an elastic definition, can be regarded as linguistic; Rossell Hope Robbins ('Middle English Research in Progress 1974-5', *NM*) musters two; and Thomas A. Kirby ('Chaucer Research in Progress 1974-5', *NM*) rises to three. These are not exhaustive lists, but compared with the literary projects they indicate an alarmingly low rate of activity. How different things can be is shown by Hewes's bibliography of works dealing with the origins of language[1]. He has combed the literature of many disciplines up to 1972 and produced a list of some 11,000 items. This is an exceptionally useful piece of work and will save future scholars untold time.

[1] *Language Origins. A Bibliography*, by Gordon Winant Hewes. Second revised and enlarged edition. Mouton. In two volumes. pp. xvi + 407, 408-890. Dfl. 225.

In what follows the material is subdivided as tidily as the subject-matter permits under the following heads: (b) general; (c) orthography/phonology; (d) grammar; (e) lexical studies (including names); (f) the literary use of language; (g) history of linguistics (including general surveys of the work of twentieth-century linguists). Within each division the order is, so far as is appropriate, first, general material, second, other material in approximate chronological order.

(b) *General*

The more general of the two works belonging here cannot, unfortunately, be commended. Williams[2] has written a students' history based on excellent academic and pedagogic principles, but repeatedly marred by misconceptions, ignorance and misleading statements. That highly productive scholar Martyn Wakelin[3] has made a book out of his doctoral dissertation, though from the ease and simplicity of his style this could hardly have been deduced. The title—*Language and History in Cornwall*—is somewhat misleading, since this is a study of the English spoken in Cornwall, and Cornish is hardly discussed except as a factor in the formation of that English. There is a brief study of the history of dialectology (effectively up to the early '60s when the author was working on the Survey of English dialects (*SED*), and on his dissertation), together with a study of present-day Cornwall, and of its history, with particular reference to the infusion of Anglo-Saxon elements. The surviving monuments of Cornish are discussed, and the dialect is studied on the basis of *SED* material. There is more on phonology than on morphology or lexis (which, indeed, is discussed only in relation to Cornish loans). The author is aware that his subject cannot be definitively treated until there has been a proper study of Cornish place names, and this deficiency is painfully obvious. But of what can be effectively discussed he has given a highly readable account.

There are admirable historical sections in two wide-ranging works which can more appropriately be considered in Section 2—a second edition of Bolinger's *Aspects of Language*; and *Language as a Human Problem*, edited by Haugen and (M.) Bloomfield.

(c) *Orthography/Phonology*

Some historical linguists intermingle specific studies with consideration of general principles, and tend to favour the latter in their titles. O. W. Robinson argues ('Concreteness in Phonology: Some Historical Arguments', *Leuvense Bijdragen*) that historical linguistics can give insight into the psychological validity of proposed models of grammar and that it suggests human beings are data-bound and concrete in their grammar-building, notably in phonology; his examples are drawn from German. H. Melchert (' "Exceptions" to Exceptionless Sound Laws', *Lingua* Vol. 35) shows that the exceptionlessness-hypothesis has a strong and a weak form, neither of which can be attributed to the Neogrammarians; and F. van Coetsem is

---

[2] *Origins of the English Language. A Social and Linguistic History*, by Joseph M. Williams. The Free Press. pp. x + 422.

[3] *Language and history in Cornwall*, by Martyn F. Wakelin. Leicester University Press. pp. 240. £10.

concerned with related issues in 'Generality in Language Change. The Case of the Old High German Vowel Shift' (*Lingua* Vol. 35). More specific and more centred on our field is Barrack's study of phonology from Proto-Germanic to Old English (West-Saxon).[4] This is a learned book, difficult to read; its weakness is that it seems more steeped in Campbell than in the feel of the Old English texts (a comment particularly relevant to the discussion of 'free variation', pp. 21 ff., and of unstressed V > ə, p. 94—a change dated far too late); but it can rise above Campbell, as the history of *cynn*, p. 105, indicates and that is no mean achievement.

I am appalled to discover that I previously failed to mention a work of the first importance, Page's study of English runes, a much-needed and definitive work.[5] Roger Lass and John M. Anderson keep up their high rate of production with a book on Old English phonology.[6] The book embodies their thinking between 1970 and 1974 and to that degree is already somewhat outgrown. Its special direction is provided by a concern to find out which pre-Old English sound-changes can be recovered as synchronic rules of Old English.

Of the next two studies I have seen only abstracts in the useful *Anglia* Supplement *English and American Studies in German* edited by Werner Habicht. The 1975 issue records Jürgen Giffhorn's study of the Old English short diphthongs, re-asserting the traditional over the monophthongal view,[7] and Blumbach's study of labials and 'tectals', designed to be the first of a series of investigations of spiranticization and de-spiranticization in Old English.[8] Richard M. Hogg ('The Place of Analogy', *Neophilologus*) applies his arguments specifically to one aspect of this problem, namely the occurrence of *sloh/slog* forms as singular partners of *slogon* by Verner's Law; in particular he shows Kiparsky to be in error. Dietz investigates a related topic ('Zur Phonologie der mittelenglischen Tektalspiranten: Die südmittelenglischen Reflexe von *Æe(o)ʒ/h*'),[9] which interprets the graphemes in relation to the sound-values, the phonetic realizations in relation to the phonemic system.

A particularly important study of written Middle English (Angus McIntosh's 'Scribal Profiles from Middle English Texts', *NM*.) was noticed in *YW* 55. p. 37 along with a related article which appeared in 1974. Paul Arakelian shows that the *Pageant of the Birth, Life and Death of Richard Beauchamp Earl of Warwick*, written in the 1490's, has a system of punc-

[4] *A Diachronic Phonology from Proto-Germanic to Old English Stressing West-Saxon Conditions.* by Charles Michael Barrack. *Janua Linguarum Series Practica*, 144. Mouton. pp. 136. Dfl.40.
[5] *An Introduction to English Runes*, by R. I. Page. Methuen. 1973. pp. xvi + 237. £4.65.
[6] *Old English Phonology*. by Roger Lass and John M. Anderson. Cambridge Studies in Linguistics 14. Cambridge University Press. pp. xvi + 326. NP.
[7] *Phonologische Untersuchungen zu den altenglischen Kurzdiphthongen*, by Jürgen Giffhorn. Wilhelm Fink Verlag. 1974. pp. 326. DM.56.
[8] *Studien zur Spirantisierung und Entspirantisierung altenglischer Konsonanten. I Labiale und Tektale*, by Wolfgang Blumbach. Dissertation Göttingen. 1974. pp. xiv + 355. NP.
[9] In *Studien zur englischen und amerikanischen Sprache und Literatur. Festschrift für Helmut Papajewski, herausgegeben von Paul G. Buchloh, Inge Leimberg und Herbert Rauter.* Karl Wahlotz Verlag. pp. 11–36.

tuation which on close study proves to be a carefully devised method of ordering and clarifying clauses, embeddings and sentences; the slash, perioslash (·/), period, periocomma (:) and comma. Each has a distinct function of delimitation for the guidance of someone reading aloud 'Punctuation in a Late Middle English Manuscript', (*NM*). P. Beade studies 'Vowel Length in Middle English: Continuity and Change' (*Leuvense Bijdragen*). He identifies a movement since early Old English to make vowel length predictable, a movement which never achieves the status of a rule because literate societies are too unstable to permit such regularity of development. This is over-simplification, though the observation that 'regular sound changes have an annoying tendency to date back to prehistoric times' is well-founded. Lois K. Smedick finds for Middle English, as Kuhn had done for Old English, that typical sentence-final rhythms are natural to the language and not due to *cursus* ('Cursus in Middle English: *A talkyng of þe love of God* reconsidered', *MIS*). This is probably the best place to mention Norman T. Gates's 'Orthographical Rhyme Forms in the Works of Samuel Rowlands' (*NM*), since the principal drift of the study is to show that English was still extremely fluid (i.e. rich in variant forms) in the closing years of the sixteenth century, but that standardization was advancing thirty years later. This perhaps goes rather beyond what the evidence from eye-rhymes in Rowlands (c.1570–c.1630) would warrant, but the abundance of eccentric and inconsistent spellings (over 300) designed to produce eye-rhymes is itself of interest. Highly welcome is Alan Ward's admirable translation of a work of high value sixty years after its first appearance in German—Ekwall's history of modern English sounds and morphology. I place it here because, in accordance with the tradition it belongs to, it devotes considerably more space to phonology than to morphology. The work has a double interest; first for its terse presentation of the essentials in remarkably brief compass, and secondly for remarks which are themselves part of the history of the language (on what the distinctive pronunciations of poetry and the stage used to be, for instance). The translator, skilful and self-effacing, has treated the text with perfect discretion, but has modernized effectively by the addition of supplementary material.[10]

(d) *Grammar*

Wolff has written a lucid introduction to diachronic English morphology.[11] He explains the basic concepts of morphology, various theories of linguistic change, the pre-history and morphematic stucture of Old English morphology and word-formation; the Middle English and Early Modern English chapters devote attention to Romance as well as Germanic materials, while the chapter on 'New English' adds neo-Latin. There is finally a review of the overall change in the system and a full bibliography. Each chapter is followed by exercises, for which a key is provided at the end.

    [10] *A History of Modern English Sounds and Morphology*, by Eilert Ekwall. Translated and edited by Alan Ward. Blackwell's English Language Series. General Editor: Eric Dobson. Basil Blackwell. pp. xvi + 134. £4.50.
    [11] *Grundzüge der diachronischen Morphologie des Englischen*, by Dieter Wolff. Anglistische Arbeitshefte, 7. Herausgegeben von Herbert E. Brekle und Wolfgang Kühlwein. Max Niemeyer Verlag. pp. x + 102. DM. 10.80.

Aspect has become fashionable. I failed to mention in 1974 a collection of 15 papers edited by Schopf.[12] The papers, by various hands and in various languages, originate at dates from 1925 to 1969, and are partly descriptive, partly historical. They are, however, well chosen; the older contributions are by no means the least valuable. Unfortunately, I have not seen a historical and descriptive study published in 1975 on one of the English aspects,[13] and I have seen only an abstract of a synchronic-diachronic dissertation on the same subject but under a different label.[14] Turning to the chronological sequence, we have a study from D. G. Miller arguing against Lehmann's view that Indo-European was an OV language, and presenting evidence that the Indo-European languages were probably at first VSO which became SOV and were in process of becoming SVO when records begin ('Indo-European: VSO, SOV, SVO, or all three?' *Lingua* Vol. 37). Paul J. Hopper has produced a study of the syntax of the simple sentence in Proto-Germanic[15] which I have not seen. J. M. Penhallurick ('Old English Case and Grammatical Theory', *Lingua* Vol. 36) points out that the conventional understanding of the term 'case-government' does not account for Old English, in which the same verb in the same relations may 'govern' various cases. A possible, but uneconomical, solution would be to regard each verb capable of 'governing' more than one case as not unitary but a set of homonyms (as on occasion is necessary, e.g. in the instance of *hieran*). Both generativists and case-grammarians have made a poor showing in this area, but the author promises a further article explaining the actual distribution of Old English case-forms on a monosemic basis.

I must make good my failure to mention in the appropriate year an excellent study of the word-formation and syntax of the Parker Chronicle.[16] Such studies of individual texts are essential to progress in the general understanding of Old English syntax; the Parker Chronicle is an obvious starting-point, and Ann Shannon's earlier study left a good deal to be desired ('A Descriptive Syntax of the Parker Manuscript of the Anglo-Saxon Chronicle from 734 to 891', The Hague, 1964). Sprockel writes clearly and is steeped in the language of the relevant text -a qualification far more important than the ability to count. This is a useful and important work. I have not seen Johnson's transformational analysis of the syntax of Ælfric's *Lives of the Saints*.[17] Modern readers are often halted by the problem of interpreting the apparently simple Old English particle *þa*, 'then, when.' Robert Foster pro-

---

[12] *Der englische Aspekt*, herausgegeben von Alfred Schopt. Wege der Forschung Band CCLII. 1974. Wissenschaftliche Buchgesellschaft, Darmstadt. pp. vi + 412. DM. 67.
[13] *The Progressive in English*, by Johannes Scheffer. North-Holland Linguistic Series, edited by S. C. Dik and J. C. Kooij. Vol. 15. pp. xii + 398. Dfl. 45.
[14] *Synchron-diachrone Untersuchungen zur 'Expanded Form' im Englischen. Eine struktural funktionale Analyse*. Linguistische Reihe, 19. Max Bueber Verlag. 1974. pp. 196. DM.19.
[15] *The Syntax of the Simple Sentence in Proto-Germanic*, by Paul J. Hopper. Janua Linguarum Series Practica, 143. Mouton. pp. 104. Dfl. 38.
[16] *The Language of the Parker Chronicle*. Volume II. *Word-formation and Syntax*, by C. Sprockel. Martinus Nijhoff. 1973. pp. xiv + 284, Dfl. 45.
[17] *A Transformational Analysis of the Syntax of Ælfric's 'Lives of Saints'*, by J. A. Johnson. Janua Linguarum Series Practica, 212. Mouton. pp. 112. Dfl. 36.

vides a by-pass by demonstrating that in many doubtful instances *þa* is used to head each of a string of clauses, usually in conjunction with another adverb. He interprets *þa* in such contexts as a marker and co-ordinator of virtually independent units, a marker of sequentiality, probably of colloquial origin, carrying little or no information about the functional relationship between clauses ('The use of *þa* in Old and Middle English Narrative', *NM*).

For Dekeyser's study of concord in nineteenth-century British English see *YW*. 55, p. 39.

(e) *Vocabulary*

As always, this division flourishes. Y. Malkiel ('Etymology and Modern Linguistics', *Lingua* Vol. 36) pleads for a return to Whitney's position that etymology is the foundation of linguistic science. My own metaphor would be that it is the fine flower, dependent on a root-system of historical phonology; but I have no doubt that it has withered for lack of sustenance. Malkiel's brilliant essay is a splendid example of what can still be produced by those whose roots are strong enough. Dyen has collected in one volume his own papers produced during a quarter-century of work on lexicostatistics;[18] the book shows, of course, immense learning and considerable linguistic subtlety, but is sometimes let down by elementary statistical errors.

R. I. Page ostensibly reviews the Toronto plan for an Old English dictionary, but his learned and witty article takes wing as an independent discussion of how to make an Old English dictionary, of some material that needs to be included, and of the problems arising (' "The proper toil of artless industry": Toronto's Plan for an Old English Dictionary', *N&Q*). Alan S. C. Ross ('O.E. "LEOHT" 'WORLD' ', *N&Q*) points out that the use under discussion is not calqued on Latin or Greek, but involves a semantic change parallelled in many languages in the same or corresponding roots. The third section of an admirable article by Alan K. Brown ('Bede, a Hisperic Etymology, and Early Sea Poetry', *MS*) discusses Bede's *dodrans* in the context of its rendering by vernacular glosses from the eighth century as *egur*, *eagor*, and tries to define that word, on the evidence of all its contexts, more precisely than has been possible hitherto. He sees it as the antecedent of modern *eagre*, 'tidal bore,' and derives it from *ea + gor*, a second element taken as related to *gyru*, 'overflowed land.' Spencer Cosmos argues against the usual view of *limwæstm*, 'bodily size', and for a revival of Bouterwerk's view that it is a periphrastic compound for 'limbs' ('Old English 'LIMWÆSTM' 'Christ and Satan' 129', *N&Q*). Marjorie Ehrhart ('Tempter as Teacher', *Neophilologus* Vol. 59) shows that a series of words in Genesis B having to do with teaching, discipleship, are Old Saxon usages rendered by their cognates, not necessarily by their translations.

Valerie Krishna studies the supra-literal meaning of archaic synonyms for 'man, knight' in the alliterative Morte Arthure, and concludes that such words (e.g. *berne*, *freke*, *hathel*) probably do less to idealize their referents than the everyday counterparts *knight*, *lord* ('Archaic Nouns in the "Al-

[18] *Linguistic Subgrouping and Lexicostatistics*, by Isidore Dyen. Janua Linguarum Series Minor, 175. Mouton. pp. 252. Dfl. 64.

literative Morte Arthure" ', *NM*). Klaus Bitterling (' "Till" "While" in Barbour's "Bruce" ', *NM*) adds some examples of this usage, while David Yerkes (' "Sir Gawain and the Green Knight" 211: "Grayn" ', *N&Q*) shows that of the two possible meanings of this word one, sc. 'spike', can be parallelled in a hitherto unnoticed example in a Percy Folio poem. Bitterling also proves the existence of the sense 'dormouse' for Middle English *glouberd*, for which *M.E.D.* has only the meaning 'glow-worm', which in one of its two quotations is impossible ('Middle English "GLOU-BERD" 'A DORMOUSE' ', *N&Q*). Alan S. C. Ross, developing further his interest in alliterative word-pairs in Middle English, seeks to unravel the native and borrowed elements in such words as *rave, reve, rove* ('wander'), *ravel* (' "Run and Reve" and Similar Alliterative Phrases', *NM*).

There is the usual crop of revisions to *O.E.D.*, now usefully grouped by the *N&Q* editors in two seasonal instalments. Roland Hall contributes in a number of fields which have long concerned him ('Cudworth and his Contemporaries: New Words and Antedatings', *N&Q*; 'More Antedatings from Locke's "Essay"', *ib*; 'John Locke's New Words and Uses', *ib*; 'Locke on Money: More Antedatings', *ib*). Four other contributors have been active in this area: L. Baier ('Antedatings and Additions for *O.E.D.*' *ib*); Philip Hines Jr. (' "Barathrum" Antedated in Fielding-Young 1742 and Postdated in Randolph 1651', *ib*); Ronald B. Hatch (' "Philosophy and "Science" ', *ib* — an explication of O.E.D. *Philosophy* sense 5); Norman Vance (' "Anything-arianism" ', *ib* — an antedating sense-addition).

A substantial article by W. B. Lockwood traces the history, etymology and applications of some bird-names, notably *puffin, smew, pochard* and related items; it is an admirable marriage of two distinct areas of expertise ('Some British Bird Names', *TPS* 1974 [1975]). Anthony Stanforth's researches into German loans in recent English have produced two valuable articles. The more general is 'Lexical borrowing from German since 1933 as reflected in the British press' (*MLR* Vol. 69); more specific, and dealing with a particularly interesting phenomenon, is 'Schein und Ruckentlchnungen aus dem deutschen im Britisch-Englischen: zur Entlehnungsgeschichte von *BLITZKRIEG* und *BLITZ*' (*ZDL*. Beihefte. Neue Folge No. 13 der *Zeitschrift für Mundartforschung*). In the normally useful *Que Sais Je*? series Forgue has produced a popular account of American English words;[19] there is room for such a volume in English as well as French, but unfortunately this work is scrappy and inaccurate.

There is has been a good deal of lexicographical activity. Major continuing projects are *M.E.D.* which in 1975 produced the first three parts of *M*;[20] *The Dictionary of the Older Scottish Tongue* — the first part of *O*;[21] *The Scottish National Dictionary* — two parts of *W-Y*.[22]

[19] *Les Mots Americains*, by Guy Jean Forgue. Que Sais-Je? 1976. pp. 128. NP.

[20] *Middle English Dictionary*, edited by Hans Kurath and Sherman M. Kuhn. University of Michigan Press. M1(M–Manere) pp. 128; M2(Manere–Medle) pp. 129–256; M3(Medle–Metal) pp. 257–384. NP.

[21] *A Dictionary of the Older Scottish Tongue*. Founded on the collections of Sir William A. Craigie. Edited by A. J. Aitken (with assistants). University of Chicago Press. Part XXVII (O–Ordinance) pp. 120. NP.

[22] *The Scottish National Dictionary*, edited by William Grant (1929–46) and David D. Murison (1946–76). Volume X Part I (W–WHEEGIL), pp. 128; and Part II

There are four modern dictionaries—the first volume of the *Oxford Dictionary of Current Idiomatic English*;[23] Freeman's *A Concise Dictionary of English Idioms*;[24] Beeton and Dorner's *A Dictionary of English Usage in Southern Africa*[25] and Meyer's dictionary of verb-preposition phrases[26] (the last of which I have not seen). The first is chiefly addressed to the foreign learner, but will also be helpful to the English scholar, particularly as each use is illustrated by quotation. The second is a substantial revision of a familiar work, addressed to both foreign and native speakers; the illustrative examples are fabricated, and explanation, though promised, is minimal. This is a practical rather than scholarly book. So, in a sense, is the Dictionary of South African English. With the laudable intention of keeping South African English internationally intelligible it condemns local usage as error; it nevertheless serves some academic purpose by indicating what 'errors' exist.

There are unfortunately no *E.P.N.S.* volumes to record. Gillis Kristensson has articles on certain Cheshire and Gloucestershire names. The first ('The Place Name Carrington [Cheshire]', *N&Q*) is able to propose a new and convincing etymology, taking the first element as from a derivative of *cæran*, 'turn, bend'; this achievement is all the more remarkable as so much has been published on Cheshire names in recent years. The second deals with Great Boulsdon and Culkerton, where it is not a question of offering a new etymology but of showing that one of the existing candidates is more convincing than had appeared ('Notes on Two Gloucestershire Place-Names', *SN* Vol. XLVII). The University of Laval continues the series inaugurated in 1969 with a useful work on place-names and language-contact which I failed to notice in the appropriate year;[27] and with an inflated dictionary of terms 'useful in place-name study' in the current year.[28]

(f) *Literary uses of English*
This too is a very active area, and one in which boundaries are difficult to define. Without claiming to be exhaustive, I would like to discuss a dozen items.

(WHEEGLE-YAT), pp. 129-240. Edinburgh. The Scottish National Dictionary Association Ltd. NP.

[23] *Oxford Dictionary of Current Idiomatic English*, by A. P. Cowie and R. Mackin. Volume 1: Verbs with Prepositions and Particles. Oxford University Press. pp. lxxxii + 396. NP.

[24] *A Concise Dictionary of English Idioms*, by William Freeman. 3rd edition revised and edited by Brian Phythian, 1973; reprinted 1975. Hodder and Stoughton. pp. 216. Boards £1.45. pb £1.05.

[25] *A Dictionary of English Usage in Southern Africa*, by D. R. Beeton and Helen Dorner. Oxford University Press. pp. xx + 196. £5.75.

[26] *The Two-Word Verb. A Dictionary of the Verb-Preposition Phrases in American English*, by George A. Meyer. Janua Linguarum Series Didactica, 19. Mouton. pp. 270. Dfl. 75.

[27] *Les Noms de Lieux et le contact des langues. Place Names and Language Contact*, edited by Henri Dorion with the assistance of Christian Morissonneau. Les Presses de l'Université Laval. 1972. pp. x + 374, end-maps. NP.

[28] *Lexique des termes utiles à l'étude des noms de lieux*, by Henri Dorion and Jean Poirier. Chronoma, 6. Les Presses de l'Université Laval. pp. 162.

A collection of papers by I. A. Richards should have been noticed last year.[29] The papers are from various dates, and in varying degrees linguistic (unfortunately those which are most linguistic are slipshod in presentation), but all show the originality, freshness and inventiveness which have characterised their author throughout his long creative life. An omission of even longer standing is Hendricks's volume of essays on semiolinguistics and verbal art.[30] He defines semiolinguistics as that branch of semiotics concerned solely with human communication by means of verbal signs, as differing from linguistics in taking as its basic unit not the sentence but the text, and having as its primary object the study of the compositional principles underlying texts. The seven essays in the volume were written between 1966 and 1971 and have been previously published. Though not designed as a unity they have a clear unity of thought, and are full of wise and original ideas. Ingrid Hantsch's *Semiotik des Erzählens*[31] has a narrower and less coherent theme than its title suggests. It deals with the satirical novel of the twentieth century, defined in such a way as not to afford a corpus of strong natural identity; it offers many interesting local insights without achieving organic unity. Nils Erik Enkvist edits a volume of four papers on text, style and syntax.[32] The first, by Erik Andersson, argues that the traditional distinction between clause and sentence should be abolished; the second, by the editor, argues for a broad sense of *context* in stylistics; the third, by Auli Hakulinen, defeats the non-reader of Finnish, who may learn from an abstract that it deals with coreferential noun phrases in complex sentences in Finnish; and the fourth by Viljo Kohonen, deals with problems of sample length in the study of major word-order patterns in Old and early Middle English narrative prose. For Roger Fowler's *Style and Structure in Language* see *YW*. 55, p. 45. There are two works in a new series, *North-Holland Studies in Theoretical Poetics*[33] which I have not seen.

More specific studies begin with E. G. Stanley's 'Verbal Stress in Old English Verse' (*Anglia* Band 93), which deals fully with two problems, that of the alliterating finite verb (*Beowulf* 2717b), and that of metrically unstressed infinitives. This close study, and the comparison with Old Saxon, reinforce the view 'that the Anglo-Saxons handled their inherited alliterative metre with peculiar precision'. There are two studies of Middle English literary uses of periphrastic verbs. Yoshio Terasawa ('Some Notes

[29] *Poetries. Their media and ends*, by I. A. Richards. Edited by Trevor Eaton. De Proprietatibus Litterarum Series Major, 30. Mouton. 1974. pp. xvi + 256. Dfl. 59.
[30] *Essays on Semiolinguistics and Verbal Art*, by William O. Hendricks. Approaches to Semiotics, 37. Edited by Thomas A. Sebeok. Mouton. 1973. pp. 210. Dfl. 42.
[31] *Semiotik des Erzählens*, by Ingrid Hantsch. Münchener Universitäts—Schriften. Philosophische Fakultät. Texte und Untersuchungen zur Englischen Philologie herausgegeben von Helmut Gneuss und Wolfgang Weiss. Band 5. Wilhelm Fink Verlag. pp. vi + 402. NP.
[32] *Reports on Text Linguistics. Four Papers on Text, Style and Syntax*, edited by Nils Erik Enkvist. Meddelanden Från Stiftelsens for Åbo Akaderni Forskningsinstitut. Nr. 1. 1974. pp. 117. NP.
[33] *The Organization of Prose and its Effects on Memory*, by Bonnie J. F. Meyer. North-Holland Series in Theoretical Poetics. pp. xviii + 249. Dfl. 35. *Pragmatics of Language and Literature*, edited by Teun A. van Dijk. North-Holland Series in Theoretical Poetics. pp. x + 236. Dfl. 45.

on ME *gan* Periphrasis', *Poetica* Vol. 1, 1974) studies the origin of the *gan* -periphrasis and its distribution in a range of works, mostly romances of the thirteenth to fifteenth centuries. The form is commoner in the north, and is almost confined to verse in the sample, being especially common in rhymed verse; it is confined to declarative sentences, and can have a structural function in the narrative. A further study will investigate *gan* as a criterion of authorship. Matsuji Tajima reviews a related issue, 'The Gawain-Poet's Use of "Con" as a Periphrastic Auxiliary' (*NM*). This northern feature appears in the rhymed lines of *Pearl* and *Gawain* but is rare in the unrhymed lines of *Gawain, Purity* and *Patience*. Only *Pearl* has it as an auxiliary of the present. Almost invariably it is used to place the infinitive in rhyming position, and its frequency in *Pearl* is attributable to the difficulty of the rhyme-scheme. Jack Conner sets out to demonstrate the unity of English metre from Chaucer to Wyatt,[34] and has many interesting and useful things to say. Sadly, as he shows no knowledge of the best work on English rhythm and metre, some of it is beside the point.

In subject-matter we then leap several centuries and arrive at Eliopoulos's study of Beckett's dramatic language.[35] The first 58 pages are concerned with discussion of preliminaries; then eleven characteristics of style (not without overlap) are listed and exemplified in pp. 59 to 101, and the whole is summarized, reiterated and concluded in pp. 102–114 (followed by a *Bibliography* and *Index*). The book might almost give the impression that it is hard to find enough to say about Beckett's dramatic language (including 'absence of language' as a 'characteristic of style').

(g) *History of linguistics*

The abundance of this section is increased, but only marginally, by some decisions I have taken about the placement of items. I consider first the works which are primarily studies, and later those that are primarily publications of the text of earlier linguistic work.

Though I have not seen it, it is clear that Sebeok's two-volume *Historiography of Linguistics*[36] is of the first importance, covering not only the usual tradition from Panini to structuralism, but giving accounts, by specialist hands, of other traditions of linguistic scholarship, especially in the Middle and Far East, and incorporating an exhaustive bibliography of the history of linguistics. Emma Vorlat has produced a re-working of her well-known doctoral dissertation, studying a much larger selection of English grammars published between 1586 and 1737, but narrowing the focus of interest to part of speech theory.[37] Unfortunately many opportunities for improvement have been missed. M. S. Hetherington offers a

[34] *English Prosody from Chaucer to Wyatt*, by Jack Connor. Janua Linguarum Series Practica, 193. Mouton. 1974 in text, but listed as 1975. pp. 104. Dfl. 20.
[35] *Samuel Beckett's Dramatic Language*, by James Eliopoulos. De Proprietatis Litterarum, series Practica, 100. Mouton. pp. 132. Dfl. 28.
[36] *Historiography of Linguistics*, edited by Hans Aarsleff, Robert Austerlitz, Dell Hymes, Edward Stankiewiez. Current Trends in Linguistics, Volume 13, in two parts. Edited by Thomas A. Sebeok assisted by Donna Jean Umiker-Sebeok. Mouton. pp. xviii + 1518. Dfl. 420.
[37] *The Development of English Grammatical Theory 1586-1737. With special reference to the theory of parts of speech*, by Emma Vorlat. Leuven University Press. pp. xiv, 478. Guilders 72.80.

sympathetic study of Sir Simonds D'Ewes, whose unpublished Anglo-Saxon dictionary was the immediate predecessor of Somner ('Sir Simonds D'Ewes and Method in Old English Lexicography', *TSLL* Vol. XVII). James Knowlson makes an approach towards treating properly, i.e. on the basis of evidence from all European cultures, the subject of universal language schemes after the decline of Latin as an international language.[38] The coverage is not complete, but it is wider than the title suggests, and this is an immense advance in a particularly difficult area. Anthea F. Shields ('Thomas Spence and the English Language', *TPS* 1974 (1975)) examines Spence's linguistic outlook and reconstructs, from his representations, what his conception of good English was. We now come to five volumes I have not seen—one in the *Studies in Philosophy* series[39] and four in *Studies in the History of Linguistics*.[40] Since the whole contents of *Historiographia Linguistica Vol. II* are 'relevant they may be mentioned together regardless of chronological order. The contents of the first issue are in the medieval-renaissance period: R. W. Hunt on '*Absoluta*: The *Summa* of Petrus Hispanus on Priscianus *Minor*'; Maria-Luisa Revero on 'Early Scholastic Views on Ambiguity: Composition and division'; Manuel Breva-Claramonte on 'Sanctius's *Minerva* of 1562 an the Evolution of his Linguistic Theory'. There is also a review article by Richard Braun on 'Die "Ideologen" des 18. Jahrhunderts und die Sprachwissenschaft' and a biographical notice by E. F. K. Koerner on 'Philip Aronstein (1862–1942)'. The second issue is more mixed. The four major articles are by James W. Ney on 'The Decade of Private Knowledge: Linguistics from the early 60s to the early 70s; D. L. Olmsted on 'Jeremiah Curton (1835–1906)· His life and work as linguist, folklorist and translator'; Vivian Salmon on 'John Brinsley: 17th-century pioneer in applied linguistics'; Stephen K. Land on 'Berkeley's Theory of Meaning'. F. F. K. Koerner completes a series with 'An Annotated Chronological Bibliography of Western Histories of Linguistic Thought, 1822–1972. Part IV Addenda', and Herbert Brekle has a review-article on 'The Port-Royal Grammar: Some bibliographical and critical notes on recent editions' (a subject of which more below). The third issue has articles by Nils Frik Enkvist on 'English in Latin Guise: A note on some Renaissance textbooks'; T. M. S. Priestley on 'Schleicher, Celakovský, and the Family Tree Diagram· A puzzle in the history of linguistics'; Paolo Ramat on 'Friedrich Engels zwischen Anthropologie und Sprachwissenschaft'; Raffaeli Simone on 'Théorie linguistique et l'historie de la linguisti-

---

[38] *Universal Language Schemes in England and France 1600-1800*, by James Knowlson. University of Toronto Press. pp. xii +302. £8.75.

[39] *Horace Bushnell's Theory of Language in the Context of Other Nineteenth-Century Philosophies of Language*, by Donald A. Crosby. Studies in Philosophy, 2. Mouton. pp. 302. Dfl. 70.

[40] *Collected Papers on the History of Grammar in the Middle Ages*, by R. W. Hunt. Studies in the History of Linguistics, edited by E. F. K. Koerner, ca. pp. 190. ca. Hfl. 40; *Studies in the History of the Grammatical Tradition in Tibet*, by Roy Andrew Miller, ib. ca. pp. 160. ca. Hfl. 35; *A Glance at the History of Linguistics, with particular regard to the historical study of phonology* (1916), by Holger Pedersen, translated by Caroline C. and Peter A. Henricksen. ib. ca. pp. 120. ca. Hfl. 28; *Chronologisches Verzeichnis französischer Grammatiken vom Ende des 14. bis zum Ausgange des 18. Jahrhunderts, nebst Angabe der bisherermittelten Fundorte derselben* (1890), by Edmund Stengel. ib ca. pp. 180. ca. Hfl. 40.

que'. Horst Weinstock contributes a moving notice 'In Memoriam Otto Funke (1885-1973)'. Outside this journal there are two other tributes to great scholars. A. J. van Essen lists over 600 publications by Kruisinga,[41] and Juri Nosek offers a 60th birthday tribute to Ivan Poldauf (happily still flourishing and writing as actively as ever) in the form of a biographical notice and a bibliography (*PP* A.18).

Three relevant items I have not seen are a study of (*inter alia*) Grimm's historical linguistics;[42] a volume by Rudelev on eminent Russian linguists from the eighteenth century to the present day;[43] and Tavoni's study of Benvoglienti.[44]

Among the editions and reprints we note the first part of Zettersten's excellent edition of Thomas Batchelor, introduced by a well-judged account of Batchelor.[45] Some account must be given of a series of facsimiles previously omitted. This is the *Grammatica Universalis*, edited by Brekle. The first issue, in two volumes, was the Port-Royal Grammar, with an excellent introduction.[46] Alongside this should be mentioned an

---

[41] *A Chronological Bibliography of the Writings of Etso Kruisinga, 1904-1944*, compiled by A. J. van Essen. Foundation for Pure Scientific Research (Z.W.O.) File Number 34-42, first interim report, 13. Institute of Applied Linguistics, University of Groningen. pp. iv + 56. NP.

[42] *Hegel und Jacob Grimm*, by Helmut Jendreieck. Philologische Studien und Quellen, 76. Ed. Schmidt. pp. 366. DM.69 (especially pp. 254-297, 344-350, 351-362).

[43] *Russke jazykovedy*, edited by V. G. Rudelev. Tambovskij gosud. Pedagogiceskij Inst. pp. 114. NP.

[44] *Il discorso linguistico di Bartolomeo Benvoglienti*, by M. Tavoni. Biblioteca degli studi mediolatini e volgari, N.S.3. Pacini. pp. 109. L.3.800.

[45] *A Critical Facsimile Edition of Thomas Batchelor 'An Orthoepical Analysis of the English Language' and 'An Orthoepical Analysis of the Dialect of Bedfordshire' (1809)*. Part I, edited by Arne Zettersten. Lund Studies in English, 45. Edited by Claes Schaar and Jan Svartvik. 1974 pp. xlvi + 186. NP.

[46] *Grammaire generale et raisonnee ou La Grammaire de Port-Royal*, edited by Herbert E. Brekle Vols. I-II. Grammatica Universalis, I: Meisterwerke der Sprachwissenschaft. Frederich Fromman Verlag. 1966. pp. xxxii + 161 followed by unnumbered Table of Contents. DM. 54.

[47] *General and Rational Grammar: The Port-Royal Grammar*, edited and translated with an introduction and Notes by Jacques Rieux and Bernard E. Rollin with a Preface by Arthur C. Danto and a Critical Essay by Norman Kretzmann. Janua Linguarum Series Minor, 208. pp. 200 Dfl. 43.

[48] *Discours physique de la Parole*, by Gerauld de Cordemoy. Nouvelle impression en facsimilé de l'édition de 1677 avec un commentaire par Herbert E. Brekle. Grammatica Universalis 2 (see Note 46). 1970. pp. xlviii + 180. DM. 68.

[49] *Versuch einer allgemeinen Sprachlehre*, by Johann Severin Vater. Faksimile Neudruck der Ausgabe Halle 1901 mit einer Einleitung und einem Kommentar von Herbert E. Brekle. Grammatica Universalis, 3 (see Note 46). 1970. pp. 36, xvi + 296. DM. 76.

[50] *Mechanismus der menschlichen Sprache nebst Beschreibung eine sprechenden Maschine*, by Wolfgange von Kempelen. Faksimile-Neudruck der Ausgabe Wien 1791 mit einer Einleitung von Herbert E. Brekle und Wolfgang Wildgen. Grammatica Universalis, 4 (see Note 46) 1970. pp. xlvi + 456. DM. 96.

[51] *Exposition d'une méthode raisonnée pour apprendre la langue latine; Les véritables principes de la Grammaire ou nouvelle Grammaire raisonnée pour apprendre la langue latine; Des Tropes, ou des différens sens dans lesquels on peut prendre une même mot dans une même langue*, by César Chesneau du Marsais. Reproduction en facsimilé des textes tirés de l'édition complète de 1797. Avec une introduction par Herbert E. Brekle. Grammatica Universalis, 5 (in three volumes). (see Note 46 1971.) pp. lviii + 267, 366, 392. DM. 92, 82, 82.

edition and translation by Rieux and Rollin.[47] It should be remarked in passing how extraordinary it is that between 1966 and 1973 ten modern editions or facsimiles of this grammar should have appeared (see Brekle, *Historiographia Linguistica* Vol. II, pp. 223–5), no doubt all triggered by Chomsky's interest; while Firth made all his students read the work from about 1930 on without provoking, I believe, a single edition. The second issue of *Grammatica Universalis* was de Cordemoy's *Discours physique de la parole*,[48] followed by Vater's *Versuch einer Allgemeinen Sprachlehre*,[49] von Kempelen's *Mechanismus der Menschlichen Sprache*[50] and a three-volume du Marsais.[51] Beauzée fills two substantial volumes and in another series is the subject of a full-length study.[52] The rather Whorfian Michaelis is the subject of issue 9[53] and Silvestre de Sacy of issue 10.[54] Meanwhile, *Amsterdam Classics in Linguistics*, which began in 1974, had put out eleven titles in 1975, which I have not seen[55] and Roman Jakobson edited the correspondence (mainly addressed to himself) of Trubetzkoy.[56]

[52] *Grammaire générale ou exposition raisonnée des éléments nécessaires du langage, pour servir de fondementà l'étude de toutes les langues*, by Nicolas Beauzée. Nouvelle impression en facsimilé de l'édition de 1767 avec une introduction par Barrie E. Bartlett. Grammatica Universalis, 8 (in two volumes) (see Note 46). 1974. pp. 52, xviii + 619, 664 and unnumbered *Approbation*. Hfl. 58. The study is *Beauzée's Grammaire Générale: Theory and Methodology*, by Barrie E. Barlett. Janua Linguarum Series Maior, 82. pp. 202. Dfl. 58.

[53] *De l'influence des opinions sur le langage et du langage sur les opinions*, by Johann David Michaelis. Nouvelle impression en facsimilé de l'édition de 1762 avec un commentaire par Helga Manke et une préface par Herbert E. Brekle. Grammatica Universalis, 9 (see Note 46). 1974. pp. 1xvi + 208. NP.

[54] *Principes de Grammaire générale, mis à la portée des enfans, et propres à servir d'introduction à l'étude de toutes les langues*, by Antoine-Isaac Silvestre de Sacy. Nouvelle impression en facsimile de l'edition de 1803 avec un commentaire par Herbert E. Brekle et Brigitte Asbach-Schnitker. Grammatica Universalis, 10 (see Note 46). pp. 40, xxviii + 366. NP.

[55] 1. *Ueber die Sprache und Weisheit der Indier. Ein Beitrag zur Begründung der Altertumskund*, by Friedrick Schlegel. (Heidelberg, 1808). pp. ca. 55. 200 Hfl. 60; 2. *A Grammar of the Icelandic and Old Norse Tongue*, by Rasmus Christian Rask. (London 1843). pp. ca. 50, 280. Hfl. 55; 3. *Analytical Comparison of the Sanskrit, Greek and Teutonic Languages, showing the original identity of their grammatical structure*, by Franz Bopp. (London 1820). 1974. pp. xxxviii + 68 Hfl. 28; 4. *Die Sprachen Europas in systematischer Uebersicht: Linguistische Untersuchungen*, by August Schleicher. (Bonn, 1850). pp. ca. 45, 280. Hfl. 55; 5. *Standard Alphabet for Reducing Unwritten Languages and Foreign Graphic Systems to a Uniform Orthography in European Letters*, by Richard Lepsiu. (2nd rev. ed., London, 1863). pp. ca. 45, 330. Hfl. 60; 6. *Linguistics and Evolutionary Theory: Three essays*, by Charles Darwin, August Schleicher and Wilhelm Bleek. (1863, 1865, 1868). pp. ca. 160. Hfl. 35; 7. *Cultivated Plants and Domesticated Animals in their Migration from Asia to Europe. Historico–linguistic studies*, by Victor Hehn, (1870). pp. 1xxv + 523. Hfl. 95 8. *Introduction to the Study of Language: A critical survey of the history and methods of comparative philology of Indo-European languages*, by Berthold Delbrück. (Leipzig, 1882). 1974. pp. xix + 148. Hfl. 35; 9. *The "Lautgesetz" Controversy: A documentation*, essays by Curtius, Brugmann, Delbrück, Schuchardt, Collitz, Osthoff, Jespersen. Edited by Terence H. Wilbur. pp. ca. 520. Hfl. 90; 10. *Einleitung in die Allgemeine Sprachwissenschaft*, by August Friedrich Pott. (1884–90). 1974. pp. x1vi + 502 Hfl. 70; 11. *Writings in General Linguistics: "On Vocalic Alternations (1881), and "Prinzipien der Sprachentwicklung*, by Mikotaj Kruszewski. (Leipzig 1884–90). pp. ca. 185. Hfl. 44.

[56] *N. A. Trubetzkoy's Letters and Notes*, prepared for publication by Roman Jakobson with the assistance of H. Baran, O. Ronen and Martha Taylor. Janua Linguarum Series Maior, 47. Mouton. pp. xxiv + 506. Dfl. 190.

Section II

The organisation of this sub-chapter of *YW* is patterned on the same principles as its fellows of previous years: interdisciplinary topics are examined first and then formal linguistic structure from semantics 'downwards'.

(a) *Varieties*

Dan Ben-Amos and Kenneth S. Goldstein have edited and introduce a collection of papers on *Folklore: performance and communication*.[57] The volume contains nine papers, apart from the introduction. Two, by Hymes and by Rosenberg, on performance as such; three, by Kirshenblatt-Gimblett, by Menez, and by Basgoz, on performance and communication; one, by Degh and Vazsonyi, on transmission and communication; and three, by Bauman, by Toelken, and by Abrahams, on cognitive aspects of folkloric communication. The main aim of the collection is to represent a recent emphasis in folklore research which, rather than dwell upon comparative, nationalist, anthropological, psychological, or structural perspectives for folklore research, draws instead upon an extension of Malinowski's ideas about context of situation. Each of the papers, in its different concerns, emphasizes the impossibility of separating the collection of data from the formation of hypotheses—there *are* none of the former without at least one of the latter. The methodology on which such folklore studies rest is that of Hymes, and usually known as the 'ethnography of speaking'. The papers variously use this kind of method to address the main analytical task for a communicative view of folklore. That task is an analysis of those utterances which transform the roles of speaker and hearer to those of performer and audience.

J. McH. Sinclair and R. M. Coulthard take some steps *Towards an analysis of discourse*.[58] Their book is a considerably revised version of a report submitted to the Social Science Research Council of two years research to establish a framework within which spoken language used in the classroom could be accommodated. After a brief introduction a short and somewhat idiosyncratic review of the literature, the authors present us with their system of analysis. Section 4 uses this analytic framework on texts, and section 5 shows how this kind of framework might be generalized to other less restrictive kinds of discourse. There are several points at which the coherence and credibility of the book suffer, possibly from over condensation; there is, for instance, a strange disjunction between disclaimers made as to the capacity of the authors' theory to state (or predict) the relative importance of discourse features for different subtypes of discourse (p.6) on the one hand, and claims of extensibility of the methods made on the other (p.112ff.).

One-sided discourse, the nature of whose analysis more resembles that adopted by Ben-Amos and Goldstein than that of Sinclair and Coulthard,

[57] *Folklore: performance and communication*, edited by Dan Ben-Amos and Kenneth S. Goldstein. (Approaches to semiotics No. 40). pp. 308. The Hague: Mouton. D.Gldrs. 92.–

[58] *Towards an analysis of discourse: the English used by teachers and pupils*, by J. McH. Sinclair and R. M. Coulthard. London: O.U.P. pp. 163. £2.50 pb.

is covered by essays on *Political Language and Oratory* edited by Maurice Bloch.[59] The volume contains ten essays ranging in subject matter from the structure of assemblies and the expression of authority in Oceanic cultures, through the articulation of responsibility and obligation in Africa, to the sociolinguistic distribution of power in the ambiguity of pronominal usage by organised groups in the May 1968 unrest in France. Bloch's introductory essay emphasises the social generality of those forms of speaking which are the vehicles for the transmission of political power, and are literally undeniable propositions for corporate change. He shows how in different cultures, there is clear correlation between types of oratory and types of authority and shows with subtlety how it is possible for highly formalised language (i.e. that deprived of the usual kinds of 'creativity') to have power over its hearers.

Basil Bernstein discusses the transmission, not of political, but of educational power, its differentia, its formalisation, its structure, its stratifying effects.[60] This is the third volume of *Class, codes and control*: it contains three papers on changes in the moral basis of schools, and four on changes in the coding of educational transmissions—to this extent the collection is clearly less 'linguistic' than its predecessors. Nevertheless, there are important points of contact between Bernstein's general sociolinguistic thesis of types of codes and their reproduction of the culture on the one hand, and on the other the extent and nature of consensus, disaffection, ritual, curricular changes, team teaching, mixed ability groups, and the ways in which knowledge is classified and framed, in staff rooms and class rooms. John T. Platt and Heidi K. Platt have somewhat pretentiously, in the light of the contents, written on *The social significance of speech*.[61] The book is intended to be *An introduction to and workbook in sociolinguistics*: as an introduction it covers too much too thinly; as a workbook it is simply neither structured nor taxing enough. Its price seems excessive. Also expensive, though in other respects less modish is Wolfgang Viereck's editing of the lexical and grammatical material of Guy Lowman's dialectological survey of mid-and southern England.[62] The volumes are well printed and minutely prepared. The second volume lists map by map the responses to the items whose working (by Lowman), relevance to U.S. dialectology, pedigree in U.K. dialectology and history, are given in the first volume. The minuteness of the whole proceeding is sometimes pointless, sometimes wasteful, and often infuriatingly uninterpreted. Some maps are unnecessary, some have more symbols than they need, some are unreadable because they incorporate too much information. The mixture of phonological and lexical material on one map is often

[59] *Political Language and Oratory in Traditional Society*, edited by Maurice Bloch. London: Academic Press. pp. 240. £6.90.
[60] *Class, codes and control. Volume 3: Towards a theory of educational transmissions*, by Basil Bernstein. London: Routledge & Kegan Paul. pp. 167. £3.50.
[61] *The social significance of speech: an introduction to and workbook in sociolinguistics*, by John T. Platt and Heidi K. Platt. Amsterdam: North-Holland Pub. Co. pp. 194. £7.70.
[62] *Lexikalische und grammatische Ergebnisse des Lowman-Survey von Mittel- und Sudengland. Band I, Textband; Band II, Kartenband*, edited by Wolfgang Viereck. Munchen: Wilhelm Fink. pp. 361, 342. DM. 240.—

quite unjustified, and opportunities to make cross-comparisons between different syntactic forms are missed. The bibliography, though long, contains errors.

Richard Bauman and Joel Sherzer have edited an extremely important set of *Explorations in the ethnography of speaking.*[63] Apart from prefatory and introductory material by the editors, the book is divided into five sections. Firstly, communities and resources for performance are dealt with: from the point of view of quantitation; from the point of view of forms of language as social markers of nothing but themselves; and from the point of view of alien varieties of one's language as the source of ritual speech. Secondly, ground rules for performance are explored in a variety of languages, cultures and situations. Thirdly, six papers deal with various aspects of the ways in which speech acts, events and situations are mutually, often dynamically, defining. Fourthly, the difficult relationship between unmarked performance and the use of performance to shape artistic (oral) structures is examined in five papers. Lastly, three papers try to move the explorations towards an ethnology of speaking. All the contributions to this volume are useful, not least because of their methodological and terminological sensibility. For any course covering sociolinguistics and anthropological linguistics, it is surely essential. The *Sociocultural dimensions of language use* nicely complements the preceding volume and, happily, shares its excellence: it is edited by Mary Sanches and Ben G. Blount.[64] This collection concentrates more on the modelling of ethnographic findings than the previous volume. The papers are gathered into two sections: on the construction of social reality, and on metacommunicative acts and events. Papers in the first section are concerned to indicate how one can determine for two different cultures the extent to which members of those cultures do or do not make sense of each other's behaviour by assuming that *internal* states are the main spring of that behaviour; how one can determine the extent to which spatial and positional behaviour is appropriate from its correlation with an abstract cultural code; how one must *demonstrate* the relationship between a performance and an episode of behaviour in the narcotic sub-culture, since the semantics of the lexicon is so flexible; how one can examine the regulation of interactional affairs by showing what happens when people break those rules (by lying, for instance); how to investigate the generation of social meaning in the classroom; how to construe children as practical reasoners; and how to account for the social encoding of knowledge in linguistically salient structures such as genealogies. The second group of papers deals with metacommunicative, not just metalinguistic, acts and events. Such acts have been little studied within formal linguistics.The papers draw their force from four different strands of interest. The first is simply an interest in self-referring expressions (metalinguistic acts); the second is the work of Bateson on those members of the community who avoid the massive use of such acts by normal members of the community, notably schizophrenics, or those

[63] *Explorations in the ethnography of speaking*, edited by Richard Bauman and Joel Sherzer. London: C.U.P. pp. 501. £9. hb, £3.60 pb.
[64] *Sociocultural dimensions of language use*, edited by Mary Sanches and Ben G. Blount. With a foreword by John J. Gumperz. London: Academic Press. pp. 404, £10.80.

so diagnosed, who in not using such acts deprive their interlocuters of information which forms the basis of obtaining a 'proper reading' of their utterances; the third is the work of Jakobson and Hymes on a suitable set of dimensions for communicative acts; and the fourth is the work of anthropologists on the *symbolic* meaning of events in culture. The goal of a cross-cultural theory of metacommunicative acts, which is one that the book hopes to have moved towards, is certainly now something whose general characteristics one has more than an inkling of.

We turn now from ethnographical concerns to those of sociolinguistic methodology and applied sociolinguistics. Derek Bickerton has provided us with an important test of the methods of implicational scaling, due originally to Decamp, in his *Dynamics of a creole system*.[65] The data upon which the book is based are variant syntactic patterns from creole speakers of Guyanese. The problem with such data is that they show continuous variation, with varying co-occurrences, across the population under consideration, and hence provide sociolinguistics with an extremely serious problem of representation and interpretation. Bickerton overcomes the problem of representation by erecting three broad lects, differentiated according to prestigiousness: the acrolect (most prestigious), mesolects, and basilects (the least prestigious). Spatial and temporal diffusion of verb phrase morphemes through these lectal strata are then shown to be interpretable on a form of coding which represents the grammars of individual speakers on a cline, any particular point on which predicts presence-absence relations amongst the syntactic features, and relates it in systematic ways to other points (grammars) to left and right. The care with which Bickerton formulates methodological difficulties, his specification of the intractibilities of the data, and the ways in which he articulates his findings with wider theoretical considerations are all models for linguists as well as sociolinguists.

Peter Trudgill tackles a completely different problem in his *Accent, dialect and the school*.[66] This little monograph, in the Arnold 'Explorations in language study' series for teachers and student teachers, by emphasising the correctness of each native speaker's use of his own variety of the language, and by examining the evidential, rational, logical, and humane bases and consequences of this correctness, argues with some passion against the view that standard English should hold any special sway in schools. For thoughtful and humane teachers, none of the book will be new. Howard Giles and Peter F. Powesland provide us with a very thorough review of the interactions between *Speech style and social evaluation*.[67] Much of the work in this somewhat atheoretical and ill-understood area of social psychology comes from the hands of these authors or from work done by Wallace Lambert and his colleagues in Canada. Their main focus of attention is how social judgements which are made about a particular person derive from or are dependent upon how

[65] *Dynamics of a creole system*, by Derek Bickerton. London: C.U.P. pp. 224. £7.25.

[66] *Accent, dialect and the school*, by Peter Trudgill. London: Edward Arnold. pp. 106. £1.95.

[67] *Speech style and social evaluation*, by Howard Giles & Peter F. Powesland. London: Academic Press. pp. 218. £6.60.

that person speaks the language that he speaks. There is some confusion about terminology (as between, for instance, accent, dialect, variety, and language), and there is no attempt to distinguish between the occasions upon which hearers do, and the occasions upon which they do not, make such judgements. Nor is there any attempt to specify the actual linguistic features or groups of co-occurrent linguistic features which are the empirical basis for such social judgements by ordinary hearers. But either these are difficulties which can be easily overcome (terminology), or the nature of their solution is at the moment impossible to find methods for (the basis for, and process of, 'judging'). The authors are to be congratulated for amassing so much material so coherently. The transparency with which they doubt the finality of their own methods is refreshing, and only serves to show that the problems are worth expending more effort on, and where and how that effort must best be deployed.

(b) *Psycholinguistics*

Colin Cherry has edited a collection of eight papers in *Pragmatics of human communication*, a volume which should have been noticed last year.[68] As Cherry himself remarks, human communication is a field of enormous breadth comprising many different techniques, theoretical perspectives and terminologies. Add to this the fact that the volume is not the outcome of a conference or symposium and that the invited contributors come from six different countries, and it is nothing short of remarkable that the volume is as coherent as it is. John Marshall and Roger Wales consider the functional *value* of communicative acts from birdsong to human language, whilst Isaak Revzin examines the ancient question of the origins of language by confronting the theory of linguistic universals and evolutionarily interpreted design features of language with recent findings of zoo-semiotics and ethnology. Dennis Dicks attempts to dissect the notion of 'conversation' under experimental conditions and Aaron Cicourel shows how misinterpretation and misconstruction occur in settings with fixed formats like medical interviews. Merrill Garrett dissects experimental problems arising from the understanding of sentences, and Kenneth Foster does the same for their production. S. Marcus shows how two languages of discovery, the scientific and the poetic, differ from each other, and J. Marschak gives some new insights into why language communicates as it does by showing how information is extracted from scientific experiments. The book offers much food for thought.

Dominic W. Massaro has edited a collection of eleven chapters from various hands (four and a half from his own) on *Understanding language*.[69] The book reviews models and results from the research on speech perception, reading, and psycholinguistics, and does so from a base of information processing metaphors. The information processing framework is never very adequately characterized, and, as Massaro himself says, the book is a mixture of the elementary and the advanced. It presents elementary

---

[68] *Pragmatics of human communication*, edited by Colin Cherry. Dordrecht, Holland: D. Reidel. (1974). pp. 178. NP.

[69] *Understanding language: an information-processing analysis of speech perception reading and psycholinguistics*, edited by Dominic W. Massaro. London: Academic Press. pp. 439. £7.90.

linguistic facts and theories in ways better done by better known works designed for that purpose, and mixes them with quite subtle critiques of certain psychological views of the communicative act. Massaro thinks that this may be useful; my view is that he does not have an audience remotely well-defined. On a similar topic, but of considerably more interest, are the proceedings of a symposium on dynamic aspects of speech perception entitled *Structure and process in speech perception*,[69A] edited by A. Cohen and S. G. Nooteboom. The main theme of the collection is the study of perceptual processes in the decoding of *connected speech*. The demands made upon speech perception models by this kind of material put them in need of considerable revision. This is pointed out with subtlety in papers on theoretical issues by M. P. Haggard, D. Pisoni and J. Sawusch, and S. E. G. Ohman. Their distinctions between modelling and theorising, their questions about what the proper source for undertaking a new experiment should be (neither hypotheses which are so 'new' that the outcome of their experiments is unintelligible, nor paradigms which are so well tried that more experiments add nothing), and their desire to work in ways which Haggard calls 'semi-empirical', are all extremely important. The second group of nine papers deal with various aspects of the ways in which prosodic characteristics of connected speech may be the *creative* basis for the hearer's perceptual processing; that is, prosodic characteristics do not simply constitute a further level of acoustic structure which has to be decoded, rather they are features which may be thought of as the power which actively drives the parallel processing of 'phonemic', syntactic, lexical and semantic 'levels of structure'. For those who have despaired at the lack of theoretical and widespread interest in prosodic and paralinguistic systems, this is a most exciting development.

E. Zwicker and E. Terhardt have edited the proceedings of a symposium on psychological models and physiological facts in hearing entitled *Facts and models in hearing*, which should have been noticed last year.[70] Considerable progress has been made in our understanding of the process of hearing by both psychologists and neurophysiologists in recent years. This collection draws together the work of researchers in anatomy, morphology, neurophysiology, bio-engineering, and psychoacoustics; the editors point out that there is always a danger, when so many disciplines are involved in the solution of some particular problem, that research will diverge rather than converge. The papers here, if not actively promoting convergence, prevent further divergence. They fall into five groups: there are three papers on the structure of the ear, seven on the nature and operation of cochlear mechanisms, seven on the auditory analysis of frequency, nine on the auditory analysis of temporal distribution, and seven on the structure and function of various non-linear effects (for

---

*[69]A*Structure and process in speech perception: proceedings of the symposium on Dynamic aspects of Speech Perception held at I.P.O., Eindhoven, Netherlands August 4-6, 1975, edited by A. Cohen and S. G. Nooteboom. Berlin: Springer-Verlag. pp. 353. DM. 48.—

*[70]Facts and models in hearing: Proceedings of the Symposium on Psychophysical models and physiological facts in hearing held at Tutzing, Oberbayern, Federal Republic of Germany, April 22-26, 1974, edited by E. Zwicker and E. Terhardt. Berlin: Springer-Verlag. pp. 360. DM. 39.—

instance the non-linear response of the basilar membrane to frequencies close to the 'characteristic frequency' of different parts of the membrane). The likelihood of persons working in the field of hearing research to come to a unified view of the *whole* of the hearing process, though a long way off, is much improved by this volume. A collection of papers for the advanced undergraduate and the beginning postgraduate on *Measurement procedures in speech, hearing, and language* has been edited by Sadanand Singh to honour the work done in this field by Professor John W. Black.[71] There are two papers on the measurement of language—actually of linguistic and phonological deficiency—there are eight papers on perception and audition, and there are five on production and acoustics. There are slight differences amongst the papers as to the extent to which they deal with measurement *procedures*, but they are all very well documented and clearly presented. This will prove to be a very useful collection. Neil O'Connor edits the deliberations of a study group on *Language, Cognitive deficits and retardation*, held under the auspices of the Institute for Research into Mental and Multiple Handicap.[72] There is an introductory essay by the editor which provides useful perspective, and there follow twelve papers which fall roughly into three categories; psycholinguistic studies of development; clinical, comparative and experimental studies of language-deficient children; and studies of teaching and learning problems. Eric Lenneberg and Neil Smith give theoretical perspectives on syntax and phonology; A. Fourcin rejects the motor theory of speech perception on evidence from spastics, while D. Ricks contrasts the nature of babbling behaviours in normal and autistic children. The relation between language skills and cognitive development is dealt with from the point of view of subnormal speakers by H. Sinclair (in a Piagetian frame of reference), and by R. F. Cromer. The extent to which comprehension *does* precede production is examined for brain-damaged subjects by J. McFie, and by W. Ule. Problems of programming and of memory storage for language in the severely retarded are dealt with by Graham Morris. The collection as a whole shows firstly that understanding of the world can occur without the expected syntactic and semantic rules having been grasped, and secondly that a facility with coding mechanisms for memorial, communicative, and self organising purposes may be independent of comprehension.

Harry Beilin has provided us with an extremely important set of *Studies in the cognitive basis of language development*.[73] Beilin's starting point is the desire to investigate the influence of cognition upon language development. He acknowledges that there is in fact considerable autonomy of linguistic systems vis-a-vis cognitive capabilities, but he is at pains to stress that the characteristic structures which are shared by both are *logical* structures. Evidence for this view is provided by a series of experiments

[71] *Measurement procedures in speech, hearing and language*, edited by Sadanand Singh. London: University Park Press. pp. 470. £10.50.

[72] *Language, Cognitive deficits and retardation*, edited by Neil O'Connor. London: Butterworths (Published for the Institute for Research into Mental and Multiple Handicap). pp. 233. £7.75.

[73] *Studies in the cognitive basis of language development*, edited by Harry Beilin with the collaboration of Barbara Lust, Hinda G. Sack, and Helen-Marie Natt. London: Academic Press. pp. 420. £11.25.

upon specific features of the child's expanding repertoire which would be likely to show logical structure in both language and cognition. These were the passive, time and number, and the connectives (taking up, respectively, two, two, and three, chapters). Beilin concludes that in general, especially at earlier stages, the mapping from cognitive structures to linguistic ones is uni-directional (cognitive to linguistic); in certain cases, however, and certainly at later stages (such as when the child has a propositional logic of sorts available to him) the mapping relation can be bi-directional and uni-directional (language to cognition). This is a theoretically and empirically sensitive corpus of work which merits the closest attention. M. A. K. Halliday has written an important book, which whilst complementing Beilin's concern for the relation between cognition and language, articulates that concern by asking of the speech of one child, in a sociocultural rather than in a psychological context, what constitutes *Learning how to mean*.[74] Though it is possible to criticise Halliday both for the limited quantity of data he uses, and for the way in which it was collected and recorded, the work is important because it sees the development of the use of different linguistic functions as a continuously increased refinement of the articulation of socially oriented meanings. Put like this, it does not sound like a particularly surprising development. Halliday's contribution is the realisation that the source of the duality of patterning (which is such an important characteristic of human languages) is not, for the individual child, a blind (whether innate or learned) acquisition of syntax, but is a powerful motivation to mean (contribute, say) more and more in a social environment which 'means' (signifies, impinges) more and more. The child's ability to do this (in the single case studied, but it is doubtless generalisable) is not linked to a single, gradually expanding, expressive vehicle. There are two distinct phases: one in which the child use a 'private' language comprising simply content and expression, a language in which only one thing can be meant at a time; the other, in which the language has content, form and expression, a language which approximates to the adult form. There is, of course a transitional phase, but the distribution of the same expressive functions across these two quite distinct forms of code gives added depth and power to Halliday's initial schema. Sinclair Rogers has edited a collection of twenty one papers from divers hands on *Children and Language*.[75] Three papers discuss the social contexts of language. Seven papers deal with the functions of language in dealing with the world, self and society. Four deal with language and thinking and four with language and meaning. The collection ends with three papers on language and the environment. The purpose of the selection, which succeeds in my view, is to give a balanced view of the relationships between the processes of using and becoming more proficient at using language, of being sociable and becoming socialised, of learning how to learn, how to think, how to ponder, how to imagine. The collection revolves tellingly around a paper of Halliday's.

[74] *Learning how to mean: explorations in the development of language*, by M. A. K. Halliday. London: Edward Arnold. pp. 164. £2.75.
[75] *Children and language: readings in early language and socialisation*, edited by Sinclair Rogers. London: O.U.P. pp. 346. £7.50.

(c) *Computational linguistics*

When we take computational linguistics to include artificial intelligence studies (see below), it often proves difficult to decide whether to incorporate particular works or collections in this category or in the preceding (psycholinguistic) one. A case in point is a collection of invited papers presented to a symposium of the Institute of Electronic and Electrical Engineers on *Speech recognition* edited by D. Raj Reddy.[76] Automatic speech recognition has had some of the fashionableness and some of the economic setbacks which attended the attempts to do fully automatic high quality machine translation. This collection marks both a stock-taking and the onset of a renaissance. A key-note address by Gunnar Fant and a tutorial paper on speech understanding systems by Allen Newell make both of these points very markedly. In addition to Newell's paper, there are three others on systems as such. (E. P. Neuberg's makes the timely point that much of the renaissance has neither to do with the discovery of new ways of extracting parameters from speech signals, nor to do with the large funding of the subject recently, but rather depends upon there being friendly systems available on large machines. Friendly systems are those which voluntarily provide the researcher with as much capacity and as much relevant help (playing the advantage rule) as he needs when interacting with the machine. This point seems to me to have general validity for all non-numerical problem solving and research applications.) There are six papers on parameter and feature extraction, three on various aspects of the acoustic specification necessary for automatic speech recognition, three on the representation of syntactic and semantic features for such systems, and four on the general algorithmic and logical structure of such systems.

The possibility of constructing computing machines which have a general capacity for intelligent behaviour is one that has been considered for some years now under the names of artificial intelligence or machine intelligence. The reader may wonder what these projects have to do with language and linguistics. A collection of essays of the first importance on *Representation and understanding*, edited by Daniel G. Bobrow and Allan Collins, will certainly leave him in no doubt about the connection, and the significance which artificial intelligence is coming to have for many fields of linguistic research.[77] The subtitle of the book is significant: cognitive science draws on stances and expertise from computer science, linguistics, education, philosophy, psychology, but in ways which do not merely reflect their intersection so much as their active integration in a study of intelligent systems. State of the art accounts of machine intelligence in the late sixties and the early seventies (by, for instance, Marvin Minsky and Donald Michie) showed that much of the blockage of further progress in the research was to be attributed to our not knowing how much information to provide the systems with, nor in what form it should be coded. Given the ground that has to be cleared in basic philosophical ways in each of the papers in this collection, the problem was much more intractable

---

[76] *Speech recognition: invited papers presented at the 1974 IEEE Symposium*, edited by D. Raj Reddy. London: Academic Press. pp. 542. £9.35.

[77] *Representation and understanding: studies in cognitive science*, edited by Daniel G. Bobrow and Allan Collins. London: Academic Press. pp. 427. £12.15.

than even those very thoughtful papers had suggested. The papers fall into four groups: theory of representation, memory models, higher level structures, and semantic knowledge in existing systems. I cover each of these in turn. There are four papers on the theory of representation. Daniel Bobrow proposes to examine competing models of how knowledge is represented by examining the ways in which a system desired to achieve some goal would *use* that representational model. These different functional evaluations of competing models can then be used as dimensions within which to represent types of representation. W. A. Woods provides us with a very fair and revealing critical account of the representation of semantic information in network form. He shows just why we should not be satisfied with the forms of semantic representation which are currently available, but he also shows how what is yet to be done may be done. The question as to whether *all* of the relevant semantic knowledge can be incorporated in one large (and, from a processing point of view, unwieldy) network, is left open, but does not seem to be critical. Joseph Becker discusses the inferability of representations inside behaving systems (this work links interestingly with Bobrow's). Others discuss the ways in which systems can synthesize a contingent knowledge structure from prior knowledge and a situation and then answer questions solely from this structure. Discussion of memory models includes the proposal that schemata might be active and that the invocation of these memory schemata would be geared to context dependent descriptions. Two other papers reach useful conclusions using the idea of frames of knowledge. David Rumelhart writes a grammar for well-formed stories, and Roger Schank shows what is involved in understanding paragraphs. Robert Abelson develops a notation for describing the intended effects of plans. Allan Collins and others describe a system which teaches people how to give reasonable answers to questions for which they do not have enough knowledge to answer with certainty. There is more of interest and importance for the thoughtful linguist in this volume than can adequately be discussed here. Abbe Mowshowitz has written an interesting book on *The conquest of will. information processing in human affairs.*[78] Whilst not disputing the advances and interest of such activities as are covered in the last two volumes mentioned, Mowshowitz thinks it important to point out the price that is being paid for technological improvements (especially in information processing) in terms of the alienation of individual responsibility. This is a fairly documented and coolly argued book whose moral stance and humane warnings deserve the widest and most careful reading.

(d) *Semantics, lexical theory, syntax*
Another volume in the excellent series published by Academic Press and, as often as not, edited by John P. Kimball, is *Syntax and semantics. Volume 4.*[79] A review of tests of ambiguity (which distinguish, for instance, between the ambiguity of *They saw her duck* and the semantic inspecifi-

[78] *The conquest of will: information processing in human affairs*, by Abbe Mowshowitz. London: Addison-Wesley. pp. 365. £5.85.
[79] *Syntax and semantics: Volume 4*, edited by John P. Kimball. London: Academic Press. pp. 281. £10.30.

city of *One more can of beer and I'm leaving*) is provided by Arnold Zwicky and Jerrold Sadock. Georgette Ioup provides telling examples of the relationship between precedence relations in surface structure and the semantic consequences of the scopes of quantifiers. Talmy Givon further illuminates the debate about causative verbs by considering data from the semantics of interpersonal communication. He draws the distinction between differing kinds of control from one person to another and the expression of this by means of verbs of 'cause'. Joan B. Hooper examines the types of assertive and non-assertive factive and non-factive verbs. Per Lysvag explores the different readings of verbs like *believe, think, seem, appear, assume, suppose, expect* in terms of the notion of hedging and the variable behaviour of the verbs in terms of their permitting *neg* raising, *so* and *it* pronominalisation. John P. Kimball discusses various ways in which speaker-hearers can be thought of as computing surface structure, and relates these parsing algorithms to semantic information. Leonard Talmy considers the syntax and semantics of motion by specifying certain universal semantic components of motion situations and seeing how they map onto the syntax of various languages. The ways in which different languages compress such expressions when they are complex are also discussed. John Grinder and Suzette Elgin provide evidence from the use of the verb *bully* which, they argue, supports the predicate raising analysis of semantic paraphrases with differing surface lexicalisations. Edwin Williams gives good reasons for rejecting a transformation (called *whiz deletion*) which, for instance, derives *The man driving the bus was drunk* from *The man who is/was driving the bus was drunk.*

Pierre Guiraud's book on *Semiology* is an extremely valuable and clear introduction to that notoriously difficult and variably interpreted study.[80] He introduces the Saussurian basis of present-day semiology, relates it to communicative functions and the notion of media, distinguishes the components of signs and their significations, and demonstrates their integration into codes and the structure of their interpretability. The last three chapters introduce a typology of codes—logical, aesthetic, and social—and discuss their functioning and their form. The clarity of the work and the willingness with which Guiraud expresses himself in ways which encourage critical reactions, are both refreshing, and ensure a lasting usefulness for the book. Jaako Hintikka has collected a second volume of his essays on the applicability of modal logics to the solution of semantic problems.[81] The revolutionary nature of the approach is less marked now than it was in the late sixties: largely due to the vigorous insistence of Richard Montague that an adequate semantics of natural language had to incorporate notions of possible worlds. The history and utility of the approach are dealt with in chapters on the work of W. V. O. Quine and R. Carnap. The main thrust of the remaining chapters, however, is the development of arguments which show that modal logics have their most successful application in the semantics of propositional attitudes, in quantification, in the problem of

---

[80] *Semiology*, by Pierre Guiraud (translated by George Gross). London: Routledge & Kegan Paul. pp. 106. £2.95 hb, £1.25 pb.
[81] *The intentions of intentionality and other new models for modalities*, by Jaako Hintikka. Dordrecht, Holland: D. Reidel. pp. 262. Dfl. 85.— hb, 45.— pb.

naming, in the answering of questions. Hintikka's work is an extremely valuable contribution to the growing certainty amongst logically minded linguists and linguistically minded logicians that the tools of modal logic are such as to indicate that it may now be possible to begin to draw a picture of *natural logic*, that is, the logic of natural language and human reasoning.

Ruth Kempson, in *Presupposition and the delimitation of semantics*, argues for two related propositions.[82] Firstly, that semantics should be a component of a general linguistic model which has only to do with truth values in sentences; secondly, that presupposition (either in the sense of the logical relations between statements which are distinct from entailments, or in the sense of speaker beliefs which lie behind utterances) is *not* properly to be considered a part of semantics, but of pragmatics, which must needs depend upon a two-valued truth based semantics. The kind of pragmatics which Kempson espouses is that of Grice. As Kempson herself says, it is impossible at this stage to decide upon one of the competing ways of representing and relating the semantic and pragmatic parts of the model as being the best. Deirdre Wilson has dealt with a very similar theme in her *Presuppositions and non-truth-conditional semantics*.[83] She concludes similarly, though by interestingly different pathways of argument and using different types of fact to advance her argument; she characterises presuppositional analysis as a theory of preferred interpretations, a theory which, insofar as it is capable of becoming coherent, is clearly not a part of semantics, but of pragmatics.

Peter Cole and Jerry L. Morgan have edited an important collection of papers on linguistic approaches to speech acts—matters which are clearly related to the many and diverse contents of pragmatics.[84] The papers are contributions by both linguists and philosophers to a theory—perhaps the only theory—which unites philosophical interests and linguistic interests in the problems of the meaning of utterances and the problems of the meaning of statements (propositions). Two themes inherent in speech acts are dealt with broadly speaking: (a) criticisms, explorations, and extensions, of the performative hypothesis (the hypothesis of J. R. Ross which, briefly, claims that every sentence is embedded in a hyper-sentence whose verb is an explicit performative verb (*declare, swear, question, . . .*)); (b) the status, extensibility, and generality of H. P. Grice's work on conversational implicature. Edward L. Keenan has edited the papers from the 1973 Cambridge colloquium on the *Formal semantics of natural language*.[85] This is a collection of the first importance. David Lewis discusses adverbs of quantification, Barbara Hall Partee examines the relations between deletion, quantification and variable binding, J. E. J. Altham and Neil

[82] *Presupposition and the delimitation of semantics*, by Ruth Kempson. London: C.U.P. pp. 235. £7 hb, £2.95 pb.

[83] *Presuppositions and non-truth-conditional semantics*, by Deirdre Wilson. London: Academic Press. pp. 161. £4.60.

[84] *Syntax and semantics: Volume 3, Speech Acts*, edited by Peter Cole and Jerry L. Morgan. London: Academic Press. pp. 406. £9.35.

[85] *Formal semantics of natural language: papers from a colloqium sponsored by the King's College Research Centre, Cambridge*, edited by Edward L. Keenan. London: C.U.P. pp. 475. £12.50.

Tennant describe sortal quantification, and R. D. Hull provides a semantics of superficial and embedded questions. There are papers by John Lyons, Pieter Seuren, Osten Dahl, and Colin Biggs on various aspects of reference and cross-reference. Five papers deal with intensional logic and syntactic theory, and papers by N. Jardine and by T. Potts question, from various points of view, the extent to which the widely held belief that model theoretic semantics (taken over from its completely uncontroversial use in formal logics) can account for natural languages is reasonable. Five papers handle pragmatic problems and the meanings of sentences in context, and four attempt to deal with the problematic relationship between semantics and surface syntax. Much of the material in this volume will be the source of inspiration which will accelerate the growth of semantic studies in linguistics and philosophy at an even greater rate. Two other collections add complementary dimensions to the work so far considered in modern semantic studies; firstly, twelve essays by linguists and by philosophers edited by D. Hockney and others, ranging in topic from 'Counterfactuals and comparative possibility' (David Lewis) to 'Verbs of bitching' (James McCawley);[86] and secondly a collection of six essays by British philosophers which are, in their different ways, optimistic about the solubility of problems of meaning within a philosophical framework.[87] David C. Bennett has examined the semantics of the *Spatial and temporal uses of English prepositions* within a stratificational framework.[88] Part one provides a discussion of the spatial uses, part two the temporal uses of English prepositions. Part three formalises these analyses showing how they can be generated and mapped onto surface structures. This is a clearly and carefully argued piece of research which dispels many of the confusions which had grown up around prepositional use. Christian Paul Casparis undertakes an empirical analysis of the 'historical present' in a framework which denies that there is any necessary connection between tense and time. He uses narrative sources and shows how the use of this tense is related to a quality of perception reproduced with a minimum of cognitive analysis.[89] Arne Juul's very valuable study *On concord of number in modern English*, which was discussed in *YW* 55 has now appeared in printed form.[90]

(e) *General*

Peter Ladefoged has written a splendidly clear and practical *Course in phonetics* which not only makes the student make noises, and shows him how they are to be written, but also gives him relevant theoretical

[86] *Contemporary research in philosophical logic and linguistic semantics; proceedings of a conference held at the University of Western Ontario, London, Canada*, edited by D. Hockney, W. Harper, and B. Freed. Dordrecht, Holland: D. Reidel. pp. 332. NP.
[87] *Meaning, reference and necessity: new studies in semantics*, edited by Simon Blackburn. London: C.U.P. pp. 210. £4.95.
[88] *Spatial and temporal uses of English prepositions: an essay in stratificational semantics*, by David C. Bennett. London: Longman. pp. 235. £4.75.
[89] *Tense without time: the present tense in narration*, by Christian Paul Casparis. Bern. Francke Verlag. pp. 212. Sw.Fr. 32.—
[90] *On concord of number in modern English*, by Arne Juul. Copenhagen: Nova. pp. 314. NP.

perspectives (the formulation of allophonic alternations in rules, the distributional patterns of stress by means of rule, the recoding of phonetic transcriptions in feature terms).[91] An especially attractive feature of the book is the profusion of very carefully specified ear- and production-training exercises. A. C. Gimson provides *A practical course of English pronunciation* together with two cassettes,[92] which is a companion handbook to his own *Introduction to the pronunciation of English* for foreign learners. The new book relies upon developing auditory discriminations as a basis for adequate production. Margaret Berry has produced a clear but not a simplified introduction to a theory of grammar which is mainly associated with the name of Halliday.[93] Her task was not an easy one since not only is the theory of increasing interest to, for instance, workers in artificial intelligence because it provides problem-free parsing methods, but it is a theory whose practitioners make quite diverse use of the same terminology. The best parts of the book are those where Berry is discussing details of the operation of the model. Geoffrey Sampson in *The form of language* has tried to follow a path between the obscurity of formalisms and the trivialisation of informality in expounding what is important about linguistics, language, and the work of Chomsky.[94] Sampson's final chapter offers some speculations to the effect that what the psychological design-features of innate abilities might be are equivalents of automaton theory. James R. Hurford examines the numerals, and enumeration procedures in different languages and determines *The linguistic theory of numerals*.[95] On the basis of English, Mixtec, French, Danish, Welsh, Hawaiian, and Yoruba, he establishes a typology of universals of numeral systems, and, in the context of that typology, calibrates other theories of number systems which exist in the literature. Ian Robinson offers a critique of Noam Chomsky's linguistics entitled *The new grammarian's funeral*.[96] It is a disconcerting book to read because in many respects it fails to see what Chomsky's arguments are arguments *about*, and because it progresses by means of an increasingly arrogant acidity, which simply destroys any element of credibility that Robinson's case might have had. George Steiner's criticisms of Chomsky arise from a much more interesting basis—the problem of translation and the 'fact' of translation between users of the same language—and more important, they have a creative impetus, to answer the question, among many others, why there are so many human languages.[97] The importance of the work of W. V. Quine is re-asserted by

[91] *A course in phonetics*, by Peter Ladefoged. New York: Harcourt Brace Jovanovich. pp. 296. NP.

[92] *A practical course of English pronunciation: a perceptual approach*, by A. C. Gimson. London: Edward Arnold. pp. 80. £2.75. Two cassettes £7.50.

[93] *An introduction to systemic linguistics: 1 Structures and systems*, by Margaret Berry. London: Batsford. pp. 209. £5.50 hb, £2.75 pb.

[94] *The form of language*, by Geoffrey Sampson. London: Weidenfeld and Nicholson. pp. 236. £6.50 hb, £3.50 pb.

[95] *The linguistic theory of numerals*, by James R. Hurford. London: C.U.P. pp. 293. £8.75.

[96] *The new grammarian's funeral: a critique of Noam Chomsky's linguistics*, by Ian Robinson. London: C.U.P. pp. 189. £4.50.

[97] *After Babel: Aspects of language and translation*, by George Steiner. London: O.U.P. pp. 507. £2.50.

a second edition of *Words and objections*.[98] Apart from the correction of errors and the updating of Quine's bibliography, the collection remains its splendid self. Dwight Bolinger's textbook on *Aspects of language* has undergone major revision in its second edition.[99] For those who do not know it, this is an excellent introductory text, neither partisan to the point of dogma, nor eclectic to the point of confusion. As Bolinger says of it himself, his book speaks 'for an enlightened traditionalism'. It is very well illustrated and contains usefully taxing exercises. The newest elements take account of the force of mentalist linguistics and of socio-linguistics. One's expectations of crispness, telling examples, fine critical judgement and humanist values—all standard ingredients of Bolinger's work—are fully satisfied by this second edition. Einar Haugen and Morton Bloomfield have edited an important collection of essays which focus upon language problems which touch human life.[100] The essays fall into three groups: the variety of language, the learning of language, and the functions of language. Morton Bloomfield provides an introduction showing how the psychological, anthropological, philosophical, educational, and literary interests in linguistic matters are the very roots of the history of linguistics. There are six essays on variety, four on learning, and six on functions. Those of Dell Hymes on linguistic inequality, of Courtney Cazden on the unlearnability (as opposed to the acquirability) of their native language by children, and of David Hays on the expression of interpersonal relationships, are particularly stimulating, but to single these out is not to imply that the remainder of the book is anything other than an excitingly coherent view of an alternative framework for the considering of language to the formalist one.

[98] *Words and objections: essays on the work of W. V. Quine*, edited by Donald Davidson and Jaakko Hintikka. (2nd. edition). Dordrecht, Holland: D. Reidel. pp. 373, NP.
[99] *Aspects of language*, by Dwight Bolinger. New York: Harcourt Brace Jovanovich. (2nd edition) pp. 682. £3.65 pb.
[100] *Language as a human problem*, edited by Einer Haugen and Morton Bloomfield. London: Lutterworth. pp. 266. £5.50.

III

Old English Literature

T. A. SHIPPEY

Comprehensive bibliographies of Anglo-Saxon studies appear annually in *ASE* and in *OEN* (the latter published for the Modern Language Association of America by the Center for Medieval and Renaissance Studies, The Ohio State University). *OEN* also contains a review of the year's work in OE studies, edited by Rowland L. Collins. An annual list of 'OE Research in Progress', compiled by Alan K. Brown, appears in *NM*.

1. Social, Cultural and Intellectual Background

The most substantial contribution to Anglo-Saxon studies this year is the first volume of Rupert Bruce-Mitford's definitive account of the Sutton Hoo ship-burial[1] —over eight hundred pages with hundreds of figures, maps, plates, fold-outs. Its most interesting statements for students of literature are probably the abandonment of the cenotaph theory—it seems there *was* a body after all—and the assertion of a 'very strong case for concluding that the Sutton Hoo ship-burial is the tomb of king Raedwald, the greatest figure of the Wuffinga dynasty'. Opinions of the ship's seaworthiness appear also to have improved, which makes a marginal contribution to the historicity of *Beowulf* (see C. Weibull, Section 5, below). However, the volume's expense will make many readers content themselves with twelve of Mr. Bruce-Mitford's already familiar papers, collected, revised, and indexed, with four new additions, in *Aspects of Anglo-Saxon Archaeology*.[2]

The early OE period is further illuminated, from a different angle, by Alan K. Brown's 'Bede, A Hisperic Etymology, and Early Sea Poetry' (*MS*), which begins with a discussion of the word *dodrans* in Bede's *De Temporibus*, goes on to show why early Insular Latin writers misunderstood it to mean 'tide' or 'flood' or 'tidal wave', and ends by comparing it with OE *eagor*, a word used to gloss *dodrans* and probably meaning the same as modern *eagre*, 'a tidal bore'. The use of this word to describe Noah's Flood in *Genesis A* may take us back to explanations of the Flood in Philippus on Job, not far from the passage that caused the muddle over *dodrans*, and offers us our first connection 'between an element of OE literature and the style of the earliest Latin poetry of the islands'. Much more speculative connections are made by D. R. Howlett, 'The Provenance,

[1] *The Sutton Hoo Ship-Burial, Vol. I: Excavations, Background, the Ship, Dating and inventory* by Rupert Bruce-Mitford and others. London: British Museum Publications. pp. xl + 792. 13 Plates. £45.

[2] *Aspects of Anglo-Saxon Archaeology: Sutton Hoo and other discoveries* by Rupert Bruce-Mitford. London: Victor Gollancz, 1974. pp. xx + 356. 112 Plates. £12.50.

Date, and Structure of *De Abbatibus'* (*Archaeologia Æliana*), who thinks that that poem may be placed at St. Peter's Church, Bywall, in 819 AD— for it has 819 lines—while it is composed chiastically and according to the Golden Section, like several other works. The same author suggests (*EPS*) that 'Alfred's *Æstel'* was something very like Alfred's jewel in the Ashmolean Museum, and that the iconography of the jewel itself can be connected with King Alfred's works of translation, see 'The Iconography of the Alfred Jewel' (*Oxoniensia* 1974). By contrast, Milton McC. Gatch, considering 'Noah's Raven in *Genesis A* and the Illustrated OE Hexateuch' (*Gesta*), feels that the Anglo-Saxon poet need have known very little about the raven except the traditional and literal explanation that he did not return to the Ark because he had found a place to rest on floating corpses. If, as has been suggested, line 1447 were emended to *se feond*, the result would be allegorically inept; the picture illustrating the Hexateuch, however, reflects 'a rather rich array of traditional variations' on typological knowledge, though its impaled eye-pecked head is unique. Discord between poets and illustrators is more definitely revealed by George Henderson's study of 'The Programme of Illustrations in Bodleian MS Junius XI', pp. 113–45 of the memorial volume for David Talbot Rice.[3] The lack of alignment between text and pictures is so great that one might almost suspect the illustrators of being 'illiterate in OE'.

Disagreements over the relationship between history, theology, and literature reach what one may hope to be a productive peak in the volume of *Tenth-Century Studies* produced to commemorate the millennium of the Council of Winchester.[4] In a brief 'Introduction' David Parsons introduces the main bones of contention: did the impetus of the Benedictine Reform fall away? Was there perhaps little to live up to, and what achievements there were institutional rather than intellectual? Very different answers are given by different contributors. In 'Church and State in England in the 10th and 11th Centuries' H. R. Loyn extols the virtues of 'the Carolingian compromise' between monarchs and monks, glancing at Wulfstan's collection of canon-law, the *Excerptiones Egberti*. His view is corroborated by the picture of manuscripts and marriages that emerges from D. A. Bullough's 'The Continental Background of the Reform'. D. H. Farmer, however, feels that 'The Progress of the Monastic Revival' was enfeebled by a continuing drain of the ablest members of small communities to the episcopate and to royal service.

Dom Thomas Symons attempts to restore a traditional view of the reformers in his '*Regularis Concordia*: History and Derivation', arguing that though the customs of the Rule are derivative, they show 'how independently and how skilfully its borrowed material has been adapted, blended, and even altered'. C. E. Hohler, in terrifyingly iconoclastic mood, will have none of this. He does not doubt that the tenth-century reformers

---

[3] *Studies in Memory of David Talbot Rice* ed. by Giles Robertson and George Henderson. Edinburgh: U of Edinburgh Press. pp. xiv + 434. 97 Plates. £12.

[4] *Tenth-Century Studies: Essays in Commemoration of the Millenium of the Council of Winchester and 'Regularis Concordia'* ed. by David Parsons. London and Chichester: Phillimore & Co. pp. xii + 270. Frontispiece and 24 Plates. £8.75. (abbreviated as *Tenth-Century Studies*).

did their best, but their best was often 'absurd'. In his study of 'Some Service-Books of the Later Saxon Church' he claims that even reformed monks were luxurious and drunken, their critical faculties numb. The assembled abbots of England ascribed Isaiah to Moses, jumbled canons and penitentials, showed 'a low level of competence at Latin and the grimmest superstition'. 'Cut off from the general cultural heritage of the West', England contributed little to the Latin liturgy beyond 'the formula, to be read over the cask by the priest, to improve the quality of beer in which mice or weasels have got drowned'. Mr. Hohler receives some little support from P. H. Sawyer's account of 'Charters of the Reform Movement: the Worcester Archive', which indicates that there were fairly major changes at Worcester between 969 and 977 (at least thirteen new recruits to the community), but that witnesses to charters were loath to call themselves monks, and that even known monks can be detected holding private property. Reform in that community, then, did not involve any great change of character.

In addition to the preceding essays and those mentioned below, *Tenth-Century Studies* contains accounts of Winchester, of church-building, of sculpture, illumination, and metalwork, which stress new magnificence and old conservatism in different ways.

Tenth-century Latinity is treated in much greater detail in Michael Lapidge's 'The hermeneutic style in tenth-century Anglo-Latin literature' (*ASE*). Although 'excessively mannered', this mode of writing enjoyed high prestige in English monastic circles, largely as a result of continental impetus, though with a traditional predilection for the writings of Aldhelm. Mr. Lapidge considers four main centres and a dozen writers, prints six poems in appendices, and demonstrates conclusively the existence of at least one kind of learning in tenth-century England. A striking exception to its influence, however, was Ælfric, who not only failed to employ the hermeneutic style but 'reacted vigorously against it'. Far away in Durham, Provost Aldred was glossing the *Durham Ritual* and applying the erudition of Jerome and Bede, on a much humbler level, to the interpretation of some dozen Biblical words and names. W. J. P. Boyd considers these in 'Aldrediana XXV: *Ritual* Hebraica' (*EPS*), and presents a picture of learning struggling back through 'murky ignorance'. It is a useful reminder of the wild variations of cultural level within England during the tenth century and in all probability during others.

2. Vocabulary

In this field as well, controversy rules. The Dictionary of OE makes a slight advance with the 'Short titles of OE texts' proposed in *ASE* by Bruce Mitchell, Christopher Ball and Angus Cameron, to be used from now on by Dictionary editors. However, the entire project has come under withering fire from R. I. Page in ' "The Proper Toil of Artless Industry": Toronto's Plan for an OE Dictionary' (*N&Q*). The idea of working from accurate transcripts, he suggests, presents many more difficulties than the lexicographers admit. What of *ælhyde* in CCCC MS 383? This has been explained as 'awl, hide', 'eel-skin' (n.) and 'eel-skin' (adj.), while it could as well mean 'fire-retainer'. What good is a transcript of words like that?

Glossary evidence is even harder to evaluate, many words are explicable only by historians or numismatists or archaeologists, and the heart of a good dictionary is not computerised comprehensiveness but generosity and good judgement in explaining meanings. Dr. Page fears that the Dictionary will provide only 'a quarry for future Ph.D. students'.

The same author illustrates some of the problems in 'More Aldhelm Glosses from CCCC 326' (*ES*), adding a number of new glosses but pointing out that since the glossator did not always bother to write the whole of a word one often has to guess what he meant, and furthermore guess something not found elsewhere. Almost as if to discourage dictionaries further, single words are considered by two writers in *LeedsSE*. Margaret Lindsay Faull surveys the evidence for 'The Semantic Development of OE *Wealh*', but can come to no firm conclusions about the date of changes from 'Celt' to 'slave' or 'foreigner'. More startlingly, Christine E. Fell insists in 'OE *Beor*' that 'beer' is as much a false translation as 'wife' for *wif*. Study of 'functional' and 'emotive' compounds in the poetry as well as many uses in prose leads her to conclude, among much else, that *beor* was a very strong drink 'made from honey and the juice of a fruit other than grapes', as the gloss *ydromellum* always suggested. Modern 'beer' is a loan-word from German, describing an imported drink made with hops. As the rhyme has it, 'Turkeys, Heresy, Hops and Beer/Came into England all in one year.'

A. S. C. Ross's 'OE *Leoht* "World" ' (*N&Q*) is content to suggest that the word's development went from 'light' to 'bright open space' to 'world', and to offer parallels from other languages. Robert C. Rigg, '*Hreowcearig* "Penitent, Contrite" ' (*ELN*), feels that the normal translations 'troubled, anxious, sorrowful' are inadequate for a word with associations with *penitentia*. Two of the four examples in poetry support his case, one (the devil in *Juliana* 536) is recalcitrant but argued down, one (*Guthlac* 1053) is abandoned as a relic of the 'pre-Christian sense'. Karl P. Wentersdorf considers *dreorig, dreorighleor, seledreorig, seledreamas* in '*The Wanderer*: Notes on some Semantic Problems' (*Neophilologus*), referring to earlier articles of his in *SN* (1972) and elsewhere (see *YW* 54, 72-3). He prefers to take *sele-* from *sæl* 'time' rather than *sele* 'hall', and would strengthen *dreorig* to mean 'anguished' or 'agonising' or 'doomed'.

Faced with disagreements and revaluations on this scale, the Toronto editors may well wish they had lived in an earlier century. M. S. Hetherington, studying 'Sir Simonds D'Ewes and Method in OE Lexicography' (*TSLL*) makes it pretty clear, in spite of James Rosier (*YW* 47, 43), that Sir Simonds did not get many new words from reading MSS, but used others' collections and assistance. His main contribution was in the technique of writing entries, though—*absit omen*—his results were never published. Nevertheless he. at any rate, 'had learned what was needed to put together a dictionary of OE'.

3. Old English: General

As in section 1, general studies this year split sharply into early and late. At the start of it all, G. A. Lester reviews 'The Cædmon Story and its Analogues' in *Neophilologus* (1974). Most of the analogues cited over the years prove to be not at all close ones, with the surely meaningless exception of the Call of Mohammed; possibly this supports the story's authenticity. Donald W. Fritz, however, digs into a new vein of similarities in 'Cædmon: a Monastic Exegete' (*ABR*, 1974) alleging that Cædmon's masticatings and ruminations were in fact typical (which is probably why Bede put them in). At the other end of the period G. W. G. Wickham looks at the famous *quem quaeritis* passage in *Regularis Concordia* and summarily evaluates 'The Romanesque Style in Medieval Drama' (*Tenth-Century Studies*). In the same volume P. A. M. Clemoes reviews 'Late OE Literature', with some suggestive remarks which might help to bridge the seemingly irreconcilable positions with regard to the Benedictine Reform already noted. Was the vernacular in fact being taught by 'set texts' in Ælfric's boyhood? Should one see the reform as aiming at diffusion of Christian education rather than peaks of scholarship? Did it not succeed at least in provoking consideration, use, disagreement? If so, the rhetorical force which Professor Clemoes sees even in *Maldon* may be taken as compensation for a certain absence of original thought. This view is supported by Robert Foster's 'The Use of *þa* in Old and Middle English Narratives' (*NM*), which considers passages mostly from Ælfric to evolve a set of 'rules' less syntactic than stylistic. Even simple narratives, it is shown, can contain subtle variations.

Returning to even older times, E. G. Stanley discourages further quest for that 'lost world of pre-Christian antiquity' in *The Search for Anglo-Saxon Paganism*,[5] a revised and indexed reprint of his nine articles in *N&Q* (see *YW* 45, 64 and 46, 68). Tha balance of views has changed in the last decade, as Professor Stanley admits, and scholars who assume that Anglo-Saxon poets knew the *Patrologia* at least as well as Migne's index will have little to learn from this book. However, the analysis of a learned empire collapsing undefeated still has charm; it offers the moral that the scholarship of mutual congratulation is unlikely to survive its beneficiaries. Mary R. Gerstein happily remains uninhibited by the wreckage of ancient theory and claws back a little of what has been lost by considering all the evidence, legal as well as literary, for 'Germanic *Warg*: the Outlaw as Werwolf'.[6] Early references from Gothic onwards lead us into a dim world of wolves, stranglers, and grave-robbers, where the modern critic is bound to feel uneasy. Nevertheless this world is much the same as that of the Exeter and Cotton gnomes, and purely *en passant* Ms. Gerstein offers valuable insights on *Beowulf*, *Dream of the Rood* line 31, the 'Nine Herbs Charm', and much else.

Finally, Randolph Quirk, Valerie Adams and Derek Davy offer a glimpse of the future in their new primer/reader, *Old English Literature: A Practical Introduction*.[7] Stress falls heavily on 'practical'. The authors' premises are clearly that undergraduates will not learn paradigms any more, and must be started on literature straight away. The format is then of text

[5] *The Search for Anglo-Saxon Paganism* by E. G. Stanley. Cambridge: D. S. Brewer and Totowa, N.J.: Rowman & Littlefield. pp. 143. £3.95.
[6] pp. 131–156 of *Myth in Indo-European Antiquity* ed. by Gerald J. Larson, co-eds C. Scott Littleton and Jaan Puhvel. Berkeley, Los Angeles and London: U. of California Press, 1974. pp. 197. £5.
[7] *Old English Literature: A Practical Introduction* ed. by Randolph Quirk, Valerie Adams and Derek Davy. London: Edward Arnold. pp. 79. hb £3.25, pb £1.50.

with facing-page commentary, amounting at the start to word-for-word translation but broadening quickly to points of grammar or idiom. Used by an energetic tutor, this book should get students on to OE poetry with adequate knowledge and unblunted enthusiasm; though since *The Wanderer* is the only poem presented whole any appetite that is whetted here will have to be sated elsewhere. With many students this is certainly the best that can be done: a *memento mori* that more fastidious scholars should not forget.

4. Poetry: General

It is this circumstance which makes John Gardner's *The Construction of Christian Poetry in Old English*[8] hard to forgive. Its purpose—to explore the various allegorical 'styles' of OE poetry—is sensibly tolerant of diversity, and its terminology of *kosmoi* and 'rhythmic encodings' could well prove fascinating, or perhaps hypnotic. However, a deadly jadedness hangs over the book, as if the author were looking only for novelties to break his own tedium. 'There is much to be said for the intellectual games of weary sophisticates,' he writes. 'When a man has looked for a hundred years at a statue of a discus-thrower, he begins to think "So what?" '. So *Elene* is reduced to an unconvincing cruciform diagram, *Beowulf* to a gloss on the first line of the *Æneid* via Fulgentius, *Christ* and *Guthlac* to poems of 'holy madness' never intended for an audience. Hatred of the word reaches its peak, perhaps when *The Dream of the Rood* is attributed to Cynewulf with a calmly unargumentative 'scholars are generally in agreement', and a pretence of support from a footnote. Any intelligent student who gets hold of this book will form a poor idea of the charms of OE, and an even poorer one of the utility of its scholarship.

Allegory recovers a little in the pages of *SLit I*, where Alvin A. Lee writes on 'OE Poetry, Mediaeval Exegesis and Modern Criticism' and James W. Earl on 'Typology and Iconographic Style in Early Medieval Hagiography'. Professor Lee compares the four levels of exegesis with the four critical phases of Northrop Frye, and concludes they have something in common, though our ancestors could give us lessons in critical toleration. One might think that such remarks as that *Maldon* and *Brunanburh* are '*unmistakably* moral and exemplary' (my italics) betray still a certain *parti pris*, but the general plea for 'critical tact' is unexceptionable. Professor Earl, meanwhile, condemns literary critics for feverishly exploiting the levels of allegory as if they were just 'sophisticated rhetorical devices', and points to the theories of reality which underlie them. Saints' lives are like icons, as saints are like relics; iconography and hagiography are related in their stasis, their conventionality, their uncertain position between truth and art. All this suggests that 'figural narrative' could stand yet deeper scrutiny. Scholars wishing to overgo their predecessors are offered the assistance of Hugh T. Keenan's 'A Check-List on Typology and English Medieval Literature through 1972' (*SLI*).

---

[8] *The Construction of Christian Poetry in Old English* by John Gardner. Carbondale and Edwardsville: Southern Illinois U. Press. pp. xii + 147. $8.95.

'The Meaning of "Formulaic" in OE Verse Composition' is confused rather than clarified by F. H. Whitman in *NM*. The author has little trouble in showing that the poets of Psalm 52, Riddle 40 and Boethius Meter 15 worked by adding alliterative 'fillers' to literal translation, and that this is an ugly and mechanical process. To insist that this is the only sense of 'formulaic', though, betrays a wish that all adherents of Parry would commit intellectual suicide, and few will respond; *Maldon is* better than *Metres*, but not because it is free of formulas. Jeff Opland's *'Imbongi Nezibongo*: the Xhosa Tribal Poet and the Contemporary Poetic Tradition' (*PMLA*) contains nothing on OE but offers valuable analogical light in its demonstration that among the Xhosa of today there are good oral poets, bad oral poets, literate poets, and memorisers, who may all be the same man at different stages of his career. Thomas Cable continues his important work on the performance of OE poetry (see *YW* 55, 81), with 'Parallels to the Melodic Formulas of *Beowulf*' (*MP*). These come from various linguistic traditions, including Gregorian chant, but fulfil his hypothetical 'rules' that accent and pitch should coincide, and that pre-existing melodic formulas should filter out unacceptable linguistic patterns. Corroboration of this theory is offered by Jane Maria Luecke's 'Measuring the Rhythmic Variation of OE Meter' (*Lang&S*). The author borrows ideas from the Solesmes school of Gregorian chant to provide a notation in which phrase-stress or pitch tends towards a fixed, isochronous pattern while word-stress re-establishes fluid but rhythmical variation.

In 'Verbal Stress in OE Verse' (*Anglia*), E. G. Stanley ponders the (insoluble) problem of the alliterating verb in *Beowulf* 2717b; and then generates a set of provisional rules for the employment of metrically unstressed infinitives in initial dips. Richard A. Leslie continues to explore the patterns of 'Plurilinear Alliteration in OE Poetry' (*TSLL*), concluding that they are the products of 'literate, sensitive poets'. Peter R. Schroeder's 'Stylistic Analogies between OE Art and Poetry' (*Viator* 1974) suggests that the poets' lack of concern for straightforward chronology resembles the 'barbaric abstraction' of early Anglo-Saxon visual art, but is replaced by greater naturalism later on. He reminds us that in art-history such terms as 'barbaric' or 'primitive' need not be disparaging.

Bruce Mitchell pleads for the priority of the former over the latter in 'Linguistic facts and the interpretation of OE poetry' (*ASE*), with special reference to *swa* in *Wanderer* 43 and the (hypothetical) pluperfects of *Wife's Lament* 11 and 15. Less rigorously, Joyce M. Hill reviews the 'Figures of Evil in OE Poetry' (*LeedsSE*), and concludes that spiritual corruption is shown by perverted imitation of the good: a useful theory, since it enables one to say that God 'rewards' His followers while Satan merely 'bribes' his, an entirely different activity. *Deaþscua* in *Beowulf* 160 is also considered in relation to patristic *umbra mortis*. A more contrastive view of good and evil emerges from David Williams's 'The Exile as Un-creator' (*Mosaic*), which makes play with etymologies and with disjunctions of many kinds. Michael S. Fukuchi takes up the interesting question of 'Gnomic Statements in OE Poetry' (*Neophilologus*), largely with reference to *Andreas*, and offers a classification of gnomes and gnomic kernels, resting on the old definition of Blanche C. Williams—'a sententious saying' but paying more attention to the sayings' functions.

5. Beowulf

In 'Sharon Turner's First Published Reference to *Beowulf*' (*N&Q*) E. G. Stanley takes criticism of the poem back to 1803. Few years have elapsed since without some addition to the corpus, and the problem for critics now is almost as much to explain their predecessors as to explain the poem. Andreas Haarder makes a thorough attempt at both in his book *Beowulf: the Appeal of a Poem*[9] beginning (with a touch of humour) at the first seven reviews of Thorkelin's edition, and following the critical stances—patriotic, apologetic, antiquarian, as well as literary—generated seemingly inevitably ever since. Much of the material discussed is unfamiliar to modern Beowulfians, and much that is not is handled freshly by virtue of the author's long perspectives; but for most readers the pay-off will be in the last three chapters, in which the question of appropriate modern responses is considered firmly if tolerantly. Professor Haarder sees *Beowulf* as a work of social self-definition, by which modern as well as Anglo-Saxon audiences are spurred to reject the monsterworld within themselves and to accept the splendours and miseries of humanity. His analysis of Beowulf's *wæfre mod* is particularly compelling, as is his restatement of the importance of the poem's many 'minor' characters. Much further evidence on the way that *Beowulf* has transcended scholars can be gleaned from the re-issue of Chauncey B. Tinker's *The Translations of Beowulf*,[10] now brought up to date by Marijane Osborn.

The reasons why *Beowulf* was and is popular are best illuminated this year by two very different articles, Kathryn Hume's 'The Theme and Structure of *Beowulf*' (*SP*), and Robert B. Burlin's 'Gnomic Indirection in *Beowulf*', in *Anglo-Saxon Poetry*,[11] the enormous *festschrift* compiled for John C. McGalliard. The former agrees with Professor Haarder in rejecting a 'hero-centered design', proposing instead as controlling theme '*threats to social order*', i.e. 'troublemaking, revenge, and war'. The view is similar to John Earle's ancient dictum—quoted by Haarder—that 'mutual dependence is the law of human society', but Professor Hume's more apparently negative stance enables her to consider all the poem's digressions, and to use comparable Scandinavian material to good effect. Professor Burlin, by contrast, considers only short secfions of the poem, noting in them how beneath apparent gnomic 'blandness' the poet is able to restate central themes and paradoxes, gaining extra force from the conflict between gnome and context. This author also sees 'societal interdependence' at the heart of the heroic ethos, and shows how the 'bardic posture' can intensify poet-audience communion.

Mary C. Wilson Tietjen reacts against 'narrow Christian didacticism' in 'God, Fate and the Hero of *Beowulf*' (*JEGP*), re-examining the references to *wyrd* to argue that though God may control the dictates of this whimsi-

---

[9] *Beowulf: the Appeal of a Poem* by Andreas Haarder. Copenhagen: Akademisk Forlag. pp. 341. £5.

[10] *The Translations of Beowulf: A Critical Bibliography* by Chauncey B. Tinker, with an updated bibliography by Marijane Osborn and a new foreword by Fred. C. Robinson. Hamden, Conn.: Archon Books, 1903 repr. 1974. pp. 180. $9.

[11] *Anglo-Saxon Poetry: Essays in Appreciation for John C. McGalliard* ed. by Lewis E. Nicholson and Dolores Warwick Frese. Notre Dame and London: U. of Notre Dame Press. pp. xvi + 387. £10.40. (abbreviated as *McGalliard Studies*).

cal force, He does not reverse them. Charles Donahue presents a new anthropological perspective in 'Potlatch and Charity: Notes on the Heroic in *Beowulf'* (*McGalliard Studies*), urging that the poem's society is essentially good and that the 'potlatches' (or reciprocal donation-scenes) are an image of a kind of charity. One might cavil at the definition of 'potlatch' (often thought to be hostile and competitive), as at the assumption that intelligent thanes would retire to monasteries (see Mr. Hohler, Section 1 above).

Karl P. Wentersdorf, having persuaded himself (*YW* 52, 70) that *oferswam* in line 2367 means 'rowed', returns to the charge with 'Beowulf's Adventure with Breca' (*SP*). The copious evidence for swimming-matches in Germanic society is dismissed as 'exceedingly thin gruel'; cases of *mid sunde* are racked for evidence of artificial support (one plank, two barrels); and it is concluded that the contest with Breca was a rowing one (for which Germanic literature offers no analogues at all). The sober Beowulf who emerges is regarded with approval. John Gardner, in his 'Guilt and the World's Complexity: the Murder of Ongentheow and the Slaying of the Dragon' (*McGalliard Studies*), rejects John Leyerle's 'annoying theory' of the hero's guilt only to take up Robert Kaske's equally annoying one that all the names in *Beowulf* mean something (usually uncomplimentary). So Ongentheow is killed by Wolf and Boar, sons of Dark-counsel, servants of Mindlack. Beowulf's guilt by association is shown by his killing of Dæghrefn, not Day-raven but 'dawn or somehow related to dawn'. Ongentheow or 'beginning ⊢ servant' is related to it too, and when Beowulf falls to the dragon 'it is Ongentheow's ghost that kills him'.

Lewis E. Nicholson, also in *McGalliard Studies*, propounds the view in 'Hunlafing and the Point of the Sword' that the *Hunlafing* of line 1143 is short for Hunferth Ecglafing, while Hrunting is the *hildeleoma*. The words 'fairly drip with irony', and so do those of all the other sword-scenes in the poem—including the 'potlatch' to the coastguard in lines 1900 ff., though Professor Nicholson is not quite sure where *that* irony lies. Eugene J. Crook is just as convinced, in 'Pagan Gold in *Beowulf'* (*ABR* 1974), that the poem's *sapientia* must be seen 'in the context of the heathen and hopeless'. Fortified by the belief that the poet had an 'intricate knowledge of the body of lore we call the *Elder Edda*', he rebukes Beowulf for involvement with pagan mythology and concludes that the re-interment of the dragon's gold reflects eighth-century clerics' rejection of compromise (but see E.G. Stanley, Section 9 below). Thomas A. Carnicelli offers a relatively forgiving view in 'The Function of the Messenger in *Beowulf'* (*SP*): though the Geats were guilty of aggression, they redeem themselves by admitting it. The speaker of 2900–3027 must be one of the ten cowards; maybe, rehabilitated, he is also one of the twelve final riders.

Criticism of this sort, much more ethical than literary, is likely to be swollen by Joseph F. Tuso's compilation on *Beowulf*,[12] which assumes that students will work from a translation (admittedly the excellent Donaldson one), but offers them all the paraphernalia of scholarship apart

---

[12] *Beowulf: the Donaldson Translation, Backgrounds and Sources, Criticism* ed. by Joseph F. Tuso. A Norton Critical Edition. New York: W. W. Norton & Co. pp. xvi + 205. hb $10, pb $2.95.

from a text—bibliography, family trees, map, index of names, some rather indigestible remarks on 'Backgrounds and Sources' and a great deal of 'Criticism'. It certainly fulfils a demand. Is this, however, a need? Diagrammatic analysis is once more exemplified by D. R. Howlett, who seizes the opportunity of writing about 'The Structure of *Ecbasis Captivi*' (*SN*) to say how similar it is to *Beowulf*: chiasmus, Golden Section, etc. C. B. Hieatt detects other divisions in 'Envelope Patterns and the Structure of *Beowulf*' (*ESC*), finding eleven 'fitts' which are also 'envelopes', but also 'envelopes' within or across fitt-boundaries. Interestingly, Ruth P. Lehmann's 'Broken Cadences in *Beowulf*' (*ES*) shows how reluctant the poet is to repeat patterns of metre and syntax, though he can do it when he wants to, for instance in the last two lines. Bruce A. Rosenberg, in 'Folktale Morphology and the Structure of *Beowulf*: A Counterproposal' (*JFI*), rejects the larger patterns found by D. R. Barnes (*YW* 51, 66), and by this reviewer (*YW* 50, 71), insisting that though Unferth may owe something to oral tradition he is nevertheless a literary addition whose main function is to 'realise' the hero's character. H. R. Ellis Davidson accepts the 'morphological' theory without comment in 'Folklore and Literature' (*Folklore*).

As if to show that nothing in the poem can be taken for granted, C. Weibull argues in the first of *Zwei Diskussionsbeiträge*[13] that the Swedes did not incorporate the Götar c. 560 AD, that the Geats could not have been Götar because raiding Frisia round the Skaw in primitive boats was too risky, and that Gregory of Tours was right in thinking Hygelac a Dane. There are four very minor articles to conclude this survey. Raymond S. J. Grant's '*Beowulf* and the World of Heroic Elegy' (*LeedsSE*) is derivative, relaxed and should not have got outside the lecture-room; Norman E. Eliason's 'Healfdene's Daughter' (*McGalliard Studies*) cautions against accepting the Malone amplification of line 62; Bruce Moore, '*Beowulf* 1417b–1421' (*Expl.*), notes the effect of the *syðþan*-clause in this sentence; Thomas J. Jambeck compares 'The Syntax of Petition in *Beowulf* and *SGGK*' (*Style* 1973) to prove that in lines 426–32 the OE hero also *cuþe duguðe ðeaw*.

6. The Junius Manuscript

Study of the poems in this codex is this year all but entirely figural, and concentrates heavily on *Exodus* and *Genesis B*. John F. Vickrey re-interprets lines 135–53 of the former in '*Exodus* and the *Herba Humilis*' (*Traditio*). He rejects the notion that the lacuna after line 141 would have contained an account of Genesis 47, and suggests instead that the *yrfeweard* of line 143 is the devil, the *wære* of 147 his broken compact with Christ. Lines 146–7, e.g., 'refer allegorically to the devil's attack on Christ . . . and morally to his attack on the souls of the redeemed'; *se yldra cyning* (141) is not Pharaoh but Melchisedek, and the broken sentence should run 'though the older king . . . had revealed the new covenant'. As for the

---

[13] *Die Geaten des Beowulfepos und Die dänischen Trelleburgen*, by Curt Weibull. Acta Regiae Societatis Scientiarum et Litterarum Gothoburgensis, Humaniora 10. Göteborg 1974. pp. 43.

antwig crux of line 145, this refers to the *fasciculus hyssopi* of Exodus 12, 22, connected figurally with the Cross and commonly glossed as 'humility', which the Israelites show by their obedience. In similar mood, but less rigorously, John P. Hermann considers 'The Green Rod of Moses in the OE *Exodus*' (*ELN*), and urges us to read neither *tane* nor *tacne* in line 281, but both, since the rod of Moses was both *tan* and *tacn*. The *grenne grund* of line 312a receives yet more explication (see *YW* 54, 72) from Kari Sajavaara's 'The Withered Footprints on the Green Street of Paradise' (*NM*), this time by way of a story in *Cursor Mundi*—Seth following Adam's footprints back to Paradise. J. R. Hall produces two pieces, '*Niwe Flodas*: OE *Exodus* 362' (*N&Q*) and 'The Building of the Temple in *Exodus*: Design for Typology' (*Neophilologus*). In the first he argues that Noah's Flood was a repetition of the Deluge preceding Creation; the poet is emphasising new floods and a new creation to point to the new man born of the new birth of baptism. As for the criticised lines 389–396, their syntax is tortuous in order to identify the building (temple, Church, Christ's body) with the builder (Solomon, Christ, the Church's founder). The digression within a digression is typologically appropriate, the poet a shaper of masterful architectonic achievement'. Joseph B. Trahern, meanwhile, identifies 'More Scriptural Echoes in the OE *Exodus*' (*Mc-Galliard Studies*) mostly from apocryphal books of wisdom; and a last *Ritter des Realismus*, Alfred Bammesberger, suggests in 'Zu *Exodus* 145b' (*Anglia*) that though Kock's emendation *antþigðu* is now rejected, the MS *ymb an twig* is little better. *And-þyngð(u)* would do, meaning 'the prosperity of the Israelites in opposition to the Egyptians'.

Genesis B criticism is just as unanimous. G. C. Britton propounds an ironic view of Satan in 'Repetition and Contrast in the OE *Later Genesis*' (*Neophilologus* 1974), and excuses verbosity on the grounds of didactic function and deliberate verbal echo. J. R. Hall agrees. His '*Geongordom and Hyldo* in *Genesis B*: Serving the Lord for the Lord's Favour' (*PLL*) considers the ironies evoked by these two words and by the parallels between Satan and Adam and Eve. Both articles are largely subsumed in Margaret J. Ehrhart's 'Tempter as Teacher: Some Observations on the Vocabulary of the OE *Genesis B*' (*Neophilologus*), which deals with the master/disciple relationship in the poem, the set of words round *geongra*, and the verbal pairs *(for)læran, (un)ræd, (un)hyldo, (for)wyrcan*. 'The infernal,' she decides, 'is a mirror image of the celestial . . . it is the wrong choice between the two that causes Adam and Eve to fall'. The (un)fairness of this is pondered by Thomas D. Hill in 'The Fall of Angels and Men in the OE *Genesis B*' (*McGalliard Studies*). He points to the re-enactment of the Fall of the angels in men's sins of overreaching and insubordination, without accepting the allegory by which Adam, Eve, and the devil would represent reason, sense, temptation. Still, though the poet was 'in no sense heterodox', he might be 'misconstrued'. Was Old Saxon analogous to modern Dutch? A vehicle for thoughts too daring to be trusted to the universal medium of Latin? Marcel Dando answers indirectly with a piece on 'The Moralia in Job of Gregory the Great as a Source for the Old Saxon *Genesis B*', in *C&M* (1974 for 1969).

The same much-delayed journal includes Robert Emmett Finnegan's long piece on '*Christ and Satan*: Structure and Theme', which argues for the unity of that battered poem by pointing to similar alternations of exposition, exemplum and exhortation in homilies. The poem reveals Christ's character in divinity and humanity and explores 'the implications of this revelation for man's moral life'. Spencer Cosmos, 'OE *Limwæstm* (*Christ and Satan* 129)' (*N&Q*) insists that the word does not imply great size. Finally, Michael Benskin and Brian Murdoch offer a long critique of and supplement to J. M. Evans's *Paradise Lost and the Genesis Tradition* (*YW* 49, 219), with particular reference to Old Irish: 'The Literary Tradition of Genesis' (*NM*).

7. Poems of The Vercelli Book

The most disturbing piece on these poems is certainly Robert D. Stevick's 'Arithmetical Design of the OE *Andreas*' (*McGalliard Studies*). Scepticism preserves one from minor numerologies, but Professor Stevick can offer some curiously round numbers. The poem *is* in fifteen sections; the first five are 600 lines; the whole poem would be very close to 1800 if complete, and that is fifteen times factorial fifteen; multiples of 12, 13 and 15 appear frequently in pairs or groups of fitts. The author does not dissipate belief by forcing interpretations or ignoring manuscript lacunae, but leaves us to ponder the implications of his argument. David Hamilton's '*Andreas* and *Beowulf*: Placing the Hero' (also *McGalliard Studies*) compares the two poems to suggest that the author of the former 'cultivated ways of making departures from the epic', for the purposes of irony and spiritual metaphor. The argument is weakened by too-ready acceptance of the belief (derived from *ASPR*) that Latin translations of the Greek *Acts of Andrew and Matthew* are 'lost' or insignificant; in places a glance at the *Recensio Casanatensis* would soon disperse any notion of modulations on *Beowulf*.

Still in *McGalliard Studies*, Alvin A. Lee goes 'Toward a Critique of *The Dream of the Rood*', though so fully that the first word functions as mere modesty. In several details he is challenged by other writers of 1975. Thus William Helder argues that 'The *Engel Dryhtnes* in *The Dream of the Rood*' (*MP*) is Christ, with patristic support and a reading of lines 9b to 12 as a sort of pluperfect flashback. Professor Lee scouts this; but later on his worry as to why the Harrowing of Hell is not mentioned till line 148 would be resolved by the pun on *byrigde*, 'tasted'/'buried', identified by F. H. Whitman, '*The Dream of the Rood* 101a' (*Expl.*). The late James Smith further explains 'The garments that honour the Cross in *The Dream of the Rood*' (*ASE*) as neither palls nor streamers but the blood and gold with which the Rood is *begoten* and *bewrigen*: 'Who is this with garments gory, Triumphing from Bozrah's way?' Kathleen E. Dubs, finally, enthuses over the words *beorn* and *hæleð* in '*Hæleð*: Heroism in *The Dream of the Rood*' (*Neophilologus*), not without syntactic confusion.

Cynewulf's smallest poem receives two treatments this year. D. R. Howlett, '*Se Giddes Begang* of *The Fates of the Apostles*' (*ES*), finds it composed according to the Golden Section, i.e. its minor portion (lines 1-8 and 85-122) is as much smaller than the major portion (9-84) as that is smaller than the whole. In '*The Fates of the Apostles*, the Latin Martyrologies and the Litany of the Saints' (*MÆ*), Daniel G. Calder finds other structures of digression and repetition, which transform the poem from a verse calendar to a personal but ritual work designed to calm the poet's soul.

Elene continues to cause embarrassment to its critics by its plain picture of coercion used against Jews. Ellen F. Wright assures us in 'Cynewulf's *Elene* and the *singal sacu*' (*NM*) that the slow revelations of knowledge in the poem bear witness to the perceived difficulty of conversion. James Doubleday, 'The Speech of Stephen and the Tone of *Elene*' (*Mc-Galliard Studies*), shows first that the family of Judas is significant, in that his 'brother' is that Stephen whose speech in Acts 6 and 7 provided a model for the Church's approach to the unconverted, while his 'grandfather', equally unhistorically, is the Zaccheus of Luke 19. But the fact that in *Elene*, unlike Acts, it is the Christians who are the persecutors can only be excused by the suggestion that Elene herself is to be seen as increasingly and deliberately 'ambiguous'. E. Gordon Whatley more boldly considers 'Bread and Stone: Cynewulf's *Elene* 611–8' (*NM*), and shows that the reference there is not to Matthew 4, 3–4, as T. D. Hill had suggested (*YW* 52, 73), but to Matthew 7,9. God is ready to give the bread of *charitas*, but Judas exemplifies the stone of *duritia cordis*. John Chrysostom is cited as evidence of the Church's designs on Jews. The same author points out the significance of Cyriacus being interpreted as *æ hælendes* rather than *æ dryhtnes* in 'OE Onomastics and Narrative Art: *Elene* 1062' (*MP*). The Jewish law is the letter, the Saviour's law is the spirit, but in the end Judas-become-Cyriacus is presented as both more tolerant and more authoritative than he is in the Latin sources. John P. Hermann considers the differences between *Elene* and the *Acta Cyriaci* in 'The Theme of Spiritual Warfare in the OE *Elene*' (*PLL*), suggesting that the heroic vocabulary needs firm re-reading. Varda Fish also looks at sources in 'Theme and Pattern in Cynewulf's *Elene*' (*NM*), but more fully and sensitively. Judas in the pit is man under the Old Law, Elene representing Grace (who has to be summoned); the poem is a triptych, based on the three conversions of Constantine, Judas, and Cynewulf, the latter progressing from letter to spirit, from mere *wordcræft* (1237) to *leoðucræft* (1250).

8 The Exeter Book

Cynewulf's other saint's life is given similar treatment by Joseph Wittig, 'Figural Narrative in Cynewulf's *Juliana*' (*ASE*). Juliana's virginity represents the Christian's indifference to the world; her passion recalls Christ's, and her dispute with the devil the Harrowing, though here details are 'deliberately inverted'; the source has been changed in places to promote identification of saint and Saviour. Though all this establishes the poem's significance, it does not make it one of the greatest in OE. R. W. Adams is more enthusiastic over 'Christ II: Cynewulfian *Heilsgeschichte*' (*ELN* 1974), arguing that its theme is not limited to the Ascension. Dolores Warwick Frese praises 'The Art of Cynewulf's Runic Signatures' in *McGalliard Studies*, for each reflects it preceding poem; astonishingly, this leads to the thought that maybe only the signatures are 'authentically "Cynewulfian"'. In the same volume Robert E. Diamond also considers the canon in 'The Diction of the OE *Christ*'. Formulaic analysis offers a percentage of verses repeated within Cynewulf's work alone; if *Christ I* and *Christ III* approached this 'it may well be that they must be regarded as possibly by Cynewulf'. Luckily their scores are far too low. John Miles Foley also disclaims 'interpretive bias' in favour of 'structural principle' in *'Christ* 164–213: a Structural Approach to the Speech Boundaries in *Advent Lyric VII'* (*Neophilologus*). He rejects Robert B. Burlin's speech-division of the lines in question in favour of the *ASPR* one.

Paul F. Reichardt, in *'Guthlac A* and the Landscape of Spiritual Perfection' (*Neophilologus* 1974), thinks that the saint's *beorg* is a mountain not a barrow. This has nothing to do with the fens of Crowland but is a symbol of 'interior spiritual achievement', like John Cassian's 'mount of saintliness'. Daniel G. Calder swallows barrows but strains at demons in *'Guthlac A* and *Guthlac B*: Some Discriminations' (*McGalliard Studies*). *A*, he feels, is an abstract but didactic poem, with a symbolic object at its centre; *B* has more sense of progress in time, and is closer to typology. Thomas D. Hill argues convincingly for patterns of 7 (and 8) days, 6 (and 7) sections in 'The Typology of the Week and the Numerical Structure of *Guthlac B*' (*MS*), but all but throws his case away in a final footnote which admits that the poem is unfinished but refuses to discuss it 'since I am only concerned with the numerical pattern which is implicit in the portion of the poem which we have'.

The *Wanderer* and *The Seafarer* seem to excite less interest this year, perhaps from exhaustion. Karen Mullen briefly refutes A. A. Prins's 'patchwork' theory (*YW* 45, 60) in *'The Wanderer* Considered Again' (*Neophilologus* 1974). Eugene R. Kintgen writes on 'Wordplay in *The Wanderer*' (*Neophilologus* 1975), concluding that *eal is wæl*. An undergraduate translation of *The Seafarer* by Lawrence L. Austin appears in *OEN*, to show that the subject need not be confined to graduates. More ambitiously, D. R. Howlett explains 'The Structures of *The Wanderer* and *The Seafarer*' in *SN*. His symmetries and centre-points are at times remarkable, but spoilt by dogged refusal to notice negative evidence (such as the perceptions of editors and clear signs of textual corruption). In *McGalliard Studies* Rosemary Woolf sharpens received notions of 'elegy', considering 'The *Wanderer*, *The Seafarer*, and the Genre of *Planctus*'. W. F. Klein's 'Purpose and the "Poetics" of *The Wanderer* and *The Seafarer*', in the same volume, offers a fuller revaluation of the two poems. The structure of the former is, in brief, tripartite: past memory, present perception, volitional futurity. All three notions are expressed by words conveying the power of the mind, and all three lead to (increasingly qualified) failure. *The Seafarer* also rests on this recognition of mental power; in an ending by turns bold and timid the author suggests that the poem's *sylf* is Othinn, the ravens Memory and Future Vision on his shoulders.

James L. Boren also puts a high value on mental power in 'The Design of the OE *Deor*' (*McGalliard Studies*), seeing the central stanza as the one on Boethius's persecutor Theodoric. Alternations of activity and passivity, artists and tyrants, lead to the first-person conclusion: Deor is like Boethius and like Weland. K. S. Kiernan offers 'A Solution to the Mæðhild-Geat Crux in *Deor*' (*ES*) by reading *slæp* as 'sleep of death' or 'slippery place'. Jon Erickson considers the grammatical peculiarities of 'The *Deor* Genitives' (*ArL*). In 'Widsith's Journey through Germanic Tradition' (*McGalliard*

Studies), Robert P. Creed defends the MS reading of line 2 of *Widsith*, translating 'he who travelled most through what-men-know/of peoples over earth'; the poet speaks at the very end of oral tradition, in which all poets share a voice.

Alain Renoir's 'A Reading Context for *The Wife's Lament*' (*McGalliard Studies*) is the obvious one of 'a Germanic tradition of suffering women', briskly reviewed. Clifford Davidson would compare it, however, with the Latin 'Cambridge Songs', all 'Erotic "Women's Songs" in Anglo-Saxon England' (*Neophilologus*). *The Wife's Lament* is about 'social and psychological displacement', while the heroine of *Wulf and Eadwacer*, poor lady, is displaced 'even in the place where she should feel herself most integrated'. Margaret E. Goldsmith will tolerate none of this licentiousness, solving 'The Enigma of *The Husband's Message*' (*McGalliard Studies*) by reading it and Riddle 60 as one poem, based on Psalms 44, 1, and meant to indicate the Reed-pen (Holy Writ), bringing the message of the Lord (Christ) to his queen (*Ecclesia*)—a solution not incompatible with references to the Cross, boats, sceptres, measuring-rods. The verb in line 49a, in her opinion, is *gehyre*. Earl R. Anderson considers '*The Husband's Message*: Persuasion and the Problem of *genyre*' (*ES*), translating the latter as 'superimpose on', and rather withdrawing his earlier suggestions (*YW* 54, 80) about prosopopoeia.

The less familiar poems of the Exeter Book, as usual, receive scant notice. Douglas D. Short, '*Leopocræftas* and the Pauline Analogy of the Body in the OE *Gifts of Men*' (*Neophilologus*), finds 'physical abilities' an inappropriate idea in that poem unless one thinks of human endowments as members of 'the metaphoric body of Christ, which is the Church'. Neil D. Isaacs, 'Up a Tree: To See *The Fates of Men*' (*McGalliard Studies*), thinks that the poem does not reflect daily life but archaic initiation rites. He discovers many shamans who climbed trees; unfortunately falling out of them, which is what happens in the poem, is a rarer ceremony. John P Hermann's '*The Riming Poem* 45b–47a' (*Expl.*) sees its 'flights' as the figurative darts of moral evil.

The Riddles clearly provide more sport. In a forceful article Ann Harleman Stewart sees 'OE Riddle 47 as Stylistic Parody' (*PLL*), because although it follows its source's format of 'ic, doch ohne y', it gives its own solution at the start—moth. Further, heroic vocabulary is used with deliberate inappositeness; and conventions of variation and parallelism are teasingly exaggerated. Fred C. Robinson makes a similar point in 'Artful Ambiguities in the OE "Book-Moth" Riddle' in *McGalliard Studies*. Jackson J. Campbell reads the first three riddles as one in 'A Certain Power' (*Neophilologus*), seeing it as an account of the postlapsarian relationship between God and Nature threatening but 'ultimately disarmingly orthodox'. Riddles 1–3 are among those discussed in Marie Nelson's 'Time in the Exeter Book Riddles' (*PQ*), which shows well how much more dynamic OE riddles are than Latin ones in their use of anaphora, variation, and envelope. The same author contributes 'OE Riddle No. 18: The "Badger": An Early Example of Mock-Heroic' (*Neophilologus*).

Four final articles offer more or less unconvincing solutions, with little respect for their texts. Christopher B. Kennedy answers 'OE Riddle No. 39' (*ELN*) as 'cloud': *earmost ealra wihta*? K. S. Kiernan expounds 'The

Mysteries of the Sea-Eagle in Exeter Riddle 74' (*PQ*), with some success on lines 3–5, but less on lines 1–2. Ambrose may have thought vultures parthenogenetic, but that is not the same as thinking eagles hermaphrodite. The same author solves Riddle 95 as 'prostitute' (*'Cwene*: the Old Profession of Exeter Riddle 95' (*MP*)), informing us eagerly that 'prostitution was something of a specialty to the Anglo-Saxons'. This slur, at least, is refuted by Edith Whitehurst Williams's aggressive 'What's So New About the Sexual Revolution?' (*TQ*). She thinks that riddles 25, 45, 61, and 12 (the obscene ones) were written by a woman, probably a nun, but anyway a 'spirited individual' expressing 'wholesome and spontaneous attitudes'. Anglo-Saxon monasteries have indeed been misrepresented!

9. Other Poems

Some excellent criticism on *Judith* is one of the year's redeeming features. Ian Pringle offers a conventionally allegorical view in '*Judith*: the Homily and the Poem' (*Traditio*), reading the poem determinedly by way of Ælfric, and concluding that it is a plea for the purification of society through the maintenance of monasteries for chaste *oratores*—a scheme which will also keep off the Vikings. But David Chamberlain notes that while Judith is much praised in the poem, neither her chastity nor her widowhood—both allegorical essentials—is so much as mentioned. His '*Judith*: a Fragmentary and Political Poem' (*McGalliard Studies*) proves easily that much of the poem is lost, and suggests strongly that the poet did not *want* to exploit allegory. The lessons of Nocturns, he observes, would be a natural place to hear selections from the Book of Judith simply as narrative; the events of 990–1010 offer an apt political context. In 'Hypermetricity and Rhetoric' in the same volume Burton Raffel dares to own a sense of disquiet in translating parts of *Judith*; the poem contains 'padding' (a thought that has clearly scandalised the *festchrift*'s editors, used to explaining everything as deliberate art). But honesty about the bad bits is a concomitant of sensitivity to the good bits; the editors should be glad to find one Diogenes left.

Maldon is appraised with similarly productive coolness by John Mc-Kinnell, 'On the Date of *The Battle of Maldon*' (*MÆ*). The use of the words *eorl* and *ealdormann* in the poem strongly implies a date 'about or after 1020', and this makes it hard to take the poem as historic, ironic, or panegyric (with or without fatal flaw). The warrior-saint Olaf was canonised in 1031, and maybe the author thought similarly of Byrhtnoth. Elizabeth S. Sklar looks at the two rhyming lines in the poem in '*The Battle of Maldon* and the Popular Tradition' (*PQ*), noting the recurrence of the rhymes (similar rhymes, anyway) in Middle English poetry.

Some advance is also made over the treacherous ground of gnomic and magic poetry. J. K. Bollard suggests that *dyrne cræfte* means love-potions, citing Ælfric's *De Auguriis*, in 'A Note on the Cotton Maxims, lines 43–5' (*Neophilologus*). In '*Maxims II*: Gnome and Poem' (*McGalliard Studies*), Stanley B. Greenfield and Richard Evert read the whole poem as developing the idea 'that true wisdom ultimately reveals the limitations of human knowledge'. Three charms are strikingly translated by Brian Swann, 'Anglo-Saxon Charms' (*Antaeus* 1974); and in 'Cursing with the Thistle:

Skírnismál 31, 6-8, and *OE Metrical Charm 9*, 16-17' (*NM*), Joseph Harris interprets both cruces as referring to the dry, brittle, seed-swollen thistle of harvest-time. Hildegard L. C. Tristram's 'Der "homo octipartitus" in der irischen und altenglischen Literatur' (*ZCP*) considers the story of 2 Enoch that Adam was made of eight (or seven) substances, and its insular descendants, concluding interestingly that the English versions are independent of and possibly older than the Irish ones. This gives strong support to L. Whitbread's suggestion, 'Adam's Pound of Flesh: A Note on OE Verse *Solomon and Saturn (II)* 336-9' (*Neophilologus*), that instead of *niehtes wunde* at that point we should read *eahta pundum* 'eight substances'.

Returning to the start of the tradition, K. W. Humphreys and A. S. C. Ross print four new texts of *Cædmon's Hymn* and three of *Bede's Death-Song* in 'Further MSS of Bede's *Historia Ecclesiastica*, of the *Epistola Cuthberti de Obitu Bedae*, and Further Anglo-Saxon Texts of *Cædmon's Hymn* and *Bede's Death-Song*' (*N&Q*). They offer little support to D. R. Howlett, who thinks that 'The Theology of *Cædmon's Hymn* (*LeedsSE* 1974) is one of Trinitarian orthodoxy: nine names, three sentences. E. G. Stanley makes it two two-clause sentences in 'The Oldest English Poetry Now Extant' (*Poetica*, Tokyo, 1974), and also considers *Wynfrith's Proverb*, with interesting remarks on the meaning of *foreldit* and the latent opposition of *dædhwæt* and **dædlæt*. The proverb sums an ideal of heroic fellowship, applied surprisingly but not incongruously to missionary endeavour.

10. Prose

The main event in this field is Michael Swanton's translations of *Anglo-Saxon Prose*.[14] Some obvious pieces are translated, like St. Edmund and *Sermo Lupi*; but there are many others which draw on to less familiar material—the Gospel of Nicodemus, the Institutes of Polity, the Distichs of Cato, two Blickling Homilies, laws, charters and the amusing 'Letter to Brother Edward'. The translations are clear and elegant, and one can imagine the book being used as background for historians, study-aid for English students, and also quite simply as bait.

Ingvar Carlson presents the first volume of an edition of the *Pastoral Care* from MS Cotton Otho B.ii,[15] arguing against D. M. Horgan (*YW* 54, 81) that this a copy of a copy of Hehstan's MS, not a direct descendant. Torben Kisbye ('Sardinia-Sarþinia: Über die Wiedergabe einiger griechisch-lateinischer Namensformen im altenglischen Orosius' (*SN*)) concludes that the work was dictated by someone who knew Vulgar Latin pronunciation and then corrected sporadically by someone with a grasp of Carolingian *Schriftlatein*. J. E. Cross finds some more sources in Caesarius, Gregory and pseudo-Augustine for 'Blickling Homily XIV and the OE Martyrology on John the Baptist' (*Anglia*). Paul E. Szarmach prints two pages of

---

[14] *Anglo-Saxon Prose* ed. by Michael Swanton, London: Dent and Totowa, N.J.: Rowman & Littlefield. pp. xxvi + 188. hb £3.25, pb £1.60.
[15] *The Pastoral Care, edited from British Museum MS Cotton Otho B.ii, Part I (ff. 1-25 v. a/4)* by Ingvar Carlson. Acta Universitatis Stockholmiensis. Stockholm Studies in English XXXIV. pp. 166.

corrections to his earlier article (*YW* 54, 81) in 'Revisions for Vercelli Homily XX' (*MS* 1974). Jerome Oetgen's 'The OE Rule of St. Benedict' (*ABR*) considers three versions derived from Æthelwold's translation, and argues th'at they were intended for the three audiences most in need of translation: laymen, nuns, schoolboys.

In 'Sermo Lupi ad Anglos: the Order and Date of the Three Versions' (*NM*), Stephanie Dien re-interprets the history of the MSS. In her view the shortest texts (BH) are not the earliest; Wulfstan's intention is most clearly represented by EI, from which references to conquest and humiliation were successively deleted as they became (except in the North) less topical. Eleventh-century thought is also considered by M. R. Godden, 'OE composite homilies from Winchester' (*ASE*). The sources of two unpublished homilies are traced (mostly back to Ælfric), and it is remarked that the compiler had a detailed knowledge of Ælfric and 'remarkable respect' for his predecessors' words, though his own interests were limited largely to admonition. Dr. Godden has also produced a new bibliography to add to the reprint of Caroline Louisa White's old book on Ælfric.[16] This is a great aid to study, but though we are told that Miss White's work has 'stood the test of time remarkably well', it is a pity that she has had to stand it for so long. *Oft dædlata dome foreldit*, as the proverbialist has so inscrutably said.

---

[16] *Ælfric: A New Study of his Life and Writings* by Caroline Louisa White, with a new bibliography prepared by M. R. Godden. Hamden, Conn.: Archon Books, 1898 repr. 1974. pp. 244. £5.10.

IV

Middle English: Excluding Chaucer

R. W. McTURK AND D. J. WILLIAMS

1. General and Miscellaneous Items

The fifth volume of the revised 'Wells' *Manual*[1] contains a section on 'Dramatic Pieces' by four contributors including the late Francis Lee Utley, and another on 'Poems Dealing with Contemporary Conditions' that aims to be complete to 1973 (and still including, understandably but uncomfortably, *Summer Sunday* in the category). The drama section is subdivided into miracles, moralities, and folk drama, with bibliographies complete to 1970, 1973, and spring 1972 respectively.

Sheila Delany's 'Substructure and Superstructure: The Politics of Allegory in the Fourteenth Century' (*Science and Society*) is a rare and welcome approach in Marxist terms to medieval literature. It is an ambitious, if necessarily sketchy, attempt to incorporate a sense of dialectics into medieval scholarship. It argues a rejection by many, during the late Middle Ages, of analogical argument and allegorical representation, and tries to relate this to an economic foundation especially in the major change from feudalism to capitalism.

Diane Bornstein's *Mirrors of Courtesy*[2] are the courtesy books and chivalric manuals in which she traces the evolution of aristocratic social ideals in the late Middle Ages. Her study consists of summaries of this material with a commentary on the change from militaristic ideals to the ideal of the gentleman brought about by the ambition and prosperity of the gentry and middle class. What is first a soldier's code, practical but propagandist for a military aristocracy, as it attempts to mitigate the practice of war, becomes a social code for an aristocracy engaged primarily in civil occupations. The book includes some illustrations from manuscripts, not always clearly identified. In 'The Love Mythos in the Middle Ages and Renaissance' (*Ball State University Forum*), Clifford Davidson looks at the evidence from the twelfth to the seventeenth centuries 'to determine the phenomenological and structural elements' in pursuit of 'a more viable approach to the literature'.

Michael Benskin and Brian Murdoch perform a useful task in 'The Literary Tradition of Genesis' (*NM*), offering both a critique (often very critical) and a supplement to the medieval parts of J. M. Evans's *'Paradise Lost' and the Genesis Tradition* (*YW* 49). The first number of *SLitI* for

[1] *A Manual of the Writings in Middle English 1050–1500*, Vol. V, ed. by Albert E. Hartung. The Connecticut Academy of Arts and Sciences. Hamden, Connecticut: Archon Books. The Shoestring Press Inc. pp. 10 + 428 (pp. 1315–1742 of the whole). $25.00.

[2] *Mirrors of Courtesy*, by Diane Bornstein. Hamden, Connecticut: Archon Books. pp. 158. 24 illustrations. $10.00.

the year is devoted to 'Typology and Medieval Literature'. In addition to articles on typology in the drama (noticed further below in section 11), there are discussions of the theological origins and development of the method, and of its use in Old English and medieval German literature and visual iconography. Hugh T. Keenan contributes 'A Check-List on Typology and English Medieval Literature'. In 'Venus in the Medieval Mythographic Tradition' (*JEGP*) Earl G. Schreiber outlines in some detail Boccaccio's account of *Venus magna* and *Venus secunda*, although he does refer to other sources too. He concludes with a warning about how such material may be used in the interpretation of literary texts.

Editing the Middle English Manuscript[3], by Charles Moorman, is an elementary book intended for graduate student editors with little or no training in palaeography, in Middle English language, or textual criticism. It tries to deal with those matters through 'simple theoretical models and general principles'. Books in this area are rare and difficult to assess. This one may well at least provide a guide to more detailed studies of the individual topics covered.

In an article on 'Editorial Theory and Practice in Middle English Texts', in the *Festschrift* volume for Ian Maxwell reviewed last year (*YW* 55. 101, n. 13) G. H. Russell advocates an approach to Middle English manuscripts comparable to Sisam's approach to Old English poetical manuscripts as expressed in *RES* (1946) and reprinted in his Studies in the *History of Old English Literature* (*YW* 34. 44).

2. Alliterative Poetry

The Awntyrs off Arthure at the Terne Wathelyn is edited again by Ralph Hanna[4], according to the methods used by Kane and Donaldson for the B-text of *Piers Plowman*. The Bodleian manuscript is used for the copy text, with variants from the other manuscripts and from earlier editions. The very full introduction includes discussion of metrical and stanzaic form, emphasizing the differences between the two parts of the poem and arguing that they were at first the work of two different poets. The same argument is pressed in discussing sources and analogues, and also, perhaps more significantly, becomes a feature of the text as printed: we find two poems, *Awntyrs* A and B, followed by a final stanza, held to be originally part of A, but later made to serve as a conclusion for all in the final compilation. Hanna remains convinced of the influence of *Sir Gawain* on *Awntyrs* A at least, and argues strongly for the contribution of *Morte Arthure* to both A and B. In examining the use of *Pope Gregory's Trentals* and legends of St Patrick's Purgatory, he suggests that there are 'imagistic connexions' between such literature and histories of Arthur, namely in the presence in both of wheels of fortune or torture.

Valerie Krishna believes that 'Archaic Nouns in the *Alliterative Morte Arthure*' (*NM*), and therefore presumably in other alliterative poems, may

[3] *Editing the Middle English Manuscript*, by Charles Moorman. Jackson: U.P. of Mississippi. pp. x + 107. illustrations. $6.95.
[4] *The Awntyrs off Arthure at the Terne Wathelyn*, ed. by Ralph Hanna III. Manchester U.P. New York: Barnes and Noble. pp. x + 190. £4.20. $10.75.

have been misinterpreted. The nouns for male persons, commonly said to have elevated, idealizing, typifying connotations (*berne, freke, gome, hathel,* etc.), denote something more general, not more particular than 'man'. They may not be set off so sharply as they have been thought to be from words like *man, knight, lord,* of low alliterative rank. Indeed, it may be rather that these last are the words that have the grandiose connotations and idealizing effects. The archaic synonyms are instead neutral and general but receive rhetorical force according to context. The suggestion may be extended to other words and concepts, such as 'cruel'. It is a good argument and interesting for its suggestion that Modern English words like 'hero' and 'knight' may give us clues to the real connotations of similar words in Middle English. In studying 'The Theme of Justice in the Alliterative *Morte Arthure*' (*AnM*), Georg R. Keiser considers John of Salisbury's doctrine of the king as the image of equity to be a decisive influence shaping the narrative. The first half shows the king as upholder and restorer of justice. His conquests in Lorraine, Lombardy, and Tuscany receive ambiguous treatment. Keiser does not agree with Finlayson that here Arthur has quite simply abandoned justice. Even at worst Arthur does not forget God, but he must discover and combat evil within himself. The kind of tragedy presented is conditioned by the poet's qualification of moral issues. Rather than showing the king simply falling because he is wicked, 'he suggests that because of his sin, the fall that Arthur, like all men, must suffer, seems more just'. Keiser's interpretation of the rest of the poem is equally responsive to nuance and gives proper place to the poem's atmosphere of heroic emotion as well as Arthur's final submission to God's will. In 'A Note on the *Alliterative Morte Arthure*, 208-9' (*NM*) Keiser suggests that the unorthodox assignment to Kay of the cup-bearer's role in Arthur's court stems from a misreading of Wace, upon whom the poet may have been relying with bookish closeness. This too may indicate the narrowness of the poet's knowledge of the material, that it did not include, for example, the Vulgate Version of the story. James D. Johnson identifies ' "The Hero on the Beach" in the Alliterative *Morte Arthure*' (*NM*), an oral-formulaic theme found in Old English but nowhere else in Middle English except *Morte Arthure* 3724-31, Gawain's impetuous rush ashore to attack Modred. As an alternative to the usual suggestions of sources for the passage, Johnson argues, at first cautiously, that the poet acquired it orally, and eventually that the use of the theme here 'must have descended directly from Old English poetry, undoubtedly via oral tradition'. John Finlayson relates 'The Alliterative *Morte Arthure* and *Sir Ferumbras*' (*Anglia*, 1974), arguing that the Gawain-Priamus episode depends not on the Old French *Fierabras* directly but on *Sir Ferumbras*, which can be dated about 1380.

'*Richard the Redeless* and *Mum and the Sothsegger*: A Case of Mistaken Identity' (*N&Q*) is Dan Embree's argument that these two fragments represent two poems. After a history of citations and editions starting with John Bale, he surveys scholarly support for the idea of unity between the fragments, demonstrating the dubiousness of its basis. In each fragment the poet sets out his aims, which appear in no way compatible with each other. Embree interprets the first as a warning to Henry disguised for safety as advice to Richard in prison. The poem's breaking off is not therefore the result of Richard's death, as Skeat thought. The *Mum*-poet's intentions show a wholly different pretext and time context, some way into Henry's reign, 1402–6 rather than 1399, and with no mention of Richard at all. A strong conclusion by Embree sums up what believers in one poem have to contend with, including an 'essential difference of style', the change of person addressed from Richard to the reader, and even the very similarity of contents which would make for awkward repetition were the two fragments from one work. Alcuin G. Blamires, on the other hand, in '*Mum and the Sothsegger* and Langlandian Idiom' (*NM*), does not at first make clear that under that title he includes both fragments, but in the course of his argument he uses the very awkwardness of the relationship between the two as itself evidence of the similarity of the work to *Piers Plowman*. He calls the fragments a poem 'composed "ad hoc"', in response to events'. Without actually pressing the idea of Langland's authorship, Blamires finds the literary accomplishment of the fragments of the same order as that of *Piers Plowman*, and finds many features both of subject matter and of method, taken in combination, to be characteristic of Langland, too.

Beryl Rowland surveys 'Classical and Medieval Ideas on the "Ages of Man" and the Middle English Poem *The Parlement of the Thre Ages*' (*Poetica*), and finds no clear relation between any of the usual divisions into ages and the three ages of the poem, although the numbers of years given to each, thirty, sixty, and one hundred, do have traditional symbolic meanings, and the poem also uses a traditional association between the ages and the Seven Deadly Sins. In another article on 'The Three Ages of *The Parlement of the Thre Ages*' (*ChauR*) Rowland approaches more closely the question why Youthe, Medill Elde, and Elde in the poem are allotted those particular numbers of years, and finds the reason in the usual exegesis of the parable of the sower, where the seed, yielding thirty-fold, sixty-fold, and one hundred-fold, is associated with degrees of sanctity or chastity. Paschasius Radbertus actually connects these degrees with three ages of man. But the protagonists in the poem have sprung from seed which fell on barren ground. Whatever degrees of perfection may belong to their ages, their activities show how far they have fallen short. The hart hunt too, according to Rowland, despite its realism, is an allegory representing the course of human existence.

McKay Sundwall sees relationships between '*The Destruction of Troy*, Chaucer's *Troilus and Criseyde*, and Lydgate's *Troy Book*' (*RES*) which may help to date the alliterative poem, and which may tend to push that date in the later direction suggested by C. A. Luttrell's findings. When Briseida is being taken to the Greek camp, the detail of Diomedes' grasping her rein, which the anonymous poet adds, occurs first in Chaucer's account. This strengthens the assumption that when the poet refers his readers to 'Troilus' for further information he means Chaucer's poem. But the collocation of an elaborate allusion to Chaucer with the detail of the bridle at the same point in Lydgate's version may indicate that the alliterative poet, while perhaps knowing Chaucer's work, drew here on Lydgate's, which would put the date of his own composition after 1420.

Ruth Morse's edition of *St Erkenwald* was not available for review.

3. The Gawain-Poet

Matsuji Tajima produces evidence that 'The Gawain-Poet's Use of *Con* as a Periphrastic Auxiliary' (*NM*) is a metrical device for placing the infinitive in a rhyming position. It almost always has this function in the rhymed lines of *GGK* and *Pearl*, and is used only in the latter poem as an auxiliary of the present as well as the preterite. It appears only sporadically in the unrhymed alliterative lines of *GGK, Cleanness* and *Patience*. David Yerkes finds in the poem *John de Reeue*, preserved in Bishop Percy's Folio MS, evidence to support Tolkien's and Gordon's view that 'spike' is the meaning of ' "Sir Gawain and the Green Knight" 211: "Grayn" ' (*N&Q*). Michael J. Curley, in 'A Note on Bertilak's Beard' (*MP*), suggests that the beaver-hued quality of this mentioned at line 845 may have been intended to suggest the gaining of spiritual freedom through payment of renounced sins to the devil, as allegorized in the *Physiologus* by the beaver's self-castration. William Matthews suggests that '*bi lag mon*: A Crux in *Sir Gawayn and the Grene Knyʒt*' (*M&H*) that is, in 1. 1729, means 'like a lawyer', and hence 'cunningly'.

Victor Yelverton Haines finds 'Allusions to the Felix Culpa in the Prologue of Sir Gawain and the Green Knight' (*RUO*, 1974), particularly in such phrases as 'tried for his tricherie, the trewest on erthe', 'Felix Brutus', and 'blysse and blunder', which he examines in detail. The references to Æneas and Romulus, both of whom participated in actions reminiscent of the *felix culpa*, call to mind Adam, whose sin permits the Redemption of the human race. The repetition at the end of the poem of references and phrases used at the beginning suggests that the poem is meant to be enclosed within a framework of allusion to the fortunate fall —a framework reinforced by the presentation of Arthur and his court, the dark origins of which contrast with its subsequent glory. James II. Sims suggests that 'Gawayne's Fortunate Fall in Sir Gawayne and the Grene Knight' (*OL*) consists in his falling into 'cowardyse and covetyse' through pride. Once he recognizes this, he functions as a 'redeemer' for Arthur's knights, who follow his example in wearing the green baldric as a symbol of the lesson he has learned and taught them. While emphasizing the important difference that the Gawain-poet makes no explicit statement of his theme, Sims finds *GGK* as a whole 'a clearer artistic portrayal of the *felix culpa* notion than Milton's *Paradise Lost*'.

Tony Hunt, in 'Gawain's Fault and the Moral Perspectives of *Sir Gawain and the Green Knight*' (*Trivium*), argues against Burrow (*YW* 46. 69) that Gawain's confession at line 1880 is a valid one, since the concealment of the girdle from Bertilak has not yet taken place. Gawain is unaware that its acceptance or concealment is sinful, and what sin there is in this respect is venial, and thus not obligatory for the confessional. Burrow, in Hunt's view, concentrates too much on the concealment of the girdle, as does the Green Knight in emphasizing the *unleute* of the concealment at the end of the poem, while the poet, like Gawain himself at that stage, is more interested in the *cowardyse* and *covetyse* which the girdle's acceptance might imply. In their final encounter, Gawain and the Green Knight are talking about different offences rather than differently of the same offence, and the poem gives a more complex picture of the many-sidedness of moral danger than Burrow's approach allows.

According to Peter Taitt, the two elements in 'Sir Gawain's Double Quest' (*RUO*) are 'a structurally exterior and literal progress' on the one hand and 'an interior and ambiguous revelation' on the other; there is a gradual movement in the poem from objective to subjective perception of events, and the reader comes to share Gawain's point of view in the course of his journey on Christmas Eve in Fitt II. This process, which is continued throughout Fitt III, with its increased emphasis on the passing of time and its externalization in the fox-hunt of Gawain's inner harassment, comes full circle at the end of the poem, where the reader, from a superior vantage-point, sees that Gawain is embarrassed by his loss of reputation rather than by his pride which, in wearing the girdle, he continues to display.

Einar Ol. Sveinsson, in 'Herra Valvin og Karlinn grái' (*Studia Islandica*) suggests a now lost poem or prose work written in England in English, French or Latin as a source for the lost saga which lies behind the seventeenth-century Icelandic ballad-cycle *Sveins-rímur Múkssonar*, part of which shows a striking resemblance to the Beheading Game as presented in *GGK*.

Alphonsus M. Campbell includes *GGK* in his examination of 'The Character of King Arthur in the Middle English Alliterative Poems' (*RUO*), finding that Arthur in this poem 'is a gay and chivalric young king . . . keen, witty and joyful'.

Christopher Tolkien edits his father's verse translations of *GGK*, *Pearl* and *Sir Orfeo*[5], including introductory and subsidiary material on the first two poems based largely on hitherto unpublished writings by Professor Tolkien, though the section on *Pearl* appeared in E. V. Gordon's edition of 1953 (*YW* 34. 78–9). The editor provides a short glossary of archaic and technical terms used in the translations, which in general read smoothly rather than colloquially—thees and thous, yeas and nays and inversions are used frequently but not consistently. Since the idea of the book derives partly from Professor Tolkien's view that 'A translation may be a useful form of commentary' it seems regrettable that his wishes have prevented the editor from providing line-numbers for *GGK* and *Pearl*. Much useful and provocative material will be found in the translations, for instance at lines 211 ('grayn') and 1237–8 ('welcum to my cors') of *GGK*, and at lines 435 and 757 ('makeles') of *Pearl*.

Göran Kjellmer ventures to answer the question *Did the "Pearl Poet" write Pearl?*[6] in the negative, after 'ranking the texts' of *Cleanness*, *Erkenwald*, *Gawain*, *Patience* and *Pearl* 'in a number of dimensions according to different variables'. These latter are the 'independent linguistic variables' of 'Lexical Frequency' (that is, the relative distribution among the poems of the words listed by Kottler and Markman (*YW* 47. 77) as the ten most frequent ones in the group), 'Clause Length', 'Sentence Length', 'Clause Linkage Types' (that is, co-ordinating and sub-ordinating

[5] *Sir Gawain and The Green Knight, Pearl and Sir Orfeo*, trans. by J. R. R. Tolkien, London: George Allen and Unwin Ltd. pp. 149. £3.95.
[6] *Did the "Pearl Poet" write Pearl?* by Göran Kjellmer. Gothenburg studies in English 30. Göteborg: Acta Universitatis Gothoburgensis. pp. 105.

'connectors' of clauses), 'Passive Forms' and 'Alliteration'. *Pearl* is found to deviate statistically from the other poems in all these variables more than does any other poem in the group and more, indeed, as a supplementary chapter shows, than does *Winner and Waster*, a completely unrelated text, though this poem is not compared with the others with regard to lexical frequency. Kjellmer finally raises the question of whether several authors lie behind the five poems examined.

William Vantuono draws attention to two occurrences of 'A Name in the Cotton MS. Nero A.X. Article 3' (*MS*)—that of J. Macy, which is found in one of the illuminated folios of *Cleanness*, and in one such folio of *GGK*. Both are written in the same ink and apparently the same hand, and it is suggested that the name is that of the illuminator, though the less likely possibilities—that the illuminator wrote either the name of the family for which the MS was made or that of the poet himself—are also considered. The latter possibility leads Vantuono to offer tentative arguments in favour of John de Masey of Sale, Rector of Ashton-on-Mersey 1364–1401, as a candidate for the title of '*Pearl*-poet'. In 'Hoccleve, "Maister Massy", and the *Pearl*-poet: Two Notes' (*RES*), Thorlac Turville-Petre argues against the view developed by Peterson (*YW* 55. 101) from the earlier, somewhat different opinions of Greenwood and Farley-Hills, that the *Pearl*-poet was identical with John de Massy of Cotton and with the 'Maister Massy' referred to by Hoccleve in the epistle to John of Lancaster accompanying his *Regement of Princes*. In Turville-Petre's view Hoccleve's Maister Massy was not a poet but a financial officer, and his name was William and not John. Edward Wilson, on the other hand, argues in the second note against the view developed by Nolan and Peterson that the texts of *Pearl* and *St. Erkenwald* contain the name of the author— I. Massi—in anagrammatic form. Nolan's argument, on which Peterson's is based, is found to be unsatisfactory in leaving surplus duplicate letters in the supposed anagram, in arriving at the latter through a selection of line-numbers based on a preconception that I de Massi was the poet's name, and in the fact that no rules are provided to determine the alleged anagram's solution. In Wilson's view, Peterson's argument is vitiated by its use of the same line-numbers in *St. Erkenwald* as those selected by Nolan from *Pearl*. The message supposedly provided at these points is not the same in both poems; the *Erkenwald* 'anagram' depends, like the *Pearl* one, on subjective considerations, and is no more provided with a key to its solution than the one in *Pearl*. In a letter to *RES*, David Farley-Hills reasserts against Turville-Petre his own view that Hoccleve's Massy was a poet, and emphasizes that this view is intended to complement Greenwood's conjecture that the *Pearl*-poet's name was Massy.

Laurence Eldredge gives a useful critical survey of 'The State of "Pearl" Studies since 1933' (*Viator*), up to c. 1970, dealing with the three problems —'Elegy or Allegory', 'Heresy or Orthodoxy', and 'Symbolism'—which Wellek regarded as pressing in 1933, and the relatively recent ones of 'Historicism', and 'Authorship'. The most important questions now, in Eldredge's view, are how the dreamer-narrator's consolation and the symbolism of the pearl can be viewed simultaneously, and whether historicism —the setting of the poem in its era—can aid an understanding of the poem's seemingly unparalleled brilliance of style and language.

Thomas C. Niemann, in 'Pearl and the Christian Other World' (*Genre*, 1974) relates *Pearl* to the genre of apocalyptic literature dealing with visits to the Christian Other World, in which the pains of hell and joys of heaven are vividly described, and the visitor, not allowed to enter heaven until he is purged of his sins, returns to earth to a life of penance and greater virtue. *Pearl*, which stresses the joyful aspects of this Other World, is then compared in particular with the twelfth-century *Vision of Tundale* and with Dante's *Divina Commedia*, both of which are posited as generic parallels to *Pearl*, rather than as sources for it. According to Niemann, this view helps to place in a proper perspective the consolatory, elegiac and allegorical aspects of the poem.

Thomas Andrew Reisner, in 'The "Cortaysye" Sequence in *Pearl*: A Legal Interpretation' (*MP*) examines the use of the word 'cortaysye' in lines 409–92 in the light of its legal sense of curtesy, that is, the right providing for a mode of accession by means of marriage to possession and title in respect of a life estate.

Attila Faj, acting on the assumption that 'the more numerous are the extra-biblical resemblances between *Patience* and a former work on the Jonah-subject, the more probable is their relation', points out a number of parallels between *Patience* and the *Naufragium Jonae prophetae* by Bishop Marbodus of Rennes (1035–1123), suggesting that these are even more noteworthy than those pointed out by Kelly (*YW* 48. 75) between *Patience* and the *Hymnus Ieiunantium* of Prudentius.

4. Piers Plowman

The most important publication of the year is certainly the B–version of *Piers Plowman*[7] in its new form at the hands of George Kane and E. Talbot Donaldson. The growth of the new edition of all three texts is becoming a process as absorbing to watch as that of the creation of the poem itself, since it too changes as it goes. The new B incorporates changes of the A-editor's mind, while relying on decisions of the C-editor which may of course be later revised. In the rewarding introduction, the section on manuscript classification yields elaborately qualified results: 'The B-version of *Piers Plowman* would be the despair of a recensionist'. But the analysis demonstrates the homogeneity of the B tradition, and the extreme frequency of convergent variation in transmission. The editors reconsider the evidence for the sequence of the three versions. With B as intermediate, they seek to show that not only is ABC the more likely sequence on literary critical grounds, but on textual grounds too. In this situation agreements between A and C 'are the determinant circumstances in the editing of the B-version'. Of prime importance too is the corruptness of the archetype of B. We see Langland working on his C revision with a text of his own B better than the archetype of the surviving manuscripts

---

[7] *Piers Plowman: The B Version: Will's Visions of Piers Plowman, Do-Well, Do-Better, and Do-Best. An Edition in the Form of Trinity College Cambridge MS B.15.17, Corrected and Restored from the Known Evidence, with Variant Readings,* ed. By George Kane and E. Talbot Donaldson. U. of London: Athlone Press. pp. x + 682. £20.00. $50.00.

but still a corrupt scribal copy, and revising and rewriting rather than trying to 'restore' his work. The corruptness of the B-archetype means that the editors reject the conservative reconstruction of this as 'a poor-spirited and slothful undertaking, of strictly limited value, moreover, with respect to recovery of the historical truth of the poem'. Instead we have a text with more thorough-going emendation than the A-edition. Some conjectural emendation is based on the editors' own analysis of the verse technique. The Trinity College Cambridge manuscript was chosen on grounds of the exceptional consistency of its spelling and the conformity of its grammar to standard later fourteenth-century usage as seen in the best manuscripts of Chaucer and Gower. The text is full of square brackets, but it reads more smoothly than the Langland we have been used to. The editors have proceeded, however, in the belief that reconstruction and conjecture must be open also to the users of their work. In being thus radical and challenging rather than definitive, this fine edition is entirely appropriate to the poetry it presents.

A text for students, consisting of *Selections from the B-text*[8] is edited, in manuscript spelling, with a prose translation but no glossary, by Stella Brook. The selections are presented as four continuous passages with indications of omissions but with Passus divisions indicated only in the notes. For example, 'The World and its Ways' consists of most of the Prologue followed continuously by the whole of Passus I and II. The Introduction is genuinely introductory, concise, helpful, encouraging. It covers all the more problematic aspects of the poem but refrains from arguing solutions and so shutting down further questioning. Comparison of the Passus to 'the chapters of a novel' is perhaps more encouraging than really informative to a new reader, but otherwise the method of presentation may well draw beginners into the poem.

The World of Piers Plowman[9] is a selection of texts designed to reflect the techniques or the concerns that shaped Langland's poem. They are not the great works by the most famous authors, but extracts from various kinds of popular versions of the higher learning. The editors have in mind the kind of compilation often owned by owners of *Piers Plowman* manuscripts and even bound along with the poem. The French and Latin pieces appear in translation, and the book is divided into sections by subject matter. For example, the first deals with notions of order from the cosmic down to the social and political and includes Fitzstephen's Description of London. A section on 'the preacher and the heretic' presents Brinton and Wycliffe.

David Aers begins his discussion of *Piers Plowman and Christian Allegory*[10] by surveying modern controversy about medieval figurative language. He considers the possible distinctions between allegory and

[8] *Langland Piers Plowman: Selections from the B-text as Found in Bodleian MS Laud Misc. 581*, ed. by Stella Brook. Manchester U.P. New York: Barnes and Noble. pp. viii + 168. £4.50. $15.00.
[9] *The World of Piers Plowman*, ed. by Jeanne Krochalis and Edward Peters. The Middle Ages. General Editor, Edward Peters. Philadelphia: U. of Pennsylvania P. pp. xxii + 265. Paper. $7.95.
[10] *Piers Plowman and Christian Allegory*, by David Aers. London: Edward Arnold pp. x + 142. £6.00. $19.00.

typology, poets' and theologians' allegory, Hellenistic and Judaeo-Christian tradition. What is lacking in the debate, according to Aers, is 'close analysis of actual allegorical practices', and this he aims to provide. 'Close analysis' is itself a term that needs closer definition than Aers gives it, but the following chapters yield interesting arguments. Medieval exegetes seem little concerned with a supposed historical commitment of Christianity. Hellenistic conceptions prevailed over the Hebraic and typological, and ultimately the unique Christian allegory or typology seems little different in practice from other kinds. Exegetes may have believed in the historicity of events but their readings, exemplified by Irenaeus and Origen, do not show this. Denis the Carthusian and Nicholas de Lyra are used to show that later exegesis is no more historical and literal than the earlier. A codified allegorical machinery is seen at work in homiletic and literary works too, a mode incapable of exploring or presenting any but simple ideas. Aers contrasts with the simplistic 'shell and kernel' or 'picture' model of allegory the 'disclosure model' outlined in Dante's letter to Can Grande, where the figure is itself an essential part of the writer's vision. At this point Aers rather unsatisfactorily abandons the general field of medieval critical theory in pursuit of his intention to show that Langland's poetry, while using picture models too, belongs to Dante's kind. Will's encounter with Imaginative certainly sounds more like a disclosure model, and Aers's reading of their dialogue is sensible and suggestive. In the last chapter, attacks on Robertson and Huppé, and on Fowler, are followed by too perfunctory dismissal of the contributions of Frank, Lawlor and Donaldson. Everyone is damned for a 'striking failure to remain aware of the poet's own imagistic process', a process here called 'organic'. An examination of the Tree of Charity and of the imagery of ploughing emphasizes a kind of allegory that develops its interpretation in time.

In *Incubus and Ideal*[11] Peter S. Taitt deals with the method and content of Langland's and Chaucer's portrayal of ecclesiastical figures. Langland's method of presentation is called 'linguistic and explicit rather than implicit and dramatic', and his irony, oddly, less deliberate and conscious than Chaucer's. Chaucer concentrates on the person, Langland on the abuse. Langland's figures are remoter but his method of portraying the sins and abuses is not.

Joseph S. Wittig is against the idea that 'The Dramatic and Rhetorical Development of Long Will's Pilgrimage' (*NM*) is a result of confused searching or the elaboration of discrete allegories. It is a consistent narrative and dramatic pattern with a precise rhetorical purpose, and is under the poet's firm control. All the apparent doubts and confusions are brilliant rhetorical impersonation designed to have the audience identify with the resistance of the human will to affective awakening, and to have it participate in that awakening. There is no frustration or uncertainty at the end, only the poet handing the problem to his listeners as the appropriate ones to solve it. Britton J. Harwood finds 'Imaginative in *Piers*

[11] *Incubus and Ideal: Ecclesiastical Figures in Chaucer and Langland,* by Peter S. Taitt. Salzburg Studies in English Literature, ed. Erwin A. Stürzl. Elizabethan and Renaissance Studies, ed. James Hogg, 44. Salzburg: Institut für englische Sprache und Literatur. pp. 228. $17.50.

Plowman' (*MÆ*) to be a personification of 'the mind's power for making similitudes', and his argument brings much light to a complex subject. He convincingly rejects mystical readings of the figure, and separates it from the concept of memory. The association with making similitudes explains Imaginative's ability to prophesy, his relation to Clergy, and the unity of his whole speech. Clergy is concerned, like the poet, with the use of similitudes to understand spiritual truth, and Imaginative's speech is especially full of metaphors, is even about metaphor. But Imaginative leaves Will 'witless nerehand' not because Langland thinks poetry useless for theology, but because he can no more provide direct, rational, 'kynde knowing' than can Clergy. William J. Birnes discusses 'Christ as Advocate: The Legal Metaphor in *Piers Plowman'* (*AnM*). Langland creates a legal and political framework for theological discussion even to the extent, it is suggested, of presenting the contrast between the Old and the New Law in the context of a contrast between English Common Law and Chancery Law in the fourteenth century. In the Harrowing of Hell, Christ is seen as a law-abiding monarch, but the debate with Satan is one of a series which Langland puts into the poem exploiting a popular theme in redemption literature.

Thomas D. Hill explains 'A Liturgical Allusion in *Piers Plowman* B XVI, 88' (*N&Q*). It is a reference designed as a point of departure from which an audience familiar with the *Ordo Missae* can orient themselves in the Tree of Charity allegory. John A. Alford provides sources and further examples for more than thirty 'Unidentified Quotations in *Piers Plowman'* (*MP*), pointing out that nearly a quarter of the Latin phrases in the three texts otherwise remain to be identified. Not all of Alford's identifications here are new.

5. Romances

Velma Bourgeois Richmond notes *The Popularity of Middle English Romance*[12] as evidenced in its juxtaposition with religious and didactic literature in manuscript collections, and in the large number of early printings of romances, and finds the origin of the more hostile attitude to the genre which has developed since the sixteenth century in the humanist view that the romances distort classical ideals by the introduction of new and largely Christian ideas. One of the twentieth century manifestations of the hostility is the critical distinction between 'popular' and 'significant' literature, which would have been meaningless in the Middle Ages. Richmond then seeks the reasons for the popularity of the romances, finding that those which treat 'Fortune's heroes' (Alexander and the Arthur of the alliterative *Morte*) modify classical values by placing them in a Christian framework, and that the supernatural is given a moral function in such a framework in *Emaré*, *Robert the Deuyll*, and *Partenay*. 'Friendship and Brotherhood' are then examined as powerfully moral themes in *Athelston*, *Amis and Amiloun* and *Valentine and Orson*, and so are the ramifications of 'The Delights of love' in *Ywain and Gawain*, the stanzaic *Morte Arthur*,

[12] *The Popularity of Middle English Romance*, by Velma Bourgeois Richmond. Bowling Green, Ohio: Bowling Green University Popular Press. pp. xii + 237. 12 illustrations.

and *Paris and Vienne*. Finally *Guy of Warwick* ('The Most Popular Hero') is given a separate chapter. 'What emerges very clearly', Richmond concludes, 'is the place of the romance in the English moral tradition'. While believing that the Middle English romances are in need of a re-habilitation, Richmond pays due tribute to those later writers—including Shakespeare, Milton, Bunyan, Johnson, Dickens, Tolkien and T. H. White —who have made use of romance modes.

Contributions of general relevance include Margaret Hurley's 'Saints' Legends and Romance Again: Secularization of Structure and Motif' (*Genre*), which refers mainly to Old French examples of the genres in question; M. Dominica Legge's 'Anglo-Norman Hagiography and the Romances' (*M&H*), which among other things mentions tail-rhyme as a feature of Benet of St Albans' life of Thomas Becket as well as of the East Anglian Middle English Romances; Kathryn Hume's 'The Composition of a Medieval Romance' (*NM*), in which Walter Map's 'Sadius and Galo' is used to help throw light on the creative processes of medieval romance writers; and T. E. Pickford's *Apollonius of Tyre* as Greek Myth and Christian Mystery' (*Neophilologus*), a combination which ensured the popularity throughout the Middle Ages of this romance, which was used by, among others, the compiler of the *Gesta Romanorum* and Gower. Two articles deal with the historical background to the Arthurian legend: Elizabeth Smith's 'King Arthur and his Rôle in Early Britain—A Summary' (*Contemporary Review*), which is perhaps even more of a summary than it is meant to be; and Von Helmut Nickel 'Wer Waren König Artus' Ritter?' (*Waffen—und Kostümkunde*), which gives a wealth of useful references. *BBSIA* contains notices and summaries of papers read at an Arthurian conference in Exeter which include treatments of the English manifestations of Arthurian romance. Ones dealing specifically with Malory are noted in the appropriate section below; mention may be made here of the following: W. R. J. Barron, 'The English Arthurian Romance: Traces of an English Tradition'; Valerie M. Lagorio, 'The Glastonbury Legends and the English Grail Romances'; Eugène Vinaver, 'The concept of Morte Arthur'; Maldwyn Mills, 'The Englishness of *Ywain and Gawain*'; Ronald Tamplin, '*Sir Tristrem* and *Sir Perceval of Galles*: the Meaning of Narrative'; Eithne M. O'Sharkey, 'King Arthur's Prophetic Dreams and the Rôle of Mordred in Layamon's *Brut* and the Alliterative *Morte Arthure*'; David C. Fowler, '*Le Conte du Graal* and *Sir Perceval of Galles*'; Dorothy Schuchman McCoy, 'In Pursuit of Common Sense: the Continuity of Ethical Conflict in the Breton Derivatives'; and R. Howard Bloch, 'The Text as Inquest: Form and Function in the Pseudo-Map cycle'.

Three articles deal in more specific terms with the similarities and differences between hagiography and romance. David N. Klausner, in 'Didacticism and Drama in *Guy of Warwick*' (*M&H*) studies the English and Anglo-Norman versions of the part of this romance dealing with Guy's pilgrimage, which is based on the legend of St Alexis, in relation to the English, Latin and French versions of the legend. Guy's pilgrimage has more dramatic, because less expected, origins than that of St Alexis, and his departure, unlike that of Alexis, emphasizes dramatically the necessity of penance, not least because his family ties are broken more forcibly than those of Alexis. Valerie M. Lagorio calls 'The *Joseph of Aramathie* English

Hagiography in Transition' (M&H), insofar as it establishes a pattern for subsequent English encomia to Joseph in his legendary rôles of apostle and preserver of the Precious Blood—a pattern especially evident in John of Glastonbury's Chronica. The English Joseph differs from its source, the Vulgate Estoire del Saint Graal, in being more of a strictly hagiographical work than a secular romance. This is shown in its 'de-emphasis of the Holy Grail', its 'omission of links with the Grail's future Arthurian destiny', and its emphasis on 'Joseph's career as an apostolic missioner'. Derek Pearsall links 'John Capgrave's Life of St Katharine and Popular Romance Style' (M&H), suggesting that the stylistic influence of romances such as Havelok supplements that of Chaucer and Lydgate in this poem, especially in the use of rhyming line-fillers, often of an 'inclusive' type (meaning 'all men', 'always', 'everywhere'). The description of the rule of Katharine's father Costus is reminiscent of Æthelwold's rule as described in Havelok. The Lincolnshire associations of Havelok make it possible that the poem was known to Capgrave, who lived at Lynn in Norfolk, near the Lincolnshire border. His Life of St Norbert, by contrast, shows little indebtedness to romance style.

A detailed analysis of the Erl of Tollous leads Urs Dürmüller to find some Narrative Possibilities of the Tail-Rime Romance[13], especially in the tail rime stanza itself, which is divisible into four 'sections' or two 'halves'. A stanza, a half or a section may constitute a narrative unit, and the term 'panel technique' is adopted for the subordination of sections and halves to the larger unit of the stanza. Passages of direct speech can be arranged according to these structural parts, and the tail-line itself is used for narrative effect and is hardly ever a mere tag or 'filler'. In the larger structure of the poem as a whole, its artistry emerges in framing and symmetry, in economy of presentation, and in variation, which may show itself in the connecting of scenes through reported speech or in parallelism of action. The same approach is then applied to other shorter tail-rime romances, and Emaré and Athelston are found to be less satisfactory in handling the stanza than Sir Cleges, King Edward and the Shepherd, Sir Gowther, Sir Launfal and Sir Thopas. Robert Reilly arranges 'The Earl of Toulouse: A Structure of Honor' (MS) in a pattern of four parts somewhat different from the three 'movements' proposed by Dürmüller, and suggests that the structural comparisons and contrasts in the poem draw attention to comparisons and contrasts of character, and to the abstract ideals which the characters represent. The triumph of the good characters over the bad shows that the poet believed in justice, fidelity, trust and truth, and rejected the opposite qualities.

Kevin S. Kiernan, in 'Athelston and the Rhyme of the English Romances' (MLQ), takes examples from Athelston to show that what earlier editors consider two six-line stanzas may sometimes represent one twelve-line stanza linked by couplet-rhyme rather than tail-rhyme, particularly if a speech extends across the boundary between two supposed six-line

---

[13] Narrative Possibilities of the Tail-Rime Romance, by Urs Dürmüller. Schweizer Anglistische Arbeiten. Swiss Studies in English, eds. Robert Fricker, Ernst Leisi and Heinrich Straumann. Band 83. Bern: Francke Verlag. pp. 245. S. Fr. 28.

stanzas. He goes on to find a diptych-like structure in the poem as a whole; six stages on one side of the diptych parallel six on the other, and a smaller diptych is found in the central passage in which a messenger is used on three occasions, the first and third of which participate in the larger diptych.

J. R. R. Tolkien's translation of *Sir Orfeo* is noted in Section 3, above; the brief introduction to his translation is the work of his editor. Mary Hynes-Berry, in 'Cohesion in *King Horn* and *Sir Orfeo*' (*Speculum*), finds that each of these two romances has its own kind of cohesion—that of *Orfeo* being 'dramatic and organic', and that of *Horn* depending on 'chronology and thematic progression as Horn develops from boyhood to maturity'. This progression involves 'a coherent sequence of dramatized moments', but is not dramatic in the sense that *Sir Orfeo* is, since the latter poem, with its focus on the meaning of love and loyalty, its emphasis through analogy and antithesis on psychology and the emotions, and its plot's dependence on Orfeo's will, calls for 'empathetic participation'. Both poems are successful in their different cohesive modes. N. H. Keeble suggests that 'The Narrative Achievement of *Sir Orfeo*' (*ES*) has been obscured by the poet's failure to direct the reader's attention explicitly to the shape or moral of his tale, which seems to unfold of its own accord. The medieval commonplace of the poet referring to his source in his opening lines has turned attention away from the tale itself to possible sources and analogues. The Fairy king is the vehicle of Fortune in the poem, and the harp serves to link Orfeo's life as a beggar with his life as a king. The narrative's moral concern provides a link between the main body of the poem and the final episode of the steward which underlines honour and integrity, the fundamental subject of the poem as a whole.

Bruce A. Rosenberg, in 'The Three Tales of *Sir Degaré* (*NM*), suggests that three folktales lie behind the major narrative elements in this romance. The seduction which results in Degaré's conception reflects Aarne-Thompson type 706 ('The Maiden Without Hands'); Degaré's narrow escape from incest with his mother reflects type 931 ('Oedipus'), and his search for his father reflects type 873 ('The King Discovers his Unknown Son'). If *Sir Degaré* is a conflation of these three folktales, then it may suggest that the romances should be judged by standards different from those reserved for 'reflexive literature . . . , which can be read, mulled over and re-read by the audience'.

Henry Grinberg discusses 'The *Three Kings' Sons* and *Les Trois Fils de Rois*' (*Romance Philology*); the former work is a late fifteenth-century prose translation of the latter, and survives in a unique contemporary manuscript, Brit. Mus. MS Harley 326. It appears to have had as its source an unknown MS from which descended only one of the seven extant French MSS of *Les trois fils* and the ten known sixteenth-century French printed editions of it.

P. F. Hissiger edits the stanzaic *Morte Arthur*[14] with Notes, a Glossary, and an Introduction in which, after some discussion of dialectal and metrical matters, he emphasizes that the poem has 'many suggestions of

---

[14] *Le Morte Arthur. A Critical Edition*, by P. F. Hissiger. The Hague and Paris: Mouton. pp. 184. Dutch Guilders 38.

ballad style'; that its hero is undoubtedly Lancelot; that its source was 'a version of the *Mort Artu* containing the meeting of the Queen-nun and Lancelot, as in MS Palatinus Latinus 1967'; that changes made to this source 'show an attempt by the poet to increase the stature of Lancelot, and to concentrate on the story of Lancelot and Guinevere'; and that the poem 'was probably the prime source of Malory's seventh and eight tales'. A Selected Bibliography helps to make the edition suitable for its intended audience—those who wish to read the poem as literature, or to study it as a source for Malory.

Glenys Goetinck's *Peredur: A Study of Welsh Tradition in the Grail Legends*[15] includes a detailed comparison of *Sir Perceval of Galles* with the legend of Peredur as reflected in a group of three Welsh romances, with Chrétien's *Perceval*, and with Wolfram's *Parzival*. *Sir Perceval* reflects a simpler and less polished version of the Perceval story than any of these earlier works. It is concluded that *Peredur* and Chrétien's *Perceval* have a common source, variant versions of which explain those features which Wolfram's *Parzival* shares with *Peredur* rather than with Chrétien's *Perceval*, and those in Wolfram's *Parzival* and in *Sir Perceval of Galles* which are not found in *Peredur* or in Chrétien.

6. Gower, Lydgate, Hoccleve

Samuel T. Cowling traces the development of 'Gower's Ironic Self-Portrait in the *Confessio Amantis*' (*AnM*) from a contradictory Amans, both 'caitif' and servant of Venus, seen at first only in general terms, not as Gower himself. The parodic confession is 'a device for developing the meaning of who he is'. Genius has a double rôle for, as well as being priest of Venus, he functions also as the poet's own genius and inspiration. Cowling discusses religious parodies, including the denial of Love by Amans. Here there is irony and ambiguity since the denial serves only to reinforce the fabric of the religion of love in the poem. Masayoshi Ito gives, under the title '*Omnia Vincit Amor*, An Interpretation of Gower's *Cronica Tripertita*' (*SELit*, 1973), seeing it as less like other chronicles than it is like *Confessio Amantis*, a story with a moral, but in which Amor means heavenly love. Masayoshi Ito also discusses 'Gower's Knowledge of *Poetria Nova*' (*SELit*), arguing that Murphy's rejection of Geoffrey of Vinsauf's influence on Chaucer should not be extended to Gower. He finds one new passage where Gower seems to be borrowing, and a number of other possible ones, and concludes that Gower knew the *Poetria Nova* probably better than Chaucer did. He may even have owned it in a manuscript with his favourite *Aurora*, like the manuscript known to have been in Durham in 1391. Patrick J. Gallacher's *Love, the Word, and Mercury* was seen too late for inclusion.[16]

Lydgate's concern for history and his ingenuity with a source is illustrated by C. David Benson in 'Prudence, Othea, and Lydgate's Death of Hector' (*ABR*). Usually Lydgate in the *Troy Book* only modifies his

    [15] *Peredur: A Study of Welsh Tradition in the Grail Legends*, by Glenys Goetinck. Cardiff: University of Wales Press. pp. viii + 336. £5.00.
    [16] *Love, the Word, and Mercury: A Reading of John Gower's 'Confessio Amantis'* by Patrick J. Gallacher. Albuquerque: U. of New Mexico P. pp. xii + 196. $7.50.

source in Guido with rhetoric and supplementary information, but he abandons this procedure for the death of Hector, using Christine de Pisan's *Epistre d'Othea* to give Hector a fatal flaw to explain his fall. Indeed the *Epistre* affects the entire *Troy Book* since Prudence is Lydgate's principal moral concern. The flaw is covetousness leading to recklessness which gives Achilles an opening to attack. But Lydgate makes no use of the spiritual lesson of the allegory, having no interest in a 'Christian message not directly connected to the literal meaning of the narrative'. He is keeping the facts of Guido's history but adding an explanation for them.

Hoccleve's chronic state of financial embarrassment is seen in a touch more detail by Thorlac Turville-Petre in the first of two notes on 'Hoccleve, "Maistir Massy", and the *Pearl* Poet' (*RES*). Massy is no poet after all but Receiver General and General Attorney to John of Lancaster, and of course another possible source of relief to the poet. On this see also Section 3, above.

7. Middle Scots Poetry

Bernice W. Kliman writes on 'Speech as a Mirror of *Sapientia* and *Fortitudo* in Barbour's *Bruce*' (*MÆ*), concentrating on the utterances of the Bruce himself to show that Barbour portrays in him a leader who combines these two qualities, the former showing itself in his use of rhetoric of the kind found in *Ad Herennium*, and the latter emerging, through his battle-speeches, in a knowledge of warfare based on Vegetius's *De re Militari*, which Barbour may have known in Latin or in Jean de Meun's French translation. Klaus Bitterling points out three instances of '*Till* "while" in Barbours Bruce' (*NM*).

R. D. S. Jack discusses '*The Thre Prestis of Peblis* and the Growth of Humanism in Scotland' (*RES*), finding the influence of humanism especially marked in the first and second of this poem's three tales. The influence manifests itself in echoes of Boccaccio and the *Gesta Romanorum*, and in foreshadowings of *Ane Satyre of the Thrie Estaitis, Magnyfycens, Youth,* and *Respublica*. The more modestly presented third tale, with its Every-man-like hero, shows that the poem as a whole both welcomes and sets a limit to humanist advances; and the 'prodigal son' motif of the first two tales may suggest that the king-figure in both of them is an amalgam of James III and James IV, and that the poem was written early in the latter's reign.

J. A. Burrow finds that Henryson's *The Preaching of the Swallow* (*EIC*) has the theme of prudence as its unifying principle. This, in his view, explains the essentially human (rather than animal) point of view in the poem, and the structural link between its introductory *descriptio* of the four seasons and the fable itself, which takes the last season of the *descriptio* as the first of its series of one scene for each season. Prudence— the modern meanings of which disguise its earlier status as one of the four cardinal virtues—is mentioned in the opening line of the poem, alluded to in the Latin quotation half way through it, and implied (though not mentioned) in the *Moralitas*. According to Burrow 'All the major parts of the poem bear upon this theme, more or less obviously'. Klaus Bitterling finds an example of 'Middle English "Glouberd", a Dormouse' (*N&Q*) in the *Glebard/globert* of line 910 of Henryson's *Fables*.

Frank Shuffleton, in 'An Imperial Flower: Dunbar's *The Goldyn Targe* and the Court Life of James IV of Scotland' (*SP*), relates the ship carrying the allegorical figures in this poem and the guns which awaken the poet-dreamer to James IV's interest in ship-building and gunnery respectively, and suggests that the poem was occasioned by a tournament held in 1508 to honour the state visit of Bernard Stewart, Sieur de l'Aubigny. This, in Shuffleton's view, helps to explain 'the good-humored self-mockery' apparent in the superficial treatment of the allegory, and the references to Chaucer, Gower and Lydgate which bear witness to a preoccupation with language appropriate to the mannered requirements of banquet-hall recitation. Walter Scheps, in 'The *Goldyn Targe*: Dunbar's Comic Psychomachia' (*PLL*), finds that the brevity of the poem throws its allegorical features into relief in such a way as to make them seem inconsistent with human experience and consequently poetically inadequate. The poem as it proceeds reveals itself as a comic treatment of the inadequacy of allegory as a literary genre, and in praising Chaucer, Gower and Lydgate for their rhetoric Dunbar is drawing attention to his own use of it in the *Targe*. 'The rhetoric is grave, the subject trivial, and what the former illuminates is the mindlessness of the latter'. If Dunbar is a great comic poet, then the *Targe* supports such a view.

Flora Alexander, in 'Late Medieval Scottish Attitudes to the Figure of King Arthur: A Reassessment' (*Anglia*), argues that such attitudes are not as uniformly hostile to Arthur as has recently been thought. Barbour regards him as a noble man destroyed by treachery; Harry the Minstrel compares Wallace, his hero, with Arthur; and the writer of the *Buik of Alexander* follows his French source in listing Arthur among the Nine Worthies. As for the two surviving Scottish Arthurian romances, the writer of *Lancelot of the Laik* criticizes Arthur no more severely, and sometimes less so, than does his French source, and while the view of Arthur in *Golagros and Gawain* is indeed likely to have been influenced by defensive attitudes to the English, Arthur's faults in that poem are less prominent than in the alliterative *Morte Arthure*, in which the king is regarded as admirable though not faultless.

Elizabeth Walsh, RSJC, studies the motif of a humble man aiding 'The King in Disguise' (*Folklore*) in the fifteenth-century romance *The Taill of Rauf Coilyear how he harbreit King Charlis*, and in various poems related to it. These are the fourteenth-century 'King Edward and the Shepherd', 'The King and the Hermit', preserved from the mid-fifteenth century; the fifteenth-century 'John the Reeve'; and 'The King and the Miller', preserved from c. 1600. These and other analogues illustrate the popularity of the motif, but *The Taill of Rauf Coilyear*, which seems to derive largely from oral tradition, is unique in applying it to Charlemagne. This is probably to be explained in terms of the relationship between Scotland and France in the fifteenth and sixteenth centuries.

8. Lyrics and Miscellaneous Verse

David L. Jeffrey, in *The Early English Lyric and Franciscan Spirituality*[17], finds evidence for the pervasive influence of the Franciscan friars' preaching mission to England from 1224 onwards on the development of the Middle English lyric. In his second chapter he finds Franciscan spirituality especially marked by a 'contrition-evoking, affective contemplation of the Cross, sometimes through the intermediary Virgin, prescribed in such a way as to promote spiritual conformity to the Passion of the Suffered-Christ', and in his third, where he refers largely to the writings of St Bonaventure, he emphasizes 'a characteristic Franciscan appreciation for the dramatic qualities of the literal story itself' where scripture is concerned, and 'an equally distinctive love of nature simply as nature'. Bonaventure's discussion of art shows that the lyric was acceptable to Franciscans as a means of demonstrating the incarnation of Christ, the pattern of human life, and the way towards union of the soul with God. Turning in Chapter Five from Italian to English examples of the lyric, Jeffrey discusses those found in the Franciscan compilations *Fasciculus Morum*, *Speculum Christiani*, and John Grimestone's Commonplace Book. In this chapter also he argues for the strong Franciscan associations of MSS Digby 86, Trinity Coll. Camb. 323 and Harley 2253, and conjectures that over eighty-five per cent of Middle English lyrics from before the Black Death may be attributed to the Franciscans. Here and in his final chapter (on 'Spirituality and Style'), he suggests that certain lyrics, notably the Harley ones 'The Way of Woman's Love' and 'Wynter' are not quite as 'secular' as has earlier been supposed—though a measure of apparent secularity was consistent with Franciscan principles. The inadequate and partly inaccurate glossing of the latter poem should put the reader on his guard against similar deficiencies in the volume as a whole. One of the Appendices makes it clear that a companion volume on *Early English Drama and Franciscan Spirituality* is to be expected from the same author.

Jeffrey has not used Edward Wilson's *Descriptive Index of The English Lyrics in John of Grimestone's Preaching Book* (1973),[18] perhaps because it was not reviewed in *YW* for the appropriate year. It makes available a total of 246 items, of which 182 are hitherto unprinted from this source, and over one hundred are unrecorded in the *Index of Middle English Verse* or its *Supplement*. The document is of great importance because of its precise localization and dating, a Franciscan compilation of 1372 from Norfolk—perhaps south west Norfolk according to A. McIntosh's graphemic analysis reported here. There is a full text of those lyrics previously unpublished and a text, or the opening, of such Latin sources as appear in the manuscript. A note of anthologies, not listed in the *Index* or *Supplement*, in which lyrics from Grimestone are printed, is given (twice!) The notes are mainly bibliographical and occasionally interpretative.

Many of the lyrics discussed by Jeffrey are included in *A Selection of*

[17] *The Early English Lyric and Franciscan Spirituality*, by David L. Jeffrey. Lincoln, Nebraska: University and Nebraska Press. pp. xvi + 306. 8 plates.

[18] *A Descriptive Index of the English Lyrics in John of Grimestone's Preaching Book*, by Edward Wilson. Medium Aevum Monographs, New Series II. Oxford: Basil Blackwell. pp. xxiv + 73.

Religious Lyrics edited by Douglas Gray[19], who points out in his Introduction that such lyrics were 'written to be used' in sermons, etc., and emphasizes the importance of the Franciscans in the development of the religious lyric and carol in England; two of them, Herebert and Ryman, are represented in his selection, and discussed in the Notes to lyrics nos. 29 and 59; Gray has also benefited from Edward Wilson's *Descriptive Index*, as his Note to no. 15 shows. Gray's Notes are particularly full and informative; the one to no. 27, 'Wofully araide', with its discussion of the probable misattribution of this poem to Skelton, gives another example of this. A Select Bibliography and a Glossary add to the usefulness of this selection, which is arranged not chronologically, 'but according to the subject-matter, roughly forming a "Scheme of Redemption" from the Fall of man to the Last Things'.

C. Meier-Ewert argues convincingly for 'The Anglo-Norman Origin of *Thou Wommon Boute uere*' (Anglia), a poem of Herebert's not included in Gray's *Selection*. Most of it is derived from a poem attributed to Bozon, *Le mel de ceel*, while its figure of the charter of Christ may derive from the long penitential poem *Douce dame pie mere*.

E. G. Stanley raises the question of 'Richard Hyrd (?) "Rote of Resoun Ryht" in MS Harley 2253' (*N&Q*), suggesting that the word *Hyrd* in the last two stanzas of the lyric 'Weping hauep myn wonges wet' is a pun, meaning both 'household' and 'herdsman', and reflecting in the latter meaning the occupational name of the Richard there referred to.

Theo Stemmler edits 'More English Texts from MS Cambridge University Library I i. III. 8' (*Anglia*), covering a total of forty-nine verse items, twenty-five of which are not listed in the *Index of Middle English Verse* or its *Supplement* and forty-four of which have never been printed before. He thus brings the total of vernacular texts discovered in this collection of Latin sermons to 101. He also corrects misreadings of some English texts in this same manuscript which have previously been edited.

Michael J. Preston provides a computer aided *Concordance to the Middle English Shorter Poem*[20], 'based on the ten generally accepted standard editions of Middle English Shorter Poetry', that is, those of Carleton Brown, G. L. Brook, Rossell Hope Robbins, Richard Leighton Greene, John Stevens and Henry A. Person. These volumes are numbered one to ten, and each entry in the Concordance is preceded by the volume number, the number of the poem as given in the volume, the stanza number where appropriate, and the line number as given in the relevant volume. This last category of information is not announced in the Preface, and it is not immediately clear that the letters a and b are used in the 'line-number' column to indicate the occurrences of words in unnumbered burdens or refrains. The Concordance itself is preceded by alphabetical

---

[19] *A Selection of Religious Lyrics*, ed. with an Introduction, Notes, and Glossary by Douglas Gray. Clarendon Medieval and Tudor Series, General Editor J. A. W. Bennett. Clarendon Press: Oxford University Press. pp. xxii + 174. Paper covers £2.25; boards £5.50.
[20] *A Concordance To The Middle English Shorter Poem*, by Michael J. Preston. Compendia: Computer-Generated Aids to Literary and Linguistic Research. General Editor R. A. Wisbey. Volume 6. Leeds: W. S. Maney and Son Ltd. In two parts; Part 1, pp. xii + 1220. Part 2, pp. 1221-2456. £29.

and numerical indexes of first lines, and followed by 'Ranking frequency lists' of Middle English and foreign word forms, by reverse or 'rhyming' indexes to both these categories of words, and by a concordance to the foreign words occurring in the poems. Based as it is on a number of different editions rather than one, this concordance cannot have quite the neatness of the one based on Malory's works and discussed in the appropriate section, though most of the difficulties arising from this situation are adequately dealt with in the Preface.

Russell A. Peck, in 'Public Dreams and Private Myths: Perspective in Middle English Literature' (*PMLA*), quotes one of the passages from St Bonaventure and some of the lyrics quoted by Jeffrey, above, in an essay pointing out that medieval society differs from modern society in having had a common mythology. Much of the thrill of medieval poetry derives from its breaking the barrier between private and public myth; modern poetry, on the other hand, lacks the latter kind of myth. This is illustrated by a comparison of 'Myrie songen the monkes binne Ely' with a poem by William Carlos Williams, and by a discussion of, among other poems, 'Erthe took of erthe', and 'Now goth sonne under wode'.

John F. Plummer III discusses 'The Poetic Function of Conventional Language in the Middle English Lyric' (*SP*), applying to 'Bytuene Mersh ant Averil' Dante's rules for stanza construction as abstracted in his *De Vulgari Eloquentia* from Provençal, French, and Italian songs. Plummer finds that the lyric in question reveals a 'tendency towards a pattern of balance-through-embracement' on the levels of structure and wording, and that the 'ideational argument' serves primarily 'as the raw material' of a 'formal, esthetic construct', so that 'the center of esthetic interest has clearly become the song as form'. Dante's views on Provençal poetry also form part of the subject-matter of L. T. Topsfield's *Troubadours and Love*[21].

S. A. J. Bradley draws attention to 'An Incompletely Noted Variant of the Middle English Lyric "Faith is Above Reason" (Index 4181)' (*N&Q*), showing that in Copenhagen Royal Library MS Thott 40, 110, the line beginning *Wytt hath wonder* begins the second quatrain of an eight-line lyric which may have been written down, if not composed, by Nicholas Barkley. Its first quatrain, beginning 'He ys quycke that semyth dede', states the mystery of God incarnate which is then summarized in the second quatrain as being the problem defeating Wit and Reason.

Alexandra Barratt discussess 'The Prymer and its Influence on Fifteenth-century English Passion Lyrics' (*MÆ*), meaning by the prymer the Hours of the Virgin, in Latin or English. Its influence may explain the fact that Passion lyrics of this period are more concerned with the whole course of the Passion than with single dramatic moments. This is illustrated by, among other poems, 'Quhat dollour persit our ladyis hert', 'O my hert is wo', 'Wofuly araide', and Ryman's 'Beholde me, hede, hande, foote, and side'. Barratt finds support for this view in the fact that five other lyrics, including two by John Audelay, show different degrees of verbal closeness

---

[21] *Troubadours and Love* by L. T. Topsfield. Cambridge University Press. pp. viii + 296. 1 map, 4 plates. £6.

to two works attributed to Bede which were frequently used in the prymer.

Kathryn Hume offers a readable study of *The Owl and the Nightingale: the Poem and its Critics*[22], reviewing the latter in her Chapters 2–5, after first briefly discussing problems of text, date and authorship. Many critics, she finds, have looked outside the poem for clues to its interpretation, treating it as intellectual, religious, or political allegory. In her sixth chapter, 'Structure and Sequential Impact', she advocates a return to the work itself, finding that 'From an elaborately inconsequential beginning which forcibly establishes the avian insignificance of the protagonists, the poem becomes gradually more serious in subjects, finally reaching the climaxes of the birds' deaths'. The ironic incongruity between the avian setting and the seriousness of some of the subjects debated by the birds provides the starting-point for Hume's discussion in her seventh chapter of the poem as a burlesque satire on human contentiousness, an approach which she defends still further in her eighth and final chapter. She is aware, of course, that the author of the poem (whom she only cautiously identifies with Nicholas of Guildford) would not have used the term 'burlesque' himself, and her book is useful not only for its survey of earlier interpretations, but also for the interesting comparisons with seventeenth and eighteenth century literature which her own approach suggests.

Betty Hill writes on 'Oxford, Jesus College MS 29' (*N&Q*), giving 'Addenda on Donation, Acquisition, Dating and Relevance of the "Broaken Leafe" Note to "The Owl and the Nightingale" '. She finds no clear evidence that John of Guildford was the author of 'at least one' of the poems originally contained in the part of this manuscript which contains 'The Owl and the Nightingale'. Lawrence L. Besserman, in 'A Note on the Owl and the Nightingale, Lines 1691–92' (*NM*), offers the interpretation 'proceed to' as a translation of *holde (þar) to* in support of the view that the poem represents an appeal for ecclesiastical preferment. S.R.T.O. d'Ardenne's 'Maitre Nicole de Guildford, An Preost on Leoden' (*RLV*, 1973) was not seen in time for inclusion this year.

Alan S. C. Ross discusses '*Run and Reve* and Similar Alliterative Phrases' (*NM*), suggesting that in the phrase *ryn and raue* in *A Middle English Metrical Paraphrase of the Old Testament* 'raue', meaning 'to wander', may be native or borrowed from Scandinavian. The *Saga-Book* of the Viking Society confirms that the large collection of Middle English alliterative phrases made by the late E. S. Olszewska (Mrs A. S. C. Ross) is available to research workers in the Library of University College London.

Thomas D. Hill discusses 'Parody and Theme in the Middle English "Land of Cokaygne"' (*N&Q*); the theme, he finds, is the comic juxtaposition of the idea of the cloistered paradise with the sensual paradise depicted in the poem. Hill adds to the remarks of earlier commentators on the passage involving Enoch and Elias at lines 5–16, and finds that the catalogue of negatives at lines 21–30 parodies 'the seven joys of heaven'; that the flying monks of lines 123–43 parody the 'flight' of the contem-

---

[22] *The Owl and the Nightingale: The Poem and its Critics*, by Kathryn Hume. Toronto and Buffalo: University of Toronto Press. pp. xii + 140. £5.50.

plative; and that the river of sweet milk in the nunnery episode of lines 147–62 parodies a river comparable to the one associated with charity in the *Visio Pauli*.

F. C. de Vries, in 'A Note on "Dame Sirith"' (*N&Q*), suggests that *wonne* of line 58 may be a misreading of *iunne*, meaning 'granted', and that lines 58–60 are meant to be spoken by the merchant's wife rather than by Wilekin the clerk.

O. S. Pickering begins a new series of Middle English texts under the general editorship of M. Görlach with an edition of *The South English Nativity of Mary and Christ*[23], based on the earliest of its three extant versions; the other two versions show expansions and alterations to the original. Pickering suggests convincingly that the poem was left unfinished by its author, and that the *Ministry and Passion*, which follows it as a sequel in one manuscript, was written by a later poet. Among the sources of the *South English Nativity*—though they may not have been direct ones —are the *Legenda aurea* and the *Gospel of pseudo-Matthew;* and while it also shows some indebtedness to the *South English Legendary* it seems to have been written at a comparatively early stage of the latter's development—perhaps in the Gloucestershire area in c. 1275–80. Pickering refers to an article of his in *Anglia* for 1973, not reviewed in *YW* for the appropriate year, for a definition of the expression *temporale* (as opposed to *sanctorale*) which he applies in his Introduction to the type of material with which this poem deals. The edition has no glossary, but the Introduction and the textual notes, in particular, are very full.

James W. Earl, in the course of his long article on 'Typology and Iconographic Style in Early Medieval Hagiography' (*SLitI*) refers to the alliterative couplet about Saint Kenelm in the life of that saint in the *South English Legenary* as 'a dramatic example of a hagiographic document preserved as . . . a literary relic . . . and a literary icon . . .'

Thomas J. Heffernan, in 'An Analysis of the Narrative Motifs in the Legend of St Eustace' (*M&H*), uses the three Middle English versions of this legend to show that while hagiography depends largely on convention it nevertheless provides scope for individual authorial interpretation. The Northern homily cycle version stresses Saint Eustace's exemplary qualities; the one in MS Digby 86, which shows the influence of romance, is concerned more with a secular heroic ideal and with the dramatic presentation of words and actions; and the 'South English Legendary version', finally, is characterised by lack of dialogue and a thoroughgoing pious didacticism.

Thomas J. Heffernan also edits 'A Middle English Poem on Lovedays' (*ChauR*) from a manuscript of the early fifteenth century. The term 'loveday'—the earliest recorded instance of which is found in the *South English Legendary*—is defined in *ChauR*'s abstract of Heffernan's contribution as 'an extra-legal meeting in which disputants might amicably resolve differences'. The poem is partly in quatrains and partly in rhymed couplets, and is often highly alliterative.

Kari Sajavaara shows that 'The Withered Footprints on the Green Street

[23] *The South English Nativity of Mary and Christ*, ed. from MS BM Stowe 949 by O. S. Pickering. Middle English Texts, 1. General Editor M. Görlach. Heidelberg: Carl Winter Universitätsverlag. pp. 120.

of Paradise' (*NM*) in the passage in the *Cursor Mundi* in which Adam tells
Seth the way to Paradise supports the idea of a relationship between the
grenne grund of the Old English *Exodus* and the path leading to Paradise.
Francis J. Sheeran discusses 'Ten Verse Fragments in *Dives and Pauper*'
(*NM*), all of which are written as prose in the manuscripts and early
editions of the Ten Commandments. They include the earliest known
English translation of the hymn *Vexilla Regis Prodeunt* and a verse para-
phrase of St Paul and, under the Sixth Commandment, a poem on how
Samson and David were deceived by women, one on Henry II's mistress
Rosamond, and one derived from a moralization of a tale in the *Gesta
Romanorum*. The group to which these last three belong suggests the former
existence of an anthology of poems used by preachers to elucidate the
Sixth Commandment.

Jane C. Fredeman discusses 'John Capgrave's First English Composition:
"The Life of St Norbert"' (*BJRL*), arguing that its subject-matter and
its composition in the vernacular were more compatible with Capgrave's
interests and circumstances prior to the time of its completion in 1440
than has previously been supposed. Though its original derives from the
standard (B) version of the *Vita* rather than the shorter (A) one, Capgrave
seems to have used a shortened revision of the former. He both condenses
and expands his source, clarifying it for a less learned audience, and making it dramatically effective. His methods are particularly well illustrated
in the episodes involving the possession and exorcism in section twenty,
and the cleric's ambush in section thirty-one.

Richard Green Allen argues convincingly for 'Crapshooting Devices in
a Medieval Manuscript' (*PBSA*)—that is, in 'Chaunce of the Dyse', a short,
illustrated, rhyme-royal poem of unknown authorship in MS Fairfax 16
(Bodleian 3896). A. S. G. Edwards discusses 'Variant Texts of *The
Parliament of Birds*' (*PBSA*), 'a late medieval poem' which is perhaps an
imitation of Chaucer's *Parliament of Fowls* and survives in three printed
editions and one manuscript, all from the sixteenth century.

John Reidy edits Thomas Norton's *Ordinal of Alchemy*[24] from its two
earliest manuscripts—British Museum MS Add. 10302 and, where that is
defective, British Museum MS Sloane 1873; variants are given from other
manuscripts representative of major groupings among the total number of
thirty-one manuscripts. The edition has a Glossary and an Index of authors
and books referred to in the *Ordinal*, and its Introduction contains, in
addition to accounts of the manuscripts and the language of the principal
one used, a section on the author's life and a fascinating discussion of the
alchemy of the *Ordinal*.

Wolfhardt H. Anders' *Balladensänger und mündliche Komposition*
(1974)[25], omitted from *YW* last year, has been succinctly reviewed this
year by Jörgen Wolter in *RES*. Geoffrey Grigson, editing *The Penguin*

[24] *Thomas Norton's Ordinal of Alchemy*, ed. by John Reidy. Early English Text
Society, Original Series No. 272. Oxford University Press. pp. lxxvi + 126. 12 plates.
£3.75.
[25] *Balladensänger und mündliche Komposition. Untersuchungen zur englischen
Traditionsballade*, by Wolfhardt H. Anders. Bochumer Arbeiten zur Sprach- und
Literatur Wissenschaft, eds. Siegfried Grosse, Karl Maurer, Hans Joachim Schrimpf.
München: Wilhelm Fink Verlag, 1974. pp. 250. DM. 48.00

Book of Ballads[26], rather unfairly implies criticism of David Buchan's approach to ballad-transmission on one page of his Introduction, while invoking his authority on the 'period of composition and re-composition' of ballads in North-East Scotland a couple of pages later. The seventy-five 'Earlier Ballads' in the Book include 'The Wife of Usher's Well', 'The Three Ravens' (though not, surprisingly and unfortunately, 'The Twa Corbies') and 'Chevy Chase'.

Martin Puhvel, in 'The Revenants in "The Wife of Usher's Well": A Reconsideration' (*Folklore*) argues that the return of the three ghostly sons at Martinmas in this ballad may reflect a confused or deliberately vague recollection of the widespread tradition of the return of departed spirits which is associated with All Souls' Day.

O. Arngart, in '*The Battle of Otterburn* and the *Hunting of the Cheviot*' (*SN*) argues convincingly that the former ballad was the earlier of the two, and that the latter borrowed from it. Arngart is here in agreement with most writers on these two ballads other than D. C. Fowler. Robert S. Thomson, in 'The Transmission of Chevy-Chase' (*SFQ*), suggests that this ballad was not composed by Richard Sheale, the minstrel whose repertoire is contained in Ashmole, MS 48, which provides its earliest text, but was 're-created traditionally' by him. His version of it—*The Hunting of the Cheviat*—is thus 'the first authentic folksong recovered from tradition'. Its loose metrical structure, which distinguishes it textually from later recoveries of the ballad, 'suggests that it was a performed song rather than a recited literary text', and its reference to Chevy Chase as the site of the battle of Otterburn may well be due to confusion by Sheale of the events of Chevy Chase with those of Otterburn, of which he probably knew from another ballad. *The Battle of Otterburn*, based on historical fact, differs from *Chevy Chase*, which 'details an imaginary situation'. The subsequent history of the latter ballad is then pursued in detail.

Three monographs which belong both here and in Section 10 below will be dealt with in that section.

9. Malory and Caxton

Richard R. Griffith seeks to identify 'The Political Bias of Malory's "Morte Darthur" ' (*Viator*, 1974) as Yorkist rather than Lancastrian, discussing in detail six passages which have been used in support of the latter alternative, and arguing that Malory's presentation of Arthur echoes the career of Edward IV more convincingly than that of Henry VI. Edward unlike Henry, was commonly associated with Arthur during his reign, and Malory's condemnation of English fickleness in his final Tale may have been stimulated by the rebellious activities against Edward IV in 1469 of Warwick the Kingmaker, who had helped Edward to the throne. While suggesting that acceptance of a Yorkist bias in *Le Morte Darthur* is helpful to the literary historian, Griffith admits that it provides no certain basis for choosing between the Warwickshire Malory of Newbold Revel (cf. Field

---

[26] *The Penguin Book of Ballads*, chosen and introduced by Geoffrey Grigson Penguin Poets. Harmondsworth, Middlesex: Penguin Books. pp. 376. UK 95p. U.S.A. $3.15.

below) and the Yorkshire one of Studley and Conyers (cf. Matthews *YW* 47. 121) as candidates for its authorship. This choice can perhaps be made with more confidence now that P.J.C. Field, in 'Sir Thomas Malory, M.P.' (*Bulletin of the Institute of Historical Research*, 1974), has argued against Whitteridge (*YW* 54. 101) that the Thomas Malory of Newbold Revel, who became an M.P. for Warwickshire in 1445, was identical with the Thomas Malory of Fenny Newbold who ambushed the Duke of Buckingham in 1450, and with a Thomas Malery (*sic*) who, shortly before this incident, had become M.P. for Bedwin in Wiltshire, perhaps with Buckingham's help, in 1449. After his desertion of Buckingham at the end of that year this same Malory, according to Field, became M.P. for the Yorkist-controlled constituency of Wareham in 1450. His low income and his actions generally are by no means inconsistent with the awareness shown in the *Morte Darthur* of financial insecurity and the need for finding a 'good lord'. A new edition of Vinaver's *King Arthur and His Knights*[27] includes the whole of the *Tale of the Death of King Arthur* with selections from the other Tales, and a Bibliographical Note containing, among other things, an endorsement of Field's views on Malory, summarized above.

Mark Lambert, in *Malory: Style and Vision in Le Morte Darthur*[28] first discusses 'Aspects of period style' common to Malory and his sources and contemporaries, but rare in nineteenth-century and later fiction. One of these is 'confirmation': the similarity of vocabulary between the words of narrator and character or of different characters. He then takes 'The Healing of Sir Urry' as typical of 'Malorian style', discusses the pun on the word 'whole' in this episode, and goes on to note Malory's increasing tendency to use names of characters with their titles in his later works, his preference for action to description in his adaptations of the French romances, and his 'syncopation' or omission of minor actions when adapting these sources. All these features, together with his fondness for 'performative utterances' (like 'I promise') which actually involve performance of an action, focus the reader's attention on the essential knightliness of what is being described. In his third and final chapter, Lambert concentrates on the two last tales in *Le Morte Darthur*, stressing Malory's evocation here of the sense of a noble past through his use of the word 'noble' and expressions like 'in those days', the link between these two tales through repetition and echo of phrase and situation, and Malory's emphasis on 'shame', rather than 'guilt' as a threat to knightly honour. 'The nobility of the bearing' of blame is what constitutes the final tragedy, in Lambert's view, rather than blame attaching to individuals.

Many of Lambert's observations find support in Tomomi Kato's very useful computer-aided *Concordance to the Works of Sir Thomas Malory* (1974)[29], based on Vinaver's revised edition of 1967. All words, including

[27] *King Arthur and his Knights: Selected Tales by Sir Thomas Malory*, ed. with an Introduction by Eugene Vinaver. A Galaxy Book. New York, Oxford, London: Oxford University Press. pp. xxii + 231. Frostispiece. £1.75.

[28] *Malory: Style and Vision in Le Morte Darthur*, by Mark Lambert. New Haven and London: Yale University Press. pp. xvi + 226. £7.50.

[29] *A Concordance to the Works of Sir Thomas Malory*, ed. by Tomomi Kato. University of Tokyo Press, 1974. pp. xiv + 1660. £48.00.

proper names, are listed alphabetically and shown in their immediate contextual setting; and figures are given after each entry denoting the book and chapter (in Caxton's numbering), and the page and line in which it occurs. The letter C ('Conversation'), when it follows these figures, indicates that the entry occurs in passages of dialogue rather than narrative, a feature which, among other things, helps to show instances of what Lambert calls 'confirmation'. Words like '(w)hole', 'promyse' and 'noble' can now be studied in all their occurrences, without risk of omission, and a glance at the entries for 'Arthur', 'Gwenyver' and 'Launcelot' seems to suggest that Malory uses names with titles to an even greater extent than Lambert implies. A word-frequency list, which concludes the volume, adds to its usefulness, showing, for instance, that the noun 'gylte' occurs only once in the whole of Malory, while 'shame' occurs 192 times and much more often in dialogue than in narrative.

Arthur Samuel Kimball, in 'Merlin's Miscreation and the Repetition Compulsion in Malory's *Morte Darthur*' (*L&P*), sees this 'romance', as he calls it, as representing an attempt to control the traumatic tensions arising from the contradiction between creativity and violence which forms the background to Arthur's conception, over which Merlin presides. This 'repetition instinct' fails to restore the purity of the creative impulse—witness, among other things, the death of Galahad—and Arthur's court seems to collapse beneath the weight of psychic chaos. D. J. Barnett, in 'Whatever happened to Gawain?' (*ESA*) suggests more usefully—though with reference, curiously, to Vinaver's *first* edition of Malory's *Works*—that Malory's portrayal of Gawain is more consistently negative than Vinaver believes (see his revised edition, 1967, III, 1433–4). While accepting Bodganow's view (*MÆ*, 1958) that the *Queste del Saint Graal*, in degrading Gauvain's character, represents a turning-point in his presentation, Barnett goes on to find the starting-point for this trend in Chrétien's Arthurian romances, suggesting that Chrétien may unconsciously have given rise to two Gauvains—the peerless one of *Erec e Enide*, and the rather less than perfect one of *Yvain, Launcelot,* and *Perceval*.

Edward D. Kennedy, in a long article on 'Malory's King Mark and King Arthur' (*MS*) gives a useful survey of the views of medieval theorists on kingship, showing how the ideal king, with his concern for the common good, was contrasted with the tyrant, who used power only for his own advantage. Malory needed to make few changes in the prose *Tristan* to present *Mark*, in his fifth Tale, as a tyrant, but seems to have made considerable changes to the *Mort Artu* and the stanzaic *Morte Arthur* in order to present Arthur, in the seventh and eighth Tales, as a king primarily concerned for the common good. Examples of this are found in Arthur's partiality to Gawain, and in his condemnation of Guenevere without permitting trial by combat. Kennedy argues, against Pochoda (*YW* 52. 98–9) that these features show, respectively, Arthur's loyalty to the bonds of kinship and his obedience to the law, qualities expected of a king. The references to Tristram's murder in Tales 7 and 8 help to suggest that Malory's contrast of Mark with Arthur was intentional. Maureen Fries, on the other hand, argues for 'Malory's Tristram as Counter-Hero to the Morte Darthur' (*NM*), believing that the Tristram Tale was deliberately designed to contrast with that of Sir Launcelot. The latter Tale has a unified and harmonious flow, appropriate to the Arthurian 'jantylnes', to which Launcelot there adheres, while the former proceeds by fits and starts, reflecting the 'grete force' on which Tristram relies, and which, for all his infidelity to Isode and his fellow knights, wins him a place in the fellowship of the Round Table. There he functions as a symbol of Launcelot's and others' partial departure from 'jantylnes', until Malory virtually dispenses with him as a character after making it clear that he did not join the Grail quest. Thus Malory makes a counter-hero of a character much like Lancelot in the French sources, in order to suggest the ultimate failure of the Arthurian ideal.

Charles W. Whitworth finds greater balancing of 'The Sacred and the Secular in Malory's Tale of the Sankgreal' (YES) than earlier critics have done, suggesting that, while Malory cuts down on the former element in his treatment of the French Queste del Saint Graal, he retains enough of it to show that both elements were fused in his conception of ideal knighthood. Whitworth develops this point with a close study of Malory's characterization in this Tale of Percival and Bors, both of whom, with Galahad, succeed in the Grail Quest.

Stephen F. Lappert finds the ambiguity of 'Malory's Treatment of the Legend of Arthur's Survival' (MLQ) at variance with most other medieval treatments of the subject, which were sceptical or frankly disbelieving. Malory prepares us for Bedivere's weakness of character in the final Tale by giving him more consistently negative treatment throughout Le Morte Darthur than is warranted by the relevant sources, and in the ambiguity of his narrative of the passing of Arthur, 'Malory also suggests the bleak hope left for Arthur and his society, of which, in Bedivere, he retains only the dregs'.

BBSIA records four papers on specifically 'Malorian' subjects that were read at the Exeter Conference mentioned in Section 5, above. These are Beverly Kennedy, 'Malory's King Arthur: Maker of his Own "Desteny" '; William Matthews, 'Who Revised the Roman War Episode in Malory's Le Morte Darthur?', Mary Hynes-Berry, 'Malory's Style: Translation as Transformation in the Grail Story'; and Robert L. Kindrick, 'Dynadan and the Code of Chivalry'.

Robert H. Wilson discusses 'Malory and the Ballad "King Arthur's Death" ' (M&H) found in Bishop Percy's Folio MS, emphasizing its indebtedness to Malory as evidenced by its inclusion of the latter's expansions on the stanzaic Morte Arthur, and concluding that it was written as a continuation to 'The Legend of King Arthur', which precedes it in the MS, by an author who also revised the ending of the 'Legend'. The simplest hypothesis is that this author used the text of the 'Legend' published by Lloyd—its probable author—in 1584 and the East edition of Malory published in 1578 (?), though he may have worked from older texts.

In Walter Nash's 'Tennyson: "The Epic" and "The Old Morte" ' (CQ) the latter phrase refers not to any work of Malory's but to a poetic 'fragment' by Tennyson composed in 1833–4, though part of the article shows how Tennyson's expansions and re-phrasings of Malory in this poem represent a striving for 'theatrical' effects of various kinds.

In 'Variant Printing in Le Morte Darthur' (Library) William Matthews reasserts Bühler's views of 1939–40 against those of Vinaver (YW 20, 67),

claiming that the numerous differences apparent in four pages between
the two surviving copies of Caxton's edition are to be explained as the
result of re-setting undertaken at Caxton's instigation—not because he
wanted to make alterations, but because he needed more copies of the
relevant sheets.

N. F. Blake edits *Quattuor Sermones Printed by William Caxton*[30] with
Notes, a Glossary and a Select Bibliography, showing in his Introduction
that Caxton printed three editions of this work rather than two, as previously suggested, and that its modern title, though hallowed by custom, is
inappropriate, since the work falls into three parts, the first of which is not
as easily divisible into four as was earlier thought. It does not seem to have
been linked with John Mirk's *Festial* until the end of the fifteenth century,
and the first edition most probably dates from between the end of June
1483 and March 26, 1484. It is a conflation of, among other works, the
Lay Folks' Catechism, and the *Pore Caitiff*, and parallels between it and
still more works remain to be discovered.

The catalogue for a Caxton exhibition in the Bodleian Library[31] argues
convincingly that Caxton's translation of Raoul Le Fèvre's *Recuyell of the
Historyes of Troye*, the first book to be printed in English, was completed
and published by Caxton at Bruges in 1474. The catalogue contains a
checklist of original Caxton editions in the Bodleian.

Donald B. Sands writes again on 'The Uses of the Proverb in the Middle
Dutch Poem *Reinaerts Historie*' (*MS*), a prose version of which was translated by Caxton as *The History of Reynard the Fox*.

10. Other Prose

Three studies belong both here and in Section 8, above. The first of
these is V. J. Scattergood's edition of *The Works of Sir John Clanvowe*.[32]
that is, of *The Boke of Cupide* (often known as *The Cuckoo and the
Nightingale*), a debate poem in the dream-vision convention in five-line
stanzas, and *The Two Ways*, a prose treatise showing some sympathy with
Lollard attitudes, and advocating avoidance of the 'broode way' leading
to hell in favour of the 'nargh way' leading to heaven. Scattergood argues
for John Clanvowe (rather than for Thomas Clanvowe, his son or nephew)
as the author of the former work, after showing that his authorship of the
latter one is hardly open to doubt.

Rachel Hands edits in facsimile *English Hawking and Hunting in the
Boke of St Albans*;[33] the hawking section is in prose, and the hunting one

[30] *Quattuor Sermones Printed by William Caxton*, ed. by N. F. Blake. Middle
English Texts 2. General Editor M. Görlach. Heidelberg. Carl Winter Universitätsverlag. pp. 100.
    [31] *William Caxton: A Small Exhibition Held in the Bodleian Library to Commem-
orate the Five Hundredth Anniversary of the First Book Printed in the English
Language*. Bodleian Library, Oxford. pp. 36. 25 pence.
    [32] *The Works of Sir John Clanvowe*, ed. by V. J. Scattergood. Cambridge, England
and Totowa, N. J: D. S. Brewer Ltd. and Rowman and Littlefield. pp. 96. £3.95.
    [33] *English Hawking and Hunting in The Boke of St Albans*. A facsimile edition of
sigs a2–fa of *The Boke of St Albans* (1486) by Rachel Hands. Oxford English
Monographs, General eds. Norman Davis, Helen Gardner, J. C. Maxwell and D. F.
Foxon. Oxford University Press. pp. lxx + 196.

in rhyming couplets. Her discussion of the authorship and sources of these and other relevant sections partly summarizes and partly supersedes a number of articles published by Hands in recent years (*YW* 48. 114–5; 53. 86, 100; 55. 125, 138–9).

Hands argues that the name of 'Dam Julyans Barnes', which appears in the *St Albans* colophon to the verse treatise on hunting, belonged originally not to that treatise, but to one which underlay the material on hawking and hunting which the *St Albans* compiler used to supplement the information provided in the two main sections. Neither this nor any comparable name can be regarded as that of the author or compiler of the whole book. The helpfulness of Hands' edition to a study of Middle English literary references to hunting is perhaps most evident in her Notes to lines 1317 ff and 1748 ff, where frequent reference is made to *GGK*.

Peter Revell publishes a descriptive list of *Fifteenth Century English Prayers and Meditations*,[34] including works in dialogue form and works on moral subjects in which the treatment is essentially that of the meditation as defined by the O.E.D., but excluding narrative works containing matter of the type found in religious meditations. Also included are 'Lyrics which in subject matter and general tone are similar in character to prose meditations'. Only works originally composed in the fifteenth century or by authors who lived largely during that period are included. The list is arranged under various doctrinal headings, and there are separate indexes of authors, of manuscripts, and of initia. Its twofold purpose of aiding the study of church history and of Middle English literature in the relevant period is thus well served.

In his *Moralities on the Gospels: A New Source for Ancrene Wisse*,[35] E. J. Dobson argues from a number of parallels between the *Moralia super Evangelia* and *Ancrene Wisse* that the latter work borrowed from the former. This leads him to reject, partly on chronological grounds, the identification of the *Moralia* with lectures given by Robert Grosseteste to the Oxford Franciscans in 1229–30. The Grosseteste attribution appears in one of the only two independent witnesses to the text of the *Moralia*; in the other one, the work is attributed to Alexander of Bath. Dobson argues in favour of this latter attribution, and for the probable identification of this Alexander with the dean of Wells who died before June 1212, and finally brings these arguments into line with his view that *Ancrene Wisse* was written after 1215, certainly not later than 1230, and probably not later than 1222.

According to the results of Bernhard Diensberg's thesis on the *Ancrene Riwle*,[36] which was seen only in summary in the supplement to *Anglia*

[34] *Fifteenth Century English Prayers and Meditations. A Descriptive List of Manuscripts in the British Library*, compiled by Peter Revell. Garland Reference Library of the Humanities (Vol. 19). New York and London: Garland Publishing, Inc. pp. xiv + 138. $15.

[35] *Moralities on the Gospels: A New Source for Ancrene Wisse*, by E. J. Dobson. Oxford, at the Clarendon Press. pp. x + 182. £6.

[36] Bernhard Diensberg, *Morphologische Untersuchungen zur 'Ancrene Riwle'. Die Verbalflexion nach den MSS Corpus Christi College Cambridge 402, B. M. Cotton Cleopatra C. VI, B. M. Cotton Nero A. XIV.* Dissertation, Bonn (Prof. K. Dietz). pp. xxiv + 786.

(1974), the Corpus dialect of the *Ancrene Riwle* and the additions and corrections of scribe B of MS Cleopatra display a system of verbal inflections which continues that of Old English (as in the Mercian dialect of the *Vespasian Psalter*) with slight modifications, while the systems underlying MSS Cleopatra (Scribe A) and Nero have been considerably modified owing to velarisation of Old English $\bar{a}$ and vocalization of Old English spirantal *g* in intervocalic position. This has resulted, in the two latter manuscript versions, in new ablaut series for strong verbs. As for weak verbs, it is found that the inflectional morphemes of Old English weak class II (*-ian*) are well preserved in the Corpus dialect by verbs of the *makien* and *fondin* types which are short-stemmed and long-stemmed respectively; that in the dialect of Cleopatra (A) c. 30% of the former type and c. 54% of the latter show the inflections of weak class I; and that in the Nero dialect the *makien*-type is as well preserved as in the Corpus dialect, while almost 85% of the *fondin*-type displays the endings of weak class I. It is pointed out finally that each of the dialects in question shows a high degree of phonological and morphological consistency, and that the phonological differences between them correspond precisely to morphological ones.

G. B. Jack finds, after systematically investigating the use of *þe* and *þat*, 'Relative Pronouns in Language AB' (*ES*), in the Corpus text of *Ancrene Wisse*, that the syntactic function of the pronoun and the animateness and number of the antecedent are the main factors affecting the selection of one or other of these two forms. *þe* is mostly used in subject position, or when the antecedent is animate; while the use of *þat*, which occurs mostly when the antecedent is inanimate, and preferably also singular, is not governed by syntactic considerations. Putting these findings for the A part of the language together with those of Kivimaa for the B part (in MS Bodley 34, *YW* 47. 43–4, 95), Jack concludes that in the use of these pronouns 'the AB language was much more like other varieties of early ME than has sometimes been thought'.

Lois K. Smedick, in 'Cursus in Middle English: *A Talkyng of þe Loue of God* Reconsidered' (*MS*) concludes from an examination of seven passages selected from this fourteenth-century rhythmical prose treatise that its rhythmical effects cannot be convincingly linked with the Latin rhetorical device known as cursus, but are to be explained rather in terms of the natural rhythm of the language in which it was written. Smedick, whose views support those of Sherman M. Kuhn (*YW* 53. 48, 72) in relation to Old English, is here arguing against an explicit connection made by Margarent Morgan (*YW* 33. 78) between this treatise and the Latin cursus.

Margarent Jennings, C.S.J. in 'Richard Rolle and the Three Degrees of Love' (*DownR*) points out that the latter are given such titles as 'insuperabel', 'inseparabel', and 'singuler' in Rolle's *The Commandment, The Form of Living* and the *Emendatio vitae*, while in his *Ego dormio* they are merely described. She concludes that in the first three works Rolle was compiling his personal thoughts on the degrees of love, without specific indebtedness to earlier authorities, even though he was 'heir to the gentleness of Francis and to the Jesus-devotion of Bernard, influenced by the epistolary warmth of Richard's *Tractatus* rather than by the mystical development of his *De Quattuor Gradibus Caritatis*', while in the *Ego dormio* he was defining three types of Christian living in a context of controversy concerning the superiority of the contemplative to the active life, 'without any reference to the mystical "ways" or to the illuminative way of love'. John W. Conlee, in 'The *Abbey of the Holy Ghost* and the *Eight Ghostly Dwelling Places* of Huntington Library HM 744' (*MÆ*) compares and contrasts the latter work with the former, which has long been associated with Rolle's works, as an example of the tradition of mystical writing descending from the twelfth-century *De Claustro Animae* in which the soul or conscience is compared with an abbey or cloister.

Michael Wilks, in 'Misleading Manuscripts: Wyclif and the Non-Wycliffite Bible' (*Studies in Church History*) shows that the tradition of a Bible translated by Wyclif dates from the generation after his death, and that the manuscripts used as evidence for such a Bible in fact offer no grounds for thinking that Wyclif was responsible for the translation. The presupposition that he was is a rare example of common ground between Fristedt and Lindberg in their recent writings on the subject. It is clear that an English New Testament was available by 1382, and that Wyclif came to know of it before he died two years later, but its provenance is unknown, and future research might consider John of Trevisa as perhaps responsible for it. For Wyclif, the sermon was the ideal type of *translatio*, or vehicle for divine truths, with its emphasis on literal sense, rather than on literal translation as the latter term is now understood.

A. R. Warner, in a study of 'Infinitive Marking in the Wyclifite Sermons' (*ES*), based on 164 pages of the latter and intended for comparison with findings made recently for a Chaucer corpus by Quirk and Svartvik (*YW* 51. 39), finds that the incidence of the infinitive 'marked' or preceded by *to* is much higher in the Wyclif corpus. While grammatical function is more important in Wyclif than in Chaucer for the selection of *to* or *for to* as a marker, the separation of the dependent infinitive from its governing verb is much less so. The two corpuses also differ in their use of marking in conjoined infinitives.

Peter Auksi, in 'Wyclif's Sermons and the Plain Style' (*Archiv für Reformationsgeschichte*) investigates Wyclif's Latin sermons in order to illustrate his partial adoption of classical rhetorical theory as interpreted by Augustine, and the plain style which results from the 'reductive and purifying' way of thinking which for Wyclif went together with the importance he attached to the example of Christ, to genuinely scriptural statements, and to the pattern of the primitive church.

C.W.R.D. Moseley discusses 'The Availability of *Mandeville's Travels* in England, 1356–1750' (*Library*), pointing out in the earlier part of his article that by 1400 some version of the *Travels* was available in each major language in Europe, that it was read as much for information as for entertainment, since few of its readers would then have recognized the modern distinction between fact and fiction, and that it was well known in Spain, Portugal and Germany by the time of Columbus.

Paxton Hart finds an 'Early, Unrecorded Use of *Suburb* as Singular' (*AN&Q* 1974) in John Trevisa's translation of Ranulph Higden's Latin *Polychronicon*, which was completed in 1387. M. C. Seymour's edition of Trevisa's translation of Bartholomew de Glanville's *De Proprietatibus Rerum* was not seen.

Walter H. Beale discusses 'Walter Hilton and the Concept of "Medled Lyf" ' (*ABR*). After investigating the tradition behind this treatise of Hilton's on the 'mixed life'—an expression which, unlike the concept it represents, was remarkably rare before Hilton used it— Beale concludes that Hilton is here symbolizing at various levels the contemplative and active lives, while at the same time following Augustine's example in maintaining that every life, no matter what mode of living is chosen, should be 'ordered in charity'.

John C. Hirsh argues in 'Author and Scribe in *The Book of Margery Kempe*' (*MÆ*) that the second of the two scribes whose contributions are relevant to this work's textual transmission rewrote the first scribe's text with the active collaboration of Margery herself. The *Book* is divided into two parts by Margery's pilgrimage to the Holy Land—a structure which she and the second scribe probably devised between them—and Capitulum 28, in particular, is used to show that 'the second scribe, no less than Margery, should be regarded as the author of *The Book of Margery Kempe*'.

P. S. Jolliffe edits 'Two Middle English Tracts on the Contemplative Life' (*MS*) from fifteenth-century manuscripts of Carthusian provenance in the British Museum. Both contain borrowings from the *Cloud of Unknowing* and related writings, and from Hilton's *Scale of Perfection;* and the longer of the two tracts contains further borrowings from the *Scale*, and draws on Rolle's *Form of Living* and on an English version of *Benjamyn minor*. The treatment of the threefold way in both tracts is indebted to Hugh of Balma's *Mystica theologia*. A small part of the longer tract, dealing with the active life, is in awkward couplets. The agreement between the two tracts, which is found to be especially evident in their treatment of the threefold way, is then discussed, and their value as repositories of earlier written material is finally emphasized.

Leonard E. Boyle and Richard M. Rouse edit 'A Fifteenth-Century List of the Books of Edmund Norton' (*Speculum*) from MS C.U.A. 114, which also contains Rolle's *Emendatio Vitae*, and may well have been written by Norton himself, who was probably a fellow of Balliol College.

Alison Hanham provides the first complete edition of *The Cely Letters, 1472-88*,[37] with an Introduction, Notes, Bibliography, Glossary and an Index of Names. In her Introduction, Hanham emphasizes the value of the whole collection of Cely papers as a record of commercial English and 'as a generally unselfconscious reproduction of the speech and writing habits of middle-class Londoners'; as she points out later, 'There is little striving for literary effect in the letters. At best the writing is governed by the rhythms of ordinary speech; at worst it lapses into long formless sentences . . . . '. The Notes are very full, and the Introduction also deals with the manuscripts, the Cely family, and the financial background to the letters.

Diane Bornstein examines four 'Military Manuals in Fifteenth-Century England' (*MS*), one of which, *Knyghthode and Bataile*, is in verse, and all of which have the fourth century *De re militari* of Vegetius as their major

---

[37] *The Cely Letters 1472-1488*, ed. by Alison Hanham. Early English Text Society, Original Series, 273. Published for the Early English Text Society by Oxford University Press. pp. xxviii + 366. 5 plates £5.75.

source. All agree with Vegetius on the importance of military training, and the prose translation of Vegetius and the *Boke of Noblesse* echo his imperialism and nationalism, adapting these to English and anti-French requirements. *Knyghthode and Bataile* and *Faytpes of Armes*, on the other hand, are characterised by 'civilian pleas for a protective army and peace'.

Paul G. Arakelian shows that the 'Punctuation in a Late Middle English Manuscript' (*NM*), that is, the *Pageant of the ... Life ... of Richard Beauchamp, Earl of Warwick*, written in the fourteen-nineties, represents a conscious attempt by the writer to order and clarify his clauses and sentences.

Sarah Lawson finds examples of '"Well and Truly": A Durable Cliché' (*N&Q*) in a notice printed by Caxton in 1477, and in 'The Boke of the Cyte of Ladyes', a translation by Bryan Anslay, printed in 1521, of Christine de Pisan's *Livre de la Cité des Dames*.

Edmund Colledge, O.S.A., discusses 'Fifteenth- and Sixteenth-Century English Versions of the "The Golden Epistle of St Bernard" ' (*MS*), editing the version found in the Amherst MS in the British Museum and showing that this fifteenth-century version is quite independent of the one found in St John's College, Oxford, MS 173, which dates from the same period. The relationship to these versions of the two sixteenth-century printed editions, which differ considerably from them and from each other, is unknown.

11. Drama

David Bevington's *Medieval Drama*[38] aims to replace J. Q. Adams's *Chief Pre-Shakesperian Dramas*, but without the evolutionary bias and with more sympathetic treatment of the plays themselves. It should succeed. It covers a wide range from ceremonials and liturgical tropes to 'Humanist Drama', with most space being given to the Corpus Christi cycles. The selection from these is presented in cycle order and, apart from the Brome *Isaac*, comes from the four major cycles. The book is divided into six parts with balanced and informative introductions to each, as well as brief introductions for each piece. Parallel translations are provided for Latin and foreign vernaculars, while Middle English is given with some tidying of the orthography and with glosses on the text pages. There is a description of some characteristics of the Middle English language. The illustrations are more decorative than useful, but the book is a valuable compendium. The first volume of Robert Fricker's treatment of early English drama[39] goes from 'the pagan heritage' and the liturgical plays to the humanist drama of the Renaissance. It is a summary history with an emphasis on the drama as theatre, and on its continued availability as such to modern sensibilities. Jörg O. Fichte's *Expository Voices in Medieval*

[38] *Medieval Drama*, ed. by David Bevington. Boston, Mass.: Houghton Mifflin Co. pp. xxiv + 1075. £10.95. $19.95.
[39] *Das ältere englische Schauspiel, Band I, Von den geistlichen Autoren bis zu den 'University Wits'*, by Robert Fricker. Bern: Francke Verlag. pp. 326. sFr. 64.

Drama[40] is concerned mainly with trends and developments in Latin liturgical drama, and with plays in German and French, but 'Essay V' is about the expositors in Chester and *Ludus Coventriae*. In the former the expositor was invented to incorporate non-dramatic material the author took over from *A Stanzaic Life of Christ* and the *Legenda Aurea*. Contemplacio in *Ludus Coventriae* is considered mainly in the Marian plays. In contrast to Chester, he has no clearly defined structural function, alternating between spiritual adviser to the audience and prophet or spokesman on mankind's behalf.

A welcome corrective to the uncritical acceptance of the idea that medieval drama influenced pictorial representation is provided by Patrick J. Collins in his modest but important study of 'Narrative Cycles in Medieval Art and Drama' (*CompD*). He accepts Pächt's thesis about pictorial narrative and liturgical drama in the twelfth century, but notes Pächt's caution here about the extent of such influence beyond a few episodes. Collins's main concern is the development of a tradition of pictorial representations, including Old and New Testaments and selected to highlight salvation history, before the rise of the dramatic cycles. The selection of episodes in that older pictorial tradition is strikingly reflected in the format of the plays.

'Audience and Meaning in two Medieval Dramatic Realisms' (*CompD*), by William F. Munson, deals with the nature of comic realism through a discussion of theories and traditions about the relation between dramatic productions and the life of their communities. The two realisms are differentiated by emphases respectively on fiction or play, illusion or traditional stereotype, and are illustrated by the example of the Wakefield and Chester shepherds' plays. Walter E. Myers considers 'Typology and the Audience of the English Cycle Plays' (*SLitI*), arguing, against Arnold Williams, that typology not only affects details but provides a unifying factor around which a play like Chester's is organized, and in such a way that the audience of the time would be well equipped to understand. By 'Typological Transfer in Liturgical Offices and Religious Plays of the Middle Ages' (*SLitI*) Theo Stemmler means the transfer of details between typologically related scenes. In the cycle dramas this becomes a creative tool for generating characterizations for such figures as Pilate, Annas, Caiaphas, and Antichrist. John C. Coldewey approaches the question, 'How do pre-Shaksperian dramas die?' by studying the case of 'The Last Rise and Final Demise of Essex Town Drama' (*MLQ*). He finds not one cause but many in complex combination: pressure from ecclesiastical and secular courts, but this is not decisive; the Vestiarian Controversy determining the simple problem of what the players shall wear; prophesying as a new and more popular kind of didactic entertainment. Most important is the fact that most of these factors took effect accidentally and not as a result of anyone's deliberate concern with the drama.

'The Five Cyclic Manuscripts of the Chester Cycle of Mystery Plays: A Statistical Survey of Variant Readings' (*LeedsSE*) is a kind of supplement, by R. M. Lumiansky and David Mills, to their edition. They present,

---

[40] *Expository Voices in Medieval Drama: Essays on the Mode and Function of Dramatic Exposition*, Jörg O. Fichte. Erlanger Beiträge zur Sprach–und Kunstwissenschaft, 53. Nürnberg: Verlag Hans Carl. pp. viii + 168.

with some discussion of their usefulness and limitations, a selection of statistical tables made in an attempt to reduce variant forms to a system. Lawrence M. Clopper makes a scrutiny of 'The Rogers' Descriptions of the Chester Plays' (*LeedsSE*) to determine their validity as evidence. He considers the problem of how the several versions came to be made, and the probable sources of their information, deciding that much appears to be accurate and that we should be reluctant to reject any part of them. In an appendix he prints the four main versions minus the lists of companies.

The Construction of the Wakefield Cycle[41] by John Gardner is not written 'for specialists in search of out-of-the-way information but for student medievalists and literary generalists, people whose chief concern is aesthetic'. His main contention is that the hand of the Wakefield Master can be seen shaping the whole cycle into a unity, and not only in the plays usually assigned to him. The readings of individual plays are sometimes ingenious, but as often carelessly over-ingenious. The interpretation of Noah as a type of Christ, and the treatment of 'exegetical overtones' in some other plays, suffer particularly from a slapdash approach. Robert J. Blanch gives 'The Gifts of the Shepherds in *Prima Pastorum* A Symbolic Interpretation' (*Cithara*, 1974[42]). He relates the gifts to the offerings of the Magi and associates the shepherds, like the Magi, with the Trinity. The symbolic meanings suggested are many (perhaps too many), but include, for the spruce box, death and resurrection; for the bottle, baptism and the Eucharist; for the ball, omnipotence and perfection. 'The idea of Order in the Wakefield *Noah*' (*ChauR*), according to Josie P. Campbell, is not one dependent on simple obedience, either of Noah to God or of wife to husband. The play shows a movement from an old order of such obedience to a new one of restored love. The article by Jean Forrester and A. C. Cawley, 'The Corpus Christi Play of Wakefield: A New Look at the Wakefield Burgess Court Records' (*LeedsSE*), is a re-examination of those records in the light of Jean Forrester's work (*YW*, 54.144). It turns out that none of the copies is altogether accurate, but suggestions are made to render future reprints more reliable. An appendix presents photographs of versions of the documents. Thomas J. Jambeck considers 'The Dramatic Implications of Anselmian Affective Piety in the Towneley Play of the Crucifixion' (*AnM*). He agrees with Kolve about the distance between the torturers' games and the reality of the suffering Christ in the York, Chester, and *Ludus Coventriae* versions, but finds the Towneley situation different. Here the audience is invited to a more intimate, personal involvement.

In 'After the Fall: Design in the Old Testament Plays in the York Cycle' (*Mediaevalia*[43]), Clifford Davidson argues that those plays concentrate on the post-lapsarian condition of humanity rather than on typologically looking forward to Christ. They set up a condition of conflict between hope and despair, with an associated development of two sets of characters in contrast, beginning with Abel and Cain. Davidson also subjects 'The

---

[41] *The Construction of the Wakefield Cycle*, by John Gardner. Carbondale: Southern Illinois U.P. pp. xii + 162. $8.95.
[42] *Cithara*. St Bonaventure, New York: St Bonaventure U.
[43] *Mediaevalia*: A Journal of Medieval Studies. The Center for Medieval and Early Renaissance Studies of the State University of New York at Binghamton.

Realism of the York Realist and the York Passion' to examination (*Speculum*), recognizing that a new emotionalism and an interest in specific detail are at the service of traditional aims and themes. He argues that a 'willing suspension of disbelief' is in order, though with less than adequate discussion of the concepts involved. Alexandra F. Johnson's account of 'The Procession and Play of Corpus Christi in York after 1426' (*LeedsSE*) shows that, although after William Malton's sermon on that date the city agreed to perform the play the day before the feast and hold the procession on the feast day itself, the earliest possible date when such a division may have occurred is 1468, and it was never consistent. Other arrangements were tried, and play and procession were always organized as separate events even when on the same day. But as late as 1481 the original agreement was not in force. Margaret Dorrell contributes a note on 'The Butchers', Saddlers' and Carpenters' Pageants: Misreadings of the York *Ordo*' (*ELN*). The errors are in Lucy Toulmin Smith's transcriptions and, as well as being misleading, have even concealed possible evidence for the date of the revision of the Resurrection text and the compilation of the Play register.

Alexandra F. Johnson brings together all the documentary evidence of 'The Plays of the Religious Guilds of York: The Creed Play and the Paternoster Play' (*Speculum*) and attempts a fascinating reconstruction of the origin and purpose of these plays, their production methods, structure, and contents, and a history of performances. She argues that, as well as being public and didactic like the Corpus Christi cycle, these plays were 'true processional', and that they borrowed some of the equipment owned by the craft guilds and used in their cycle. Although originally the city did not own the plays, it seems that the citizens were deeply committed to them and the council was drawn into greater and greater involvement with their production.

The 'Symbolic Character and Form in the *Ludus Coventriae* "Play of Noah"' occupy Daniel P. Poteet II in claiming the excellence of the play (*ABR*). In arguing that critical approaches based on other Noah plays are inappropriate, he also suggests that the aesthetic of this static and symbolic piece is typical of the rest of *Ludus Coventriae*. There is a scrupulous avoidance of conflict between good and evil in favour of a clear symbolic contrast between Noah's faithful, obedient family and the spiritual blindness of Lamech, the first bigamist and archetypal figure of lechery. Sherwyn T. Carr connects *Ludus Coventriae*, the Cherry Tree Carol, and *Sir Cleges* in an investigation of 'The Middle English Nativity Cherry Tree: The Dissemination of a Popular Motif' (*MLQ*). Although the motif originates with the Gospel of Pseudo-Matthew, *Ludus Coventriae* is first in connecting it with the nativity.

The *English Morality Play*[44] by Robert Potter is an engaging book with an unusual approach. He is often concerned with modern production and revival, and deals with English Renaissance plays as well as European examples. But he is most interesting on the idea of morality plays as such,

[44] *The English Morality Play: Origins, History, and Influence of a Dramatic Tradition*, by Robert Potter. London and Boston: Routledge and Kegan Paul. pp. x + 286. $21.75.

and on the world which earlier English examples present to their audience. He objects to the conventional division of the drama into miracle, mystery, and morality, emphasizing instead a 'fundamental unity of purpose' in celebrating religious truths, presenting a theory of history and a generalized and optimistic explanation of the human condition. The plots of the moralities are 'ritualized, dialectical, and inevitable'. They are calls to a specific religious act of repentance leading to forgiveness. Potter argues against the influence of the *Psychomachia* on the early English plays. Vices and virtues instead lead man into sin or educate him to repent. The figure of human nature the plays present partakes of two conflicting theories: on the one hand, of man as microcosm, and ruler of the earth, on the other, of man as imprisoned in futility. By 'The Community of Morality Plays' (*CompD*), Merle Fifield intends a connexion among the plays and their sources across national boundaries, especially between England, France, and the Low Countries. This involves a certain amount of redefinition of the term morality.

John Conley, in 'Aural Error in *Everyman*?' (*N&Q*), discusses the idea of the translator, with his shaky Dutch, translating words by guess from their sound, and suggests 'a moderately speculative example'. Conley also asks a question about 'The Phrase "Oyle of Forgyuenes" in *Everyman*: A Reference to Extreme Unction?' (*N&Q*). The phrase occurs in the last line of Confession's speech to Everyman, and according to Conley is simply a traditional metaphor for mercy manifested by penance. Shinichi Takaku seeks a reason for 'The Disappearance of Death in *Everyman*' (*SELit*, 1974). Everyman's turning to Jesus in Death's absence from the stage, and his repeated calling, keeps Death (now associated with the Devil) from returning to the scene.

Kathleen M. Ashley considers neglect of 'Titivullus and the Battle of Words in *Mankind*' (*AnM*) a symptom of a prevalent critical view of the play as lacking thematic coherence. Titivullus is the 'star in a play concerned with the crucial distinction between God's word and the words of the Devil and the World'. In its central theme of words as vehicles of salvation or damnation, the play is a debtor to the homiletic traditions of the Lent and pre-Lent seasons. In demonstrating the likelihood of this source, the article makes a convincing case for the coherence of the play around the battle of words. Lorraine Kochanske Stock is also concerned with 'The Thematic and Structural Unity of *Mankind*' (*SP*), but she emphasizes rather its eschatological elements, the playwright's use of the Job story and the parable of the wheat and tares, and the intention to urge the audience to reform.

The problem of the absence of an adequate central figure leads Eugene D. Hill to investigate 'The Trinitarian Allegory of the Moral Play of *Wisdom*' (*MP*). The source of the allegory is in Augustine and Bernard, and although the central figure is largely absent from the stage, the intention of the play is to focus increasingly closely on the human soul. Hill suggests areas for further study, especially with a view to determining the milieu which produced the play.

V

Middle English: Chaucer

JOYCE BAZIRE and DAVID MILLS

1. General

A bibliography for the current year will be found in 'Chaucer Research, 1975. Report No. 36' by Thomas A. Kirby (*ChauR*). *Encomia* vol. 1, no. 2, contains references to articles specifically connected with Chaucer and to others providing background material.

Some of the short essays in *Geoffrey Chaucer*[1] deal with familiar topics for the intended general and student readership. Thus George D. Economou's 'Introduction: Chaucer the Innovator' emphasizes the fabliaux, especially of the Miller and the Reeve; Emerson Brown Jr defends the study of old books for an understanding of 'Chaucer and the European Literary Tradition'; Esther C. Quinn examines the balance of sacred and profane in her account of 'Religion in Chaucer's Canterbury Tales: A Study in Language and Structure'; and Elizabeth D. Kirk's comparisons of 'Chaucer and his English Contemporaries'—Gower, Langland, and the *Pearl*-poet—also stress Chaucer's use of 'ordinary language'. We found Stavros Deligiorgis's 'Poetics of Anagogy for Chaucer: the *Canterbury Tales*' incomprehensible. Worthy of further note is Hope Phyllis Weissman's 'Antifeminism and Chaucer's Characterization of Women', which moves from a consideration of the antifeminist stereotypes, Emily and Alisoun, to the Wife of Bath's development from the constricting 'Eve-stereotype' towards the equally constricting 'Courtly Lady stereotype'. In 'The Theme of Art and Life in Chaucer's Poetry' Robert W. Hanning traces the conflicting impulses of artistic order and chaotic reality in Chaucer; for *Troilus* he notes the link between Pandarus's loss of control over the love-affair and the narrator's loss of control over the narrative, while in the *Tales* the initial suggestion of art, embodied in narrator and Host, as a force for order in an ordered society is progressively challenged. The mixture of philosophical optimism, sceptical pessimism, and Neoplatonism is noted in Winthrop Wetherbee's examination of 'Some Intellectual Themes in Chaucer's Poetry', which suggests 'a sustained and largely ironic parallel' in structure between Boethius's work and *Troilus*, and sees in the *Tales* a replacement of the explicit philosophical framework of the *Knight's Tale* by the expression of values through the characters, a consideration of contemporary issues under the major topic of human freedom.

Part I of A. Kent Hieatt's *Chaucer, Spenser, Milton*[2] deals with Chaucer

[1] *Geoffrey Chaucer: a collection of original articles*, ed. by George D. Economou. New York: McGraw-Hill Book Co. pp. xi + 148. Pb $2.45.
[2] *Chaucer, Spenser, Milton: Mythopoeic Continuities and Transformations*, by A. Kent Hieatt. Montreal and London: McGill-Queens U.P. pp. xviii + 292. $20.

and Spenser, isolating the Chaucerian themes and poetic fables most influential in Spenser's thought and art. Hieatt examines the operation of free human choice in love and friendship within 'an apparently indifferent but ultimately harmonious macrocosm, ruled over by a well-disposed Nature or a "Prime Mover" ' in the *Parlement of Foules* and the *Knight's Tale*, and finds the same general concern in the tales of the Merchant and Franklin. He stresses the destruction of harmonious friendship by anarchic love which opens and closes the *Knight's Tale*, and the dialectic presentation of different attitudes to love and marriage in different and complexly related narratives. Since Spenser relied on the 1532-61 Thynne editions, he did not encounter the concluding questionings of the Franklin's *gentilesse*, and found the *Squire's Tale* in a position in which he was encouraged to complete it.

In *Oppositions in Chaucer*[3] Peter Elbow adds to his earlier studies (*YW* 48.98; 53.111-2) an account of the *Nun's Priest's Tale* as the culmination of Chaucer's ability to realize and transcend contradictory viewpoints in discussing freedom and necessity, moving in the process from simple irony to complex irony. The theme and method are briefly traced into other Chaucerian topics, and the book concludes with a comparison between the Pardoner and Chaucer—both with capacity for complex irony, but the Pardoner unwilling to relinquish it as Chaucer does at the end of *Troilus* and the *Tales*.

In a sketchy account of *The Renaissance Chaucer*[4] Alice S. Miskimin considers the importance of Chaucer in the Renaissance in relation to changing attitudes towards the nature of poetic statement, the rôle of the poet and the function of poetry. The effects of these attitudes are seen in the different treatments of the Troilus-story by Chaucer, Henryson, Shakespeare, and Dryden; the ambiguous and retrospectively ironic effect of dreams and the function of the *Siege of Thebes* are also discussed. Additions by Renaissance editors to the Chaucer canon reflected and transmitted a misunderstanding of Chaucer's achievement, and linguistic changes cut him off from his Renaissance 'successors'. (Reviewed by Priscilla Bawcutt, *ELN*, 1975, pp. 140-2, John M. Steadman, *JEGP*, 1975, pp. 574-6, A. V. C. Schmidt, *N&Q*, 1976, pp. 250-2.)

Bert Dillon's *A Chaucer Dictionary*[5] provides a reference work for proper names, excluding place-names (covered by Magoun, *YW* 42. 74), but including those of months, books, allegorical figures, as well as legendary and real people. The work is also intended as an aid for exploring Chaucer's literary milieu. Where necessary, Chaucer's source for details concerning the entry is recorded, together with references to works cited in the Bibliography. Finally, the occurrences of the names are given.

In addition to discussing *Troilus* and the *Legend* in particular in the light of his subject, Henry Ansgar Kelly provides a background for other

[3] *Oppositions in Chaucer*, by Peter Elbow. Middletown, Connecticut: Wesleyan U. P. pp. 180. $12.
[4] *The Renaissance Chaucer*, by Alice S. Miskimin. New Haven and London: Yale U.P. pp. xii + 315. £7.50.
[5] *A Chaucer Dictionary: Proper Names and Allusions Excluding Place Names*, by Bert Dillon. Boston, Mass.: G. K. Hall. 1974. pp. xvii + 266. $25.

works of Chaucer in *Love and Marriage in the Age of Chaucer*[6] in which he draws on his paper of 1973 (*YW* 55. 164). From his initial comments on the theory of courtly love and his refutation of Lewis's opinion that adultery was one of its necessary characteristics, Kelly goes on to consider early French works, such as the *Roman de la Rose*, and then those of Boccaccio, with reference to Criseyde particularly. A discussion of Ovid's works leads to an examination of Chaucer's *Legend* and Gower's *Confessio*. In 'Clandestine Marriage' Kelly comments on the legal and ecclesiastical attitude to marriage without witnesses and the relationships between men and women in the marriage. Although Chaucer was bound by his story, the union of Troilus and Criseyde may be regarded in the light of these private contracts. The final section is concerned with the 'moral and religious status' of the couple, against not only an ecclesiastical and biblical background, but also, for example, that of the age of Rolle.

Ann S. Haskell's 'A Pirandellian Perspective of Chaucer' (*NM*) traces a similarity in the anti-illusionism of Chaucer and Pirandello, concentrating particularly on 'aesthetic distancing and the closely related subjects of autonomous characters and liaison figures'. Three instances are noted by George D. Economou of 'Chaucer's Use of the Bird in the Cage Image in the *Canterbury Tales*' (*PQ*), all associated with *De consolatione philosophiae* and the *Roman de la Rose*. Paul M. Clogan looks at 'Literary Criticism in William Godwin's *Life of Chaucer*' (*M&H*).

The second part of Paul Strohm's '*Passioun, Lyf, Miracle, Legende*: Some Generic Terms in Middle English Hagiographical Narrative' (*ChauR*) exemplifies Chaucer's use of the terms, especially his original use of *legende* in a secular sense in the *Legend of Good Women*; while the contrast of the tales of the Second Nun and the Man of Law serves to show the usefulness of the terms in determining the reader's expectations. In querying 'Could Chaucer Spell?' (*EIC*), F. W. Bateson considers evidence suggested by such matters as Chaucer's reading to an audience, certain spellings, elision, and differences in manuscript readings, and concludes that 'by intention he was a phonetic speller, if not an especially good one'. A. V. C. Schmidt takes up some points in the article, to which Bateson replies (*EIC*). Writing 'On Chaucer's Stressed Vowel Phonemes' (*ChauR*), W. Bruce Finnie criticizes studies by Percy G. Adams on the grounds that they ignore quantitative and certain qualitative differences in the Middle English vowel phonemes and present *r* as part of a preceding assonating vowel.

Dolores Palomo contributes two comparisons. Looking at 'Chaucer, Cervantes, and the Birth of the Novel' (*Mosaic*), she considers Chaucer's contribution to the structure of the novel, disengaging—especially via the narrator—art 'from the criterion of objective truth', and discusses the place of realism in his work as foreshadowing Cervantes. In 'Alpha and Omega: Of Chaucer and Joyce' (*Mosaic*) she starts from the non-novelistic response required by these authors and explores similarities in their contemporary situation and in their literary technique.

Some of Chaucer's works are briefly considered by Edgar Hill Duncan in 'Short Fiction in Medieval English: II. The Middle English Period'

---

[6] *Love and Marriage in the Age of Chaucer*. by Henry Ansgar Kelly. Ithaca and London: Cornell U.P. pp. 359.

(*SSF*, 1974). Kevin J. Harty's examination of 'Chaucer and the Fair Field of Anglo-Norman' (*Les Bonnes Feuilles*) concerns those of Chaucer's works which seem to have Anglo-Norman analogues. Examples from Chaucer are used by Margaret F. Nims in '*Translatio*: "Difficult Statement" in Medieval Poetic Theory' (*UTQ*, 1974). Some Chaucerian examples are given by Russell A. Peck in 'Public Dreams and Private Myths: Perspective in Middle English Literature' (*PMLA*).

2. Canterbury Tales

Robert A. Pratt's *The Tales of Canterbury*[7] (originally published in 1966) has been reissued. It contains a most useful Introduction, which indicates Chaucer's background, historical, literary and linguistic, together with some fairly brief criticism of his works, apart from the *Tales*. Pratt comments both on the scientific knowledge and Chaucer's use of it. He also devotes space here to Chaucer's careful presentation of the pilgrims and their characterization in the *Prologue*, the framework, and the tales themselves, both directly and indirectly. This part concludes with a brief discussion of the settings of the tales and what these add to the general atmosphere of the tales. Pratt then comments on the order and language of the tales and suggests further reading-matter. The tales themselves are annotated at the foot of the page with glosses at the side. At the end are textual comments and a basic glossary. A. C. Cawley has revised his Everyman edition of the *Canterbury Tales*[8] (first published in 1958).

After listing the titles for the tales in extant manuscripts and the recorded manuscripts of the fifteenth century, Robert A. Pratt notes that 'Chaucer's Title: "The tales of Caunterbury" ' (*PQ*) was superseded in the later fifteenth century by 'The Canterbury Tales', first recorded in 1471. William Elford Rogers believes that a study of the 'Individualization of Language in the Canterbury Frame Story' (*AnM*, 1974) might consider the frequency of Romance and Latinate words and the sentence-structures of each character's speech. (A list of Romance and Latinate loans for each character is supplied in an appendix.) Rogers gives a useful discussion of the Reeve's use of imagery and compares the language of the Host, Wife, and Pardoner. Ingeborg M. Ullmann's *Der Erzähler der 'Canterbury Tales'*[9] concentrates on the function of a narrator with particular references to the *Tales* and its framing-device. A critical review of the various explanations of the discrepancy between the actual number of pilgrims and the number stated in the *General Prologue*—Caroline D. Eckhardt's 'The Number of Chaucer's Pilgrims: A Review and Reappraisal' (*YES*)—suggests that Chaucer planned a thirty-three division work, corresponding to the actual number of pilgrims, to give an added—if concealed—devotional dimension

---

[7] *The Tales of Canterbury*, ed. by Robert A. Pratt. Boston: Houghton Mifflin. 1974. pp. xliii + 587.

[8] *Canterbury Tales*, ed. by A. C. Cawley. London: J. M. Dent & Sons. New York: E P. Dutton. pp. xx + 612. £2.50, pb £1.25.

[9] *Der Erzähler der 'Canterbury Tales': Das literarische Werk in seiner kommunikativen Funktion*, by Ingeborg M. Ullmann. Europäische Hochschulschriften. Reihe xiv. Angelsächsische Sprache und Literatur, 15. Berne: Herbert Lang. Frankfurt/M: Peter Lang. 1973. pp. 232.

by the use of a holy number. She concludes that the reference to *nyne and twenty* reflects Chaucer's ironic attitude towards the Narrator. Eugene Green's discussion of 'The Voices of the Pilgrims in the *General Prologue* to the *Canterbury Tales*' (*Style*) shows in detail that although an impression is created of 'recollected conviviality', yet this impression is the result of Chaucer's using conventions that are to be found in his earlier works.

'Part I' of Peter S. Taitt's *Incubus and Ideal: Ecclesiastical Figures in Chaucer and Langland*[10] contains a descriptive commentary—which includes little new—on the ecclesiastical figures in Chaucer, both the pilgrims themselves and the characters in the tales. Following a similar treatment of such figures in Langland, Taitt compares ways in which the two authors present these characters, under headings such as 'Irony' and 'Word Play'; his findings are drawn together in 'Part IV: Conclusions'. Complementing his study of the lay members of the pilgrimage (*YW* 55. 155), George J. Engelhardt turns to 'The Ecclesiastical Pilgrims of the *Canterbury Tales*: A Study in Ethology' (*MS*), in which his view of the pilgrims is reinforced by the individual tales. One of his most interesting sections concerns the Prioress, her nun-chaplain, and the priest, together with their tales. In the several studies of all the ecclesiastical pilgrims Engelhardt has presented much that is enlightening concerning the characters.

Maintaining that, although Chaucer incorporated in his poetry features popular in sermons, his interest lay rather in the preacher's dramatic performance and the reaction of the audience, Susan Gallick takes 'A Look at Chaucer and His Preachers' (*Speculum*). In the light of this, she examines the prologues of the Reeve and Wife, and the tales of the professional preacher, the Pardoner, and of the Nun's Priest, together with the pilgrims' reactions to them. Starting from the Host's words at C 292–300, Gerhard Joseph proposes a thematic link in C between the *Physician's Tale*, with its examination of the destructive effects of Nature's gifts, and the *Pardoner's Tale*, with its examination of the similar effects of Fortune's gifts; both emphasize the absence of the gifts of Grace, the third and most important of the gifts mentioned by the Parson at I 450–55, from which the article, 'The Gifts of Nature, Fortune, and Grace in the *Physician's*, *Pardoner's* and *Parson's Tales*' (*ChauR*) derives its title. Gloria Cigman's addition to The London Medieval and Renaissance Series, *The Wife of Bath's Prologue and Tale and the Clerk's Prologue and Tale from The Canterbury Tales*,[11] contains introductory and interpretative material useful for schools, as well as glosses and a commentary. Allan Rodway's *English Comedy*[12] includes a short section on the tales of the Miller, Reeve, and Wife of Bath. Chandler B. Beall suggests a possible source for 'And Gladly Teche' (*ELN*) in the Clerk's portrait.

In a long article, 'Man's Free Will and the Poet's Choice: The Creation

[10] *Incubus and Ideal: Ecclesiastical Figures in Chaucer and Langland*, by Peter S. Taitt. Salzburg Studies in English Literature. Elizabethan & Renaissance Studies. Universität Salzburg: Institut für englische Sprache und Literatur. pp. i + 228.

[11] *The Wife of Bath's Prologue and Tale and the Clerk's Prologue and Tale from The Canterbury Tales*, ed. by Gloria Cigman. The London Medieval and Renaissance Series. U. of London P. pp. vi + 194. £3.30, pb £1.95.

[12] *English Comedy: Its Role and Nature from Chaucer to the Present Day*, by Allan Rodway. Chatto & Windus. pp. x + 288.

of Artistic Order in Chaucer's *Knight's Tale'* *(Anglia)*, Joerg O. Fichte explains how he bases his interpretation of the tale on three propositions: that the teller's qualities make him a fitting mouthpiece for Chaucer in a tale concerning order and disorder in human affairs; that the characters' lack of understanding and wisdom produces disorder; and finally that the fourteenth-century concept of God is reflected in Theseus's speech, which indicates how order may be achieved; and order, Fichte notes, is shown in the actual balanced structure of the tale. After showing that the tournament of the *Knight's Tale* is of a kind archaic in Chaucer's time, Bruce Kent Cowgill proceeds to gather evidence in 'The *Knight's Tale* and the Hundred Years' War' *(PQ)* which suggests that the tale represents an indictment of that War.

After discussing several other Middle English instances, Kevin S. Kiernan —'The Art of the Descending Catalogue, and a Fresh Look at Alisoun' *(ChauR)*—then turns to several ways in which Chaucer uses this means of description, and shows its effectiveness in the description of the Miller's Alisoun. In *'The Miller's Tale*: "By Seinte Note"' *(ChauR)*, Mary P. Richards contrasts Absolon's inappropriate behaviour with St'Neot's conduct, as evidenced in three recensions of the saint's life, and refutes a previously suggested connexion with King Alfred. Answering the question 'Why Does the Miller's Tale Take Place on Monday?' *(ELN)*, John C. Hirsh cites the belief in the evil effect of certain Mondays.

By means of a comparison of two scenes in Gower's and Chaucer's versions of the tale of Constance, Paul Theiner shows, in 'The Man of Law Tells His Tale' *(SMC)*, that Chaucer's was a more diffuse narrative. Such complexity Theiner believes to be both intentional and also consistent with the character of the teller. Thomas H. Bestul's 'The *Man of Law's Tale* and the Rhetorical Foundations of Chaucerian Pathos' *(ChauR)* is devoted to rhetoric and its emotive function in that particular tale.

In 'Alysoun of Bath and the Vulgate "Perfect Wife"' *(NM)*, James L. Boren suggests an influence by antithesis from *Proverbs* 31 (which contains 'a distinctive portrait of an exemplary woman') on Chaucer in his creation of the Wife. Dolores Palomo explores 'The Fate of the Wife of Bath's "Bad Husbands"' *(ChauR)*, which seems inexplicably uncertain, and concludes that indirectly Chaucer has indicated that Jankyn was incited by the Wife to kill the fourth and later paid for this with his life. In support of this argument she reinterprets many points in the tale and prologue, both small details and extensive passages (e.g. noting that among Jankyn's *wikked wyves* were six who caused their husbands' deaths), and examines Alison's earlier life in a more understanding manner. Tom Mason examines 'Dryden's Version of *The Wife of Bath's Tale'* *(CQ)* to see how close it is to the original.

As the *Miller's Tale* is pivotal in its own triad, so also the *Friar's Tale* is pivotal in its group—not only part of the quarrel with the Summoner, but also a parody of the tale of the Wife, during whose prologue the quarrel erupted. Penn R. Szittya, in 'The Green Yeoman as Loathly Lady: The Friar's Parody of the Wife of Bath's Tale' *(PMLA)*, notes verbal echoes of the Wife's tale in the Friar's and cites parallels between the Yeoman and the hag. Finally the suggestion is made that *maistrie* (not only in the marital context), and the master-servant paradox, are the chief thematic bonds, which link more tales than the 'marriage debate'. Thomas W. Ross suggests explanations for 'Chaucer's *Friar's Tale*, D. 1377 and 1573' (*Expl.*). Janette Richardson argues the case well for 'Friar and Summoner, the Art of Balance' (*ChauR*). Unalike in externals, the two pilgrims are alike in their moral baseness. This balance between them is preserved in their tales in that each represents in his own protagonist not only his rival's flaws, but also unwittingly his own peculiarities; and in each case it is one of these peculiarities that brings about the protagonist's downfall. Developing the point of links between the Friar and Summoner in personal antagonism and in their tales, N. R. Havely, in *The Friar's, Summoner's, and Pardoner's Tales from The Canterbury Tales*,[13] shows some links also between these pilgrims and the Pardoner, and points up resemblances in structure and style to be noted among the three tales. In general pattern this edition follows that of Gloria Cigman (*ut sup.*). As there are several editions of the *Pardoner's Tale*, the discussion of the other two tales provides the part of most value.

In 'The Prince and his People: A Study of the Two Covenants in the *Clerk's Tale*' (*ChauR*), Lynn Staley Johnson examines the nature of the relationship of Walter and his people and that between Walter and Griselda, and then the two covenants, commenting on these last in the light of the Old and New Covenants in the Bible. Itala Tania Rutter writes on 'The Function of Dioneo's Perspective in the Griselda Story' (*Comitatus*, 1974).

John Bugge's 'Damyan's Wanton *Clyket* and an Ironic New *Twiste* to the *Merchant's Tale*' (*AnM*, 1973) suggests 'deftly veiled references to the unveiled genitalia in both *twiste* and the *clyket-wiket* combination' in the tale. C. W. R. D. Moseley believes that the tale contains echoes of *Gawain* and refers to Mandeville in 'Some Suggestions about the Writing of *The Squire's Tale*' (*Archiv*), and proposes that it represents a draft composed while Chaucer stayed at some provincial court. R. Ann Thompson notes ' "Our revels now are ended": an allusion to *The Franklin's Tale*?' (*Archiv*), and Roy J. Pearcy comments on 'A pun in the "Franklin's Tale" 942: ' Withouten coppe he drank al his penaunce" ' (*N&Q*). Joel R. Kehler writes 'Notes on the Epigraph to Conrad's *The Rescue*' (*ELN*)–a quotation from the *Franklin's Tale*—and remarks on its significance.

In 'For Love and not for Hate: the Value of Virginity in Chaucer's *Physician's Tale*' (*AnM*, 1973), Jeanne T. Mathewson stresses Virginius's absolute power over Virginia and the telling inappropriateness of the reference to Jephthah's daughter, concluding that Virginius, Appius, the Physician, and the Host are all false judges, prizing Virginia's beauty, youth, and virginity in different ways but 'exhibiting standard masculine unawareness of her humanity'. The representation of the near-sacrifice of Isaac in the mystery cycles is suggested as a source for the *Physician's Tale* (especially 207–53) by Anne Lancashire in 'Chaucer and the Sacrifice of Isaac' (*ChauR*). She also indicates that R. B.'s *Appius and Virginia* drew on it as well, and Chaucer probably used it again in the *Man of Law's Tale*.

In 'Life Without Death: The Old Man in Chaucer's *Pardoner's Tale*'

---

[13] *The Friar's, Summoner's, and Pardoner's Tales from The Canterbury Tales*, ed. by N. R. Havely. The London Medieval and Renaissance Series. U. of London P. pp. vi + 165. £3.65, pb £1.85.

(*ChauR*), Elizabeth R. Hatcher suggests that in his eternal geriatric misery the Old Man represents the consequences of a successful slaying of death by the rioters and serves as a warning to their folly. In 'Sacrament and Sacrifice in the *Pardoner's Tale*' (*AnM*, 1973) Rodney Delasanta stresses the sacrificial parody which is involved in the sacramental parody of the Eucharist that earlier critics of the tale have noticed. John C. McGalliard provides a perceptive analysis of 'Characterization in Chaucer's *Shipman's Tale*' (*PQ*); there are indications that the monk is no 'Boccaccian stereotype of the immoral priest', the wife's dialogue reveals different attitudes to the two men, as well as a skill in approach, and there is no reason to regard the merchant in any but a favourable light.

James Winny's edition of *The Prioress' Prologue and Tale*[14] follows the pattern of this series of Cambridge editions. The introduction includes information about analogues, the force of the narrative, and anti-Semitism placed in its medieval context. When 'Reopening the *Prioress's Tale*' (*ChauR*), John C. Hirsch considers the religious, exegetical, and liturgical influences on the tale together with that of 'affective piety', and concludes by suggesting Chaucer's attitude towards the Jews. Peter G. Beidler suggests in 'Conrad's "Amy Foster" and Chaucer's Prioress' (*NCF*) that Conrad may have used the Prioress and her tale when creating Amy.

Ann S. Haskell's 'Sir Thopas: The Puppet's Puppet' (*ChauR*) traces a metaphor of puppetry in *Thopas* and argues for the extended irony of the puppet pilgrim Chaucer, himself manipulating a puppet-'hero', which gives an image of wide resonance. The shallowness of the Monk's reading is demonstrated by F. P. Lock in 'Chaucer's Monk's Use of Lucan, Suetonius, and "Valerie"' (*ELN*), where he shows that, despite reference to authorities, the interpretation of Julius Caesar's death as a tragedy of Fortune is the result of the Monk's own mistaken reading. Diane Bornstein comments on 'Chaucer's *Monk's Tale*, 2095-2142' (*Expl.*).

In *Chaucer und die Armut*[15] Claus Uhlig defends the thematic function of the description of the widow's cottage in the *Nun's Priest's Tale*. He examines the treatment of the theme of poverty in the *Man of Law's Tale*, where it serves solely to characterize the teller, and in the *Wife of Bath's Tale*, tracing the two different views of the hardships and virtues of poverty to Boethius and defending Chaucer against the possible charge of inconsistency. In the *Nun's Priest's Tale* the widow represents *moderatio*, the virtuous poverty which is rejected by Chaunticleer, establishing a comic contrast between the human in a rural setting and the animal in a courtly setting. (Reviewed by Derek Pearsall, *YES*, 1976, 216-17.) [AJH]. The two works, 'The *Speculum Stultorum* and the *Nun's Priest's Tale*' (*ChauR*), both seem to demand a moral interpretation, as Jill Mann suggests (providing incidentally a useful exposition of the former). She considers, however, that such an interpretation is frustrated both by the story and by the animal nature of the protagonists. Although Chaucer's debt to Nigel of Longchamps is illustrated most clearly in the tale by the constant demand

[14] *The Prioress' Prologue and Tale*, ed. by James Winny. C.U.P. pp. ii + 64. 75p.
[15] *Chaucer und die Armut: Zum Prinzip der kontextuellen Wahrheit in den Canterbury Tales*, by Claus Uhlig. Mainz: Akademie der Wissenschaften und der Literatur. Wiesbaden: Franz Steiner. 1974. pp. 51. DM. 12.60.

upon the reader to modify his reactions, such a debt is also to be noted elsewhere in the *Tales*. In the interesting discussion of 'The "Nun's Priest's Tale"': An Ironic Exemplum' (*ELH*), A. Paul Shallers first touches on the 'many contradicting but convincing' interpretations of the tale, before turning to a brief history of the animal fable in England—asserting Chaucer's use of the 'fable-exemplum form'—and a description of the *Renart*-poems. Chaucer, he maintains, blurred distinctions made by these two types of story, giving us 'characters that are animals and men simultaneously', and the shifting focus enables us to see both a moral and an ironic image of mankind. 'Chaucerian Attitudes towards Joy with Particular Consideration of the *Nun's Priest's Tale*' (*MÆ*), by Nancy Dean, opens with a commentary on the several kinds of joy illustrated in Chaucer and also with quotations from other medieval works; and the discussion of the subject in the *Nun's Priest's Tale* is undertaken against the background of opinions expressed in the tales of the Monk and Man of Law.

When discussing 'The Manciple's Manner of Speaking' (*EIC*, 1974), V. J. Scattergood shows how that pilgrim's prologue and tale 'form a cogent and unified exploration of the problem of self-restraint, particularly self-restraint in speech'; the subject is also treated more briefly elsewhere in Chaucer, who realized its application to the poet's art.

3. Troilus and Criseyde

In 'Criseyde's Dream of the Eagle: Love and War in *Troilus and Criseyde*' (*MLQ*) Joseph E. Gallagher notes Criseyde's fear of destructive violence—of the warrior and of war—so readily exploited by Pandarus. Her dream both suggests the duality of the courtly warrior as martially aggressive and amatorily passive, and also proposes a metamorphosis of violence into love which Troilus later fulfils. Private love cannot overcome public war, and Troilus's martial ferocity survives to the end, but love has permanently effected a metamorphosis in his sensual appetite, so that his love endures beyond his betrayal and his aggression is never turned towards Criseyde. The precise settings of the poem provide the reader with an artificial memory involving the recognition of past, present, and future events in the manner of Prudence, argues Susan Schibanoff in 'Prudence and Artificial Memory in Chaucer's *Troilus*' (*ELH*). These settings are recalled by Troilus in V. 565–81, but with more limited awareness than the reader and with an emphasis upon the happy aspect of the associated events. But the reader's and Troilus's viewpoints converge towards the end of the poem, until Troilus goes beyond human prudence to a divine prudence which can reject *the blynde lust*. Peter Christmas's discussion of 'Troilus and Criseyde: The Problems of Love and Necessity' (*ChauR*) attempts to show how a reading emphasizing the psychological contradictions of the three principal characters can bring together the critical issues of free will versus determinism and the connexion between the story and its palinode; the *Nun's Priest's Tale* provides a useful analogy for the treatment of determinism.

Thomas B. Hanson claims that 'The Center of *Troilus and Criseyde*' (*ChauR*) was shifted from Criseyde's surrender in the alpha-version to the actual consummation in the beta, and suggests that while the first part of the alpha-version is patterned on the stages of sin, that of the beta is patterned on the *gradus amoris*. In 'Hector the Second: The Lost Face of Troilustratus' (*AnM*), K. S. Kiernan argues that Criseyde's admiration of Hector, and Hector's concern and actions on her behalf in *Troilus*, an expansion of Hector's rôle from Boccaccio, illuminate Troilus's deficiencies of character and action which sentimental critics have overlooked. McKay Sundwall's 'Deiphobus and Helen: A Tantalizing Hint' (*MP*) indicates a possible foreshadowing in II. 1702–8 of the love of Deiphobus and Helen.

Gretchen Mieszkowski regards the reference to ' "Pandras" in Deschamps' Ballade for Chaucer' (*ChauR*) as evidence that Deschamps knew of *Troilus*, but was aware of the function of Pandarus not from Chaucer but from *Le Livre de Troilus*. McKay Sundwall, in 'The *Destruction of Troy*, Chaucer's *Troilus and Criseyde*, and Lydgate's *Troy Book*' (*RES*), feels that the allusion to Diomede grasping the bridle of Criseyde's horse in the *Destruction* confirms the influence of *Troilus* in that poem and sets its date as not earlier than 1385–7, although recent re-dating of the *Destruction* indicates that the influence could be indirect, via Lydgate.

Ronald Primeau's 'Chaucer's *Troilus and Criseyde* and the Rhythm of Experience in Keats's "What can I do to drive away" ' (*KSJ*, 1974) attempts to establish *Troilus* as an influence in Keats's poems of 1819. In 'The Moon and Venus: Troilus's Havens in Eternity' (*PLL*) Gertrude C. Drake argues that Troilus's post-mortal ascent is first to the moon, a thesis supported not only by medieval astronomy but also by the numerous references to the moon in the poem; and that while Chaucer tellingly does not specify Troilus's final location, Dante gives some basis for believing it to be Venus.

Thomas A. Van comments in 'Chaucer's *Troilus and Criseyde*' (*Expl*) on two implied comparisons connected with Criseyde which somewhat catachrestically make her 'resemble a religious, and even Christ'. In 'Das Andredepronomen in Chaucers *Troilus und Criseyde*' (*Archiv*), Dieter Schmidt examines some distinctive uses of the singular and plural forms of the pronoun of address. [AJH].

4. Other Works

Although Edward I. Condren accepts John N. Palmer's date of 1368 for the death of Blanche (*YW* 55. 165), he does not accept the argument that the *Book of the Duchess* was completed in that year. In 'Of Deaths and Duchesses and Scholars Coughing in Ink' (*ChauR*) he takes up four points of his own hypothesis (*YW* 52. 120) to which Palmer objects, concerning the date of the poem, the Black Knight as representing Chaucer, the identification of *kyng*, and a possible satire of Gaunt.

Francis P. Magoun Jr and Tauno F. Mustanoja comment on 'Chaucer's Chimera: His Proto-Surrealist Portrait of Fame' (*Speculum*); while Pat Trefzger Overbeck suggests that the god of Love may have been intended as 'The "Man of Gret Auctorite" ' in Chaucer's *House of Fame*' (*MP*).

In tracing the thematic contrast of the ordered state under natural law and its chaotic counterpart under selfish leadership in the *Parlement of Foules*, Bruce Kent Cowgill's 'The *Parlement of Foules* and the Body Politic' (*JEGP*) stresses the traditionally political rôle of Scipio, the rational guide, and the familiar garden image of the earthly commonweal. Hence the royal eagle perverts nature, whose law inclines men to reason, and leads society to chaos and non-communication; the denial of procreation becomes an image of the obstruction of justice in human society, for which the Peasants' Revolt could supply a fitting context. The poem represents the logical extension of individual depravity in the *Roman de la Rose* to its social consequences. In 'Priapus and the *Parlement of Foulys*' (*SP*), Emerson Brown Jr suggests that at 253–9 Chaucer has developed the picture of the comic Priapus into the comedy of man's vain attempts to dignify sexuality, and that the comedy of Priapic sexual frustration may be thematically extended to the pretensions and frustrations of the bird-debate. 'The pattern of time in *The Parlement of Foules*' (*JMRS*) is indicated, suggests Robert L. Entzminger, by the *Somnium* as 'the source of both the logic behind the adventures Chaucer's persona struggles to interpret and the aesthetic coherence of the poem he utters'. The contrast that the narrator's dream forms with Scipio's verifies rather than refutes it, and at the level of human history is found the same 'Providential design' that directed cosmic time in the earlier dream.

Robert O. Payne's critical study of the 'G' Prologue, 'Making his own Myth: The Prologue to Chaucer's *Legend of Good Women*' (*ChauR*), sees the later version as a more efficient statement of key issues found in Chaucer's earlier career. This version of the education of a love-poet resolves many of the problems connected with the use of the narrator which are seen in the earlier visions; it fuses most completely narrator, dreamer, and poet, and achieves a close link between real and vision worlds. The Prologue looks back to Chaucer's 'old books', echoing their imagery, diction and structural plan; and its reconstruction of Alceste, like that of the Dreamer-narrator, reflects Chaucer's own concern for the rôle and identity of the poet. Mary Shaner finds 'A Possible Source of Chaucer's Error in the "Legend of Hypermnestra" ' (*N&Q*) in Lactantius Placidus's *Commentarius in Statii Thebaida*, where the rôles of Danaus and Ægiptus are similarly reversed.

Friendship, the subject of *Scogan*, is appropriate to Chaucer's relationship to a particular member of Richard II's household, to the general social situation of the civil servant, and to literary conventions. In 'Chaucer's *Envoy to Scogan*: The Social Uses of Literary Convention' (*ChauR*), R. T. Lenaghan evaluates the poem in terms of the commonplace antithesis of love and friendship, and the generally current ironic mode. A. I. Doyle and George B. Pace publish 'Further Texts of Chaucer's Minor Poems' (*SB*), the *ABC* (Melbourne MS), *Truth* (Nottingham U. Library MS ME LM1), and the probably Chaucerian *Against Women Unconstant* (Fairfax 16, Bodleian). The article includes descriptions of the manuscripts, and also lists unpublished manuscripts and unreprinted printed texts of the Short Poems with claim to manuscript authority.

In 'Chaucer, Messahala and Bodleian Selden Supra 78' (*Manuscripta*), Michael Masi suggests that this Bodleian manuscript may have been the source for the *Treatise on the Astrolabe*. In their discussion of 'Chaucer's *Treatise on the Astrolabe*: A Handbook for the Medieval Child' (*Children's Literature: The Great Excluded*, 1974) Thomas J. Jambeck and Karen K. Jambeck compare Chaucer's *Treatise* with its Latin original to show what modifications Chaucer made to adapt an adult scholarly work for a child reader, changing vocabulary and syntax and offering practical examples and repetition. The work suggests that, contrary to modern belief, the fourteenth century was aware of the special nature of the child.

VI

The Earlier Sixteenth Century

MICHAEL RHODES

1. General

With the publication of three essays by Paul Oskar Kristeller under the title *Medieval Aspects of Renaissance Learning*,[1] Duke University Press initiate a new series, Duke Monographs in Medieval and Renaissance Studies. The three essays are 'The Scholar and his Public in the Late Middle Ages and the Renaissance', 'Thomism and Italian Thought of the Renaissance', 'The Contribution of Religious Orders to Renaissance Thought and Learning' and have, to some extent, been revised and enlarged for their appearance here. (The first originally appeared in German in a *festschrift* for Walther Bulst in 1960, the second under the title '*Le Thomisme et la pensée italienne de la Renaissance*' in 1967 and the third in *The American Benedictine Review* (1970). We are much indebted to Professor Edward P. Mahoney for the excellent translations of the first two essays.

In the first essay Professor Kristeller outlines the relationships between three types of scholarly, philosophical and rhetorical literature during this period, the scholastic, the humanistic and the vernacular, observing how their distinct characteristics are essentially determined by the three diverse groups of readers for which they were primarily intended and that for his purposes (*pace* Benedetto Croce) 'the concept of literary genres is altogether indispensible'. These he nominates as principally the textbook, the commentary, the *Quæstio* and the treatise, while acknowledging the importance of the oration, the letter, the dialogue and translation in humanistic literature. Distinguishing the characteristics of the three kinds of literature, Professor Kristeller instances the general indifference to stylistic polish in favour of precise terminology and ingenious argumentation of the specialist-directed literature of scholasticism, the historical and philological erudition displayed in the often elegant style of humanistic literature and the charm and spontaneity of the vernacular. Within the scope of a single essay he offers a comprehensive and lucid general survey that may be read with pleasure and enlightenment by specialist and layman alike. However the second of these essays is likely to appeal more to the former. Averring that Thomism 'like Platonism and Aristotelianism, represents one of the great traditions of Western thought', Professor Kristeller follows a short account of its Italian history with a discussion of its influence upon Italian thought during the Renaissance, instancing the

[1] *Medieval Aspects of Renaissance Learning*, by Paul Oskar Kristeller. Duke Monographs in Medieval and Renaissance Studies No. 1, Duke University Press. pp. xii + 175. $7.50.

decisive rôle Thomist arguments occasionally played. The documentation here is formidable and most illuminating. In the third essay he argues that while the learning of the Renaissance was on the whole more secular than that of the Middle Ages, the religious orders were nonetheless more involved in it than is generally appreciated. However, Professor Kristeller concedes that they made little contribution to the vast legal and medical literature of the period, since 'clerics were excluded from the medical and notarial profession, and even the lawyers and legal professors were for the most part laymen'. However conclusive his argument may be with regard to the latter it must surely remain puzzling that this should be so with medicine. The essay is accompanied by a most useful general bibliography and two highly informative appendices which cite many little known authors and draw attention to several rare bibliographical sources and manuscripts in the libraries of religious orders. (There is an excellent review of this important book by Brian Stock in the TLS for February 20th 1976, p. 204.)

In his dual biography of Thomas Wolsey and Thomas Cromwell, *The Cardinal and the Secretary*,[2] Neville Williams undeniably achieves his principal objective, 'a reassessment of the two men', which he considers long overdue. He aims to redress an imbalance in the general estimate of these often maligned administrators, whose faults and vices are more often rehearsed than their real abilities noted or the strength of their influence appreciated. Both 'left indelible marks on the history of England and, combined, their personalities and careers counted for far more than the life and character of the monarch they loyally served until each was overthrown'. His concise summary of the differences between and the similarities of these two somewhat enigmatic figures is illuminating. The complexities of both ecclesiastical and court intrigues and of the relationships between King, cardinal and secretary, are conveyed with enviable lucidity and persuasive impartiality. Particularly striking is his adroit use of a combination of historical and literary sources. Considerable research has been concentrated into this succinct account of the lives of Wolsey and Cromwell, whose devious conduct appears to have been as much forced upon them by others and by circumstances as originating from within. The touches of detail concerning their private lives, their domestic affairs, and the influence these occasionally exerted upon their transaction of state business make for compelling reading. As a backcloth to a study of early Tudor literature this is revealing and instructive. However, it may be that in describing Wyatt's poem 'The pillar perish'd is whereto I leant' as 'a jewel of a sonnet' and as 'verse of unsurpassing beauty', Neville Williams is allowing his involvement with his subject to cloud his critical judgement. Compared with its Petrarchan model (*Rotta è l'alta colonna, e 'l verde lauro*) Wyatt's version appears both stilted in its rhythms and forced in its metaphors. The rather excessive sentiments may owe more to the plaintive tone of the original than to the reality of Wyatt's feelings on the fall of Thomas Cromwell (always assuming that this is indeed the occasion for the poem). It is the closing three lines that are biographically interesting. Was there anything in the closing stages of the relationship between the

[2] *The Cardinal and the Secretary*, by Neville Williams. Weidenfeld and Nicolson. pp. 278. £5.25.

secretary-politician and the poet-diplomat to account for the abrupt transition to a mood of self-castigation, with its suggestion of betrayal, where indeed Wyatt departs from his model? Regrettably the following works were not seen: *The Letters of Marsilio Ficino Vol. 1, Utopias of the Classical World* (which includes many references to More's *Utopia*), *Nature's Work of Art: the human body and image of the world* by Leonard Barkan, Guido Walman's translation of *Orlando Furioso*.

2. Prose

The publication of a new translation of More's *Utopia* is invariably stimulating since it provides a fresh occasion for investigating the subtleties of More's argument and its presentation. Robert M. Adams's version[3] is accompanied by 'background materials on communism and the humanistic circle' (itemised further on) with passages selected from the critical studies by J. W. Allen Russell Ames, R. W. Chambers, J. H. Hexter, Karl Kautsky, C. S. Lewis A. E. Morgan and Frederic Seebohm, together with essays by Harry Berger Jr, Robert C. Elliott and Elizabeth McCutcheon. There is also a thoughtful essay by the editor himself which compares More's *Utopia* with Machiavelli's *The Prince*, works which he describes as having a relationship similar to that between Voltaire's *Candide* and Johnson's *Rasselas*. Professor Adams's opening to his Translator's Note, 'Translations, according to a cynical, sexist wheeze, are like mistresses; the faithful ones are apt to be ugly, and the beautiful ones false' in some measure sets the tone of his translation. Favouring an up-to-date idiom and colloquial vigour before a literal rendering, Professor Adams is in some respects following in the wake of Paul Turner's high-spirited edition published ten years earlier by Penguin Books. However, Professor Adams has retained the chapter headings of Book II whereas Turner dispensed with these, opting for a 'more relaxed type of subject-changing formula'. The retention of these chapter headings facilitates the location of the various aspects of Utopian life and philosophy Raphael outlines and discusses but it is intrusive when the primary aim is to produce a tone of casual manner and colloquial ease. In his translation, Professor Adams aims to achieve clarity, completeness, colloquial ease, and a sense of contour in the prose, and in his efforts he has consulted such predecessors as Robynson, Ogden and Edward Surtz, each of whose versions suffers from various shortcomings. There is no denying that Professor Adams 'knows and cares for English idiom' or that he translates with boldness, investing his version with colloquial vigour and lucid syntax. However when consistently applied his solution to the difficulties in translating *Utopia* is not without its disadvantages: ultimately it produces its own kind of 'flatness' (a fault for which he critizes Ogden), imposing upon the style a uniformity of tone as of a monologue. The colloquial ease has been attained somewhat at the expense of the delicate tonal nuances. Nevertheless, this lively and thoughtful translation has many and real merits. Under the heading 'Backgrounds' Professor Adams has usefully assembled diverse and instructive material,

---

[3] *Utopia, Sir Thomas More* trans. & ed. by Robert M. Adams. Norton Critical Editions. N.Y. pp. xii + 239. $10.

extracts from Ovid, Plato, etc. and letters from More to Giles, Giles to More and Busleiden. Budé to Lupset and Erasmus to Ulrich von Hutten. These extracts help to realise the aim of this series, 'to furnish materials for the intelligent study of important works of literature', to provide a reliable and definitive text and so 'broaden and deepen the reader's understanding of the work'.

Of the two issues of *Moreana* for 1975 which have been received, the one for February opens with Diane Valeri Bayne's 'Richard Hyrde and the More Circle', an interesting account of some of Hyrde's educational ideals and his views on women and their education. The discussion centres on his introduction to a translation made by Margaret Roper in 1524 of Erasmus' *Precatio dominica* and his own translation of Vives' *De institutione feminæ Christianæ* in 1523. Bayne notes that the first of these has received scant attention despite Foster Watson's claim that it is 'the first reasoned claim of the Renascence period, written in English, for the higher education of women' and the speculation by E. M. G. Routh that 'Hyrde's essay might well have been composed by More himself, and is evidently inspired by his teaching'. She indicates the extent to which More's own views on the education of women influenced others and deserves our gratitude for drawing attention to these obviously informative and neglected works. Her article is followed by a description and discussion of the Boy-Bishop festival in Tudor England by Richard L. DeMolen. His main purpose is to refute the widely held view that this festival was simply an occasion for high-spirits, a variant upon the Feast of Fools, and to demonstrate that it was not as he claims A. F. Leach has described it, a form of 'relaxation and reaction' designed to compensate and relieve students for the 'restraint and repression of the year'. DeMolen sees the feast of the Boy-Bishop as 'a religious ceremony, per se, which acknowledged the innocence of childhood and promoted virtues as were commonly associated with the Child Jesus'. He supports his case with illustrations from a wide range of source material. In the May issue of *Moreana*, Charles Clay Doyle in discussing the neglected sources of some epigrams by Thomas More assigns hitherto unknown sources to two of them; the one, *In scurram pauperem*, to a jest current in Latin and possibly also in the vernacular, the other, *De chirurgo et anu*, to a narrative from Æsopic tradition. In 'Gilbert Burnet and his Whiggish *Utopia*', John F. Logan examines, at times with some amusement, the seventeenth century Bishop of Salisbury's confrontation with More's *Utopia* when translating it in 1684. He reminds us, in the process, of the considerable influence that Burnet's views had upon later historians, translators and biographers while demonstrating how Burnet's own changing attitudes to his subject and his problematic work conform with his religious and political preoccupations in the years 1679, 1684 and finally between 1712-1715. Richard S. Sylvester reviews *The Correspondence of Erasmus Vol. I [1484-1500]* translated by R. A. B. Mynors and D. F. S. Thomson with his customary acumen, fairness and cogency. However Germain Marc'hadour's review of *The Literature of Renaissance England* ed. by John Hollander and Frank Kermode is disappointing. Too much space is wasted on what are very minor considerations. Finally, of the more substantial articles, there is an intriguing and in one instance a highly entertaining review by Mahmoud Manzalaoui of a translation of *Utopia* into Arabic by Dr. Angèle Boutros Samaan.

3. Poetry

In the preface to his *Sir Thomas Wyatt, Collected Poems*,[4] Joost Daalder expresses the hope that, 'the present volume will provide the general reader with as accurate a modernized text as can at this stage be constructed, and that the annotation will help him to understand and so enjoy Wyatt's poems'. It remains, nevertheless, uncertain whether he includes in his 'general reader' the undergraduate student. The 'Chronological Table' of the main events in Wyatt's life (which might, perhaps, have mentioned the somewhat ironic fact of his stewardship of the Tower of London for which he received an annual stipend of twenty pounds) is followed by an Introduction to the poems. The avowed purpose of the latter is 'to remove some possible obstacles to a just appreciation of Wyatt's poetry'. The editor sees as one of these obstacles the perpetuation of a mistaken critical approach of the past. He observes, 'The song-like poems, it is true, have on the whole given pleasure rather than offence to those who like flowing verse, but such readers have been inclined to disapprove of many poems (often, but certainly not always "translations") which they expected to be iambic, and then proceeded to condemn as irregular'. (The expectation is hardly justified.)' Addressing himself to the question of Wyatt's imitations and supposed sources, he advises the general reader that, 'the extent of (Wyatt's) debt to foreign models has been much exaggerated' and adds 'Many of his poems have been virtually ignored because they could not be compared with Petrarch and other continental authors'. In writing upon Wyatt's character, Joost Daalder summarises, with evident approval, what he sees as Surrey's assessment of Wyatt as 'restless, profound, moral, a generally excellent poet and particularly a Christian one, possessed of sharp judgement, and free from deceit himself, though the innocent victim of deceit practised by others'. Presumably, the first trait is deduced from Surrey's well-known 'Wyatt resteth here that quick *could* never rest'. But here Surrey, having in mind the circumstances in which Wyatt's death took place, may well be making sly reference to the incessant demands of the royal master upon the time and energies of a man generally acknowledged to be one of his most able diplomats. Further on, he indicates Wyatt's letter to his son (from Paris, 15th April 1537), referring specifically to the comment concerning domestic peace and remarking, 'Wyatt characteristically says that the result of strife between man and wife is unrest, and equally characteristically he blames in his own case the woman rather than himself'. But this is not so. Moreover it might have been wiser to have quoted the relevant passages themselves (since they are short) and so left the general reader to interpret their tone for himself. There is, after all, a distinct possibility that Wyatt's observations with their hint of 'after-thought' are not without a touch of drollery. From Daalder's description of Wyatt's character one would not deduce that the author of 'Ye old mule' was blessed with a sense of humour.

In his Preface, Daalder declares that, 'It has been impossible to draw attention to the numerous errors throughout MT.[5] A list of them would

---

[4] *Sir Thomas Wyatt, Collected Poems*, ed. by Joost Daalder. O.U.P. pp. xxix + 255. hb £4.50, pb £2.25.

[5] *Collected Poems of Sir Thomas Wyatt*, ed. by Kenneth Muir and Patricia Thomson. Liverpool University Press (1969).

take up many pages'. While there are indeed a number of differences in the readings of the poems in the two editions, the criticism is excessive. Nor is it entirely clear what these 'numerous errors' are. For instance, within the first eighty poems of the two editions, there are, as far as I have detected but seven variant readings that are not mentioned in the footnotes. These are as follows: VIII 1.116 him hath (*MT*)/hath him (*JD*);[6] XII 1.1 an hert/ in heart; XXX 1.10 Or . . . rightwisely/In . . . righteously; XXI 1.8 Lyveth and rest/Liveth at rest; XLV 1.5 Too much of it were/Too much it were; XLVI 1.5 When that he sawe me/When he saw me; LVII 1.17 that I shall more attain/that I shall that attain. With the exception of the difference in XLV, the readings as given in MT are supported by the *Egerton MS*. No doubt Daalder has very good reasons for his changes, but the general reader might reasonably assume that these unannotated divergencies between the two editions are indeed instances of 'the numerous errors throughout MT' mentioned. Futhermore, an appendix simply listing these 'corrections' of MT would reassure the reader that no 'errors' had crept into Daalder's own edition.

Despite these criticisms, this is a welcome edition of Wyatt's poems. The clarity of their arrangement and general presentation is both helpful and pleasing to the eye. His footnotes manage to be both informative and elucidatory without becoming obtrusive while the Appendix will assist the reader to identify those poems by Wyatt which bear notable resemblance to poems by Petrarch, Scrafino, Sannazaro and others. Regrettably, Alastair Fowler's *Conceited Thought: the interpretation of English Renaissance poems*, Edinburgh University Press, has not been seen.

---

[6] Hereafter the reading in Joost Daalder is given second.

VII

Shakespeare

DAVID DANIELL, ANGUS EASSON
and ANDREW SANDERS

1. Editions

The Riverside edition of the complete works[1] is splendid; the only real objection might be its bulk and weight, necessitated by the value it gives. Besides the official canon, it includes *The Two Noble Kinsmen*; 'Shakespeare's' additions to *Sir Thomas More* (it seems we must wait for Richard Proudfoot's Oxford apocrypha before we can have the full text: though to compensate, the passages are also reproduced in type facsimile plus photos of the three pages concerned); and *The Lover's Complaint* and a complete *Passionate Pilgrim*. The text is excellently edited and presented, with a minimum of stage directions and scene indications; the notes, at foot of page, are brief but above all helpful, glossing words, noticing differences from sources, offering information, while textual notes are marshalled at the end of each play, with information, for instance, on who established present act/scene arrangement (these notes are particularly full for difficult texts like *Hamlet*, while bonuses include the closing Induction of *The Taming of a Shrew* and extensive passages from Q1 and Q2 of *The Merry Wives of Windsor*). Each play has a historical and critical introduction, assigned to the various critical contributors, who include Frank Kermode and Anne Barton, while Harry Levin provides a general introduction and Charles Shattuck writes on the plays in performance (films included). Other sections are Annals 1552–1616 and Shakespeare records, documents and allusions. The pleasure and usefulness to be had from the volume are enhanced by a map of London, a range of portraits and pictures, and pleasing contemporary woodcuts as tailpieces to individual plays. This edition provides nearly all that the general reader and student could need, while it incorporates necessary material for advanced study.

There are two new volumes in the New Arden series. Agnes Latham's edition of *As You Like It*[2] is going to become known as 'one of the good Ardens.' Her comments are, as one would expect, more than competent and very sensible: they also have a direct address which is warm and witty. She brings the preliminary matter to life in a most attractive way; even the dry stuff of textual history, admittedly not a serious problem in this play, takes on flesh: ' . . . the Duke cannot reproduce Lyly's prose because he is not a prose speaker. His bent for set similes is a point of characterization.

[1] *The Riverside Shakespeare*, ed. by G. Blakemore Evans. Boston: Houghton Mifflin, 1974. pp. xvi + 1902. £13.60.
[2] *As You Like It*, edited by Agnes Latham (The Arden Shakespeare). London, Methuen; New York, Barnes & Noble. pp. xcv + 135. £4.

He is a trifle old-fashioned, with a beard of formal cut. For the most part the effect of the prose in this play is one of informality, of people talking rather than actors declaiming . . .' These sentences come, surprisingly, from the first of the introductory sections, that on text: qualities of human understanding mark all the sections of the long Introduction, covering text, date, sources, people and themes, and stage history. In particular, the fourth section is both comprehensive and unpretentious, and a great relief after some of the outrageous allegorizing that has recently gone on about this play. Miss Latham is particularly good on Touchstone and Jaques, especially together, but then she is alert and wise and witty on everyone, more interested in people than in themes, unfashionably using the idea of 'character', and firmly aware of the play as a play.

The notes are refreshing, often saying more than they appear to do, e.g. at I.i.114 or II.vii.70, though occasionally one is left wanting more, e.g. at V.iv.190-1. Sources she discusses well, but leaves us to consult them in Bullough.

J. M. Lothian left his New Arden edition of *Twelfth Night*[3] unfinished at his death in 1970: T. W. Craik both completed the work and undertook the complete revision that Professor Lothian would no doubt have made. But the result is not altogether happy. No ascription allows us to see who wrote what and when, and this can be puzzling. Out of the first six pages of Introduction, on the problem of the printer's copy, no fewer than five reproduce or discuss R. K. Turner's recent views that the Folio was not set up from a prompt book, anticipating Turner's own edition, but really belonging to the world of private scholarly debate. The section on Date and Title, though putting down Hotson and others, sums up without coming to a readily understandable conclusion. One comes to feel, indeed, that the editors are writing for a few learned friends. The account of past criticism gives an impression of activity but little love, like a history of an arranged marriage. A scene by scene Critical Analysis reads, uncomfortably, like a schoolmaster's report on the work of a promising pupil, and the long account of *Twelfth Night* in the Theatre is confusingly organised and seems designed to be presented to an academic committee. Under Sources, five pages on *Gl'Ingannati*, and a brief note on other Italian plays, come in the Introduction, and the Apolonius and Silla story from Barnabe Riche makes Appendix 1. When this, and so much else, is printed in Bullough, including an excellent translation of *Gl'Ingannati* (corrected here in foot-notes), one wonders why it was thought necessary. Appendix II, however, printing music for the songs, is an excellent idea.

The annotations are adequate but uninspiring, and sometimes do not help overmuch, as at I.iii.68-78, or are overhelpful, as at I.iii.50.

Quiller-Couch's rhapsodic Introduction to the New Cambridge edition of *Twelfth Night* might be felt to be unsatisfactory, but it is sad that the New Ardens should celebrate this play, above all, with a dusty pedantry.

---

[3] *Twelfth Night*, edited by J. M. Lothian and T. W. Craik (The Arden Shakespeare). London. Methuen; New York, Barnes & Noble. pp. xcviii + 188. £5.

Other editions:
The Macmillan Shakespeare for schools has now added *As You Like It, 1 Henry IV, Julius Caesar, Richard III* and *Romeo and Juliet*[4]. The excellent New Clarendon series, some of the best smaller editions there are, have added or reprinted *As You Like It, Coriolanus, Henry V, A Midsummer Night's Dream, Othello* and *Romeo and Juliet*[5]. Other titles added to existing series include *Coriolanus, King Lear*[6], *Henry V*[7], *Hamlet*[8]. Single titles are *Richard II* and *The Tempest*[9]. The first in a new series is *Othello*[10]. Two facsimiles are of the Quarto of *Othello*[11], and of the Kelmscott 1893 facsimile of *The Poems*[12]. The *Sonnets* have also appeared from the Royal Shakespeare *Theatre*[13].
Recent translations include ten plays finely done into modern German by Erich Fried[14]. This seems an appropriate place to mention The Cooper Monograph No. 18, *Rudolf Alexander Schröders Ubersetzungen von Shakespeares Dramen*[15], by Balz Engler, a scholarly and most useful study of the work of this great translator. It is interesting to see how long Schlegel-Tieck held the stage, and an exposition of the difficulties in superseding that great Romantic monument to 'unser Shakespeare'. Balz Engler's long and detailed account of translation work over so long a period, by so practised a hand, makes fascinating reading. Klaus Bartenschlager discusses wordplay as a problem in German editions, in 'Shakespeares Wortspiele als Problem einer deutschen Shakespeare-Edition' (*SJH*).

[4] *As You Like It*, ed. by P. Hollindale; *1 Henry IV* ed. by P. Hollindale; *Julius Caesar*, ed. by D. R. Elloway; *Richard III*, ed. by R. Adam; *Romeo and Juliet*, ed. by J. Gibson. (The Macmillan Shakespeare). London: Macmillan Education Ltd. 55p each.
[5] *As You Like It*, ed. by I. J. Bisson; *Coriolanus*, ed. by B. H. Kemball-Cook; *Henry V*, ed. by R. W. Fletcher; *A Midsummer Night's Dream*, ed. by F. C. Horwood; *Othello*, ed. by F. C. Horwood and R. E. C. Houghton; *Romeo and Juliet*, ed. by R. E. C. Houghton. (The New Clarendon Shakespeare). Oxford: The Clarendon Press. 65p each.
[6] *Coriolanus*, ed. by A. Ingleden; *King Lear*, ed. by R. Blott (The New Swan Shakespeare). London: Longmans. £1.60 each.
[7] *Henry V*, ed. by S. H. Burton. (The Heritage of Literature). Longmans. £1.50.
[8] *Hamlet*, ed. by M. Davis. (The Kennett Shakespeare). Arnold. £1.45.
[9] *Richard II*, ed. by F. J. Farrell; *The Tempest*, ed. by P. D. L. Way. Collins 70p.
[10] *Othello*, ed. by W. R. D. Moseley. (The South Bank Shakespeare). University Tutorial Press. 90p.
[11] *Othello*, the Quarto of 1609 (facsimile). Oxford: Oxford University Press. £5.50.
[12] *The Poems*, ed. by F. Ellis. (Facsimile of the Kelmscott edition, 1893): Paradine. £65.50. limited edition. hb £8.25.
[13] *The Sonnets*, published by Shepheard Walwyn. The Royal Shakespeare Theatre.
[14] *Richard II, Heinrich V, Ein Sommernachtstraum, Zwölfte Nacht oder Was Ihr wollt, König Cymbelin, Zwei Herren aus Verona, Viel Getu um Nichts, Die lustigen Weiber von Windsor, Antonius und Kleopatra, Perikles, Fürst von Tyrus*. Berlin: Verlag Klaus Wagenbach. DM 6.80 each.
[15] *Rudolf Alexander Schröders Ubersetzungen von Shakespeares Dramen*, von Balz Engler. (The Cooper Monographs, 18). Bern; A. Francke AG. pp. 231. SFr. 39.

2. Textual Matters

The setting of the Folio is pursued by John O'Connor's 'Compositors D and F of the Shakespeare First Folio' (*SB*), whose work has concentrated on identifying D satisfactorily. In the process he assigns some pages to B and C previously thought to have been set by D and F, and develops criteria that can be used with the other compositors. He corrects and argues against Cairncross on mechanical evidence of first speech prefixes in the plays and use of catchwords to distinguish D and F, while adopting Howard-Hill's criterion for identifying C. An appendix gives pages set by D and F. On the final page of *SB* are two small corrections to Millard T. Jones's Table of Variants in Q1 *Othello*, noted last year. On concordances, James M. Welsh, 'A Misrepresented Reading in Folio *Tempest* 285 (I.ii. 175)' (*SQ*), shows that 'Heuens' is the true reading of the Chatsworth copy, though the Lee facsimile used by Howard-Hill reproduces it incorrectly. Peter Bettinger, 'Die Zahlwörter bei Shakespeare' (*ZAA*), considers problems of number words and compounds in these compilations. Ulrich Suerbaum writes on editorial concerns in his 'Der "Neue Shakespeare": John Dover Wilson und die moderne Textkritik' (*SJH*), while a modern editor, William C. Woodson, in 'The 1785 Variorum Shakespeare' (*SB*), on the basis of his experience with *Macbeth* for the New Variorum, suggests that Isaac Reed's 1785 revision of Steevens's 1778 Variorum may have importance in the transmission of text, citing seven substantive changes of Reed's. Belated justice is done by J. H. P. Pafford in 'W. R. Chetwood and the Fictitious Shakespeare Quartos' (*N&Q*); a list of 1750, implying Quarto publication for certain plays that appear only in Folio, repudiated by Steevens (1766) and attributed by him to Chetwood (1785), is primarily a list of supposed performances, not publications, and may not be by Chetwood at all. There is no forgery and the list may be ignored. The copyright of Shakespeare's collected works and individual plays in the eighteenth century, in which Tonson held a large share, is traced by Terry Belanger in 'Tonson, Wellington and the Shakespeare copyrights' (*Oxford Bibliographical Society*); shares not owned by Tonson belonged mainly to Richard Wellington, and Belanger traces them back where possible into the seventeenth century.

Jeanne Addison Roberts, in 'The Merry Wives Q and F: The Vagaries of Progress' (*ShakS*) gives a restrained, sound, detailed and accurate account of the history of critical attempts to deal with the problems of the rival texts of this play from Pope to H. J. Oliver's Arden, 1971. The final paragraph, in which the current position is most lucidly summarized, should be an epigraph to all future editions. A. S. Cairncross suggests emending *Antony and Cleopatra* III.x.10 to read 'Yonder ribaud Nagge of Egypt' (*N&Q*) and identifies 'spinner' at *A Midsummer Night's Dream* II.ii.21 and *Romeo and Juliet* I.iv.60 as the cranefly, or Daddy-long-legs. Warren D. Smith in his *Shakespeare's Playhouse Practice* (see below), p. 32, notes that in the only instance where words are read aloud twice, *Cymbeline* V.iv.138–45 and V.v.435–42, 'both printings in the Folio are identical, even to spelling punctuation, hyphenation, and spacing of the letters', and he suggests that the prophecy was set up from the property scroll in each case. Virgil Lee, in 'Puck's "Tailor": A Mimic Pun?' (*SQ*) attempts a comprehensive explanation of *A Midsummer Night's Dream* II.i.54 by means of mime. He should be referred to Maureen Duffy's *The Erotic World of Faery* (1972) p. 91. R. L. Smallwood (*SQ*) in a brief note defends the Q2 reading 'pallat' at *Romeo and Juliet* V.iii.107-8, with support from *King John* and the Bishop's Bible [*sic*]. Robert K. Turner in 'The Text of *Twelfth Night*' (*SQ*) works over in detail his reasons for believing that the Folio text 'was printed from a scribal copy of Shakespeare's working draft of the play'. He thus differs from Dover Wilson and Greg, who argued for a revised prompt-copy as the source: but received opinion long ago moved from that position. Balz Engler and Rolf Scheibler discuss wide issues in the publication of modern texts in 'Der Herausgeber und die theatralische Dimension des Textes' (*SJH*) and Ernst Leisi gives a lucid account of basic linguistics in 'Der Beitrag der Sprachwissenschaft zum Shakespeare-Verständnis' (*SJH*).

3. Biography and Background
Pride of place must go to Samuel Schoenbaum's *William Shakespeare: A Documentary Life*[16], which is superb in three ways: in significance, in accuracy and in presentation. It is a big handsome book in page size, in page lay-out, in type, in the consistently high quality of the facsimiles (over two hundred of them), in the supporting captions, ascriptions, notes and constant bibliographical references. Professor Schoenbaum and the Clarendon and Scolar Presses are to be congratulated.

They are also to be thanked. Here is an up-to-date scholar's biography, at last: but here are also the biographical documents—all of them, from registry entries to possible or impossible likenesses, from the Stationers' Register to legal documents. Many of the latter are fold-out—marriage-licence, indentures, leases, letters patent, will. No longer is there excuse for not knowing the records—we can now send our enquirers to 'look it up in Schoenbaum'. If it is not there, it is not worth having; a large claim, but a true one. (Simon Forman on the Laniers does not appear.) And as Professor Schoenbaum says, 'the records themselves are more numerous than is popularly supposed'. He has also found space for early maps, plans and prospects, sketches of houses and theatres, and the like. If these items are not, strictly speaking, biographical, they certainly hold interest for the biographer. They also allow in a good deal of unobtrusive scholarship, such as the long captions supporting the large reproduction of much of Hollar's Long View of London, and the reasons for preferring it to Visscher, also reproduced in part. Several items like the quotations from Malone do not at first sight seem to have needed facsimile treatment; but in fact the steady accumulation of the sense of the original, whether of script or printed page, begins to tell its own story. Occasionally one regrets that a document is not given entire; but among Professor Schoenbaum's heroes pre-eminently stand Malone, Halliwell Phillipps and E. K. Chambers, and it is possible to supplement abbreviated items by reference to 'EKC'. The significance of this book is primarily that future readers of books about Shakespeare, and there will be myriads, will be able to distinguish for themselves between

[16] *William Shakespeare: A Documentary Life*, by Samuel Schoenbaum. The Clarendon Press, Oxford in association with The Scolar Press. pp. xix + 273. £12.

fiction and fact. A popular acceptable standard measure of truth has been established. Readers enchanted by 'Shakespeare's other Anne', Anne Whateley, 'so nubile and so blushingly chaste' as Schoenbaum puts it, and so celebrated in recent popular biographies, will be able to confirm that in fact she existed only in 'the carelessness of a bumbling scribe'.

Professor Schoenbaum is exceptionally useful in his treatment of the 'mythos', deer-stealing legends and the like, matters without contemporary records, but persistent in later legend. He shows the unlikelihood of their being truth, but allows a little weight to their hold on popular imagination. On Charlecote, he rightly quotes with approval Lady Fairfax-Lucy's sense of the common touch in the story.

He is a model of how to tackle 'that class of document, more precious than the rest', the works of William Shakespeare, taking from them almost no evidence at all. He occasionally gently supports a point of common life, like the familiar horn-book and the 'cross-row' from *Richard 3*, or Lyly's grammar from *Merry Wives*. What also deserves mention is the readability of Schoenbaum's text. Partly this comes from the sense that everything recorded is supported—there are no flights of fancy; partly from the hints of a wry smile hiding in the paragraphs. 'Beside the remotely inscrutable Shakespeare of the bardolators—smiling and still, out-topping knowledge—we may set another Shakespeare who was in many ways like other, more ordinary men.'

After Schoenbaum's biography, Parvin Kujoory's 'From Fact to Fiction: Shakespeare's Biographical Development through the Eighteenth Century' (*SJW*) must seem rather small beer; though the *Documentary Life* was not available to him, it is strange indeed to find no mention of Schoenbaum's earlier *Shakespeare's Lives*. Kujoory weaves together his information skilfully enough, but treats people like Sidney Lee and C. I. Elton as though they had real authority; he is largely dependent upon E. K. Chambers. Anthony Dent has a useful brief run over 'Game and the Poacher in Shakespeare's England' (*History Today*).

A group of articles on ideas and themes provide contexts for Shakespeare. Ronald Broude's 'Revenge and Revenge Tragedy in Renaissance England' (*RenQ*) surveys the subject generally and relevantly, with brief references to *Titus Andronicus* and *Hamlet*. Karl Adalbert Preuschen in 'Zur Verwendung Mythologie in der Englischen Literatur des 16. Jahrhunderts, Dargestellt am Beispiel des Phaëthon-Mythos' (*SJH*) examines the motif of Phaethon, including its use in *Romeo and Juliet* and *Richard II*. More directly concerned with Shakespeare is Paul A. Jorgensen's 'A Formative Shakespearean Legacy: Elizabethan Views of God, Fortune, and War' (*PMLA*), which surveys sources and tradition, confining itself to discussion of the two tetralogies of history plays. Fortune dominates the *Henry VI* trilogy, but the conclusion of *3 Henry VI* suggests that Shakespeare is shaping the drama in the direction of God finally prevailing, a tendency emphasised by God's dispensation in the fall of Richard and Richmond's victory. The second tetralogy shows, if anything, a great emphasis upon secondary causes, especially human responsibility, in determining the military outcome of political issues.

Interesting matters are raised and investigated by Joel Hurstfield in

'The Politics of Corruption in Shakespeare's England' (*ShS*), beginning from the question whether the greatness of the plays 'mirrored the achievements of Gloriana or was in fact born out of the strains, the doubt and the despair . . . so marked a feature of the last years of Elizabeth'. He fastens on the idea of political corruption and asks what, since every major politician was believed to be corrupt, was meant by the concept? Were the *men* corrupt? If so, were there conditions in Tudor England which favoured growth of corruption? He defines political corruption, offers a sketch of the shift of power in the sixteenth century and of the political machine, showing that with the assumption that salaries would naturally be supplemented by gifts and gratuities the vital question is not 'Is this corruption?' but '*When* does this become corruption?' Out of this might come a conflict between illusion and reality, exemplified in the mature histories, in *King Lear* and *Coriolanus*. Less relevant (indeed the Shakespeare references are peculiarly strained, as though some connection had to be made despite all probability) is Richard L. Molen's 'Richard Mulcaster: An Elizabethan Savant' (*ShakS*). In a useful survey of Mulcaster's career, the suggestion is unnecessary that Shakespeare may have attacked Mulcaster in *Love's Labour's Lost* because of the popularity of the Merchant Taylors boy actors.

Finally, A. L. Rowse's *Shakespeare the Man*[17] gives the appearance of having been written by three people. Much of the book is the work of a very competent, experienced and authoritative Tudor historian. Rowse's account of life in Warwickshire and London, as it might have affected Shakespeare, is exactly what one wants to put in the hands of an enthusiastic lover of Shakespeare. Page after page produces insights, in neatly turned phrases, which bring the local scenes to life in a way that is not quite so well done anywhere else. Most of the book, however, is about Shakespeare The Man, and is written with the assurance of total dogmatism, announcing from some lofty height that This Is How It Was. There are innumerable oddities here: for examples taken at random, Rowse gives us Shakespeare 'the sexiest writer in the language', or the Bard himself fleshing out the Epilogue to *2 Henry IV* in person, with Rowse, our man at the Globe, reporting, 'Then he knelt to pray for the Queen'. But though to use the plays as so much biography-fodder has not been legitimate for decades, some outline of Shakespeare is in fact just visible through the encrustation. Yet the same book also contains the work of a man writing about literature whose ignorance is matched by his arrogance. He shows no shadow of understanding of how an Elizabethan sonnet sequence might work (a fact independently demonstrated for example by the prose versions in his editions of the *Sonnets* in 1964 and 1973). He has however 'solved' the 'problem' of the Sonnets with that absurd farrago of 'proof' about Simon Forman and Emilia Lanier. Truth simply retires hurt from such 'findings' and such accompanying Rowse comments as 'Perhaps I should add now merely that it will be found quite impossible to impugn any of them, for they are the definitive answers'. This is a sorry business.

[17] *Shakespeare The Man*, by A. L. Rowse. Macmillan. pp. xi + 284. £4.95.

4. General Criticism

The purpose of James G. McManaway's and Jeanne Addison Roberts's bibliography[18] is to draw attention to the best and most important publications since 1930; there is a scattering of representative works of earlier date as background and entries are almost exclusively in the English language. Certain features are unhelpful: editions are listed almost entirely under Collected Editions, so it is impossible to know which titles are available to date in e.g. the New Arden or the New Penguin editions; a study of the index (generally useful) shows for instance that except by checking elsewhere you could not discover that New Arden offered e.g. *Henry VIII* and that R. A. Foakes edited it; single editions listed at the head of sections on individual plays do not include any that appeared in collected editions, except the New Variorum. Extra information is given that makes other omissions the more irritating: it is convenient to know that the holograph of Capell's edition is at Trinity College, Cambridge or to be referred to the Shakespeare Library, Birmingham Reference Library for a particularly rich collection of translations—yet this same section on translations lists only two French and one German versions of the works: either listing of more languages or indication under individual plays of what is available would have been useful. This is clearly intended as a basic, even preliminary guide, and at that level it does its work well. A quick check against Peter Ure's *Julius Caesar* casebook shows a high rate of coincidence; the section on *Julius Caesar* is well cross referenced to the general sections (odd to find the Roman plays amongst the Tragedies); but chapters in books receive little attention—it would be difficult if not impossible to know that G. Wilson Knight's *The Imperial Theme* (listed under The Tragedies) contained anything on *Julius Caesar*. A number of special topics (e.g. Sources, Stage History, Audience, Allusion) are covered. Plays listed include *Sir Thomas More*, *The Two Noble Kinsmen* and *Cardenio*.

Volume eight on the Romances (*Cymbeline; The Winter's Tale; The Tempest—Pericles* appeared with *Other Classical Plays*) crowns Geoffrey Bullough's monumental series on the sources[19]. The basic pattern is as in earlier volumes reviewed here: an Introduction to each play, discussing the examples that are to follow and, even where no extract is to follow, often summarising or considering evidence—Prospero's 'historical' background from Thomas's *History of Italy*, for instance, and a summary of Eslava's *Noches de Invierno*, made so much of in James Smith's book praised last year. The discussion is always scholarly yet open to possibilities: Bullough feels *Die Schöne Sidea* to be as feeble as Frank Kermode styles it in his Arden *Tempest*, yet adds that 'remembering the mess made of other English plays by the German players, one dares not be so positive'. The extracts from *Sidea* make it seem up to *Mucedorus* level. The sources, as before, include also possible sources and analogues. Bullough obviously

[18] *A Selective Bibliography of Shakespeare: Editions, Textual Studies, Commentary* by James G. McManaway and Jeanne Addison Roberts. Charlottesville: U.P. of Virginia (for The Folger Shakespeare Library), pp. xx + 310. hb $12.50, pb $3.95.
[19] *Narrative and Dramatic Sources of Shakespeare (vol. 8): The Romances*, ed. by Geoffrey Bullough. London and New York: Routledge & Kegan Paul & Columbia U P. pp. xiv + 423. £6.50.

firmly excludes *The Two Noble Kinsmen* from the canon. The volume concludes with a substantial essay on the sources, the fruit of experience, even while it points on to what may still be done through such study.

Bullough is aware of a two-fold obligation: to investigate Shakespeare's ambience of story, drama, ideas, beliefs and current events; and to consider how he has used this material as poet and craftsman in the theatre to produce the plays. Bullough's treatment throughout is above all sane, level-headed and perceptive.

Brian Vickers, in this first volume of his Critical Heritage series[20], cannot of course be limited to formal criticism, but gives the bulk to excerpts from 'all the major adaptations'. The Introduction covers briefly the important allusions, and charts the changes of taste and acting style as the decades after the First Folio went by. Vickers is both detailed and economical in his account of the causes and effects of the Restoration adaptations, and the supporting material is unexpectedly impressive, considering that no fewer than fourteen adaptors are represented. He demonstrates clearly the wide difference between principle and practice. 'Neoclassical' purities vanish, confusedly, before multiplicity of characters, violence, theatrical spectacle and the new importance of music. A necessary, and sharp-tongued, page deplores the ignorance of Shakespeare shown by ultra-modern partisans on both sides of the adaptations war. More significant are the pages of the Introduction in which Vickers charts the extraordinary growth of the false notion of Shakespeare's ignorance, and its use to establish the idea of Shakespeare as the prime exhibit in the later Nature *versus* Art debate. The volume is particularly revealing about Dryden's Shakespeare criticism, both in the smaller items in the Introduction and the major ones printed later. It is manifest that 'if unsure of his facts Dryden was in no doubt as to his opinions' (i.e. his opinion at the time of writing; he could hold the opposite). Dryden worked to a neo-Aristotelian scheme, as did Rymer and many others. But Rymer's rigidity, ferociously applied, made criticism 'mandatory, even exclusive' and set up the need for reply. Dryden's attempt to argue from first principles is uneasy, but he is safer with 'the simple empirical appeal: the example of Shakespeare would refute the theory'. Vickers concludes, 'That was an argument which was to become extremely important in its implications, as subsequent volumes will show'. This intelligent, alert and disturbing volume starts with Jonson, Digges and Wright (1655), all in seven pages. The remaining 410 pages all date from after 1660. This demonstrates a 'tunnel-period' with a vengeance. There are the expected, and unexpected, adaptations to be admired, and squirmed at: ((*Enter* Viola *dancing a Saraband awhile with Castanietos*) which comes, of course, from *Much Ado . . . with Measure for Measure*) but there are also generous quotations from nine critical essays between 1662 and 1691, intelligently placed. One has two ungenerous quibbles over so useful a book: it would have been good to have indicated just how much of the selected text was, in fact, being included; and there might have been room for at least a couple of pages of contemporary accounts, other than Pepys, showing the reception

[20] *Shakespeare: The Critical Heritage* (vol. 1) 1623–1692, ed. by Brian Vickers. London and Boston: Routledge & Kegan Paul. pp. xi + 448. £6.50.

of these amazing shows.

With our next volume, the third in the series, Brian Vickers in fact reaches the half-way stage[21]. The narrow time-span of this volume suggests that he will not be far into the nineteenth century by the conclusion: a pity, because he has an excellent eye for the illuminating and the energy to dig out the obscure. This can be illustrated, for instance, by John Holt (otherwise unknown) on *The Tempest*, who, if prone to take dramatic comment as the author's own opinion ('Thou *Nature* art my *Goddess*' as evidence that Shakespeare 'wrote *to* Nature, and prided himself in it'), yet is able to bring sense to the text, correcting the punctuation of scene i by precise knowledge of sea terms, recognizing the emotional charge of Ariel's 'Full fathom five' upon Ferdinand, and very properly berating Pope and Warburton for the change of 'maid' to 'made' in *'If you be* Mayd *or no?'* Vickers sees the period as uneventful for textual criticism: Hanmer's edition was nugatory, while Warburton's of 1747, which had no rules or glossary, was rightly attacked for arrogance, pretentiousness, and misuse of the editor's prerogative (still, Warburton made people think about editing and provoked Thomas Edward's highly amusing and penetrating *Canons of Criticism, and Glossary*). Adaptations declined in quality and quantity, while Shakespeare performances greatly increased, pushed on by the 1737 Licensing Act, which led to the revival of plays previously neglected but already 'allowed'. The critical attitudes that do emerge are more liberal, Vickers points out in his introduction; alternative judgements to neo-classicism were invoked more frequently, while there were fierce attacks on French influence and on the Unities. No doubt it was stage playing that helped and above all Garrick's acting, so that much theatrical criticism shows freshness and cogency. An article by Vickers, 'Die ersten Shakespeare-Kritiker' (*SJH*) draws upon his work for the eighteenth-century volumes, discussing critics of the period, notably Theobald and Johnson.

An intriguing, persuasive, if perhaps rather off-centre study is Juliet Dusinberre's *Shakespeare and the Nature of Women*[22]: intriguing because the Puritans are its hero, persuasive through the handling of evidence, and off-centre by not being so much about Shakespeare as about the depiction of women in English Renaissance drama generally and about the status of women in that society. There is a section on 'Disguise and the Boy Actor', which draws very largely on Shakespearean examples, but it is perhaps symptomatic of the mistitling of the book that the final brief section should be headed 'Shakespeare' in bold capitals: it offers a summary, but is also an assertion that this has been the book's true subject. Feminism and Puritanism are Dusinberre's interests: she claims first that the 'feminism of Shakespeare's time is still largely unrecognised', then that the Puritans played a large part in the changed attitudes to women in the period. This is good in rescuing an idea of Puritanism; it is at least worth considering that to 'connect Shakespeare with the Puritans is not to detract from the dramatist but to restore to the idea of Puritanism the brilliance and energy which went into creating it'. Doubts rise more insistently at the claim that

[21]*Shakespeare: The Critical Heritage (vol. 3): 1733–1752*, ed. by Brian Vickers. London and Boston: Routledge & Kegan Paul. pp. xii + 487. £8.50.
[22]*Shakespeare and the Nature of Women*, by Juliet Dusinberre. London and Basingstoke: Macmillan. pp. 329. £7.50.

there were common links between dramatists and women, since both were attacked: there is plenty of evidence that attack does not necessarily link people whose interests might seem immediately closer even than these two classes. A further problem is that though it is good to question the modern caricature of Puritanism, these very attacks that supposedly linked playwrights and women were often from people identifiable as Puritans, so that it is difficult to be sure that it is Puritanism (rather than, say, Protestantism) which is producing the changes. In her discussion of topics like virginity and vice, chastity and art, women as property, one is sometimes led to wonder whether discussion is about the drama, about women, or about feminism. Cleopatra has her own moral law and the integrity of the player; but this excellent insight about the character seems unilluminated by Puritanism. Yet Dusinberre writes with vigour and a constant flow of ideas; she ranges admirably over Marston, Middleton and the rest; and if she is not always to be agreed with, she is not dull.

Amongst general articles, three stand out. A revised version of a lecture, Harry Levin's 'The Primacy of Shakespeare' (SQ) considers the problem of value in literature, beginning with the thought that the 'history of taste is the name we give to criticism after it has become obsolete, and that obsolescence is the measure of progress'. He traces the development of Shakespeare as the dominant figure of English, even Western, literature and concludes that 'the forthrights and meanders of criticism . . . would seem to have brought us progressively nearer to Shakespeare', which 'does not mean that the latest words are the wisest, but that wisdom accumulates in a continuous enterprise'. Yet more lively and perhaps even more timely is Richard Levin's 'Refuting Shakespeare's Endings' (MP), which attacks with vigour and perception an absurd tendency to read Shakespeare's finales as deeply ironic—so deeply ironic that only our generation has perceived his intention. Levin gives examples of such endings from Romeo and Juliet, Twelfth Night and Macbeth (critics not named; so we are teased to identify them). He demonstrates that the standards or themes by which these critics judge and find the overt ending wanting derive from the critic rather than the play. Levin's appeal is to a totality, a rhythm in the play, 'a basic dramatic fact which the refuters of the ending consistently ignore' and in attacking the notion that plays are 'about' central themes, Levin pleads for the sane and joyful spirit in our reading of Shakespeare, to understand that he 'did not wish to be misunderstood, that he wanted the audience to grasp his meaning and took some pains to ensure this, especially in the crucial final moments of the play'. René Wellek may claim too much for what he is doing in 'A. C. Bradley, Shakespeare, and the Infinite' (PQ), but defence of a critic whom we find illuminating again and again is welcome. Wellek stresses the importance of Bradley's intellectual milieu, particularly Oxford objective idealism and connections with German aesthetic theory: for Bradley the idea of tragedy is drawn from the metaphysical concept that all finite existence is a 'partial manifestation of the infinite'. Since in this view the hero must be active, not passive, to be tragic, Bradley must begin with character analysis. Wellek then proceeds to defend Bradley as a critic aware of theatre and with a knowledge of performance applied to criticism. It is useful to note here two review articles concerned with Shakespearean criticism: John F. Andrews in

' "The *Ipsissima Verba* in My Diary"?' (*ShakS*) looks at R. A. Foakes's edition (1971) of *Coleridge on Shakespeare*. Andrews feels that Collier's transcription of the lectures in 1811-12 is considerably more authoritative than that represented by the 1856 edition: while many of the problems he raises about Foakes's edition are hardly substantial, they need to be asked, especially given some of Collier's manuscript revisions and the editorial problems they indicate: did Coleridge say, 'That Falstaff was no Coward but pretended to be one merely for the sake of trying experiments on mankind!!' or perhaps '. . . pretended to be one merely for the sake of incurring the contempt of mankind'? In 'Shakespeare Today' (*ES*), M. Mincoff finds the current critical situation gloomy or at least depressing. He considers ways of getting Shakespeare wrong, amongst them the imposition of a common theme on a group of plays.

Robert Ellrodt performs several services in his subtle and suggestive 'Self Consciousness in Montaigne and Shakespeare' (*ShS*), not least by providing a bibliography of post-1940 work on the topic in his footnotes. He also demonstrates a way of proceeding that is at once cautious and persuasive: he is not concerned with sources or debt, but the ways in which the minds of French essayist and English dramatist had worked in self-scrutiny, though he suggests the effect a reading of Montaigne may have had on *Hamlet*, above all in soliloquy where thought is perceived self-consciously in the moment of thinking: an example is the Hecuba soliloquy where with 'Why what an ass am I', Hamlet discovers 'that he has been acting the comedy of indignation', and further links are made with *Troilus and Cressida* and *Measure for Measure*. Of less interest is Ernest Schanzer's 'Shakespeare and the Doctrine of the Unity of Time' (*ShS*), which has the substance of a note on the scattered skirmishes Shakespeare made against the tyrannical upstart, the doctrine of the unity of time. James Edward Siemon's useful 'Disguise in Marston and Shakespeare' (*HLQ*) begins by premising the 'importance of rôle playing to psychic and moral health' as a constant theme of Shakespearean drama. Rôle playing is a means to achieve self-definition (or to fail of it); in playing a rôle, it will in time become our reality; and the relationship of rôle to reality is unstable (Siemon here is close to Peter Ure's argument on *Macbeth*, reviewed last year). Siemon discusses in particular Coriolanus, Edgar, and *Measure for Measure*.

In *Levende talen* F. L. W. M. Buisman-de Savornin Lohman writes 'De historische achtergrond van *Measure for Measure* en *All's Well*' concerning some historical background to the plays, curiously linking them with odd authorship theories. William Babula is the author of the Salzburg study '*Wishes Fall Out As They're Willed*': *Shakespeare and the Tragicomic Archetype*[23] in which a simple pattern of the imposition of a just order on events is followed from mediaeval cycles *via* Tudor historical plays and Greene to *All's Well, Measure for Measure*, and *Pericles*. In two notes on verbal connections, Eliot Slater looks at 'Word Links with "The Merry Wives of Windsor"'(*N&Q*), enforcing by statistical association H. J. Oliver's suggestion in the New Arden that the play was written close to *2 Henry IV*

---

[23] '*Wishes Fall Out As They're Willed*'; *Shakespeare and the Tragicomic Archetype*, by William Babula. Salzburg: Universität Salzburg. pp. 133.

(before *Henry V*) rather than after *Twelfth Night* and *Hamlet* as suggested by Chambers. In 'Shakespeare: Word Links between Poems and Plays' (*N&Q*), Slater builds from his earlier attempt to find statistical evidence bearing on the authenticity of *A Lover's Complaint* (*YW* 1973). He sets out to enlarge the evidence of MacD. P. Jackson and Kenneth Muir for authenticity and to add precision by examining vocabulary in the *Complaint* with the aid of statistical tests. By using above all unique and rare words he suggests that the play/poem link strengthens the association of *Venus and Adonis* and *The Rape of Lucrece* with the early plays (and marginally boosts *Titus Andronicus's* authenticity), while the link associates the Sonnets with *Love's Labours Lost* and *Henry V*, and the *Complaint* with *Hamlet, Troilus and Cressida, All's Well that Ends Well* and *Cymbeline*. Given that the method enforces what is already known about the narrative poems, it adds weight to the authenticity of the *Complaint*. A rather different consideration of language is Philip E. Cranston's ' "Rome en anglais se pronounce *Roum*. . . ' ": Shakespeare Versions of Voltaire' (*MLN*), which touches on the polemical uses Voltaire made of Shakespeare and looks at the version of Hamlet's 'To be or not to be' and the less familiar translation from *Julius Caesar*, used in a comparison with Corneille's *Cinna* (to the Englishman's disadvantage, though Voltaire had praised the play itself on an earlier occasion).

After two articles in *SJW*: Martin Lehnert on 'Poetisch-Dramatische Gestaltungsprinzipien in Shakespeares Werken', Rolf Rohmer on 'Das "poetische Prinzip"–einst und jetzt', it is convenient to note Anne Ferry's chapter on Shakespeare in her book on seventeenth-century love poetry[7]. This offers a series of low-level paraphrasing readings of some of the sonnets: when Ferry says 'rough' paraphrase, she means it—that of the second quatrain of sonnet 30 is far from the mark of what Shakespeare says, which may be difficult, but is worth trying for. Too often Ferry shows an imprecision in her use of language ('pun' when Shakespeare is playing with shades of meaning, not different meanings; 'joke' when Shakespeare is both distanced from yet genuinely recalling an emotion). Her refusal to use a good text of the Sonnets suggests abdication of critical responsibility.

The spirit of Maurice Morgann and his defence of Falstaff is abroad in Rupin W. Desai's *Sir John Falstaff, Knight*[25]. While it has the charm of personal conviction and a strong appeal to the idea of literature as a living force, it will not do. Desai does not consider or allow for the conventions of drama (and claims that Falstaff saves Hal and is seriously wounded at Shrewsbury—hence his apparent death), or that in Part 2 Falstaff speaking to the Chief Justice for 'all those trampled into the dust by the vaunting of authority' will not hold water. Falstaff himself uses the word 'counterfeit' of his apparent death and far from stabbing Hotspur only to see whether he may be alive still he has already stated 'I'll swear I killed him'. When the Chief Justice is 'rebuked', perhaps we might think it is he rather than

---

[24] *All in War with Time: Love Poetry of Shakespeare, Donne, Jonson, Marvel*, by Anne Ferry. Cambridge, Mass. and London: Harvard University Press. pp. 287. £6.95.
[25] *Sir John Falstaff, Knight*, by Rupin W. Desai. Fennimore, Wisconsin: Westburg Associates. pp. 133. pb $10.

Falstaff who supports 'all those trampled into the dust'—like the Hostess by men such as Falstaff. In 'Shakespeare and History' (*CritQ*), John D. Jump takes up the old puzzle of the title of *Julius Caesar* and suggests the need to think of it as a *history* play, on the analogy of the English histories, which take their titles from monarchs whose reigns they represent (monarchs naturally important in their plays but not necessarily the most important characters in them). Jump then examines whether the likeness between *Julius Caesar* and the English History plays is merely superficial, considers Shakespeare's position on historical interpretation (see Paul A. Jorgensen above), and speculates that after *Henry V* Shakespeare, dissatisfied with his hero, wanted to write another history but with freer hand, 'unburdened by providential interpretation in favour of the Tudors'. Zdeněk Stříbrný's The Idea and Image of Time in Shakespeare's Second Historical Tetralogy' (*SJW*) continues from an earlier article on the first tetralogy. Shakespeare, though able to show time as the whole movement of history, is against the futility of man within time: Hotspur's 'life, time's fool' is not Shakespeare's. Marilyn L. Williamson argues well on the character of Henry V in 'The Courtship of Katherine and the Second Tetralogy' (*Criticism*), seeing the wooing as consonant with Shakespeare's total portrait of Henry, in repeating a basic pattern in the tetralogy and in completing tendencies developed earlier in *Henry V*. For Williamson, the courtship is play-acting or rôle-playing about a settled issue, Henry's manoeuvre being to get Katherine to justify his demanding her as one of the treaty terms: to do so he sets up a situation that pretends 'both are free as ordinary men and women to love and marry by choice'. Henry is separated from the rest of humanity; he cannot even talk to his intended wife (he has to act out their wooing) and he has become 'all that he mocked earlier—a pompous Hotspur, without the saving bluntness and sincerity'. One might remind Williamson of what she herself says about the effective theatricality of the scene and be unhappy about the simple equation between Hotspur and Hal, but the case has coherence.

J. Leeds Barroll's study of Shakespeare's tragic characters[26] is an 'attempt to make as explicit as possible' the protocol or theory of characterisation that the tragedies require us to hold. His concern is with how Shakespeare 'may have made his dazzling persons, not with the admittedly wonderful fact that he made them at all'. Problems appear with the early statement that 'I take it that the whole point of our valuing Hamlet over...Hieronymo...is that Hamlet does indeed seem real to us and is therefore important to us as a person'; continue with the application of quotation to discussion (Vincentio's questioning of Julietta doesn't surely suggest how she must 'make sure that her affections reach back to their "anthropological roots"'?) and with the plain fact that much of it is unreadable. Barroll makes good claims for recognition that a concern with Renaissance modes of psychology ought not to exclude post-Freudian interpretation; but even allowing for absence of context the following kind of writing is a deadly blow to understanding: 'the model which we propose as the basis for

---

[26] *Artificial Persons: The Formation of Character in the Tragedies of Shakespeare*, by J. Leeds Barroll. Columbia, S. Carolina: University of South Carolina Press. pp. ix + 267.

Shakespeare's own possible individuation of character, for his creation of individual processes, might show the dramatist engaged in an effort to present a cognitive situation, a hypothetical and fictitious perception structured according to psychological systems inherent in the myriad possibilities of transcendentalist ontology. Such a fictitious perception would presumably involve transcendentally formulated dilemmas or problems corollary to the proposition which might inform one particular hypothesis of 'person' ''. A thin good book is perhaps trying to break out of a fattish bad one. Pleasant, then, to turn to Peter Egan's *Drama within Drama*[27], whose brevity comes close to wit. This book is uncluttered by the show of scholarship, and despite a few inaccuracies and sillinesses (he is astonishingly wrong on what Dr. Johnson meant by 'revising' *King Lear* for his edition) it is excellently argued and reads well. Egan endeavours 'to show how Shakespeare has bodied forth the artistic purpose of each play through its characters' attempts to control or alter reality directly through the exercise of dramatic illusion', which in turn shapes or qualifies the relationship intended by Shakespeare between the art of the play itself and the real world of its audience. On *King Lear* he happily rejects both Christian Redemption and 'Lear as Endgame'; a subtle consideration of Edgar and Gloucester's leap leads to a tracing of Lear's own course up to the way in which 'the unmoving, pietà tableau' of Lear and Cordelia is isolated and framed for our 'communal' recognition as the play's ultimate dramatic image. The range of dramatic illusion in *The Winter's Tale*—Camillo as dramatist, the illusion of Florizel's arrival with his bride greeted with joy by Leontes only to be shattered by reality—is explored fruitfully, though one might question whether in the statue scene our responses are in every way on the same level with those of the watchers ushered into Paulina's gallery: it is part of the art that the audience is slightly in advance of their perception. Prospero is presented as the essentially human, though having godlike powers, with a clash between his artistic ideal of a perfect world and the morally imperfect nature of his fellow beings. Again, one might object that Prospero's art does serve to intensify and confirm the love of Ferdinand and Miranda, even if it fails to change human nature. Yet this does not challenge the persuasiveness and essentially exploratory nature of Egan's work.

Frances A. Yates's 'new approach' to the Last Plays[28] is deeply disappointing. Delivered as the Lord Northcliffe Lectures in 1974, these lectures now appear with an additional chapter on Ben Jonson. Yates does not claim any of this as finished work, proposing it as suggestive: little indeed of what she says that is new will stand up to close examination. Her main argument has been 'that the hopes of a younger generation which the play seems to express may allude to hopes in relation to a real historical generation, Prince Henry, and, after his death, Princess Elizabeth and her husband.' Yet after allowing for Emrys Jones's reading of *Cymbeline* and agreeing

---

[27] *Drama within Drama: Shakespeare's Sense of his Art in King Lear, The Winter's Tale, and The Tempest*, by Robert Egan. New York and London: Columbia University Press. pp. ix + 128. $11.25.
[28] *Shakespeare's Last Plays: A New Approach*, by Frances A. Yates. London: Routledge & Kegan Paul. pp. xi + 140. £5.50.

with R. A. Foakes's interpretation of *Henry VIII*, what evidence has Yates to offer? She claims that these plays were amongst those performed at the betrothal and marriage ceremonies, but has not a scrap of evidence that Shakespeare wrote them specially for these occasions or even necessarily with these events in mind beyond a general and public interest promoted by them. To argue that Shakespeare had a special relationship to court policies, Yates has to rely on assumptions that quickly harden into 'facts'. 'Read literally', we are told, *'Cymbeline* is a tissue of impossible events and situations' (yet what is it but a play,—largely taken from history and other stories?—few of Shakespeare's plays would stand so literal a test). In the summary of the plot, Imogen 'wakes to life again on the corpse of Cloten, a scene so strange that it seems to demand some allegorical explanation' ('Hah? I like not that'); on p. 50 Geoffrey of Monmouth speaks of an eagle prophecy, and on p. 51 a leading feature of the play is 'the eagle prophecy', but Geoffrey's were uttered by an eagle, very different from Jupiter descending on his eagle (speculative connections here are made real ones). Yates further suggests that *Cymbeline* was written in 1611 and revised in 1612 for Elizabeth's engagement: no evidence is offered for revision (she similarly suggests the masque in *The Tempest* may have been added, quoting from the Arden edition without making it clear that Kermode rejects the idea) and when details of the play don't fit the historical situation, behold! 'Shakespeare did not have time to rewrite the whole play'; by p. 59 this suggested revision has become fact. Similar details might be cited in her discussion of *The Tempest*. Only the chapter on Ben Jonson offers new possibilities, where she suggests that *The Alchemist* is a satire on Rosicrucianism, particularly on Dr. Dee, but then she has to posit that *The Tempest* has Shakespeare consciously defending Dee and his reputation.

Clifford Davidson's 'Death in his Court: Iconography in Shakespeare's Tragedies' (*Studies in Iconography*) considers the 'emblematic' nature of *tableaux* in the plays and their likely relation to the Elizabeth receptiveness to Emblem Books. Davidson cites possible examples in *Othello* and *King Lear* which he sees as visual parallels to the imagery contained in Shakespeare's verse, and he argues that sixteenth-century audiences would have been able to interpret the iconography, and even the shape, of the Globe. Less plausibly he suggests that as swords or daggers are taken to represent Tragedy (i.e. as in Ripa's *Iconologia* of 1630), and the skull is taken as an emblem of death, we should note the significance of their iconographic function in *Macbeth* and *Hamlet*.

In *Shakespeare's Playhouse: The Poet's Method*[29], by Ronald Watkins and Jeremy Lemmon, has as its object 'to reconsider Shakespeare's plays in the light of the conditions in which he continually worked, and in which his dramatic art was formed'. The book irritatingly tilts at windmills, asserting in the opening sentence that the least admired of Shakespeare's qualities is his skill as a playwright, and quoting *The Times* to support the error that 'Shakespeare's Method is irrecoverable'. On the whole, the

---

[29] *In Shakespeare's Playhouse: The Poet's Method*, by Ronald Watkins and Jeremy Lemmon. Newton Abbott: David & Charles. pp. 207. £4.50.

attempt to illuminate dramatic methods by reconstruction of probable playhouse procedure is successful, if elementary, but the reading is curiously old-fashioned, and the bibliography gives weight to T.W. Baldwin (1927), Percy Simpson (1911) and Ronald Watkins (1950) but has no mention of Richard Hosley, Richard Southern, and many others.

Joseph Kau suggests in 'Daniel's Influence on an Image in *Pericles* and Sonnet 73: An *Impresa* of Destruction' (*SQ*) that the device of the Fourth Knight in *Pericles* comes from Daniel's rendering of Giovio (as *The Worthy Tract of Paulus Jovius*, 1585) since his Latin is Shakespeare's, where the usual proposed source, Whitney, has slight differences. The same influence is proposed for Sonnet 73. Jerome W. Hogan offers 'Three Shakespearian Echoes' (*N&Q*) from *Hamlet, Richard II* and 1 *Henry IV* in the seventeenth century, while John Feather notes that 'A Shakespeare Quotation in 1628' (*N&Q*) from 2 *Henry IV*, noted by Thorn-Drury, is quoted (apparently memorially) from Q rather than F. Donald T. Siebert's 'The Scholar as Satirist: Johnson's Edition of Shakespeare' (*SEL*) is critical, not textual, and about Johnson rather than Shakespeare in its discussion of the impulse to satirize by verbal manipulation. Robert D. Eagleson, in 'Eschatological Speculations and the Use of the Infinitive' (*SQ*) looks at part of Hamlet's 'To be or not to be' soliloquy and part of Claudio's 'I, but to die' speech, and comments briefly on the unique use of infinitives in both. Franz H. Link examines two clebrated difficulties, those of time in *A Midsummer Night's Dream* and *The Merchant of Venice* (*SJH*). Toshiko Oyama gently follows 'Form and Rhetoric in Shakespearean Comedy' (*ShStud*) and Isamu Murakoa finds simple examples of commonplaces occurring in both 'Shakespeare and George Herbert' (*ShStud*).

The *Shakespeare Newsletter* does great service in allowing room for the lunatic fringe, and lets in a splendidly dotty piece from Roger Prior (which actually gets two appearances) which finds Emilia Lanier, no less, (née Bassano) in the names in *The Merchant of Venice*: Bassano-Bassanio, 'Lanier is clearly audible in Solanio' and so on; Salerino is an anagram of Rosaline—see *Romeo, Love's Labour's Lost* and so on. But even more astounding is the account of the remarkable Dr Jean Jofen, who got enough signatures (forty) for a seminar at the MLA meeting where she expounded her notion that Bacon, Oxford, Nashe, and Marlowe not only together wrote the anti-church literature in the Marprelate controversy but went on to write the works of Shakespeare.

Michel Grivelet in the *Annual Lecture of the British Academy*[30] follows the idea of Proteus both in the plays and in the attribution of Protean qualities to Shakespeare himself. Francis Fergusson in 'Romantic Love in Dante and Shakespeare' (*SR*) writes of three traits in the vision of romance which Dante and Shakespeare share.

Finally, some essential reading. *College English* has a deeply depressing piece, 'I Actually Know Not Too Much on Shakespeare' about the result of American methods of teaching Shakespeare at State University level. Shakespeare, it emerges, is known to these students supremely as the author of *Romeo and Juliet; Macbeth, Hamlet, Julius Caesar, Othello* and the *Sonnets* score not too badly. The rest of the plays and poems are

[30] *A Portrait of the Artist as Proteus*, by Michel Grivelet. Shakespeare Lecture, 1975. Published for the British Academy by Oxford University Press. pp. 20. 75p.

nowhere, though there are modest statistics giving the number of students who have read Shakespeare's novels and short stories. The author seriously counsels despair. One sees why, when Roy L. Weitel in the same journal suggest elementary exercises in imaginative writing for these students, based entirely on the limited egos of his young performers, in the hope of enabling them to grasp a little more of Shakespeare. The conclusions are even more depressing: the resolute self-absorption is encouraged, and Shakespeare is even further out in the cold. *Shakespeare Newsletter*, however, has a cheeringly good idea with a number on teaching Shakespeare, with most distinguished contributors. Yet it must all seem slightly irritating to British teachers in that, as so often, the 'new' trans-Atlantic ideas are simply the formalisation and classification of what many of them have been doing, unsung, for generations. Henrich Straumann (*SJH*) however offers 'Shakespeare im Unterricht—Zwölf Üblegungen zu einem Podiums-gesprach'.

To aid us all, *Shakespeare Newsletter* has most useful pages giving a 'consumer-research' type of survey on Shakespeare Handbooks; and Joel Hurstfield, Astor Professor of English History at University College, London, giving an invitation from the heart of the historical-records country: 'it would be a wonderful experience for all of us if some of the best Shakespeare scholars and their graduate students would come down into the mine and join us working at the coal-face'. Two outstandingly encouraging items finish this section. Warren D. Smith's *Shakespeare's Play-house Practice*[31a] is a most splendid little book. It dodges neatly through the minefield of modern theories of discovery spaces and stage platforms and so on and engages firmly with its real subject, which is what we can gather of playhouse practice simply by reading the plays with a practising actor's eye It is vastly illuminating, for example, on how Shakespeare helped to avoid unwanted prompts from a prompter who couldn't see the actor; how actors could 'ascend' or 'descend' in three lines or less, why exit-cues are so firmly placed and usually supported by couplets—the answer to the latter point is that even the best actors playing on a bare stage *in repertory* can make mistaken exits, with more disastrous results than any other error. This is one of those rare books which at every point tells you more about the plays than about the author, or other critics. Richard Levin's paper at the MLA conference is abstracted in *ShN*, a very short but lucid piece which brings joy to the heart of a professional Shakespearean. To abstract the abstract further, he points to three popular approaches to Shakespeare which have generated most of the current 'new readings' the thematic 'the play is not about what it appears to be because it is really about something very different'; the encoded; 'the characters and actions of the play are not in themselves significant but merely a collection of clues'; and the 'trick to be seen through' (naturally by a significantly exclusive élite, i.e. the critic concerned, and one or two others who can see the inner ironies whereby everything means its opposite; and thus Shakespeare is making fools of everyone else).

[31a]*Shakespeare's Playhouse Practice: a Handbook*, by Warren D. Smith. Published for the U. of Rhode Island by the U.P. of New England. Hanover, New Hampshire. pp. xii + 119.

5. Shakespeare in the Theatre

Peter Thomson has properly always regarded his review of the Royal Shakespeare Company's Stratford Season in *Shakespeare Survey* as the place to discuss the state of theatre and the Company's policy, since these factors determine repertoire, productions and achievement. In surveying 'The Smallest Season: The Royal Shakespeare Company . . . in 1974' he paradoxically deals with the longest season yet. But gloom was the main note, since of 23 projects announced by Trevor Nunn in the second half of 1974, only 3 were housed at the Memorial Theatre. Thomson records with sadness and a sense of outrage that 'it has become a London company with a branch in Stratford' (the present reviewer thinks that may not be all bad and welcomes especially the renewal of *English* touring in 1977). Fare was sparse in the summer: only one play in August, and another added in repertoire for September and October. The policy, Thomson says, seems to be a running down of the repertory system, which has bad effects on box office and audience morale. *Macbeth* came too late to be reviewed, but in general Thomson's verdicts were close to those of Speaight's recorded last year (surely both these reviewers might catch up the end of the season in their subsequent review?). One notices the closer analysis of text and theatrical implication in Thomson. He is still dubious about directors' theatre: the more he describes what goes on, the more the academic view at least seems to allow a sense of the play's total dimension. When Thomson compares John Barton and Nahum Tate as men desiring to make a play better, we may claim that the academic would want Shakespeare's play so far as script goes, whatever degree of interpretation: otherwise we reach the position of Peter Stein producing *Das Rheingold* (Paris, 1976), on record as saying he'd prefer *The Ring* without music—and proceeding as though he couldn't hear it. The Stratford season began with Barton's *King John*; Thomson stressed that though himself no purist this was Barton's play rather than Shakespeare's (which the audience might properly assume they were seeing) and more appropriate to presentation in, say, the Open Space. Additions came from Bale, the *Troublesome Reign*, and John Barton, Shakespeare's last two acts being unrecognizable. Stage images were used undiscriminatingly. The play was set on a raked stage, with an inversely sloping ceiling, pitted with stars; the lights displayed round the acting area; practical curtains to allow front playing during scene changes. The set was designed (as later in the season) to remind us we were in a theatre: but why? 'The unruly original has been turned, by directorial interference, into a well-made play!' As John, Emrys James grinned and fretted (simultaneously where possible). Three laughs were gained at the expense of the play: if 'the actors are playing on the director's side of the text, the playwright loses'. The much praised *Richard II* played success-fully again. *Cymbeline*, the third play, was not rewritten though 1150 lines were cut (see Frank Kermode, reviewed last year). Cornelius was a magical master of ceremonies and Thomson praises the bedroom scene (unlike Speaight last year), with the use of the trunk in Iachimo's obscene violation of Imogen's bedroom (Ian Richardson's Iachimo strongly commended) and the reunion of Posthumus and Imogen (Susan Fleetwood bringing to the heroine a sense of grace in relation to the audience and a mutual trust between actress and director). The season's other acceptably traditional production was Peter Gill's *Twelfth Night* (with a new cast: where, Thomson demands, is the proud sixties talk of a company style?), the dominant image being Narcissus. Praise for Jane Lapotaire's Viola, Nicol Williamson's Malvolio, and the discomforting outsider of Ron Pember's Feste. *Measure for Measure*, directed by Keith Hack, presented a Vienna where 'a garishly perverted sexuality was in league with an established church; and the chief ally of the corruption was the Duke.' Indeed, a programme analysis by Edward Bond stressed the theme of 'seeming', with the duke as figure-head, supporting Angelo's corruption. The audience watched a performance of the events of the play, conceived in Victorian stock terms (the same *actor* played Mistress Overdone and Francisca), but though the theatrical imagination that conceived the production was impressive, it operated at a distance from the text and had not adequately communicated itself to the actors.

Shakespeare *Quarterly*, now completing reorganization under new editorship, has put off reviews of productions until 1976, but its Annual Bibliography carries as usual, under section VI, Reviews of Current Stage and Screen Productions. German productions are described for 1974 in the West by Christian Jauslin (*SJH*) and for 1973 in the East by Armin-Gerd Kuckhoff (*SJW*), who includes photographs of *A Midsummer Night's Dream*. The latter periodical also includes Roman Szydtowski's 'Shakesepare in Polen' and Günther Klotz's '*Othello* and *Mass für Mass* in Budapest' (1973).

Gámini Salgádo has made an entertaining collection[31], though given the (proper) largeness of his interpretation of performance and of what is Shakespeare he might have found room for the 1809 *Hamlet* performed by dogs and need not have been so contemptuous of Lacey's *Sawny the Scott* [*sic*] (the account of Peg Woffington's last appearance, for instance, has little to do with her part as Rosalind, while Ira Aldridge's *Titus Andronicus* —good though it is to have the account—could present Aaron as 'a noble and lofty character'). A further restriction is its almost entire devotion to English players and London performances. The book is divided into two sections—chronological accounts up to 1700, very generous in interpretation of performance, then play by play to 1890, with an odd tail-piece. This latter arrangement is based on Alexander's chronology, dividing by genre as well as period, so that oddly *The Merry Wives of Windsor* comes before any of the Falstaff histories. One must always regret what is not included—Helen Faucit's account of her Hermione opposite Macready, which combines so splendidly acting and criticism: the more missed when so many accounts of performance are anecdote or imprecise description (a constant problem of stage criticism). Problems of presentation (given that the book is for the ordinary reader) lie in the incomprehensibility of some early extracts (Helmes on *The Comedy of Errors*;, Scolokar on *Hamlet* meaningless as it stands), while the notes offer dubious assertions, e.g. that Jonson's 'creaking throne' means *Cymbeline*. Small errors are frequent: George I should be George II, p. 92; the captions are reversed, p. 103;

[31] *Eyewitnesses of Shakespeare: First Hand Accounts of Performances 1590-1890*, by Gamini Salgado. London: Sussex University Press (Chatto and Windus) pp. 360. £6.

Charles Dickens should be Junior, p. 115; the date of Kynaston was wrong, p. 174 (given correctly with the illustration, p. 60); Kean played Othello to Booth's Iago, p. 265. The collection provides amusement and makes a 'good read'; there is pathos in Macklin's last attempt at Shylock ('God help me—my memory, I am afraid, has left me') and insights like Lamb's fine analysis of Dorothy Jordan's Viola. The book achieves its aim, but one regrets it was not more rigorous (without losing its charm) in pursuit of the elusive traffic of the stage.

Two pieces from a book not previously noted in this chapter[32] are John Lawlor's 'Continuity and Innovation in Shakespeare', an after-dinner talk, which asks how we can hope to get, consistently, at the veritably Shakespearian, at that which is central in each play? In a slight piece, appropriate to its occasion, he finds Shakespeare's not a drama of ideas but above all of the theatre. J. A. Lavin's 'Shakespeare and the Second Blackfriars' is an important attack upon assumptions about a particular theatre drawn from a play or about a particular play's shape derived from the theatre in which it was to be performed. He exemplifies this by demolishing the assertion that the acquisition of the Blackfriars Theatre (1609) by the King's Men brought about a complete change in Shakespeare's methods and style, concluding that the different companies show a capacity to deal with almost any play put into their hands and act them in virtually any surroundings. The construction of theatres is considered by D. A. Latter in 'Sight-Lines in a Conjectural Reconstruction of an Elizabethan Playhouse' (ShS), whose investigation endorses Southern on the placing of prickposts and gives them a use, finds 3000 a possible audience capacity (so confirming de Witt's account), and offers dead ground before the arras for the gallants to sit in, facing the groundlings.

Various aspects of eighteenth-century theatre are covered by Babette Craven's 'Derby Figures of Richard III' (TN), which suggests that three figures in the accompanying plate represent Garrick, Kemble and Kean, not the first alone; and by Judith Milhous's two-part 'An Annotated Census of Thomas Betterton's Rôles, 1659–1710' and John W. Velz's 'An Early Eighteenth-Century Cast List for Shakespeare's Julius Caesar (suggested benefit of 1719), both in the same publication. For the nineteenth century, Maarten van Dijk considers 'John Philip Kemble as King John: Two Scenes' (TN), Hubert's temptation and the death scene. Mary M. Nilan contributes an interesting account in 'Shakespeare Illustrated: Charles Kean's 1857 Production of The Tempest' (SQ), including some details of effects like Ariel as ball of fire and upon a dolphin's back (contamination from another play, presumably), and of the antiquarian rage (the furies which torment Trinculo 'are copied from Furies depicted on Etruscan vases'). Shorter considerations of actors are John A. Mills's ' "The Modesty of Nature": Charles Fechter's Hamlet' (1861) and Edward Carroll Powers's 'Tommaso Salvini: An American Devotee's View' of Salvini as Othello (both ThS, 1974). A footnote is provided by Y. S. Bains in 'Theatre and Society in Early Nineteenth-Century Toronto' (Nineteenth Century Theatre Research), where plays 1809–1828 include Cibber's Richard III, Macbeth,

[32] The Elizabethan Theatre III, ed. by David Galloway. Connecticut: Archon Books and Macmillan of Canada. pp. xvi + 149. $10.

and Garrick's *Katherine and Petruchio*. More wide-ranging is John Osborne's illustrated 'From Political to Cultural Despotism: the Nature of the Saxe-Meiningen Aesthetic' (*ThQ*), which includes consideration of Shakespearean production and a design for *The Merchant of Venice*. Two articles on Charles Lamb as critic take up his knowledge of the stage and his later influence: Joan Coldwell writes on 'The Playgoer as Critic: Charles Lamb on Shakespeare's Characters' (*SQ*), noting his dislike of Cooke's overplaying the monster as Richard III and concluding that 'the real value of his criticism lies not in its method but in the insights it gives to Shakespeare's characters'; while James A. Davies in 'Charles Lamb, John Forster, and a Victorian Shakespeare' (*RES*) traces Lamb's influence on Forster as theatre critic.

More recent theatre history is taken up by George Rowell on 'Tree's Shakespeare Festivals (1905-1913)' (*TN*), including a reminder of *Hamlet* without scenery, and information on finance and casts; by Henry Kahane in 'Max Reinhardt's Total Theatre: A Centenary Lecture' (*CLS*), which touches Reinhart's handling of actors in Shakespeare; and by Richard France in 'Orson Welles's Modern Dress Production of "Julius Caesar"' (*ThQ*), which usefully gives a detailed account of what he calls, perhaps hyperbolically 'unquestionably Welles's highest achievement in the theatre' and a dazzling piece of propaganda. He describes the setting (bare stage except for arrangement of wooden platforms), the back stage wall painted the colour of dried blood; lighting, with 'Nuremburg' beams directed straight up from the floor; music (Blitzstein); and costumes (Italian Fascist). Welles played Brutus and George Coulouris Mark Antony; the text, with Welles's concern to show fascism as a dateless state of mind, was much hacked and transposed—an entry for Caesar at the very beginning and complete omission of Octavius in order to stress Mark Antony's opportunism. Particular care was paid to a drawn-out 'Cinna the Poet' scene. France notices also Welles's engrossment of the production and his amateurish boredom during a prolonged run. Two other articles may be mentioned: Fritz Däbritz's 'Shakespeare auf dem Puppentheater', with photograph (*SJW*), and Howard Brenton's 'Petrol Bombs through the Proscenium Arch' (*ThQ*), in which he notes that his play *Revenge*, intended first as a rewrite of *King Lear*, still has elements of Shakespeare in it.

Films are the concern of two pieces of no great concentration, though of some interest. Marvin Felheim in 'Criticism and Films of Shakespeare' (*CompD*) is concerned more with film criticism than Shakespeare and inspires little confidence in his opening statement that the 'union of film and Shakespeare was as natural and ordained a combination as bread and butter'. What he says shows that for him Shakespeare is interesting only as material for treatment; discussion is hampered by lack of reference to particular films. More enjoyable is Dilys Powell on 'The Film of the Book' (*EDH*), which concentrates on sound versions, particularly *Henry V* and *Hamlet*. She praises also the Russian *Hamlet* and has a pleasingly personal judgement of Orson Welles's *Othello* as 'the essence of Shakespeare'.

The Library of Congress, which has been receiving batches of papers from Margaret Webster, the theatre director, since 1967 reports their final acquisitions, following her death (*Library of Congress Quarterly Journal*);

amongst material held are about 50 prompt books (titles not specified) and letters and papers of Ben Webster and May Whitty, her parents.

6. Individual Plays and Poems

All's Well That Ends Well

W. Speed Hill writes 'Marriage as Destiny: An Essay on *All's Well That Ends Well*' (*ELR*) in which he says that 'an analysis of the familial basis for the marriage of Bertram and Helena shows a play at once more coherent in itself and more of a piece with other Shakespeare plays than is commonly acknowledged'. The marriage symbolises an acceptance by each of their respective parental histories. Hill is very good on Helena and Bertram, and writes a useful, intelligent constructive piece in which the notion of Problem Play is never once touched: this is 'a marriage comedy'. Nicholas Jacobs adds a gloss on IV. v. 1–3 (*N&Q*) showing 'villainous saffron' as, among other things, hinting at a medication against syphilis.

Antony and Cleopatra

In his stimulating 'Literature without Philosophy: *Antony and Cleopatra*' (*ShS*) Morris Weitz argues for the legitimacy of philosophical criticism as part of the discipline of literary criticism, and asserts that in the play there are a number of philosophical themes but no thesis or universal philosophical claim. Weitz considers that one important theme, that of generation and corruption, suggests that *Antony and Cleopatra* can be seen as Shakespeare's 'pre-Socratic' tragedy. He justifies his theory with generous quotation of the play's verbal and intellectual paradoxes and its 'inverted images', and he concludes that Shakespeare is suggesting that generation implies destruction and self-destruction. The play, Weitz tells us, does not show a clear dichotomy between Romans and Egyptians, for both share similar imagery; it neither presents a philosophical assertion nor a denial. Ultimately, however, its total 'nobleness' transcends the baser, destructive elements in its characters. While accepting that Dryden in no way 'adapted' Shakespeare, Leslie Howard Martin in '*All for Love* and the Millenarian' (*CompL*) touches at several points on Shakespeare's play and on earlier dramatisations of the story. Dimiter Daphinoff, in 'Zur Behandlung der Quellenfrage in der englisch-deutschen Studienausgabe der dramatischen Werke Shakespeares' (*SJH*), contributes a long and important discussion of the value of source-study, with special reference to *Antony and Cleopatra*.

As You Like It

Kent Talbot van den Berg in 'Theatrical Fiction and the Reality of Love in *As You Like It*' (*PMLA*) follows recent views of this comedy as 'self-reflective', that is, 'the characters' experience in the play reflects our own experience of the play'. He goes on to propose that the relation between the two worlds becomes in fact a metaphor of love — 'the rôle-playing of Rosalind and Orlando becomes a remarkably comprehensive theatrical symbol of love's complexity'. Van den Berg is helpful in summarising recent studies of the complexities of reference in the play, though not al that he mentions are fully acceptable, and useful in that he restores Rosalind to the centre of the play's activity: 'fiction and reality, like true lovers, preserve their separate identities so that they can mutually enhance each other'. In 'The Way to Arden: Attitudes Toward Time in *As You Like It*' Rawdon Wilson (*SQ*) finds James Smith and others wrong in their time-and-space interest in the journey to and from Arden. For Wilson, the way to Arden is 'the way of the mind's journey; a mental voyage of discovery which leads to the recognition of self and the importance of feelings. Thus Time becomes not merely the measurement of motion and change . . . but also the symbolic function of each stage of the journey.' Though a little overstrained, this is not unhelpful. David G. Byrd points out in a brief note 'Shakespeare's Familiaritie between Sir Rowland and Duke Senior in *As You Like It*' (*SQ*) that the friendship between the two was already in Lodge. Harry Morris, however, goes one step further into the bleaker realities of the play, he says, in '*As You Like It*: Et in Arcadia Ego', (*SQ*). He 'observes the presence of death in the Forest of Arden' by means of full-scale reference to Poussin, Panofski and others, extending into this play his work on the icons of *memento mori* in *Hamlet*. The reference to the final emblem in Whitney (1586) is impressive, though the notion is surely adequately covered by the one-and-a-half lines on the subject in Agnes Latham's New Arden edition, p. lxxvii.

The Comedy of Errors

In *TSLL*, James L. Sanderson analyses Patience in this play with somewhat wearisome reiteration and no perceptible point. He links it with *Pericles*, and comes to the conclusion that G. Wilson Knight was right—it is 'a glorious little play'. In pleasant contrast, Kurt Tetzeli von Rosador in ' "Intricate Impeach": Die Einheit der *Comedy of Errors*' (*SJH*) writes on the unity of the play; he is acute, and alert to many aspects of Shakespeare criticism, including production values from both the 18th century and today, and including a good knowledge of comedy techniques contemporary with Shakespeare. He rates the play very highly indeed, with the support of a refreshingly thorough examination.

Coriolanus

Andrew Gurr's '*Coriolanus* and the Body Politic' (*ShS*) discusses the common Tudor emphasis on the concept of the body-politic, a metaphor for national progress based on common consent, and the opposition to the idea presented by James I's belief in Divine Right. The question of where true sovereignty was located was evidently of interest to Shakespeare in 1607, the year of riots in the Midlands, for, Gurr suggests, he saw the fallaciousness of an organic analogy. The Commonwealth depicted in *Coriolanus* is not united by love, but by war, and war requires generals rather than tribunes. 'The tragedy', Gurr concludes succinctly, 'starts from political realities'.

In 'The Metamorphoses of Coriolanus' (*SQ*) Ralph Berry considers stage versions of the play as a touchstone of the political attitudes of the times. Starting with Kemble's production of 1789, and ending with the 1972 version, he notes a gradual transition from a crude political understanding to a sympathetic stress on the human faults of the protagonist. The ambiguity of Caius Martius is considered by Michael Gassenmeier in his 'Odi et Amo: Das Dilemma Von Shakespeares Coriolan' (*Anglia*), asking whether the ambivalences come from matters external to the play, such as current political theory, or from Coriolanus' various understandings of himself. Gassenmeier, in a long, alert, and valuable treatment, relates them to Coriolanus' relationship with Aufidius.

Hamlet

Ralph Berry's ' "To Say One": An Essay on *Hamlet*' (*ShS*) investigates Hamlet's move towards a unity of self, and to some sort of identity with his father. Berry argues that the Prince exhibits a profound concern with his public image, and this requires him to act or to feign. The point is reiterated, rather less interestingly, in Lillian Wilds's *Shakespeare's Character-Dramatists: A Study of a Character Type in Shakespearean Tragedy Through Hamlet*[33], which discusses *Titus Andronicus, Richard III*, and *Richard II* as precursors of *Hamlet* in a line of plays containing characters who function as 'dramatists' or as 'actors'. She sees *Hamlet* as 'an organic ordering of experience in terms of the theatre', and the Prince, Polonius, and Claudius as rôle-players and scene-makers. The study concludes with a somewhat thin coda which contrasts Shakespeare's practice with those of Kyd and Marston. In another Salzburg study, *Denmark, Hamlet and Shakespeare*[34], Cay Dollerup attempts to show that there is 'an authentic Danish atmosphere' in the play. It is a lengthy and laborious piece of work, but the speculations unwittingly suggest that Shakespeare knew rather less about Denmark than might originally have been supposed.

In his 'Three Notes on *Hamlet*' (*ES*) Horst Breuer discusses Hamlet's comparison of himself to Hercules (I.2.153), concluding that it reflects on the Prince's physical build; the lines in Act I Scene 4 (17–38), which he believes should be interpreted as a general observation rather than a personal statement; and the Prayer Scene, which, he argues, develops a leading motif, that of the damnation of the villain. Mother M. Christopher Pecheux notes in her 'This Fell Sergeant Death' (*SQ*) the possible inspiration of the line in the medieval representations of Death as the bailiff of God, while Laurence Rosinger suggests in 'Hamlet and the Homilies' (*SQ*) that Shakespeare was influenced by Elizabethan Homilies on Matrimony and Adultery. G. A. Wilkes, in his ' "An Understanding Simple and Unschooled": The "Immaturity" of Hamlet' (*Sydney Studies in English*), considers and disputes the approaches of T. S. Eliot and, more especially, of L. C. Knights to Hamlet's character. Much of the 1975 *Shakespeare Jahrbuch* from Weimar (*SJW*) is occupied with *Hamlet*. Martin Lehnert in 'Poetisch-dramatische Gestaltungsprinzipien in Shakespeares Werken' (*SJW*) writes a wide-ranging and useful discussion of the principles behind the making of poetic drama, with reference to Hamlet's advice to the players, a matter taken up again in Anselm Schlösser's 'Über Hamlets

[33] *Shakespeare's Character-Dramatists: A Study of a Character Type in Shakespearean Tragedy Through Hamlet*, by Lillian Wilds. Salzburg: Universität Salzburg pp. 236.
[34] *Denmark, Hamlet and Shakespeare*, by Cay Dollerup. Salzburg: Universität Salzburg. pp. 358.

Schauspieltheorie und deren Verwirklichung im *Hamlet*' *(SJW)*. Willi
Schrader contributes a short but useful piece 'Was ist uns Hekuba?' *(SJW)*
and Georg Seehase's 'Konflikt und Harmonie in Shakespeares Dramen'
(SJW) refers both mainly to *Hamlet*. Thomas Sorge writes on the grave-
diggers in 'Hamlet und die Totengräber' *(SJW)* with particular reference to
the complex relation between Hamlet and the audience. Two pieces of
special importance both concern matters about which many scholars are
ignorant: Ursula Klein's 'Zur *Hamlet*-Rezeption ein Vergleich' *(SJW)* is a
long and fully argued comparison of interpretations of Hamlet from
Schlegel to the Marxist Armin-Gerd Kuckloff, and Thomas Wieck in
'Shakespeare testfeld für das Theater unsere Epoche' *(SJW)* sees him as
the testing-ground for contemporary theatre.

In *ShStud*, Hisae Niki makes a simple comparison in 'The Mixture of
the Comic and Serious in *Hamlet* and *Kanadehon Chushingura*', an 18th
century Japanese play. Martin Stevens in 'Hamlet and the Pirates: A
Critical Reconsideration' analyses again the familiar notion of Hamlet's
cold-blooded murder of Rosencrantz and Guildenstern, seeing it as 'the
last link in a chain of self-willed events'. Paul Hamill in 'Death's Lively
Image: The Emblematic significance of the Closet Scene in *Hamlet*'
(TSLL) labours the obviously emblematic nature of the two pictures, and
Hamlet himself, at some length.

Two *Hamlet* studies are of unusual interest, and both come from old
Shakespearean hands. Harold Jenkins in 'Hamlet and the Fishmonger'
(SJH) opens up that hoary old puzzle, and actually gives us something
both new and valuable. Endearingly observing in passing that 'it is important not to let the fishmonger supply us with red herrings' he gives a useful
run over the various theories, finally citing M. A. Shaaber's demolition of
what must be called the prostitute-theory. He demonstrates, with a subtle
but convincing twist, that what is on Hamlet's mind is Ophelia's power to
conceive and breed easily, then further showing how this locks in to the
movement of the play at that point. Hamlet's choice between fishmonger's
daughter and Jephtha's daughter has for the first time real point. W. W.
Robson, however, returns to an even more hoary problem in his 'Did The
King See The Dumbshow?' *(CQ)*. In the course of a long discussion, he
arrives at the customary resting-place, that the controlled and resourceful
Claudius was overcome not by the representation of his crime, but by
Hamlet's behaviour during the spoken playlet. Robson, being less than
half-way through, then moves on to follow up recent suggestions about the
intentional unreality of the Ghost, and the obviously inappropriate melodrama of making the play-scene anything but quiet. He argues, *via* the
extraordinary nature of the method of poisoning and the complete silence
of the king about Hamlet's knowledge of his secret, that the King saw the
dumbshow, but did not recognise the representation of his own crime, and
so the Ghost's story was untrue, at least in this particular, 'and the whole
action of *Hamlet* must be seen differently'. The play-scene, he concludes,
is one forceful example of the trick of this play of not subordinating the
various points of view to a single synoptic vision.

Henry IV
    Roy Battenhouse's 'Falstaff as Parodist and Perhaps Holy Fool' *(PMLA)*

gives a fat knight unrecognizable in the plays Shakespeare wrote. Like his article on Henry V reviewed last year it seeks to offer an entirely new reading and thereby perverts any common understanding of the character. By presenting Falstaff as 'holy fool', Battenhouse attempts to show that the knight is conscious stage manager in a persistent attempt to educate Hal. If the holy fool is 'a comic symbol for the supernatural order of charity' it could mean 'that while as "allowed fool" Falstaff is shamming vices and enacting parodies, his inner intent is a charitable almsgiving of brotherly self-humiliation and fatherly truth-telling'. Gross distortion follows from this: certainly Gadshill can be seen as comment on the falling out of Bolinbroke and the Percies, but how are we to see Falstaff letting himself play the rôle he does at the robbery?–particularly since Battenhouse says it is the Prince and Poins who suggest the robbery. Falstaff may be an improviser (his reaction to Hal's exposure of the Gadshill buffoonery makes that clear), but he is not a deviser: Battenhouse claims that Falstaff plants the bill with its deal of sack on himself, for Hal to find, while to motivate all this fatherly truth-telling he invents a morally-sensitive Falstaff present as Mowbray's page in the lists at Coventry. If Margaret B. Bryan's ' "Sir Walter Blunt. There's Honor for You" ' (*SQ*) is bold enough to seek the play Shakespeare wrote she is yet not so startingly original, particularly in a plunge through Renaissance concepts of honour, as she may think. Still she focuses reasonably on Blunt, a character 'who says nothing about honor', in whom 'the conception of honor as selfless integrity' can be found, though more dubious is her suggestion that such honour cannot exist in the world of men. Richard S. M. Hirsch offers 'A Second Echo of "Edward II" in 1.iii. of "I Henry IV" ' (*N&Q*), a link between Marlowe's II. ii. 237–8 and lines 230–33, where Malone had already noted borrowing between the same two scenes.

John W. Blanpied writes in *ELR* on ' "Unfathered heirs and loathly births of nature": Bringing History to Crisis in *Henry IV, Part Two*.' In relation to *Part One*, he says, 'The very displacements from our expectations serve to enforce upon the play's anxious concern with its own creative processes, which in turn become a significant level of dramatic action. In this sense the "history" of the play can be seen as a metaphor for the play itself rather than the reverse.' Concentrating on showing how IV. iv and v. bring to their culmination the complex sequence of dramatic developments in the history plays, Blanpied ends his long and densely-worked piece by showing how the scenes also conclude the dramatic metaphor 'English History' in Shakespeare's career. Another long, detailed and learned essay–itself the argument of a full length study now nearing completion–Sherman H. Hawkins' 'Virtue and Kingship in Shakespeare's *Henry IV* (*ELR*) tackles the problem of 'a clear judgment between virtue and lineage' as it is in all the histories, but especially *Henry IV*. Hawkins proceeds by references to Cicero, Plato and Aristotle, 'The three authorities who most influenced ethical theory in Renaissance princely institutions'. The argument is too complex to be reproduced here: but it can be said that a new and impressive group of subjects has been added to the curriculum of the education of the Prince.

Henry V

An interesting piece by Jean-Marie Maguin, 'Shakespeare's Structural Craft and Dramatic Technique in *Henry V*' (*Cahiers Elisabéthains*), suggests that the play's structure is not that suggested by the traditional five act division. Rather, there is a movement that stresses a pattern of doom for the French, of success for the English (the Chorus important as one of National Spirit rather than Universal History), the scene in the French camp before Agincourt marking the end of a movement that began at Harfleur. The French 'are shown to be linguistically as well as militarily conquered by the English'. Pierre Sahel argues in 'Henri V, Roi Idéal?' (*EA*) a link between Henry's situation and the conduct of Machiavelli's Prince, concluding that if Henry's political realism does not accord with traditional moral standards, then Shakespeare is accepting this as Renaissance actuality.

Henry VI

George Walton Williams in 'Fastolf or Falstaff' (*ELR*) writes a minor piece supporting the not uncommon view that Shakespeare wrote 'Fastolfe' in *Henry VI Part One*, as in all the sources, but a later hand, between the original draft and Folio intervened to change it to follow the popularity of the fat knight. John W. Blanpied argues in ' "Art and Baleful Sorcery": The Counterconsciousness of *Henry VI Part 1*' that a monumentalised past is peculiarly the subject of this play, 'and is bodied forth so palpably as to seem almost the chief character.' The past, for Blanpied, is not just political but includes the very conventions of drama and speech that the play makes use of—and then finally abandons and surpasses. Jörg Hasler in 'Gestische Leitmotive in Shakespeares *Henry VI*' (*SJH*) discusses valuably the movement and dramatic relationships of gesture in the *Henry VI* plays, in the relatively simple but important sense of sitting, standing, kneeling and so on.

Henry VIII

Two excellently suggestive pieces indicate renewed interest in this neglected play. Frederick O. Waage's '*Henry VIII* and the Crisis of the English History Play' (*ShakS*) seeks to detach it from the Last Romances and argues that the final scene (nearest in spirit to the Final Plays) is not an organic growth, but an appendage (a conclusion that Lee Bliss also reaches in 'The Wheel of Fortune and the Maiden Phoenix of Shakespeare's *King Henry the Eighth*' (*ELH*), both therefore radically at odds with R. A. Foakes in the Arden edition). The dichotomy between moral and political is here at its sourest, Waage maintains, and is emphasised by Shakespeare's inability to mythologise history, perhaps a reaction to Prince Henry's death (rather different in its implications from Frances Yates's explicit linking of Shakespeare to the Henrician crusade noted above). Shakespeare was avoiding any of the obvious and universally acceptable contemporary connotations of the reign—Waage takes into account all three plays on Henry VIII reprinted in 1613—as he was avoiding any transformations of history, until the very end, that could flatter the king or the king's cause. Rather than building towards glorious climax, the play undercuts, through images of the theatre and its show of pageantry, both ceremony and the meaning of history. Lee Bliss complements this study by suggesting that we have neither a heroic view of Henry as a champion of the Church of England nor as a misled youth who finally attains self-knowledge and the virtues of an ideal monarch. The play is concerned rather with moral complexity of the 'historical' political world and with the problematic king himself. Henry's is a shifting and shifty character, consistent only with the whole world of conflicting perspectives and ambiguous motives evident from the first scene. Katherine is the one figure of integrity and it is Wolsey who comes to moral regeneration; this pair 'surrounds' Anne's coronation, the play beginning 'to move on two levels: the public glory, now presented rather than reported, is surrounded by powerful scenes of private disillusionment and rejection'. Two good explorations.

Julius Caesar

John W. Velz and Sarah C. Velz make the point in 'Publius, Mark Anthony's Sister's Son' (SQ) that the popular connotations of 'sister's son' make emendation unnecessary, as the phrase as it stands gives special evidence of callousness. Sidney Homan makes most of his point in his title: 'Dion, Alexander, and Demetrius—Plutarch's forgotten Parallel Lives—as mirrors for Shakespeare's Julius Caesar' (ShakS). He argues persuasively for Shakespeare's use of the comparison between Grecians and Romans that follows each set of parallel lives, and indeed his use of the parallel lives themselves—Dion with Brutus, Alexander with Caesar and Demetrius with Antony. Certainly the habits of reading that Homan suggests for Shakespeare fit well with what we know of his methods elsewhere.

King Lear

Richard Matthews claims in 'Edmund's Redemption in King Lear' (SQ) that the delayed 'conversion' of Gloucester's bastard in the last scene of the play has been either neglected or, as by Bradley, regarded as a flaw. Matthews sees Edmund as moving rapidly through four stages of awareness, acting finally through a 'compulsion of love' to save others, thus presenting a parallel to the experience of Lear himself.

In her 'The Cat is Grey: King Lear's Mad Trial Scene' (SQ) Adrienne Lockhart discusses Edgar's words (III vi. 41–46) which stress a need for justice, but which include a doggerel rhyme which has puzzled commentators. She suggests that a clue to its meaning is to be found in Heywood's Dialogue and that Edgar is quoting a proverb dealing with the problem of discrimination and judgement. O. B. Hardison Jr. relates the play not to English folklore but to Classical myth ('Myth and History in King Lear') (SQ), finding a parallel to the story of Ixion. Hardison traces the mediaeval and Renaissance interpretation of the myth, and sees it symbolic of a fall after a desire for pomp and as a fable of ingratitude. The storm in the play, he argues, reflects the thunderbolt which cast Ixion into Hell, and the play's imagery of wheels and centaurs indicates that Shakespeare found the myth giving coherence and reason to his historical material.

H. F. Lippincott writes on 'King Lear and the Fools of Robert Armin'

(*SQ*) and contrasts Armin's picture of court fools in *Foole upon Foole* with Shakespeare's. Lippincott suggests that Shakespeare drew instead on Archee Armstrong, James I's fool and that he was looking back beyond Armin to a mediaeval idea. He also argues that Poor Tom takes on the rôle of the wise fool after the middle sections of the play. In '*King Lear* and John Brown's *Athelstan*' (*SQ*) J. D. Hainsworth suggests that the latter play may have influenced Garrick's revival of *Lear* in 1756.

Alan C. Dessen's 'Two Falls and a Trap: Shakespeare and the Spectacles of Realism' (*ELR*) argues that 'looking at Elizabethan drama through the spectacles of realism can lead the modern critic or director into a trap from which he may have difficulty in extricating himself'. By way of a brief examination of *Titus Andronicus* II. iii, illuminating the 'Peacham drawing' and demonstrating the advantages of non-representational staging, he turns attention to *King Lear* IV. vi. He focusses on the true miracle, 'not Gloucester's survival from an illusory fall, but Edgar's meaningful assertion of the bond between child and father'; his argument is well expounded, and too complex for fuller explanation in this brief space. H. A. Mason in *CQ* asks 'Can We Derive Wisdom about Old Age from *King Lear*?' and offers 'two small suggestions', both in fact powerful landmines: one is that we should 'go all the way with the Bastard. He represents the claims of Nature that we deny in our decent solicitude for the aged . . .' The other is that the mutual kneeling of Cordelia and Lear, asking for forgiveness, shows that 'even under ideal conditions we cannot have rôles that are just . . . we are guiltlessly guilty towards each other and we need both to forgive and be forgiven.' Richard D. Fly writes in *TSLL* 'Beyond Extremity: A Reading of *King Lear*' with an ambitious aim, claiming that it is possible for him 'to gain a perspective on the play's formal and thematic peculiarities which has not been properly examined or understood'. What follows, however, is valuable: a demonstration that *Lear* shows in all its parts a persistent urge to 'top extremity'. Stephen J. Brown in 'Shakespeare's King and Beggar' (*YR*) illuminates III. iv., showing that King Cophetua and the Beggar Maid are frequently referred to in Shakespeare, being 'part of the vocabulary of his imagination'; but here the idea is actualized, making 'a heroic image of power with an ironic image of powerlessness' and pointing forward to the ironic mode of contemporary drama, to Genet and Beckett.

Arnold Shapiro in ' "Childe Roland", *Lear* and the Ability to See' (*PLL*) briefly illuminates Edgar's words and Browning's poem. Alan R. Young in 'The Written and Oral Sources of *King Lear* and the Problem of Justice in the Play' (*SEL*) analyses and comments on Shakespeare's deliberate distortion of the basic patterns of both oral and written traditions in the final scenes, though we are still, as he says, far from understanding why. Dieter Mehl analyses 'King Lear and the Poor Naked Wretches' (*SJH*), rather simplistically.

Love's Labour's Lost

Antony J. Lewis attempts to show in 'Shakespeare's Via Media in *Love's Labour's Lost*' (*TSLL*) how the play blends extremes, producing 'the temperate life best for all seasons'. Thomas L. Berger in a note in *SQ* called 'The Lack of Song in *Love's Labour's Lost*' says that at I. ii. 127–31 there should be no song, thus refuting Long and Seng. Malcolm Evans, however, in his elaborate and lengthy 'Mercury Versus Apollo: A Reading of *Love's Labour's Lost*' (*SQ*) suggests in his closely argued article that the concluding sentence in Q, 'The words of Mercury are harsh after the songs of Apollo' is Shakespeare's own comment on the printed text 'in which the play, removed from the social context of the theatre and the Apollonian world of sound, inevitably assumes what in its own terms are the qualities of writing, the words of Mercury'. Evans is learned in his pursuit of the Mercurial and Apollonian throughout the play: 'the words of Mercury, both written words in books and rhetorical penned speech, entail a psychic withdrawal from the realities which are figured in the very substance and decorum of speech' and the play becomes matter for Plato and Aquinas. They seem large powers to gain a little patch of ground.

Macbeth

Despite its slick terminology Richard S. Ide's 'The Theatre of the Mind: An Essay on *Macbeth*' (*ELH*) offers a general discussion of the bi-partite structure of the play, a structure which Ide sees as combining a psychological tragedy with a 'symbolic pattern of retribution'. He considers that Shakespeare merges the 'natural hurlyburly' with the 'psychological hurlyburly', and moves between the stances of a 'cosmic playwright' and one who presents the 'inner theater of Macbeth's psyche'. Ide suggests that the play lets us recognise that there is a pattern, and that Macbeth's psychic state becomes a symbol of his damnation.

Frederic B. Tromly's 'Macbeth and His Porter' (*SQ*) sets out to counter the traditional interpretation of the Porter scene, but it treads generally familiar ground. Tromly sees the Porter as a 'metaphor' for Macbeth, one who makes the murderer seem more human by suggesting the frequency of human criminality.

Measure for Measure

A. D. Nuttall's attractive but discursive article in *ShS* '*Measure for Measure: the Bed-Trick*' states that 'The whole play of course unites an elegant intricacy of plot with the greatest possible inconsistency of ethical principle' and, *via* a reworking of the position of the marriages, affirms his first thesis, that 'the stories of *Measure for Measure* and *All's Well That Ends Well* are essentially and systematically disquieting, and that our disquiet is exacerbated by the presence in the plays of psychological complexity'. But this is to be held at the same time as his second thesis, that the plays are also the exact opposite, fairy tales, and 'the endings are genuine catastrophes, the forgiveness is experienced as real forgiveness, and the concluding matrimony a joy'. Arthur C. Kirsch in 'The Integrity of *Measure for Measure*' points firmly in a long and curiously waspish piece to the Christian texture of this play, with ample quotation from Scripture and elsewhere, and insists upon imposing the play as a sermon upon us: 'the degree to which we are entangled by Isabella, Claudio and Angelo is a measure of our own necessarily mortal conditions, and our hope for their comic deliverance is an extension of the capacity for hope and forgiveness in our own lives. We experience, we do not merely observe the process by which they are brought to self-knowledge and regeneration'

David Rosenbaum in a minute note in *Expl* assigns 1 Gent's speech at 1. ii. 138 to the Bawd. Eamon Grennan in 'Keats's *Contemptus Mundi*: A Shakespearean Influence on the "Ode to the Nightingale"' (*MLQ*) adds *Measure for Measure* III. i. 5–41 and 119–133 to the long list of possible influences, with some plausibility in view of Keats's known markings in his copy of Shakespeare.

Nigel Alexander's *Shakespeare: Measure for Measure*[35] is a disappointment. A short, sparse commentary on the play is preceded by eccentric and opinionated pages which, among other things, praise at length Bertrand Evans' 'brilliant' approach to the earlier comedies, and then focus far too much attention on Frances Yates' notions of the significance of the figure of Astraea for James's court, as a means of solving the 'problems' of this play – these 'problems' themselves being dogmatically, and curiously, stated. An example of the logic is the following: 'Shakespeare changed his sources to insist upon Isabella's virginity, thus associating her with Astraea'. Alexander often refers to critical material or snatches of scenes as 'important', but such 'importance' in fact appears only if a very narrow view is taken. The book is in the Studies in English Literature series, and one wonders a number of things: why Edward Arnold makes the book so unpleasant, with poor paper and tiny type; why a book appears which so contradicts David Daiches' General Preface, where he remarks that in this series 'biographical and historical facts . . . are generally subordinated to critical discussion', though here over half the book, and much of the commentary, is occupied in applying external facts to the play. There are some distinctly odd remarks. *Pericles, Cymbeline, The Winter's Tale*, and *The Tempest* are 'arguably the finest plays he ever wrote'. 'Other courtly pageants of the year 1604 have faded and left no wrack behind. *Measure for Measure* remains to puzzle the will.' This sentence, as well as being peculiar, is misleading. Even if we do accept the play as a 'courtly pageant', it remains true that 1604 was rather a good year for the survival of scripts, in fact.

By contrast, the modestly titled 'The Unity of Measure for Measure' by Lawrence W. Hyman (*MLQ*) is a major contribution to our understanding of the play. In this fine piece, Hyman speaks out for the possibility of a new taste for *Measure for Measure*, correcting that of even recent Christian allegorists. The difficulty has sometimes been that the play feels split down the middle. Hyman, setting out to demonstrate the unity, follows through an equation between life and shame, with its corollary that 'a strict adherence to virtue and chastity—whatever form it takes in Angelo or in Escalus or in Isabella—leads to death'. He goes on to show very well that Isabella's involvement in the arrangement of the bed-trick, involving deceit as well as lust, holds together the movement of the play, which so apparently falls apart at the Duke's lines to Claudio at III. i. 160ff, and that the play thereafter exemplifies the paradoxical equation of shame and life. Thus, though there are other tones as well, there is a strong unity: everyone lives in the second half of the play. Not only is the possibility of life literal, as it is for Claudio and Barnadine, but there is a resurgence of

---

[35] *Shakespeare: Measure for Measure*, by Nigel Alexander. London: Edward Arnold. pp. 61. hb £2.20, pb £1.20.

life in a wider sense for Mariana, Angelo and Isabella'.

The Merchant of Venice

R. F. Hill's 'The Merchant of Venice and the Pattern of Romantic Comedy' (ShS) points out the singularity of this play as a comedy of love. The perspective on sexual love is ambivalent, as Hill illustrates from the rest of the comedies, but here 'ambivalence has been toned down almost to the point of disappearance' with a uniquely early union, and high altruism replacing self-interest. There is an unusual balance between male friendship, the love between friends, and that between the sexes. The result is a comprehensive picture of love, in its largest dimension.

The Merry Wives of Windsor

Jeanne Addison Roberts in 'Falstaff in Windsor Forest: Villain or Victim?' (SQ) decides he is both: the fat knight turns out to be 'a very delicately balanced ambiguity, easy to shatter and difficult to maintain', which makes him sound uncomfortably like Humpty Dumpty. A study of some of the iconography of the last scene—including an astonishing quotation from Beryl Rowlands, who writes of 'the strange Devonshire custom known as "skimiting riding" ' in apparent ignorance of The Mayor of Casterbridge—well supports the valuable general point.

A Midsummer Night's Dream

This play has now grown up. We are no longer to look for what the critic discussed below calls 'the old pixie-dust trivialization of the play'. It now has 'intellectual substance', and indeed is to be read as 'a study in the epistemology of the imagination'. Such an approach, however, is not compulsory. The lover of Shakespeare who objects to having his play transformed into a study of anything at all, least of all the epistemology of something else, and who sighs, illicitly, for a shimmering of fairies' wings is going to find life hard in the stern world of American criticism: but let him hold on—England's Puck has a trick or two yet, and to do with love-juice too. In the most unfortunately titled 'A Midsummer Night's Dream. The Fairies, Bottom, and the Mystery of Things' (SQ) Ronald F. Miller takes the recent ideas of the Solemn High Seriousness school of critics of this play, and pushes them all a little further. Commenting on the quartet waking at IV. i. 191–98, he says 'So moving is this association of the fairies with immanent benevolence that, for a moment, all formal amigui-ties—all questions of the reality of the fairies—fade to insignificance before the greater mysteries underlying mortal existence'. But, one protests, this is simply word-spinning. What can there be there that is not done, and infinitely better too, by Shakespeare in his play? Many pages are given to an anlysis of Bottom, who then gets his revenge because Miller comes to the conclusion that criticism of this play is folly. So, to quote a wise character from another play, 'To what end are all these words?' Leon Guilhamet in 'A Midsummer Night's Dream as the Imitation of an Action (SEL) attempts to resolve the question of the unity of action by means of a Neoplatonic commonplace, Harmonia est discordia concors.

Much Ado About Nothing
In 'Hercules Shaven: A Centering Mythic Metaphor in *Much Ado About Nothing*' Andrew B. Crichton writes about 'the careful use of a sub-mimetic system concerning Hercules which parallels a mimetic heightening of beards' (*TSLL*).

Othello
Michael Black includes two perceptive discussions of the play in his study *The Literature of Fidelity*[36], arguing in his first chapter that the often accepted view of Othello as the noble soldier manipulated by an unscrupulous Iago is both sentimental and mistaken. Black believes that we are disturbed by both Iago and Othello because we identify with them and their actions, acknowledging their faults in ourselves. Both men, he suggests, have a 'peculiar kinship' underneath their personal identity which is indicated in the related styles of speaking given them by Shakespeare. Black develops his argument in his second chapter, and ends by drawing a parallel between Othello's possessive love and that of Lawrence's Gerald Crich, and by contrasting to it the parable of the Prodigal Son, the idea of the prodigal father in *Lear*, and the restored love of Natasha and Prince Andrei in *War and Peace*. These gestures of 'reaching across', or 'dropping defences', Black argues, serve to show how rich is the pearl that Othello throws away.

Rodney Poisson's 'Othello's "Base Indian": A Better Source for the Allusion' (*SQ*), suggests that the American Indian's ignorance of the value of gold and pearls was 'almost proverbial' in the sixteenth century, citing its instance in Nashe, and tracing its source to letters sent by Amerigo Vespucci. Richard S. Veit shares Coleridge's indignation at the conventional reading of the same line in his ' "Like the base Judean": A Defense of an oft-rejected reading in *Othello*' (*SQ*). Veit insists that word clusters in Othello's last speech give it a decidedly 'Middle Eastern' image pattern, and that the presence of the Judean gives coherence to what would otherwise seem to be a 'sequence of ramblings'.

Othello's nobility is reasserted in Jean Klene's 'Othello: A fixed figure for the time of scorn' (*SQ*). Klene refers to the Renaissance insistence on the maintainance of a good reputation in the man of honour, and suggests that Shakespeare's play with the word 'honest' emphasizes this, as does the rendering of his, as opposed to Cinthio's hero, as an 'honorable murderer'. Iago, by contrast, Klene insists, is seen throughout as a destroyer of honour. C. F. Burgess, in 'Othello's Occupation' (*SQ*) claims that the idea of the soldier and the military theme in the play have been critically neglected in favour of a stress on a love-story. Contrastingly, and somewhat questionably, Pierre Janton argues in 'Othello's Weak Function' (*Cahiers Elisabéthains*) that 'with Desdemona Shakespeare created a figure of Eros', a symbol of 'unquenchable life' with whom Othello cannot cope sexually.

Coping sexually is very much the theme of Warren Staebler's 'The

[36] *The Literature of Fidelity*, by Michael Black. London: Chatto and Windus. pp. 216. £4.50.

Sexual Nihilism of Iago' (*SR*), a strangely old-fashioned piece, not immune from private fancy, which overvalues the sexual obsessions of that villain. There is more going on even under the dominantly sexual language of Iago than Staebler allows: *Othello* as a play is here merely a vehicle for Iago, and Iago for the critic's single-minded interest. Lynda E. Boose in 'Othello's Handkerchief: The Recognizance and Pledge of Love' (*ELR*) discusses in detail the possible significances of the celebrated piece of linen which gave such offence to Thomas Rymer, taking it as both a universally-understood token of virginity, and as having a special symbolic history in this play. 'As symbolic nexus, Othello's magical handkerchief not only spans the major issues of the play but also reaches into man's deepest cognitions about his sexuality, his myths, his religion, and his laws'. E. K. Weedin Jr develops the idea in 'Love's reason in *Othello*' (*SEL*) that that play above all anatomizes the operation of reason in man.

Pericles

Pericles as tale is the concern of two articles. In 'Shakespeare's Gower and the Role of the Authorial Presenter' (*PQ*), Walter F. Eggers distinguishes the authorial presenter from ordinary inductions and prologues, and explores the convention, concluding that Shakespeare returns 'to the rudiments of drama—the presentation of a simple story—to mark the limits of dramatic representation and transcend them'. Again, Annette C. Flower in 'Disguise and Identity in *Pericles, Prince of Tyre*' (*SQ*) stresses that the play's 'mouldiness and narrative basis are deliberately exploited', both in Gower's tale and in its dependence on being 'told' by its own characters. This promising start is not fully borne out by what follows, though there is a good argument about the way Pericles's disguises have never been to conceal the truth, but serve rather as rôles which isolate and emphasise one aspect of that truth, until all rôles are integrated into full identity. In a brief note, 'North's Plutarch and the Name "Escanes" in Shakespeare's "Pericles" ' (*N&Q*), MacD. P. Jackson links the name with the Greek orator Aeschines, three times given in Plutarch's life of Pericles.

The Phoenix and the Turtle

After three pages summarising critical views of the poem, Vincent F. Petronella turns in 'Shakespeare's *The Phoenix and the Turtle* and the Defunctive Music of Ecstasy' (*ShakS*) to its literary genesis, its symbolic and stylistic elements, in order to understand better what forces are at work beneath the marmoreal surface of this enigmatic elegy (the function of those three pages never emerges). For Petronella, the poem is 'a vision of an overwhelming disaster', confronting us with 'the death of both body and soul', since the grim fact is that 'truth and beauty have been destroyed beyond the point of revival'.

Richard II

S. Schoenbaum has an enjoyable, unpretentious yet scholarly article, ' "Richard II" and the Realities of Power' (*ShS*), in which he illuminatingly looks at the matter of Richard and at the revival of a play about Richard on the eve of Essex's rebellion. He points to long-standing interest in Richard and his reign, plus the lack of consensus among the various writings. The king's character is examined in *The Life and Death of Jack Straw*, a poor play but interesting for a young Richard of compassion and the sun; in *Woodstock* with its 'wanton tyrant'; and the play Simon Forman saw (not, despite A. L. Rowse, Shakespeare's). In considering the 'Essex' performance (he accepts that it was Shakespeare's play, though stressing this is inference rather than certainty), Schoenbaum sees Shakespeare neither as seditious supporter of Essex nor as darling of the Court, yet with political sense, evident in the play's first scene, where the king shows as much political acumen as weakness. Schoenbaum sees skill in Richard's handling of events at Coventry, a view challenged by Diane Bornstein's 'Trial by Combat and Official Irresponsibility in *Richard II*' (*ShakS*), which presents too much undigested material on the code of the duel: she concludes that criticism of Richard is implied by his allowing the combat. She does not comment upon Shakespeare's reversal of the combatants' order of entry (see Arden edition, head-note to I. iii), though she quotes from William Segar (1590). Still, Bornstein is useful, where Larry S. Champion's 'The Function of Mowbray: Shakespeare's Maturing Artistry in *Richard II*' (*SQ*) is obscure and unconvincing. He argues that the audience focus on Richard's treatment of Mowbray in scene three and on 'the King's' attempt to maintain in public an image of equity and objectivity.' Mowbray's actions are made functional to the development of Bolingbroke's character. David M. Bergeron points out in 'The Hoby Letter and *Richard II*: A Parable of Criticism' (*SQ*) that the idea that this letter of 1595 refers to Shakespeare's play (or any play at all) was challenged in 1936, 1950 and 1958, yet is still referred to by recent critics and editors as an authority and so needs to be challenged yet again. The same writer offers a very unconvincing argument in 'The Deposition Scene in *Richard II*' (*RenP* 1974) that the part of Act IV missing in early Quartos and only printed in 1608 was new material and not the restoration of lines acted but excised in print. Peter Mortenson and Jo Ann Davis suggest 'A Source for "Richard II", II. i. 40–68' (*N&Q*), finding the sea-girt island fortress and the sceptred isle in Greene's *Friar Bacon and Friar Bungay*, scenes iv and xvi. Richard E. Barbieri posits a borrowing from the play in Donne's *Devotions*, no. 8 ('John Donne and *Richard II*: An Influence?' (*SQ*)), an idea of a mirror- though the implications of Donne's image are rather different from Shakespeare's and goes on to speculate that Donne saw the play, possibly even the 'Essex' performance.

Richard III

Michael Neill starts badly with a punning title in 'Shakespeare's Halle of Mirrors: Play, Politics and Psychology in *Richard III*' (*ShakS*). 'The tragic paradox of Richard's position is that only action can validate the self he proclaims' but action must be acting. The argument includes theatricality, self-division, mirror-images, self-reflexive ironies, and the not-quite-fashionable-any-longer sneer at a Shakespearean ending. This article presents two worlds, one of a dense, all-knowing, all-suggestive omnipotence, that of the critic, and the other of blessed relief at the lucid words of Shakespeare in the very many inset quotations. It is good to get into the fresher air of Emrys Jones' 'Bosworth Eve' (*EinC*), one of the more balanced pieces on *Richard III* to appear for some years. Jones, partly concerned to counter recent 'diminishing' criticism of the play, argues that the great weight of the ending is in the entire movement of the last two acts. He shows that the wooing of Elizabeth, which uncharacteristically freezes the headlong pace of military urgency in a long moment out of time, develops a historical irony in which references to Richmond are subtly underscored. He then lucidly and persuasively shows why it is the *eve* of Bosworth that is 'the occasion richest in imaginative potential and significance' with special reference to Shakespeare's use of the feast of All Souls and—unexpectedly—the possible presence of a traditon of the dream of Constantine, very appropriate for the Tudor feeling for dynastic drama and the sense of great historical watershed. James A. Riddell in a brief note in *ES* suggests convincingly that Hastings' phrase 'my foot-cloth horse' refers to the nobility of the beast.

Romeo and Juliet

Charles B. Lower writes on *'Romeo and Juliet* IV. v.: A stage Direction and Purposeful Comedy' (*ShakS*). He finds both the received text of the lamentations of Old Capulet, Paris, Juliet's Mother, and Nurse, and the Q1 SD *All at once cry out and wring their hand[s]*, funny. On this subjective reaction Lower then builds a large edifice of criticism and five pages of notes. James Black writes well on 'The Visual Artistry of *Romeo and Juliet*' (*SEL*) and especially on the recurrence of stage groupings.

The Sonnets

In 'A Note on Sonnet 73, 1.12' (*SQ*) Alan Taylor Bradford challenges the orthodox interpretation of the line, and seeks the definition of natural death in Henry Cuffe's *The Differences of the Ages of Man's Life*. Here he finds a recognition, parallel to that in the sonnet, that all nutrition involves consumption, and that mortality is inherent in nature.

The Tempest

Glynne Wickham in 'Masque and Anti-masque in "The Tempest" ' (*E&S*) continues his exploration of image in drama, taking up the Jacobean masque as something beyond the spectacular quality of the Last Plays. Peter Hall's National Theatre production (noticed last year) stressed the masque element, but the iconography of the designer was haphazard and largely incorrect. An iconographical approach brings out the anti-masque/masque relationship between Act III's Banquet and the heavenly vision of Act IV. Wickham, reprehending Hall for showing Juno as Elizabeth herself, shows that the goddess appears as deity of Union and patroness of marriage. The masque is related to Court figures and ultimately both the late Queen and Princess Elizabeth, Anne and James 'are all to be seen on the stage together as flickering images in the mirror of the masque's received conventions'. Harry Epstein offers a well-written if not over-original view in 'The Divine Comedy of *The Tempest*' (*ShakS*): from the human perspective, Prospero appears immense, but from the transcendent, it is impossible to take him seriously. It is his renunciation of the rôle of providence that begins Prospero's reintegration into the human community. Decidedly original and a neat piece is L. T. Fitz's 'The Vocabulary of the Environment in *The Tempest*' (*SQ*), written with humour, which queries the popular image of the island as semi-tropical. Prospero seems only to have a 'hunting and gathering economy' and the world of his magic is made more attractive than the world of the 'bare island' to emphasise the value of what Prospero has brought to the island. Jacqueline E. M. Latham in ' "The Tempest" and King James's "Daemonologie" ' (ShS) is what she claims: useful if inconclusive (a pity she was unable to draw on James Smith). She concentrates on Caliban and his complexity, arguing that if King James is followed he would be human, since a devil having no sex can have no sperm and hence an incubus that impregnates a woman must have obtained the sperm from a man, dead or alive. Peter Milward looks briefly at Gonzalo's 'Merry Fancy' (ShStud) and Klaus Büchler writes a short piece on stage directions of various kinds (SJH) under the title 'Explizite und implizite Bühnen- und Spielanweisungen in Shakespeares Tempest'.

Titus Andronicus

Pierre Legouis, in one of this distinguished scholar's last pieces, (ShS) illuminates III. i. 298–9, about Tarquin begging at the gates, strengthening a little the possibility that Shakespeare was acquainted with Dionysius of Halicarnassus. Jørgen Wildt Hansen (Anglia) in 'Two notes on Seneca and Titus Andronicus' suggests a passage from Hercules Furens behind IV iii. 49–51, and restores Seneca as an influence on II. iii. 93–108. Lawrence N. Danson in 'The Device of Wonder: Titus Andronicus and Revenge Tragedies' (TSLL) suggests we need something other than revenge as the 'central tragic fact' in this play, and with some insight and learning arrives at 'a nexus of concerns' whereby both the playwright and his characters are faced with the problem of breaking out of rhetoric, 'that high gift which has become a prison' and achieving the action which will suffice, this being, inevitably, death. But in the end it is not clear quite how all this insight and learning and comparison with other tragedies actually says anything new about Shakespeare's play. G. Harold Metz in a confused and confusing article 'The History of Titus Andronicus and Shakespeare's Play' (N&Q) newly relates our play, the ballad, and the 18th century chapbook.

Troilus and Cressida

Richard D. Fly has two bites at this play, saying roughly the same thing in two different journals. In SQ he writes on 'Cassandra and the Language of Prophecy in Troilus and Cressida', seeing this play as 'a particularly instructive instance of the dramatic interplay between dynamic language and informing vision' for 'in this play Shakespeare exploits the overdetermined nature of his characters' speech to create and sustain a vision of imminent and radical catastrophe'. This Fly explores in a detailed commentary on the language of disintegration and final darkness which becomes curiously more vivid than the play, which itself becomes subordinated to this one 'vision'. In SEL he writes ' "Suited in Like conditions as our Argument": Imitative Form in Shakespeare's Troilus and Cressida' where the technique itself functions as the vehicle of theme and vision, which is of disintegration. It is refreshing to move back in critical time to Robert Grudin's 'The Soul of State: Ulyssean Irony in Troilus and Cressida' (Anglia). Grudin, apparently happily unaware of the most recent work on the play, analyses the 'puzzle' of the character of Ulysses, whose counsel and actions 'seem deeply at odds with each other'. An unpretentious account of his part in the play leads to a useful presentation of his capacity for irony. Better still is 'Cressida and the World of the Play' by Grant L. Voth and Oliver H. Evans (*ShakS*),showing richly how Cressida moves from awareness to self-deception and back to awareness. This excellent piece has much that is good to say about the language of the play. But best of all is John Bayley's 'Time and the Trojans' (*EinC*), developing the familiar observation that the action of the play is isolated in a perpetual present. What Bayley calls 'novel time' is quite lacking, either in the sense of past or in the linking of characters to environment. Among many results of this is the prominence given to Thersites and the sense of characters as victims of the moment and its impulses; Cressida is seen as a victim of what other people want.

Twelfth Night

Richard Henze writes in the tradition of *belles lettres* about a collection of opposites he has noticed in this play in '*Twelfth Night*: Free Disposition on the Sea of Love' (*SR*) offering his piece as 'a solution to this puzzle of interpretations'. D. Allen Carroll, however, really does illuminate in 'Fabian's Grudge Against Malvolio', a note in *SQ*. He presents useful material supporting the equation Fabian = roisterer, and he has discovered a John Fabian who was probably well-known in real life as a member of the party of misrule, with ample cause to resent the authorities.

Two Gentlemen of Verona

It is good to see attention directed to this play, but sad that it is so often patronizing as well as overblown. Peter Lindenbaum's 'Education in *Two Gentlemen of Verona*' (*SEL*) says the play shows 'a radical change in the definition of a "perfect man" from a mere courtier to, in effect, an unfallen being, and in this process of redefinition, Proteus, Julia, Valentine . . . have all been educated to see man, and particularly Proteus, for what he is as imperfect and fallen'.

Venus and Adonis

David N. Beauregard writes '*Venus and Adonis*: Shakespeare's Representation of the Passions' (*ShakS*) delineating the affections arising from the concupiscible and irascible powers of the sensitive soul. W. R. Streitberger writes on 'Ideal Conduct in *Venus and Adonis*' (*SQ*) on the courser and jennet episode as a double-edged *exemplum*.

The Winter's Tale

Glynne Wickham's 'Romance and Emblem: A Study in the Dramatic Structure of *The Winter's Tale*' (in *Elizabethan Theatre III*: see 'Shakespeare in the Theatre' above) argues that it is an emblematic play (not allegory, nor parable), a dramatic narrative in course of which allusion is made more or less frequently but always obliquely to other characters and another story, the interpretation being a matter for the discerning spectator. This, Wickham feels, may help explain puzzling features of, above all, the Last Plays and is developed in his essay on *The Tempest* noticed above For him the correspondence between the double setting of the play, the events depicted and the passage of time on the one hand and the course of

Anglo-Scottish relations on the other is striking. He claims it as Shakespeare's contribution to the celebrations marking Prince Henry's investiture as Prince of Wales. A range of evidence is drawn from pageants, masques, speeches and two statues (illustrated) of Elizabeth and Mary, Queen of Scots. This is provocative and Wickham handles his argument well. The use of these statues links interestingly with Marie-Madeleine Martinet's 'The Winter's Tale et "Julio Romano" ' (EA), which finds the element of trompe-l'oeil important in Julio's work, considers the relation between the aesthetic of Romano and the theme of the play, and concludes that the reference to the painter is not an anachronism nor to be taken literally; it is a deliberate shift of register which makes an effect in keeping with the whole of the play. The interaction between speech and character is traced by Carol Thomas Neely in 'The Winter's Tale: The Triumph of Speech' (SEL), until in the final scene 'language compels gesture, and the two, interchangeable now, bring reconciliation to perfection'. François Laroque concentrates upon the sheep-shearing in 'Feasts and Festivity in The Winter's Tale' (Cahiers Elisabéthains, 1974), suggesting the use of folk material to give a precise and realistic image of festival customs, of the world of popular festive traditions as mirror to the stage, and of the feasts for the characters to indulge repressed passions and desires. A useful note is Siegfried Koss on 'Gab es ein Küstenland Böhmen?' (SJH). A feeble piece is ' "Browzing of Ivy": The Winter's Tale' (ArielE), by Leo Rockas, who in the course of his wanderings comes to suggest that Antigonus is transformed to Autolycus and the bear to Time as Chorus. Patricia Southard Gourlay writes in ELR ' "O my most sacred lady": Female Metaphor in The Winter's Tale' (is there no end, one wonders, to sexism? even the very figures of speech now have their gender); Shakespeare in this play, she argues, uses femaleness to bring together a rich assortment of meanings. The women in the play embody those ambiguities of Leontes' own nature which he feared and despised, but without which his masculine force is a wasteland.

Sir Thomas More

Michael L. Hays offers two interim reports on the manuscript and attribution. In 'Shakespeare's Hand in Sir Thomas More: Some Aspects of the Paleographic Argument' (ShakS) he stresses that paleographic arguments are central to any attribution of Addition IIc in hand D to Shakespeare, but in assessing the data as basis for an examination, he finds little in the evidence so far on which to make a case. The larger field of descriptive bibliography, which he feels now the most fruitful line of exploration is opened out in 'Watermarks in the Manuscript of Sir Thomas More and a Possible Collation' (SQ). He suggests possibilities of conjugate sheets and raises the question of the separation of C and D as hands.

VIII

English Drama 1550–1660, Excluding Shakespeare

BERNARD HARRIS and BRIAN GIBBONS

1. Editions

The major activity this year seems to have been the continued provision of plays in a great variety of editions. The Malone Society has maintained its publications policy and has made available four relatively scarce dramatic texts.[1] David Carnegie's edition of Goffe's *The Raging Turke* and *The Couragious Turke* offers good examples of early seventeenth-century academic drama, properly most appreciated for their literary quality, as the surviving number of copies seems to confirm. Judith Levinson's text of that interesting play *The Famous History of Captain Thomas Stukeley* has a valuable introduction, including a note on the Gaelic used in the work. G. M. Pincess has edited the MS of *The Faithful Friends* with an effective account of the difficulties presented by such a manuscript. Three additions, all considerable, have been made to the important series of modernised texts of plays of this period.[2] G. K. Hunter details the vexed problems of the textual history of *The Malcontent*, furnishes the play with a scholarly commentary which the difficulties of this dramatist make necessary and welcome, and includes as part of the critical introduction an interesting section on the relationship between tragi-comedy and satire. Akihiro Yamada's edition of *The Widow's Tears* has a substantial study of Chapman's source, and relates the play to Chapman's comedies more generally; these are certainly neglected now and deserve the attention drawn to them. J. R. Mulryne's edition of *Women Beware Women*, now, like *The Malcontent*, being re-established as a stage-piece, is the most comprehensive and authoritative edition of this work, based on long research in the source-material and printing history, and has an analysis of the structure and dramatic effectiveness of the play drawn from practical experience in production.

Middleton is clearly the focus of much attention at present. In a representative volume Kenneth Muir has edited *A Chaste Maid in Cheapside*,

---

[1] The Malone Society. Thomas Goffe, *The Raging Turke* (1631) and *The Couragious Turke* (1632), ed. by David Carnegie. 1968 (1974). *The Famous History of Captain Thomas Stukeley* (1605), ed. by Judith C. Levinson. 1970 (1975). *The Faithful Friends*, ed. by G. M. Pincess. 1970 (1975). O.U.P. for The Malone Society. By subscription.
[2] The Revels Plays. John Marston, *The Malcontent*, ed. by G. K. Hunter. pp. lxxxv + 171. £6. pb £3.50. George Chapman, *The Widow's Tears*, ed. by A. Yamada. pp. lxxxv + 152. £9.50. Thomas Middleton, *Women Beware Women*, ed. by J. R. Mulryne. pp. lxxix + 201. £6. pb £3.50. Methuen.

Women Beware Women and *The Changeling*, in a conservative manner,[3] and from the same publisher has come R. G. Lawrence's choice of three Jacobean and Caroline tragedies, as companions to his previously published selected comedies; he has chosen *Women Beware Women*, *Perkin Warbeck* and *The Cardinal*.[4] He reads the plays partly as 'comments on politics and society, dramatic mirrors for magistrates', but offers this fruitful approach without confining the plays in doing so. The Muir and Lawrence volumes represent a return to principles of intelligent and sensitive anthologising which must commend them to scholarly student purchasers in these immoderate times. Among editions of single texts Dora Ashe deals efficiently with the textual problems of *Philaster* and offers shrewd judgments on that play.[5] Elsewhere, Elizabeth Brennan has provided a chance to reconsider *The Devil's Law-Case* (overdue for professional attention), D. J. Palmer has made a fresh presentation of that hardy annual *The Shoemaker's Holiday*, and R. V. Holdsworth put in a claim for Middleton and Rowley's *A Fair Quarrel*.[6] In another popular series G. Salgado's choice in the rich field of Jacobean comedy provides texts of *The Dutch Courtesan*—probably Marston's best contribution to the genre—Middleton's *A Mad World, My Masters*, Jonson's *The Devil is an Ass*, and the more widely available *A New Way to Pay Old Debts*.[7] The two series of dissertation reprints relevant to this chapter coming profusely from Salzburg—hereinafter described simply as Salzburg Studies—have continued their welcome contribution to edited texts.[8] Robert Carl Johnson has made 'A critical edition of Thomas Preston's *Cambises*', and A. Harriette Andreadis has edited Lyly's *Mother Bombie* with an updated introduction taking account of recent critical studies. (This is a commendable achievement; the editions are respectively nos 23 and 35 in 'Elizabethan & Renaissance Studies'.) Brownell Salomon has published a critical, old-spelling edition of Thomas Heywood's *The Fair Maid of the West, Part I*, with a fully informative introduction and a refreshing wit sometimes lacking in editors of popular comedies; Cathryn Anne Nelson's two-volume 'Critical edition of *Wit's Triumvirate, or The Philosopher*' provides a modern text of a manuscript currently in preparation for The Malone Society and is closely annotated in a thoroughly useful manner. (These editions are respectively nos 36 and 57 in 'Jacobean Drama Studies'.)

---

[3] Thomas Middleton, *Three plays*, ed. by Kenneth Muir. (*A Chaste maid in Cheapside*, *Women beware Women*, *The Changeling*). Dent. pp. xix + 217. £2.95. pb £1.50.
[4] *Jacobean and Caroline Tragedies*, ed. by R. G. Lawrence. (Thomas Middleton, *Women Beware Women*; John Ford, *Perkin Warbeck*; James Shirley, *The Cardinal*). Dent. pp. xii + 264. £3.95.
[5] Regents Renaissance Drama series. Francis Beaumont and John Fletcher, *Philaster*, ed. by Dora J. Ashe. Arnold. pp. xxxii + 152. £4.
[6] The New Mermaids. John Webster, *The Devil's Law-Case*, ed. by Elizabeth Brennan. pp. xxix + 157. pb £1.25. Thomas Dekker, *The Shoemaker's Holiday*, ed. by D. J. Palmer. pp. xxv + 101. pb £0.95. Thomas Middleton and W. Rowley, *A Fair Quarrel*, ed. by R. V. Holdsworth (1974). pp. xlv + 130. £1.35. pb £1. Benn.
[7] Penguin English Library. *Four Jacobean City Comedies*, ed. by G. Salgado. pp. 423. pb 80p.
[8] Salzburg studies in English literature, under the direction of Erwin Stürzl: Elizabethan & Renaissance studies, and Jacobean drama studies, both ed. by J. Hogg. Universität Salzburg. Not for sale.

2. Stage Studies

Although substantially a volume of general history, *The Revels History of Drama in English* by its deliberate emphasis deserves attention and commendation for its decision to concentrate on the theatrical context of drama.[9] The third volume covers the years of the formation of the professional theatre until the end of Shakespeare's participation. This is an awkward decision to make but at least it provides opportunity to consider the post-Shakespeare theatre through to the Restoration without the literary inhibition imposed by the date 1640. J. Leeds Barroll sets up an introductory account of 'The social and literary context' of this theatre, with an admirable summary of the complex documentation associated with the Office of Revels, and thus determines the appropriate approach for the reader of this book: Alexander Leggatt performs a similar service through the complexities of 'The companies and actors', a vivid and evocative essay; Richard Hosley on 'The playhouses' accompanies his review with many excellent illustrations and many persuasive technical proposals, basing his comments, with typical refusal to speculate beyond evidence, on the Swan, First Globe, and Second Blackfriars playhouses: Alvin Kernan's 'The plays and the playwrights' naturally finds its centre in Shakespeare's plays, but manages to relate them positively to the drama of his major contemporaries, perhaps with most success to the rival worlds of *Bartholomew Fair* and *The Tempest*—rich contrast indeed. The book is provided with a chronological survey, good illustrations—especially of theatre design, and selective bibliographies. Richard Hosley has made a response to C. Walter Hodge's account of their mutual theatrical interests in 'The Second Globe' (*TN*), concluding that 'the area of disagreement between us grows ever smaller', that is, at least in the search for truth. J. W. Binns in 'Women or transvestites on the Elizabethan stage?: an Oxford controversy' (*Sixteenth Century Journal* V, 2 1974) marshals the terms of the controversy between Gager, Gentili, and Rainolds and distinguishes their importance in treating of both the academic and popular stage. J. L. Simmons's note on 'Volpone as Antinous: Jonson and "Th'Overthrow of Stage-playes"' (*MLR*), though primarily a gloss on Antinous by reference to Gager's *Ulysses Redux*, throws light on the contemporary dispute over the moral defence of drama. Inga-Stina Ewbank discusses 'Language and Spectacle in the Theatre of George Peele' (*The Elizabethan Theatre V*), considering the mutual illumination of visual and verbal imagery, so that language in Peele can serve the same function as in pageants, not so much the evocation of meanings and creation of patterns in its own right, as the emphasis on a visual reality existing already before the eyes of the spectator. In 'Civic pageants and historical drama' (*JMRS*) David M. Bergeron takes his authoritative studies further in this analysis and survey of their relationships and argues that we should 'view civic pageants as a special type of history and thereby expand our awareness of the shapes and forms that historical drama assumed in the sixteenth and seventeenth centuries.' In a brief note on '*Hannibal and Scipio* (1637): how "The places sometimes changed"' (*TN*) T. J. King makes a new comment

---

[9] *The Revels History of Drama in English: Volume III 1576-1613*, ed. by C. Leech and T. W. Craik. Methuen. pp. xxxiii + 526. £10.50. pb £4.50.

on this recurrent exchange, arguing, interestingly, that though court amateurs 'provided occasional scenic innovations during the reign of Charles I', professional actors continued to follow 'the conventions of the Elizabethan "open stage" '. Norman Rabkin's review of Stephen Orgel's *The Illusion of Power: Political Theater in the English Renaissance (SEL)* suggests that despite its brevity (pp. 94) and price ($6.50) it should be seriously sought as 'an essay about theater at court': it was not available for review.

3. Textual Studies

David J. Lake's book on the canon of Middleton's plays inevitably draws our eyes to the verdict on the authorship of *The Revenger's Tragedy*; the answer is in favour of Middleton.[10] It would be a pity if the statistical methods employed were to receive unqualified approval before rigorous scrutiny of other factors, which the dispute over the authorship of *The Revenger's Tragedy* has long occasioned, has been enjoyed by some other plays in an admittedly largely unexciting canon. The book is a substantial intervention in the present conduct of textual studies, and may well be influential in the future; let us be cautious before following the example of those nineteenth-century confidences which have led to so much con fusion in the present century. The same critic's 'Dekker and "The Telltale"': some difficulties' *(N&Q)* is an analysis derived from his work on Middleton; the play's inclusion in the Dekker canon is disputed, and the work returned to anonymity. This seems an acceptable opinion. J. R. Mulryne's 'Half-sheet Imposition and Running-title transfer in *Two New Plays by Thomas Middleton*, 1657' *(Lib)* is a specialist account of these aspects in the printing process of *More dissemblers besides women* and *Women Beware Women'*. Robert K. Turner, in 'Act-end notations in some Eliza-bethan plays' *(MP)*, provides a helpful list of manuscript and printed plays which afford evidence on this subject; it will be extremely useful to editors of the plays involved. Despondency with the present achievement of much twentieth-century textual and bibliographical criticism will be increased by Constance Brown Kuriyama's article on 'Dr Greg and *Doctor Faustus*: the supposed originality of the 1616 text' *(ELR)*. She traces in precise terms the difficulties an editor faces in accepting Greg's arguments—the exception being Roma Gill's heretical stance—and argues for the despon-dent conclusion that adherence to Greg's proposals hampers the literary critic of the play, who is left with 'no edition which he can use with ease and confidence'. It is a chilling comment on the benefits of the new biblio-graphy in terms of making available its knowledge in the service of clarify-ing the issues for potential readers.

4. Books and Articles

Joseph W. Houppert has written an informed, lively and succinctly stated book on Lyly[11]. The author keeps the claims of modern criticism in

[10] David J. Lake, *The canon of Thomas Middleton's plays: internal evidence for the major problems of authorship.* Cambridge U.P. pp. xi + 302. £6.50.

[11] Joseph W. Houppert, *John Lyly.* Boston: Twayne's English Authors series. pp. 169. $7.50.

view but does not allow them to intrude overmuch on his own direct, brief, vigorous discussion of Lyly's work. These plays do present a problem; they lost the life of action on the stage in their own day, and have not recovered it; but Houppert's book, written in a manner suited to the purposes of the series concerned, will certainly encourage readers to explore and appreciate this intricate art.

Among other studies of the early period of drama Renate Stamm's book on certain aspects of the Senecan influence is an example of the successful approach to these matters in terms of theatrical physiognomy, and has useful chapters on *Cambises, The Spanish Tragedy* and *Edward II.*[12] There is little of biographical interest to record, other than an account by Mark Eccles of research, impeccable, detailed, corrective, into the life of 'George Wilkins' (*N&Q*). Charles W. Whitworth, in ' "The Wounds of Civil War" and "Tamburlaine" ': Lodge's alleged imitation' (*N&Q*) supports older opinion in arguing that Lodge's play came before Marlowe's; there was always a strong case. B. P. Fisher glosses ' "Phyteus" in Marlowe's "Tamburlaine" ' (*N&Q*), and J. C. Maxwell (whose death is a great loss to all of us engaged in these studies) elucidates a puzzle in 'Peele's "Edward I" ', 1238–9' (*N&Q*). Gareth Roberts shows that 'The "Beasts of Death" in Marston's "Sophonisba" ' (*N&Q*) is owed to Lucan. G. Fitzgibbons picks up 'An echo of "Volpone" in "The Broken Heart" ' (*N&Q*), and Michael Neill suggests that 'New light on "The Truth" in "The Broken Heart" ' (*N&Q*) may be thrown by recollection of the celebrated Ratcliffe affair of 1600. Joel H. Kaplan adds 'Apuleius as a Chapman source' (*N&Q*), offering Book VIII of *The Golden Ass* as relevant to the creation and character and role of Tharsalio in *The Widow's Tears*. James A. Riddell has provided a list of 'Seventeenth-century identifications of Jonson's sources in the classics from marginalia in a copy of the 1616 folio of Jonson's *Works*' (*Ren Q*).

In the Elizabethan and Renaissance studies of the Salzburg series Philip C. Kolin has made a survey of 'The Elizabethan stage doctor as a dramatic convention' (No 41), and Lawrence Michael Bonaquist has analysed 'The tripartite structure of Christopher Marlowe's *Tamburlaine* plays and *Edward II*' (No 43). Nicolas Kiessling argues, in 'Doctor Faustus and the sin of demoniality' (*SEL*), that there is 'no structural, thematic, textual, or cultural reason why we should agree with Greg's thesis'. In 'Old Marston or New Marston: the *Antonio* plays' (*EIC*) T. F. Wharton finds them works in which Marston's 'habitual irresponsibility is most pronounced, and their stylistic opportunism simply demonstrates his incapacity to handle plot and agent in any integrated design.' In the Jacobean drama studies of the Salzburg series Andrew Clark contributes a two-volume enterprise 'Domestic drama: a survey of the origins, antecedants and nature of the domestic play in England 1500–1640' (No 49), Leonard Goldstein devotes two volumes to 'George Chapman: aspects of decadence in early seventeenth century drama' (No 31), Peggy Faye Shirley writes on 'Serious and tragic elements in the comedy of Thomas Dekker' (No 50), Charles A. Hallett on 'Middleton's cynics: a study of Middleton's insight into the moral psychology of the mediocre mind' (No 47), Winifrid K.

---

[12] Renate Stamm, *The Mirror-technique in Senecan and pre-Shakespearean tragedy.* The Cooper Monographs, vol. 23. Bern. pp. 162. sFr. 35.

Eaton considers 'Contrasts in the representation of death by Sophocles, Webster and Strindberg' (No 17), Robert W. Witt 'Mirror within a mirror: Ben Jonson and the play within' (No 46), and Ingeborg M. Sturmberger 'The comic elements in Ben Jonson's drama' (No 54); Lucette Andrieu's two-volume study of 'Dommage qu'elle soit une P . . . de John Ford: vitalité et devenir scénique de la tragédie' (No 52) is a substantial and well-illustrated account of recent productions. John Creaser's article on 'Volpone: the mortifying of the fox' (EIC) is a general study of that play as well as a learned note on the nature of Volpone's sentence and his reception of it. A. R. Braunmuller's account of ' "A greater wound": corruption and human frailty in Chapman's Chabot, Admiral of France' (MLR) is a detailed, sombre reading of that saddening drama, arguing that 'the central conflicts of the play turn on personal rather than societal or idealistic bases'. Ronald Broude has made a lengthy analysis of a familiar topic in 'Revenge and revenge tragedy in Renaissance England' (RenQ) and manages to deal with the complex issues in a clarifying and effective manner. Although Charles R. Forker's 'The love-death nexus in English Renaissance tragedy' (ShakS) is naturally focused on Shakespeare, there are many relevant observations on Webster, Tourneur and Marston. Robert F. Whitman's 'The moral paradox of Webster's tragedy' (PMLA) reviews some salient opinions of Webster's critics and invokes the terms 'Apollonian' and 'Dionysian' in discussing the form of this tragedy as 'concepts much too useful to neglect'. Larry S. Champion's 'Ford's 'Tis Pity She's a Whore and the Jacobean tragic perspective' (PMLA) sees it as 'a tragedy of a whole society as much as it is the tragedy of an individual', the affections of Giovanni and Annabella are unrighteous but are also 'intensely sincere, and the spectators are constantly required to weigh that sincere immorality against the lust, avarice, treachery, vindictiveness and hypocrisy of the society whose morality the lovers have rejected'. Margot Heinnemann's 'Middleton's A Game at Chess: Parliamentary-Puritans and Opposition drama' (ELR) is a learned account of the religious and political context of that celebrated theatrical event. J. B. Savage has demonstrated 'The intellectual traditions of Comus' (ELR) showing that 'the intention of the masque is to reveal the moral inadequacy of the happiness that the empirical world of Comus is solely capable of offering'. Finally Richard S. Peterson has made an important study of 'The iconography of Jonson's Pleasure Reconciled to Virtue' (JMRS), showing how 'ancient myth lends visual as well as verbal coherence to characterization, plot, and scene itself'; the text is well supported by plates of extremely high quality.

IX

The Later Sixteenth Century, Excluding Drama

JOHN ROE

This chapter is arranged as follows: 1. General; 2. Sidney; 3. Spenser; 4. Sir John Davies; 5. Poetry; 6. Prose. A selective review of books may be found in *SEL*.

1. General

As Frances Yates tells us in the preface to her magnificent book on Astraea,[1] the essays which comprise the work mark the culmination of a lifelong interest. The cornerstone of the book, the chapter entitled 'Queen Elizabeth as Astraea', was duly praised by D. J. Gordon in these columns when it first appeared in *JWCI* in 1947. Miss Yates describes how related interests, for example French monarchy symbolism, grew from there. The importance of the imperial theme, as well as showing off the monarchy to effect in pageants, processions, and tournaments, lies in its anti-papal nature. The author goes outside England, specifically to Dante, to find imperial spokesmen to match the anti-papal pronouncements of Englishmen like John Jewel. Her interest in visual and iconographic manifestations is, as usual, rewarding. She elaborates her theme also by quotations from the great contemporary poets, Shakespeare and Spenser, and some of the lesser talents like Peele and Sir John Davies—though in this connexion it is a pity that the latter should still be confused with Davies of Hereford. But if Protestant Englishmen thrived on the existence of a figure who could so triumphantly oppose the Pope, Catholic voices could just as easily sound a contrary note. In Nicholas Sanders' *The Rape of the Churche* Miss Yates observes that 'the pure, imperial virgin becomes the lewd worldly power, the *civitas diaboli*, the Antichrist which was against the *civitas Dei*'. In pursuing the wider implications of the imperial theme (the sections devoted to France discuss the comparative claims of the French monarchy to embody the idea, describing in detail the religious processions of Henry III), the author suggests that 'Religious royalism already has in (Elizabeth's) reign the two flavours of ultra-Protestantism or of sub-Catholicism which recur again and again in English history'. The argument and its illustrations are well researched and compelling.

Renato Poggioli's *The Oaten Flute*[2] is another book which has been

---

[1] *Astraea: The Imperial Theme in the Sixteenth Century*, by Frances A. Yates. Routledge and Kegan Paul. Plates. Pp. xvi + 234. £6.95.

[2] *The Oaten Flute: Essays on Pastoral Poetry and the Pastoral Ideal*, by Renato Poggioli. Cambridge, Mass.: Harvard U.P. Pp. xii + 340. $15.

long germinating, but sadly for different reasons. At the time of its author's death its material had been composed but not yet arranged; it comes to the press under the selecting and editing hand of A. Bartlett Giamatti, who has retained fourteen out of a total thirty chapters. Originally a Slavic scholar, Poggioli's interest in pastoral drew him inevitably towards the Renaissance (though much of the book remains beyond the scope of this review). 'The Oaten Flute', the opening chapter of the book, establishes the author as an intelligent, inspired investigator into the theme of pastoral, which he defines as the perfect expression of the evasive, the short-lived, or the would-be. He believes that its essence is neither classical nor Christian. What makes it compelling is its poignancy. Poggioli emphasizes its delicacy (it has little to do with Bacchus or Silenus) and its affinity with the elegiac. 'The Oaten Flute' ends by affirming the melic character of pastoral—its natural, not unnatural, tendency towards opera and ballet. However slight in itself, it dominates whatever genre it unites with. These essays are likely to rank with Bruno Snell's *Landscape of the Mind* as an original exploration of their theme.

Alice S. Miskimin's study of the Renaissance Chaucer[3] blends survey with speculation. She gives a fascinating, detailed account of how Chaucer and 'Chaucer' came in and out of focus in the fifteenth and sixteenth centuries. Her informative sections on the growth and evolution of the Troilus legend and the history of the printed texts, while not reversing accepted notions, assemble much previously disseminated material into a convenient whole. The chapter on Chaucer and Spenser argues effectively that the word *maker* was steadily upgraded from its position below *poet* to mean divine creator for the Elizabethan. Dr Miskimin likes to play the fashionable games of Renaissance literary criticism, and has chapters on the poetic 'I' and the 'imaginary audience'. Though stimulating and done tactfully for the most part, this sometimes has the disabling effect of making hard facts seem less so.

A Swiss-German publishing venture has produced a guide on the literature of the English Renaissance.[4] The book divides into two sections, one on prose and the other on poetry. The first section opens with an account of Humanism and ends with the Reformation; the second discusses the Renaissance and cites poetic examples, ending not quite with *The Faerie Queene* but with a note on satire. Given the limits the authors set themselves, the proportions are more or less right. Sidney's *Arcadia* receives too much space while other works too little, e.g. 'George Chapman vollendete Marlowes Fragment allerdings in anderem Geist'. The list of names heading a sub-section on prose fiction looks odd: Lodge, Deloney, Dickenson, Forde. But the German student will find the guide helpful on the whole, especially since the notes and bibliography convey a sound sense of direction.

David Cressy's *Education in Tudor and Stuart England*[5] forms part of a

[3] *The Renaissance Chaucer*, by Alice S. Miskimin. New Haven and London: Yale U.P. Pp. xii + 316. $15.
[4] *Literatur der Renaissance*, by Ludwig Borinski and Claus Uhlig. Düsseldorf and Bern: Bagel and Francke. Pp. 188. Sfr. 17.80.
[5] *Education in Tudor and Stuart England*, by David Cressy. Edward Arnold. Pp. x + 142. hb £5.95, pb £2.95.

publisher's series called *Documents of Modern History*. The editor has drawn on original sources to give a cross-section of views, extending from start to finish of the Renaissance, by educationalists and others. The generally well-chosen extracts include Ascham, Mulcaster, and Hoole, with an occasional literary exploiter like Nashe, as well as anonymous statements on matters like school governance. The editor groups his spokesmen under different sections (schoolmasters; organization and control of education; opportunity; education of women; and so forth), and prefaces his texts with a short history of the development of education and of changing attitudes towards it.

In 'A Note on the Life and Death of Nicholas Fuller (1543–1620)' (*N&Q*), Marc L. Schwarz gives the pertinent facts on this Puritan Parliamentarian and exposes the fiction of the length of his prison sentence. Fuller was in jail for nine months, not twelve years as Anthony Wood supposed from Thomas Fuller's misleading account.

2. Sidney

The peculiarity of Sidney studies this year lies in the prominence achieved by other members of the family. Robert Sidney receives the first of what will undoubtedly be many appraisals in 'A Manuscript of Poems by Robert Sidney: Some Early Impressions' (*BLJ*) by Hilton Kelliher and Katherine Duncan-Jones. Reporting the acquisition of the manuscript ('the largest body of original verse written in the author's autograph that is known to have survived from the Elizabethan period') by the British Library, the authors print a number of the poems and reproduce in facsimile two sonnets and part of a 'pastoral'. They make some bibliographical and critical observations, including a description of the manuscript's physical condition (good) and an account of its fortunes in the nineteenth century, the details of which would do credit to Wilkie Collins. To Katherine Duncan-Jones falls the distinction of being the first scholar of this century to comment extensively on the poems' literary merit and character. While Robert shares some of his brother's stylistic interests (managing them less ably than Philip), his insistent melancholy is closer in mood to Ralegh, and Miss Duncan-Jones suggests that the relationship between the two men 'may . . . prove to be of value in determining the vexed question of dating surrounding Ralegh's own poems'. She notes the dominance, with melancholy, of feelings of loneliness and despair in these love poems, and thinks that the several horrific details of physical decay may allude indirectly to the death of Philip himself. Speculating on the identity of the lady behind them, certainly not the poet's wife, she sees Elizabeth in 'Lisa' and Carey in 'Charis', and supports her 'tentative hypothesis' with biographical fact.

Next it is the turn of Sidney's sister in G. F. Waller's 'The Text and Manuscript Variants of The Countess of Pembroke's Psalms' (*RES*). Mr Waller promotes the Countess as a poet in her own right: 'between Sidney's versions and the Countess's latest revisions lie a great many variants and independent or parallel versions, all making up a rich and fascinating story of nothing less than the growth of the Countess of Pembroke's literary vocation and poetical skills'.

Sidney's niece joins the family roll-call with Graham Parry's 'Lady Mary Wroth's *Urania*' (*PLPLS*), occasioned by the acquisition for the Brotherton Collection at Leeds of a rare copy of this 1621 edition. Writing with a facility equal to that of his subject, if not in precise keeping with its spirit (e.g. 'Distressed and questing gentry appear at every turn'), Dr Parry remarks the difference in ability between Lady Mary and her uncle: 'Urania has lost the philosophic garb of the *Arcadia* and has become the central figure in an infinitely convoluted history that lacks the intellectual strength of Sidney's work'.

And so to Philip Sidney himself, whose poems have been added to the Cornell concordances.[6] Elizabeth Story Donno, in 'Old Mouse-eaten Records: History in Sidney's *Apology*' (*SP*), skilfully attempts to redress the balance between the three arts discussed in the treatise. Sidney believed that poetry and history shared a civilizing aim, as the correspondence with Languet and his brother shows; so that his robbing the 'opposition' of its arguments was an insignificant debating tactic. Miss Donno confines herself to Sidney's writings, and does not discuss the attacks on poetry carried out by historians.

The *Apology* has been edited for Indian students of English literature by Visvanath Chatterjee,[7] whose introduction and notes show an excellent grasp of idiom. Where his appreciation may be questioned is in his emphasis on Sidney's Romantic sensibility, but he displays a clear understanding of the Elizabethan critical background. Eiji Ochi lacks Mr Chatterjee's fine sense of English idiom, and as a result writes not always clearly on the engaging subject of love and discipline in 'Intrigues of Love and a Romantic Perfection of it: In the Case of *Arcadia*' (*USSE*).

Alan Sinfield reflects on the relationship of 'Sidney and Du Bartas' (*CL*), wondering how and how well they knew each other. Contemplating their references to each other in their works and in their correspondence with third parties, he concludes that 'at least in 1584, Sidney and Du Bartas knew of each other as prominent Protestant writers and probably as friends of Du Plessis-Mornay'. The conviction emerging from his essay, that the two shared 'an ardent religious faith', makes Mr Sinfield one of a growing number of critics who have affirmed Sidney's austere Christianity. A different sort of Frenchman from Du Bartas takes us back to the sphere of family interconnections in Gustav Ungerer's 'The French Lutanist Charles Tessier and the Essex Circle' (*RenQ*). Mr Ungerer prints two of the airs Tessier composed for Lady Penelope Rich, which perpetuate, in a lighter vein, Sidney's resentful pun on her married name. And here is as good a place as any to notice Dwight C. Peck's 'An Alleged Early Draft of "Leicester's Commonwealth" ' (*N&Q*).

3. Spenser

Several hands have joined together to produce *Contemporary Thought on Edmund Spenser*[8] ('contemporary' meaning modern), partly to honour

[6] *A Concordance to the Poems of Sir Philip Sidney*, ed. Herbert S. Donow, with programming by Trevor J. Swanson. Cornell U.P. pp. xvi + 624. £8.

[7] *Sir Philip Sidney: An Apology for Poetry*, edited by Visvanath Chatterjee. Bombay: Orient Longman. Pp. x1viii + 96. Rs. 10.

[8] *Contemporary Thought on Edmund Spenser*, edited by Richard C. Frushell and Bernard J. Vondersmith. Carbondale, Illinois: Southern Illinois U.P. Pp. xvi + 240. $15.

the memory of Edwin A. Greenlaw, a newly discovered record of whose seminar proceedings in the 1920s receives introductory comment from the editors. Since that was half a century or so ago, none of the contributors can quite recreate the spirit of a *Festschrift* which the editors (who pay homage to Greenlaw's pioneer work on the *Variorum* Spenser) appear to have wanted. Foster Provost comes closest in his review of twentieth-century criticism of *The Faerie Queene*, which applauds Greenlaw's concern to relate the poem to Tudor history. (Professor Vondersmith supplements this chapter with a bibliography of related studies between 1900 and 1970.) The clear voices of the century resound again—Renwick, Lewis, Hough, Woodhouse, Bennett, et al.—but the not so clear, such as the numerologists, receive short and uncertain shrift in a closing paragraph or two. With a sidelong glance at the *Variorum* A. C. Hamilton writes a sensible, discerning piece on annotation which seems to be a prolegomenon to his own annotated *Faerie Queene*. In 'Spenser Recovered: The Poet and Historical Scholarship', Rudolph B. Gottfried amuses himself with James Russell Lowell's fanciful essay of 1875 before turning to an attack on Angus Fletcher, explaining that we still have not banished the bogey of subjectivism. Unlike A. Kent Hieatt, whose chapter follows his, S. K. Heninger Jr is not one to make concessions to the modern predicament in the matter of appreciating the poet's purpose: 'We must take at face value Spenser's announcement of a foreconceit in the title, and we must accept literally the confidences about method he reveals in the letter to Raleigh (sic)'. Professor Heninger's brow-beating imperatives belie his subtle grasp of sixteenth-century scholarly premises. The closing chapter, 'Spenser's Pluralistic Universe: The View from the Mount of Contemplation' by Carol V. Kaske, attempts too much in too little space (the author promises a 'companion-piece'). Her theme is syncretism, and she examines the degree to which Spenser successfully combines the Christian, natural, and classical worlds. More than one of the contributors refers to a book published after 1970 and so excluded from Professor Vondersmith's list. Such discontinuity between the parts reinforces an impression that this volume, a valuable but not invaluable addition to Spenser scholarship, is slightly at odds with itself.

A. Kent Hieatt incorporates the substance of his contribution to the above collection into his extraordinarily wide-ranging work on Chaucer, Spenser, and Milton.[9] His aim is to find myths common to all three poets and through them to show that the concerns dominating our culture from the Middle Ages to the late Renaissance are, however altered in form, just as alive and urgent now. Marriage—with its insistence on mutual responsibility—is the main surviving myth. The author draws heavily on Cartari's emblems and relates them persuasively to some of the key moments in Spenser, with their help interpreting the violence of Britomart's unconsciousness. But it must be said that incidental points of scholarship like these are more impressive than the argument they are meant to serve. The propositions uniting Chaucer, Spenser, and Milton are so spacious that almost anything could be squeezed into them, while the subtler parts of

[9] *Chaucer, Spenser, Milton: Mythopoeic Continuities and Transformations*, by A. Kent Hieatt. Montreal and London: McGill and Queen's U.P. Plate. Pp. 292. $20.

Professor Hieatt's investigation are as remote in tone and nature from his announced theme as an epic poem is from a marriage manual. That theme is put as follows: 'What comes through in *The Faerie Queene*' is 'the sensation of loving and hating, the pathos of subjection to an emotion which is not yet shared by its object, the sense of what it is to be either considerate or thoughtless towards the sharer of an intimate relationship, what it is to woo or be wooed, or to be excited about frivolous or superficial sex'. Happy marriages, according to Professor Hieatt's Spenser, avoid such pitfalls; but according to Anthony Powell's irreverent novelist St. John Clarke, 'there is nothing sadder than a happy marriage'.

Mark Rose treads something of A. Kent Hieatt's path, but in a deliberately less scholarly fashion. His book[10] also, aimed at the less responsive student, has human appeal: 'The prerequisite for understanding *The Faerie Queene* is not knowledge of theology or history but some knowledge of people based on experience'. His recounting of the adventures of Book I (much of his study is paraphrase), in terms that make large concessions to —not to say large assumptions about—his audience, will achieve some converts but at the cost of misrepresenting the faith.

A more satisfactory approach to students' needs is A. Bartlett Giamatti's *Play of Double Senses*.[11] Though joining the infamous list of those who have given the wrong version of Rosemond Tuve's name, it engages with its subject in an able and interesting manner. Professor Giamatti is well qualified to fill in the traditional picture—especially the Continental—behind Spenser's version of epic. His chapter on 'Mutability and Health' employs the classic distinctions between medieval and Renaissance attitudes to enter into the complexities of Spenser's poem, which take up the second half of the book: 'Where Spenser surpasses his earlier English predecessors is in his knowledge that the forces of mutability are not only fatal to the city without, to the public man, but also to the mansion within, the private world'. The significance of the book's title emerges fully in the chapter, 'Pageant, Show, and Verse', where loss of faith in temporal power is shown to be replaced by faith in a more permanent power.

It would be remiss, on the subject of the Renaissance epic, not to say a word in favour of Barbara Reynolds's highly readable translation of the first half of the *Orlando Furioso*.[12] Taking her cue appropriately from Byron, Miss Reynolds handles the ottava rina form skilfully, bringing out the spirit and verve of the original in a manner that excuses the many inevitable occasions when meaning is inexactly rendered. She introduces the literary and historical background to the poem, and provides a useful list of characters and devices (including the family tree of the House of Este) as well as an explanatory index. This book will help anybody who wishes to inquire into the European context of Spenser's epic.

Few of this year's articles on *The Faerie Queene* have been written out of Robert Graves's spirit of 'terrible necessity'. Characteristically contrived

---

[10] *Spenser's Art: A Companion to Book One of The Faerie Queene*, by Mark Rose. Harvard U.P. Pp. xiv + 159. £3.85.

[11] *Play of Double Senses: Spenser's Faerie Queene*, by A. Bartlett Giamatti. Englewood Cliffs; New Jersey: Prentice-Hall. Pp. xiv + 140. pb $3.95.

[12] *Ariosto: Orlando Furioso (The Frenzy of Orlando)*, translated by Barbara Reynolds. Harmondsworth: Penguin. Pp. 828. pb £1.50.

is 'Battles that Need not be Fought: *The Faerie Queene, III.i*' (*ELR*) by Lesley W. Brill. Outside Castle Joyous Britomart errs in engaging in a needless battle which delivers her into the hands of Malecasta. The usual distinction is offered between the 'narrator', like Britomart of incomplete vision, and Spenser (who always sees what's coming). J. C. Gray's promisingly entitled 'Bondage and Deliverance in the "Faerie Queene": Varieties of a Moral Imperative' (*MLR*) is not in fact about perversions but describes the poet's expert interweaving of the themes of heavenly and earthly love.

Michael F. N. Dixon tries to define and place 'fairy', in 'Fairy Tale, Fortune, and Boethian Wonder: Rhetorical Structure in Book VI of *The Faerie Queene*' (*UTQ*). In the end, Spenser celebrates an 'idealized human' order with its implicit limitations. Other interesting definitions come from Geoffrey A. Moore in 'The Cave of Mammon: Ethics and Metaphysics in Secular and Christian Perspective' (*ELH*). Distinguishing ethics from metaphysics (i.e. behaviour from the absolute terms in which it is judged), Mr Moore identifies the classical attitudes invoked by Guyon's trial and discusses the problems they constitute for an Elizabethan Protestant. His very subtle, but generally sound, distinctions make relevant use of Dante's account of Ulysses' temptation to *esperienza*.

Gordon Braden's love of James Joyce has to do with his 'riverrun: An Epic Catalogue in *The Faerie Queene*' (*ELR*). The river's easy flow inspires Mr Braden with a sense of the naturalness of formal restraint; his style, like his treatment, is full of surprizing eddies. But we go seriously to sea with Jerome S. Dees in 'The Ship Conceit in *The Faerie Queene*: "Conspicuous Allusion" and Poetic Structure' (*SP*), who identifies the poet as a mariner, uncertain about the stars and the weather, anxious for the reader to come on deck and share the responsibility for the dangerous, epic voyage.

Two essays gaze out from the poem to the wider contemporary context. Lila Geller comes up with an interesting account of the sixteenth century's understanding of the relationship between birth and character, in 'Spenser's Theory of Nobility in Book VI of *The Faerie Queene*' (*ELR*). Spenser's 'minority view' (which insists that birth determines whether a character can perform nobly) is tempered by his belief in Providence, which may intervene, raising the lowly to noble status. In 'History, the Epic, and *The Faerie Queene*' (*ES*), Robert E. Burkhart shows how Spenser achieved the important Renaissance aim of expressing essential events through his imagination (the epic being the poetic genre most aware of history).

Turning to the minor poems, we find F. C. de Vries debating the meaning of a puzzling phrase, in 'Cuddie's "Headlesse Hood": A Note on "The Shepheardes Calender"' (*N&Q*). He takes the words to mean 'brainless condition'. In 'Colin Breaks His Pipe: A Reading of the "January" Eclogue' (*ELR*), John W. Moore Jr moves the emphasis of *The Shepheardes Calender* from mistress to god (and eventually from god to God) arguing that Colin breaks his pipe not because of betrayal by Rosalind but because of rejection by Pan. The solution is to abandon, in turn, this temporal, erotic deity for the true Deity; but Colin cannot know this so soon as the end of "January".

Judith Dundas provides a rare account of the Butterfly poem in '*Muiopotmos*: A World of Art' (*YES*), an essay which pits ethics and aesthetics against each other in a bid to explain how 'what might have been a *memento mori* poem should have turned into a celebration of life'. Of course the two are not really rivals: 'Spenser has made beauty the touchstone of value'. As well as emblem literature she investigates popular, proverbial wisdom, and concludes her deft, never solemn, argument remarking, 'Spenser has used the mock-heroic mode, not to belittle pretension, but to cherish the insignificant'.

The redeeming power of Christ is the point of all four hymns, according to Einar Bjorvand in 'Spenser's defence of poetry: some structural aspects of the *Fowre Hymnes*' (included in Maren-Sofie Røstvig's *Fair Forms: Essays in English Literature from Spenser to Jane Austen*). Challenging the view that the heavenly hymns simply refute and supersede the earthly pair, he detects 'a structural pattern that allows even the first two hymns to form by parallelism and contrast, foreshadowing and antithesis, a glorification of God in his Trinity of supreme love, beauty, and wisdom'. He demonstrates the pattern ably via the close verbal links between the passages on Cupid (merciless) and Christ (merciful) in the two hymns on love; but he perhaps overplays his hand in his account of the numerological significance of the thirty-third stanza in either poem. So might think G. K. Hunter who squares up to the numerologists in ' "Unity" and Numbers in Spenser's *Amoretti*' (*YES*). Acknowledging the discoveries made by numerology in respect of the ordering and patterning of the sonnet sequence, he insists that only a few poems can yield the calendrical significance claimed for them all.

Finally, in a note on 'Spenser and Champier' (*N&Q*), James Neil Brown remarks that the Lyons poet Symphorien Champier may have provided Spenser with an insight into how to Christianize Orphism, after the manner of Ficino.

4. Sir John Davies

Sir John Davies is the minor poet on whom this year posterity has chosen to smile favourably. The favour in question is Robert Krueger's judicious critical edition[13] ('in old spelling—not necessarily the spelling of Davies—but one that he would have been able to read without surprise'). The editor permits himself a reasonable degree of normalization. Discussing the incorrect attributions of Grosart's 1876 edition of the poems (the last complete version), Mr Krueger points out that the problems of editing Davies are less those of wrongful identification than of not discovering everything he wrote. Collected under 'Poems not hitherto ascribed to Davies' are eleven epigrammatic sonnets on the marriage of Sir Edward Coke, which are provided with a persuasive commentary—like all the poems. Supplementary remarks on attribution are made in the bibliography. Acknowledging Ruby Nemser's work on *Nosce Teipsum*, Mr Krueger has graciously invited her to share the introduction and commentary with him. They are not impressed by T. S. Eliot's view that Davies's

[13] *The Poems of Sir John Davies*, edited by Robert Krueger. With an introduction and commentary by Robert Krueger and Ruby Nemser. Oxford: Clarendon P. Pp. 1xviii + 452. £15.

gift was 'for turning thought into feeling', and assert that where emotional effect occurs, as in the love poetry, the result is inferior. But James L. Sanderson shows more sympathy with Eliot's interpretation, especially as regards the 'deep, emotional sub-structure' of *Nosce Teipsum*, in his own helpful introduction to the man and the works, *Sir John Davies*.[14] Giving the relevant social, historical, and poetic contexts, he includes an assessment of Elizabethan satire in the chapter 'Our English Martial'. On the question of attribution he is reluctant to identify the *Ten Sonnets to Philomel* as Davies's; but he will not have seen Mr Krueger's strong arguments for doing so. Like the latter and Miss Nemser, Mr Sanderson is cautious in his estimate of the poet's literary status. He resists some of the more far-fetched interpretations of the ending to *Orchestra*, but takes seriously Krueger's argument (available in an earlier essay) 'that the animosity which had led Davies to attack (Richard) Martin lingered on', causing him to remove from the 1622 edition the stanzas referring obliquely to his former friend. However, this explanation excites the impatience of J. R. Brink in 'The 1622 Edition of Sir John Davies's *Orchestra*' (*Library*). He maintains that the reasons for the change are partly organic (he deplores the 'somewhat artificial' list of poets ending the edition of 1596) and partly nostalgic (by 1622 time had modified the poem's final vision into an 'Elizabethan court of his youth'). Mr Brink believes that the stanzas concluding the 1622 edition were printed in the wrong order, and he rearranges their sequence—adding fuel to the controversy.

5. Poetry

Derek Attridge chooses an unpromising subject, that of Elizabethan quantitative experiments in verse[15]. Far from attempting to reform our opinion of such poetry, he declares that much of it is 'unquestionably bad', and that the theory behind it 'existed as an obstacle to the flowering of the Elizabethan poetic genius'. On the other hand, the question why it claimed the interest of Sidney, Spenser, and Campion deserves a full answer. Dr Attridge asserts that, contrary to the opinion of Daniel in the *Defence of Rhyme*, quantitative metre cannot be separated from the Humanist enterprise, or from the taste for 'artificiality'. He makes an attractive point in his chapter, 'The Elizabethan pronunciation of Latin', where he compares Erasmus's successful standardization of Greek pronunciation with the difficulties stemming from 'a much more deeply ingrained pronunciation of Latin'. Believing not only that Latin pronunciation took its character from English but also that Roman metres were susceptible of being moulded by native rhythms, Dr Attridge illustrates ably from individual examples. The author handles his subject with assurance, incidentally improving our understanding of the relationship of quantity to poetry as a whole.

Philip E. Blank Jr concentrates his discussion of metre and related topics on the poetry of Barnabe Barnes.[16] His methodical classification of

[14] *Sir John Davies*, by James L. Sanderson. Boston: Twayne. Pp. 170. $7.50.
[15] *Well-weighed Syllables: Elizabethan Verse in Classical Metres*, by Derek Attridge. Cambridge U.P. Pp. viii + 258. £7.70.
[16] *Lyric Forms in the Sonnet Sequences of Barnabe Barnes*, by Philip E. Blank Jr. The Hague and Paris: Mouton, 1974. Pp. 162. Unpriced.

the poems according to their forms tends to bury them beneath statistics. However, form is not to be denied: 'Barnes alone among Elizabethans includes the forms in great variety and number to set forth an assortment of lyrics in a sonnet sequence on the model of Petrarch and other Continental masters . . . deficiencies in previous scholarship about the forms are particularly evident'. He demonstrates the flexibility of the 'Italian-English' sonnet form, for example, by showing how the balance of paradox in a poem can be modified according to whether it is read in the foreign or native manner (either being subtly permitted). Several of the book's distinctions are too small to amount to much.

Salzburg Studies have sent a critical edition of Gascoigne's *The Steele Glas* and *The Complainte of Phylomene*.[17] The editor, William L. Wallace, describes the combination of Roman and English satiric traditions in *The Steele Glas*, and the significant changes of detail from Ovid in *The Complainte*. He has taken care in the preparation of his texts, but displays a casual approach to the surrounding apparatus. Among numerous errors he fails to note that time has changed Walkhamstowe to Walthamstow, and that Arthur not William Golding translated the *Metamorphoses*.

Also from Salzburg comes Joseph D. Scallon, S. J.'s study of the poetry of Robert Southwell, S. J.[18] The man, priest, and missionary excite Father Scallon more than the poet, who is cheerfully acknowledged to be inferior to any of the religious Metaphysicals. Undue originality would only disturb the poems' strictly orthodox theological basis, as this study makes clear. More questionable is Father Scallon's conviction that, far from being an outsider, Southwell shared the English government's fears of 'atheism'. Untroubled by the execution, he says: 'We are told that Queen Elizabeth lamented his death, especially after she had seen his book in which he tried to teach poets to use their talents as they ought'. But the source for this is unpromising: Diego de Yepes's *Historia particular de la persecucion de Inglaterra* (Madrid, 1599).

Edith Whitehurst Williams writes very interestingly on the Old English Legacy of 'A Farewell to the Court' and 'Like to a Hermite', in 'The Anglo-Saxon Theme of Exile in Renaissance Lyrics: A Perspective on two Sonnets of Sir Walter Ralegh' (*ELH*). Aware of the presence of French-derived words in the poems, she nonetheless affirms that 'theme and tone are dominated by vocabulary drawn from the native stock'.

The topic of satire engages R. B. Gill in 'A Purchase of Glory: The Persona of Late Elizabethan Satire' (*SP*). Gauging the extent to which an author releases himself into the persona he creates, Mr Gill, in his informative survey, compares the relaxed 'swagger' of Hall and Guilpin with Marston, whose 'seeming belief in the pose gives his dark moral judgments an intensity that most other Elizabethan satirists lack'.

Two authors try separately to rescue a poem of Chapman's from the school of 'irony'. A. B. Taylor, in 'Sir John Davies and George Chapman: A Note on the Current Approach to *Ovids Banquet of Sence*' (*ELN*),

---

[17] *George Gascoigne's The Steele Glas and The Complainte of Phylomene*, edited by William L. Wallace. Salzburg: Institut für Englische Sprache und Literatur. Pp. 246. £4.80.

[18] *The Poetry of Robert Southwell, S. J.*, by Joseph D. Scallon, S. J. Salzburg: Institut für Englische Sprache und Literatur. Pp. xiv + 236. £4.80.

quotes Davies's straightforward commendation of the poem to show that it held nothing sinister for contemporaries. Louise Vinge also cites Davies, in 'Chapman's *Ovids Banquet of Sence*: Its Sources and Theme' (*JWCI*), and casts an unusually critical eye at the person of Corinna. She looks extensively into the concepts and intention underlying each of the senses to reaffirm what has lately been disputed. 'Chapman's poem develops Renaissance Platonism by trying to give sensual love a place in its system, and by striving to reconcile the dualistic concepts of divine and bestial love'. Also on Chapman, Raymond G. Schoen notes the influence of Jean de Sponde, both on the title-page of the *Odysseys* and in the text, in 'Chapman and Spondanus' (*N&Q*).

Different areas of Drayton provoke interest. In 'The Date of Michael Drayton's First Elegy' (*N&Q*) William B. Hunter quarrels with attempts to assign the poem to the early 1620s, proposing instead 1614–15 (he supports his claim with references to Stowe's *Annales* and John Smith's *A Description of New England*). Katherine D. Carter provides a useful distinction between two kinds of praise, in 'Drayton's Craftsmanship: The Encomium and the Blazon in *Englands Heroicall Epistles*' (*HLQ*). While employing the encomium according to rhetorical custom, Drayton departs from the *blason* tradition of the French, and uses the blazon to highlight individual features in the 'author' of the epistle.

An effect similar to this in Samuel Daniel strikes Ronald Primeau, in 'Daniel and the *Mirror* Tradition: Dramatic Irony in *The Complaint of Rosamond*' (*SEL*). Mr Primeau examines the lady's statements, finding that she protests too much; from this he argues the superior subtlety of Daniel's characterization to that of the contemporary complaint genre.

Benedicta J. H. Rowe's concern is with an original example from the *mirror* tradition, in 'John, Duke of Bedford, in "The Mirror for Magistrates", Tragedy 30' (*N&Q*). Noting that the author was acquainted through Holinshed with the Burdet family, she speculates that the tribute (a belated one) which Burdet pays Bedford in the poem was inspired by family memories. Manuscript signatures help Steven W. May to find the poet, in 'The Authorship of "My Mind To Me A Kingdom Is" ' (*RES*). He identifies him as Edward de Vere, not Sir Edward Dyer, and prints the two parts of the song in the 'best version', also listing twenty-nine manuscripts that contain either or both of them. Jean Fuzier remarks the prolific nature of rural and street songs, noting their appeal to composers such as John Dowland, and prints several of them, in 'London and Country Cries: Elizabethan Life in Song and Music' (*CahiersE*). In the same journal, Eliane Cuvelier proposes Lodge's 'Truths Complaint Over England' as a source for Shakespeare ('Sur la Métaphore du Jardin dans *Richard II* et un poème de Thomas Lodge'). I have not seen a copy of Elizabeth W. Pomeroy's *The Elizabethan Miscellanies: Their Development and Conventions*.

6. Prose

Only Abraham Fraunce's reputation as a prose writer warrants placing here an edition of the hybrid *Amintas Dale*,[19] handsomely prepared by

[19] *Abraham Fraunce: The Third Part of the Countesse of Pembrokes Yvychurch Entitled Amintas Dale*, edited by Gerald Snare. Northridge, California: California State University. Pp. xxiv + 182. $8.

Gerald Snare. The editor speculates on the interest in quantitative metres in Fraunce's day, but unlike Derek Attridge (see under *poetry*) comes up with nothing more novel than Jonson's 'Abram Francis in his English Hexameters was a Foole'. Suggesting from its balance of effects (erotic, divine, pastoral, and satiric) that *Amintas Dale* was aimed carefully at the London buying public, Mr Snare shows a particular interest in the satirical tale of Daphne, and gives good reasons for identifying the three Cambridge scholars (led astray by astrology) as Gabriel, Richard, and John Harvey— the episode alluding to a contemporary literary battle. The notes give English translations of the sometimes extensive foreign passages quoted by Fraunce's polyglot commentator Elphinus. Literary feuding is the theme of Clifford Chalmers Huffman's elegantly presented 'Gabriel Harvey on John Florio and John Eliot' (*N&Q*). Mr Huffman has inspected Harvey's annotations to his copy of *Florio his First Fruites*; his understanding of the relationship between the three writers permits him to remark incisively the possibility of personal amity between literary opponents.

An attractive extra to A. F. Allison's bibliography of Robert Greene[20] (prepared for the *Pall Mall Bibliographies* series) is the microfiche of title-page facsimiles attached inside the back cover. This feature indicates, as the general editor acknowledges, that the series is aimed at booksellers and collectors as much as scholars. Correspondingly, the volume on Greene (I have not seen the one on Thomas Lodge) covers no publication after 1640. This clear, helpful, and well-prepared bibliography lists Greene's works alphabetically by title, and notes critical disagreements over authorship or purpose. Each entry contains the following: the short-title, imprint, and date; microfiche reference; collation; list of contents; selected catchwords and occasionally running titles; note of copies seen; and bibliographical references. D. Nicholas Ranson, in 'The Date of Greene's "Vision" Revisited' (*N&Q*), proposes to move its assumed date of composition from early to later in 1590. He also challenges Waldo F. McNeir's emendation of a word to 'Aeconomical' as untypical usage.

Scholars' Facsimiles and Reprints have reproduced the 1591 printing of Southwell's beautiful and moving *Marie Magdalens Funeral Teares*.[21] Vincent B. Leitch provides a short introduction, with details of the background to the original printing, and discusses the Magdalen tradition in literature. He describes the work as an Ignatian meditation, observing that the narrator's emotional, intellectual, and imaginative responses take precedence over those of Mary. .

Comic formulae in romance or prose fiction attract the attention of R. S. White and Charles Larson. Mr White, in ' "Comedy" in Elizabethan Prose Romances' (*YES*), argues that the principles of morality, justice, and delight which govern Elizabethan comic drama were taken from the prose romances rather than from 'lost' plays; he supports his contention by noting the frequent use of the word 'comedy' in prose fiction. Charles Larson strives gallantly to resolve the dilemma posed by the terrible incidents that beset Jack Wilton, in 'The Comedy of Violence in Nashe's *The*

[20] *Robert Greene, 1558-1592: A Bibliographical Catalogue of the Early Editions in English (to 1640)*, prepared by A. F. Allison. Folkestone: Dawson. Pp. 76. £9.
[21] *Robert Southwell: Marie Magdalens Funeral Teares (1591)*, a facsimile reproduction with an introduction by Vincent B. Leitch. Delmar, New York: Scholars' Facsimiles and Reprints. Unpaginated + [14], 68 fol. $15.

Unfortunate Traveller' (CahiersE). Previous commentators have tried, not wholly successfully, to find reassuring categories for the violent action; Mr Larson adds to them the medieval category of the *danse macabre* (and notes also the resemblance of Nashe's methods to those of Rabelais) for the battle episodes. Detachment from individual suffering—and so peace of mind—is achieved by alienation: easiest in the case of foreign villains like Zadoch and Cutwolfe, whose brutal fates are appropriate. But Mr Larson's argument that outrage can be modified by stylistic ingenuity, though fair, is given contrived expression. Nancy R. Lindheim looks at tradition in the prose romance, in 'Lyly's Golden Legacy: *Rosalynde* and *Pandosto'* (*SEL*). Lodge and Greene adapted Lyly's device of antithesis to their own ends: Lodge, eager to resolve the conflict between appearance and reality, moved 'towards an affirmation that in the romance world the forms of Nature combine to harmonize the two halves of this antithesis'; but Greene used Euphuism to depict 'a world of moral anarchy'. Miss Lindheim's subtleties are attractive, though they sometimes defeat her style.

Finally, James Binns appears to have made an exciting discovery, in 'Henry Dethick in Praise of Poetry: the First Appearance in Print of an Elizabethan Treatise' (*Library*). He argues that *Oratio in laudem artis poeticae*, by John Rainolds, is really an adaptation of Dethick's *Oratio in laudem poësos*, which is noticed by him for the first time. Giving a date of 1572–6, he infers from his discovery the influence of Latin composition on Elizabethan attitudes to poetry—especially as regards sacred themes. He notes in particular Dethick's *Feriae sacrae libri octo* of 1577, and prints an English translation of the dedicatory letter to this work.

The Earlier Seventeenth Century, Excluding Drama

ROBIN ROBBINS

The chapter is arranged as follows: 1. General; 2. Poetry; 3. Prose. A selective review of books may be found in *SEL*.

1. General

It is not always understood by students of literature how a Puritan could be a royalist, or an aristocrat a parliamentarian: the complexes of emotional, political, theological, and intellectual loyalties are concisely disentangled by William Lamont and Sybil Oldfield in their introductions to the extracts of prose and poetry in *Politics, Religion and Literature in the Seventeenth Century*.[1] Its eight main sections illustrate monarchism, the preliminary conditions and events of the 1630s, the Cavaliers' and Puritans' images of themselves and each other, the characters of Charles I and Cromwell, the foulness of war, and the continuation of conflict into the 1680s. Though specious misprints in some of the verse will trip the less wary, and there is no index of authors drawn on, this collection offers vivid enlightenment for the non-specialist student.

2. Poetry

From a microfilm at Illinois of the Vatican Manuscript, Philip Clarence Dust has transcribed the *Carmen Gratulans Adventu Serenissimi Principis Frederici Comitis Palatini ad Academiam Cantabrigiensem*,[2] unprinted before save for its two poems by George Herbert. The introduction discusses the manuscript (to have seen which might have benefited the many conjectural readings), its authors, historical and literary contexts, and the content of the poems themselves, saying little that is original or interesting, and some things that are simply wrong. The text is furnished with (sometimes questionable) translations, apparatus (not always explaining what

---

[1] *Politics, Religion and Literature in the Seventeenth Century*, ed. with introduction and notes by William Lamont and Sybil Oldfield. London: Dent; Totowa, N.J.: Rowman & Littlefield. pp. xvii + 248. £4.50, $12.50. pb £2.40, $6.75.

[2] *The Carmen Gratulans Adventu Serenissimi Principis Frederici Comitis Palatini ad Academiam Cantabrigiensem*, ed. with introduction, translation and commentary by Philip Clarence Dust. Salzburg: Institut für Englische Sprache und Literatur. pp. cxviii + 311. pb, no price given.

needs explanation, and in the case of the Greek poems disastrously at variance with the text itself), a commentary on matters biographical, textual and literary, various appendixes, and indexes of authors and first lines. Because of the weakness of historical argument in the introduction, and patent unfamiliarity with Renaissance scripts—especially Greek—this edition is unripe for publication.

Joseph A. Galdon offers in *Typology and Seventeenth-Century Literature*[3] a clear explanation of the view of universal history habitual to writers such as Donne, Browne and Milton. The typological interaction of past, present and future is well exemplified in the 'Nativity Ode', bestriding time in joyful immediacy. The second half of the book examines appearances of the second Adam, Eve and the Garden, Exodus, Jacob, Noah, and the Temple, in Milton and the metaphysical poets. While drawing for the most part on earlier scholars, Mr Galdon sometimes sheds his own light, seeing 'Upon Appleton House', for example, as a progression from Creation to Flood, and a passage from death to salvation.

Melissa C. Wanamaker argues in *Discordia Concors*[4] that Johnson's definition is more central to an understanding of the wit of metaphysical poetry than has been grasped. After surveying changing concepts of wit, culminating in the Augustan separation of judgement and fancy, and defining two main branches of *discordia concors* as the yoking of opposites and the perception of unity in multiplicity, she examines Donne's metaphor and paradoxical argument, Herbert's scriptural mode of allusive metaphor, Vaughan's recurring images and sudden paradoxes, and Marvell's acceptance of the universal contrariety that will only be resolved into harmony after death by divine grace. She contends that rather than praising detailed correspondence or deploring discrepancy in Milton's similes, we should appreciate both simultaneously, the complex of concord and discord being a deliberate expression of the contradictions encircled and reconciled in his cosmic epic.

Anne Ferry's *All in War with Time*[5] examines four poets' preoccupation with transience: while Shakespeare claims hyperbolically that time is defeated by art, Donne plies other weapons—scholastic propositions, the lovers' bed, their control and shaping of the expression of feeling, their refinement of passion, and firmness of spirit. Poems which pretend to return to the tradition of overt exaltation of the power of art actually celebrate the here and now, or mock a gullible posterity which expects mythic 'eternizing' verse. Jonson is shown likewise to arouse expectations of a Petrarchan poet-lover in order to defy them, throwing into prominence the gross physical figure of the real man. Ms Ferry brings out vividly how the struggle between love and time culminates in Marvell's poetry, where conventions are not merely incorporated but questioned, transformed, parodied or rejected.

---

[3] *Typology and Seventeenth-Century Literature*, by Joseph A Galdon. The Hague & Paris: Mouton. pp. 164. Dfl. 48, $19.25.

[4] *Discordia Concors: The Wit of Metaphysical Poetry*, by Melissa C. Wanamaker. Port Washington, N.Y., & London: Kennikat P. pp. x + 166. £8, $9.95.

[5] *All in War with Time: Love Poetry of Shakespeare, Donne, Jonson, Marvell*, by Anne Ferry. Cambridge, Mass., & London: Harvard U.P. pp. |xii| + 287. £6.95, $11.50.

Gerald Hammond's introduction to *The Metaphysical Poets: A Casebook*[6] unfolds the history of the term metaphysical, and recounts the fluctuations in relative and absolute popularity of the poets so labelled. In the historical sections the extracts range in quality and helpfulness from scrappy superficiality to the solidity of Addison's discussion of wit and judgement, from the maturity of De Quincey to the gush of Emerson. 'The best in modern criticism' comes with one exception from America: though all of the highest quality, only Miles and Selvin's factor analysis will jolt the student who has already looked at the usual books. The 39 *Essential Articles for the Study of John Donne's Poetry*[7] edited by John R. Roberts represent most of the deservedly well-known modern critics while not overlapping with the other easily available collections to which the editor draws attention in his preface, along with some outstanding book-length studies. The selective yet comprehensive bibliography makes this volume a good guide as well as introduction for the student. The sections on Donne's reputation, relation to the development of English poetry, use of tradition, prosody and rhetoric, and religious poetry, are fair and useful selections, though it is disputable whether the *Anniversaries* deserve as many articles as the *Songs and Sonets*, of which only four are discussed—and three of those the most over trodden by critics and students.

The theme of Dwight Cathcart's *Doubting Conscience*[8] is Donne's use of the methods of 'cases of conscience' in poems where there is conflict between the precepts of moral or religious orthodoxy and the immediate human demands of the protagonists situation, between general laws and special cases. Donne's argument's are properly neither syllogistic nor inductive, consisting rather of accumulations of alternative probabilities, just as casuists assembled a plethora of opinions from which by selective argument to concoct often shocking conclusions. In charting this confident application of reason to the unreasonable in poems such as 'The Extasie', this careful and lucid study illuminates Donne's poetic modes.

Raoul Granqvist's *The Reputation of John Donne 1779-1873*[9] presents a thorough account and discussion of attitudes to Donne's poetry and prose from Johnson to Browning which show how each generation has read him selectively, praising those elements in his richly various writings, life or beliefs which agree with its own prejudices, while ignoring or denouncing the rest. A general shift is mapped from eighteenth-century disapproval of his formal irregularity, through romantic approval of the passion in the poems, and of the man presented by Walton, to the more sophisticated relishing by Coleridge and the Lamb circle of 'difficult'

---

[6] *The Metaphysical Poets: A Casebook*, ed. by Gerald Hammond. Macmillan, 1974. pp. 254. £2.95. pb £1.25.

[7] *Essential Articles for the study of John Donne's Poetry*, ed. by John R. Roberts. Hamden, Conn.: Shoestring P.; Hassocks, Sx.: Harvester P. pp. xiii + 558. £10.50, $17.50.

[8] *Doubting Conscience: Donne and the Poetry of Moral Argument*, by Dwight Cathcart. Ann Arbor: U. of Michigan P.; Don Mills, Canada: Longman Canada. pp. [xi] + 199. $10.

[9] *The Reputation of John Donne 1779-1873*, by Raoul Granqvist. Uppsala: Acta Universitatis Upsaliensis: Studia Anglistica Upsaliensia 24. pp. 212. Kr. 61, £6.55.

poetry, and pious Victorian cultivation of the devout moralist.

Donne's persisting popularity towards the end of the seventeenth century appears from the fresh account by Mabel Potter (*HLB*) of the Dobell manuscript's contents, its sometime owner, William Balam, his literary quotations and comments on authors from Homer to Obadiah Sedgwick, and his annotations, emendations and paraphrases of Donne himself. In a general account, Paavo Rissanen (*NM*) finds the same search for love and security in the later as in the earlier poems. Raman Selden (*CritQ*) sees the paradox inherent in the legend of the incarnation, and its sanction of the mixed style, as central to the deep structure of almost all Donne's best poems, such as 'The Extasie', and expressed in 'the frequently occurring interpenetration of corporeal and spiritual terminology'. Arthur F. Marotti's essay in *The Rhetoric of Renaissance Poetry*[10] examines the movement of ideas in 'The Extasie', contending that it embodies a celebration and justification of the poet's marriage. James L. Spenko (*ELN*) perceives the thematic development and return of 'The Undertaking' and 'A Nocturnal upon St Lucy's Day', and their numbers of stanzas—seven (perfection) and five (the first spherical number)—as conscious and significant exploitations of the circle as symbol both of perfection and hope of eternity. Alan MacColl (*ES*) explains the analogy in lines 15–18 of 'Loves Growth' by a belief, expressed in a sermon, that not only the moon and planets but all stars owed their light to the sun. Frank Kerins (*N&Q*) draws attention to a Shakespearian sonnet entitled 'The Flea' by John Davies of Hereford, which adopts and amplifies Donne's conceit of the mingling of bloods in the insect as coition. Gerald Gallant and A. L. Clements (*SEL*) unweave three voices in 'The Dampe': those of the cynical, true, and Petrarchan lovers. Leishman's evaluation of the relationship of the *Elegies* to Ovid is modified by A. J. Peacock (*Hermathena*), who finds not only a greater indebtedness to the *Amores* but an eclectic drawing on, and reworking of, other poems such as the *Ars Amatoria*, and other poets, such as Tibullus. William Rockett (*SEL*) unearths the Epicurean roots of *Elegy III*'s 'Change is the nursery Of musicke, joy, life, and eternity'. The poet's stance in the *Satires* is found by A. F. Bellette (*UTQ*) to be more complex than Horace's graceful negligence or Juvenal's savage indignation, since he is concerned with the problem of his own weakness and corruptibility. Clayton D. Lein (*ELR*, 1974) shows 'The Storme' to be 'a sustained variation upon a standard rhetorical theme' exemplified in Virgil, Seneca, Lucan, and, especially, Ovid, who furnish Donne not only with the convention but with many of his details. Nevertheless, his intense concern with sin, disease and death transforms the epic storm into a cosmic battle between chaos and creation, with himself as hero. Robert Bozanich (*PMLA*) discusses Donne's sense of the vanity of his life, especially in the letter to Goodyer of September 1608, and more at large in the sermons, drawing attention to the indebtedness of the *Anniversaries* to Ecclesiastes and the comment thereon by Lorinus, exemplified in the contempt for this world to which we are exhorted in *The First Anniversary*, and the image of the soul stringing

---

[10] *The Rhetoric of Renaissance Poetry from Wyatt to Milton*, ed. by Thomas O. Sloan and Raymond B. Waddington. Berkeley, Los Angeles & London: U. of California P., 1974. pp. vi + 247. $11.

together heaven and earth in the second. Antony F. Bellette (*SEL*) develops and qualifies Martz's account of the patterns of the *Anniversaries*. It is suggested by Paul A. Parrish (*PLL*) that 'A Funerall Elegie', in its reiteration of *The First Anniversary*'s theme of the world's sickness, and its anticipatory hints of the second's emphasis on the soul's health in heaven, 'serves as an effective transitional piece between the longer Anniversary poems'. Jonathan Goldberg (*SEL*) illuminates the manifold nature of Venus profane and religious in *Paradoxes and Problemes* and *The Second Anniversary* by an analysis of allusions by Milton and Marvell. Antony F. Bellette (*SP*) shows how in some of the *Holy Sonnets* the expectations raised by the form's potential for discipline of feeling, and resolution of conflict, are thwarted as order disappears in the fragmented syntax and rhythms of violent, unanswered questioning, and how in others their initial discontinuities and conflicts are resolved in strong but stable endings, while the more contemplative sonnets' opening questions and exclamations imply the affirmations of their endings. The structure of 'Goodfriday, 1613' appears to be symmetrical round the figure of Christ crucified. On 'Batter my heart' and 'Show me deare Christ', William Kerrigan (*ELR*, 1974) examines the doctrinal background of God as rapist and Christ as willing cuckold. Dominic Baker-Smith (*RES*) demonstrates that Donne's avowed precedents for a private litany, together with his information about their status in the liturgy, were available to him in the *Antiquae Lectiones* of Henricus Canisius, the relevant part of which was published in 1608, thus supporting the dates assigned to the poem and the associated letter to Goodyer.

As Ian Donaldson reminds us in the introduction to his new edition of the *Poems*[11] Ben Jonson regarded his non-dramatic verse as 'the ripest of my studies' by which he wished and expected to be remembered. Its recent rise in critical esteem is marked by the publication of two respectable yet modestly priced editions on the same day. Mr Donaldson presents the Herford and Simpson text modernized in spelling and modified in punctuation, with explanatory notes at the foot of each page. Also provided are a table of dates, a brief introduction to the personal, public and traditional aspects of the poems, a select bibliography of editions, criticism and scholarship, and of notable usefulness—a collection of source material, being extracts from classical authors too long to include in the notes. George Parfitt's *Ben Jonson: The Complete Poems*[12] is also much indebted to Herford and Simpson, and provides a table of dates (including first performances of plays), and a list of further reading (slightly more up to date in respect of its compiler's own articles). In addition Mr Parfitt prints the second version of *Horace, of the Art of Poetry*, *Timber*, and the *Conversations with William Drummond*. Mr Donaldson's conveniently placed notes are fuller, and his print, paper and layout are much better; the Penguin is less easy and pleasant to read but contains more.

[11] *Ben Jonson: Poems*, ed. by Ian Donaldson. O.U.P. pp. xxii + 410. £6.50, $24.50. pb $2.75, $6.95.
[12] *Ben Jonson: The Complete Poems*, ed. by George Parfitt. Harmondsworth, Middx.: Penguin. pp. 634. pb £2.75.

Judith Kegan Gardiner's *Craftsmanship in Context*[13] identifies the changes in attitude and technique of Jonson's poetry. His ideal of a social order remained constant, but whereas the *Epigrammes* display a simplistic, uncompromising moral stance, *The Forrest* expresses in some places more awareness of life's complexities and difficulties, and in *Underwood* the persona is capable at times of irony regarding himself, compassion for others, and an altogether more realistic view of human nature's strengths and weaknesses. By close analysis, Ms Gardiner shows simultaneous developments in the poet's characteristic verse forms, imagery and diction, which are compared with thematic and technical changes in the plays. This may evoke in a reader more sober certainty than waking bliss, but must be commended for its careful readings and patient particularizations, its retention of critical balance through all the uneven, sometimes monotonous corpus of this scholarly glutton.

Praise of Jonson's epigrams by Robert Hayman (1628), and a second allusion to him in the anonymous *Apollo Christian* (1617) are pointed out by Jerome W. Hogan (*N&Q*). On *Epigramme XLVI*'s 'wast wife', Robert Earley (*MLN*) shows that the tentative *OED* definition (followed by Parfitt) of 'wast' as 'worthless' is wrong; as Donaldson points out, the knight is a widow-hunter, but whereas he glosses the word in question as 'old, cast-off', Mr Earley prefers 'decayed', perhaps by disease as well as age like the analogous targets of Martial, Thomas Freeman and John Heath. Peter E. Medine (*SEL*) plausibly suggests that the Shelton of 'On the Famous Voyage' is Thomas Shelton, shady translator of *Don Quixote*, elsewhere disapproved of by Jonson, and shows how the lampooning of two writers broadens into satire against Jacobean life and learning in general. Harris Friedberg (*ELR*, 1974) examines the use in Jonson's eulogies of disclaimers of his own ability and of the names of his subjects, and the search in 'To Penshurst' for 'a language of praise that will discriminate the invisible values . . . and yet tie those values to a world of fact.' The function of 'A Celebration of Charis' is taken by R. V. Leclercq (*TSLL*) to be the praise of immortal beauty, and its subject Charis both as Venus heavenly and earthly and as the three Graces, Beauty, Love and Pleasure. He argues that the first five poems are mirrored inversely by the last five with increasing contrast till the idealized lady of 'His Excuse for Loving' becomes the pragmatist of 'Another Lady's Exception'. The addressee of 'An Epistle to a Friend to Perswade Him to the Warres' is identified by Judith K. Gardiner (*N&Q*) as the 'Colbie XXXV yeres' with whom Suckling obtained a licence to leave the country for the Dutch wars in 1629. Similarities to the 'Ode to Himselfe' written after the failure of *The New Inn* in that year also support a revision of Herford and Simpson's putative dating of 1620. The structure and content of the Cary-Morison ode are compared and contrasted by Mary I. Oates (*PLL*) with Pindar's, showing Jonson's imitation to be selective and purposive, and finding in the prosodic genre itself a metaphor for the careers, 'the lines of life' both cut short and continuing, that are celebrated.

---

[13] *Craftsmanship in Context: The development of Ben Jonson's Poetry*, by Judith Kegan Gardiner. The Hague & Paris: Mouton. pp. [vii] + 208. $11.25.

Roger D. Sell introduces his learned and useful but lamentably mis-printed edition of *The Shorter Poems of Sir John Beaumont*[14] with an account of the author's upbringing, poetic acquaintance in London, retirement to Leicestershire after conviction for recusancy, and brief spell of Court favour, setting in this context the genesis of the poems. The critical introduction highlights the poetic and moral ambivalences of one who looks back to Southwell emotionally, but in practice forward to Waller, who combines didactic pretensions with the worldliest of values, often within one poem. *Bosworth-field* (1629) constituted the first edition, and thence the copy-text, of most of the shorter poems; others are reprinted here from their first appearances in print, and a few come directly from manuscripts. Mr Sell places his textual apparatus at the end as a list of emendations; it is only a fifth as long as his 'Notes of witnesses and copy-texts other than *1629*, and lists of variants'; neither is easy to use. The commentary dwells less on the glossing of allusions than on relishing Beaumont's epanorthosis, polyptoton, anaphora and asyndeton. Else-where (*NM*), Mr Sell presents evidence of recusant loyalties in the Beaumont family—even in the father, later renowned as a vicious persecutor of recusancy.

The Newberry Library copy of Wither's *Emblemes*[15] has been reproduced on good paper in the actual (pot folio) size with as much clarity as the uneven original press-work allows: Rollenhagen's engravings come out beautifully. The late Rosemary Freeman briefly places Wither's work in its tradition, relates it to his source, characterizes his outlook and techniques, and draws attention to the game he includes for selecting emblems (the dials and pointers are here, alas, merely photographed in two dimensions). Charles S. Hensley provides a full bibliographical descrip-tion of the first edition, with briefer notes on the later republications of some of the emblems. From the Folger presentation copy are reproduced Wither's dedicatory verses to the physician who cured his dysentery.

The ambivalences Christian and classical, religious and amorous in Herrick's semi-liturgical poems are examined by A. B. Chambers (*SP*), who makes the dubious inference from the date 1647 on the title-page of *His Noble Numbers* that the pious pieces were once intended to be placed first. However, not only was this title-page printed seriatim after *Hesperides* (being the last leaf of the last gathering of that work), and the title-page to *Hesperides* with the entire preliminary gathering last of all, as shown by the errata (1647 indicating, perhaps the actual date of the type-setting, and 1648 the customary anticipation of publication), but the poet himself in 'The Argument of his Book' puts the two last things, hell and heaven, appropriately enough in the last two lines.

Quarles's strictures on 'strong lines' in the preface to *Argalus and*

---

[14] *The Shorter Poems of Sir John Beaumont*, ed. with introduction and commen-tary by Roger D. Sell. Åbo: Åbo Akademi, 1974. pp. vi + 344 + [ii]. Fmk40.

[15] *A Collection of Emblemes, Ancient and Moderne (1635)*, by George Wither, with introduction by Rosemary Freeman, and bibliographical notes by Charles S. Hensley. Columbia, S.C.: U. of S. Carolina P. pp. xix + [xix] + 270 + [ix] + ix. $19.50.

Parthenia are taken up by David Freeman in his contribution to *A Fest-schrift for Edgar Ronald Seary*.[16] After exploring the many characteristics the term could cover, such as obscurity, ellipsis, disjointedness, harshly irregular rhythm, and clashing of sounds, he examines Quarles's practice in their light, finding in most of his work an aspiration to elevated religious lyricism that resulted often in lax prolixity, but in the later *Hosanna* achieved condensation, paradox, pun and conceit in lines that deserve the epithet. Karl Josef Höltgen (*N&Q*) describes the monument at Hambleden to Quarles's sister Martha and her husband Sir Cope D'Oyley, outlines the connections between the two families, and by pointing out in the twenty lines of the two verse-epitaphs nine unmistakable echoes of Quarles's printed elegies makes his authorship of the epitaphs practically certain.

The Poetry of George Herbert, by Helen Vendler,[17] comprises for the most part close readings of individual poems, and comparisons among those—both more and less successful—which employ similar devices. One such device is the 'reinvented poem', in which the argument progresses by recurrent correction of the self's facile, egotist first thoughts and responses, or of received doctrine by a redescription and reassessment of experience. Comparisons are drawn also between Herbert's poems and later imitations and adaptations, bringing out by contrast the individuality and complexity which less competent and religiously more orthodox versi-fiers could not accommodate. As the chapter on liturgical and homiletic poems shows, though Herbert satirizes the habitual quibbler, it is his conflicts with comfortable, received sentiments and teachings, as well as his internal struggles, that generate the tensions which are the very life of his more powerful poetry. Though not always pushing an analysis through to its end, and sometimes offering a reading that owes more to cleverness than felt response or the text itself, this study displays the complex riches to be gained from sensitive and strenuously intelligent reading of *The Temple*.

The dramatic searching of Herbert's poems and the certain faith of the poet are reconciled by Stanley E. Fish, in his essay in *The Rhetoric of Renaissance Poetry*,[10] in a formula suggested in *A Priest to the Temple*: the pedagogical use of knowing naivety, of Socratic questioning that pro-vokes—even implies—the desired answer. The five poems titled 'Affliction' are discussed as a group by Bill Smithson (*SEL*), who concludes after some level-headed exegesis that in a rearranged order they express a deepening conception of grief as not only a source of strength but a means of know-ing God, and a transference of attention from self to Christ. This assump-tion of constant spiritual progress, however, is one that Herbert, with his acute experience of lapses and regressions, might not have shared. Taking from the two sonnets he sent his mother, from the 'Love' sonnets I and II the 'Jordan' poems, and 'The Forerunners', Herbert's vows to reapply the 'beauteous words' of erotic verse to things divine, Misako Himuro (*SELit*)

---

[16] *A Festschrift for Edgar Ronald Seary: Essays in English Language and Litera ture presented by colleagues and former students*, ed. by A. A. Macdonald, P. A O'Flaherty and G. M. Story. Memorial U. of Newfoundland. pp. [ix] + 224.

[17] *The Poetry of George Herbert*, by Helen Vendler. Cambridge, Mass., & London Harvard U.P. pp. [xi] + 303. £9.50, $15.

examines in detail the use of such language, showing that the stock devices and epithets of the Petrarchan sonneteer are not merely transferred but transformed. Mr Himuro makes sensible reservations concerning other likely sources of such imagery, biblical, patristic, medieval and renaissance, and contrasts Herbert's free use of Petrarchan models such as Pembroke's 'Song' with Southwell's inability to escape their psychological limitations. That the eucharist provided Herbert with a pattern as well as with much of his imagery has been perceived before: the idea is extended and pursued slightly further by Elizabeth McLaughlin and Gail Thomas (SEL), who derive 'Love bade me welcome', for example, from the exhortation to the negligent, and assert the relationship of book, building and liturgy, especially the service of consecration of a church, all centring on the altar and the love-sacrifice. The authors' failure, however, to show any exact or extensive correspondences is symbolized by their confusion of lectern with font. Interesting details of the large and hospitable household in which the poet grew up are gleaned by Amy M. Charles (ELR, 1974) from Mrs Herbert's kitchen book for twenty-one weeks in 1601, which records expenditure on books, clothes, and a stream of visitors.

Setsuko Nakao's Study of Richard Crashaw[18] is an uncritical introduction for 'the sober succinct taste of traditional Japanese sensibility' which depends largely on poorly assimilated secondary sources. Innocent of literary criticism, it concludes with a special plea for Crashaw's alleged 'solution to the conundrum of existence', a bibliography, and a brief account of previous Japanese discussions of Crashaw. Michael McCanles argues in his contribution to The Rhetoric of Renaissance Poetry[10] that Crashaw tries to arouse the emotion of the sublime in his reader 'through hyperbole and paradox in which image and statement mediate a trans-human reality primarily by manifesting their own inadequacy for doing so'.

John Cleveland,[19] a brief study by Lee A. Jacobus, claims backhandedly that its subject's greatest strength was his knowledge of his audience. After a chapter of biography, Mr Jacobus proceeds to show that 'Clevelandism'—a chasing after extremities of wit at the expense of continuity and deep feeling—is a structural as well as a verbal characteristic which excludes the erotic from Cleveland's amatory pieces, and allows only fragmentary felicities in the political poems. His preference for humour over accuracy, for a quick hit over coherence, becomes effective when the only purpose is ridicule, as in the satires: in 'The Rebell Scot' (on whose metrics Mr Jacobus makes questionable observations) fun for its own sake gives way to wit that is a sharp, well aimed weapon of war. Though unamiliarity with classical literature, along with historical, semantic and yntactical solecisms, undermines confidence in Mr Jacobus, he has sensible things to say, and reminds us that although Cleveland has been justly belittled by serious writers from Dryden onwards as 'not a poet of high meaning but one of effect', some of his effects are amusing and clever.

[18] A Study of Richard Crashaw, by Setsuko Nakao. Tokyo: The Renaissance Institute, Sophia University. pp. iii + 124. pb, no price given.
[19] John Cleveland, by Lee A. Jacobus. Boston, Mass.: Twayne. pp. 162. $7.95, 3.80.

Helen Duffy and Paul S. Wilson (*N&Q*) note possible involvement with the Thorold family on the part of both Cleveland and his editor Samuel Drake, suggesting that the latter was responsible for the Osborn manuscript as well as *Clievelandi Vindiciae*.

Tay Fizdale (*ELH*) rightly insists on detaching the imaginative fiction of Marvell's 'Bermudas' from its historical sources, but in trying to define its elusive tone by treating it as a criticism of spiritual pride falls into misdirected subtlety. The Renaissance Neoplatonist inspiration of body and soul dialogues such as Marvell's is distinguished by Rosalie Osmond (*ELR*, 1974) from the medievalism of Prynne and William Crashaw, and from the politics and theology of Howell's *Vision*. Edith W. Hetherington and Norriss S. Hetherington (*ELN*) point out that in stanza 58 of 'Upon Appleton House' Marvell was thinking probably not of a compound but of a simple microscope (which, of course, goes without saying for most seventeenth-century references). On the Cromwell poems, Annabel Patterson (*ELR*) directs attention to the literary problems encountered by Marvell in the 'Horatian Ode', 'The First Anniversary' and the elegy, in the first two of which the poet revises the traditions of epideictic, rejecting with allusive echoes the idolatry of Stuart panegyrists. Milton's *Defences* are fruitfully drawn on to clarify Marvell's attitude to the possible assumption of the crown by Cromwell, and Lucan to explain the elegy. Franklin G. Burroughs (*ELN*) draws parallels between the situation of Cromwell returning from Ireland and that of Caesar addressing the Senate in the Seventh book of May's *Continuation of the Pharsalia*—each disclaiming usurpation, and professing clemency, obedience, and future service abroad—, and points out Marvell's significant reuse of the *gain/maintain* rhyme. Since 'Tom May's Death' shows clearly that neither his and Lucan's dislike of Caesar nor his desire for a popular republic were shared by Marvell, the ambivalence of the 'Ode' is not resolved by knowledge of his borrowings. Nicholas Guild (*PLL*) argues that monarchy is so discredited early in 'The First Anniversary' as heavy, malignant, slow and brittle, that Marvell cannot be advocating Cromwell's assumption of the crown, and points out that the simile of the sun's setting and rising again refers not to Charles but quite obviously to Cromwell's coach accident. A useful bibliography partly annotated, of work on all aspects of Marvell up to 1973 is provided by Gillian Szanto (*ELR*).

Another such bibliography has been compiled for Henry Vaughan by Robert E. Bourdette Jr (*ELR*, 1974), comprising an annotated survey of scholarship and criticism up to 1973. Claude J. Summers and Ted-Larry Pebworth (*JEGP*) explicate Vaughan's 'Regeneration' and his discovery of a church out of doors with reference to the ejectment of the Anglican clergy, as well as elucidating the significance of the biblical echoes and epigraph.

3. Prose

The rise of anti-Ciceronianism is briefly surveyed anew by Gary F. Grund (*TSLL*), who draws attention to the appearance of Seneca's more and familiar epistolary form, along with the Senecan style with its criteria of brevity, clarity, simplicity, pleasantness, and propriety, in the epistolar works of Hall, Howell, Breton and Markham. It was according to Senecan values that James I and VI advised his son Henry, 'In your language be plain, honest, natural, comely, clean, short and sententious ... let the greatest part of your eloquence consist in a natural, clear and sensible form of delivery of your mind.' G. P. V. Akrigg (*UTQ*) claims for the King competence as a sonneteer, pungency as a satirist (less plausibly), and vivid energy as a prose-writer with a talent for aphorism and image; one who thought—and perhaps too much acted—as a man of letters. Richard S. M. Hirsch (*ELN*) reveals that Richard Johnson rehashed his 1613 pamphlet *Look on Me London* from Whetstone. The *Vindex Anglicus* is shown by Gerhard Graband (*NM*) to have been as dependent on other dictionaries (and therefore largely a repository of 'dictionary words') as its predecessors by Cawdrey, Bullokar and Cockeram, and the later compilations by Blount and Phillips.

William A. Armstrong's introduction and notes to Bacon's *Advancement of Learning, Book I*[20] (though not as full as those of Arthur Johnston's Oxford Paperback English Text, which also gives Book II and *New Atlantis*—see *YW* 55.276) should be useful to students. The introduction gives a concise history of attitudes to learning, treating of the hold that Christian obscurantism derived from the theory of the world's decay, and of the contempt for practicality and manual labour propagated by classical philosophers from Plato onwards and thence assimilated into humanism, and draws attention to Bacon's unusual preference for the pre-Socratic thinkers. A summary and explanatory discussion of Book I remarks the revisions made for the Latin version, and asserts the book's independent status as a comprehensive and fundamental defence not only of science but of all other forms of learning. A bibliography, a summary of Book II, and a glossary are appended, the awkwardly devised textual apparatus (recording departures from Ellis and Spedding) appears at the foot of the page, but the more immediately necessary notes are hidden away at the end.

A work as (justifiably) dependent on previous scholarship as James Stephens's *Francis Bacon and the Style of Science*[21] suffers from following too hard on the heels of Lisa Jardine's book (*YW* 55.277) to have taken advantage of it. Mr Stephens begins by considering Bacon's growing awareness of the need to accommodate his work to the capacities of his audience, lengthily summarizes the already well known rhetorical tradition, and argues that Bacon derived most help in coming to terms with problems of audience and convention from Aristotle's *Rhetorica*. His view of human nature (essentially the faculty psychology of his time) led him gradually to admit the usefulness of persuasive devices so long as they remained subordinate to the content to be communicated, and did not remove the degree of obscurity which would protect his work from vulgar understandings. Mr Stephens then examines the aphorism—fit either for plain statement or to be a vehicle of persuasion—and the figurative lan-

[20] *Francis Bacon: The Advancement of Learning, Book I*, ed. William A. Armstrong. Athlone P. pp. [vi] + 153. £4, $10.75. pb £1.50, $4.
[21] *Francis Bacon and the Style of Science*, by James Stephens. Chicago & London: . of Chicago P. pp. xi + 188. £7.50, $10.95.

guage of analogy and metaphor which Bacon attempts to make respectable as a means of making new ideas comprehensible. Though this book is repetitive, and harder reading than this summary may suggest, it does contribute to our understanding of Bacon's stylistic aims.

Charles Webster's *The Great Instauration*[22] sets Bacon in a wide and rich context of ideas, reducing his prominence while not dismissing his importance. An unexpected channel through which his ideas flowed with force and significant effect was millenarianism: his justification of the pursuit of knowledge in *Valerius Terminus* (keenly read in manuscript though not printed till 1734) and in *Instauratio Magna* with the argument that Adam's fall was caused by too much inquisitiveness into not natural but moral philosophy, and with citations of the prophecy of Daniel 12:4 (emblematized on the title-page of the *Instauratio*) so chimed in with the predilections of the Puritans as to make him their chief prophet of reform in learning, as Foxe was in religion. *New Atlantis* seized their imagination not only with its broadly utopian cast but with its specific emphasis on improving the life of man by improving diet and medicine, so counteracting the corruption contracted at the Fall. Bacon's anti-authoritarian discounting of dictatorial schools of theory in favour of every fit man's inductive gathering of knowledge and contriving of improvements was obviously sympathetic to those who believed that the Bible itself was to be read and interpreted by the individual: consequently his view of the necessary coincidence of truth and utility, and his investigatory methodology and programme 'explicitly conceived in the biblical and millenarian framework', found ready acceptance and energetic implementation among the Puritan intellectuals (who included, of course, Milton) whose role in the scientific revolution it is Mr Webster's chief purpose to describe.

As with the Bayeux tapestry, the problem is to extract the history from the embroidery in Daphne Du Maurier's *Golden Lads*,[23] a romance of the Rowse-with-stoups-of-Rhenish-wine variety about Anthony and Francis Bacon which blinks the former's double-dealing as a secret agent, and quite fails to comprehend his homosexuality. The incidental comments on Francis are largely conjectural; the pictures are pleasing, if not all necessary or authoritative. James S. Tillman (*PLL*) takes up Bacon's characterization of his enterprise as 'Georgics of the mind', noting his recurrent images of husbandry, fruit, harvest and storehouse, as he develops rules of practice for labourers in the garden of knowledge. His view of intellectual history is examined by Achsah Guibbory (*JEGP*), who brings out Bacon's belief in a past cyclical pattern of improvement and decay, out of which men must co-operate to break into a new pattern of progress, a linear ascent by means of the accumulation of understanding, which, paradoxically, will complete the cycle of time by returning man to his state of knowledge before the Fall.

The man who wrote 'Hope not for minde in women' has again been

---

[22] *The Great Instauration: Science, Medicine and Reform 1626–1660*, by Charles Webster. Duckworth. pp. xvi + 630. £13.50, $29.50.

[23] *Golden Lads: A Study of Anthony Bacon, Francis and their friends*, by Daphne Du Maurier. Gollancz. pp. 288 + 30 of plates (6 coloured). £5, $10.

shamed, this time by Elizabeth Savage's reproduced thesis edition of the *Devotions*.[24] In her introduction she summarizes previous criticism, distinguishes his use here of scripture for private ends from the exegetical analyses in the sermons, and relates the work to the *Ars moriendi* tradition, and its structure, attitudes, techniques, content and style to the Ignatian *Spiritual Exercises*. The bibliographical account of the first five editions adds little of significance of Keynes, and mistakenly takes the scarce variant title-page of the first to indicate a separate issue, thus unnecessarily raising the question of priority. The text, based on that of the first edition, is supplied with an apparatus which, as well as seventeenth-century variants, records the lapses of more recent editors when it would have sufficed to acknowledge their improvements. The full and helpful commentary is accompanied by a glossary, bibliography, and indexes scriptural and general.

The Menippean tradition behind, *Ignatius* is sketched by Eugene Korkowski (*SP*), showing how it was used to satirize not only overweening intellectuals in general but theologians in particular, and pointing out the Jesuits were the target of *La Satyre Menipée* (1594), twice Englished before Donne wrote *Ignatius*. There was, furthermore, a flurry of Menippean productions during the Jesuit campaign against J. J. Scaliger between 1607 and 1621 with which Donne's work shares several characteristics, suggesting, when taken in conjunction with the 'Printer's' references to previous examples, that he was consciously working in the genre. Bruce Henrickson (*PLL*) argues that in his sermons Donne took a Thomistic way in working out a reconciliation of reason and faith, keeping the former subordinate to, but not by definition at odds with the latter. Ernest Sullivan (*SB*) reveals that all seven of the manuscript corrections found by John Sparrow in one or other of the first two issues of *Biathanatos* (*YW* 53.237) occur together in one copy at Yale, shows that they must have been made after the sheets had been folded for binding but before the reissue by Humphrey Moseley, and produces further evidence implying that 'the corrections represent an effort by the younger Donne, acting through the publisher, to improve the readings in some copies of the first issue.'

A rare recusant emblem book, Henry Hawkins's *Devout Hart*[25] has been reproduced by the Scolar Press to their usual high standard. Karl Josef Höltgen introduces it with a brief account of Hawkins's life, patrons and sources, and has communicated privately his discovery that Hawkins had not, after all, 'renounced the prospect of marriage', but was a widower. In two successive articles, Wolfgang Lottes (*RES*) provides information about Hawkins's family, life, and other works (all translations or adaptations), and a detailed study of *Partheneia Sacra*'s debts to its sources and model; of its ninefold structure in each emblematic part; of the quality of the illustrations, and of the engraver. Hawkins is shown to have exercised some skill and thoughtfulness in his reuse of others' materials and forms.

---

[24] *John Donne's Devotions upon Emergent Occasions*, ed. with introduction and commentary by Sister Elizabeth Savage S.S.J. Salzburg: Institut für Englische Sprache und Literatur. 2 vols. pp. cxxiii + 269. Paperback $17.50.

[25] *Henry Hawkins: The Devout Hart, 1634*, with an introductory note by Karl Josef Höltgen. Scolar P. pp. [xxi] + [i] + 314 + [v]. 20 plates. £10.

Thomas Hooker's *Writings in England and Holland, 1626-1633*[26] is a collection of sermons, prefaces and the like by the early New England congregationalist. George H. Williams outlines Hooker's life up to his arrival in New England in 1633; Norman Pettit discusses his theology; Winfried Herget gives details of the transcription (few of the printed sermons are in Hooker's own words: see also *YW* 53.238) and transmission of the corpus, and Sargent Bush Jr treats tentatively of the disputed canon. The volume concludes with a descriptive bibliography, a scriptural index, and an index of names.

Robert Burton's use of Æsop is detailed by David G. Hale (*N&Q*) without identifying the particular edition he read. B. D. Greenslade (*N&Q*) notes a reference to the recent publication of Hobbes's *Leviathan* in a letter dated 6 May 1651. Roger G. Clarke (*JEGP*) re-examines the sermons preached by Henry King between 1625 and 1665 in the light of differing accounts of the changes in seventeenth-century prose style by Croll, Jones and Adolph, finding less an adoption of new rhetorical characteristics and abandonment of old ones than a change of proportions in their use. David Novarr (*EA*) offers a useful introduction to Francisque Costa's study of Walton[27] not noticed in *YW* at the time of its publication. Achsah Guibbory (*ELN*) points out that the figure of Janus appears in the writings of Sir Thomas Browne as an emblem not merely of ambivalence or time but also of wisdom. Allison Coudert (*JHI*) gives the intellectual and personal context of Henry More's distaste for the Kabbala.

Hard on the heels of the reprint of William Lilly's autobiography (*YW* 55.280) comes *Familiar to All*[28], a full modern study by Derek Parker of the man and his craft, which charts the entertaining, varied life, and explains the content and relative worth of his publications with lucidity and knowledgeable assurance. We are shown the effect attributed to almanacs in the Civil War, and the consequent significance of Lilly's conflict with George Wharton. *Christian Astrology* is demonstrated to be a notable gathering and organization of astronomical lore. Lilly's political instinct is brought out in his triumphant survival of the Restoration, and his humorous relish for controversy in the witty demolition (in his seventy-third year) of rival John Gadbury. It is regretable that in omitting detailed references Mr Parker (or his publisher) seems not to expect readers intelligent or interested enough to follow up his many tantalizing allusions and extracts. Though he glosses over Lilly's thieving and impersonating, makes some errors of fact (it was at no such place as 'Holmby Hall, Oxford', for example, that Cornet Joyce seized Charles I), and too readily declines to estimate the value of his library, since prices are written into some of the extant volumes, Mr Parker gives a clear picture of an important element in seventeenth-century English culture.

[26] *Thomas Hooker: Writings in England and Holland, 1626-1633*, ed. with introductory essays by George H. Williams, Norman Pettit, Winfried Herget and Sargent Bush Jr. Cambridge, Mass.: Harvard U.P. pp. ix + 435. pb £7.50, $10
[27] *L'Œuvre d'Izaak Walton (1593-1683)*, by Francisque Costa. Études Anglaises No 48. Paris: Didier, 1973. pp. 527. 70fr.
[28] *Familiar to All: William Lilly and Astrology in the Seventeenth Century*, by Derek Parker. Cape. pp. 272. £5.50.

Sir Thomas Urquhart is known chiefly as translator of the first three books of Rabelais: Richard Boston introduces us in *The Admirable Urquhart*[29] to his other writings, the most interesting of which is his *Discovery of A most exquisite Jewel*, presenting his own theory of a universal language in which words are systematically related to things (Mr Boston relates this to Roget, but ignores Urquhart's predecessors in this field, such as Lodowyck), and 'a vindication of the honour of Scotland', containing—among others—the biography of 'the admirable Crichtoun' (reprinted here), which well exemplifies its author's intoxication with words. His *Logopandecteision*, though claiming also to be 'An introduction to the Vniversal Language', is substantially a polemic against his creditors, repetitive, but wildly fertile in parody and insult. How his passionate involvement in useless learning fitted him to out-Rabelais Rabelais in his command of the pedantic, the colloquial and the bawdy, in his thirst for the obscure and gust for coinage, is shown in a comparison of his thirty-eight loving synonyms for the penis with Rabelais's thirteen. His store of synonyms is—partly—explained by his use of Cotgrave's *Dictionarie*. Substantial extracts from the Rabelais, and representative parts of the *Logopandecteision* make this finely produced volume a pleasant introduction to one who exceeded all others (a theme phrase) not only on paper but, allegedly, in life, being present at the first fatality of the Civil War at Tolly, fighting in its first battle, the 'Trot of Turriff', and, at the news of the Restoration, dying 'in a fit of excessive laughter'.

[29] *The Admirable Urquhart: Selected Writings*, ed. and introduced by Richard Boston. Gordon Fraser. pp. 205 (4 plates). £5.50.

Milton

C. A. PATRIDES

1. General

We know about some of the books Milton owned because he himself names them; but circumstantial evidence can expand a possible list of his library considerably if rather uncertainly. Jackson C. Boswell has now ventured what he rightly describes as a 'conjectural catalogue' of Milton's library and ancillary reading,[1] yet sagely looks to the time 'when Miltonic scholarship has turned up enough new evidence to justify a revised edition'. The present catalogue, containing over 1500 entries, will prove very useful to scholars; and, given its authoritative range, should make its periodic revisions indispensable.

Seven lectures delivered in November 1974 during the tercentenary celebrations at Leipzig's Karl Marx University are now printed in the East German ZAA. The first lecture, Georg Seehase's 'John Milton: der Dichter der englischen bürgerlichen Revolution', sets the stage with a survey of Milton's reportedly anti-feudalist activities. Later, Helmut Findeisen in '"Man Naturally Born Free" zu Miltons Prosaschriften' points to the obvious fact that the Miltonic and Communist ideologies are hardly identical; Dorothea Siegmund-Schultze in 'Milton und Toland' lists some reprehensible materialist tendencies; while Horst Höhne in 'Peter Hacks' Adam und Eva, Milton und das Verarbeitung der Mythen' demonstrates how a recent comedy (1972) reduced the epic in order to make it palatable to Communists. The remaining three lectures, equally amusing, are noticed below.

A single volume of Milton Studies a year suffices to earn our gratitude; but in 1975 two volumes were made available: one under the supervision of two guest editors, Albert C. Labriola and Michael Lieb;[2] the other, under that of the usual editor, James D. Simmonds.[3] Most of the essays are noticed below, but here one may record three general studies: in the Labriola-Lieb volume, B. Rajan's suggestive examination of 'The Cunning Resemblance' or the deployment of parody in several of Milton's poems; and in the Simmonds volume, G. Stanley Koehler's wide-ranging survey of

---

[1] Milton's Library: A Catalogue of the Remains of John Milton's Library and an Annotated Reconstruction of Milton's Library and Ancillary Readings, by Jackson Campbell Boswell. New York and London: Garland Publishing, Inc. pp. xv + 264. $28.
[2] Milton Studies VII–'Eyes Fast Fixt': Current Perspectives in Milton Methodology–edited by Albert C. Labriola and Michael Lieb. Pittsburgh: University of Pittsburgh Press. pp. xii + 311. $19.95.
[3] Milton Studies VIII, edited by James D. Simmonds. Pittsburgh: University of Pittsburgh Press. pp. 291. $18.95.

'Milton and the Art of Landscape' and John Spencer Hill's speculative contemplation of 'Poet-Priest: Vocational Tension in Milton's Early Development'. Ralph W. Condee's *Structure in Milton's Poetry* delineates the poet's eventual mastery of the technique of 'functional structure', i.e. the progressive movement of the given poem 'from initial perturbation to ultimate resolution.[4] This movement is embodied at its best in *Paradise Lost* and with varying success in the minor poems, *Samson*, and the shorter epic. Condee's thesis is concerned with the total development of Milton's poetry as it advances toward the fusion of 'extra-poetic experience, traditional form, and poetic structure'. There is no evidence that Condee is even remotely interested in the current obsessions, and his structuralism derives from Aristotle, Crane, and Woodhouse, rather than from Lévi-Strauss, Barthes, or Donald Bouchard. Such an approach is in many ways old-fashioned, but resting as it does on a thorough familiarity with classical literature, it is likely to remind us of the grievous loss we suffer in our pursuit of alien gods. *Structure in Milton's Poetry* is a serenely articulated, economically argued, and brilliantly suggestive invitation to reconsider the quintessence of Milton's achievement.

Idolaters of Milton do not always respond sympathetically to Blake. Whether vexed by a misconstrued remark in *The Marriage of Heaven and Hell* or stunned by the exuberant rhetoric of *Milton*, they venture generalisations sometimes phrased with telling irritation. Now, however, Joseph A. Wittreich Jr has rendered such jejune responses obsolete. Thoroughly familiar with Milton and Blake alike, and sympathetic to both in equal measure, Wittreich provides in *Angel of Apocalypse: Blake's Idea of Milton* the most authoritative even, indeed, the most definitive—discourse on the subject to date.[5] Written with impressive clarity and argued with persuasive conviction, *Angel of Apocalypse* begins with a ringing declaration of Blake's 'profound sense of tradition' and advances to a detailed explication of Milton's presence in it. Three sustained chapters comment at length on Blake's portrayals of Milton, on his Milton illustrations, and on his view of Milton as a revolutionary, while the epilogue suggestively encourages extensions by others of the theory of influence examined here. Blake's portrayals of Milton are observed to be apocalyptic in their thrust and ambiguous in their nature, resulting in a mythologised Milton regarded as worthy of apotheosis because he had felt, yet tried to cast off, 'the anxiety of influence'. The Milton illustrations are discerned to be at once interpretive and corrective, involving in the designs for *Paradise Lost* an emphasis on the poet's visionary experience, and in those for *Paradise Regained* a proclamation of the poet's redemption of the Christian precepts which the 'terrifying theology' of the longer epic had perversely tried to reinforce. The revolutionary Milton, moreover, is said to be not the destructive political fanatic but the constructive artist who re-creates the

---

[4] *Structure in Milton's Poetry: From the Foundation to the Pinnacles*, by Ralph Waterbury Condee. University Park, Pa., and London: Pennsylvania State University Press, 1974 (actually published in 1975). pp. v + 202. $12.50; £7.55.
[5] *Angel of Apocalypse: Blake's Idea of Milton*, by Joseph Anthony Wittreich Jr. Madison: University of Wisconsin Press. pp. xxiii + 332. $15.

creative past, liberating himself through the very tradition which appears only to confine. Wittreich's sensitive study of a major poet's imaginative response to a major poet includes, among many other felicities, forty-five plates.

In another enterprise, *Milton and the Line of Vision*, Wittreich collects eight essays by as many contributors in order to provide not simply eight points of view but 'a collective essay in criticism.[6] The stated emphasis is on 'poetic relationships'—those of Milton with his predecessors, and those of Milton's successors with Milton—in order to examine the nature and dimensions of 'the line of vision', i.e. 'the tradition of prophecy' which Wittreich in his own contribution opposes to the 'line of wit' represented by Donne, Dryden and Pope. But a collection of essays, however coherent in theory, does not always unite in practice. Donald R. Howard, in the opening essay on Chaucer, undermines the editor's intent by suggesting a poetic influence on Chaucer's part which, not surprisingly, transcends all categories, be they lines of vision or of wit. Kathleen Williams discourses next, and most persuasively, on 'Milton, Greatest Spenserian'; yet she, too, eschews categories by reminding us *inter alia* of Pope's part in 'the line of vision', witness in particular the 'magnificent prophetic evocation' of his *Dunciad*. But even if 'the tradition of prophecy' is far broader than we are initially led to credit, the eight essays should be accepted as excellent contributions on the more immediate aim of the collection to elucidate 'poetic relationships'. The essays on Chaucer and Spenser—like the subsequent ones on Sidney (by S. K. Heninger, Jr.), Milton himself (by the editor), Blake (by Jackie DiSalvo), Wordsworth (by James Rieger), the Shelleys and Byron (by Stuart Curran), and modern American poetry (by Joan Webber)—are alike major contributions to our understanding of the towering presence of Milton within English poetry. They will generate further studies; and so far, certainly, we will be (as we already are) much indebted to Wittreich's editorial labours.

Equally concerned with poetic relationships is A. Kent Hieatt whose study of 'mythopoeic continuities and transformations' embraces Spenser and Milton (see above). Hanns Hammelmann's *Book Illustrators in Eighteenth-Century England* (Yale University Press) lists the principal works relevant to Milton's poetry.

Helen Barolini casually joins 'Milton in Rome' (*SAQ*) but revisits territory only too familiar. Robert T. Fallon in 'John Milton and the Honorable Artillery Company' (*MiltonQ*) denies that the poet was ever a member of the military unit. William Kerrigan in 'The Heretical Milton: From Assumption to Mortalism' (*ELR*) energetically speculates that Milton's deviation from orthodoxy was dictated by his artistic aims, and argues in profuse detail the consequent transformation of mortality 'into a perfection of Ovidian metamorphosis'.

The oddest edition of Milton's poetry for some time is D. J. Enright's strictly personal collection of excerpts.[7] Not only are the major poems

[6] *Milton and the Line of Vision*, edited by Joseph Anthony Wittreich Jr. Madison: University of Wisconsin Press. pp. xxi + 278. $17.50.
[7] *A Choice of Milton's Verse*, selected by D. J. Enright. London: Faber. pp. 128. £3.50; pb £1.25.

reduced ruthlessly, but among the shorter poems *L 'Allegro* and *Il Penseroso* are represented by some fifty lines each, and *Lycidas* is clipped by one third. What purpose is served by such indiscriminate slaughter?

2. The Minor Poems

The *Cambridge Milton for Schools and Colleges*, begun in 1972 under the general editorship of J. B. Broadbent (*YW* 53.243), now focuses its attention on nine minor poems variously alloted to five editors.[8] Winifred Maynard provides a straightforward introduction to the *Nativity Ode*, promptly followed by Broadbent's well-attested fondness for dangling quotations from a variety of sources, brief remarks, unlikely yet intriguing juxtapositions, and the like. David Aers next annotates *The Passion, Upon the Circumcision*, and *On Time*; Winifred Maynard pauses to consider *At a Solemn Music*; Leona Sage attends to *L 'Allegro* and *Il Penseroso*; Peter Mendes covers familiar ground in relation to *Arcades* and *Comus*; while Broadbent applies his multiple references to *Lycidas*. In all, the quotation from Rilke below the title page of this self-effacing volume is not nearly as relevant here as it is to the erratic volumes already devoted to *Paradise Lost*: 'Wehe, wo sind wir? Immer noch freier . . . '

The *Epitaphium Damonis* provides the starting point of an adventurous 'psycho-biographical perspective' by John T. Shawcross in 'Milton and Diodati: An Essay in Psychodynamic Meaning' (*MiltonS*). The total evidence of Milton's life, we are assured, suggests 'a latent homosexuality which on occasion might emerge and a homoerotic personality'. But the evidence is in fact marvellously bent to serve a predetermined theory, best evident in a note about Satan's whisper to Beelzebub—'Sleepst thou Companion dear . . . ?' (*Par. Lost*, V, 673)—where the tone and language suggest, at least to Shawcross, 'a homosexual attitude'. Good God!—unless he too . . . ?

Mother M. Christopher Pecheux remarks perceptively on the central rôle of 'The Image of the Sun in Milton's *Nativity Ode*' (*HLQ*). The same poem also concerns two of the contributors to *Fair Forms*:[9] Maren-Sofie Røstvig, who dwells on 'the conceptual richness of the structures selected by Milton as appropriate', and H. Neville Davies, who attends to 'the symbolism of the stanza numbers'. The predictable interest in both cases is numerology. Far more responsibly, Philip Rollinson in 'Milton's Nativity Poem and the Decorum of Genre' (*MiltonS*) invokes several precedents to establish that the poem is not an ode but a literary hymn.

The twin lyrics have elicited two essays: Stanley E. Fish's argument, in 'What It's Like to Read *L 'Allegro* and *Il Penseroso*' (*MiltonS*), that while the one poem permits 'freedom from care', the other imposes a 'continually exerted pressure'; and Stephen C. Behrendt's discriminating exposition, in 'Bright Pilgrimage: William Blake's Designs for *L 'Allegro* and *Il Penseroso*' (*ibid*.), of a major poet's response to a major poet.

[8] *John Milton: Odes, Pastorals, Masques*, general editor J. B. Broadbent. Cambridge: Cambridge University Press. pp. xii + 240. pb £1.25.
[9] *Fair Forms: Essays in English Literature from Spenser to Jane Austen*, edited by Maren-Sofie Røstvig. Cambridge: D. S. Brewer.

Marcia Landy in an essay not yet noticed here, 'Language and Mourning in *Lycidas*' (*AI* for 1973), reads the poem as 'a series of transformations' which lead by way of the poet's exploration of language to its re-creation in the reader's experience. W. K. Thomas in 'Mouths and Eyes in *Lycidas*' (*MiltonQ*) endeavours to dismiss every 'troublesome metaphor' by seeing in 'blind mouths' (l. 119) only rhetorical spokesmen, and in 'eyes' (l. 139) merely flower buds. Alberta T. Turner examines 'the convention of academic miscellanies' to which *Justa Edouardo King*, the volume which included *Lycidas*, belongs (*YES*). Karl E. Felsen annotates that vexing two-handed engine yet again (*MiltonQ*), while Edward Le Comte in *Poet's Riddles*[10] revises an essay on the same topic (from *SP* for 1950 and 1952) even as he revisits an essay on the haemony passage in *Comus* (*PQ* for 1942).

Charlotte F. Otten also studies 'haemony', and in the light of the period's herbals identifies it as the potent plant 'andros-haemon' (*ELR*). J. B. Savage in '*Comus* and its Traditions' (*ELR*) places the poem within the context of the formal masque and studies its Platonic contours. Stewart A. Baker in 'Eros and the Three Shepherds of *Comus*' (*Rice University Studies*) argues with stylistic elegance that the masque advances though a process of 'transformation and transvaluation' to an exploration of the rôle of the poet, of poetry, and of language. Kathleen M. Swain notes 'an Ovidian Analogue for *Comus*', i.e. the tale of Picus and Canens in *Metamorphoses*, XIV, 320–434 (*MiltonQ*). Rosemary K. Mundhenk in 'Dark Scandal and the Sun-Clad Power of Chastity: The Historical Milieu of *Comus* ' (*SEL*) revisits the Castlehaven scandal (see Barabara Breasted's essay as noticed in *YW* 52.237) to argue the immediate appropriateness of the masque's celebration of chastity. Annabel Patterson in '*L'Allegro, Il Penseroso* and *Comus*: The Logic of Recombination' (*MiltonQ*) notes, and interestingly endeavours to account for, the echoes of the two companion poems in the masque. *Comus* also elicits two essays in Earl Miner's collection *Illustrious Evidence*:[11] 'The Music of *Comus*', where Louis L. Martz discourses on the masque's several levels of 'meaning', and 'Problem Solving in *Comus*', where Stanley E. Fish is concerned as usual with the reader's—i.e. Fish's own—response. Finally, Julian Lovelock's 'casebook' on *Comus* and *Samson Agonistes*[12] reprints some early criticism on the masque, notably Leigh Hunt's inconsequential thoughts (1815), as well as five modern essays by A. S. P. Woodhouse, J. B. Broadbent, Rosemond Tuve, C. L. Barber, and A. E. Dyson.

So far as the sonnets are concerned, William B. Hunter, Jr, fixes the date of Sonnet VII in December 1631 (*ELN*); Dixon Fiske studies 'The Theme of Purification in Milton's Sonnet XXIII' (*MiltonS*) and concludes that its subject is the poet's second wife, Katherine Woodcock; while Charles E. Goldstein in 'The Hebrew Element in Milton's Sonnet XVIII'

---

[10] *Poets' Riddles: Essays in Seventeenth-Century Explication*, by Edward Le Comte. Port Washington, N.Y.: Kennikat Press. pp. xiv + 189. $10.
[11] *Illustrious Evidence: Approaches to English Literature of the Early Seventeenth Century*, edited by Earl Miner. Berkeley: University of California Press. pp. xxiii + 135. $9.50.
[12] *Milton: 'Comus' and 'Samson Agonistes'—A Casebook*, edited by Julian Lovelock. London: Macmillan. £2.50; pb £1.25.

(*MiltonQ*) reads the sonnet 'Avenge, O Lord' as 'a kind of traditional Hebrew lament or call for revenge'—which, one is tempted to propose, is neither here nor there.

3. 'Paradise Lost'

The epic is now available in a 'Norton Critical Edition', edited by Scott Elledge.[13] Compressed within the edition's covers are an introduction, the text of the poem with extensive notes, selections from the prose inclusive of *De doctrina christiana*, extracts from the Bible, 'Background Notes on Important Concepts and Topics in *Paradise Lost*', extracts from critics, and a bibliography. The editor's problems must have been daunting. In the event, the Biblical selections encompass passages from a variety of books, some in the Authorised Version, others in the New English Bible; the 'Background Notes' move quickly through The Universe, Physiology and Psychology, Reason, and the like; while the critics are represented by Northrop Frye, Stanley Fish, Albert Cook, Christopher Ricks, *et al.*, with a backward glance at Voltaire, Jonathan Richardson, Dr Johnson, and Coleridge. Ambitious as the new edition is, teachers would be well advised to test its usefulness against their particular needs.

Is *Paradise Lost* a poem 'in which theology is basic'? The claim is perhaps unfashionable, and will in all likelihood irritate many readers of Milton. Yet it is advanced with utter conviction by Austin C. Dobbins in *Milton and the Book of Revelation*.[14] The first sustained study of the epic's apocalyptic burden to date, the book is dedicated to the propostion that the events pertaining to the 'heavenly cycle'—the exaltation of the Son, the War in Heaven, the creation of Sin and Death, and the earthbound activities of the infernal trinity are based on the Bible, particularly (but not exclusively) on the Book of Revelation and its interpretation by major theologians of the time. The conclusions are articulated lucidly enough, starting with the first chapter's demonstration that the controversial word 'begot' (V, 603) refers to the Son's literal exaltation in Heaven. So, thereafter, other major dimensions of the poem are explicated in the light of Renaissance commentaries on Revelation; and it is telling that nearly one quarter of this slim volume is comprised of detailed references to primary and secondary sources. The emphasis on Milton's partiality to 'traditional Christianity' will not please everyone; and Christopher Hill, himself partial to the radicals of Milton's age, has already registered his dissent (in *English*, Spring 1976). At the very least, however, Dobbins has alerted us to a neglected dimension of the poem's background, while at best, he has written a study which readers of Milton will disregard to their disadvantage.

Neither the classical nor the Hebraic burden of *Paradise Lost* has been studied to date with the sophistication each deserves. It is certainly to be

[13] *'Paradise Lost': An Authoritative Text, Backgrounds and Sources, Criticism*, edited by Scott Elledge. 'A Norton Critical Edition': New York: W. W. Norton & Co. pp. xxiv + 546. $15. pb $4.95.
[14] *Milton and the Book of Revelation: The Heavenly Cycle*, by Austin C. Dobbins. Studies in the Humanities, No. 7, Literature. University, Ala.: University of Alabama Press. pp. vi + 170. $6.75. pb $2.95

regretted that the investigation of the poem's classical background in depth by Davis P. Harding, in *The Club of Hercules* (1962), has not been extended by others. The Biblical background, it is true, has elicited the attention of the formidable Harris F. Fletcher; but his studies, published half a century ago (1926–30), require drastic reconsideration. A gentle effort in that direction is now ventured by Kitty Cohen, who interestingly remarks on some of the Hebraic connotations in the poem's vision of Hell, Heaven, Paradise, and post-lapsarian history.[15] But the subject, enormously complex as it is, demands stupendous learning and talents of co-ordination which Mrs Cohen does not possess. Her generalisations are particularly perilous, not least when she proposes that *Paradise Lost* contains elements distinctly 'more hebraic than Christian'. Are we to understand that Milton's Christianity was misplaced en route?

The number of *ZAA* devoted to Milton includes three lectures on the epic. Anselm Schlösser in '*Paradise Lost* als Erbeproblem' isolates aspects of the poem which a Communist may not find utterly abhorrent; Günther Klotz in 'Biblische Figuration und irdische Notwendigkeit zu Miltons *Paradise Lost*' eclectically studies some of those same aspects; while Leonard Goldstein in 'The Good Old Cause and Milton's Blank Verse' invokes Marxist dialectic to argue ever so deviously that Milton's rejection of rhyme was a 'fundamentally political' gesture. Rhyme, it appears, was the legacy of those capitalist/feudalist rascals.

The two volumes of *Milton Studies*[2, 3] jointly contain ten studies of *Paradise Lost*. John M. Steadman in 'The Epic as Pseudomorph: Methodology in Milton Studies' remarks on the extent to which our various techniques of interpretation are necessarily 'interrelated and complementary'. Ernest Häublein in 'Milton's Paraphrase of Genesis: A Stylistic Reading of *Paradise Lost*, Book VII' analyses in profuse detail the poet's paraphrastic techniques in the light of the Vulgate, the Geneva Bible, and the Authorised Version. Jason P. Rosenblatt in 'The Mosaic Voice in *Paradise Lost*' delineates the implications for the poem of the Moses-Christ typology. Michael Lieb in '*Paradise Lost* and the Myth of Prohibition' attempts a sojourn in the poem's mythic dimensions. Albert C. Labriola in 'The Aesthetics of Self-Diminution: Christian Iconography and *Paradise Lost*' studies the poem's deployment of several basic iconographic patterns. Leonora L. Brodwin in 'The Dissolution of Satan in *Paradise Lost*' tries— but fails—persuasively to argue that the poem's eschatology is 'unquestionably Socinian'. John T. Shawcross dwells briefly on 'The Rhetor as Creator in *Paradise Lost*'. Nicholas R. Jones in '"Stand" and "Fall" as Images of Posture in *Paradise Lost*' perceptively studies the two words within their physical/metaphysical context. Beverly Sherry in 'Speech in *Paradise Lost*' fully demonstrates the deterioration of language after the Fall. Desmond M. Hamlet in 'Recalcitrance, Damnation, and the Justice of God in *Paradise Lost*' valiantly defends Milton's God by shifting our attention to divine justice; but, alas, Milton's God keeps on *talking*.

Among the general studies of the epic, Michael McCanles in '*Paradise*

---

[15] *The Throne and the Chariot: Studies in Milton's Hebraism*, by Kitty Cohen. The Hague and Paris: Mouton. pp. xii + 194. Dutch Guilders 44.

Lost and the Dialectic of Providence'[16] considers Milton's aspiration to
merge several modes of discourse within a providentially-sustained vision.
Peter A. Fiore in ' "Account Mee Man": The Incarnation in *Paradise Lost*'
(HLQ) glances in passing at the extremely complex background to one of
Milton's central tenets. Margaret E. Shaklee in 'Grammatical Agency and
the Argument for Responsibility in *Paradise Lost' (ELH)* speculates on the
possibility that the poem's grammatical structures reflect moral norms.
S. A. Demetrakopoulos in 'Eve as a Circean and Courtly Fatal Women'
(MiltonQ) shrouds Milton's heroine in fashionable terminology not calculated to carry conviction, e.g.: 'When Eve is active, independent, an
individual in her own right, she becomes cosmically castrating, the original,
archetypal *vagina dentata'*—and so on. Dennis Berthold in 'The Concept of
Merit in *Paradise Lost' (SEL)* reconsiders the poem's twenty-one uses of
the word both in their immediate contexts and in the prose; but he can
hardly compete with the delightful wordplay in the late Merritt Y. Hughes's
'Merit in *Paradise Lost' (HLQ* for 1967). Melinda G. Kramer in 'Taking the
Solitary Way through Eden: An Allegorical Reading of *Paradise Lost' (The
Gypsy Scholar*, 1974) does not fulfil the threat in her title but does read
the poem after an endearingly naïve fashion.

Claude E. Wells in 'Milton's "Vulgar Readers" and "The Verse" '
(MiltonQ) tries to come to terms with the belligerent statement prefixed
to *Paradise Lost*. Jason P. Rosenblatt in ' "Audacious Neighborhood":
Idolatry in *Paradise Lost*, Book I' *(PQ)* examines the Pauline burden of
Milton's thought. James A. Freeman considers the classical antecedents to
Pandemonium *(CompL)*. Four studies are concerned with Book III:
Leland Ryken in 'Milton's Dramatization of the Godhead in *Paradise Lost*'
(MiltonQ) argues that the poem's deity is consistently 'indefinite' because
Milton adhered to the Biblical model of blurring the allocation of any
given divine 'role' to the Father or to the Son; George E. Miller in 'Stylistic
Rhetoric and the Language of God in *Paradise Lost*, Book III' *(Lang&S)*
concludes that a study of Milton's rhetorical figures suggests that he
created 'a distinctive poetic style for his God'; Franklin R. Baruch in
'Milton's Blindness: The Conscious and Unconscious Patterns in Autobiography' *(ELH)* considers the opening lines of Book III as revealing Milton's
use of personal details to advance his artistic vision; and Michael Lieb
revisits a familiar battleground in '*Paradise Lost*, Book III: The Dialogue in
Heaven Reconsidered' *(Renaissance Papers 1974)*—but his casual remarks
leave us as we were before, puzzled.

R. D. Bedford in 'Similes of Unlikeness in *Paradise Lost' (EIC)* argues
persuasively that the poem's imagery attests the Fall even while it anticipates the redemptive process. Georgia R. Christopher in 'The Verbal Gate
to Paradise: Adam's "Literary Experience" in Book X of *Paradise Lost*'
(PMLA) glances at the 'protevangelium' of Genesis 3.15 which other
scholars have noted far more astutely. Marjorie B. Garber enriches our
current interest in the visual arts with a comparative study of 'Fallen
Landscape: The Art of Milton and Poussin' *(ELR)*. John T. Shawcross

---

[16] In his *Dialectical Criticism and Renaissance Literature*. Berkeley: University of
California Press. pp. xvii + 278.

revisits 'The First Illustrations for *Paradise Lost*' in 1688 (*MiltonQ*) *pace*
Suzanne Boorsch (see *YW* 53.247); while Judith F. Hodgson in 'Satan
Humanized: Eighteenth-Century Illustrations of *Paradise Lost*' (*Eighteenth-
Century Life*, 1974) reconsiders the artists from Medina to Fuseli to
suggest how their presentation of Satan dislocated the period's 'aesthetic
hierarchy'. But students of Milton's illustrators will be especially interested
in William Feaver's well-written and handsomely illustrated study of *The
Art of John Martin*.[17] The author, remarking on the concurrent exhibition
of Martin's work at London's Hazlitt, Gooden & Fox (*Observer*, 2 Nov.),
notes that the illustrations of *Paradise Lost* 'were extraordinarily successful because in them [Martin] transcended his copybook neoclassical
sources and engineered visions of infinity'.

Four diverse items may also be recorded. Aleida Assman in 'Vom ver-
lustigten Paradeiss zum Verlorenen Paradies' (*Archiv*) authoritatively surveys the major German translations to our day, from Theodor Haak's
(*c.* 1670) and Jacob Bodmer's (1724) to Hans Heinrich Meier's (1969).
Christopher Bentley in 'The Earliest Milton Word-Index' calls attention
to *A Verbal Index to Milton's 'Paradise Lost'* (1741), almost certainly
compiled by Alexander Cruden (*MiltonQ*). Concetta C. Greenfield in 'S.
M. Eisenstein's *Alexander Nevsky* and John Milton's *Paradise Lost*: A
Structural Comparison' (*MiltonQ*) discourses on the two works in terms of
montage, applying the Russian director's celebrated remarks on Milton (in
The Film Sense, translated by Jay Leda, 1943). Galbraith M. Crump's
The Mystical Design of 'Paradise Lost' (Bucknell University Press) was not
available for review.

4. 'Paradise Regained' and 'Samson Agonistes'

The fourth volume of the *Variorum Commentary on the Poems of John
Milton*, devoted to *Paradise Regained*,[18] is the third to be published (for
Volume I on the Latin, Greek and Italian poems, see *YW* 51.233; and for
Volume II on the minor poems in English: *YW* 53.241). The editor of the
present venture is Walter MacKellar, who knows which readings of the
poem to endorse, and which to bypass in stony silence. He is assisted by
Edward R. Weismiller who is expressly responsible for a hundred-page
essay on 'Studies of Style and Verse Form in *Paradise Regained*'. The essay
is at once broadly bibliographical and distinctly personal.

A. B. Chambers in 'The Double Time Scheme in *Paradise Regained*'
(*MiltonS*) authoritatively studies the poem's rectilinear and circular contours.

Wedges and Wings, Burton J. Weber's study of *Paradise Regained*,[19]
looks at the arrangement of the materials in the poem and asks, 'Can

---

[17] *The Art of John Martin*, by William Feaver. pp. 360, with 166 illustrations
Oxford: The Clarendon Press. £7.
[18] *A Variorum Commentary on the Poems of John Milton*, general editor Merrit
Y. Hughes. Vol. IV: *Paradise Regained*, edited by Walter MacKellar. New York:
Columbia University Press; London: Routledge. pp. xxiv + 379. £9.50.
[19] *Wedges and Wings: The Patterning of 'Paradise Regained'*, by Burton J. Weber
Carbondale and Edwardsville, Ill.: Southern Illinois University Press. London and
Amsterdam: Feffer and Simons, Inc. pp. xiii + 130. $10.

temperance account for the divisions of these arguments? Magnanimity?
The Platonic tripartite soul?' His answer is repeated from a previously
published essay (see *YW* 52.242): each day's temptation—and each sub-
division of each temptation—constitutes 'a test of the full neo-Platonic
tripartite soul'. Four chapters are now added to elucidate the 'wedges' in
the pattern, while two more chapters delineate the 'wings' of broader
issues. The contrast with his earlier book on *Paradise Lost*, also noticed in
these pages (*YW* 52.239), is clearly marked. Gratuitous polemics have now
been displaced by a thoughtful and constructive reconsideration of the
views of other readers, while the style has been lifted from the uninspiring
structures so generously evident before. The argument now advances
lucidly, often abandoning the overall theory to focus with commendable
perception on the details. Despite its relentlessly pursued thesis, Weber's
book raises questions which will oblige further study of an irritatingly
magnificent poem.

'New Objections to a Pre-Restoration Date for *Samson Agonistes*' are
raised by Edward Le Comte in *Poet's Riddles*.[10] Frank Kermode dis-
courses generally on 'Milton in Old Age' (*SoR*) but more particularly on
Samson in terms of Milton as 'separate to God'. Camille W. Slights in 'A
Hero of Conscience: *Samson Agonistes* and Casuistry' (*PMLA*) studies
Samson's moral progress in the light of the period's 'cases of conscience'.
Christopher Grose in ' "His Uncontrollable Intent": Discovery as Action in
Samson Agonistes' (*MiltonS*) talks somewhat cryptically on patterns and
modes of action said to pervade the play. Heather R. Asals invokes Luther
'In Defense of Dalila' (*JEGP*); but the argument that Dalila is the agent of
Samson's regeneration cannot seriously be entertained without numerous
qualifications. John J. M Tobin in 'The Trojan Harapha' (*ELN*) proposes
that Harapha and Samson echo Dares and Entellus in the *Aeneid*, Book V.
Finally, Julian Lovelock's *Casebook*[12] provides some early criticism on the
play, notably by Dr Johnson and Landor; resurrects Sir Richard Jebb's
outdated piece (1907–8); and reprints three recent essays—by Don C.
Allen, Mary Ann Radzinowicz, and Stanley E. Fish—of which only one
deserved to be so honoured.

5. Prose

Keith W. Stavely's study of *The Politics of Milton's Prose Style* is a
major endeavour to delineate the changes in Milton's style within the ever-
increasing gulf between political reality and his own imaginative vision.[20]
Stavely first immerses himself briefly—much too briefly—in the troubled
waters of seventeenth-century prose style, and next follows Milton's
passage from the 'emotional monomania' of the tract *Of Reformation* to
the rational argument pointedly enacted in the style of *The Readie and
Easie Way*. In between, we are assured, Milton habitually espoused 'ideational' theses in opposition to, or at the expense of, reality. The divorce
tracts, for instance, are in this respect 'not pamphlets but poems', to the

[20] *The Politics of Milton's Prose Style*, by Keith W. Stavely. Yale Studies in
English, 185. New Haven and London: Yale University Press. pp. ix + 136. £4.25.

extent that they 'absorb patterns of daily life into the one true ideal universe'. Such a conclusion is hardly calculated to elicit one's enthusiastic assent, save where 'reality' is explicated after the simplistic fashion evident here, or where embattled prose is expected to eschew the imposition of literary patterns. Stavely, in other words, pursues his argument rather too relentlessly; and undermines it precisely where his own extremely literate prose suggests 'one true ideal universe' which we must, and will, explore further.

Charles Larson in 'Milton and "N.T.": An Analogue to *The Tenure of Kings and Magistrates*' (*MiltonQ*) records one of the earliest justifications of regicide, N.T.'s *The Resolver*, published three weeks before the appearance of Milton's tract. Annabel Patterson in 'The Civic Hero in Milton's Prose' (*MiltonS*) traces the convolutions, and the implications, in Milton's deployment of 'heroic allusions'. More particularly, James Egan in 'Milton and the Marprelate Tradition' (*ibid.*) argues that the pseudonymous tracts of 1588–9 proved 'a versatile satiric paradigm' for Milton's rebuttals of his opponents. Leo Miller notes that a copy of *Areopagitica* (1644) inscribes its price as 4d. (*N&Q*).

Dayton Haskin, S. J., in 'Milton's Strange Pantheon: The Apparent Tritheism of the *De doctrina christiana*' (*Heythrop Journal*), approaches the treatise strictly as a theologian in order to understand 'certain features of Milton's manner of theologizing'. The ambition is to provide 'a frame of mind akin to Milton's own' largely through a sustained comparison with the work of Karl Barth: a useful strategy, especially as regards Milton's departures from his stated strict adherence to the Reformation principle of *sola scriptura*. Robustly polemical in his estimates of those who regard *De doctrina* as Arian (e.g. Maurice Kelley) or subordinationist (e.g. William B. Hunter and C. A. Patrides), Haskin pleads for a recognition of Milton's unique position inclusive of his pantheon of 'three Gods, but no Trinity' Finally, while *Paradise Lost* is here ignored on purpose, Haskin suggest the interesting possibility that the epic might have influenced the treatise not the other way around.

XI

The Later Seventeenth Century

JAMES OGDEN

This chapter has four sections: 1. General bibliography, anthologies, literary history and criticism; 2. Dryden; 3. Other poets, dramatists and prosateurs; 4. Background. The treatment of philosophy in section 3 and of background studies is highly selective and depends mainly on what was supplied for review.

1. General

'The Eighteenth Century: A Current Bibliography for 1974' (*PQ*) is excellent and indispensable, though it was not available until March 1977. Readers of this chapter in *YW* 55 should consult *PQ* for specialist book reviews and fuller coverage of bibliography, philosophy and background studies; readers of *PQ* should consult this chapter in *YW* 55 for fuller coverage of work on Restoration literature, especially learned articles. George Hammerbacher's 'Restoration and Eighteenth Century Research Bibliography for 1974' (*RECTR*) lists, annotates and indexes 246 items. '*CN* was as usual a good source for book reviews, abstracts of dissertations and articles, and conference reports. A 'Special Satire Double Issue' included 'Satire: A Selective Critical Bibliography', which surveys recent books and articles on satire generally and on particular figures and topics, among them Butler, Restoration Drama, Oldham, Rochester, Dryden and poems on Affairs of State. Some 'Recent Studies in the Restoration and Eighteenth Century' were ably reviewed by Paul Fussell in *SEL*. In opposing impure diction he is taking arms against a sea of troubles, but his list of fashionable learned expressions should help lexicographers. I would add that 'quote', as a noun, seems no longer to be 'colloq'.

T. R. Steiner's *English Translation Theory 1650–1800*[1] offers a comprehensive survey and an anthology of primary texts. Steiner argues that before Dryden the emphasis of French theorists was on the needs of the audience, that of English ones on capturing the spirit of the original; he synthesised these ideas and laid a foundation for future theoretical work in England. The idea that the translator by identifying with his author could make his translation a work of art was widely held but not systematically expounded. The seventeenth-century authors anthologised are Denham, Cowley, Dryden, Roscommon, Laurence Echard and Sir Edward Sherburne.

[1] *English Translation Theory 1650–1800*, by T. R. Steiner. Assen and Amsterdam: Van Gorcum. pp. viii + 159. pb Dfl. 40.

Three studies of comedy and satire deserve mention. A long chapter on Augustan comedy in Allan Rodway's *English Comedy*[2] covers among other things Restoration drama and Dryden's satires, maintaining that in the eighteenth century 'satire *for* bourgeois values replaced satire against them, and sentimental comedy supplanted the Restoration drama of wit that had tried to sustain a society of rational gallantry and gaeity'. John R. Clark's 'Anticlimax in Satire' (*SCN*) was more rewarding. He shows with many good examples that anticlimax is both a rhetorical figure and a narrative strategy. As a strategy it takes the form either of unexpected climax or continuation after the climax; either *coitus interruptus* or *coitus reservatus*, he says. *Mac Flecknoe* is discussed in some detail. Edward Bloom's 'Apotropaic Visions: Tone and Meaning in Neoclassical Satire' (*HLQ*, 1974) argues that satire is essentially didactic; 'the measure of *good* satire—as distinct from inconclusively cruel satire—is good intention well and amply argued'.

(a) *Poetry*

The Yale *Poems on Affairs of State* was completed with a seventh volume, covering the years 1704–14 and hence belonging to the next chapter. Claude Rawson has weighed the faults and beauties of the whole enterprise in a masterly review article (*TLS* 25 June 1976). George de F Lord edited a generous selection from the seven volumes for students and general readers.[3] The textual apparatus has been left out and the comment ary cut down, but annotation is still copious and the book has a scholarly introduction, a select bibliography, detailed indices, and fifteen illustra tions. Concentration on Dryden, Swift and Pope can mislead us about both politics and poetry, and the idea of the anthology is to show no only the salient political events which occasioned satirical poetry, but als the various forms and styles it adopted. The behaviour of Charles II an his brother was such that even monarchists had to prune the divinity tha had been thought to hedge kings, while Whigs incessantly satirised real c fancied follies and knaveries of the great; thus 'the myth of a hierarchic community ordained by God' was replaced by the more familiar 'standard that were individualistic and secular'. Tory poets were loyal to the mo literary forms, especially mock-heroic, while Whigs resorted to all kinds c burlesques, ballads, doggerel and songs. So *Absalom and Achitophel* ar *The Medal* are not in the anthology, but it enables us to supplement ou reading of them with many other poems on the Popish Plot and the tri of Shaftesbury. We also find good selections from the satirical poetry c Marvell, Rochester and Defoe, but not Defoe's *Hymn to the Pillory*, whic is considered in the introduction, and nothing from *Satires upon the Jesui* These are regrettable omissions, but all in all this is a very good antholog and very good value in paperback.

Affairs of state were often enough affairs of courtiers and oran

[2] *English Comedy: its Role and Nature from Chaucer to the Present Day*, by Alla Rodway. Chatto & Windus. pp. x + 288.

[3] *Anthology of Poems on Affairs of State: Augustan Satirical Verse, 1660-171* ed. by George de F. Lord. New Haven, London: Yale University Press. pp. xxxii 800. 15 illustrations. £19.25, pb £3.80.

wenches, and John Adlard's *The Fruit of that Forbidden Tree*[4] is a collection of Restoration erotic verse. The authors most often drawn on are Etherege, Rochester and Sedley, but many of the poems come from drolleries and miscellanies, and some from manuscripts, notably a pornographical piece which has found its way to the Royal Library, Stockholm. The poems are generally witty or at least nicely phrased, all tending to promote what Adlard calls 'the humanising value of pleasure'. In his introduction he briefly places Restoration libertinism in its Renaissance context, but the poems appear without explanatory notes. Texts are accurate, but he does not always show when they are abridged, and regularly omits titles.

Dona F. Munker's ' "That Paultry Burlesque Stile": Seventeenth-Century Poetry and Augustan "Low Seriousness" ' (*SCN*) is scholarly and entertaining. Dr Munker queries whether the tradition of high seriousness and heroic couplets should remain the touchstone for Augustan verse satire. She surveys the Classical, medieval and Renaissance sources of the alternative tradition of colloquial satire in octosyllabic and lyrical forms. *Hudibras* and the octosyllabics of Rochester and Swift show that sophisticated satire could develop from this tradition, though Dr Munker's analysis of Rochester's 'The Mistress' seems oversophisticated. He does not say 'kind jealous doubts... make us blest at last', which she understands as announcing that jealousy is a substitute for the genuine gratification of passion, but 'kind jealous doubts, when past... make us blest at last', which I understand as admitting that jealousy helps.

(b) *Drama*

Geoffrey Marshall's *Restoration Serious Drama*[5] is a study of heroic plays, tragedies, tragi-comedies and other hybrid forms. Marshall assumes we do not like these plays and contends that since they are about perennial human problems our distaste must be owing to their manner, not their matter. He shows convincingly that many reasons we may give for not liking them are unsound, for example, we should not argue that their ritualistic quality is at odds with general truth to life, because modern drama is ritualistic yet we believe its characters are real. But it is one thing to remind us that our standards are relative, another to suggest that our judgments are unnecessary, particularly in a book which contains a measure of special pleading. Marshall says it is foolish 'to read *The Conquest of Granada*, respond with distaste, and conclude that Dryden was incompetent as a serious dramatist. The only evidence for that conclusion is our own distaste.' But what if our conclusion is that when relevant comparisons have been made—with Marlowe, Racine, grand opera—Dryden is *limited* as a serious dramatist? The evidence would not be just modern distaste anyway; Dryden's contemporaries and eventually Dryden himself had doubts about his plays. Points like these might still be made, I think, if the play in question were one which plainly did deserve a place in the repertory, such

[4] *The Fruit of that Forbidden Tree: Restoration Poems, Songs and Jests on the subject of Sensual Love*, ed. by John Adlard. Cheadle Hulme: Carcanet Press. pp. 39. £2.80, pb £1.10.
[5] *Restoration Serious Drama*, by Geoffrey Marshall. Norman: University of Oklahoma Press. pp. xx + 247.

as *Aureng-Zebe*; but here Marshall would perhaps object to my being 'judgmental'. His book is stimulating but finally unsatisfactory, because he tries to make us respect all Restoration serious drama and cannot bring himself positively to recommend specific plays.

In *Comic Character in Restoration Drama*[6] Agnes v. Persson's thesis is that a comic character is generally one who is unaware of his own deficiencies. The varying degrees of ignorance and the fields in which it appears are illustrated mainly from the comedies of Shadwell, Dryden, Etherege, Wycherley and Congreve. Dr Persson seems to have read more widely in theoretical works on humour than in Restoration drama and recent criticism. Her opening theoretical chapter is the strongest, and while the rest of the book is not without interest she does less than justice to Etherege and Farquhar and does not mention Vanbrugh at all.

Among critical essays on drama Harold Love's 'State Affairs on the Restoration Stage, 1660–1675' (*RECTR*) was the most important. Love points out that Loftis's *The Politics of Drama* (*YW* 44, 245) made little reference to plays written before 1680, while political drama in England can be seen as beginning with Tatham's *The Rump* (1660), the first English play about named living political figures. It points forward to Crowne's *City Politiques*. In tragedy there was a vogue for plays about incredibly wicked usurpers, with more or less explicit reference to Cromwell. The third Dutch war (1672–4) gave a new impetus to political drama, Dryden's *Amboyna* inaugurating a move towards crude propaganda. Payne's *The Siege of Constantinople* (1674) aimed at convincing Charles II of the need to treat Parliament ruthlessly; because of the Emperor of Constantinople's scrupulous fairness in dealing with his people, and of the Machiavellian treachery of his Chancellor—the first stage portrayal of Shaftesbury—the city falls to the Turks. Payne's play points towards *The Female Prelate, Lucius Junius Brutus* and *Venice Preserved*. Gordon K. Thomas's essay, 'The Knight Amid the Dunces' (*RECTR*), studies eight plays based on *Don Quixote*, including Crowne's *The Married Beau* and the three parts of D'Urfey's *The Comical History of Don Quixote*.

A number of articles dealt with theatre history. Colin Visser's 'The Anatomy of the Early Restoration Stage: *The Adventures of Five Hours* and John Dryden's "Spanish" Comedies' (*TN*, two parts) examines the theatrical devices and method of staging of Tuke's play and their influence on *The Rival Ladies, An Evening's Love* and *The Assignation*. Davenant's production of *The Adventures of Five Hours* 'demonstrated for the first time the full scenic potentialities of the theatre at Lincoln's Inn Fields. . which was the prototype of all the theatres of the Restoration'. Judith Milhous's 'An Annotated Census of Thomas Betterton's Roles, 1659–1710 (*TN*, two parts) amplifies and corrects the account of Betterton in the recent *Biographical Dictionary* of Restoration and eighteenth-century stage people (*YW* 54, 293). She has documented '183 *certain roles*, 131 of which Betterton created', and shows that the liking of this 'astonishingly versatile' actor for Shakespearean and tragic parts has been overemphasised. Kenneth Richards's 'The French Actors in London, 1661–62' (*RECTR*

---

[6] *Comic Character in Restoration Drama*, by Agnes v. Persson. De Proprietatibus Litteratum, Series Practica, 99. The Hague and Paris: Mouton. pp. 151.

argues that the first visiting troupe from the continent after the Restoration was probably Les Comédiens des Mlle. d'Orléans, and they probably performed Chapoton's *Descente d'Orphée* and Corneille's *Andromède*. Richards's 'The Comedians of the King of England at Ghent, 1663' (*EA*) argues that a troupe of that name was probably French, not English as has been thought; if so 'no English acting company of the Restoration period is known to have played abroad'. 'The Architect of Dorset Garden Theatre', according to Diana de Marly (*TN*), was not Wren but may have been his associate Robert Hooke, though probably a speculative builder was responsible for many features of its eccentric design. Maximilian E.Novak's 'The Closing of Lincoln's Inn Fields Theatre in 1695' (*RECTR*) shows that this theatre was temporarily closed after the failure of the anonymous *She Ventures and He Wins*. L. J. Morrissey's 'Theatrical Records of the London Guilds 1655–1708' (*TN*) shows how public processions in London, especially Lord Mayor's Shows, gradually lost their connexion with the theatre. William P. Williams throws new light on 'Sir Henry Herbert's Licensing of Plays for the Press in the Restoration' (*N&Q*).

2. Dryden

(a) *General*

John A. Zamonski's *Annotated Bibliography of John Dryden: Texts and Studies, 1949–1973*[7] is a welcome supplement to Monk's *John Dryden: A List of Critical Studies 1895–1948*. Zamonski lists books, articles, notes and dissertations, under the headings of canon and bibliography, biography, comprehensive or miscellaneous studies, drama, prose, poetry, and translations; and supplies brief descriptive notes, cross-references, and an index. But I have one or two complaints. Many books listed under the sub-heading 'School Texts' are nothing of the kind. Despite the title, a fair number of books and articles published in 1973, and mentioned in *YW* for that year, are excluded; up to 1972 Zamonski is pretty comprehensive. I would have expected to find reference to *YW* in the list of annual bibliographies consulted; if he had used it Zamonski might not have omitted an article by George Watson (45, 256), books with chapters on Dryden such as Sellin's *Daniel Heinsius and Stuart England* (49, 226) and Chalker's *The English Georgic* (50, 247, 263), and books on broader topics which make extensive reference to Dryden, such as Weinbrot's *The Formal Strain* (50, 263–4).

Various biographical points were clarified in two learned articles. Edward L. Saslow's 'Dryden in 1684' (*MP*) attempts a more exact chronology of Dryden's literary work that year, and argues that a letter from Dryden to Lawrence Hyde dates from March and petitions for an appointment as Commissioner of Appeals. G. C. R. Morris's 'Dryden, Hobbs, Tonson and the Death of Charles II' (*N&Q*) raises the question of why the lines in *Threnodia Augustalis* about how Charles's illness baffled his doctors should specify only '*Short*' in 1685 but '*Short* and *Hobbs*' in

[7] *An Annotated Bibliography of John Dryden: Texts and Studies, 1949-1973*, by ohn A. Zamonski. Folkestone: Dawson. pp. 147. £9.

1701. One of the surgeons attending Charles was the Thomas Hobbs who later attended Dryden; probably Hobbs mentioned his attendance on Charles and Dryden put Hobbs's name into the poem 'to remedy an historical injustice'. It is a nice point, I think, whether the change makes the lines more or less worthy of inclusion in *The Stuffed Owl*.

Edward Pechter's *Dryden's Classical Theory of Literature*[8] is broader in scope than its title may suggest. Pechter emphasises that Dryden was responsive to various literary modes; in theory and practice he generally favoured both this and that, not either this or that. The classical quality of this outlook is shown by parallels with Aristotle, Plutarch and others, and its effects are traced in Dryden's criticism and some of his poems. His criticism shows him to have been fully aware of differences between opposites such as Virgil and Ovid, French and English drama, judgment and fancy, which he sought to balance rather than reconcile or transcend; while *Mac Flecknoe* shows his 'endeavor to find a comprehensive mode in which epic grandeur and naturalness could coexist'. Dryden's criticism is surely rather less balanced, and *Mac Flecknoe* perhaps rather more, than Pechter allows. Dryden did think Virgil a greater poet than Ovid, not merely a different sort of poet; and if *Mac Flecknoe* 'affirms the continuing health and vitality of tradition' it cannot show that 'everything has turned to shit'. Pechter's own book balances sweeping statements against subtle analysis, or maybe liveliness against laboriousness.

'The Temper of John Dryden' was seen differently by Thomas H. Fujimura (*SP*). He pitches into those who see Dryden as an arch-conservative, fearful of change and submissive to authority. Dryden's temper is 'essentially vigorous, aggressive, and independent'; barring Milton he is 'the most innovative writer in the Restoration'. Misunderstanding arises from taking his well-known confessions of diffidence out of their contexts, and ignoring other revelations, for instance his remark that Homer's vehemence was 'more suitable to my temper' than Virgil's phlegmatic quality. Perhaps more significant still is Dryden's use of military and athletic metaphors (though Fujimura is surely wrong to suppose the phrase 'take the glove' has to do with boxing), and his general tendency to see writing as essentially a struggle with contemporaries, foreigners and predecessors. His belligerent tone aroused antagonism and he was continually involved in bitter debates. But Fujimura's proof that Dryden was an aggressive personality and a forceful writer does not entirely dispose of the notion that he was an arch-conservative; the truth is that he was, like all great writers, a complex man.

(b) *Poetry*

James D. Garrison's *Dryden and the Tradition of Panegyric*[9] starts from Dryden's idea of panegyric as a branch of epic. Garrison shows that Classical and Renaissance writers thought of panegyric as a ceremonious oration addressed to a monarch or other powerful ruler, celebrating his power but suggesting his limitations. The tradition of English verse pane-

---

[8] *Dryden's Classical Theory of Literature*, by Edward Pechter. Cambridge University Press. pp. viii + 225. £5.
[9] *Dryden and the Tradition of Panegyric*, by James D. Garrison. Berkeley, Los Angeles, London: University of California Press. pp. xiv + 263.

gyric was founded on poems addressed to James I by Daniel and Jonson, developed by Cowley and Waller, and challenged by Marvell in his poems addressed to Cromwell. Dryden was more conscious than Cowley and Waller of the oratorical origins of panegyric, and adopted their innovations not to obscure but to emphasise its ancient themes. For him panegyric remained a genre seeking to unite the people behind an ideal monarch; his panegyrics were partly a substitute for the Stuart epic he long aspired to write. He ingeniously adapted panegyric to the purposes of satire, but even in his satires he was conciliatory. His ironic versions of panegyric exposed the danger of perverting traditional ideals to factional ends, though by showing fools and knaves as panegyrical orators he undermined the genre he was still struggling to take seriously when he wrote *Britannia Rediviva*. This is a scholarly critical book which in an unpretentious way makes a real contribution to our understanding of poetry and power in the seventeenth century.

More ambitious and difficult is Michael McKeon's *Politics and Poetry in Restoration England*.[10] All recent readings of *Annus Mirabilis* are divided into the 'poetic' and the 'political' and found wanting. If I have digested his spongy prose properly, poetic readings see the poem as valid for all people at all times, but err through dogmatic acceptance of its ideology; political ones see it as a clever attack on sedition, but err through reduction of its ideology to a set of commonplaces. He counters the former by assuming the original audience's 'sensitivity to the depoliticizing effects of Dryden's generality', the latter by assuming its 'appreciation of Dryden's ingenuous and nonironic indulgence in prophecy and eschatological speculation'. He offers a 'rhetorical analysis' of the poem, in which his account of how its rhetorical strategies would work is, as he sees it, confirmed by detailed research on public responses to the Restoration, the Dutch War, and the Great Fire, on the contemporary definition of national and party interests, and on the various prophecies about the 'wonderful year' itself. Thus *Annus Mirabilis* is found to have 'a historical representativeness which is larger than its poetic commonplaces and its political ideology'. McKeon believes his methods will give us a much improved understanding of all poetry; as he also believes 'traditional distinctions between classics and ephemera are neither absolute nor desirable' many more books are in prospect, but on the evidence of this one it is doubtful whether the improved understanding will be widely shared.

A survey of critical articles on Dryden's poetry can appropriately begin with 'Dryden's Poetics: The Expressive Values in Poetry' (*JEGP*) by Thomas H. Fujimura, who contends that Dryden's critics have made too much of his thought and imagery, and too little of his diction and prosody. Dryden himself would not have disputed the primacy of thought, but its mode of expression was the source of delight. By what he called 'the choice of words, and the harmony of numbers' Dryden in his best verse was able to 'assert and suggest poetically rather than state ideas directly'. In 'The Narrator as Rhetorician in Dryden's *The Hind and the Panther*'

[10] *Politics and Poetry in Restoration England: The Case of Dryden's 'Annus Mirabilis'*, by Michael McKeon. Cambridge, Mass., and London: Harvard University Press. pp. xii + 336. 10 illustrations. £11.25.

(*JNT*, 1974) J. M. Armistead sees the narrator's function in this poem as like that in mannerist painting of the *Sprecher* or controlling presence. The narrator 'is active within the poem itself, adjusting its structure and our aesthetic distance, shaping and molding our responses as it figures forth the Roman Catholic view... in argument, allegory, and myth'. This approach sidesteps but does not obviate the problem that troubled Dr Johnson: the various beasts are not much like the various churches, so neither Dryden nor the narrator can develop their portraits without forgetting the allegory altogether. In 'The Ascetic's Banquet: The Morality of *Alexander's Feast*' (*TSLL*) John Dawson Carl Buck remarks that while one early critic saw the ode as a celebration of vicious emotionalism, Earl Miner has seen it as showing a wise and ironic tolerance for the failings of a great man. Buck believes that the early critic's 'moral rigor' is 'sound but misdirected', and that Miner 'underestimates the moral seriousness of the poem's ironies'. It opposes the emotionalism of Timotheus and Alexander, 'and even St Cecilia herself does not provide an adequate model of the kind of asceticism which Dryden wanted to enforce'. Thus a critic tires his brains to get a sobering thought. In 'Dryden's Version of the *Wife of Bath's Tale*' (*CQ*) Tom Mason sees Dryden as differing from modern academic authorities on Chaucer, in thinking highly of the Wife's tale as a tale. His version moves, through all its episodes, towards the crone's lecture to her reluctant husband, where she argues so strongly for a central and truly human point of view that he resigns his life to her. The poem is a masterpiece of 'true wit' in the Augustan sense of combining humour and sympathy.

Two pieces of textual criticism are worth noting. In 'Dryden's Heroique Stanza's on Cromwell: A New Critical Text' (*PBSA*) Vinton A. Dearing and three assistants give ten early manuscripts and ten early printings of the poem, a critical text and apparatus, and the reasoning on which the text is based. Though it is essentially an essay in the theory of textual criticism, the article does give some better readings than the California and Oxford texts. In 'Shaftesbury Cursed: Dryden's Revision of the *Achitophel* Lines' (*SB*) Edward L. Saslow disputes the theory advanced by Dearing in the California edition. On bibliographical and literary grounds Saslow believes the Achitophel portrait originally included the lines praising Shaftesbury as a judge, and that they were left out of the first edition simply to make room for more abusive passages (lines 152–8 and 167–72 in modern editions).

(c) *Drama*

Richard Leslie Larson's *Studies in Dryden's Dramatic Technique*[11] extended the Salzburg 'Poetic Drama and Poetic Theory' series. Larson focuses on scenes of persuasion and accusation in the heroic plays, tragicomedies, and tragedies. Such scenes were of course not unknown in earlier seventeenth-century drama, but became much more common after

---

[11] *Studies in Dryden's Dramatic Technique: The Use of Scenes Depicting Persuasion and Accusation*, by Richard Leslie Larson. Salzburg Studies in English Literature: Poetic Drama & Poetic Theory, 9. Salzburg: Institut für Englische Sprache und Literatur. pp. iii +317.

the Restoration. Dryden saw them as a way of arousing what he called 'concernment' and of developing his themes; he used them increasingly till in *All for Love* and *The Spanish Friar* he built whole plays on them. A note that 'Professor Larson's present duties have prevented him from updating his Harvard thesis, presented in 1963' puts scholarship in perspective.

All for Love was edited and annotated in accordance with the policy of 'The New Mermaids' series by N. J. Andrew.[12] As similar editions are already available (*YW* 48, 235–6; 53, 258) the value of this one depends heavily on its introduction. Andrew holds that in his *Antony and Cleopatra* (1677) Sedley criticises Charles II by drawing parallels between him and Antony, and that in *All for Love* Dryden defends Charles by attacking Sedley in the preface, by attributing to Antony the Aristotelean virtue of magnanimity, and by relating the love of Antony and Cleopatra to the Platonic idea of divine love. But 'there remains a gap between intention and achievement: the reader may feel that, behind the verbiage, Dryden's argument is not tight enough to convince him that Antony and Cleopatra's relationship is of such a lofty philosophical order'. This reader felt that Andrew's argument was not tight enough, relying too much on questionable parallels, and tending to reduce the play to a dubious piece of ratiocination. In any case it is doubtful whether an introduction to an edition is the place for a discussion of this sort; students will need to be warned that what Andrew says is 'clear' or 'obvious' is often conjectural. His summary of Dryden's life is similarly tendentious in its emphasis on Dryden's 'bitterness' after 1688.

Although Dr Leavis reprinted his essay on '*Antony and Cleopatra* and *All for Love*',[13] comparing them 'only as an approach to Shakespeare', Dryden's play was not only re-edited but also made the subject of more critical articles. J. Douglas Canfield's 'The Jewel of Great Price: Mutability and Constancy in Dryden's *All for Love*' (*ELH*) is based on a thorough study of analogous plays in the Renaissance period. Others had stressed mutability, but Dryden balances mutability and constancy, especially by means of jewel imagery associated with Cleopatra, who is constant from the beginning and, as Antony finally realises, 'the jewel of great price'. I am not sure whether this interpretation increases my respect for the play or confirms my worst suspicions of it. Leslie Howard Martin's '*All for Love* and the Millenarian Tradition' (*CL*) urges that this tradition encouraged Dryden to see Octavius, the future Augustus, as an emblem of the inevitable triumph of order over chaotic passion. Octavius is omitted from the *dramatis personae* so that his distasteful personality is not obtruded and his emblematic function is clear; Restoration audiences might feel that the world was well lost but could hardly forget the traditional associations between Augustus, peace and prosperity.

An Evening's Love and *Aureng-Zebe* were also seen in relation to sources and analogues. In 'John Dryden's Indebtedness to Pedro Calderón de la Barca in *An Evening's Love or The Mock Astrologer*' (*RLC*) Angel

---

[12] *All for Love*, by John Dryden, ed. by N. J. Andrew. The New Mermaids. Benn. pp xxx + 114. pb £1.25.

[13] *The Living Principle: 'English' as a Discipline of Thought*, by F. R. Leavis. Chatto & Windus. pp. 264. £4.

Capellan, who does not mention Loftis's book (*YW* 54, 253–4), says existing studies of Dryden's debt to Calderón are unsatisfactory. He argues that Dryden freely borrowed from Spanish plays and could have read them in Spanish. A careful study of Calderón's *El astrólogo fingido*, Thomas Corneille's *Le feint astrologue*, and *An Evening's Love* shows that at various points Dryden borrows from Calderón rather than Corneille, and on the whole improves on both. In '*Aureng-Zebe* in Context: Dryden, Shakespeare, Milton, and Racine' (*JEGP*) William Frost compares Dryden's play with *King Lear, Samson Agonistes* and *Mithridate*. *King Lear* and *Aureng-Zebe* are similar in some ways, but the conflict that in Shakespeare arises from Lear's abuse of political and family authority in Dryden is further complicated by the old Emperor's passion for his son's fiancée. Dryden saw the old Emperor as like Milton's Samson in his capacity for infatuation, and like Dalila in his failure to arouse reciprocal passion. But the twist of the plot which brings about the happy ending was suggested by *Mithridate*. *Aureng-Zebe* lacks the scope and surrealistic symbolism of *Lear*, but 'as a symbol of lively rational communication the couplet . . . is unsurpassed'.

(d) *Prose*

There is little to report under this heading. H. Neville Davies's 'Dryden's *Rahmenerzählung*: The Form of ' "An Essay of Dramatick Poesie" ' comes in a collection of essays in structural analysis.[14] By imitating and echoing the structure of *The Decameron* and *The Cobler of Caunterburie* (1590), a popular collection of tales based on Chaucer and Boccaccio, Dryden draws a parallel between Renaissance Florence and Restoration London, and subtly defends London as a cultural centre. William Empson's 'A Deist Tract by Dryden' (*EIC*) is one signed 'A.W.' that was first printed in Charles Blount's *The Oracles of Reason* (1693). Empson believes Dryden wrote it between 1675 and 1678, and shows that it adopts ideas about deism and modes of argument that are also found in his acknowledged works, especially *Religio Laici*. References to Sir Charles Wolseley reflect Dryden's friendship with him and sympathy for his deistical ideas. The article reopens Empson's controversy with Philip Harth on the interpretation of *Religio Laici* (*YW* 51, 245). Earl Miner's 'Mr Dryden and Mr Rymer' is noted in 3 (*c*) below.

3. Other Authors

(a) *Poets*

A selection from Cotton was edited by Geoffrey Grigson for the Penguin 'Poet to Poet' series.[15] The text is based on the manuscript in Derby Public Library, the posthumous *Poems on Several Occasions*, and the modern editions by Beresford and Buxton. Spelling and typography

---

[14] *Fair Forms: Essays in English Literature from Spenser to Jane Austen*, ed. by Maren-Sofie Røstvig. Cambridge: Brewer. pp. 248. £5.
[15] *Charles Cotton*, selected by Geoffrey Grigson. Poet to Poet series. Penguin Books. pp. 198. pb 90p.

have been modernized, and the poems appear in 'an order corresponding conjecturally to the successive periods of Cotton's life'. A chronology and an introduction give some idea of what these periods were. Grigson believes that the best of the humorous poems are 'Winter' and the 'Quatrains' for morning, noon, evening and night, that 'the word for them is not burlesque, but *badinerie*', and that they belong to Cotton's late twenties, after his return from France. The best of his serious poems are 'Contentation', 'To... Mr Izaak Walton, on his Life of Dr Donne', and 'The Retirement', and these date from after 1668, when Walton gave him a book of poems by Malherbe, Racan, Maynard and other French poets. Though we are warned that the series aims to show how one poet responds to another, it is disappointing that Grigson does not include selections from Cotton's most famous and in their time popular poems, the Virgil travesty and *The Wonders of the Peak*. But Cotton being undeservedly neglected any selection is welcome, and may encourage further exploration of his work. On textual and chronological matters Grigson could have been helped by Alvin I. Dust, who in 'The Manuscript of Cotton's 'Contentation'' (*Lib*) answers 'unwarranted suggestions and untenable conclusions' by Stephen Parks (*YULG*, 1969) about the textual history of this poem, dated by Dust between 1676 and 1683, after 'The Retirement' and the epistle to Walton.

I noted only two articles concerning Butler. Michael Wilding's 'Flecknoe's "Diarium": A Source for "Hudibras" ' (*N&Q*) suggests that Richard Flecknoe's *The Diarium* (1656), a genially satirical and scurrilous account of everyday life in England, in octosyllabic couplets or 'Burlesque Rhyme or Drolling Verse', anticipates many of Butler's effects in *Hudibras*. James L. Thorson's 'A Broadside by Samuel Butler' (*BLR*, 1974) describes a compilation by Benjamin Tooke of extracts from *Hudibras*, forming a satirical attack on the practice at treason trials of packing juries with Whig sympathisers.

There were three articles on Rochester. Reba Wilcoxon's 'Pornography, Obscenity, and Rochester's "The Imperfect Enjoyment" ' (*SEL*) maintains that the poem is not pornographical or obscene, because 'it effects psychic distance through complex linguistic devices; it is intellectually and emotionally enriched by a classical and seventeenth-century literary tradition; and it explores an emotional relationship between human beings and sets up a norm for that relationship'. Ronald W. Johnson's 'Rhetoric and Drama in Rochester's "Satire against Reason and Mankind" ' (*SEL*) warns that we do not see the poem's major irony unless we understand the relation of its apparent rhetorical to its real dramatic structure. 'The poem appears to be one thing, an indictment of those who regard mankind as superior to beasts on the basis of reason; but the poem is quite another thing, an indictment of those who regard mankind as inevitably dishonest on the basis of common sense.' If I have followed Johnson's tortuous but interesting reasoning, the rhetorical indictment of reason is based on common sense, but then it is unclear what the dramatic indictment of common sense is based on; unless he means the rhetorical attack on reason and the dramatic one on mankind are both based on common sense. K. E. Robinson's 'A Glance at Rochester in Thomas Durfey's "Madam Fickle" ' (*N&Q*) notes an incident in the play which recalls the Epsom Wells brawl, and some parallels between the character of Lord Bellamore and Rochester. In 'Editing the Poems of John Oldham: Desiderata' (*N&Q*, 1974) and 'John Oldham: Some Problems of Biography and Annotation' (*PQ*) Harold Brooks posed questions to most of which, he tells me, he has not yet found satisfactory answers. Who was 'Cosmelia', to whom Oldham addressed love poems? Who was '*Irish Emma*', alluded to in the 4th 'Satyr Upon the Jesuits'? Is the 'Satyr upon a Woman, who. . . was the Death of my Friend' an attack on Lady Grey, wife of Baron Grey of Warke? What precisely is meant by the toping term 'six in hand'? Is it true that Parliamentary troops at Chichester stole the chalice from which they received the sacrament? What is meant when '*J-n* and the rest' fly over 'the Pyramid' in Juvenal III?

The lack of a modern scholarly edition of Garth makes especially welcome a volume of facsimiles.[16] It contains *The Dispensary, to which is added Several Verses omitted in the late Editions, and a Compleat Key* (Dublin 1725, with six illustrations from the London 1726 edition); *A Short Account of the Proceedings of the College of Physicians* (1697) and *Claremont* (1715). *A Short Account* helps us to relate *The Dispensary* to its occasion; *Claremont* is a verse-epistle celebrating the Earl of Clare and his estate.

Finally some items on minor or minimus poets. Peter K. Shea's 'Alexander Pope and Aphra Behn on Wit' (*N&Q*) notes a parallel to Pope's 'True Wit is Nature to Advantage drest' in Aphra Behn's epistle 'To Henry Higden, Esq' (1687). Jule Anne Byars's ' "The Tory-Poets": Anonymous? (*N&Q*) queries the attribution of this satire to Shadwell. However, John Ross's 'Adenda to Shadwell's "Complete Works": A Checklist' (*N&Q* proposes that seven poems, five pamphlets, three plays and some miscellaneous items can with varying degrees of certainty be attributed to Shadwell in whole or part; *Englands Great Deliverance* (1689), a political tirade, is printed in full. James M. Osborn's 'Thomas Rymer as Rhymer' (*PQ*) reprints and discusses Rymer's light verse, much of it addressed to ladies whose identities are more or less hidden behind conventional names. Osborn does not remark that the lines 'My Heart is Loves mere *Tennis ball*,/Here toss'd, there bandy'd up and down' (in the song, 'Some say for *Olinda* dye') echo 'We are merely the stars' tennis balls, struck an bandied/Which way please them' (*The Duchess of Malfi*).

(b) *Dramatists*

A chapter on 'Bayes versus the Critics' in Robert F. Willson's book on burlesque drama, *Their Form Confounded*,[17] sees *The Rehearsal* in relation to earlier examples of the genre. Willson argues persuasively that while Dryden's heroic plays are the main objects of burlesque, we can

[16] *The Dispensary by Samuel Garth, with A Short Account of the Proceedings of the College of Physicians, London, in Relation to the Sick Poor (1697) and Claremont (1715),* with an introduction by Jo Allen Bradham. New York: Scholars' Facsimiles & Reprints. pp. [165].

[17] *Their Form Confounded': Studies in the Burlesque Play from Udall to Sheridan,* by Robert F. Willson, Jr. De Proprietatibus Litteratum, Series Practica, 88. The Hague and Paris: Mouton. pp. xv + 170. pb Dfl. 48.

still enjoy Buckingham's play as an attack on bad theatre in any age, but takes no account of recent work suggesting that the heroic plays are themselves basically ironic, and that there is political satire in *The Rehearsal.* I noted only two articles on Etherege. Arthur R. Huseboe's 'The Mother of George Etherege' (*N&Q*) supplements the biographical sketch in Bracher's edition of Etherege's *Letters.* Etherege's mother, Mary Powney, was born in 1612 and died in 1699, and he may have started writing plays to raise money when she was in difficulties after the death of her second husband in 1622. Harold Clifford Brown Jr.'s 'Etherege and Comic Shallowness' (*TSLL*) analyses the 'shallowness, in philosophy and in cultural schizophrenia' of some Restoration rakes, especially in Etherege's plays. While Dryden's rakish heroes reflect the 'shallow taste' of his audience, unlike the Mob of Gentlemen he was not himself pathologically shallow and did not portray this condition. But we are to think of Rochester and Etherege's Dorimant not as libertines, not as reformed rakes, and certainly not as immoral characters, but as victims of a neurosis, bordering on schizophrenia and according to Brown widespread in America today.

In *The Four Plays of William Wycherley*[18] W. R. Chadwick's aims are to look at the plays as stage pieces, to examine their themes and techniques, and above all to trace Wycherley's development as a dramatist. *Love in a Wood* is seen as an experimental mixture of Spanish plot, Jonsonian humours, romantic lovers and witty exchanges, not a unified play. *The Gentleman Dancing-Master* is simpler and more coherent, and may have been written for the great farceurs Nokes and Angel, though it is not merely a farce; Hippolita's vacillations in the main plot constitute 'a fascinating analysis' of her struggle for a genuine rather than an arranged marriage. *The Country Wife*, thematically and technically the triumphant outcome of the first two plays, 'sets out to attack a society that accepted marital contracts based on interest rather than love' and shows the resulting hypocrisy and cruelty. Wycherley probably wrote much of *The Plain-Dealer* before *The Country Wife*, and rewrote it later, making its satire broader and darker but damaging its structure. It makes a general indictment of society but leaves an impression of 'confused bitterness'. An excess of detailed analysis and the lack of an index betray the book's thesis origin, but it makes fresh and helpful observations in an unpretentious way and certainly deserves publication. Chadwick is quite good at taking the plays out of the study onto the stage, but if disguising the country wife as a young gentleman shows that 'in the hands of fools a complete disguise is worse than a partial one' I would add that in the theatre it should have the ironic effect of actually making her look more attractive.

The Country Wife became the first Restoration play to appear in 'The Revels' series.[19] It has received the same scrupulous editing as its fore-

[18] *The Four Plays of William Wycherley: A Study in the Development of a Dramatist*, by W. R. Chadwick. Studies in English Literature, lxxxiii. The Hague and Paris: Mouton. pp. 208. 1 plate.
[19] *The Country Wife*, by William Wycherley, ed. by David Cook and John Swannell. The Revels Plays. London: Methuen; New York: Barnes & Noble. pp. lxxviii + 175. 3 plates. £6. pb £3.50.

runners. The introduction includes accounts of Wycherley's life, the Restoration theatre, and 'Restoration Comedy' in general; a critical study of the play; and discussions of sources, date of performance, stage-history, and the provenance of the text. Annotation is as usual thorough, and here especially helpful with words and phrases which may seem clear but which conceal subtle shades of meaning. Appendices give the scene from *The Plain-Dealer* in which *The Country Wife* is discussed, and biographical notes on the cast for the first performance. Work on the text is almost faultless, though from the general sense of II.i.138 and the editors' account of Q1's method of indicating asides it seems they should have marked an aside for Pinchwife there. In the critical part of the introduction the section on 'The Characters' is forceful, but that on 'The Structure' seems to me self-indulgently prolonged. The play also received critical attention in Anthony Kaufman's essay, 'Wycherley's *The Country Wife* and the Don Juan Character' (*ECS*). Horner shares with the Don Juans of Tirso de Molina and Molière an abnormal hostility towards women, arising from 'inner feelings of masculine inadequacy... which require perpetual denial'. His malaise can also be seen in Pinchwife, Sparkish and Sir Jasper Fidget, and in Manly in *The Plain-Dealer*. He is 'a prisoner of sex' but we enjoy the play because the Don Juan myth lets us realise our dreams of freedom. Kaufman's essay is interesting and scholarly, but as even he seems not to know of them it may be worth noting here that Armand E. Singer has published in *WVUPP* substantial supplements to his *Bibliography of the Don Juan Theme*.

Congreve is the subject of a good short study by Harold Love,[20] the first in a new series of critical books on dramatists which aims to put some emphasis on social and theatrical background. Love accordingly begins with a chapter on the Restoration theatre, the qualities of Congreve's leading actors and actresses, and the character of the audience—which he argues was more middle-class than has usually been supposed. Part of the argument of a concluding chapter on adverse critics of Congreve is that they have not seen his plays as theatre. In between are chapters on the four comedies, where Congreve is seen as centrally concerned with how the individual is to attain happiness in a society given over to dissimulation. *The Old Batchelour* rather frivolously suggests he must be cleverer than the rest. *Love for Love* is a romantic comedy proposing that the way is through trust and love, though the play is to be valued more for its vitality than its abstract ideals. *The Way of the World* looks more realistically at the problem of 'how we are to resist the deadening force of the world'; in Lady Wishfort's case 'the limitations of resource are redeemed by a grandeur of aspiration', and in Millamant and Mirabell's by our sense that they 'have been developed to their utmost point of perfection'. Love sees an almost Shakespearean richness of ambiguity in Congreve's last two comedies.

Articles on Congreve dealt with biographical, textual, and critical problems. J. M. Treadwell's 'Congreve, Tonson, and Rowe's "Reconcilement" ' (*N&Q*) brings forward evidence that Nicholas Rowe's poem,

[20] *Congreve*, by Harold Love. Plays & Playwrights Series. Oxford: Blackwell. pp. viii + 131. £3.

'The Reconcilement between Jacob Tonson and Mr Congreve', refers to the close friendship between Congreve and his publisher in 1695. T. C. Duncan Eaves and Ben D. Kimpel's 'The Text of Congreve's *Love for Love*' (*Lib*) shows that lines from this play cited in 1700 in an indictment of some players for using profane and obscene expressions are much more profane and obscene than corresponding lines in the early printed texts. David D. Mann's 'Congreve's Revisions of *The Mourning Bride*' (*PBSA*) compares the first quarto text with that of the *Works* (1710), which was revised by Congreve. Changes mostly help to emphasise the main theme, the triumph of love over lust, and so point to affinities between *The Mourning Bride* and Congreve's last two comedies. Anthony Kaufman's 'Characterization in Congreve's *The Old Bachelor*' (*NM*) argues persuasively that Heartwell and Fondlewife are characters of some complexity. Behind the facades of satyr-satirist and puritan they show signs of introspection and ironic self-awareness. Heartwell is aware of 'the painful reality of his sexual appetite', and Fondlewife of his need to believe in his wife's pretence of fidelity; in both we see a sensibility beyond that of the younger characters. This psychological realism anticipates both Congreve's later achievements and the typical concerns of the novel. Brian Corman's '*The Way of the World* and Morally Serious Comedy' (*UTQ*) claims that in his last play Congreve's adroit manipulation of Restoration comic conventions enabled him to achieve moral seriousness and compose the greatest comedy of the age. Mirabell and Millamant are intellectually and morally finer, and more credible, than heroes and heroines of earlier Restoration comedy. Their situation presents real moral issues; they know their own feelings and are aware of the consequences of marriage. Congreve's villains, though they cannot dominate the action, are not the usual cardboard figures and do pose a real threat to the happiness of his hero and heroine. His moral seriousness even leads to his unconvincing attempt to suggest how the Fainalls may 'live easily together'; in earlier comedies, their difficulties would have been left unresolved.

Finally two important contributions to the study of Restoration tragedy. Tate's *History of King Lear* was edited by James Black for the 'Regents Restoration Drama Series'.[21] The text has been reliably edited and annotated in the manner of the series, though I noted some editorial or printing errors (read 'Thy' for 'They' at II.v.34, point for comma at II.v.77, 'and' at II.v.120, 'Then' for 'When' at V.iv.71, 'virtue' at V.vi.160) and the editor should have marked an exit for Edgar at I.i.256. In his introduction Black shows that the play was a popular success because Tate transformed Shakespeare's tragedy into typical Restoration drama, though 'it has as much affinity with the later sentimental drama as with heroic tragedy'. I suggest that this affinity may explain why the play was apparently more popular after 1700 than it had been before. The introduction ends with a survey of its theatrical history, and there is an interesting appendix on 'Tate's Shakespearean Text' and other possible sources. This edition fulfils a major aim of the 'Regents' series, making available a

[21] *The History of King Lear*, by Nahum Tate, ed. by James Black. Regents Restoration Drama Series. University of Nebraska Press, 1975; Arnold, 1976. pp. xxxvii + 111. £4.50, pb £2.25.

text which is difficult of access, with the sort of editorial help the modern reader wants. Unlike Tate's play, Lee's *Lucius Junius Brutus* can be considered a genuine if 'marginal' tragedy, according to David M. Vieth's 'Psychological Myth as Tragedy: Nathaniel Lee's *Lucius Junius Brutus*' (*HLQ*). It cannot be fully understood, Vieth maintains, as Whig propaganda, or as Aristotelian tragedy, or even as 'affective' tragedy in the manner of Otway; its characters should be seen as 'semi-symbolic projections of a unitary psychological situation' or 'psychological myth', that of fatherhood and sonship.

(c) *Prose writers*

Firstly, two amiable eccentrics, William Lilly and Sir Richard Urquhart. Derek Parker has used Lilly's autobiography, his correspondence with Ashmole, some of his pamphlets and almanacs, and his own astrological expertise, to write a lively biography,[22] drawing attention to the effects of astrology on social and political life in the middle years of the century. The stars have not helped Parker to foresee the reprinting of the autobiography last year (*YW* 55, 315–16). *The Admirable Urquhart* is a selection from Urquhart's prose works.[23] Predictably but unfortunately most space goes to extracts from the famous but readily accessible translation of Rabelais. There are also extracts from *Logopandecteision, or an Introduction to the Universal Language*, 'The Admirable Crichtoun' from *The Jewel*, and a well-illustrated introduction by Richard Boston. The favourite exercise of Urquhart's mind was verbocination, and the universal language was to have improved on all others in having more words, parts of speech, cases, genders, moods and tenses; but Boston suggests Urquhart anticipates the principles of Roget's *Thesaurus* and computer languages. Certainly he was more Rabelaisian than Rabelais, and for Gargantua's 'petite dille' finds thirty-eight synonyms to Rabelais's thirteen. Urquhart's logomania was near allied to creative genius; its outcome was that rare achievement, a translation which cannot be superseded.

An interesting book on Bunyan by Monica Furlong[24] should perhaps be seen as a contribution to religious rather than literary studies. She says 'the poetry' of *Pilgrim's Progress* and parts of *Grace Abounding* 'should chiefly commend Bunyan to us', but *Grace Abounding* is treated as a biographical source, and chapters on *Pilgrim's Progress, Badman* and *The Holy War* are too much given over to summaries; readers of *YW* may well find the chapter on his literary influence more helpful. The chapters on Bunyan's life and beliefs, on his progress through and beyond Puritanism, are the most interesting; Ms Furlong suggests that it was only when he saw that man cannot be pure that he attained both peace of mind and, in the second part of *Pilgrim's Progress*, a new level of creativity. The relevance of the beliefs to the writing is also considered in Claude Fleurdorge's

---

[22] *Familiar to All: William Lilly and Astrology in the Seventeenth Century*, by Derek Parker. Jonathan Cape. pp. 272. 10 plates.

[23] *The Admirable Urquhart: Selected Writings*, ed. by Richard Boston. Gordon Fraser. pp. 205. £5.50.

[24] *Puritan's Progress: A Study of John Bunyan*, by Monica Furlong. Hodder and Stoughton pp. 223. 6 illustrations. £5.50.

'Marques textuelles de l'idéologie' (*Cahiers Elisabéthains*), which shows by detailed analysis of the Worldly Wiseman episode in *Pilgrim's Progress* how opposed ideas of moral law and religious faith affect Bunyan's prose. Wolfgang Iser's *Der Implizite Leser*, including an important chapter on Bunyan (*YW* 53, 268), has been translated into English.[25] A facsimile of Walter Charleton's *The Ephesian Matron*[26] will make this curious tale more widely available. According to Achsah Guibbory's introduction, Charleton makes it illustrate Hobbes's low view of human nature, and implies that only Christianity, not Epicureanism, can help us control our passions. For a discussion of the many versions of the tale Dr Guibbory rightly refers us to a fine essay by Peter Ure (*DUJ*, 1956)—which has been reprinted in Ure's *Elizabethan and Jacobean Drama* (*YW* 55, 236). Neither Guibbory nor Ure says much about the Chaucer quotations in this edition of Charleton's version, so it seems worth adding that three are wrenched from *The Book of the Duchess*, one is from the spurious 'Praise of Women', and one seems to be a cento or parody.

The tercentenary of the death of Clarendon was marked at Oxford on 2 December 1974 by a lecture by Professor Trevor-Roper.[27] Clarendon is viewed sympathetically as an English patriot whose ideas, had they been acted upon immediately, might have saved his country some of its revolutionary excesses. He thought the established church should be essentially tolerant and ecumenical, and strove to keep the monarchy on an Anglican base; but after his fall that base was undermined by the policies of Charles II and James II. Just as his *History of the Rebellion*, 'the historical Bible of the Tory Party', had to wait till 1704 for publication, so his policy had to wait till Queen Anne's time for its final triumph. In the splendid gallery of the *History* there is no portrait of Charles II; the explanation, according to W. G. Roebuck's 'Charles II: The Missing Portrait' (*HLQ*), is that Clarendon hoped Charles would recall him from exile. If he had been resigned to his fate he might well have concluded with a realistic and unflattering portrait of Charles; as it is, he witholds either the final condemnation or the final accolade. In 'Clarendon, Sir Robert Howard, and Chancery Office-Holding at the Restoration' (*HLQ*) P. H. Hardacre reprints a letter of Clarendon's about an office which he gave Howard for a small consideration, and which Howard sold at a vast profit.

A selection from Aubrey's *Brief Lives*, with introductions and notes, was edited by Richard Barber.[28] 'The basis for selection has been to include only those lives for which a reasonably authentic contemporary portrait could be found'. Some 93 lives are thus chosen, whereas Oliver Lawson Dick included a good many more in his edition. Only one is found in Barber but not in Lawson Dick, that of Lacy the comedian, with

---

[25] *The Implied Reader*, by Wolfgang Iser. Johns Hopkins University Press. pp. 303. 6.30.

[26] *The Ephesian Matron*, by Walter Charleton, 2nd edition, 1668, with an introduction by Achsah Guibbory. A.R.S., 172-3. Los Angeles: Clark Memorial Library. p. xiv + [xiv] + 80. By subscription.

[27] *Edward Hyde, Earl of Clarendon*, by Hugh Trevor-Roper. Oxford: Clarendon Press. pp. 29, pb 75p.

[28] *Brief Lives*, by John Aubrey, ed. by Richard Barber. Folio Society. pp. 324. 4 illustrations. £5.95.

Wright's portrait showing him in three of his acting roles. Barber complains Lawson Dick has 'rewritten' Aubrey, so it can be noted that in Barber's version of the life of Milton Dryden's remark that Milton 'pronounced ye letter R very hard' is detached from its proper context and attributed to 'John Bryden'. However, in his version of the life of Richard Corbet we are told Corbet's father was the Vincent Corbet whose epitaph was written by Jonson, an interesting detail omitted by Lawson Dick. Neither edition is wholly satisfactory; Lawson Dick's is more complete and has an index, but Barber's has the portraits and some helpful explanatory notes. From reading *Brief Lives* and maybe Anthony Powell's biography we are unlikely to form an accurate idea of the range and quality of Aubrey's intellectual interests. Michael Hunter's *John Aubrey and the Realm of Learning*[29] should help here. Aubrey made substantial notes for and partly wrote works on archaeology, topography, natural history, 'things praeternatural', education, religion and many other topics, but failed to put his notes in order and left most of his works in manuscript. He has not been well served by his editors (as Hunter shows in an appendix; see also *YW* 53, 270–1) and some of his work remains unpublished. Hunter has gone back to the foul papers, makes many apt and striking quotations, and supplies the necessary organisation. He relates Aubrey to the seventeenth-century scientific movement, arguing that while he cannot be said to have made a major contribution to the advancement of science, his scientific interests did help to win him an important place in the growth of English historical writing. He was an innovator in using non-literary sources whose value had been underestimated, seeking conclusions about the past from the accumulation of data about antiquities, architecture, technology, folk-lore and place-names. In this book we see Aubrey much better as an individual and in relation to contemporaries, though the impression remains that his achievement depended more on historical imagination than on scientific method.

Thomas Rymer is the focus of attention in Earl Miner's 'Mr Dryden and Mr Rymer' (*PQ*). Rymer took from Dryden the ideas of literary periods and literary progress, but came to believe that in tragedy the way forward lay in going back to the Greeks. His return to primitive truth for the sake of reform makes him essentially a Protestant Humanist; Dryden's feeling that 'the memorable day was his own' helps to give him a truly catholic taste. Rymer also borrowed, and improved, the method of critical analysis pioneered by Dryden; he may have murdered to dissect, but his analyses often yield valuable results. He never wholly lost Dryden's respect. The description of him as a 'literary Quixote', vaguely attributed by Miner to 'Disraeli', is from Isaac D'Israeli's *Amenities of Literature*.

The storm over Jeremy Collier's *Short View of the Immorality and Profaneness of the English Stage* rumbles on in the learned journals. In 'Jeremy Collier's Courage: A Dissenting View' (*YES*) Benjamin Hellinger says the view that Collier showed courage in attacking distinguished writers 'has become standard in literary history', though the only authority quoted is the *D.N.B.* Hellinger dissents on the grounds that Collier was

29 *John Aubrey and the Realm of Learning*, by Michael Hunter. Duckworth. pp. 256. 18 plates. £12.50.

keen controversialist, did not care who he attacked, had nothing to lose, could rely on some support, and as a known Jacobite was unlikely to be accused of Puritanism. In 'Jeremy Collier's "False and Imperfect Citations" ' (*RECTR*) Hellinger shows that most of Collier's quotations from plays are accurate enough, and that on the whole he tries to be fair, but he is often guilty of misrepresentation, owing to 'literary obtuseness, extremely narrow piety, and an easily stimulated imagination'. In 'No Cloistered Virtue: or, Playwright versus Priest in 1698' (*PMLA*) Aubrey Williams argues that Collier did not win the argument. Congreve and others maintained that comic dramatists need not approve of the vice and folly of their characters, and that obscene or profane expressions should be seen in their contexts. They felt with Milton that the 'survey of vice' was 'necessary to the constituting of human virtue'. Many censured plays remained in the repertory, and Collier and his friends bemoaned the futility of protest. In 'Jeremy Collier and the Jonson revivals of 1700' (*Trivium*) Graham Nicholls notes that after the first decade of the Restoration Jonson's plays lost popularity, but when Collier pronounced them morally sound Christopher Rich was encouraged to produce *Volpone, The Alchemist* and *Epicoene* at Drury Lane in 1700.

I have space only for brief mention of work on philosophy and the history of ideas. James Knowlson's *Universal Language Schemes*[30] shows how these were expected to promote the advancement of learning, and considers inter alia John Wilkins's *Essay towards a Real Character and a Philosophical Language*. Knowlson's confession that he has 'not yet seen' Barbara Shapiro's 1969 biography of Wilkins (*YW* 52, 265) is a surprise in a learned work in a specialised field. *The Locke Newsletter*[31] as usual carries articles, notes, queries, bibliographies, and reports of work in progress. Klaus P. Fischer's 'John Locke and the German Enlightenment' (*JHI*) argues that Locke had little influence on German thought. Roland Hall contributed three articles on Locke and one on Cudworth to *N&Q*, mainly lists of new words and antedatings; of these, 'John Locke's New Words and Usages' interestingly discusses his ideas about words and reasons for coining new ones. John North's 'The *Principia* in the Making' (*TLS*) is a review article on the latest volumes of Newton's *Mathematical Papers*[32] and *Correspondence*.[33] A number of articles dealt with religious ideas. Allison Coudert's 'A Cambridge Platonist's Kabbalist Nightmare' (*JHI*) tells how Henry More, partly because of a nightmare, decided that the Kabbala enshrined dangerous ideas, though some of his friends sought to use them to convert Jews and pagans and to unite the Christian church. Caroline Robbins's 'Faith and Freedom (*c*. 1677-1729)' (*JHI*) examines 'modern attitudes' in the various modes of religious and rationalist thought of the period. Irène Simon's 'Robert South and the Augustans' (*E&S*)

---

[30] *Universal Language Schemes in England and France 1600-1800*, by James Knowlson. University of Toronto Press. pp. [x] + 301. 5 plates.

[31] *The Locke Newsletter*, ed. by Roland Hall, No. 5. York: Dept. of Philosophy, University of York. pp. 104. Free to Locke scholars.

[32] *The Mathematical Papers of Isaac Newton, Volume 6: 1684-1691*, ed. by D. T. Whiteside. C.U.P. pp. 614. £25.

[33] *The Correspondence of Isaac Newton, Volume 5*, ed. by A. Rupert Hall and Laura Tilling. C.U.P. pp. 439. £20.

shows that South's sermons, with their attacks on both enthusiasm and deism, prefigure the ideas of man and society of conservative thinkers in the eighteenth century.

4. Background

'European Architectural Heritage Year' produced two books on Wren. Bryan Little's *Sir Christopher Wren*[34] is 'A Historical Biography' in the sense that Wren's career is seen in relation to political events and economic circumstances. Little describes Wren's private life in as much detail as scanty sources allow, and brings out some of his interests outside architecture quite well, but does not do justice to his scientific work, not even mentioning the experiments in blood transfusion, for instance. The emphasis falls on Wren as an architect, but Little has ill-advisedly tried to fit everything into a rigid chronological scheme, one chapter for about every six years, so that the main lines of development are obscured among family matters, business, politics, and the routine of the Surveyor General's office. This clumsy arrangement is often reflected in individual sentences; he packs in so much detail that the sense is lost, and bad proof-correcting compounds our difficulties. The illustrations bring some relief and more problems. Sixty-seven photographs crowd onto thirty-two pages, and some are awkwardly trimmed, notably that of the design for the rebuilding of London, which does not show the riverside. Some captions are unhelpful, if not positively wrong; plate 49 is called 'The 'Penultimate' Design, before 1675', but from the discussion on pp. 98–9 it seems the term 'Penultimate' should refer to a design for St Paul's much less like the one carried out. In short, Wren's ideas of structure and style have had little influence on the making of this book. It is informative, but it is not the authoritative work that is wanted; meanwhile, both the general reader and the specialist will get more satisfaction from Sir John Summerson's *Sir Christopher Wren* (1965). Eric de Maré's *Wren's London*[35] 'does not pretend to contain prime scholarship', but is well written and not unoriginal in concentrating on the most dramatic decades of London history. De Maré describes the medieval city as it was just before the Great Fire, the trauma of the fire itself, and the rebuilding programme, to which Wren would have given his genius if it had been acceptable. The many illustrations are beautifully reproduced.

The Genius of the Place[36] is a splendid anthology of literature and art illustrating the history of English landscape gardening. The texts are from original editions and manuscripts, presented 'with the minimum of editorial interference'. Some texts and a few paintings and prints are familiar and accessible, but a great many are not; among the authors from our period are Evelyn, Milton, John Woolridge, Cotton, Temple and Timothy Nourse, and their writings are accompanied by paintings by Danckerts, Rubens,

[34] *Sir Christopher Wren*, by Bryan Little. Robert Hale. pp. 288. 67 illustrations. £6.
    [35] *Wren's London*, by Eric de Maré. Folio Society. pp. 128. 35 illustrations in colour, 50 in monochrome. Free to members; price for additional copies £3.75.
    [36] *The Genius of the Place: The English Landscape Garden 1620-1820*, ed. by John Dixon Hunt and Peter Willis. Paul Elek. pp. xx + 390. 101 plates. £12.50.

Sieberechts and others, and their own prints and sketches. The editors supply a scholarly introduction, headnotes, and a select bibliography. They claim that landscape gardening is 'the one art that England [has] contributed to Europe since the Renaissance'. It reflects changing ideas of art and nature, themselves often reflecting the work of theorists and landscape painters; or possibly it gives rise to these ideas and activities. In the seventeenth century the enclosed and excessively artificial Tudor garden gave way to something more ambitious and natural, though French formality remained the dominant influence. Milton thought 'a happy rural seat' could do without 'nice Art', and the guiding principle of English landscape gardening was formulated by Pope: 'Consult the *Genius* of the *Place* in all'. Such ideas led to the displacement of Classical temples by Gothick ruins, to Capability Brown's artificial avoidance of artificiality, and finally to the search for the picturesque outside gardens altogether. By the early nineteenth century landscape gardeners are being satirised by Peacock. This stimulating book will obviously help students of the visual arts, and it is to be hoped it influences planners of our environment, but it must also appeal strongly to anyone with an interest in English culture. As background reading for literary students it should have high priority.

The late Sir Jack Westrup's book on Purcell[37] reached a seventh edition and achieved paperback status. There are minor revisions to the text and bibliography, and new information on Purcell's family is incorporated in an appendix; Westrup maintains that Thomas Purcell was the composer's father.

[37] *Purcell*, by J. A. Westrup. The Master Musicians. Dent. pp. xii + 323. £3.60, pb £1.80.

XII

The Eighteenth Century

K. E. ROBINSON

This chapter is in five sections: 1. General; 2. Poetry; 3. Prose; 4. The Novel; 5. Drama.

1. General

The period continues to be indebted to the annual *PQ* bibliography and the selective notices and reviews in *The Scriblerian*. This year's review article in *SEL* is by Paul Fussell. 1975 produced little of outstanding general literary importance, but it was rich in historical works. There are several of biographical interest. The Duke of Newcastle continues to attract attention: Kelch's study of Newcastle's finances is followed this year by Reed Browning's impeccable biography, *The Duke of Newcastle*.[1] Its chief merit is its sense of proportion: Browning admits the justice of much of the negative view of Newcastle but tries to redress the balance by showing his handling of both foreign and financial affairs to be "professional", by proving him a good subordinate minister, and by separating the man from his role. Newcastle was 'generous and soft-hearted. . . . He worked hard, enjoyed life in his own anxious fashion, and never forgot his family'. Anyone whose interests are primarily literary might be disappointed that there is very little about the Hanover and Kit-Kat Clubs. Browning's account of the continuity between the politics of Newcastle and Rockingham initiated a debate with Paul Langford in the *TLS*, whilst Rockingham himself and the Rockingham Whigs are the subject of two studies with an equally keen sense of proportion, backed by immense scholarship: *The Marquis: A Study of Lord Rockingham 1730-1782* by Ross J. S. Hoffman[2] and Frank O'Gorman's *The Rise of Party in England: The Rockingham Whigs 1760-82*.[3] Hoffman may be allowed the last words: 'uncreative, Rockingham was a practical improver of other men's work and had the kind of critical eye that makes a man a good judge of a horse'. Rockingham's nephew, Earl Fitzwilliam is, too, the subject of a well-balanced study, by E. A. Smith[4] who attempts to place his life in the context of the Whig party between 1748 and 1833. Smith concentrates upon the conflict between political principles and the demands of party politics. This will be an important work for anyone interested in Burke.

[1] *The Duke of Newcastle*, by Reed Browning. Yale University Press. pp. xiv + 388

[2] *The Marquis: A Study of Lord Rockingham 1730-1782*, by Ross J. S. Hoffman Fordham University Press. pp. 379.

[3] *The Rise of Party in England: The Rockingham Whigs 1760-82*, by Frank O'Gorman. Allen & Unwin. pp. 662.

[4] *Whig Principle and Party Politics. Earl Fitzwilliam and the Whig Party 1748-1833*, by E. A. Smith. Manchester University Press. pp. 411.

Sheila Biddle chronicles the relationship of Bolingbroke and Harley.[5] Her two opening chapters supply incisive portraits of the two men to back up her sense that 'political or personal differences alone would have been sufficient to divide them'. The remainder of the book concerns itself with the puzzle of 'the great Affection they bore to each other' in the early days of their relationship. The quotation is from Swift who plays a large part in Miss Biddle's work. Apart from an account of his relations with both politicians, we are here provided with a remarkable opportunity to judge Swift's claims as a historian. Miss Biddle finds for Swift as 'an acute judge of character, remarkable both for his honesty and insight' despite inaccuracies and inevitable incompleteness. Further, whatever his failings, 'much of the time he was, quite simply there'. Pope, Arbuthnot et al. also figure in Miss Biddle's narrative, which is one of the most useful of the books in this section for 1975. Another biography of interest for light on the literary world is William L. Sachse's *Lord Somers: A Political Portrait*[6] in which a chapter is devoted to Somers' role as patron and connoisseur. Much in these books emphasises the improbability of J. H. Plumb's contention that 'the monarchy of the first four Georges provided the mainspring of political life', a view resuscitated in the second edition of his *The First Four Georges*[7]. And in contrast with these books Audrey Williamson's study of Wilkes[8], like her earlier study of Tom Paine, is very partisan. Miss Williamson's reply to a hostile *TLS* review by Gita Curtis stresses the research behind the biography, but it does nothing to convince the present reviewer that it is not unduly partial.

The rash of books on Marlborough continues with Bryan Bevan's *Marlborough the Man*.[9] Unfortunately, Bevan's pretensions to throw light on Marlborough's enigmatic character are unsubstantiated: he seems more concerned with circumstantial detail than analysis. A far more interesting Marlborough emerges from *The Marlborough-Godolphin Correspondence* edited by Henry L. Snyder,[10] a Marlborough much less sure of himself and more passionate than the man of the biographies The letters are painstakingly annotated, lucidly introduced and well indexed. It is disappointing that there is scarce reference to literary figures, but some recompense is made by Robert D. Horn's *Marlborough: A Survey, Panegyrics, Satires and Biographical Writings, 1688-1788*[11] which lists, describes and supplies locations for some 582 works dealing with Marlborough. The letters from Henry St. John to Charles Boyle, Earl of Orrery are also printed for the first time: there are fifty-three, penned between 1709-11, edited for The Royal Historical Society by H. T. Dickinson.[12] Finally, in this batch of books relating to specific individuals, there is Philip Roberts' edition of

[5] *Bolingbroke and Harley*, by Sheila Biddle. Allen & Unwin. pp. 307.
[6] *Lord Somers: A Political Portrait*, by William L. Sachse. Manchester University Press. pp. 475.
[7] *The First Four Georges*, by J. H. Plumb. Spring Books. pp. 208.
[8] *Wilkes. "A Friend to Liberty"*, by Audrey Williamson. Allen & Unwin. pp. 254.
[9] *Marlborough the Man. A Biography of John Churchill First Duke of Marlborough*, by Bryan Bevan. Robert Hale. pp. 320.
[10] *The Marlborough-Godolphin Correspondence*, edited by Henry L. Snyder. Oxford: Clarendon. 3 volumes. pp. xxxix + 1794.
[11] *Marlborough: A Survey. Panegyrics, Satires and Biographical Writings 1688-1788*, by Robert D. Horn. Garland. pp. xxii + 588.
[12] *Camden Miscellany*, volume XXVI, edited by H. T. Dickinson. Royal Historical Society.

The Diary of Sir David Hamilton, 1709-14[13] which is most noteworthy for the light it casts on Swift's relationship with the Queen (already described in Roberts' *PQ* note). Swift's accession to a Deanery provoked Anne to remark 'that all the Deanerys in Ireland were of the Lord Lieutenant's gift but the Bishopricks of Hers'. Roberts supplies all one could want in the way of an introduction and explanatory notes. On a less political note, Laurence Stone has edited two volumes of essays on *The University in Society*.[14] In the first volume Sheldon Rothblatt explores eighteenth-century Oxbridge, arguing that the emphasis on examinations in the early nineteenth century has moral implications as a reaction against the loose living of student life in the previous century. In the second volume Nicholas Phillipson writes on the interrelation between the university and its environs, centring upon the Edinburgh of the Scottish Enlightenment, after the Union. Phillipson holds that when the Scottish sense of identity was at a low ebb the Edinburgh literati assumed authority with the blessing of the local gentry.

Two very important books remove us from the heady arena of big politics and academe to the realities of life for the less fortunate in the eighteenth century. *Albion's Fatal Tree: Crime and Society in Eighteenth-Century England*,[15] a collection of essays by Douglas Hay, Peter Linebaugh, E. P. Thompson, John G. Rule and Cal Winslow, takes the inspiration for its title from Blake and is touched throughout with a Blakean sympathy. The focus is upon 'law both as ideology and as actuality'. It examines the connection between the apparent rise in crime figures and the growing number of statutes redefining the range of activities which could be said to be criminal. 'The ideology of the ruling oligarchy, which places a supreme value upon property, finds its visible and material embodiment above all in the ideology and practise of the law'. I shall mention only those papers of especial interest in the present context. Douglas Hay writes on "Property, Authority and the Criminal Law", carefully defining key terms in the legal rhetoric of the day: 'It was a society with a bloody penal code, an astute ruling class who manipulated it to their advantage, and a people schooled in the lessons of Justice, Terror and Mercy. The benevolence of rich men to poor and all the ramifications of patronage, were upheld by the sanction of the gallows and the rhetoric of the death sentence'. In a second essay Hay investigates the implementation of, and resentment towards, the Game laws on Cannock Chase. Peter Linebaugh looks into "The Tyburn Riot against the Surgeons," the relations of the Old Bailey judges with the physicians and surgeons around the corner in Warwick Lane and Cripplegate providing him with a source of plebeian wrath. Linebaugh contrasts the view of death as having "medical utility" with 'the complexity of plebeian con-

---

[13] *The Diary of Sir David Hamilton 1709-14*, edited by Philip Roberts. Oxford: Clarendon. pp. xlviii + 138.

[14] *The University in Society. Volume I: Oxford and Cambridge from the fourteenth to the early nineteenth century; Volume II: Europe, Scotland and the United States from the sixteenth to the twentieth century*, edited by Laurence Stone. Princeton University Press. pp. 964.

[15] *Albion's Fatal Tree. Crime and Society in Eighteenth-Century England*, by Douglas Hay, Peter Linebaugh, John G. Rule, E. P. Thompson and Cal Winslow. Allen Lane. pp. 352.

ceptions of death and the gravity with which the fact of death was held.'
E. P. Thompson rounds off the collection with an outline of the implications of the anonymous threatening letter regarded as a form of social
protest, taking his sample from *The London Gazette*, 1750-1820. Thompson was originally going to include a paper on the origin of the Black Act,
but his research grew into a larger study, *Whigs and Hunters*,[16] caught
sight of in his exchange with Pat Rogers in the *TLS* last year. Thompson
works through the system of forest government in Windsor and Hampshire
to delineate the deer-hunters there and closer to London. As Thompson
puts it, as the book progresses it gets 'ever closer to the measures and
ideology of the Whigs, to the men who made the Black Act and to the law
which they made.' Thompson is well aware that both his evidence and the
account it yields are partial; but here lies one of the remarkable characteristics of his book. It recreates something of the plebeian view of the Act
with a method which clearly has important historiographical implications.
Both these books offer invaluable material for anyone at all interested in
the century: both are richly spiced with literary reference. The second
appendix of *Whigs and Hunters*, for example, elucidates Pope's connections
with the Blacks through Charles Rackett, suggesting a degree of sympathy
with their plight and antipathy to the regime which produced it.

There are, too, several historical papers which deserve mention. The
reaction to Sacheverell's impeachment is the subject of Lee Horsley's
illustrated "*Vox Populi* in the Political Literature of 1710" (*HLQ*). In the
reaction the Whigs, traditionally sympathetic to 'the Voice of the People,'
became 'the victims of *vox populi*, defeated by an enormous surge of
popular support for the Tories'. The situation pleased neither party: the
Whigs argued that the people were being deluded, whilst the Tories,
pleased on the one hand, were 'embarrassed by the disorderly demonstrations in their cause'. The literature which Horsley examines against this
background includes Swift's *Examiner* essays and Defoe's *A Vindication
of Dr. Henry Sacheverell, Hymn to the Mob* and Captain Tom pamphlets.
In a study complementary to, but lacking the rich detail and analytic
imagination of, the two Thompson books, Janelle Greenberg comments
on the "Legal Status of the English Woman in Early Eighteenth-Century
Common Law and Equity",[17] calling attention to the disjunction between
legal rights and social reality. According to J. H. Plumb: the eighteenth
century opened up a new world for children with the growing demise of
patriarchal attitudes. Plumb gives details of educational and social change.
So do two related books on children's literature, Gerald Gottlieb's *Early
Children's Books and their Illustrations*[18] and Joyce Irene Whalley's
*Cobwebs to Catch Flies: Illustrated Books for the Nursery and School-
room 1700-1900:*[19] both contain a wealth of illustrated material.

[16] *Whigs and Hunters. The Origin of the Black Act*, by E. P. Thompson. Allen
Lane. pp. 313.
[17] From *Studies in Eighteenth-Century Culture, Volume IV*, edited by Harold E.
Pagliaro. University of Wisconsin Press. pp. xxii + 326.
[18] *Early Children's Books and their Illustrations*, by Gerald Gottlieb. Morgan
Library. n.p.
[19] *Cobwebs to Catch Flies: Illustrated Books for the Nursery and Schoolroom
1700-1900*, by Joyce Irene Whalley. Elek. pp. 163.

There is plenty of evidence for the social historian in Ronald Paulson's latest book on Hogarth,[20] which concentrates on the paintings, especially the "modern moral subjects" or "comic history-paintings". The text is essentially introductory, but it does correct errors in, and add to, his *Hogarth: His Life and Times*. In addition to a large number of high quality illustrations, John Hayes' book on Gainsborough[21] provides an introduction to the man and the artist, letting him speak in his own words as much as possible. Both books are, in the present financial climate, reasonably priced in relation to the number of plates they contain. 'Damn the man, how various he is': such was Gainsborough's comment on Reynolds' portraits. Another aspect of that variety is the *Discourses*, the Wark edition of which is now reissued in a photographic reprint with additions and corrections to several annotations and two supplementary appendices containing Blake's marginalia to and Hazlitt's essays on the *Discourses*.[22] Robert Wark is also responsible for producing a fine catalogue of the Huntington Rowlandson collection,[23] illustrating all the drawings. The variety of Fuseli's achievement as realised at the Tate exhibition is reviewed by Peter Conrad (*TLS*). Conrad finds it entirely appropriate that the exhibition should have been arranged according to the divisions of his literary material: 'he is more a dramatist than a painter—his people have a troubling reality of character for all their lack of pictorial refinement.' Despite its two hundred or more illustrations, the catalogue[24] is disappointing: its introduction merits Peter Conrad's charge of "canting apology". From the turbulence of Fuseli we turn to a master of pastoral serenity, Thomas Bewick, the wood-engraver, whose *Memoir* is edited by Iain Bain in a handsome volume for the Oxford English Memoirs and Travels Series.[25] The tactfully annotated text follows Bewick's manuscript draft in the British Library, including the apparently digressive sections which contribute appreciably to the *Memoir*'s charm. It is complemented with finely printed head and tail pieces and some very useful remarks on Bewick's technique. Those concerned with eighteenth-century book illustrators generally now have an invaluable aid in Hans Hammelmann and T. S. R. Boase's biographical dictionary, *Book Illustrators in Eighteenth-Century England*,[26] listing 263 artists with details of their work. The history of the art of landscape gardening benefits from an anthology of literary and visual material edited by John Dixon Hunt and Peter Willis (*The Genius of the Place: The English Landscape Garden 1620-1820*).[27] The anthology is a fascinating mixture of items ranging from theoretic pronouncements to

---

[20] *The Art of Hogarth*, by Ronald Paulson. Phaidon. pp. 206.
[21] *Gainsborough. Paintings and Drawings*, by John Hayes. Phaidon. pp. 232.
[22] *Discourses on Art*, by Sir Joshua Reynolds, edited by Robert R. Wark. Yale University Press. pp. xxxv + 349.
[23] *Drawings by Thomas Rowlandson in the Huntington Collection*, by Robert R. Wark. Huntington Library. pp. 398.
[24] *Henry Fuseli*, by Gert Schiff and Werner Hofmann. Tate Gallery. pp. 143.
[25] *A Memoir*, by Thomas Bewick, edited by Iain Bain. O.U.P. pp. 258.
[26] *Book Illustrators in Eighteenth-Century England*, by Hanns Hammelmann and T. S. R. Boase. Yale University Press. pp. 184.
[27] *The Genius of the Place: The English Landscape Garden 1620-1820*, by John Dixon Hunt and Peter Willis. Elek. pp. xx + 390 + 101 plates.

practical hints, all given shape by an introduction which sketches in the general lines of development and the formative influences and headnotes to the extracts. It has not been possible to consult a copy of Peter Willis's *Furor Hortensis*.[28]

Literary satire, more specifically "The Satirists' London", is the concern of Ian Donaldson (*EIC*) who explores the truthfulness of various writers' accounts of various aspects of London life. It is a shame that he ducks the more interesting theoretical questions implied by his study to focus simply upon 'some of the ways in which satirists. . . . may suppress, distort and manipulate the evidence'. Most of the material has to do with the Thames and crowds: Johnson, Pope, Smollett and Blake all figure (as does T. S. Eliot who is introduced to evidence the claim that the problems facing the eighteenth century are perennial). Arthur J. Weitzman's "Eighteenth-Century London: Urban Paradise or Fallen City?" (*JHI*) suffers from the same failure to impact a cohesive argument on familiar material. Weitzman chronicles the place of London in eighteenth-century literature and the Romantic reaction. Paul C. Davies (*EIC*) pursues a less familiar line, the manifestation of the Augustan predilection for discrimination in the attitude to smell. 'It is because the sense of smell is less easily deceived than the sight that it becomes an important adjunct to the Augustan's main literary enterprise, the discrimination of truth from falsehood.' Swift, Pope and "the learned Smelfungus" provide the central texts. Smollett, Davies notes, is an exception to the rule that the sense of smell atrophies in the literature of the second half of the century with the rise of sensibility. The most interesting of the papers on satire is C. R. Kropf's 'Libel and Satire in the Eighteenth Century' (*ECS*). Kropf points out the possibilities for *ad hominem* satire allowed by the legislation. Almost anything was permissible, providing that the victim was not named: the most outrageous *double entendre* was safe for what mattered legally was its 'most innocuous sense'. What is more, if a writer was pressed to justice, the Courts allowed a plea of reasonable provocation, a fact of which Pope made a careful note. To attack a state official was, however, quite another thing, hence Swift's careful covering of his tracks as author of *Gulliver's Travels*.

Thomas R. Preston's *Not in Timon's Manner*[29] traces a tradition of 'benevolent misanthropy, . . . hating man and loving the individual' and attempts to demonstrate how it 'provided a mode of literary satire accommodated to the prevailing antisatiric ethos of what has been called the "Age of Sensibility".' Preston sees this tradition as allowing for both that age's pessimism about the possibility of man's moral transformation and its optimism about the individual's capacity for moral progress through benevolence. Three general chapters chart the development, a little over-schematically perhaps, in preparation for a chapter each on Smollett and

[28] *Furor Hortensis. Essays on the History of the English Landscape Gardens in memory of H. F. Clark*, edited by Peter Willis. Elysium Press. pp. 107 + 32 plates.
[29] *Not in Timon's Manner. Feeling, Misanthropy, and Satire in Eighteenth-Century England*, by Thomas R. Preston. University of Alabama Press. pp. 217.

Johnson. A final chapter sketches the demise, the decay of feeling into affectation, morbidity, and finally criminality, which led to the disappearance of the benevolent misanthrope as satirist. Preston's survey is useful, but it lacks the depth of understanding and sense of wider significance characteristic of R. F. Brissenden's *Virtue in Distress* which covers related ground.

Just as Hay and Thompson remove us to the realms of less familiar history, so Ivanka Kovačevic presents us with less familiar literature by way of discussion and anthology in *Fact into Fiction*.[30] She investigates reactions to the industrial scene between 1750 and 1850 as a background to the genesis of the so-called social novel and the growth of social conscience. The introductory chapters account for the way that 'the triumphant feeling of achievement faded in the face of grave apprehensions concerning the many negative effects of industrialisation on the life of the nation' (the section on "self-help" is particularly helpful); but the most important part of the book lies in the anthology of pieces difficult to obtain outside the larger libraries. These include pieces by William Paley and Hannah More, both with a prefatory note. Back with the more familiar, the title of Thomas Noel's *Theories of the Fable in the Eighteenth Century*[31] is self-explanatory. Originally a comparative literature thesis, Noel's study casts its net widely over European animal fable, in which the educational and literary are inseparable. Its acme in England was John Gay's *Fables*, but as Noel is interested in theory not practice Gay gets scant attention. Dodsley, Goldsmith and Beattie are discussed in a short chapter, but here, as elsewhere, Noel does not rise above uninspiring precis.

John Chalker's inaugural lecture, *Violence in Augustan Literature*,[32] takes examples from Smollett, Pope and Swift to show that the Augustan treatment of violence reveals 'the nature of man as precariously balanced and open to urges towards violence. . . recognising the necessary place of violence and. . . finding proper means for its expression'. The occasion seems to have thrust neatness upon Chalker: one would have liked to see more of the distinctiveness of individual writers' treatments. Despite its many supportive references to modern writers, this is no match for Claude Rawson's best work on allied topics. Rawson provides a review (*ELH*) of recent work on the vexed question of order in Augustan literature. Finally in this section, Donald F. Bond has contributed a bibliography for the eighteenth century to the Goldentree series.[33]

2. Poetry

The most important general book in this section is undoubtedly D. F Foxon's *English Verse 1701-1750*,[34] a two volume bibliography o separately printed poems. The first volume catalogues not much short o

[30] *Fact into Fiction. English Literature and the Industrial Scene, 1750-1850*, by Ivanka Kovačevic. Leicester University Press. pp. 424.
[31] *Theories of the Fable in the Eighteenth-Century*, by Thomas Noel. Columbi University Press. pp. 177.
[32] *Violence in Augustan Literature*, by John Chalker.University of London. pp. 2€
[33] *The Eighteenth-Century*, compiled by Donald F. Bond. AHM. pp. xvi + 184
[34] *English Verse, 1701-1750; A Catalogue of Separately Printed Poems wit Notes on Contemporary Collected Editions*, by D. F. Foxon. Cambridge Universit Press. 2 volumes. pp. xxx + 1225.

10,000 items alphabetically under author, title (where the author is not known) or first line (where neither the author nor title is available). Each item carries a bibliographical description. The second volume contains the tools with which the first can be used: (i) a first line index, (ii) a remarkably detailed chronological index, (iii) an index of imprints, sorted chronologically by location and publisher; (iv) a section on "bibliographical notabilia" covering such categories as piracies and fictitious imprints, (v) an account of descriptions of anonymous authors, and (vi) a subject index. Both the more general sections (iv and vi) contain a wealth of classified information. The first volume corrects and adds minor and major details to the bibliography of many writers: the whole is a monument to painstaking scholarship. John Holloway and Joan Black supply texts of some of the more ephemeral material in their *Later English Broadside Ballads*,[35] an almost entirely eighteenth-century selection printed from contemporary copies in the Madden Collection. A short introduction includes a brief account of distribution, printing and the characteristic ballad situations and narratives; but the emphasis is firmly upon bringing largely unknown material to the light. Annotation is kept to an absolute minimum and there is no bibliographical apparatus, though an end-note to each ballad gives the occasional detail. The woodblock illustrations are faithfully reproduced. Foxon's bibliography is an object lesson in the sort of contexture bibliographical detail and imaginative indexing which would have added to this collection; but it will remain useful in the absence of a comparable modern edition. More of Foxon's material is supplied in the final volume of the Yale edition of *Poems on Affairs of State*, edited by Frank Ellis.[36] This hefty volume, covering the years 1704-14, is especially well annotated, and a random check on the index has exposed no omissions. Now that the Yale series is complete, a single volume selection has been published, edited by George deF. Lord, available in paperback.[37]

Turning to critical work on the poetry, John Wilson Foster (*ECS*) demonstrates the influence of surveying and topography on 'the visual organisation of landscape poetry'. As distinct from the Renaissance, the eighteenth century was characterized by its ability 'to organize a spatial field objectively and methodically'. Foster centres upon 'Windsor Forest' as marked by this organisation but finds in it, too, a tendency to equate 'prospect with paradise' significant of the earlier mode. Later developments show the increased method breaking down the proper relationship between 'literalness and figurativeness, topic and meditation'. The synthesis of another pair of opposites, of particular and universal, is the province of a fascinating paper by David Parker (*Neophilologus*). He argues that many eighteenth-century poets used the direct article ambiguously in periphrases such as 'the fleeting nation' in an attempt to reproduce the ambiguity of Latin devoid of the article. This ambiguity allows the poet to represent 'the specific as a manifestation of general order, the general as an extrapolation

---

[35] *Later English Broadside Ballads*, edited by John Holloway and Joan Black. Routledge & Kegan Paul. pp. 296.
[36] *Poems on Affairs of State. Augustan Satirical Verse, 1660-1714, Volume VII: 1704-1714*, edited by Frank H. Ellis. Yale University Press. pp. x1 + 732.
[37] *An Anthology of Poems on Affairs of State: Augustan Satirical Verse, 1660-1714*, edited by George deF. Lord. Yale University Press. pp. 832.

from a single individual reality'. Heinz-Dieter Leidig[38] studies the reception of Lucan's *Pharsalia* from the Renaissance to the end of the eighteenth century. He is particularly concerned with the Lucan as a work of mixed genre; and his account of the eighteenth century is at its best on James Wellwood who included an essay on the historical poem in his edition (1719) of Rowe's translation of the *Pharsalia*. Leidig shows that the acceptance of Lucan is linked with a softening of legislative criticism. Emerson R. Marks, too, writes on an aspect of poetic theory (*PQ*). He explores the odd fact that the relative uniformity of taste in the eighteenth century is not matched by any consistency in the theory of poetic diction. Eighteenth-century critics found it difficult to elucidate poetic diction without reference to versification, but here, again, the results are disappointing. Only Samuel Say's essays on prosody merit a kind word. Sr. M. Pauline Parker (*ECS*) discusses the hymn as a literary form: she concludes that the hymn evidences 'the same traditional genius, popular yet artistic,' as the secular folksong.

Further evidence of John Sena's work on Garth is to be found in his note (*AN&Q*) on the poet's birthplace, correcting the eighteenth-century biographers' notion that he was a Yorkshireman. Garth was a native of Bolam in County Durham. Sena's work on Garth is sadly not matched by Jo. Allen Bradham's in her facsimile edition of *The Dispensary*.[39] Miss Bradham's choice of a pirated ninth edition (1725) for her text renders her efforts of little use to scholars. The introduction in which Garth is systematically devalued does nothing to offset her bibliographical obtuseness. Gay's text fares rather better. With Faber's edition very difficult to obtain and Underhill's Muses' Library edition of doubtful use, a much needed edition of Gay's poetry and prose is now available from the hand of Vinton A. Dearing with the assistance of Charles E. Beckwith.[40] Despite the furor caused amongst reviewers because the dramatic works are not included (see e.g. *TLS*), this edition provides a reliable text for an author whose poetry is consistently under-rated. It is essentially a tool for future critical work for its own introduction leaves a lot to be desired, though, in fairness, it does seem that critical material was cut because of unspecified exigencies. Its usefulness as such a tool is limited by a confusing arrangement of notes and the absence of an index; but a number of reviews, notes and letters suggest that it has already prompted critics to take stock of their knowledge of the poetry. Donald Greene's *TLS* review is an odd affair. Greene seems uninterested in the non-dramatic poetry; indeed, what little space is allowed to the poetry denies without substantiation whatever claims have been made for it. It is not surprising that Greene should have been taken to task, by David Nokes (*TLS*), though Nokes's claim that 'whenever Gay adopts the mock-pastoral style he develops a network of reciprocating ironies that defy literal interpretation' is not very inspiring.

[38] *Das Historiengedicht in der englischen Literaturtheorie: die Rezeption von Lucans "Pharsalia" von der Renaissance bis zum Ausgang des achtzehnten Jahrunderts.* by Heinz-Dieter Leidig. Herbert and Peter Lang. pp. 243.
[39] *The Dispensary*, by Samuel Garth, edited by Jo. Allen Bradham. Scholars' Facsimiles & Reprints. pp. xi + 154.
[40] *John Gay. Poetry and Prose*, edited by Vinton A. Dearing with the assistance of Charles E. Beckwith. Oxford: Clarendon. 2 volumes. pp. 656.

Greene's reply (*TLS*) asserts the poems to be pedestrian. In *The Scriblerian* Arthur Sherbo contributes a survey of criticism on Gay, ranging those who see him as lightweight against those who see him as heavyweight. Sherbo is conspicuously unwilling to commit himself unless it be in agreeing with Sutherland (*Pope and his Contemporaries*) that Gay takes 'his art seriously and wears his morality lightly'. The relation of Gay's art to his moral interests exercises Robert J. Merrett who addresses himself to Gay's 'consistent satire of the distortions of justice and literary perception' to deny Battestin's notion that aesthetic sensibility is the source of Gay's moral effectiveness.

Those critics who concentrate on aesthetic sensibility and find it lacking in Swift's poetry are the object of Dona F. Munker's attack in *SCN*. She defines and defends 'the light-minded aberrations' of a 'low style' which was an extension of the seventeenth-century burlesque and shared its raillery, concentration upon commonplace experience, empirical knowledge and detached irony. Hazlitt was not one of these critics: Colin J. Horne (*EIC*) puts the record of Henry Sams (*EIC*) straight. Whereas Sams had lumped together Hazlitt with Thackeray and Macaulay as a Swift-hater, Horne reminds us that Hazlitt thought of Swift as 'in the first rank of agreeable moralists in verse'. W. R. Irwin's concern with the poetry (*PQ*) is similar to Munker's. Irwin opines that Swift gave 'light verse' a status it had not previously enjoyed, stressing the centrality of the device of the 'willful posture of an observer refusing to be involved'. Carole Fabricant (*ELH*) joins in the search for complexity behind the playfulness. She is primarily interested in verses upon the houses and estates of Swift's friends which describe a 'landscape of alienation,' more precisely 'the city's depersonalizing of human relationships, its conversion of human values into monetary ones'. In other words Miss Fabricant gives a fresh slant to the commonplace that Swift exposed a chaos lurking beneath the ordered façade of contemporary society. A. B. England (*SEL*) finds evidence of this same questioning of the reality of order in Swift's deliberate subversion of the 'orderly structures which appear on the surface of his work'. Similarly, Donna G. Fricke (*Eighteenth-Century Life*) focuses upon 'character-portraitures of fallen women' in Swift and Hogarth to display a sense of disorder. Fricke finds neither artist to have had much sympathy for Moll or Corinna. There is a less happy attempt to link Hogarth and Swift in Jeanne K. Welcher's contribution to *Ventures in Research* edited by Richard R. Griffith.[41] Peter J. Schakel's approach is very different. In *Criticism* he finds that the allusions to the *Aeneid* and Ovid's *Art of Love* in "Cadenus and Vanessa" suggest contrastive ideals: the allusions to Ovid look out to an ideal lover, those to Virgil refer to the heroic figures of Dido and Aeneas. Swift's interests are more general than autobiographical: the allusions are part of an explanation of 'the human need for self-acceptance and self-sacrifice in love.' Finally, there are two bibliographical papers on Swift. David Vieth (*N&Q*) reminds us that the eighteenth-century texts of "The Lady's Dressing Room" print "*Statira*" for the "*Satira*" of modern editions in the couplet 'To him that looks behind the Scene, *Statira*'s but some pocky Quean'. Modern editions miss

[41] *Ventures in Research*, edited by Richard R. Griffith. C. W. Post Center. pp. 225.

the allusion to Lee's *The Rival Queens* and the force of the pun on 'Quean'. George Mayhew (*PQ*) suggests possible identities for the 'F.A.' who supplied the first published version of 'On the Day of Judgment' and the 'Mercutio' whose version appeared in the *St. James's Chronicle* a year later: Dr. Francis Andrews LLD., Provost of Trinity College, Dublin, and Theophilus Swift. Mayhew's evidence confirms the authenticity of the later version.

It is almost inevitable that the name of Pat Rogers should appear in these columns in the context of Pope studies. This year he appears as the author of *An Introduction to Pope*[42] which benefits from being slightly less flippant and journalistic than much of his recent work (though there is still a slickness and playfulness which leads to obscurity—see, for example, his toying with Eliot at the opening of chapter ten). In the space of a mere 175 pages Rogers covers the whole corpus of Pope's writings and supplies a chapter-by-chapter reading list and a table of dates. His book is business-like but nothing more. The blurb on the cover emphasises the book's inclusiveness, but it may be that students would be better directed to a list of papers and/or parts of books. The bibliographies are useful, but there is a significant omission in Leavis's *Revaluation*. Howard Erskine-Hill's *The Social Milieu of Alexander Pope: Lives, Examples and the Poetic Response*[43] is a model of its kind, carefully researched, without pretension and lucidly written. Erskine-Hill compiles brief biographies of six men who figure in Pope's work: Caryll, Kyrle, Digby, Ralph Allen, Sir John Blount and Peter Walter. Each of these represents a social type, and the investment of their income is used to illuminate Pope's interest in the relation of wealth and morality. This background material occupies almost three times the space allowed for criticism, but it does more than provide a foundation for the criticism. Less tangibly, it creates a rich contexture for Pope and his values. In this way Erskine-Hill's book is comparable with Thompson's *Whigs and Hunters*.

Amongst the papers on Pope, several deal with poems not often discussed. Dustin Griffin (*MLQ*) considers the revisions in the 1717, 1727 and 1736 editions of the 'Ode on Solitude'. In the second of these Pope reverted to the 1709 manuscript text 'in evry variant'; but the 1736 edition is deemed the most original. Felicity A. Nussbaum (*PQ*) examines Pope's depiction of the 'inconstant, self-centred and affectedly witty' women of 'To a Lady' within a structure of 'increasing detail and deepening moral seriousness'. Extensions to the Pope canon are suggested by David Nokes (*YES*) who presents strong circumstantial evidence that probably in September 1738, Pope penned two epigrams on William Kent, one of which is included in the Twickenham edition as of doubtful author-ship. His evidence centres upon a British Museum manuscript in a hand resembling Warburton's. In *The Scriblerian* Harold Love presents a photo graph and a text of a new Pope letter, to Dorothy Boyle, Countess of Burlington, probably dating from 1739. 'Eloisa to Abelard' occupies David K. Jeffrey (*BSUF*) who argues that the poem is essentially dramatic

[42] *An Introduction to Pope*, by Pat Rogers. Methuen. pp. 180.
[43] *The Social Milieu of Alexander Pope: Lives, Examples and the Poetic Response* by Howard Erskine-Hill. Yale University Press. pp. xiv + 344.

its drama arising not from 'the conflict of opposing arguments but from the development of Eloisa's visions'. He charts this development and its imagery as they appear through Eloisa's perspective. The *Essay on Criticism* attracts a paper and a note. The latter, by Peter K. Shea (*N&Q*) records a similarity between Pope's '*True Wit* is *Nature* to Advantage drest,/What oft was *Thought*, but ne'er so well *Exprest*' and lines from Aphra Behn's commendatory poem to Henry Higden's *A Modern Essay on the Tenth Satyr of Juvenal* (1687). The paper, by Douglas B. Park (*PMLA*), holds that the *Essay*'s controlling metaphor is not 'an Aristotelian one of balance, but the Neoplatonic and Christian one of creating powers radiating from God into his creation, and of the created being's then attempting to rise back to a more perfect realisation of its Source in which all seeming divisions and discords are reconciled in perfect harmony'. The late J. C. Maxwell (*N&Q*) annotates the *Essay on Man*, IV, 167–70: the similarity between a passage from Remark (o) of Mandeville's *The Fable of the Bees* and Pope's '. . . give Humility a coach and six' may suggest that, like Mandeville, Pope had in mind the Archbishop of Canterbury, William Wake. In a second note (*N&Q*) Maxwell points out that in lines 129–32 of 'The First Satire of the Second Book of Horace Imitated' Pope turned not to Horace but Juvenal's eleventh satire (86–99), possibly in Congreve's translation.

Amongst the essays more particularly on the satires, Barbara Lauren (*SEL*) tries to show, by reference to the *Epistle to Burlington*, that a 'passionate commitment to satire is not inconsistent with a retired stance'. Pope focuses upon the proper reaction to provocation, not upon provocation itself. The major provocation of the *Epistle to Burlington* is the subject of two notes by Robert Folkenflik (*EA*) and Pat Rogers (*N&Q*). Folkenflik sees Timon as supported by allusions to Mulciber and Satan and Rogers remarks that the description of Timon's library could echo *Tatler* No. 158. *The Dunciad* as usual attracts most attention. Teona T. Gneiting (*ECS*) investigates the pictorial imagery, tracing Pope's iconography not to Du Fresnoy but to Veronese, Titian and Raphael. Another paper concerned with the Renaissance, with Renaissance classicism in *The Dunciad*, comes from R. G. Peterson (*SEL*). Peterson is especially concerned with a 'thin but distinct thread of Apollonian imagery' instituted by the motto and running through the whole poem. John V. Regan (*ECS*) focuses on the Orphic element in the poem. He examines the importance of the Latin couplet from Ovid's account of the death of Orpheus printed as an epigraph to the 1743 *Dunciad*. Regan believes that, whilst not diminishing the destructive elements of the myth, the allusion draws attention through an Orphic inspired narrator to the legend's essential hopefulness, 'the existence of a divine providence which brings order out of disorder, victory out of defeat, and good out of evil'. William Kinsley (*MLR*) takes a very different tack. He is convinced that the lines IV, 71–90 find Pope using physico-theology which he postulates . . . as a positive value threatened by the dunces with perversion into an immoral gravity, a symbol of the love of Dulness, or, in short, a physico-demonology'. Finally, on *The Dunciad*, there are two papers on the dunces. Pat Rogers (*SEL*) restores an allusion to Settle's *The Seige of Troy* in I, 187–88 of the 1728 *Dunciad*; and George C. Brauer (*Cornucopiae*) comments on Pope's dislike of the arid

neoclassicism entailed in modish numismatics in IV, 375–86.
Robert Halsband (*ECS*) adds to C. R. Kropf's account of satire and the
libel laws with a note on Pope's witty transmutation of Lady Mary Wortley
Montagu from a pioneer of smallpox innoculation into 'the propagator of
the great-pox, or syphilis' which elicited an acid satiric reaction without
either party considering legal action. On the same topic Richard Reynolds
(*ECS*) contends that since the courts had begun to examine intention
rather than the words *in mitiore sensu*, Pope's wit was actionable. Cedric
D. Reverand II (*DUJ*) tries to turn Pope's altercation with Blackmore into
a professional rather than a private affair to explain why Pope continued
to attack '*Everlasting Blackmore*' even after his death in 1729. In a more
positive strain, Charles Beaumont (*TSLL*) argues that Pope's letters, conversations, poetry and first-hand knowledge of Chiswick and Prior Park
show him sympathetically conversant with Palladio's principles. Pat Rogers
(*DUJ*) investigates a Burlington circle in Yorkshire, centering upon alumni
of St. John's and the 'lesser squirarchy', and including Hugh Bethel. In
The Scriblerian Sarah Burroughs provides a photograph and an explanatory text of a commemorative tablet erected by Pope for his life-long
nurse Mary Beach. Three papers cover various aspects of the letters. Pat
Rogers (*MP*) records substantive deviations in printed texts from the
manuscripts of eighteen letters to Fortescue between 1720 and 1743; A
C. Ellis Jr. (*PBSA*) reports on the first state of the first impression of the
Pope-Swift *Letters*, and Peter E. Martin (*N&Q*) remarks on an editorial
error which proved a source of confusion for garden historians. Finally, on
Pope, George Havens and Ahmad Gunny (*RLC*) write on Pope and Voltaire
The increasing interest in Mandeville brings a facsimile of *Wishes to a
Godson with Other Miscellany Poems* from The Rota;[44] and another poe
long out of print, Edward Young, is honoured with a useful selection o
his poems by Brian Hepworth[45] which is blotted only by a tendency to
slickness in the introduction. Parnell, Young and Thomson are the centra
figures in Robert J. Merrett's account of 'Religious and Linguistic Sensi
bility in Augustan Poetry'.[46] Jargon aside, Merrett does show how thei
poetry moves away from a strict mimetic theory and towards the expres
sive, towards 'poetic rage.' Young is also represented in Pierre Danchin's
review of Pettit's edition of *The Correspondence* (*ES*). Danchin register
his disappointment that social distance prevents 'any real, deep-felt com
munication' in many of the letters. The letters seem to him to show the
friendship with Richardson to be founded more on business and mutua
esteem than on common literary interests. Martha Collins (*ELH*) aptly
addresses herself to Collins' 'acute awareness of his role as poet and hi
self-conscious hesitance to assume that role', whilst John L. Greenway
discusses Ossian and his imitators as 'legitimizing the values of sentimenta
primitivism through a mythic narrative (the Ossianic poems) which showe
that sentimental views of human nature, virtue, and vice were really presen

---

[44] *Wishes to a Godson with Other Miscellany Poems*, by Bernard Mandeville. Th
Rota. pp. 39.
[45] *The Transactions of the Samuel Johnson Society of the Northwest*, edited t
Thomas R Cleary. University of Victoria Press. pp. iv + 134.
[46] From *Edward Young (1683-1765)*, edited by Brian Hepworth. Carcanet Pres
pp. 136.

at the dawn of Northern, *non*-classical civilisation'.

Two of the papers on Johnson's poetry deal with his Latin work. Maurice J. O'Sullivan Jr. *(PQ)* demonstrates how Johnson's first published work, a translation of Pope's *Messiah* into Latin hexameters (1728) throws light on his development as poet and critic. Johnson learned through imitation, altering (and thereby criticizing) Pope's diction. In an important article R. G. Peterson *(ECS)* sets Johnson beside minds intoxicated with classicism (Lipsius, Pope and Ruskin) to argue that Johnson 'lacked an emotional commitment to the classical past . . . . He rejected the authority of antiquity . . . whenever it went against reason and common experience.' Johnson's Latin verse lacks classical tone; instead it is intensely personal (in a way that Catullus is not). It offers 'a self-revelation paralleled only by such notorious exhibitionists as Augustine, Montaigne, Rousseau, Boswell, in his *Journals*, and some of the Romantics'. Two papers on *The Vanity of Human Wishes* are less rewarding. Paul D. McGlynn *(SEL)* simply sets out to show the 'elementary rhetorical units of the poem as a microcosm of Johnson's broad philosophical structure', concentrating on the catalogue; but he asserts more than he proves. William Kupersmith *(SP)* defends the poem's structure, suggesting a structure derived from classical rhetoric. Similarly, Jack Werner's edition of verse from a manuscript notebook of Boswell's early poetry promises more than it can fulfill. Its bizarre title, *Boswell's Book of Bad Verse*,[47] is matched only by its ridiculously dilettante pretensions to scholarship.

Tom Davis's edition of Goldsmith's *Poems and Plays*[48] also fails to match up to the claims it makes for itself. The shortcomings are both textual and critical. The major textual difficulty has to do with the punctuation: the plain fact is that we do not know enough about the 'form in which Goldsmith intended his work to appear' which Davis purports to reproduce. His argument that this intention was simply 'a correct eighteenth-century style of pointing' poses a host of unanswered (and unanswerable) questions. Roger Lonsdale's pragmatic assumption that 'a discreet modern-ization of the text is only an equivalent to the regularization which these poets expected when their poetry was printed in their own lifetime' produces a much more articulate text for the modern reader. It is not merely that there is a difference of editorial principle here: Davis's certainty about his procedures is built on some shaky logic. There are errors of fact, too. In his note on 'An Author's Bed-Chamber' Davis remarks that 'Goldsmith introduced lines 7-18 of this poem in a letter to his brother'; but it was only a version of the lines, as Lonsdale records. There is a similar slip in the note to 'On the Death of a Mad Dog' which implies that the poem is an imitation of La Monnoye's *Le fameux la Galisse*: only three stanzas of Goldsmith's poem are involved. These are small errors, but their effect is cumulative. They undermine one's confidence in the edition as a whole, especially when they are seen alongside other inconsistencies such as the frequent reference to *The Citizen* as *Chinese Letters* (as distinct from Chinese Letters') and the indiscriminate mixture of arabic and Roman numerals when referring to particular letters. Davis's critical position may

---

[47] *Boswell's Book of Bad Verse*, edited by Jack Werner. White Lion. pp. 214.

[48] *Oliver Goldsmith. Poems and Plays*, edited by Tom Davis. Dent. pp. xxv + 258.

be summed up by the following quotation from his introduction: 'Goldsmith was a great writer in his day because he judged the market so exactly; he is considered a great writer now because the popularizing is presented in his best work with careful intelligence and irony.' A. Lytton Sells is also guilty of not being able to make up his mind about how to refer to the 'Chinese Letters', an uncertainty symptomatic of many disappointing failings in his *Oliver Goldsmith. His Life and Works.*[49] His study falls into two parts, a biographical and a critical. The biography is neither as full nor reliable as Wardle's and its popularizing style seems to demand certainty where none exists. It gets off to a very bad start with a bland avoidance of the difficulties of dating Goldsmith's birth, opting for a date not normally favoured: 'Oliver was born, apparently on 10 November 1728.' The critical part betrays a very ordinary literary historical mind with a penchant for plot summary and source hunting: he can admire Goldsmith for being 'prudently brief', but sadly cannot emulate him.

The vexed question of Thomas Warton the Elder's two distinct poetic voices, the friend of Pope and Prior and the melancholy, contemplative poet fond of nature, solitude and early Milton, is the subject of an authoritative article by David Fairer (*RES*). Fairer solves the problem by reference to the Warton papers: 'from these it is now clear, not only that Joseph Warton sometimes heavily edited and improved his father's verses, but that he and his brother wrote at least ten of the poems themselves.' Fairer's findings reduce Warton to a 'mediocre litterateur with some talent for satire and occasional verse'. In contrast his sons become more significant in the literary history. Norman Nicholson has pared down Cowper's work in a rather different way, editing a selection with a largely biographical introduction[50]. In an accretive mood, Betty Rizzo (*RES* and *N&Q*) supplies the lyrics for a hitherto lost song, 'The Prize Carnation,' by Christopher Smart, adds two 'frame stanzas' to a known Smart song, 'The Distressed Damsel' and suggests Smart as author of 'The Hymn of Eve' from Arne's oratorio, *The Death of Abel.*

Blake studies continue to appear in abundance. There are two aids to the uninitiated in G. E. Bentley's Critical Heritage volume,[51] which includes twenty useful illustrations, and Martin K. Nurmi's[52] lively and sensible introduction in the Hutchinson University Library series. For the more specialized reader there is Joseph Anthony Wittreich's *Angel of Apocalypse: Blake's Idea of Milton*[53] which is good for its sketching of the background of prophetic writings in the sixteenth and seventeenth centuries and survey of reactions to Milton in the eighteenth. It is interesting, too, for its careful location of allusions to Milton's prose in *The Marriage of Heaven and Hell*, but in more essential ways it is unhelpfully

[49] *Oliver Goldsmith. His Life and Works*, by A. Lytton Sells. Allen & Unwin. pp. 423.
[50] *A Choice of Cowper's Verse*, edited by Norman Nicholson. Faber and Faber. pp. 96.
[51] *William Blake: The Critical Heritage*, edited by G. E. Bentley. Routledge & Kegan Paul. pp. 320.
[52] *William Blake*, by Martin K. Nurmi. Hutchinson University Library. pp. 175.
[53] *Angel of Apocalypse: Blake's Idea of Milton*, by Joseph Anthony Wittreich Jr University of Wisconsin Press. pp. xxiii + 332.

contentious. Those wanting to sample Wittreich's book might look at his *HLQ* article on 'Blake's Portrait and Portrayals of Milton.' It has not been possible to consult a copy of Donald Ault's *Visionary Physics: Blake's Response to Newton.*[54] Last of the books on Blake is a fine study by Raymond Lister of Blake's techniques as an artist, *Infernal Methods.*[55] Lister stresses that this is a book about how rather than why Blake created what he did: his account of how is detailed yet sufficiently lucid for the uninformed layman to understand. A separate chapter is given to each of the different media; and in each Lister painstakingly distinguishes between the traditional and the innovatory. The text is complemented with fifty-two fine illustrations.

Amongst the papers on Blake's lyrics, Mary R. and Rodney M. Baine (*SEL*) explore 'The Tyger' in the context of Blake's other tigers. As the illustration to the poem shows, Blake wanted to present the tiger not only as fearsome but as 'ugly and stupid'. Traditionally it symbolized 'bloodthirsty cruelty;' within Blake generally it denotes 'cruel rapacity'. The Baines conclude that in the tiger we see 'fallen man, dominated by his spectrous selfhood.' From the real tiger we turn to the real 'Holy Thursday' and Thomas E. Connolly (*BS*). Connolly remarks that the Holy Thursday on which Charity School children gathered at St. Paul's was neither Maundy Thursday nor Ascension Day but a Thursday between. B. H. Fairchild, Jr. (*BS*) writes more generally on the lyric intensity and mellifluousness of the *Songs* and Michael Phillips (*RES*) provides details for 'The Reputation of Blake's *Poetical* Sketches 1783–1863'.

The Baines are seen at work again (*ELN*) on *America* 5 and *Marriage* 19 for which Swedenborg is found to have provided the moral symbolism and a hint at Uranus. David Worrall (*BNYPL*), more widely interested in the Prophetic Books, traces the influence of Darwin's botany and cosmology, whilst Daniel Stempel (*Mosaic*) demonstrates Blake's strong antipathy to those who tried to make 'their systems permanent by mathematic power' Stempel compares and contrasts Blake and Leibniz: they share a beatific vision but it is finite for Leibniz, infinite for Blake. Mollyanne Marks (*SEL*) believes that irony served Blake in *Urizen* as a way of mediating between a 'visionary evocation of eternity and self-consciously didactic picturing of the fallen world in which he found himself'. Like Stempel she stresses Blake's avoidance of the systematic, 'the absurdity of writing a poem which attempts the rigid ordering of experience it mocks'. Miss Marks finds in *Urizen* seeds of the self-doubt at the centre of *Jerusalem*.

Two papers deal with Blake's reaction to earlier radicalism, centering on Milton. Jackie DiSalvo[56] sees in *The Four Zoas* a critique of Milton's attitude to sexual love and the 'bourgeois' conception of the family, linking Blake with the Ranters and Diggers. 'Blake condemns the bourgeois family both for its repression of the individual and for its destruction of the community.' E. P. Thompson (*TLS*) entertains the possibility that the

[54] *Visionary Physics. Blake's Response to Newton*, by Donald Ault. University of Chicago Press. pp. 229.
[55] *Infernal Methods. A Study of William Blake's Art Techniques*, by Raymond Lister. G. Bell. pp. x + 101 + 66 plates.
[56] *Milton and the Line of Vision*, edited by Joseph Anthony Wittreich Jr. University of Wisconsin Press. pp. 237.

Muggletonians might form a link between Blake and the radical theology of Milton's time.

Of the remaining papers, G. E. Bentley Jr. investigates a little biography in 'Ozias Humphry, William Upcott, and William Blake' (*HAR*); Martin Butlin (*BS*) reports on a new portrait and F. B. Curtis (*BS*) looks into Blake's relationship with the London booksellers and authors (especially those connected with Joseph Johnson). Ron Taylor (*BNL*) charts the mass of recent work with a checklist. Finally, two publications aid further work: a fine facsimile of *The Marriage of Heaven and Hell* edited by Geoffrey Keynes,[57] available at a reasonable paperback price (though one hopes that the binding will be superior to that of the comparable facsimile of the *Songs*), and an issue of *BNL* by John E. Grant and Robert E. Brown collecting the materials for analysis of Blake's vision of Spenser's *Faerie Queene*.

3. Prose

The year produced a larger than average crop of work on the periodicals. Phyllis J. Guskin (*N&Q*) clears up the authorship of *The Protestant Post-Boy* (1711-12): in *The Political State of Great Britain* (1727) Abel Boyer reveals that he and Philip Horneck were responsible. James F. Woodruff (*RES*) extends our knowledge of *The Tatler Revived* (1750), mentioned by Boswell as a 'competitor for fame' with the *Rambler*. Woodruff shows that it was longer lived than the standard references allow. Problem-solving of this sort seems still very much a part of work on the periodical: James Tierney (*PBSA*) describes some of the problems and the progress. Our knowledge of the circulation of periodicals is extended, albeit slightly, by Michael Harris (*OBSP*) who gives details of the ledger of one Charles Delafaye who was employed as a clerk in the office of the Secretary of State. Delafaye, capitalizing upon his franking privileges, distributed newspapers (including the *Tatler, Guardian* and *Post Boy*) to clients in England and Ireland. His Huguenot background brought connections with the Continental press. Not surprisingly *The Spectator* attracts most attention. Donald Kay contributes a book-length study of *Short Fiction in the Spectator*[58] in which his efforts centre mainly upon cataloguing the fictions under the following headings: (i) the Character, (ii) the dream vision-cum-allegory, (iii) the fable, (iv) the domestic apologue, (v) the satirical adventure tale, (vi) the oriental tale and rogue literature, (vii) the fabliau, (viii) the exemplum, and (ix) the mock sentimental tale. Kay devotes a separate chapter to each type, prefaced by a chapter on the storytelling tradition and periodical antecedents to *The Spectator*. He sees *The Spectator* as 'using the short story superbly as a means to an end: "the mind ought sometimes to be diverted, that it may return to thinking the better" '. Kay's focus necessarily limits his usefulness on the connections between short fiction and the novel. According to Edward W. Pitcher (*SSF*) the didactic success of short fiction in both *The Spectator* and *The*

---

[57] *The Marriage of Heaven and Hell*, edited by Geoffrey Keynes. O.U.P. pp. 82
[58] *Short Fiction in The Spectator*, by Donald Kay. University of Alabama Press. pp. 145.

Tatler depended upon the reader being convinced that 'the story actually came from the mouth of a real person, and that it had been related honestly, or that knowledge of the incidents could be confirmed'. Steele's *Guardian* No. 12 is the object of Louis J. Milic's exercise in 'propositional reduction' in *Style and Text*. Milic reduces sentences to a paraphrase from which everything inessential to the cognitive meaning is omitted in blatant disregard of the theoretical difficulties entailed, though some of his remarks on Steele's style may be found useful. The same writer (*Eighteenth-Century Life*) examines the decline in Steele's reputation, arguing that Steele deserves more recognition as pioneer of the periodical essay and creator of Sir Roger de Coverley. Addison is represented in a very welcome selection of *Essays in Criticism and Literary Theory* edited by John Loftis.[59] A set of original folio half sheets in the Huntington Library serves as copy text for Loftis's modernized text which is discreetly annotated and introduced, prefaced with a table of dates and rounded off with a bibliography. Addison's style, or rather Bishop Hurd's view of it, is the province of Samuel J. Rogal (*Costerus*) who offers a very heavily documented account of Hurd's criticisms of Addison's 'grammar and usage'. The most interesting study of the periodical in 1975 was of a French review of English letters, Matthieu Maty's *Journal Britannique*.[60] Uta Janssens places Maty in the tradition of Huguenot interest in English letters, charting his life and character as a key to the attitudes informing his articles and critiques and relating the *Journal* to the larger context of eighteenth-century journalism. Believing that 'pour penser avec liberté, il faut penser seul', Maty departed from his predecessors' policy of farming out work on a large scale. The *Journal* was written in London and sent to The Hague to be printed. Miss Janssens analyses its contents and in appendices supplies an analytical index of articles and books reviewed and a list of contributors.

There is remarkably little to report on Defoe's prose this year. The two volume Everyman *Tour through the Whole Island of Great Britain* (1962) is now reprinted in a single volume edition,[61] and James T. Boulton's *Selected Writings of Daniel Defoe* (1965) has been reprinted by the Cambridge University Press.[62] Maximillian E. Novak (*N&Q*) extends the Defoe canon with the attribution of a pamphlet, *Two Arguments Never brought yet. . .*, on internal evidence. J. A. Downie (*ECS*) reports on Defoe's relations with Harley and Godolphin in the context of the General Election of 1708 in Scotland, and, in a second paper (*N&Q*) draws out some of the implications of Pat Rogers' discovery that Defoe was in the Fleet in 1702, arguing that if Defoe was prepared to be less than truthful

[59] *Joseph Addison. Essays in Criticism and Literary Theory*, edited by John Loftis. AHM. pp. viii + 189.
[60] *Mattieu Maty and the Journal Britannique 1750-1755. A French View of English Literature in the Middle of the Eighteenth Century*, by Uta Janssens. Holland University Press. pp. x + 215.
[61] *A Tour through the Whole Island of Great Britain*, by Daniel Defoe, edited by G. D. H. Cole and D. C. Browning. Dent. pp. xxxii + 437.
[62] *Selected Writings of Daniel Defoe*, edited by James T. Boulton. Cambridge University Press. pp. xii + 286.

to Harley about his financial standing immediately before the publication of the *Shortest Way*, 'it surely casts grave shadows on the validity of the voluminous Defoe-Harley correspondence in its entirety, more especially concerning Defoe's activities in Scotland'. The books on Defoe by Richetti and Zimmerman are best reviewed in the novel section of this chapter.

Mandeville fares rather better. Scholars' Facsimiles and Reprints publishes a facsimile edition of the first edition (1709) of *The Virgin Unmask'd*, introduced by Stephen H. Good[63] who deftly places the text in the larger corpus of Mandeville's work. H. T. Dickinson introduces *The Mischiefs that ought Justly to be Apprehended from a Whig-Government* (1714) for the Augustan Reprint Society.[64] Dickinson adds no essentially fresh evidence, but he finds the evidence more positive than Kaye did. If *The Mischiefs* is by Mandeville, it reveals a 'new political dimension' in his works, according to Dickinson. Hector Monro's *The Ambivalence of Bernard Mandeville*[65] puts its critical antennae into the most occasional corners of Mandeville's work, but its central focus is upon *The Fable of the Bees* and particularly its ironic difficulties. Monro carefully sketches in the two antithetical attitudes to *The Fable's* argument that private vices are public virtues, finding neither adequate. Indeed, Mandeville, aware of both alternatives, took neither but pursued a path of witty ambivalence, 'not really interested in the moral, theological or philosophical implications'. The critical debate into which Monro plunges himself demands a much more rigorous account of where and how Mandeville is sincere, where and how he works through indirection with a Swiftean manipulation of social assumptions; but there is some useful background material to be mined here. Harry Landreth (*HOPE*) approaches the same problems through Mandeville's economic thought. He concludes that Mandeville believed government must 'interfere in the economy to bring about public benefits from private vices', a harmonious society being the product of 'dextrous management. . . by a skilful Politician'.

The text of the 1906 Everyman edition of *Gulliver's Travels* has been reissued, refurbished with an introduction, up-to-date selective bibliography, and the suppressed passage on the Lindalians, all gathered by Clive T. Probyn.[66] The introduction gives a sensible review of the literary, social and critical background; the text is taken from the 1735–38 edition, with little textual apparatus. There is also a new edition of *A Tale of a Tub and Other Satires* from Everyman, using Herbert Davis's text and introduced and annotated by Kathleen Williams (with additions by Clive Probyn).[67] Like the *Gulliver's Travels* volume, this is a very responsible edition: its notes and the short bibliographical aid ought to prove particularly helpful for the undergraduate. Philip Pinkus presents two pamphlets

[63] *The Virgin Unmask'd (1709)*, by Bernard Mandeville, edited by Stephen H. Good. Scholars' Facsimiles & Reprints. pp. xi + 214.

[64] *The Mischiefs that ought Justly to be Apprehended from a Whig-Government*, by Bernard Mandeville, edited by H. T. Dickinson. Augustan Reprint Society No. 174. University of California Press. pp. xiv + 40.

[65] *The Ambivalence of Bernard Mandeville*, by Hector Monro. Oxford: Clarendon. pp. 283.

[66] *Gulliver's Travels*, by Jonathan Swift, edited by Clive T. Probyn. Dent. pp. 318.

[67] *A Tale of a Tub and Other Satires*, by Jonathan Swift, edited by Kathleen Williams with additions by Clive T. Probyn. Dent. pp. xxix + 279.

on Swift,[68] both disappointing. Much of the material is well-worn, and where it is not, Pinkus seems to be more interested in arguing a line than in looking for the truth. The presentation is shoddy. Finally, amongst the books, A. L. Rowse writes on himself and Swift in his biography, *Jonathan Swift, Major Prophet*.[69] Rowse fails to distinguish fact from apocrypha (despite referring to Ehrenpreis in his suggestions for further reading) and he too often creates a Swift in his own image. Amongst the articles are several on the less popular works. The *Project for the Advancement of Religion* attracts John Kay (*UTQ*): against the background of the early eighteenth-century argument that hypocrisy is preferable to open immorality, he holds that neither a persona nor a literal meaning is appropriate. The *Project* is designed 'to promote the interests of the Established Church and the Clergy'. It now seems possible, thanks to the sleuthing of C. P. Daw (*HLQ*), that Swift's 'Strange Sermon' was *Mutual Subjection*, delivered Ash Wednesday, 26 February 1717/8. Also concerned with a sermon, E. W. Rosenheim Jr. (*PQ*) addresses himself to the fusion of Swift the preacher and Swift the polemicist in his 'Sermon upon the Martyrdom of King Charles I': 'for all the talk about Swift's postures and personae, we recognize, in such a work as the sermon. . .the voice of a simple and genuine human being who, though not without irony and humour and exaggeration, manages powerfully to convey authentic passion.' From Daw the detective we turn to the statistician Roberta S. Borkat (*Eighteenth-Century Life*) who demonstrates that the statistics yielded by the modest proposer's methods are self-indicting, arguing for 'charity and respect for human life'. In a more familiar critical mode, John F. Wickham examines the emergence of Swiftean satire in *The Battle of the Books*. There is a much more original piece in Claudia R. Stillman's (*LCP*) account of the *Journal to Stella* as governed by the tone 'of dream fantasy'. Freud in hand, Miss Stillman emphasizes the dream-like interest in language.

Of the three essays to report on the *Tale*, none offers anything to rival the chapter in DePorte's *Nightmares and Hobbyhorses*. Eugene Bud Korkowski (*SEL*) describes some figures of containment as a way of emphasizing Swift's fideistic dismissal of 'unaided reason', whilst Ricardo Quintana (*MP*) places two paragraphs from Section IX in the context of their contemporary philosophical debate. The paragraphs, beginning with a definition of happiness as 'a Perpetual Possession of being well Deceived', draw on Bacon's philosophical realism and, in an essentially anti-Cartesian spirit, Descartes' epistemological uncertainties. Swift emerges as a champion of the 'human freedom to choose, freedom to act'.

The lion's share of the articles goes, predictably, to *Gulliver's Travels*. William Bowman Piper (*RUS*) tries to set the proper tone by isolating the two requisites for any reader of the *Travels*: 'plain good sense' and a willingness to read analytically, word by word. Swift, he argues, does not allow us the comfort of generalisations. In an analogous spirit, Pat Rogers (*MLR*) tries to restore some historical particularities to *Gulliver's Travels*,

---

[68] *Swift's Vision of Evil: A Comparative Study of A Tale of a Tub and Gulliver's Travels. Volume I: A Tale of a Tub. Volume II: Gulliver's Travels*, by Philip Pinkus. Victoria University Press. pp. 276.

[69] *Jonathan Swift: Major Prophet*, by A. L. Rowse. Thames Hudson. pp. 240.

especially to Book III. Rogers works from Bolinbroke's allusion to the *Travels* when he 'raillyes Swift upon his Southern Journey' and from apparent references to the South Sea trade within the text to argue that Swift was hinting at connections with the South Sea Bubble. The wild schemes of the third voyage are closer to the 'bustling, uncerebral world of entrepreneurs and inventors' than 'the elitist science of the 1690s.' It is a shame that Rogers does not evidence the assertion that although 'in strict usage the South Sea trade was that conducted with South America and the islands of the Pacific. . .in ordinary speech any sailor who passed the Equator (in whichever ocean) was travelling the South Seas'. Donald T. Torchiana (*PQ*) also attempts to relocate *Gulliver's Travels* in its contemporary situation. He is convinced that Firth's account of the correspondence between the Yahoos and the 'savage old Irish' has been underestimated. Firth's arguments are reviewed and Torchiana adds the opinions of a few of Swift's friends on the native Irish. Comparing the depiction of the Irish by English travellers with the Yahoos, Torchiana stresses Swift's 'unrelenting drumfire against Ireland'. Drumfire against projectors is the focus of J. M. Treadwell's contribution on *Gulliver's Travels* (*TSLL*). The projectors are of two sorts, the 'speculator-projectors of the early 1720s' attacked in the satire on Laputa and the disinterested, benevolent projectors like Gulliver (and Swift himself who is 'dangerously simple-minded in his *Project for . . . the Reformation of Manners*'). Gerald J. Pierre (*TSLL*) believes he has found a model for Gulliver in Sir William Temple in his final years at Moor Park as well as a source for the polarized Houyhnhnms and Yahoos in Temple's contrasting of the civilised Chinese and primitive Tartars. Amid so much recent criticism on *Gulliver's Travels* it is good to have Phyllis J. Guskin (*SP*) remind us of the remarkable modernity of Abel Boyer's incisive account.

Clayton D. Lein (*ECS*) points out that Swift's consistent underestimation of the population of Ireland at a million and a half constitutes part of a political argument that English rule was stunting population, an argument designed to obviate heavier taxation. Lee Sonsteng Horsley (*YES*) discusses Swift's connection with political writers. She finds that like such writers Swift was adroit at using the vernacular metaphors, cliches and idioms of ordinary conversation. Swift, however, 'gave these familiar figures new life and complexity of suggestion, lifting them beyond the confines of contemporary political controversy'. On the other hand, political bias amongst historians and its threat to the ideal of an impartial history chronicling 'the principles governing the conduct of societies' worried Swift, particularly in *Gulliver's Travels*, according to Myrddin Jones (*DUJ*).

The account of the year's work on Johnson must begin with matters arising from Donald Greene's *TLS* review of the John Wain biography. Greene has a genius for stirring the conscience of the critics. He himself focuses upon the differences between Boswell's 1769 diary and the 1791 *Life*, in response to David Pole's criticism of his revaluation of the *Life*. Millicent Rose (*TLS*) comments on the illustrations which show 'the Johnson of nineteenth-century legend, Boswell-based, sentimentalized and false'. Some details of Miss Rose's distinction between Johnson's summerhouse as it appeared in its original Streatham setting and as it appeared from the 1820s are corrected by Derek Chittock (*TLS*): it was moved to Ashgrove in Knockholt by Susanna Arabella Thrale, probably after 1813. Greene's review stimulated Michael Holroyd (*TLS*) to defend Hugh Kingsmill's 1933 biography which 'demonstrated for the first time how much of Johnson lay outside Boswell's view'. Donald Greene (*TLS*) counters with a deserved rap on the knuckles.

There is nothing contentious about either the Folio Society's edition of *Rasselas*,[70] with fine lithographic illustrations by Edward Bawden, or Margaret Lane's *Samuel Johnson and his World*.[71] The latter is especially welcome for its illustrations which include the greater part of the portraits. The portraits are studied by Herman W. Liebert in his contribution to *English Portraits of the Seventeenth and Eighteenth Centuries*.[72] He judges the Nollekens bust the best likeness and the Reynolds the best portraits, 'manly, simple, sincere, and deeply interpretative of character'. But the most important book on Johnson in 1975 was Richard B. Schwartz's *Samuel Johnson and the Problem of Evil*,[73] centering on the Jenyns-Johnson engagement. It is designed to show that 'close examination of Johnson's review reveals the struggle and frustration but also some interesting philosophic alignments and an impressive ability to reassert orthodoxy in the light of advanced, contemporary comment'. Schwartz demonstrates that Johnson saw the problem of evil as insoluble, though he thought it was possible to arrive at a fuller understanding of the nature of evil and suffering thereby enjoying 'a palpable degree of mitigation and palliation, for much of our terror and pain is based on the proverbial fear and apprehension in the face of the unknown'. One of the incidental achievements of this work is its evidencing of Johnson's philosophic interests: just as Schwartz's *Samuel Johnson and the New Science* (1971) released Johnson from the view that he was antipathetic to contemporary science, his present study challenges Johnson's 'alleged philosophic philistinism', plotting his ideistic relationship with Hume and Berkeley. The appendices include a facsimile of Johnson's review.

Paul K. Alken (*MP*) uses the *Life of Savage* and reactions to it over the centuries to test 'the assumption that any text's form, meaning, and intention are most clearly reflected not by the words on its pages, but in the responses it elicits from readers'. Although the enterprise seems dubious, some might find Alken's paper useful for its recounting of the reactions. Howard D. Weinbrot's examination (*MP*) of the relationship between John Clarke's remarks on *Paradise Lost* in his *Essay on Study* and Johnson's discussion of the same poem is a much more respectable affair. Weinbrot contends that Johnson adapted the notions that Milton was wrong to have Satan utter blasphemies and that the 'materiality of angels is absurd' and developed and altered the charge that Milton's verse is prosaic. In a related essay, James L. Clifford (*PQ*) presents a William Lauder, embittered by personal failure and a crippling accident, seeking

[70] *Rasselas*, by Samuel Johnson. Folio Society. pp. 132.
[71] *Samuel Johnson and his World*, by Margaret Lane. Hamish Hamilton. pp. 224.
[72] From *English Portraits of the Seventeenth and Eighteenth Centuries*, by J. Douglas Stewart and Herman W. Liebert. University of California Press. pp. v + 95.
[73] *Samuel Johnson and the Problem of Evil*, by Richard B. Schwartz. University of Wisconsin Press. pp. x + 118.

revenge upon mankind by, amongst other things, blackening Milton's character. Johnson was moved by Lauder's misfortunes and Clifford sets himself to explore Johnson's involvement. He describes the history of Lauder's charges against Milton as an 'unlicensed' plagiarist, Johnson's gathering realisation that he had been duped by Lauder and his public avowals of dissociation. Richard R. Reynolds (*YES*) tries to arbitrate between the attitudes of Paul Fussell and Ashcroft Underwood (in his foreword to G. A. Lindeboom's biography of Boerhaave) on Johnson's *Life of Boerhaave* by examining Johnson's use of his sources and comparing his account with those of his contemporaries. Reynolds finds in Johnson's favour: Johnson makes 'extensive and judicious use of autobiographical notes left by Boerhaave. Where the notes leave gaps Johnson draws on Schulters.' Herbert Croft's *Life of Young*, the reactions to its 'subtle derogation' of Young's character and Johnson's reasons for farming out the *Life* to Croft, occupy the attention of Henry Pettit (*PQ*). Pettit feels that no-one knew better than Croft that he had missed the Johnsonian essence, yet he deserves recognition for 'an unusually creditable record of the poet's life'.

In an article on Johnson's edition of Shakespeare, Donald T. Siebert (*SEL*) takes issue with Walter Jackson Bate's view of Johnson as a 'satirist manqué'. The Preface, for example, allowed Johnson to 'write satire and yet avoid being typed as a satirist, a person too often thought of as a misanthropic ranter or irresponsible joker'. The Preface is a 'defence of scholarship and criticism and of Johnson's position as a scholar critic'.

Rasselas is the focus of papers by Earl Wasserman (*JEGP*) and Gwin J. Kolb (*PQ*). The latter investigates the intellectual background of the 'Discourse of the Soul.' Howard D. Weinbrot reports on Johnson's manuscript notes on a very different discourse, Dr. Thomas Lawrence's *De Natura Animali Dissertatio*. Finally, on Johnson, Robert Scholes (*PQ*) gives body to the critical truism that Jane Austen read Johnson. He looks particularly at 'the diction used by the two writers in making discriminations of character', concentrating upon such terms as 'elegance, breeding, and principle'. He concludes that there is a 'closeness—almost unity—of thought and attitude . . . in the important matters of manners and morals, love and marriage'.

The autobiographies of Hume and Gibbon are treated by Robert H. Bell and Martin Price respectively. Bell (*PQ*) studies the application of Hume's theory of personal identity to his autobiography: it helps 'to reconcile the apparent contradictions between the 'self' Hume presents in his autobiography and the 'Hume' we see in his earlier writings'. 'My Own Life' allows little room for conflicts such as 'philosophical melancholy and delerium,' yet it remains consistent with a theory which allows a natural propensity to imagine an identity. Price (*PQ*) opines that Gibbon's memoirs may claim to be the first great autobiography in English because of their style, an 'instrument of a sensibility, a way of fixing a vision of the self, that is related to the vision of a great history'. Price discovers within the memoir 'a dialectic response to another view of the self', as typified by Rousseau's *Confessions*: the memoirs enjoy a 'double vision'. An instance of Gibbon's indebtedness to Johnson is recorded by Robert C. Olson (*N&Q*).

4. The Novel

Two books which will become necessary reading have annoying flaws. The strengths of Paul Zweig's *The Adventurer*[74] are also its weaknesses: like Leavis's *Great Tradition* (which it is so much written against) it has an illuminating yet claustrophobic narrowness of focus. Zweig's prototypical adventurer is Odysseus who (*pace* George Dimock) means trouble: he heads a tradition of the 'profoundly ambivalent character whose gift for violence and extreme action creates a problem for those who need to make use of him.' The modern descendants are the creations of Norman Mailer. The hero of Zweig's alternative tradition is essentially an *Untermensch*. The most interesting discussion of a particular eighteenth-century work is that of *Robinson Crusoe* which Zweig demonstrates to lie outside his particular tradition. Far from being an under-dog, Crusoe is middle-class to the marrow and he bears with him a restrictive Protestant ethic. Crusoe's characteristic activity is the erection of protective barriers; 'if he has strains of a wild man, they are there only to be domesticated, like the island itself, through a campaign of hard work and wall-building.' (This chapter ought to be read alongside Pat Rogers *EIC* article from last year.) Eric Rothstein's *Systems of Order and Inquiry in Later Eighteenth-Century Fiction*[75] is flawed in less stimulating ways, by an often obstructive language and not knowing when to stop (it can be both repetitive and over-ingenious). Yet its argument that the major eighteenth-century novels are structured according to 'systems of order' and deal with 'systems of inquiry' (or 'epistemological procedures') current in the period deserves to be taken seriously. The novels monitor the compatibility of the various systems of organisation with the real world. Rothstein's account of *Tristram Shandy* typifies the failings of the book when it descends to detailed criticism. Like all the novels he considers, Sterne's functions through analogy and contrast. The more general remarks upon these devices, pivoting on the internal structure of Book VI and its relation to the whole novel, are useful, but to see Walter, Toby and Tristram as 'a trio representing thought, action, and (taking Tristram as author) creative force' is to systematize unduly. Rothstein's conclusion that Tristram's 'methods' (as author) might 'reduce or cripple reality as his father's and uncle's have reduced and crippled him' is, however, attractive. *Rasselas, Amelia, Humphry Clinker* and *Caleb Williams* all serve Rothstein's thesis, all with the same mixture of sense and ingenuity. Rothstein's study would be at its most stimulating if one were to read the section on a particular author in the light of general remarks; read as a whole it becomes tedious. Josephine Grieder's *Translations of French Sentimental Prose Fiction in Late Eighteenth-Century England*[76] attempts much less but succeeds admirably within its limits. As well as a list of the works translated, with English titles, Miss Grieder supplies chapters on the sources, commercial significance and public response to the tales. She lays the responsibility for the

[74] *The Adventurer. The Fate of Adventure in the Western World*, by Paul Zweig. Dent. pp. 275.
[75] *Systems of Order and Inquiry in Later Eighteenth-Century Fiction*, by Eric Rothstein. University of California Press. pp. 256.
[76] *Translations of French Sentimental Prose Fiction in Late Eighteenth-Century England*, by Josephine Grieder. Duke University Press. pp. 136.

craze for French novels at the door of entrepreneur booksellers, its demise with the Gothic, 'the legitimate heir to the established traditions of sentimental fiction'. Dan J. McNutt has compiled a complementary bibliography of this heir, *The Eighteenth-Century Gothic Novel.*[77] The problem of identity continues to entertain the critics of Defoe. Two books deal with Defoe's interest in characters who are engaged in a quest for the self in a hostile environment. John J. Richetti's *Defoe's Narratives*[78] is a lucid, altogether sensible reading of the novels as 'dramatizations of what can be called the individualist dilemma . . . the tangled relationships between the free self and the social and ideological realities which that self seems to require', but it suffers in comparison with Everett Zimmerman's more taxing *Defoe and the Novel.*[79] Where Richetti reaffirms critical views with which the modern critic of Defoe would be familiar (albeit with uncommon insight and tact), Zimmerman is not afraid to see the larger possibilities. Richetti's book would be an excellent starting point for anyone unfamiliar with Defoe criticism. Defoe's own search for order and identity led, according to Zimmerman, to his consistent interest in characters whose autobiographies enact and describe their fight to realise their integrity in the face of pressures which undermine their identity. Zimmerman finds a development of authorial stance from *Crusoe* to *Roxana*. Crusoe's journal is weak in self-exploration: it represents Crusoe's (and Defoe's) willingness to shield himself from difficulties ('the disorder within') behind a precarious identity derived from his own shaping of reality. In contrast, the weather imagery in *Roxana* exhibits a Defoe much more psychologically aware and more sensitively engaged in placing the heroine's account of herself. Her difficulties in reconciling inner values with the world outside herself lead inevitably to ambiguities which Zimmerman sees as putting an end to Defoe's activities as a novelist. Zimmerman recognises that Defoe's concern about 'self-protective diversions' is related to Swift's interest in images of containment in *A Tale of a Tub*: both Swift and Defoe lay bare the dilemma of the man 'who, because of his sense of inner vacuousness or incoherence, desperately tries to give a shape to his life through conventional piety and the rituals of business'. No doubt there will be objections to this likeness, at least as it stands, but it is a likeness which needs to be pondered. Zimmerman is often, it seems to me, slightly off-target, but he is seldom unstimulating.

Edward Kelly's Norton Critical Edition of *Moll Flanders* is complemented with a similar edition of *Robinson Crusoe* edited by Michael Shinagel.[80] Shinagel sees his way clearly through the complex editing problems, basing the text on a collation of all six of the authorized editions published by William Taylor in 1719. The section devoted to 'Backgrounds and Sources' (including Dampier, Cooke and Woodes Rogers) together with the sections

[77] *The Eighteenth-Century Gothic Novel: An Annotated Bibliography of Criticism and Selected Texts*, by Dan J. McNutt. Dawson. pp. xxii + 330.
[78] *Defoe's Narratives. Situations and Structures*, by John J. Richetti. O.U.P. pp 256.
[79] *Defoe and the Novel*, by Everett Zimmerman. University of California Press. pp. 200.
[80] *Robinson Crusoe. An Authoritative Text, Backgrounds and Sources, Criticism*, edited by Michael Shinagel. Norton. pp. x + 399.

covering the reception of the novel from the eighteenth to the twentieth century makes this a very attractive edition, especially at its paperback price. Amongst those competing for a place in future anthologies of Defoe criticism, Homer O. Brown's 'The Displaced Self in the Novels of Daniel Defoe', originally published in 1971 (*ELH*), is close to the topic pursued by Richetti and Zimmerman. Similarly close, David Leon Higdon (*ES*) stresses that at the end of her narrative Moll moves beyond her 'limited view of the world' built on 'accounting of her 'life by time' ' into an awareness of a sense of pattern: 'she acquires a sense of 'life by value' which enables her to relate present, past, and future.' Defoe's narrative technique in *Roxana* 'suggests a developing artistic self-consciousness' and a movement towards the psychological novel, according to Wallace Jackson (*SN*). 'His last novel is . . . not only his most ambitious, but suffers far less from ambiguous character delineation' than does *Moll Flanders*. Rodney M. Baine (*SEL*) argues that since the title page of *Roxana* is not by Defoe, its placing of the novel's action '*in the Time of Charles II*' is misleading. The latter part takes place in the London of George I: Baine relates its picture of aristocratic London society to George's court and the Prince of Wales. He finds no firm candidate for the model for Roxana, but there are partial parallels with several: Lady Mary Wortley Montagu, the Italian Marhesa Paleotti; Mary Ker, the Countess of Roxburgh and Elizabeth Hervey.

There is much less to report on Richardson. Anthony Kearney's volume on *Clarissa* in the Arnold Studies in English Literature[81] series is disappointing. Basically a character study, it does not rise above a rudimentary introduction even in the chapters on 'Design and Movement' and 'Styles and Voices.' The final chapter suggests some questions and problems, but it would have been better to give at least one or two of them a more detailed airing (Hill's view, for example, that *Clarissa* is a critique of 'property marriage'). A. D. McKillop first attributed *The Apprentice's Vade Mecum* to Richardson: he now edits it for the Augustan Reprint Society.[82] In the periodicals, Elizabeth R. Napier (*ELH*) sees *Clarissa* as a 'power struggle' in which there is an inversion of the 'power structure', Clarissa gaining mastery over Lovelace: 'patterns of symbolism and narrative structure, manipulated in the first half of the novel by Lovelace as elements of an inner, private fiction, suddenly range out of his control and pass into the hands of Clarissa.' K. Smidt (*CQ*) is generally concerned with Richardson's art as a novelist, whilst James S. Munro (*MLR*) attacks the question of Richardson's indebtedness to Marivaux, a 'hardy perennial of Richardson criticism'. He believes it possible that the two writers derived inspiration from a common source, the French seventeenth-century romance which 'in the study of nascent love, forges analytical tools which both Marivaux and Richardson later adapt for their own purposes'. In two notes on Richardson, J. C. Hilson and Rosalind Nicol (*N&Q*) conjecture that Richardson may have taken the germ of Sir Charles Grandison's character, as well as found a hint for his name, from the dedication to the

---

[81] *Samuel Richardson: Clarissa*, by Anthony Kearney. Arnold. pp. 72.
[82] *The Apprentice's Vade Mecum*, by Samuel Richardson, edited by A. D. McKillop. Augustan Reprint Society. University of California Press. pp. 97.

'Earl of Grandison' in the first volume of John Ogilvie's translation of Pietro Giannone's *The Civil History of the Kingdom of Naples* which Richardson printed in 1729. Abraham Ruchat's contribution to *L'Etat et les Delices de la Suisse*, perhaps in William Windham's translation provides a possible source for the account of the crossing of Mont Cenis in the same novel.

The Wesleyan edition of Fielding is larger by two works, *Tom Jones*, edited by Fredson Bowers with an introduction and notes by Martin C. Battestin,[83] and *The Jacobite's Journal and Related Writings*, edited with an introduction and notes by W. B. Coley and a textual introduction by Bowers.[84] It is fitting that Coley's *The Jacobite Journal* should appear in the same year as J. Paul Hunter's *Occasional Form: Henry Fielding and the Chains of Circumstance*,[85] for Hunter's general aim is to place Fielding's career and his major works in relation to historical forces operating on his mind and art, 'chronicling his anxiety and adjustment to circumstance'. He is alive to the 'difficulties in getting to know Fielding', not merely historical difficulties but those posed by his masks, by 'the conjunction of comic and didactic art' and by 'the fusion of rhetoric and self-revelation'. These problems stem from Fielding being 'betwixt two ages cast'. Hunter argues that writers of Fielding's generation 'lacked an inherited identity' and an 'objective standard or norm'. Fielding's conception of the artist was classical, but his materials and methods were hostile to the didactic intent of such a conception. Hunter describes his development from the reflexive plays, themselves a turning away from the public modes of fiction, to his organization of 'modern disbelief, uncertainty, and outrage into a rhetoric of discovery' in *Joseph Andrews* and definition of 'how new heroic ideals can be rescued from the deflated ideals of the past' in *Tom Jones*. With some qualifications he considers *Amelia* to be a turning of 'discovery back into failure'. Hunter's detailed critical accounts of the plays and novels are particularly rich when he is dealing with the country/city antithesis: Fielding's alternative to urban life was 'not the civilized garden of Pope... but the country of mind and spirit, and its closest approximation in reality was Somersetshire.' Another fine book on Fielding, *Henry Fielding's Tom Jones: The Novelist as Moral Philosopher* in the Sussex *Text and Context* series comes from a professional philosopher, Bernard Harrison.[86] Harrison capitalizes on Empson's notion of 'double irony' which he takes to mean that 'no one viewpoint is ever 'guaranteed,' ever wholly adequate as a basis from which to grasp the nature of human reality'. Fielding's novel deals with, and embodies, the notion that 'certain kinds of knowledge of a man's inwardness, of what he is, are easier to convey through the ironic juxtaposition of viewpoints than through the creation of an illusion of

[83] *The History of Tom Jones*, by Henry Fielding, edited by Fredson Bowers with an introduction and notes by Martin C. Battestin. Oxford: Clarendon. 2 volumes. pp. 1250.
[84] *The Jacobite's Journal and Related Writings*, by Henry Fielding, edited by W. B. Coley with a textual introduction by Fredson Bowers. Oxford: Clarendon. pp. 515
[85] *Occasional Form: Henry Fielding and the Chains of Circumstance*, by J. Paul Turner. John Hopkins University Press. pp. 252.
[86] *Henry Fielding's Tom Jones: The Novelist as Moral Philosopher*, by Bernard Harrison. Sussex University Press. pp. 144.

direct knowledge of a character's stream of consciousness'. He presents a Fielding concerned to explore the relationship between character and conduct through the interplay of different perspectives on what a character says and does. The most impressive aspect of Harrison's book is his ability to make the moral philosophy inseparable from the contexture of the novel. This is nowhere more evident than in his account of the ambivalence of sexual desire (which Brissenden deals with so brilliantly in *Virtue in Distress*) in relation to Fielding's elucidation of some of the problems benevolism faced in distinguishing between appetite and a response to the needs of others. Battestin's *The Moral Basis of Fielding's Art*[87] is now available in paperback.

The three papers most worthy of mention on Fielding are all on *Tom Jones*. The best is Maren-Sofie Rostvig's 'Tom Jones *and the Choice of Hercules*' in her *Fair Forms: Essays in English Literature from Spenser to Jane Austen*.[88] The choice, coming down to Fielding from the Renaissance, is between virtue and vice, an active and contemplative life. Miss Rostvig shows both Fielding', and Johnson invoking Milton's 'The world was all before them, where to choose/Their place of rest, and providence their guide' (in Fielding, when Tom is expelled from Paradise Hall); and she discloses 'the thematic importance of the concept of choice' in the novel's narrative structure. Fielding's story is compared with some iconographic and literary forms of the Hercules myth, particularly the version 'transmitted by the Earl of Shaftesbury and by an artist like William Hogarth'. Henry Knight Miller (*PQ*) claims that recent experiments in fiction have made it more possible to appreciate Fielding's narrative digressions in *Tom Jones* within a romance perspective, even if the effect is sometimes anti-romantic. He centres upon the Man of the Hill and Mrs. Fitzpatrick's story which present 'the morally isolated hero and heroine' with the temptation of confusing the merely 'Actual' with the ultimately 'Real'. Robert Folkenflik (*UTQ*) finds the encounter of Tom Jones and the Gypsies in Book XII chapter 12 'neither a mere digression nor primarily part of a subplot, but centrally related to the main events, larger meanings and literary traditions of *Tom Jones*'. Tom needs to meet both high and low to come to know himself, and the gypsies, low and outcasts and depicted as 'morally better than the over-refined...householders of Hanover and Grosvenor Square', provide episodes which 'sum up and symbolize what the novel has been telling us throughout' as a preparation for the city sequence. On *Joseph Andrews*, T. C. Duncan Eaves and Ben D. Kimpel (*MP*) comment on two names whose appropriateness depends on lost usage. They quote from Ned Ward's *London Spy* for 'Slip-Slop' as meaning 'kissing' and *A General History of the Lives and Adventures of the Most Famous Highwaymen...* for 'Tow-wow' female pudendum.

The most important Sterne item is undoubtedly Arthur H. Cash's biography *Laurence Sterne, The Early & Middle Years*.[89] It is impossible

[87] *The Moral Basis of Fielding's Art. A Study of Joseph Andrews*, by Martin C. Battestin. Paperback edition. Wesleyan University Press. pp. 195.
[88] *Fair Forms: Essays in English Literature from Spenser to Jane Austen*, edited by Maren-Sofie Rostvig. D. S. Brewer. pp. 248.
[89] *Laurence Sterne. The Early and Middle Years*, by Arthur H. Cash. Methuen. pp. 333 + 14 illustrations.

in a review of this sort to do full justice to Cash's achievement; suffice it to say that no-one concerned with Sterne can afford to ignore his by and large immaculately evidenced and lucid text (especially good on the difficulties posed by Sterne's failure in the Church and domestic strains) with its complementary illustrations. The only reservations I have stem from Cash's relative unfamiliarity with the landscape within which he has to place Sterne (see Donald Davie's *TLS* review). Hipperholme, where Sterne spent his schooldays, is, for example, described misleadingly as 'half-way up a mountain'. Although Hipperholme is in the midst of the Pennines, it would have been better to give the relevant heights: the centre of Hipperholme village is 500 feet, the School 600 feet above sea-level and the summit of the hill on which it stands is slightly above 1300 feet. But these are minor difficulties. Cash's biography takes the life as far as the publication of *Tristram Shandy*. Helene Moglen's *Philosophical Irony in Tristram Shandy*[90] is an altogether competent, if unadventurous, account of the 'sources of Sterne's vision and its expression through the novel's form, characters and themes'. Miss Moglen reviews Sterne's attachment to Locke, 'the hero of *Tristram Shandy*' and she offers chapters on stylistic and thematic irony; but the best part of her study comes with her account of how Sterne's ability to see the ramifications of Locke's 'subjective realism' in 'every area of man's intellectual, emotional and aesthetic life' makes him a precursor of 'some aspects of the thought of Bergson, James and Freud'. I have not yet seen a copy of Robert Alter's *Partial Magic*[91] which includes work on Sterne.

Sterne's indebtedness to Burton exercises H. J. Jackson (*PQ*). Jackson is interested in the justice of Ferriar's accusation of plagiarism, believing that Sterne expected at least some of his readers to compare parts of *Tristram Shandy* with Burton. The quotations in volumes V to IX 'function as allusions, adding an ironic dimension to the novel'. Sterne deliberately misquoted to create a Tristram who is, amongst other things, 'a pedantic but unstable scholar'. Richard H. Davies (*N&Q*) traces further debts, to Picart, Nathaniel Wanley and John Wallis; and W. G. Day (*N&Q*) adds a borrowing from Bishop Hall's *Epistles*. A probable source for the 'Key' to *A Political Romance* is suggested by Michael Fardon (*RES*) in 'the disputes between the editors of Sterne's copies of Rabelais'. Finally, Van R. Baker (*N&Q*) supplies information on Sterne's widow, daughter, son-in-law and grandchildren in France.

Henry Mackenzie's *Man of Feeling* is treated by M. Rymer (*DUJ*) and Mackenzie's work generally benefits from a modest introduction in the Twayne English Authors series.[92] Its author, Gerard A. Barker gives a brief survey of Mackenzie's life and literary activities with chapters on each of the three novels, the tales, the dramatic and critical writings. He emphasizes Mackenzie's awareness of the limitations of, and dangers lurking in, the sentimental response, being especially worth reading on *Julia de Roubigne*. Apart from the Sells biography, Goldsmith receives little attention. Oliver

[90] *Philosophical Irony in Tristram Shandy*, by Helene Moglen. University of Florida Press. pp. 193.

[91] *Partial Magic*, by Robert Alter. University of California Press. pp. xvi + 248.

[92] *Henry Mackenzie*, by Gerard A. Barker. Twayne. pp. 189.

W. Ferguson (*PQ*) defines Goldsmith's clerical ideal from his work generally: 'a rural setting which, combined with the preacher's simple way of life, creates a benedictory mood; and an hospitable fireside presided over by unaffected good humour and spontaneous benevolence.' Dr. Primrose differs from the clergymen who provide the definition only by virtue of being an 'amiable humourist'. The comic does not undercut Primrose; it simply makes him fictionally interesting. Ferguson recognises that his reading of Primrose's character assumes that Goldsmith's estimate of him in the Advertisement can be taken at face value.

There is a little more to report on Smollett. Rosenblum (*ELH*) depicts Smollett as a 'conservative satirist', his typical hero is a figure who 'demonstrates a belief in the orderly society . . . the bad society is essentially the . . . one which recognizes no values and has lost the sense of obligation and distinctions upon which social class depends.' In a similar vein John F. Sena (*PLL*) considers Matthew Bramble in the tradition of the physician-satirist. Amongst those dealing with points of information Paul-Gabriel Bouce (*YES*) links Smollett's description of the Duke of Newcastle's levee in *Humphry Clinker* with an anonymous poem, *The Levee: A Poem Occasion'd by the Number of Clergy at the Duke of Ne——le's Last Levee*, dated 1756 and reviewed in the *Critical Review* for December of that year. Bouce concludes that it is very unlikely that the Duke is drawn from life, as John Butt once held. In *N&Q* F. Felsenstein reports on an early abridgement of *Peregrine Pickle*, undated but probably printed 1774–75 for an adult audience, and Lewis M. Knapp and Lillian de la Torre remark on two letters (c. 1826) which bear on Smollett portraits. Richard C. Cole (*PBSA*) comments on Smollett and the eighteenth-century Irish book trade and, finally, in the textual issue of *SN* O. M. Brack Jr. discusses the difficulties posed by Smollett's revision of *Peregrine Pickle* for the second edition. He approaches the revision against the background of 'evidence concerning Smollett's writing habits gathered primarily from the *Travels* with some assistance from the letters and his other revised works'. Brack finds against Buck's view of the revisions as 'hack' work; instead they represent an attempt to tighten up the novel.

5. Drama

The *RECTR* annual bibliography remains an indispensible guide to current work in the period, and the *SEL* review article by Paul Fussell also contains items of interest. The most important publications this year are in the nature of tools for research. Volume VI of the Revels History covers the period 1750 to 1880,[93] and in general provides an unignorable guide. It is almost inevitably of mixed quality, but it would be misleading to emphasize the passing failings at the expense of the work as a whole. The strongest contribution is Richard Southern's account of the architecture; the weakest is the account of the actors by Frederick and Lise-Lone Marker (though their introduction to the London theatres is very sure-

[93] *The Revels History of Drama in English: Volume VI 1750–1880*, by Michael R. Booth, Richard Southern, Frederick and Lise-Lone Marker and Robertson Davies. Methuen. pp. lxii + 304.

footed). Michael R. Booth sketches in the social and literary milieu, arguing with sense that if the drama of the period covered by the volume is seen in terms of the theatre rather than the texts, the conventional view of it as marking a decline becomes unacceptable. Robertson Davies supplies a decade by decade breakdown of playwrights and plays (see below, Chapter XIII, note 33). The quality of the third and fourth volumes of the *Biographical Dictionary*[94] of everyone connected with the theatre between 1660 and 1800 is uniformly high. These superbly detailed volumes take the *Dictionary* from Cabanel to Dynion. Together the Revels History volume and the *Dictionary* overshadow all else that appeared in 1975, but it is worth mentioning in passing two wide-ranging books with touch upon, and given context to, the eighteenth century, Cesare Molinari's finely illustrated *Theatre through the Ages*[95] and David Oenslager's *Stage Design: Four Centuries of Scenic Invention*,[96] a compilation of scenic drawings from the Italian Renaissance to twentieth-century America. Neither stops long enough in the century to warrant a review.

Two books have appeared dealing with the eighteenth-century reception of earlier drama. Robert Potter's *The English Morality Play: Origins, History and Influence of a Dramatic Tradition*[97] chronicles the awakening of interest in the morality play against the background of a gathering sympathy for the Gothic. Potter's account moves from the ignorance of Rymer and Flecknoe, through Theobald's incipient awareness to Riccoboni's *Historical and Critical Account*, as published by Dodsley (1741) to Warton's *History of English Poetry*. The span of Brian Vickers' remarkably useful *Shakespeare. The Critical Heritage*[98] is extended to 1752 with the publication of the third volume. This includes Garrick's *Essay on Acting* (1744) and Foote's *Treatise on the Passions* (1747) as well as allowing room for gobbets from adaptations (here, for example, Garrick's *Romeo and Juliet*) and pieces from Cibber, Murphy, Johnson et al. Relatedly, James S. Malek (*RECTR*) concerns himself with the dramatic response to the eighteenth-century recreation of an earlier tradition in Macpherson's *Ossian*. Malek discovers at least six plays which are significantly indebted to Macpherson, some of which 'were undoubtedly written to capitalize on late eighteenth-century interest in melancholy and the exotic'. Although the Ossianic poetry 'provided adequate plot material and interesting characters'. Malek's researches show the language to have been 'a hindrance.' Gordon K. Thomas (*RECTR*) plies a similar method in his 'Knight amid the Dunces'. The knight is Don Quixote; the dunces are none other than Pope's *bêtes noires*. Thomas investigates eight plays based on

[94] *A Biographical Dictionary of Actors, Actresses, Musicians, Dancers, Managers and Other Stage Personnel in London, 1660-1800*. Volumes III and IV, by Philip H. Highfill, Jr. Kalman A. Burnim and Edward A. Langhans. Southern Illinois University Press.

[95] *Theatre through the Ages*, by Cesare Molinari, translated from the Italian by Colin Hamer. Cassel. pp. 324.

[96] *Stage Design. Four Centuries of Scenic Invention*, by Donald Oenslager. Thames and Hudson. pp. 303 including 217 illustrations.

[97] *The English Morality Play: Origins, History and Influence of a Dramatic Tradition*, by Robert Potter. Routledge & Kegan Paul. pp. 286.

[98] *Shakespeare: The Critical Heritage*. Volume III 1733-1752, edited by Brian Vickers. Routledge & Kegan Paul. pp. 487.

Cervantes written for the London stage between 1694 and 1742; those which focused on lovers' intrigues, 'putting a stock English comedy in Cervantine dress', were the most successful. Several papers centre upon more out of the way material. Continuing his work on the early theatre in Scotland, Terence Tobin (*RECTR*) has compiled a very useful checklist of plays presented in Scotland between 1700 and 1750. His list shows, amongst other things, that although 'professional theatre in Scotland was a struggling provincial operation', 'despite the objections of civil and ecclesiastical authorities the activities of the playhouse increased'. Civil authority in the form of the 1737 Licensing Act helped to plunge Richard Baker's afterpiece *The Mad-House* into obscurity; the Act was abetted by the fact that Baker's subversive play could not hope to compete with the plays on which it was modelled and from which it borrowed, Fielding's *Pasquin* and *Historical Register* and Gay's *Beggar's Opera*. Valerie C. Rudolph (*RECTR*) treats the play 'as an eighteenth-century equivalent of Swift's *Tale of a Tub* and as a forerunner of *Marat/Sade*'. Although Vanbrugh's revision of Fletcher's *The Pilgrim* enjoyed a more lasting popularity in the eighteenth century, it did so only through further revisions, the last being by Thomas King (not Kemble) in 1787. Leo Hughes and A. H. Scouten (*MP*) describe the successive alterations in the Drury Lane promptbook which cut more than two hundred lines in an apparently unsuccessful attempt to rid the play of those elements which led one reviewer to accuse it of being 'tainted with gross indelicacy'. In *TN* John W. Velz reports on an early cast list for *Julius Caesar* and John Thieme remarks on the term 'spouting' which by 1756 had acquired 'the specific technical meaning of "theoretical declamation" '. There were 'spouting' clubs and 'spouting' companions; behind the rise of the clubs lay 'the hero-worship of Garrick' at its height about 1770.

From 1766 to 1776 Garrick not only took part in the evening's fare for the Drury Lane performances on behalf of The Theatrical Fund but addressed the audience in a prologue or epilogue which invited its continued support for the fund. His address was essentially the same for the decade in which he was involved. J. D. Hainsworth (*RES*) demonstrates something of Garrick's 'minute attention to precise theatrical occasion' in his 'concern to adapt the address to a particular occasion'. Hannah More remarked on the care which went into the 1774 address: George Winchester Stone Jr. (*PQ*) shows that same care at work in the 1761 production of *Cymbeline*, which set the tone for the Kembles, McCreadys and Keans of the world. As distinct from the late seventeenth and early eighteenth-century performances based on D'Urfey's adaptation, Garrick's production was 'strikingly close to the Shakespearean original'. It was not merely that Garrick provided a more faithful acting text: his 'inspired acting and direction' showed the way for scene painters and costumers as well as the actors and managers. James E. Tierney (*YES*) gives the texts of two unpublished and one partially published letter by Garrick. Garrick's Richard III was immortalized in the 1790s in a Derby figure; Babette Craven (*TN*) points out, however, that two more figures, assumed to represent Garrick, in fact show Kemble and Kean in the same role. Kemble's performance as King John is studied by Maarten Van Dijk (*TN*). Like Thomas Sheridan, by whom Kemble was instructed, he made 'an internal struggle between guilt and desire' the basis of his interpretation of the scenes with Hubert. This conflict 'was demonstrated pantomimically by action and facial expression'. Van Dijk offers a detailed analysis of the scenes and the critical reaction to them. Richard B. Kline (*RECTR*) casts a fresh light on a contretemps earlier in the century, that between the Whig Anne Oldfield and the Tory Mrs. Manley. Relations between the two women had so improved by 1720 that Anne Oldfield was probably involved in Mrs. Manley's benefit on 27 April. Her contact with Mrs. Manley, and through her with Prior, 'demonstrates . . . that even in that age of violent faction, the curse of party was subject to amelioration and reconciliation'.

There is little to report on many individual dramatists this year. In two notes on Rowe Alfred W. Hesse (*N&Q*) tries to counteract the scarcity of biographical material with a close reading of the Rowe Estate Act of 1706; and Marilyn Klawiter (*N&Q*) suggests that two scenes from the fourth act of Cibber's *The Comical Lovers* are elaborated versions of part of the third act of Dryden's *An Evening's Love: or, The Mock Astrologer.* Samuel Foote's Shadrach Bodkin in *The Orators*, a disreputable Methodist, seems to David Dillon-Smith (*N&Q*) to represent James Wheatley who suffered the first judicial sentence pronounced against a Methodist preacher.

John Gay fares a little better. Yvonne Noble's selection of criticism for *The Beggar's Opera* in the Twentieth-Century Interpretations series[99] contains known and new pieces. Empson's piece from *Some Versions of Pastoral*, Maynard Mack's from *The Augustans*, Martin Price's from *To the Palace of Wisdom*, John Loftis's from *Comedy and Society from Congreve to Fielding*, Roger Fiske's from *English Theatre Music in the Eighteenth Century*, Ian Donaldson's from *The World Turned Upside Down* and Bertrand Bronson's from *Facets of the Enlightenment*, are all represented in the known and Miss Noble's introduction, together with Eric Kurtz on the musical mock pastoral and Harold Gene Moss on Christian satire, constitutes the new. The selections from Loftis and Fiske are slight: this is especially sad in Fiske's case, not merely because his book is far from thin but because it means that the music gets short measure. Eric Kurtz's study of the music is fundamentally literary. He emphasizes the playfulness of the pastoral, 'a literary game in which one pretends, in a sophisticated way, to be simple, in order artfully to celebrate artlessness', to argue that both literary and musical pastoral 'call attention to their conventions, and test them by exposing their artifice'. In doing this the *Opera* draws on an established tradition, as Kurtz tries to establish in an exploration of Gay's borrowing from Purcell's *Fairy Queen*. Whereas Kurtz's interest in the formal playfulness of pastoral leads him to undervalue the seriousness of Gay's concerns, Harold Gene Moss's excursion into Christian elements misses much of the play's exuberance. Moss centres on the themes of love and time within the context of his view that *The Beggar's Opera* 'functions with respect to tragedy as the *Dunciad* does with respect to the epic poem. Both authors work their materials against the background of a higher style, both develop extensive allusions to Christian materials that fall into an orderly satirical scheme, and from both works arises an enduring sense of

[99] *Twentieth Century Interpretations of The Beggar's Opera: A Collection of Critical Essays*, edited by Yvonne Noble. Prentice-Hall. pp. iii + 92.

human frailty when man and society are tested by absolute Christian standards ' Moss makes full (some will find it too full) use of Empson's notion that Macheath is a 'supreme sacrificial hero' and, like Empson, he is alive to irony; but unlike Empson, he seems temperamentally unsuited to the *Opera*'s 'comic mixture'. Miss Noble's introduction deftly places Gay in his historical and critical context. Like Kurtz, Dieter Schulz (*DVLG*) is interested in the songs. He distinguishes two types, those which are integral to the dialogue and are primarily addressed to one actor by another and those which interrupt the action and are addressed to the audience. The songs are further divided into three categories in the light of various formal aspects of the play (theme, character, structure, imagery, etc.). In *The Scriblerian* Peter A. Martin describes two contemporary reactions to *Achilles*; whilst Donald Greene's reaction to the plays can be found in his *TLS* review of the Clarendon edition of Gay's poetry and prose.

In addition to the section on Fielding's drama in J. Paul Hunter's *Occasional Form*, Jean B. Kern (*PQ*) concentrates on Fielding as a dramatic satirist. In the absence of a critical theory, Fielding derived inspiration for his dramatic experiments in satire from sources partly dramatic, partly journalistic and partly poetic. Miss Kern stresses that there is a movement away from the plays in which the various techniques merely provide decoration for the comedy to those in which the techniques are sufficiently developed to exert a controlling influence. It is generally agreed that the controlling influence behind Steele's *The Conscious Lovers* is sentimentalism, but Michael M. Cohen (*RECTR*) differs in finding that the scene in which Bevil talks Myrtle out of a duel violates a fundamental principle of sentimentalist thought, 'that when a character has strayed from the normal natural path of goodness, the way he must be reclaimed is *by example*. He sees his true course reflected in the virtuous behaviour of the person serving as his example, and returns to that course not as a reformation, but as an expression of his real nature.'

Goldsmith is not represented outside the two books already mentioned, Tom Davies' Everyman edition of the *Poems and Plays* and A. Lytton Sells' critical biography. The Davies edition is less worrying for the drama, though it seems odd that Colman's epilogue to *She Stoops to Conquer* should have been omitted simply because it is 'rather perfunctory'. To be consistent it ought to have been omitted only if Goldsmith intended it so to be; but here we come up against the difficulties that I have already hinted at. In the absence of an autograph manuscript or firm evidence of Goldsmith's precise relation to the Larpent copy it is impossible to be sure what Goldsmith intended, especially in punctuation. Oddly, Davies' failure to outline the uncertainties and difficulties makes one less certain of his text. The new Oxford Standard Authors edition of Sheridan's plays[100] is, by contrast, wholly reliable. Its editor, Cecil Price, uses the text of his very fine Clarendon edition. In *TN* Price is at work again describing the Clare Sheridan MSS in the British Theatre Museum. They include several prompt copies of *School for Scandal*, letters from Sheridan and Joseph Richardson, and notes on the programmes given and receipts taken at Drury Lane in

[100] *Sheridan. Plays*, edited by Cecil Price. O.U.P. pp. xxxi + 442.

the seasons 1747–62, 1770–71, and 1776–82 (with receipts alone for 1803–05). Turning to the plays, Hans-Peter Breuer (*MP*) evaluates *The Rivals* in the light of its stage history. He discovers that, as 'a comedy of character . . . in which the major roles need only be adequately portrayed for a good representation, but which would lend itself to cuttings that could emphasize any of the several different starring parts if need be,' *The Rivals* was excellent material for a stock company. The history of the text underlines these practical exigencies.

XIII

The Nineteenth Century

LAUREL BRAKE, J. A. V. CHAPPLE and J. R. WATSON

The chapter has five sections: 1. Romantic Verse and Drama is by J. R. Watson; 2. Victorian: General and 3. Victorian Verse and Drama are by Laurel Brake; 4. Nineteenth-Century Prose Fiction and 5. Selected Prose Writers are by J. A. V. Chapple.

1. Romantic Verse and Drama

The most useful bibliographical aid to the romantic period is 'The Romantic Movement, A Selective and Critical Bibliography' (*ELN*), edited by David V. Erdman and others. The summer number of *TWC* reviews new books, and also has two surveys of articles published – Eric R. Birdsall's 'Wordsworth Scholarship: An Annual Register', and Jane Matsinger's 'Coleridge Scholarship: An Annual Register'. An annual bibliography of theatre research is provided by L. W. Conolly and J. P. Wearing in *Nineteenth Century Theatre Research*.

The collection of modern essays in criticism edited by M. H. Abrams under the title *English Romantic Poets*[1] has been reissued. Some of the essays of the previous edition have disappeared, such as Charles Williams on Wordsworth and Ronald Bottrall on Byron; in their place are fourteen essays taken from major critical works published during the last fifteen years. These include Hartman and Sheats on Wordsworth, Wasserman on Shelley, and Stillinger and Sperry on Keats. Geoffrey H. Hartman's *The Fate of Reading*[2] contains a number of essays which have been reviewed in these columns during the last five years. An unnoticed one is 'Poem and Ideology: A Study of Keats's "To Autumn" ' (from *Literary Theory and Structure*, edited by Brady, Palmer and Price), a moving celebration of the poem as un-epiphanic. One new essay, 'Self, Time, and History', deals with past and present in literature, with an illuminating reference to the 'Boy of Winander' episode, as printed in the 1805 *Lyrical Ballads*.

Karl Kroeber's *Romantic Landscape Vision*[3] is an important book for anyone who is concerned with the relationship of literature to the visual arts. It is one of those few books which really do carry the theory and practice of criticism one stage further, though it does so in a direction

[1] *English Romantic Poets*, ed. by M. H. Abrams. O.U.P. pp. viii + 485. pb £3.50.
[2] *The Fate of Reading*, by Geoffrey H. Hartman. Chicago and London: Chicago U.P. pp. xvi + 352. $15, £8.25.
[3] *Romantic Landscape Vision: Constable and Wordsworth*, by Karl Kroeber. Madison: U. of Wisconsin P. pp. xii + 144. $10.

which may not always be available: it relies heavily on the perception of time in relation to painting, on the presentation of contrasting rhythms in man and nature which are found in Constable and which make him comparable with Wordsworth in detail. Thus *The Hay Wain* is juxtaposed with the 'spots of time' in *The Prelude*, and 'Tintern Abbey' and *The Cornfield* show the interaction of man and nature. From these particular comparisons Kroeber moves to a more general account of the development of Wordsworth and Constable, with a final, very sensitive account of *The Leaping Horse* and 'Home at Grasmere'. The whole book (parts of which have appeared before as articles: see *YW* 52.304 and *YW* 55.363) celebrates what Kroeber calls the 'ecological moment', a point in time which helps to define the romantic movement and to make it precious, because in it man saw the last of the old patterns of organic relation with the natural world, was aware of them, and felt the interactive rhythms of nature. Another book which bridges two arts is Frank D. McConnell's *The Spoken Seen*,[4] which argues that certain aspects of the art of film have their origins in the basic assumptions of romantic literature. Although the book is concerned primarily with the art of the film, it requires a look back at romantic ideas of reality, language, and the function of the artist. It begins with Keats and ends with James Cagney, but it discusses the specific examples with a sensitive understanding of the theoretical concerns involved.

David Newsome's *Two Classes of Men*[5] is a delightful and stimulating study of Platonism and English Romantic thought. It takes its 'two classes' from Coleridge's remark that all men are either Platonists or Aristotelians, and it considers some related questions, primarily about Platonism and its influence on the intellectual assumptions of the period. Platonism, says Newsome, 'was to become the lifeblood of Romanticism'. Specifically, the book deals with the importance to Wordsworth and Coleridge of the idea of pre-existence, and other neo-Platonic attitudes to childhood; it goes on to reject the over-simple distinction between Coleridge and Cambridge (Platonist) and Newman and Oxford (Aristotelian); and traces the continuing influence of Platonism on the early Victorians.

Erland Anderson's *Harmonious Madness: A Study of Musical Metaphors in the Poetry of Coleridge, Shelley and Keats*[6] is somewhat overloaded with background material about the London musical world of the age, and also with critical theories of poetry and music. Of the poets studied, Coleridge apparently uses music to indicate harmony, and disharmony is associated with despair; Keats and Shelley use it more obviously, to embody beauty and transcendent reality respectively. This means that part of the book is all too predictable. Another musical study is Jean-Pierre Barricelli's 'Romantic Writers and Music: The Case of Mazzini' (*SIR*), which deals particularly with Mazzini's *Filosofia della Musica*.

In 'A Defence of (the Teaching of English Romantic) Poetry' (*Archiv*), Helmut Viebrock writes movingly and penetratingly about 'wholeness of

[4] *The Spoken Seen* by Frank D. McConnell. Baltimore: The Johns Hopkins U.P. pp. xiv + 195. pb. $2.95.
[5] *Two Classes of Men*, by David Newsome. John Murray, 1974. pp. x + 169. £3.75.
[6] *Harmonious Madness: A Study of Musical Metaphors in the Poetry of Coleridge, Shelley and Keats*, by Erland Anderson. Salzburg: Romantic Reassessment, 12. pp. iii + 321. $12.50.

vision', found in Wordsworth and other romantic poets, which has a transforming and expanding power for the mind. Another article which emphasises unity is L. J. Swingle's 'Romantic Unity and English Romantic Poetry' (*JEGP*), which discusses the romantic idea that apparent opposition between man and the external world is really a fundamental harmony.

Cyrus Hamlin's 'The Temporality of Selfhood: Metaphor and Romantic Poetry' (*NLH*) is a learned discussion of metaphor in the period, with particular reference to German and English literature, questioning the importance of symbol and stressing the place and time of creation and the representation in poetry of the creative act itself. More questions of representation occur at the centre of Heinrich Bosse's subtle 'The Marvellous and Romantic Semiotics' (*SIR*), with particular reference to German romanticism and to Novalis.

A graceful but too short article by Frank Doggett, 'Romanticism's Singing Bird' (*SEL*, 1974), discusses the notion of poet as singing bird in Shelley, Keats, Swinburne and Hardy, among others. In 'John Sell Cotman's *Dismasted Brig* and the Motif of the Drifting Boat' (*SIR*), Adele M. Holcomb distinguishes between the shipwreck itself in romantic art and the subsequent portrayal of the damaged ship, drifting helplessly on an open sea. In 'Romantic Poetry and the Unstamped Political Press, 1830–1836' (*SIR*), N. Stephen Bauer outlines the diffusion of the poetry of the major romantics in the popular and radical press, with a list of quotations from them. The radical bookseller, Joseph Johnson, who knew many of the great romantic writers, is the subject of a long and informative study by Leslie F. Chard II, 'Joseph Johnson: Father of the Book Trade' (*BNYPL*).

The first volume of the new 'Cornell Wordsworth', which will supersede the great five-volume de Selincourt edition, contains *The Salisbury Plain Poems*[7] and is edited by Stephen Gill. These poems are a felicitous choice for the first volume, for they illustrate very well the editors' hope that the new series will make available (in the first instance) the long poems which Wordsworth wrote in his early years and then left unpublished or incorporated into other works. The various *Salisbury Plain Poems* are particularly difficult to disentangle and almost impossible to read in de Selincourt's edition; this new one prints them in successive versions. To ensure the ultimate and complete correctness, the reading text is printed first, and this is followed by photographic reproductions and transcriptions of the manuscript. The result is a volume which is an unqualified success: a new edition which is fundamentally new, as well as being scholarly and reliable.

Also indispensable is Mark Reed's *Wordsworth: The Chronology of the Middle Years, 1800–1815.*[8] This follows the pattern of the previous volume, though the additional information available means that this second part is much bulkier; it contains a chronological list of the poet's writings, followed by a list of activities, with appendixes discussing complex issues of dating, notably on *The Prelude* and on 'Home at Grasmere'.

[7] *The Salisbury Plain Poems of William Wordsworth*, ed. by Stephen Gill. The Cornell Wordsworth, Vol I. Ithaca, N.Y.: Cornell U.P. Hassocks, Sussex: Harvester P. pp. xviii + 310. £10.

[8] *Wordsworth: the Chronology of the Middle Years, 1800-1815*, by Mark L. Reed. Cambridge, Mass.: Harvard U.P. pp. xiii + 782. $25.

Richard E. Brantley's *Wordsworth's "Natural Methodism"*[9] is well argued, but over-anxious. It shows Wordsworth's debt to Evangelical Anglicanism, and in so doing it tends to read some passages, especially of *The Prelude*, in a dogmatic way. However, there is much of value here, especially the rebuttal of the widely-held view that Wordsworth was pagan, replacing theological concepts with natural ones. Brantley rather overstates his case, in my view, pinning Wordsworth closely to a Christian orthodoxy, and to early Methodist structures of belief. The argument is supported by all kinds of evidence − Wordsworth's library, fragments of his letters and occasional sayings, and every reference in the poetry that could possibly be construed as religious; the poet turns into a local preacher. The Everyman *William Wordsworth, Selected Poems*[10] is decently done, with a good introduction by Walford Davies that leads the reader gently but firmly away from a simple view of Wordsworth as a poet of nature. The selection swims against the tide, for it omits everything written before 1797 in order to include *The White Doe of Rylstone*. It is good to see *Peter Bell* in full, but *The Prelude* is represented only by 'crucial passages', so that it is not easy to see this selection superseding the complete Wordsworth for teaching purposes.

Herbert Wurmbach's monograph[11] enquires into the rendering of mystical experience in Wordsworth's work examining in detail passages from *The Prelude* and *The Excursion* in which the so-called *spots of time* are given poetic expression. The second part of the book argues persuasively that the function of nature in Wordsworth can better be grasped in the light of the mystical doctrine of mediation. Finally, based on material from the Prefaces and statements in the poems themselves, Wordsworth's conception of imagination is examined and shown to be closely related to the mystical doctrine of the ground of the soul. I have been unable to see Eugene L. Stelzig's *All Shades of Consciousness: Wordsworth's Poetry and the Self in Time.*[12]

In 'What did Wordsworth mean by "Nature"?' (*CQ*), Laurence Lerner has produced an article which is as challenging as its title. He points to some strange moments in Wordsworth's poetry of nature, and illuminates them by reference to the Polixenes-Perdita encounter in *The Winter's Tale*, ending with the controversial view that *The Prelude* is an agnostic poem about man and nature. Another major article is Wallace Jackson's 'Wordsworth and His Predecessors: Private Sensations and Public Tones' (*Criticism*), in which Jackson distinguishes between eighteenth-century poetic techniques of description leading to states of mind (with special reference to the theories of Archibald Alison) and a romantic poetry of an emerging self-consciousness. Charles R. Woodward makes out a slender case (except

[9] *Wordsworth's "Natural Methodism"*, by Richard E. Brantley. New Haven and London: Yale U.P. pp. xvi + 205. £5.50.

[10] *William Wordsworth, Selected Poems*, ed. by Walford Davies. Dent. pp. xxvi + 227. £2.50. pb £1.20.

[11] *Das mystische Element in der Dichtung und Theorie von William Wordsworth*, by Hubert Wurmbach. Anglistische Forschungen Heft 106. Heidelberg: Carl Winter Verlag. pp. 179. n.p. [H.C.C.]

[12] *All Shades of Consciousness: Wordsworth's Poetry and the Self in Time*, by Eugene L. Stelzig. The Hague: Mouton. pp. 211. DFl. 49.

in relation to *The Borderers*) for Wordsworth's work to be included in any
consideration of the underside of romanticism, in 'Wordsworth and the
Romantic Agony' (*TSL*). Robert Holkeboer and Nadean Bishop discuss
'Wordsworth on Words' (*TWC*) in a sophisticated approach to the question
of the poet's understanding of words as the clothing of thought rather
than as ornament. Alan G. Hill, in 'Wordsworth, Comenius, and the Meaning of Education' (*RES*), suggests that the origins of Wordsworth's thinking
on education may lie not with Rousseau and the eighteenth century but
with Comenius, the seventeenth-century Moravian bishop and educational-
ist. Wordsworth's interest in the Italian language, and his Italian teacher
Isola, are described by E. R. Vincent in 'Wordsworth, Isola, Lamb' (*Essays
in Honour of John Humphreys Whitfield*).[13]

Jonathan Ramsey's 'Seeing and Perceiving in Wordsworth's *An Evening
Walk*' (*MLQ*) sees the poem as more than the transcription of appearances,
and as involving relationships between natural objects, even though the
poem fails to depict successfully a mind in harmony with nature. Wordsworth's use of Shakespeare, and the deliberate policy behind it, is the
subject of W. J. B. Owen's '*The Borderers* and the Aesthetics of Drama'
(*TWC*), which argues that to the discerning reader the play benefits from
its Shakespearean echoes and use of sources and analogues.

The structuring of episodes and of the poem as a whole is the subject of
John T. Ogden's 'The Structure of Imaginative Experience in Wordsworth's
Prelude' (*TWC*), a valuable thesis which sees the individual episodes as
having a pattern which is found again in the whole work. Michael C. Jaye
considers two unpublished drafts from Dove Cottage MS.71 of a section of
Book I of *The Prelude* in '*The Prelude, The Excursion*, and *The Recluse*:
An Unpublished *Prelude* Variant' (*PQ*). In 'Wordsworth's Card Games'
(*TWC*), J. R. Watson compares the description of the games in Book I of
The Prelude with Pope's, and sees a connection between the cards and the
discharged soldier in Book IV. The 'Was it for this' question in *The Prelude*
was the subject of a correspondence in the *TLS*, effectively concluded by
H. Erskine-Hill (Sept 26). Book V of *The Prelude* was the subject of
Michael Ragussis's 'Language and Metamorphosis in Wordsworth's Arab
Dream' (*MLQ*), in which Ragussis notes the origins of the stone and the
shell in Ovid, and sees the survival of poetry and geometric truth as lying
in their status as created worlds of universal truth. Also concentrating on
Book V is David Wiener's 'Wordsworth, Books, and the Growth of a Poet's
Mind' (*JEGP*), which examines the complex stimulating and developing
influence of the books which Wordsworth read. Robert Schell finds an
unexpected gap in Wordsworth scholarship in his helpful 'Wordsworth's
Revisions of the Ascent of Snowdon' (*PQ*), which demonstrates that in the
early version of MS. W, Wordsworth drew attention to the powers of
nature rather than to the creative imagination. Thomas Weiskel's 'Wordsworth and the Defile of the Word' (*GaR*), is a complex and sustained
discussion of dialogue and imagination in *The Prelude*.

Kenneth R. Johnston's 'Home at Grasmere: Reclusive Song' (*SIR*), is a
careful examination of the affirmations and tensions of the poem, seen

also as reflected in the structure and imagery. It is an important article, with understandings for Wordsworth's poetry which reach beyond the single poem and even suggest fruitful ideas for romantic poetry in general. In 'Wordsworth and Goethe in Literary History' (*NLH*), Geoffrey H. Hartman considers the impact of the 'northern enchantment' on the two poets, and in particular the idea of the northern ballad on Wordsworth's 'The Danish Boy'. James B. Twitchell finds an elaborate analogy between the hart in 'Hart-Leap Well' and the figure of Christ in' "Hart-Leap Well": Wordsworth's Crucifixion Poem' (*TSL*). Twitchell suggests that this emphasises 'the really dreadful arts of man', and that the poem may be Wordsworth's bitterest. In 'Wordsworth's Symbolic White Doe: "The Power of History in the Mind" ' (*Criticism*), Barbara Gates argues that the doe is a variable symbol of the power of history in the mind, which can relate to different characters in different ways.

Geoffrey J. Finch, in 'Wordsworth's Solitary Song: The Substance of "true art" in "The Solitary Reaper" ' (*ArielE*), concentrates on the way in which Wordsworth sees the girl as transfigured, feeling both identity with her and separateness from her at the high point of the poem's aesthetic experience. In 'The Use and Abuse of Structural Analysis: Riffaterre's Interpretation of Wordsworth's "Yew-Trees" ' (*NLH*), Geoffrey H. Hartman refers to an earlier article in *NLH* 1973 by Michael Riffaterre; Hartman provides a long and complex reading of the poem, with a phenomenological interpretation which questions Riffaterre's structuralist method.

Changes at Grasmere, and family bereavement, are two reasons why Wordsworth did not write *The Recluse*, according to James A. Butler in 'Wordsworth's *Tuft of Primroses*: "An Unrelenting Doom" ' (*SIR*). Judith B. Herman sees a connection with Plutarch in 'The Roman Matron with the Bird-cage: A Note on "The Sailor's Mother" ' (*TWC*), a neat observation which increases an understanding of the poem. In 'The Design of Wordsworth's Sonnets' (*ArielE*), G. M. Harvey discusses the 'symbiotic' qualities of Wordsworth's rhetoric, which allow Wordsworth to be involved in the subject yet also detached from it, emotional in feeling yet also intelligent in thought.

Several Wordsworth items appear in the February number of *N&Q*. In ' "The Dedication Scene" in "The Prelude" and "The Book of Common Prayer" ' Emily Lorraine de Montluzin suggests similarities in wording and idea, especially between the passage in the poem and the service of Baptism. Unpublished letters include an interesting one on epitaphs printed by Russell Noyes and two less important ones printed by James A. Butler; and an echo of *Paradise Lost* is found by C. R. La Borsiere in 'Wordsworth's "Go back to antique ages, if thine eyes" ', and ' "Paradise Lost", XII, 23–47'.

Several articles deal with the reception of Wordsworth. N. Stephen Bauer gives an account of 'Early Burlesques and Parodies of Wordsworth' (*JEGP*) noting a surprising number, the first of which appears as early as 1801. Nathaniel Teich considers Wordsworth's role and purpose in changing the taste of his contemporaries (particularly in relation to simplicity) in 'Evaluating Wordsworth's Revolution: Romantic Reviewers and Changing Taste' (*PLL*). Elsewhere Teich discusses a pamphlet by Edward Copleston, *Advice to a Young Reviewer* (1807) in 'Wordsworth's Reputation and

Copleston's *Advice* to Romantic Reviewers' (*TWC*). Sharon Bassett's 'Wordsworth, Pater and the "Anima Mundi": Towards a Critique of Romanticism' (*Criticism*) deals with Pater's appreciation of Wordsworth's individual vision and his sense of coherence in the world, and with Pater's own necessary limitation of this to the world of art.

Wordsworth appears devious and mean in his relations with Haydon in Stanley Jones's 'B.R. Haydon on Some Contemporaries: a New Letter' (*RES*). A meeting in Oxford during his later years is described by B. W. Martin in 'Wordsworth, Faber and Keble: Commentary on a Triangular Relationship' (*RES*).

As 'A Source for the Folklore of the Ass in Wordsworth's "Peter Bell" ' (*N&Q*), Kent Beyette suggests John Brand's *Observations on Popular Antiquities* of 1813. Another article on the ass theme is Leah Sinanoglou Marcus's 'Vaughan, Wordsworth, Coleridge and the *Encomium Asini'* (*ELH*), a delightful and informative account of a long tradition of donkey poetry with special reference to Coleridge's 'To a Young Ass' and Wordsworth's *Peter Bell*. It is particularly convincing in linking the pretended bungling of *Peter Bell* with Christian lowliness, seen in the choice of the ass for the entry into Jerusalem. Another article which combines Wordsworth and Coleridge is S. V. Pradhan's elegant and scholarly 'Fancy and Imagination: Coleridge Versus Wordsworth' (*PQ*): this sees the two poets as complementary, with Coleridge's interest being more philosophical and Wordsworth's more those of a practitioner.

Stephen Prickett's little book *Wordsworth and Coleridge: The Lyrical Ballads*[14] suffers from a compression of thought into less than sixty pages. Nevertheless, Prickett makes out a good case for the unity of *Lyrical Ballads*, with 'Tintern Abbey' giving an affirmative answer to the 'metaphysical terror' of 'The Ancient Mariner' at the beginning of the 1798 volume. Between these two poems, Prickett emphasises particularly the philosophical and contemporary background to the poetry, and Wordsworth's radicalism. The result is a short account which is nicely stimulating without being over-complex and difficult; the bibliography is prepared for 'the ordinary student', and the text will help such a student to gain an entry into *Lyrical Ballads* and into the Preface.

E. S. Shaffer's *'Kubla Khan' and the Fall of Jerusalem*[15] is a formidable and impressive book, a splendid piece of scholarship with a convincing thesis and a radically new approach to 'Kubla Khan'. Sharp as a razor, and sometimes as dangerous (there are slashing asides which cut down some established names), the book justifies its astringency by the precision and breadth of its reference. According to Shaffer, Coleridge read the German higher critics, especially J. G. Eichhorn, and was directed by them to the subject of the Fall of Jerusalem; unwilling to write an epic, he wrote 'Kubla Khan' instead as a symbolic summary, a fusion of the ballad and the sublime ode. The book is much wider than this summary, or its title, suggests: it goes on to deal with Hölderlin, Browning and George Eliot in

[14] *Wordsworth and Coleridge: The Lyrical Ballads*, by Stephen Prickett. Arnold. pp. 64. pb £2.20.
[15] *'Kubla Khan' and the Fall of Jerusalem*, by E. S. Shaffer. Cambridge: Cambridge U.P. pp. x + 361. £8.80.

its survey of the higher criticism and its influence on secular literature. It is thus of interest to Victorian scholars as well as those in the romantic period: the section on George Eliot, for example, supersedes Basil Willey's account in *Nineteenth Century Studies*. Another good book, without Shaffer's impressive display of learning, is Reeve Parker's *Coleridge's Meditative Art*.[16] This also studies Coleridge's Christian reading, and especially the influence of Richard Baxter's *The Saints' Everlasting Rest*. Parker is also very good on Wordsworth's influence, especially through the 'Salisbury Plain' poems and subsequently as an exemplar of all that Coleridge had failed to be; in expressing this, as Parker points out, Coleridge draws on Milton, especially on 'Lycidas' for the image of the drowned poet. Throughout the book, Parker is ingenious and almost always convincing, blending a straight consideration of influences with a sensitive intuition of Coleridge's relationships and needs. A related study is an article by Avery F. Gaskins, 'Nature, the Conversation Poems and the Structure of Meditation' (*Neophilologus*), which argues that the Conversation Poems display a consistent use of the formal structure of seventeenth-century meditations.

The influence of 'To the River Lodon' on Coleridge's 'To the River Otter' is noted by A. Harris Fairbanks in ' "Dear Native Brook": Coleridge, Bowles, and Thomas Warton the Younger' (*TWC*). In another article, Fairbanks shows Coleridge's low opinion of a poem which others thought well of, in 'Coleridge's Opinion of "France: an Ode" ' (*RES*). William H. Scheuerle's 'A Re-examination of Coleridge's "The Eolian Harp" ' (*SEL*) finds the poem consistent, and suggests that the statement of faith is necessary, for Coleridge, to the full perception of the One Life.

James Twitchell's 'The World above the Ancient Mariner' (*TSLL*) emphasises the unseen world of the poem, and particularly its Neoplatonic daemonography, as expressions of man's inward nature. Another work concerned primarily with 'The Ancient Mariner' is Christian La Cassagnère's introduction to the *Poèmes en bilingue*[17] edition of Coleridge, which is a brilliant exposition of the archetypal themes.

Leslie Brisman, in 'Coleridge and the Ancestral Voices' (*GaR*) deals primarily with 'Kubla Khan' but also with 'The Ancient Mariner', seeing the imagination as concerned with origins and opposites, including the person from Porlock in its purview. Michael J. Kelly traces some echoes, which I find rather speculative, faint and coincidental, in ' "Kubla Khan" and Cowper's *Task*: Speculation amidst Echoes' (*BNYPL*).

Eugene L. Stelzig suggests an actual North Devon landscape as the origin of the scene in 'Kubla Khan' in 'The Landscape of "Kubla Khan" and the *Valley of Rocks*' (*TWC*). Joseph Sgammato points out, in 'A Note on Coleridge's "symphony and song" ' (*TWC*), that symphony was at one time supposed to be another word for a dulcimer. In 'The Mystery of Eros: Sexual Initiation in Coleridge's "Christabel" ' (*PMLA*), Jonas Spatz counters recent arguments that for Coleridge sex was a necessary evil, and sees 'Christabel' as concerned with a necessary coming to terms with

---

[16] *Coleridge's Meditative Art*, by Reeve Parker. Ithaca and London: Cornell U.P. pp. 270. $12.50, £6.85.
[17] *Samuel Taylor Coleridge, Poèmes*, traduction par Henri Parisot, chronologie, introduction et bibliographie par Christian La Cassagnère. Paris: Aubier-Flammarion. pp. 313. 10.50 fr.

sexuality. Constance Hunting's 'Another Look at "The Conclusion to Part II"' of *Christabel*' (*ELN*) catches echoes from the main poem in the lines about the little child; some seem fanciful, but others help to make out a good case for the lines as referring to the poem's action and not to Hartley Coleridge.

Mary Lynn Johnson engages in what is substantially a tidying-up operation in her account of 'Gillman's Discovery of the "Lost" *Times Review* of *Christabel*: An Aid to Reflections on Community among Scholars' (*TWC*)—the last reference being to some gentlemanly behaviour by Professor Erdman. A sequel to the two parts of 'Christabel', which actually appeared in 1815, before the poem itself, is printed by Donald H. Reiman in 'Christobell; or; The Case of the Sequel Presumptive' (*TWC*); Reiman suggests that the author was a certain Anna Jane Vardill.

In 'The Form of Coleridge's Dejection Ode' (*PMLA*), A. Harris Fairbanks considers the implications of the poem's status as an ode, and its relationship to the conversation poems: in the process he includes an interesting defence of the poem's revision from the original verse letter.

In 'Narrative Technique in the "Biographia Literaria" ' (*MLR*), Richard Mallette emphasises the speaking voice of the narrator, and his use of metaphors of plant life and natural process; Mallette shows how Coleridge gains the reader's confidence in the opening chapters and then reveals himself as the apostle of the new age, especially in his critique of Wordsworth. Continuing his studies of the Coleridge milieu, 'The Cool World of Samuel Taylor Coleridge', P. M. Zall gives an entertaining account of a flamboyant journalist and editor, James Perry—or as Zall calls him 'James Perry, *Vox Pop.*' (*TWC*); in another of the same series, Zall describes Perry's brother-in-law Richard Porson in a lively, even hilarious, account entitled 'Richard Porson, Don or Devil' (*TWC*). In 'Coleridge and Jeffrey in Controversy' (*SIR*), David V. Erdman and Paul M. Zall show how Jeffrey orchestrated early attacks on the Lake Poets, and contributed to them in the *Edinburgh Review*: but they suggest that there was a difference between Jeffrey's private opinion and his public stance. There is a small overlap between this and Erdman's long essay on 'Coleridge and the "Review Business" ' (*TWC*). This discusses Coleridge's relations with the *Edinburgh*, the *Quarterly* and *Blackwood's Edinburgh Magazine*, in relation to the remarks on critical journals and the essay on Wordsworth in *Biographia Literaria*. It also suggests that Coleridge may have been the author of a review of 1821. Marginalia referring to a review in the *Quarterly* which acted as a catalyst for *Biographia Literaria* are discussed by James D. Wilson in 'A Note on Coleridge and *The Quarterly Review*' (*TWC*).

Coleridge's references to Petrarch, and the influence of Petrarch on his work, are discussed by Giuseppe Gaetano Castorina in 'Coleridge e Petrarca' (*Critica Letteraria*). A survey of recent Coleridge scholarship is Denise Degrois's 'Quelques ouvrages sur S. T. Coleridge (éditions et études critiques)' (*EA*). A complex bibiographical problem is laid out by Mary Lynn Johnson, who discusses the many annotated copies of *Sibylline Leaves*, in 'How Rare Is a "Unique Annotated Copy" of Coleridge's *Sibylline Leaves*?' (*BNYPL*). I have not seen L. D. Berkoben's *Coleridge's Decline as a Poet*.[18]

[18]*Coleridge's Decline as a Poet*, by L. D. Berkoben. The Hague: Mouton. pp. 171. Fl. 36.

Kenneth Curry's *Southey*[19] in the 'Routledge Author Guides' series is a very good brief account, since Southey lends himself particularly well to this series with its emphasis on the biographical survey and the historical background. The book is informative about Southey's interest in contemporary history, his knowledge of social questions, and his acquaintance with other literary figures. Curry is perhaps too kind to Southey: the quarrel with Byron, for instance, is seen as some kind of unfortunate occurrence, which seems a little too easy; and in general Southey appears as reliable, kindly and thorough. Six unpublished letters of Southey are printed in *N&Q*, two by Peter Mann and four by Nicholas Horsfall. A poem by Southey and Coleridge, 'The Devil's Thoughts' (1799) is shown by William Ronald Runyan to have influenced a tradition in 'Bob Southey's Diabolical Doggerel: Its Influence on Shelley and Byron' (*TWC*). A neglected part of Southey's prose is discussed and listed by Kenneth Curry and Robert Dedmon in 'Southey's Contributions to *The Quarterly Review*' (*TWC*). Richard Hoffpauir studies Southey's epic poetry, suggesting that it is often propaganda for Southey's opinions, in 'The Thematic Structure of Southey's Epic Poetry' (*TWC*).

A nice subject is beautifully laid out by Clare Lamont in her masterly British Academy lecture, 'The Poetry of the Early Waverley Novels' (*PBA*). Scott's use of songs, lyrics and ballad snatches is shown, among other things, to present sudden insights and to affect our understanding of character, especially in *The Bride of Lammermoor*.

In 'George Crabbe and the Workhouses of the Suffolk Incorporations' (*PQ*), Ronald B. Hatch contrasts the descriptions of poorhouses in *The Village* and *The Borough*, showing the poet's dislike of the new large workhouses. L. J. Swingle, in 'Late Crabbe in Relation to the Augustans and Romantics: the Temporal Labyrinth of his *Tales in Verse*, 1812' (*ELH*), argues that Crabbe is different from the Augustans in his concern with change, and living in his time; but Swingle also argues interestingly that Crabbe is different from the Romantics in his concern for the individuality rather than the unity of things in time. Thomas C. Faulkner prints four unpublished letters of Crabbe, and one of his successor as rector of Trowbridge, in 'Letters of George Crabbe and Francis Fulford' (*RES*).

Claude A. Prance discusses sources for Lamb's verses on eminent composers in 'Charles Lamb's "Free Thoughts" ' (*The Charles Lamb Bulletin*). One double number of this *Charles Lamb Bulletin* is a special bicentenary number, containing 'The History of Charles Lamb's Reputation' by George L. Barnett, 'A Note from Lamb to Coleridge' by Kathleen Coburn, a suggestion from Kenneth Curry that Southey's essay form in *The Doctor* owes something to Lamb, and a cautionary tale from Carl Woodring, 'Lamb Hoaxes and the Lamb Canon'. The pages from Haydon's diary about the 'immortal dinner' are reproduced in this number; there is also an account of Lamb's imaginative involvement with Hogarth in 'Perfect Sympathy: Lamb on Hogarth', by John I. Ades. George Whalley in 'Lend Your Books to Such a One' discusses the Coleridge marginalia in the books lent to him by Lamb. P. M. Zall provides a felicitous tribute to

[19] *Southey*, by Kenneth Curry. Routledge & Kegan Paul. pp. xii + 191. £4.95.

'The Memory of Barry Cornwall', and other articles include 'Lamb, Dickens and the Theatrical Vision', by Peter A. Brier, and 'An Elian Enigma' by Ralph M. Wardle, concerning the Lycidas manuscript mentioned in 'Oxford in the Vacation'. R. A. Foakes, in 'The Authentic Voice: Lamb and the Familiar Letter', gives a graceful account of Lamb as a letter-writer.

The fourth volume of Leslie A. Marchand's new edition of *Byron's Letters and Journals* is entitled *Wedlock's the Devil*.[20] It deals with two busy years, 1814 and 1815, including the marriage in January 1815. It was in this period that Byron befriended Coleridge, and arranged for the publication of *Christabel*; he also wrote warmly to Leigh Hunt about *The Story of Rimini*, and to Thomas Moore and Samuel Rogers. Among the newly-printed letters are two to James Wedderburn Webster, warning him against becoming involved with Lady Caroline Lamb; throughout the volume Byron appears as warm-hearted, generous, witty and impulsive, as well as a man of pleasure and bonhomie.

John S. Chapman's *Byron and the Honourable Augusta Leigh*[21] is well-executed, by a scholarly and able writer; but on the whole it is a peculiar and unsatisfactory book. It is peculiar because it brings to the Byron-Augusta relationship all the serious scholarship which might have been kept for something more worth while: one is accustomed to the gossip-column approach, but hardly to this methodical sifting of evidence. Chapman's own uneasiness is found in some arch and affected humour in the early part of the book: later he becomes brisker and clearer, only to conclude with irrelevance. His verdict on the question of incest is 'not proven'; disappointing but almost certainly correct. Some of the same ground is covered by Malcolm Elwin's *Lord Byron's Family*,[22] which deals with Annabella, Ada and Augusta during the years of the poet's exile. Elwin's use of the Lovelace Papers in his books has clarified the situation considerably, chiefly to the great discredit of Lady Byron; in this volume Elwin seems to have hardened towards her, and her behaviour appears as a series of selfish and self-justifying actions, aimed at blackening Byron's reputation and preventing his access to Ada.

John D. Jump's *Byron, a Symposium*[23] is a decent but not very lively collection of commemorative essays and lectures on the 150th anniversary of the poet's death. It begins with A. L. Rowse's 'Byron's Cornish Ancestry', an account of the Trevanion family; John D. Jump himself writes on 'Byron's Prose', noting the poet's ability to relate to the recipients of his letters. Francis Berry writes amiably and discursively on 'The Poet of Childe Harold', and Gilbert Phelps, in 'The Byronic Byron', has some sensible things to say about Byron's use of Augustan and Romantic modes. P. M. Yarker, my predecessor in these columns, deals with the satires up to and including *Beppo* in 'Byron and the Satiric Temper', leaving A. B. England to write on 'The Style of *Don Juan* and Augustan

[20] *'Wedlock's the Devil': Byron's Letters and Journals*, Vol IV, ed. by Leslie A. Marchand. John Murray. pp. vi + 369. £5.75.
[21] *Byron and the Honourable Augusta Leigh*, by John S. Chapman. New Haven and London: Yale U.P. pp. xxiv + 282. $10.
[22] *Lord Byron's Family*, by Malcolm Elwin, ed. by Peter Thomson. John Murray. pp. x + 252. £7.50.
[23] *Byron, a Symposium*, ed. by John D. Jump. Macmillan. pp. xvi + 188. £6.95.

Poetry', in which he suggests that Byron has rhetorical affinities with Pope, but that essentially he challenges the Augustan view of coherence. W. Ruddick writes on 'Don Juan in Search of Freedom: Byron's Emergence as a Satirist', emphasising the influence of Thomas Moore and Fielding in the formation of Byron's narrative style. Anne Barton, in ' "A Light to Lesson Ages": Byron's Political Plays', gives a neat account of Byron's political drama, ending with a stimulating comparison to Brecht; and P. D. Fleck (in an essay also printed in *The Byron Journal*) writes of dream-fulfilment in 'Romance in Byron's *The Island*'.

If this collection seems faded and dull, students and scholars will find ample compensation in Bernard Blackstone's *Byron: A Survey*.[24] Blackstone's account is wonderfully fresh and incisive, deriving in part from his 'topo-critical' approach which involves the examination of Byron 'on his own ground' from Scotland to the eastern Mediterranean. It unites east and west in its understanding of influences, and only occasionally does Blackstone get carried away with his own virtuosity—'Byron, deep in Jones and Waring, Weston and the Koran, conflates Ossian and the topographically alien and remote but psychologically akin diagrams of Jami and Firdausi'. For the most part, unregarded poems spring to life under Blackstone's eyes, such as *The Curse of Minerva*, or the 'Lines to Mr Hodgson' or the lines 'Written after Swimming from Sestos to Abydos'; and Blackstone's understanding of the Levant, with its peculiar mingling of Classical and Islamic influences, opens up new insights throughout. There is a small price to pay: from the eastern Mediterranean Wordsworth and the other English romantics seem a very long way off and rather small, while Blackstone is better, I think, on the romantic than on the satirical poems: yet here too there are flashes of illuminating commentary, as in the discussion of Canto II and the eating imagery, and the final admiration of Byron's different levels, 'all authentic though contradictory'.

John D. Jump's selection, *Byron: Childe Harold's Pilgrimage and other Romantic Poems*[25] contains the four cantos of *Childe Harold*, *The Giaour*, *The Prisoner of Chillon, Mazeppa*, and a few of the short romantic lyrics. There is a sensible introduction, particularly the section describing cantos III and IV of *Childe Harold*, and there are short and informative notes at the end. In the *Romantic Reassessment* series, Daniel P. Deneau presents two judicious essays on *Byron's Narrative Poems of 1813*.[26] The first is entitled 'Byron's Giaour and Its Critics: a Review and Reassessment', and takes a moderate stand between those who would write off the poem and those who would over-praise it; Deneau sees Byron's major difficulty as the manipulation of the fisherman-narrator. The second essay, 'Byron's Selim and Zuleika: A Reading of *The Bride of Abydos*' is another moderate and unpretentious reading which takes the two characters in turn and discusses their functions within the tale. Elizabeth Longford's *Byron's Greece*[27] is a pleasing picture record of Byron's visits, on the tour with

---

[24] *Byron, a Survey*, by Bernard Blackstone. Longman. pp. xviii + 371. £7.5⊂ pb £4.50.
[25] *Byron: Childe Harold's Pilgrimage and other Romantic Poems*, ed. by John D Jump. Dent. pp. xxii + 233. £3.25. pb £1.65.
[26] *Byron's Narrative Poems of 1813: Two Essays*, by Daniel P. Deneau. Salzburg Romantic Reassessment, 55. pp. 92. $12.50.
[27] *Byron's Greece*, by Elizabeth Longford. Weidenfeld & Nicolson. pp. 183. £4.95

Hobhouse and later on his last journey. *The Byron Journal* for 1975 opens with Paul Fleck's essay on *The Island*, found also in the Jump *Symposium*. An orthopaedic surgeon, A. B. Morrison, writes on 'Byron's Lameness', and John Jump provides some 'Reflections on Byron's Prose', emphasising the spontaneity and the nobility of temper in the letters and journals. There are two most delightful and informative essays in the *Journal*: one is Robert Escarpit's study of Byron's French translator, Amédée Pichot. Entitled 'Misunderstanding in France', it is a penetrating though brief discussion of the effect of Pichot on Byron's European reputation, and of subsequent Byronic influence in France, ending with André Malraux. The other is Leslie A. Marchand's 'Byron's Hellenic Muse', a graceful discussion of the effect on Byron of both modern and ancient Greece.

A catalogue of 'The Byron Sesquicentenary Exhibition Held in 1974 at the Humanities Research Center of the University of Texas at Austin' by Sally Leach is printed in *TSLL*. In 'The Accuracy of Lord Byron' (*CQ*), George Watson considers the co-existence in Byron's poetry of a certain kind of accuracy and the careless speed of his composition. In 'Byron, Norway and Ibsen's *Peer Gynt*' (*ES*), B. J. Tysdahl surveys the reputation of Byron in Norway in the nineteenth century, and the use of Byron by Wergeland and Ibsen. The importance to Byron of the sceptical and dualistic *Historical and Critical Dictionary* of Pierre Bayle is studied by Roy E. Aycock in *YES*, and John Clubbe has a review article, 'Byron in His Letters' in *SAQ*.

Several articles deal with Byron's *Cain*. In 'Byron's Mysteries: The Paradoxical Drive Toward Eden' (*SEL*), William P. Fitzpatrick discusses *Cain* and *Heaven and Earth* in terms of the lost paradise; he argues that in the attempts to regain paradise, the characters re-enact the Fall in subsequent generations. Stephen L. Goldstein's 'Byron's Cain and the Painites' (*SIR*), deals with the evolutionary material in the poem, and traces the similarity between Byron's ideas about geology and those of Richard Carlile, editor of the *Republican*. The scepticism of *Cain* is also the subject of Leslie Tannenbaum's 'Lord Byron in the Wilderness: Biblical Tradition in Byron's *Cain* and Blake's The Ghost of Abel' (*MP*), which deals with Blake's reaction to Byron's ideas. Leslie Brisman, in 'Byron: Troubled Stream from a Pure Source' (*ELH*), sees Byron as rejecting myths of the origins of good and evil, especially paradise myths, in *Cain, Lara,* and *Manfred*. In another article on the narrative poetry, ' "Galvanism upon Mutton", Byron's Conjuring Trick in The Giaour' (*KSJ*), Peter B. Wilson sees Byron's heroic stance as a hindrance rather than a help, and his energetic rhythms as acting upon 'the dead meat of melodrama and exhausted poetic diction.' A splendid example of Byronic influence is found by Sona Stephan Hoisington, in '*Eugene Onegin*: An Inverted Byronic Poem' (*CL*).

Gerald C. Wood's 'Nature and Narrative in Byron's "Prisoner of Chillon" ' (*KSJ*) draws attention to the importance of nature in the poem, and sees the subject as man's alienation from the unity of nature. In 'The Supernatural Structure of Byron's *Manfred*' (*SEL*), James Twitchell sees the structure of the drama as originating in Byron's interest in the ancient Neoplatonic mystics of Alexandria, especially Iamblichus, and examines this in some detail. In 'Byron's *Don Juan*: The Obsession and Self-Discipline of Spontaneity' (*SIR*), Michael G. Cooke stresses the nature of the poem as fragment, and the patterns which Byron develops in his continual searching and developing. Two echoes of Scott are found in *Don Juan* by J. C. Maxwell and William A. Stephenson (*N&Q*). Other minor notes in *N&Q* are N. Stephen Bauer's 'Byron at Harrow', which quotes some lines supposed to have been written by Byron in the churchyard, and speculates on their authenticity; and Bertha Keveson Hertz's 'A Putative Byron Poem', which identifies Disraeli as the author of a piece of Byron apocrypha.

Judy Little's *Keats as a Narrative Poet*[28] is not entirely convincing in its theory that imagery is a major structural element: too often this becomes a matter of 'rising imagery' to the exclusion of other factors. But Ms Little is good on the influence of Hazlitt, and this gives the book more substance than the link between imagery and structure is able to do alone. Florence Physer Krause writes about Keats as well as Shakespeare in 'Negative Capability and Objective Correlative in Shakespeare's Sonnets' (*TSL*) relating Keats's ideas, as other critics have done (see *YW* 53.315), to the performance of Kean as Richard III which Keats reviewed.

Frank W. Pearce extends Robert Gittings's argument about traces of Coleridge in Book IV of *Endymion* in 'Keats and the Ancient Mariner: Book III of Endymion' (*KSJ*). C. T. Andrews gives a medical description of the start of Keats's pulmonary tuberculosis in 'Keats in the Island of Mull' (*KSMB*), together with a detailed description of the poet's journey. Also related to the Scottish tour is Angus Graham-Campbell's 'Beauly Priory and the Eve of St. Agnes' (*KSMB*), which suggests a visit to the Priory near Inverness as a source for the Beadsman and for certain other elements of *The Eve of St. Agnes*. In 'Narrative Structure and the Problem of the Divided Reader in *The Eve of St. Agnes*' (*ELH*), Michael Ragussis takes the *via media* between the romantic and the anti-romantic interpretations of the poem.

In 'Keats's *Contemptus Mundi*: A Shakespearian Influence on the "Ode to a Nightingale" ' (*MLQ*), Eamon Grennan argues that a Shakespeare play which influenced this and other Keats poems was *Measure for Measure*, and in particular its awareness of death and the value of life. Eugene J. Harding suggests 'tread' as 'A Possible Pun in Keats's "Ode to a Nightingale" ' (*KSJ*). Harry M. Solomon discusses the end of the 'Ode on a Grecian Urn' with reference to Shaftesbury's *Characteristics*, and then cleverly extends his argument to suggest that the whole poem can be read in the light of Shaftesbury's aesthetics, in 'Shaftesbury's *Characteristics* and the Conclusion of "Ode on a Grecian Urn" ' (*KSJ*). Another interpretation, by James Shokoff, emphasises the way in which the poet learns from the urn about man's human limitations in 'Soul-Making in "Ode on a Grecian Urn" ' (*KSJ*). In 'Keats's Odes and two *New Monthly Magazine* Sonnets to an "Antique Grecian Vase" ' (*KSMB*), Neil G. Grill finds two urn poems of 1819 and points to a just-possible influence on Keats. Donald Pearce's 'Thoughts on the Autumn Ode of Keats' (*ArielE*) discusses the repose and the intensity of the poem. He sees the poem as prophecy rather than pastoral, with special reference to the absence of rhetoric in

[28] *Keats as a Narrative Poet*, by Judy Little. Lincoln: U. of Nebraska P. pp. viii + 167. $8.50.

the poem, which is seen as 'a complex, subversive affirmation of the values of process and spontaneity over those of system, hierarchy, stasis, order'. Katherine M. R. Kenyon writes charmingly of Keats in Winchester in 'Keats and the Ode to Autumn Walk' (*KSMB*), describing the corn-growing area, and the threshing barn which still survives.

Pierre Vitoux reconstructs 'Keats's Epic Design in *Hyperion*' (*SIR*), arguing that the poem is concerned with the acceptance of change and that there is a rehandling of the legendary features to suggest a single warlike episode (the second rebellion) followed by a peaceful fusion of the old world and the new. A. J. Woodman disentangles some mistakes about Classical allusions in 'Greek Sources of "Writ in Water": A Further Note' (*KSJ*). C. P. Ravilious notes the possible use of a joke book, *The New Joe Miller* (1800), in a letter of Keats (*N&Q*).

Neville Rogers's Oxford edition of *The Complete Poetical Works of Percy Bysshe Shelley*[29] continues with the second volume, covering the years 1814-1817. It contains some of the beautiful short lyrics, together with *Alastor, Laon and Cythna* (or *The Revolt of Islam*), the 'Hymn to Intellectual Beauty' and 'Mont Blanc'. In the preface Rogers defends his editorial policy against those whom he calls the 'Fundamentalists', who print from a single extant text or manuscript. In Rogers's view this is inappropriate for Shelley, where different versions exist in manuscript, and first published versions are different again. Rogers's declared aim, in text and notes, is to elucidate the coherence and unity of Shelley's system: in the reconstruction of 'Mont Blanc', for example, he adds two lines and two parentheses in search of clarity, but in ways of which a 'Fundamentalist' would no doubt disapprove. James E. Barcus's *Shelley, the Critical Heritage*[30] begins with a grotesque and jocose review of 1810, and ends with a baffled Emerson in 1848. Between there are some striking items of violent anti-Shelley criticism, and some sentimental adulation, notably by Margaret Fuller Ossoli, who led the appreciation of Shelley in America. Barcus's emphasis on the American reception of Shelley is stronger than is usual in these volumes: among his items is a delightful piece by Hawthorne, showing Shelley matured into an Anglican clergyman.

Stuart Curran's *Shelley's Annus Mirabilis*[31] is a splendid study of the year or so from the autumn of 1818 to the beginning of 1820. It is subtitled 'The Maturing of an Epic Vision', and it sees Shelley as moving through various forms and modes towards a comprehensive and encyclopaedic epic vision. The most spectacular of Curran's chapters is the one in which he deals with the mythological background to *Prometheus Unbound*; this brilliantly brings forward patterns of Eastern and Western myth and uses them to illuminate the poem. The learning displayed in this section is parallelled by Curran's skill in exposition, and at first sight the remainder of the book is something of an anticlimax; yet at the end Curran argues that Shelley has, through the diversity of poetic forms which he used

---

[29] *The Complete Poetical Works of Percy Bysshe Shelley, Vol II, 1814-1817*, ed. by Neville Rogers. pp. xxx + 421. Oxford: Clarendon P. £10.

[30] *Shelley, the Critical Heritage*, ed. by James E. Barcus. Routledge & Kegan Paul. pp. xvi + 432. £9.50.

[31] *Shelley's Annus Mirabilis*, by Stuart Curran. San Marino, Calif.: Huntington Library. Folkestone, Kent: Dawson. pp. xxii + 255. £7.

during this crucial year, provided a unity in diversity which is epic in conception.

William Keach, in 'Reflexive Imagery in Shelley' (*KSJ*) argues that Shelley uses this type of image to articulate some of his deepest poetic concerns. Mirror-images and masks are also the subject of James C. Evans's 'Masks of the Poet: A Study of Self-Confrontation in Shelley's Poetry' (*KSJ*). In another general article, 'Godwin and Shelley: Rhetoric versus Revolution' (*Studia Neophilologica*), Rolf P. Lessnich deals mainly with *Caleb Williams* and *The Cenci*: he sees Godwin as an optimist who was less revolutionary than his critics supposed, and Shelley as following Godwin in preferring rhetorical persuasion to revolutionary violence. Thomas A. Reisner, in 'Shelley's "Lapland Roses" ' (*N&Q*), finds the source of a Shelley image in Thomson's *Seasons*. Jean Perrin considers a recurring obsession in Shelley, which he calls 'the Actaeon complex' and sees as emerging from the Wandering Jew figure, in 'The Actaeon Myth in Shelley's Poetry' (*E&S*).

In 'Author, Narrator, and Hero in Shelley's *Alastor*' (*SIR*), Norman Thurston deals particularly with two problems: the relation of the poem to the preface (which he describes as 'oddly misleading'), and the relevance of the second half of the poem. Through an examination of the 'Arab maiden' episode, he suggests that the poet seems unable to form a meaningful human relationship, and that the narrator is left without hope. John F. Slater, in 'Self-Concealment and Self-Revelation in Shelley's "Epipsychidion" ' (*PLL*), attempts to rescue the poem from the criticisms of Eliot and Leavis by relating the autobiographical elements to a dialectical movement between concealment and revelation.

James B. Twitchell explains Act IV of *Prometheus Unbound* in terms of an attempt to set forward states and levels of consciousness, in 'Shelley's Metapsychological System in Act IV of *Prometheus Unbound*' (*KSJ*). E. B. Murray provides alternative readings of a Shelley crux in 'Gnashing and Wailing in *Prometheus Unbound*' (*KSJ*). More important than either of these is Gerald McNiece's central article, 'The Poet as Ironist in "Mont Blanc" and "Hymn to Intellectual Beauty" ' (*SIR*), in which McNiece gives a close and strenuous reading of the two poems as concerned with a higher reality, and of Shelley as searching for a new religion of humanity. John A. Hodgson gives a persuasive and pessimistic reading of 'The Triumph of Life' in which life consumes and destroys man, in 'The World's Mysterious Doom: Shelley's *The Triumph of Life*' (*ELH*). Robert C. Casto presents two versions of an 1822 Shelley translation from Goethe, one a line-by-line rendering, the other a completed versification, in 'Shelley as Translator of *Faust*: The "Prologue" ' (*RES*).

Charles E. Robinson uncovers a diverting story in 'Mary Shelley and the Roger Dodsworth Hoax' (*KSJ*), in which a man called Dodsworth was supposed to have been frozen in a glacier for 166 years and then brought to life again in 1826; Mary Shelley's essay on Dodsworth treats the idea with more sympathy than the journalists of the day, who used the supposed Dodsworth as a hoax on Samuel Rogers. Diana Pugh argues convincingly that Shelley's death was due to the bad design of his boat rather than to a collision, in 'Captain Roberts and the Sinking of the *Don Juan*' (*KSMB*). The rejection of the insurance claim on Shelley's death is described by

Lord De L'Isle in 'Phoenix and the Poet: Percy Bysshe Shelley' (*KSMB*). The special *TWC* number on Hazlitt naturally contains much that is of interest to the student of romantic poetry. There is a bibliography of Hazlitt studies, 1965-72, by W. P. Albrecht, and relations between Moore and Hazlitt are studied by Ralph M. Wardle. Other articles deal with Hazlitt's prose. Thomas Moore's novel *The Epicurean* is seen as attempting to find serious answers to the haunting questions of life in 'Thomas Moore's *The Epicurean*: The Anacreontic Poet in Search of Eternity', by Mark D. Hawthorne (*SIR*). I have seen only Volume I of Hoover H. Jordan's *Bolt Upright: the Life of Thomas Moore*,[32] published in the *Romantic Reassessment* series. It is a very good volume: it takes the story briskly to 1819, dealing with Moore's early years in Dublin, the duel with Jeffrey, and the meeting with Byron.

In 'Stalking the Essential John Clare: Clare in Relation to His Romantic Contemporaries' (*SIR*), L. J. Swingle makes out a strong case for considering Clare's early poetry as his most individual and characteristic. G. Crossan prints an unannotated bibliography of Clare in *BB*.

Volume VI of *The* Revels *History of Drama in English*[33] deals with the years 1750 to 1880. It is an attractive, freshly written, informative work, a reference book as well as an historical account; it is compiled by five authors, beginning with a chronological table and 'A guide to London theatres, 1750-1880' by Frederick and Lise-Lone Marker. There are then three substantial sections: the first section, by Michael R. Booth, is entitled 'The social and literary context', and has two chapters. The first chapter is an account of 'The theatre and its audience', which among other things has some interesting glances at the role of Queen Victoria in helping to restore the theatre to respectability; the second chapter, 'Public taste, the playwright and the law', deals with censorship, public opinion, the income of actors, and other related matters. The second section, 'Theatres and actors', begins with a description of theatre architecture by Richard Southern, and continues with the Markers' account of 'Actors and their repertory'. There are several stars here: Garrick, John Philip Kemble, Kean and Macready, Madame Vestris, followed by Samuel Phelps and the beginning of Irving's career. Brief though the notices of these great figures are, they are crisp and memorable, and are supplemented (as each part of the whole book is) by a scholarly bibliography. The final section, 'Playwrights and plays', is by Robertson Davies. It is a chronological survey which gains much from the observation of a developing pattern of drama, in which the literary elements became gradually less important as spectacle and music increased. (See above, Chapter XII, note 93).

A one-man job which covers part of the same ground is Joseph Donohue's *Theatre in the Age of Kean*,[34] an excellent short study of the drama of the romantic period. Although Kean did not make his début at

[32] *Bolt Upright: the Life of Thomas Moore*, by Hoover H. Jordan. Vol I. Salzburg: Romantic Reassessment, 38. pp. vi + 318. $12.50.
[33] *The* Revels *History of Drama in English, Vol VI: 1750-1880*, by Michael R. Booth, Richard Southern, Frederick and Lise-Lone Marker, and Robertson Davies. London: Methuen. New York: Barnes & Noble. pp. 1xii + 304. £10.50. pb £4.90.
[34] *Theatre in the Age of Kean*, by Joseph Donohue. Oxford: Blackwell. pp. x + 201. £5.75.

Drury Lane until 1814, Donohue sees the age as beginning in the late 1780s and ending in the 1830s: with economy and skill he portrays the conditions of dramatic performance: the new large-sized theatres, the roles of the theatre-managers, and the styles of the actors, especially of Kean himself. A further section is devoted to the plays, to romantic tragedies and new melodramas, and a final section deals with the critics, together with the dramas of the great romantic poets.

Besides these histories of the drama, there are two good specialist studies. Christopher Murray's *Robert William Elliston, Manager*[35] is a jolly book about Elliston's career at Drury Lane from 1819 to 1827, written with fire and wit, and allowing the occasional anecdote without ever becoming trivial. There have been studies of Elliston before, notably by George Raymond (in the 1840s and 50s) but Murray finds space enough to write about Elliston's career as an impresario and manager in a scholarly and informative manner. As he points out, Elliston was Dickensian in his vitality and exuberance, and the account of his theatrical endeavours in London, Birmingham and elsewhere is given in this book with a nice sense of enjoyment and objectivity. This biography nicely complements the 1974 publication by the Society for Theatre Research of *Drury Lane Journal: Selections from James Winston's Diaries, 1819-1827*.[36] Winston was Elliston's actor manager, and his diaries are an intriguing view of the quarrels, crises and triumphs of a back-stage entrepreneur: actors malinger, there are fights, strikes, and other disputes over money; one entry briefly reads 'Band all drunk'. Throughout, the diary is brief, matter-of-fact, and very entertaining.

I regret that I have been unable to see *The Sublime Pleasures of Tragedy: A Study of Critical Theory from Dennis to Keats*, by W. P. Albrecht.[37]

In 'The Stage History of *Werner*' (*Nineteenth Century Theatre Research*) Helen Damico traces the fortunes of Byron's play, and particularly its performances by Macready and Phelps; she also carries the history on to Irving, and gives a brief survey of *Werner* in America. Other articles deal with conditions of performance: the care taken by theatre managers to keep on the right side of the law is described by L. W. Conolly in 'The Censor and Early Nineteenth-Century English Pantomime' (*N&Q*); a book by a certain Leman Thomas Rede, written for those who aspired to an acting career, is described by Michael R. Booth in 'A Note on *The Road to the Stage*' (*NCTR*); in 'The Second Sans Souci Theatre (1796–1835)' (*TN*), Robert Fahrner describes Charles Dibdin the Elder's theatre for his one-man entertainment; and Y. S. Bains gives an account, with a list of performances from 1809 to 1828, of 'Theatre and Society in Early Nineteenth-Century Toronto' (*Nineteenth Century Theatre Research*).

[35] *Robert William Elliston, Manager*, by Christopher Murray. Salisbury: Compton Russell, for The Society for Theatre Research. pp. xii + 196. £3.50.
[36] *Drury Lane Journal: Selections from James Winston's Diaries, 1819-1827*, ed. by Alfred L. Nelson and Gilbert B. Cross. London: The Society for Theatre Research, 1974. pp. xvi + 176. n.p.
[37] *The Sublime Pleasures of Tragedy: A Study of Critical Theory from Dennis to Keats*, by W. P. Albrecht. Lawrence, Ka.: U. of Kansas P. pp. 205. $10.50.

2. Victorian: General

The most inclusive bibliography for the period is the MLA list, but a fairly comprehensive Victorian Studies Bibliography compiled by Richard C. Tobias can be found in the June number of *VS*. Tobias also edits the annual annotated guide to Victorian prose and poetry in *VP*. In *SEL* John E. Jordans surveys recent studies in a long review article. Specialist bibliographies are available in *VPN, ELT, BIS*, and *NCTR*.

Lionel Madden and Diana Dixon have compiled an annotated bibliography of studies between 1901 and 1971 on *The Nineteenth-Century Periodical Press in Britain* with 2600 entries and an index, as a supplement to *VPN*. Although the editors exclude categories found in the *New CBEL*, their list is fuller than that volume's, and they do include doctoral dissertations and more specific bibliographical detail.

Chadwyck-Healey continues its admirable project of the publication of publishers' files on microfilm and an index in book form with the appearance of the Swan Sonnenschein letters.[1] The same disclaimer regarding the limitations of the index appears here as in earlier volumes, but we are referred to a fuller introduction by Brian Maidment on the microfilm itself.

By contrast the material referred to in *Index and Guide to the Bentley Archives*[2] compiled by Michael L. Turner is recognizably edited; an introduction and five indexes—annotated author with titles, titles alone, periodical references, Dinner sale references, and by publisher's series—exemplify the standard of index that readers and libraries require if they are to buy these books separately from the microfilm for local use. Bentley's periodicals include *Bentley's Miscellany* and *Temple Bar*, and their author-list William Godwin, Isaac and Benjamin Disraeli, Dickens, Mrs. Henry Wood, E. Lear and many authors of popular novels.

Victorian People and Ideas[3] is a purpose-built historical background for students of literature. Altick disclaims originality and admits to simplifying and audacity, but the omissions and generalizations of the work result from manifest knowledge rather than ignorance. Analyses of the variety of classes which comprises the audience and of the spirit of the age, definitions of utilitarian and evangelical, accounts of religious movements, science, technology, and democracy, and an examination of the nature of art adequately outline the multitudinousness of the society. As an introduction for secondary-school students, or a general handbook for undergraduates, it is excellent.

S. Peter Bell collects eight essays on Victorian Lancashire[4] from unpublished theses on the subject. Their topics provide pertinent back-

[1] *Index to the Archives of Swan Sonnenschein & Co. 1878-1911*. Bishops Stortford, Herts: Chadwyck-Healey. Teaneck, N.J.: Somerset House. pp. 130 (unnumbered). £15, $37.50 pb.25 reels and index £310 and $775.

[2] *Index and Guide to the list of the publication of Richard Bentley & Son 1829-1898*, compiled by Michael L. Turner. Bishops Stortford, Herts: Chadwyck-Healey. Teaneck, N.J.: Somerset House. pp. 337. £10.50, $26.50. Index and 54 microfiches £58, $145.

[3] *Victorian People and Ideas*, by Richard D. Altick. Dent, 1974. pp. xii + 338. £4.50.

[4] *Victorian Lancashire*, ed. by S. Peter Bell. Newton Abbot: David & Charles. 1974. pp. 196. £3.50.

ground for the works of Elizabeth Gaskell, and for other scattered literary references to the industrial North. Two pieces, on provincial (Furness) newspapers by P. J. Lucas and on entertainment—the fairs, theatres and music halls—by M. B. Smith, are literary as well as social history.

In *Victorian Lincoln*[5] we have Francis Hill's fourth and final volume in the history of that city. The patient and careful accretion of detail from primary sources does not deny this history a notable gracefulness and readability. While there may be relatively few readers specifically interested in Lincoln, its developments reflect the more general historical movements (described by G. M. Young for example), but in a county town with its own local history. One might read it with Tennyson in mind, but *Victorian Lincoln* also evokes Casterbridge. It goes far in clarifying the particular and gradual ways in which the larger part of nineteenth-century society experienced the cataclysmic changes of its time; it is a valuable kind of history.

In the Introduction to *Village Life and Labour*[6] Raphael Samuel defines the aim of the History Workshop Series as exploring 'the inner life of the workplace' and the nature of 'people's history'. The book contains four essays, 'Village Labour' and ' "Quarry Roughs": life and labour in Headington Quarry, 1860–1920' by the editor, 'The Place of harvesters in nineteenth-century village life' by David H. Morgan, and 'Country work-girls in nineteenth-century England'. In 'Village Labour' Raphael Samuel surveys a range of occupations and work patterns geographically and chronologically. There is much here on the seasonal work of woodlanders, women's jobs, 'tramping', and the fluidity of occupational boundaries which readers of Hardy will welcome. David Morgan scrutinizes the patterns and economics of harvesting and mass gleaning which constituted the major source of income for many rural families. Containing rich detail including a glossary of harvest terminology, it alerts the reader to this vigorous culture which remained largely ignored by major British novelists before Hardy. Informative sections on farm work, rural industry, and the gangs of women and children employed cheaply to do field work comprise Jennie Kitteringham's piece on nineteenth-century girls' work in the country; and details of the hierarchy of farmwork, conditions and hours, plaiting, and lace-making are carefully extracted from the adverse judgments of middle-class nineteenth-century historians and their society. The last and longest essay is Raphael Samuel's portrait of a community of 'quarry roughs', Headington Quarry near Oxford, which remained untouched by the spirit of Victorian improvement. Drawing primarily on oral descriptions of life there, the account is both wide-ranging and detailed. Much of what Samuel describes provides an illuminating context for Jude as stonemason ('the most aristocratic of Quarry's tradesmen'). Careful notes, indexes of subject and of places, as well as eighteen plates of country people at work, help to make this readable and fascinating book useful for reference.

Many critics of nineteenth-century literature will be interested in th

---

[5] *Victorian Lincoln*, by Francis Hill. Cambridge U.P. pp. 341. £9.50, $28.
[6] *Village Life and Labour*, ed. by Raphael Samuel. Routledge. pp. xxii + 27¦ £6.95. pb £3.50.

interpretative problems of the historian as presented by Malcolm I. Thomis in his stimulating book.[7] He undertakes to examine the assumptions of the Hammonds' pioneer study in 1917, *The Town Labourer*, and to assess and review the vast scholarly debate of their successors concerning the facts, nature, and significance of the social upheaval. Full notes and a select bibliography ensure that this book makes an effective companion to Victorian literature: the presentation of the trade unions in *Hard Times* and *Mary Barton*, and the Luddites in *Shirley*, as well as more subtle aspects of society are illuminated by Thomis's balanced assessments.

A. G. Lough publishes a life of John Mason Neale, 1818–1866,[8] an Anglican priest who was also an editor and journalist, and an author of stories for children, novels, hymns, histories, and a commentary on the Psalms. Neale moved to the Tractarian camp while at Cambridge in 1839 when he founded the Cambridge Camden Society, and his future work on the implications of Anglicanism's links with the Catholic Church is presumably what occasioned the considerable literature about him; but for our readers the interest of this biography is its detailed picture—much from unpublished journals and letters—of the nineteenth-century life which includes a study and living pattern at Cambridge in the 1830s in which *Pickwick*, phrenology, passionate church-visiting, and Tractarianism figure and which testifies to the passions aroused by religious controversy, and Anglo-Catholicism.

Michael Sanderson edits a rich collection of ninety-three documents which concern the universities in the nineteenth-century.[9] The extracts in the six chapters are glossed by an effective apparatus. Sanderson's book, the work of a social historian, is a history of higher education which traces among other things the fight for inclusion of science in university education but ignores the battle for English studies. Nevertheless, the book is a useful complement for J. Gross's *The Rise and Fall of the Man of Letters* and D. J. Palmer's *The Rise of English Studies*.

Another collection of documents is J. T. Ward's,[10] which attempts to encompass various major areas of development—the land, inland transport, industrial life, social policy and attitudes, and religion. In these sections there is much of interest, notably twenty extracts on the railway, a plethora of descriptions of northern and Scottish industrial life to which we can compare our knowledge of London and Manchester, and material on the New Poor Law and factory reform. The extracts are impressively wide ranging but the details of sources are both scanty and ill-presented, nor is there a bibliography, an index, or anything but a perfunctory introduction. By contrast some of the headnotes are usefully expansive.

Silent Sisterhood[11] studies the married middle-class woman between

[7] *The Town Labourer and the Industrial Revolution*, by Malcolm I. Thomis. Studies in Economic and Social History. London and Sydney: Batsford, 1974. pp. 247. £4.50.
[8] *John Mason Neale—Priest Extraordinary*, by A. G. Lough. Newton Abbot, Devon: A. G. Lough. pp. 152. £2.20 plus postage from author.
[9] *The Universities in the Nineteenth Century*, ed. by M. Sanderson. Birth of Modern Britain Series. London and Boston: Routledge & Kegan Paul. pp. xiv + 262. £5.25.
[10] *The Age of Change 1770-1870*, by J. T. Ward. A. & C. Black. pp. 199. £4.75.
[11] *Silent Sisterhood*, by Patricia Branca. Croom Helm. pp. 170. £5.95.

1830 and 1880. Eschewing literature as a source Patricia Branca supplements the dearth of information on the subject by using health manuals, and family and women's magazines. Her painstaking economic definition of middle-class women as those with an annual family income of £100–£300 shows that this category has been mistakenly treated as one with the upper-middle or upper classes. Outstanding chapters concerning female health and Victorian medical knowledge and technology show the middle-class woman's nervousness to be well founded. Many orthodoxies about this 'first modernized woman'—her idleness, submissiveness, and her distaste for sex—are challenged in this lively book which is marred only by a persistent stridency of tone.

Phrenology and Victorian social thought is the subject of *Conquest of Mind*.[12] De Giustino charts the development of the movement and its leaders, Drs Gall and Spurzheim, and George Coombe (1788–1858) who published in 1828 *The Constitution of Man*, a best seller on phrenology. At once philosophy, psychology, and popular science, phrenology appealed to George Eliot, Herbert Spencer, Harriet Martineau, and Marx among others; but primarily this book treats political and social history rather than literary background. Arguing that the works of two phrenologists—Coombe's (1828) and Chambers's *Vestiges of Creation* (1844)—paved the way for *Origin of Species* (1859), de Giustino shows that phrenology comprised not merely 'head-reading' but a wide range of ideas. The interesting last chapters treat the impact of phrenology on penal reform and national education; part of its battle for secular education was displacement of the rote of the classical syllabus in schools by the 'more useful' teaching of English language and literature.

Madness and Morals[13] is an absorbing collection of 115 nineteenth-century documents concerning ideas on insanity, arranged thematically and chronologically with a bibliography. Certain of the themes such as Heredity and Character, Feminine Vulnerability, and Moral Insanity pertain closely to concepts of character in the literature and biographies of the period, and to the lives of its authors. Religious enthusiasm, phrenological readings of character (with illustrations), and the power of the Will are some of the subjects of individual documents, the sources of which are clearly stated in headnotes for each excerpt.

In a copiously illustrated and scholarly publication of Studio Vista's,[14] Mark Girouard does for the Victorian (primarily London) pub what he did so consummately in *The Victorian Country House* (*YW* 52.294). Treating pubs as serious architecture, rather than as folk art, he tries to establish dates of building and alteration, architects, craftsmen, clients, and their particular social, political and economic situation. The sociology of the pub through the century as described here is richly informative about the nuances of society as a whole, while the concentration of photographs helps the reader to relate the pub to the other architecture and decorative

[12] *Conquest of Mind*, by David de Giustino. London: Croom Helm; Totowa, N.J.: Rowman and Littlefield. pp. viii + 248. £6.
[13] *Madness and Morals*, ed. by Vieda Skultans. London and Boston: Routledge & Kegan Paul. pp. xv + 260. £5.50.
[14] *Victorian Pubs*, by Mark Girouard. Studio Vista. pp. 223. £9.95.

design of the period. The Wellers, Thackeray's Vauxhall Gardens, John Barton's union meeting, and Squeers's recruiting parlour all gain in concreteness through knowledge of their context.

Readers acquainted with the details of the Victorian literary market-place will find much of interest in Jeremy Maas's parallel description of dealing in Victorian art.[15] Rather than a biography, the book is a wider study of the Victorian art world; and although sometimes verging on frivolous detail, it includes memorable material on Gambart's long-lived patronage of Rosa Bonheur and Holman Hunt, and his dealings with Madox-Brown, Alma-Tadema, Rossetti, Millais, Frith, and Lambinet (cf *The Ambassadors*). The interacting rhythms of the social, financial, political, and arts worlds are expertly caught, and the book reads as an informative companion to the novels of Thackeray in particular. Maas claims that Gambart's life had to be 'hewn out of granite', and he draws on diverse sources including many of the Victorian art journals.

The close alliance between the art and literary worlds in Victorian England is manifest in Edward Burne-Jones's life[16] in which Ruskin, Rossetti, George Eliot, and above all Morris figured prominently, and Malory was 'the prime influence'. While always interesting, Penelope Fitzgerald's biography is uneven, veering from felicitous interpretation of important moments and ample unpretentious explanations of iconography and significance in the pictures to dark and opaque references which anticipate future events (such as 'Mackail's mortal blow' p. 174 and 'every kind of domestic difficulty' p. 119). And while grateful for her careful individualizing of Georgiana, the artist's wife, this reader also notes a peculiar thinness concerning Burne-Jones's many crushes, and the occasional distraction of personal judgments such as 'The perpetual delusion that through political means we can better the human condition'. The author draws on much unpublished material, and notes, an index, a select bibliography, and illustrations make this an attractive and useful volume.

Morris & Co[17] is an annotated and illustrated catalogue by B. G. Fryberger, D. W. Donaldson, R. Imhoff, J. Osborne, and P. Stansky of an exhibition of items from the collection of Sanford and Helen Berger at Stanford University in 1975. Boside a full chronology of the artist's life and work and a bibliography of D. Donaldson, it includes a brief essay on the firm, and an introduction by Betsy Fryberger, who suggests that if Morris is judged by his designs rather than his writing, he should be regarded as the great classical designer of his age rather than the pioneer.

Isobel Spencer's *Walter Crane*[18], the first book-length critical study since the artist's death at 69 in 1915, treats the full range of his artistic activity, its ideological basis, and his work for education and socialism, but eschews detailed biography. This book is sumptuous with 150 good illustrations, frequent full-page plates, and a readable and scholarly text.

[15] *Gambart, Prince of the Victorian Art World*, by Jeremy Maas. pp. 320. Barrie & Jenkins. £8.50.
[16] *Edward Burne-Jones, A Biography*, by Penelope Fitzgerald. Michael Joseph. pp. 320. £7.50.
[17] *Morris & Co*. Stanford, Calif: Dept of Art, Stanford U. Stanford Art Book 15. pp. 76. $7.
[18] *Walter Crane*, by Isobel Spencer. Studio Vista. pp. 208. £8.50.

Chapters on Crane's painting, his decorative art which included ceramic, wallpaper, and textile design, stained glass, mosaic, and gesso, his socialist art, and work for educational texts, extend our understanding of the scope of his achievement, so that a figure comparable to William Morris, his comrade and mentor, emerges. Crane's development is linked with that of the book trade and printing as well as that of art and the craft movement. In the conclusion the 'healthy benevolence' of Crane's work is placed beside the 'sinister refinement' of Beardsley's and the 'ghoulish fantasy' in Arthur Rackham's, and the implications of Crane's distaste for aestheticism, art nouveau, and Impressionism are explored. Notes, a bibliography, and a full index supplement the text and illustrations.

The world of black-and-white illustrations which Walter Crane entered is well depicted in Forrest Reid's book (1928)[19] with its ninety-one illustrations which Dover reprint in an economical but durable format. The works of fifty-eight British artists including the Pre-Raphaelites, Whistler, Watson, Du Maurier, Houghton, G. F. Watts, the Dalziels, Crane himself, and the Moxon Tennyson are surveyed in some detail as parts of a movement rather than a decade. An introductory chapter contains interesting advice on locating and assessing material, and periodicals figure centrally. Our attention is alerted by the text and the index to editions with illustrations which might have escaped attention: reprinted are G. Du Maurier's illustrations for *Wives and Daughters* (*Cornhill*), *Harry Richmond* (*Cornhill*) and *Esmond* (1868).

Dover also reprints the 1864 edition (published Dec. 1863) of Millais's twenty black-and-white illustrations of *The Parables of Our Lord* with a new introduction by M. Lutyens[20] in which she describes the period's technique of engraving through woodcutting, and the history of these particular drawings (1857–63) and engravings, which involved photography and a lengthy correspondence between artist and engraver. Though the engravings vary in conception and technical quality, the whole is attractive, and a good example of the Victorian and the contemporary gift book.

In his introduction to Chesterton's short illustrated monograph (1904) on the painter G. F. Watts (for whom Meredith, Arnold, Mill, Browning, Tennyson, Bulwer, Morris, Rossetti, and Carlyle sat),[21] Quentin Bell readily admits that Chesterton's judgment in preferring Watts's later to his earlier work does not coincide with ours. But he points to the admirable quality of Chesterton's defence of Watts's heroics—his wit, ingenuity, high spirits, and enthusiasm—a response which other readers will endorse. Emphases on the closeness of Watt's sceptical idealism to the age, his humility as a form of self-confidence, and his capacity to distinguish art from ethics relate the single figure to the period in a stimulating way— though for Chesterton Watts remains an isolate among Victorian artists.

The spectrum of Victorian wit and humour—domestic, social, aesthetic,

---

[19] *Illustrators of the Eighteen Sixties*, by Forrest Reid. New York: Dover; London: Constable. pp. 295. pb. £2.80.
[20] *The Parables of Our Lord*, illustr. by J. E. Millais, engraved by the Brothers Dalziel, and introd. by Mary Lutyens. New York: Dover; London: Constable. pp. xxxvi + 76. £1.50 pb.
[21] *G. F. Watts*, by G. K. Chesterton, introd. by Quentin Bell. Duckworth. pp. 76. £4.95.

working-class and donnish, nonsense, Punch, parody and jokers—is only cursorily discussed by Roland Pearsall in a breezy book.[22] Although Pearsall avers that the book is not an anthology of mirth, he fails to provide an adequate conceptual framework, and it functions best for the scholar as a meandering collection of telling and amusing examples. At best the book provides a sketchy background to techniques and illustrations of Dickens, Thackeray, Meredith, Gilbert, Carroll, Lear, Wilde, du Maurier, Calverley, and J. K. Stephen.

In 'The Formal Nature of Victorian Thinking' (*PMLA*) G. L. Bruns reveals shared ways of conceiving among Victorian prose writers, including Carlyle, Arnold and Ruskin, who thought of themselves as part of history (rather than a cosmos), of an irreversible succession of events and processes. Even Nature is intelligible because it is historical, not transcendent.

Noting the ambivalent welcome of rational explanation and distress at the decline of myth in Victorian studies of myth, J. Burstein (*VS*) concludes that they illuminate the Victorian as well as the primitive mind; the contributions of earlier mythography, evolution, and the notion of intellectual progress to Victorian mythography are explored, primarily in connexion with G. Grote, Walter Pater, F. M. Muller, and George Eliot.

In a widely-ranging and provocative article in *VS*, M. Peckham attempts to define the term counterculture and to identify various counterculture structures in Victorian England; sexual repression, and two romantic types—redemptive explanations (Christian, social) and redemptive feelings (aestheticism, eroticism)—originate in selection from the rejected culture; but a third type, genuinely alienated, rejects both explanation and existential redemption, and accepts tension as the inescapable human condition.

M. Timko identifies engagement—the battle and the quest—as the central cultural symbol of the Victorian period. In a stimulating effort to resist the tendency of Hillis Miller, R. Langbaum, and F. R. Leavis to obliterate differences between periods, Timko stresses the problem of epistemology, the Kantian and Darwinian ideas which separate the Victorians from the certitudes of the Romantic generation. To this end Timko considers the Victorian meaning of the concepts of 'self-consciousness', 'nature', and 'civilization' rather than internal 'culture'. He notes the lack of a central tradition in the many genres of the period. Whatever the form, the Victorians use a common 'mediatorial' method which aims to bring fact and value into a meaningful relation (*NLH*).

In this year of the micro edition of the *DNB*, readers are referred to Laurel Brake's piece in *MLR* in which she examines the accuracy and reliability of the *DNB* through close consideration of one biography (of Pater)—its author, editing, and variations.

In *PBSA* D. J. DeLaura draws attention to a fact available since 1906 but unacknowledged by modern bibliography—that J. A. Froude translated anonymously Goethe's *Elective Affinities* for the Bohn's Library edition of 1854. Reasons for Froude's anonymity probably include both Goethe's reputation for ill-treatment of women, and the criticism and inadequacy of marriage in *Elective Affinities*. De Laura concludes that

[22] *Collapse of Stout Party*, by Ronald Pearsall. Weidenfeld & Nicolson. pp. 228. £4.95.

Froude knew the Goethe well before 1848, and that the translation was begun and possibly even finished at this time.

To correct the view that the Victorians disliked satire, G. C. Kinnane comments on *Ginx's Baby*, a novelette by John Edward Jenkins, as evidence that satirical literature was widely circulated, and often, in this case, very successfully. Kinnane reasons that both its Dickensian quality and the nature of its victims—'all institutions of official benefaction'—contributed to its popularity (*N&Q*).

C. Markgraf contributes an annotated bibliography of writing about J. A. Symonds to *ELT*. This periodical announces that it is ending its annual updating of bibliographies, and it publishes a final updating and index to the status of bibliographies of individual authors including Dowson, Gosse, George Moore, Arthur Symons, and Mark Rutherford.

B. W. Martin publishes a letter of 1842 to Keble from Frederick William Faber, an Oxford Movement clergyman and poet, as an introduction to a piece on the key influence of the High Church on Wordsworth's *Ecclesiastical Sketches* and ideas (*RES*).

R. W. Peattie contributes a useful annotated checklist of periodical art notices (most of them unknown) by W. M. Rossetti from 1850 to 1878 to *VPN*. An introduction reveals his methods of research and attribution.

Drawing on Gladstone's previously unexplored 'Notes of my Pictures' (1843) and the diaries, M. Pointon describes the statesman as an art patron and collector between the 1840s and 1875 (*VS*).

The priority of natural or artificial (domestic and Malthusian) selection in the formation of Darwin's concept of evolution is assessed by M. Ruse in *JHI*.

T. V. Schmidt reproduces some manuscript notes by Richard C. Jackson in Lionel Johnson's *The Art of Thomas Hardy* (1894) now in the library of the Catholic University.

In *DR* the confrontation of the late Victorian dandy as part of the Regency revival and his successful rival the new woman bemuses J. Stein who considers the work of Beerbohm (including Zuleika Dobson) and of Wilde in which the women are both dominant and threatening.

While acknowledging the shortcoming of J. A. Symonds's historiography, R. Titlebaum prefers to view *The Renaissance in Italy* as a landmark of Victorian liberalism, heavily dependent on the Darwinian theory of evolution (*ESA*). M. Vicinus reviews Victorian popular culture in *VS*. Assessing the state of this field of interest, she laments the absence of an analytic framework based on clearly articulated theory and suggests possible approaches.

The literary theories of the journalist and critic, Andrew Lang, implied in his promotion of the new romance typified by R. L. Stevenson and Rider Haggard, are considered by J. Weintraub in *ELT*. Beside close examination of Lang's notions of romance and fiction, Weintraub reveals their underlying reliance on the terminology and ideas of anthropology.

M. A. I. Whitaker in *Mosaic* stresses interesting parallels between *Morte Darthur* and Beardsley's illustrations for the Dent edition, while noting an alarming discrepancy between text and illustration. While Malory wrote romance, Beardsley was more sympathetic to satire. His pen is double-edged—he 'unconsciously satirises Arthurian romance' and 'ironically subverts the Victorian idealisation of women by substituting for the angel in the house the fatal Venus'.

This last group of articles relates to Victorian periodicals. In *SB*, S. Bennett reports on the development of John Murray's Family Library (1829–34) edited by J. G. Lockhart, which was an early and commercially unsuccessful venture in the general cheapening of books under way between 1800 and 1850. The Family Library also represents an unprecedented effort to publish across class lines at a time when divisions were growing, so that Murray may well have regarded the series as counter-revolutionary. Although Bennett concentrates on the commercial aspects of the venture, he includes a list of the fifty-three volumes in the series.

In *VPN* B. L. Crapster provides a biography of Thomas Hamber (1828–1902), a Tory editor of three London dailies from 1857 to 1870, who was overlooked by the *DNB*. In the same periodical W. Houghton reports on the progress of *The Wellesley Index*, Volume Three, to appear in 1977, which will include thirteen periodicals including the *Westminster* and the *National Review*, and on plans for Volume Four, to appear in 1882 (!).

The publishing history of *Lady Audley's Secret* and other novels emerges from S. Keith's demonstration of the usefulness of the weekly 'List of New Books' in the *Athenaeum*.

Tomahawk, a weekly periodical, and its cartoons by Matt Morgan between 1867 and 1870, are examined by T. M. Kemnitz as an alternative to and a context for *Punch* in *VS*. In *SEL* J. Nadelhaft revealingly traces the characteristics for which *Punch* criticizes the aesthetic Syncretics in the 1840s; and the Romanticism of the Syncretics themselves is found to be similar to the critical assumptions and values of the Aesthetes, particularly the ideal of self-perfection through the arts or self-culture.

A. S. Levine demonstrates how Sir Henry Cole (1808–1882) an administrator of Arts policy, used journalism to create specific public opinions in a *VPN* piece on Cole's career as a journalist. Creating journals for specific purposes and destroying them once they had served, Cole made important innovations in his *ad hoc* periodicals.

In *VPN* John North charts the complex background of *The Waterloo Directory of Victorian Periodicals*, Phase I, which comprises a single-subject-inclusive alphabetical directory with 30,000 entries. Phase II, a shelf-list, now under way, is a long-term project.

Identification of seven unrecorded contributions (1853–55) to the *Inquirer* and one to the *Spectator* (1861) by Walter Bagehot is the subject of R. H. Tener in *SB*. A review of Arnold's 'Empedocles', and articles on politics and university reform are discussed in some detail. Tener also continues his series of articles in *VPN* on R. H. Hutton with a piece on his editing of the *Economist* (1857–61) and the *Spectator* (1861–97) which includes evidence for attributions and a glimpse of relations between Hutton as reviewer and Arnold, Swinburne, Lewes, and Mrs. Oliphant, the reviewed.

The notion that Victorian novelists were the primary source of information about working-class conditions for the middle class is attacked by R. P. Wallins in *VPN*. He argues that periodicals of the 1830s and 1840s such as *Blackwoods*, *Fraser's* and *Westminster Review* provided readers with Blue Book information, only later to emerge in fiction, and in more detail than in the newspapers. Throughout the thirties and forties, fiction trailed developments in the periodicals.

In *VPN* D. Wertheimer reports on some forty contributions to *The Parthenon* (1826–40) which include a series of biographies of mathematicians by the Shakespearian scholar James Orchard Halliwell (1820–1889).

3. Victorian Verse and Drama

(a) Poetry

By rejecting the traditional rigid division between kinds of ballad and the resulting hierarchy, J. S. Bratton[23] makes a place in the ballad tradition for Victorian music-hall songs and the flourishing poetry of the period regarded as poor relations of the literary tradition, as well as for the last of the folk ballads. Background chapters of considerable interest on the literary ballad and the popular culture preface chapters on heroic ballads, those of the common man, propaganda, and comic music-hall and drawing-room ballads. The subject embraces many aspects of Victorian literature and culture. The text is fascinating because it contains many examples and interesting commentary on kinds, conventions, and variations. In conclusion the author parallels the ballad revival in the eighteenth century with Cecil Sharp's anti-bourgeois selectiveness in this century, both of which exclude this material as does Child in the nineteenth century. J. S. Bratton views these Victorian ballads as the folk-songs of the period.

Readers of these pages should not fail to read *The Finer Optic*;[24] Carol T. Christ identifies a common concern with particularity or detail and the subjective among Victorian poets which coexists with the Arnoldian emphasis on broader moral and theological issues, and explores attempts by the poets to transcend it. In this period, the observation of minute particulars reflects both the quest for scientific empirical evidence concerning universal order, and the solipsistic peculiarity of the subjective vision. In her map of the development of English poetry between Coleridge's idealism and Pater's relativism, she errs only in occasional over-writing and an inadequate knowledge of Pater whose outlook she dubs 'cheerful'. This is a serious informed essay on an aspect of Victorian poetry which admirably reveals the whole.

The Contrary View[25] is a collection of reviews by Geoffrey Grigson, many of which discuss nineteenth-century authors.

In *Sex and Marriage in Victorian Poetry*,[26] comment on marriage and divorce in the work of Tennyson and Browning is preceded by a rather allusive historical and literary rundown on the variety of forms taken by consciousness of sexuality in the period. Johnson identifies a conflict between attitudes which view sexuality secularly as biological and social,

[23] *The Victorian Popular Ballad*, by J. S. Bratton. Macmillan. pp. vii + 275. £7.95.
[24] *The Finer Optic*, by Carol T. Christ. New Haven and London: Yale U.P. pp. xii + 171. £4.75.
[25] *The Contrary View*, by Geoffrey Grigson. Macmillan, 1974. pp. xi + 243. £4.95.
[26] *Sex and Marriage in Victorian Poetry*, by Wendell Stacey Johnson. Ithaca and London: Cornell U.P. pp. 266. £6.85.

and those which regard it religiously as awesome, demonic, mythic, and mysterious. Fairly detailed discussions of these themes in poetry by Meredith, E. B. Browning, Hopkins, Patmore, Rossetti, Arnold, Clough, and Swinburne form an ungainly queue; they are qualitatively uneven with the sections on the last three being quite good.

Johnson's failure to select sufficiently also mars the chapters on Tennyson and Browning, and in the latter especially the race from poem to poem and the time-serving summarizing of the commentary on *The Ring and the Book* tend to obscure the undoubted moments of perceptive or interesting criticism in this over ambitious work.

M. Vicinus's book[27] which consists of fifty-four plates of northern operatives' broadsides (1750 to 1880), woodcuts, and an introduction can be seen as a companion volume to the same author's study *The Industrial Muse* (*YW* 55.387), and as background to J. S. Bratton's *The Victorian Popular Ballad*. The history and types of broadside, and the commentary on their printers, writers, sellers, and subject matter found in the introduction give the reader a good sense of the context of what follows. Instruction and delight are equally strong elements of this collection.

Discussing social protest in some minor poets of the nineteenth century in *ArielE*, W. G. Bebbington quotes liberally from Ebenezer Elliott (1781–1849), the Sheffield Corn-Law rhymer; Ebenezer Jones (1820–60) who strove for the ' "light" popular utterance' of Shelley, Byron, and Hood; Ernest Jones (1819–69), the editor of *The People's Paper*; Joseph Skipsey (1832–1903), the most poetic of these, who wrote about miners; and Gerald Massey (1828–1907).

In a judicious deliberation on the nature and history of Monodrama (*PMLA*), A. D. Culler distinguishes between prosopopoeia or impersonation, monodrama, and dramatic monologue. Culler contends that the passions explored in the monodrama are universal and abstract, while in the dramatic monologue they are connected with individual character so as to involve both sympathy and judgment. Utilising this distinction, he interprets 'Ulysses' as a monodrama which invites neither sympathy nor judgment but wonder at the range and variety of human emotion.

Rooting the rise of the dramatic monologue in the decay of drama and our understanding of it, Philip Hobsbaum, in a major article in *HR*, traces its development from the decline of drama beginning with the 1606 production of *Macbeth* in which monologue begins to dominate at the expense of action to 1830 when Shakespearian theatre finally floundered. Out of the misapprehension of eighteenth-century and early nineteenth-century dramatists that brilliant individual speech which obliterates context is praiseworthy came the monologue. The collection of 'gems', often as elocution exercises, and 'operatic' acting by Garrick, Barry, and Kean also separated text from context. Hobsbaum examines Joseph Warton's 'Dying Indian' (1747), the first dramatic monologue, for qualities of the developed form to be found in 'Fra Lippo Lippi', 'Tithonus', and 'Ulysses', all of which the author discusses: only by being a faulty playwright could Browning become a great poet. R. E. Brecht seeks to show that Arnold's

[27] *Broadsides of the Industrial North*, by Martha Vicinus. Newcastle upon Tyne: Frank Graham. pp. 79. £5.

final arrangement of the seven 'Switzerland' lyrics possessed a significant unity and deliberate dramatic progression which derive from the underlying paradox of demand made by the present and the past (*VP*). In an erudite and convincting piece, E. Gahtan argues that Sophocles' *Philoctetes* deserves the 'oft diffused honour' of being the most relevant source of the Sophoclean reference in 'Dover Beach', and a quarry for 'Tristan and Iseult' and 'Empedocles' as well (*VN*).

F. Giordano Jr reads 'Self-Dependence' (*ELN*) as representative of Arnold's spare, philosophical poetry. Linking it to the Romantic tradition of the excursion lyric, he shows in an analysis of rhythm and rhyme that Arnold is satirizing a Romantic aberration rather than dramatizing a subjective experience. Through revelation of the poem's (and its type's) technical craftsmanship, Giordano hopes to dismiss the common judgment of these poems as 'prosaic'. Remembering Arnold's dismissal of Dryden and Pope as 'classics of our prose', W. V. Harris examines 'intriguing parallels' with Pope and Johnson in 'Resignation' and 'Empedocles on Etna' (*VP*).

The subleties of method in W. Houghton's discussion in *VPN* of the authorship of two reviews make this piece valuable. Houghton challenges the attribution of one review to Patmore in the Critical Heritage volume on Arnold's poetry, and corrects a *Wellesley Index* (Vol I) attribution to Patmore of another Arnold review which the Critical Heritage got right. In an interesting article in *CLS* M. Jarrett-Kerr studies diverse references to Eastern religion and thought in Arnold's writings and reading-list, and charts his early interest and later disenchantment with oriental mysticism.

The Arnoldian, which began life in 1973 as the *Arnold Newsletter*, appears three times a year free; edited by Allan B. Lefcovitz from the U.S. Naval Academy in Annapolis, Maryland, it includes brief articles and bibliographic, biographical, and interpretative items dealing with Arnold, his family, and his circle. Volume Two (1974/75) contains reports of research in progress and news, articles on Arnold and the new journalism, Sainte-Beuve, and religion and counter-culture, P. Honan's modern Fox How diary, and reviews, as well as the pieces on poetry described here. Reading 'Empedocles' on its own terms, J. S. Hagen treats it as a play and stresses that the protagonist is a character in action rather than a philosopher in thought. The considerable Arnold collection in the Beinecke at Yale is surveyed by G. Wynne, and in a short piece W. R. McDonald describes Arnold's poetic theory as a continuous curve between 1853 and 1880, from his exclusive emphasis on action and total effect to his upgrading of matter and style and his tolerance of parts in the touchstone theory; because the later Arnold counted matter and style equally with action, he could regard the touchstones as *typical* of their context.

In Volume Three H. Ridley reports on his discovery among the Butler family papers at Trinity, Cambridge, of two new letters of 1872 from Arnold to H. M. Butler, the headmaster of Harrow between 1860 and 1885. S. O. A. Ullman who is editing 'Tinker 21'—what Tinker and Lowry called 'The Yale Manuscript'—details some of the editorial problems presented by the thirty-seven sheets written between 1843 and 1856 which include unpublished poems and drafts of poems that were eventually published (all in Allott's annotated edition of the poems), as well as short passages of prose which bear on the poetry. Concerning these Ullman observes that, well before Yeats, Arnold saw the centre yield and things fall apart.

A. M. Fraser reveals a proposal of marriage in 1869 by George Borrow to Lucy Brightwell by way of a hitherto unpublished letter of 1897 written by Simms Reeve (N&Q).

Joint Lives[28] is a catalogue of an exhibition of items associated with the Brownings from the Berg Collection of the New York Public Library. Quotations from the autograph letters on show, first editions, engravings and photographs, and manuscripts and proofs, give the reader a good idea of the range and strength of this collection.

Beside *Men and Women* as published in 1855, the Everyman selection of Browning[29] includes short sections of earlier and later poems, among them 'Porphyria's Lover', 'My Last Duchess', 'The Bishop...at St Praxed's', 'Caliban upon Setebos', and 'Numpholeptos'. The editor reviews the original reviews and successfully undertakes a short generic analysis of the love poems, the heroic poem (of interest here on 'Childe Roland'), and the dramatic monologue. The notes are helpful and accurate, if occasionally elementary. It is a reliable but highly selective student edition, perhaps of greater use in the sixth form than in the university.

The new biography of Browning[30] clearly sets out to be definitive and to replace Maisie Ward's life, but reviewers have resisted this and remain divided on the books' relative strengths. If anything, *The Book, the Ring and the Poet* is too full. A two-page disquisition on Mazzini prefaces Browning's voyage to Naples in 1844, and it ends rather unconvincingly with 'Whether Robert knew Mazzini personally at just this time . . . is not clear. In 1862, he was to accost him rather familiarly at Cheyne Row . . .'. There is too a certain drama of style which can be both distracting in its expansiveness ('Robert Browning's greatest exploit was his own romance. It was thoroughly in the spirit of his poetry: a passionate rather than a rational act; and the daring rescue of a pessimist by an optimist.' p. 172), and effective in a juxtaposition ('Such was the history of the profoundly unhappy woman who, at three o'clock on Tuesday, May 20, 1845, lay with beating heart and fluttering breath, awaiting Robert Browning.' p. 171). This inclusiveness does, however, leave room for ample attention to the poetry, but there is a disquieting tendency on both authors' parts to interpret the poems autobiographically, as Irvine does Pippa for example; for Honan the Pope's judgments are instantaneous, like Browning's, and Browning's view of things, like the Pope's admits of no Purgatory (p. 435). These readings are reductive, and display an anxious vigourousness, even a raciness, which mar the book as a whole. This biography is readable and formidable in its scope and learning, but it cannot claim tonal perfection. Two reviews of this biography, by P. Drew in *BIS*, and M. B. Cramer in

[28] *Joint Lives: Elizabeth Barrett and Robert Browning*, by John D. Gordan, foreword by Lola L. Szladits. New York: NYPL and Readex Books pp. viii + 40. $5.

[29] *Browning: Men and Women, and Other Poems*, ed. by J. W. Harper. Everyman University Library. London: Dent; Totowa, N.J.: Rowman and Littlefield. pp. xx + 244. £3. pb £1.40.

[30] *The Book, the Ring, and the Poet*, by William Irvine and Park Honan. Bodley Head. pp. ix + 609. £6.

SBC, are outstanding: Drew contends that it fails to distinguish between the peripheral and the central facts of Browning's poetic career, while Cramer comparing it to Maisie Ward's life concludes that their most essential differences seem to stem from their opposing assessments of Betty Miller's *Portrait*. In an altogether successful but different kind of biography,[31] F. E. Halliday deftly and concisely relates Browning's work to his life and time. The book is consistently insightful, well-written, and well-conceived, nor does Halliday shrink from discussing the poetry. The book makes an ideal introduction to Browning.

Suggesting that Browning's interest in thematic unity was strengthened by his ordering of the poems for the 1863 edition, Lawrence Poston III in *Loss and Gain*[32] studies *Dramatis Personae* as a unified collection of poems, meant to be read from start to finish. The title refers to the theme of extracting faith from doubt around which variations centre. Sections on Browning's exploration of private loss, and religious visions of aspiration and of debasement are succeeded by an analysis of the imagery (of hand, face, mouth, light and dark), structure, and themes by which unity is achieved. The philosophic centre of the volume is 'A Death in the Desert' although its dramatic culmination lies in 'Mr. Sludge, "the Medium" ' These two poems, 'Caliban Upon Setebos', and 'James Lee's Wife' receive close attention. This approach is uncommon in the U.K. and merits consideration.

Using E. B. Browning's recently discovered annotated copy of Sophocles, M. Meredith considers her appreciation of Greek tragedy, particularly her response to the female character and her identification with Philoctetes, the wounded and isolated hero (*SBC*).

Boyd Litzinger collects thirty-two letters (only half of which have been published before) from Browning to the Lehmanns,[33] who were members of the cultured upper-middle-class society frequented by Browning in London after Elizabeth's death in 1861. In an informative introduction Litzinger stresses the breadth of the Lehmanns' interests. Browning's patronage of his son Pen figures largely in these letters as it does in *SBC*, where Litzinger reveals Browning's efforts to facilitate Pen's election to the Athenaeum in 1888. Patrick Waddington publishes two polite if elegant letters of early 1871 from Browning to the French mezzo Pauline Viardot-Garcia, one in French (*ELN*).

S. H. Aiken reveals an elaborate pattern of allusion to Carlyle's *Sartor Resartus* and *Heroes and Hero Worship* in 'How it Strikes a Contemporary' which constitutes an appeal to Carlyle's authority for the poem's argument that the poet is an authentic hero (*VP*). Illustrating T. S. Eliot's definition of the objective correlative in *BSN*, J. D. Boyd treats 'Meeting at Night'

[31] *Robert Browning: His Life and Work*, by F. E. Halliday. Jupiter Books. pp. 203. £3.95.

[32] *Loss and Gain*, by Lawrence Poston III. U. of Nebraska Studies, n.s. no. 48. Lincoln: U. of Nebraska, 1974. pp. 65. n.p.

[33] 'The Letters of Robert Browning to Frederick and Nina Lehmann, 1863–1889', ed. by Boyd Litzinger in *Baylor Browning Interests* (no. 24). Waco, Texas: Armstrong Browning Library. pp 39. $3.

and 'Parting at Morning' as a single poem of remarkable conciseness. L. J. Swingle thoughtfully relates the same poems to some complexities inherent in the romantic quest, among them the hero's discovery upon attaining his goal that it is merely a goal rather than The Goal. Browning's interest in the choices of consciousness goes beyond the Romantics' characteristic interest in the journey and the experience of arriving. The Romantic celebrated the powers of the mind, but Browning worries about them (*BSN*).

In *VP* R. G. Collins's interpretation of 'Bishop Blougram's Apology' from the perspective of the last section reveals a greater dramatic element and establishes Browning as 'far more of an objective artist' in this poem than is usually recognized. Collins denies Blougram the moral superiority accorded him by F. E. L. Priestly, and reads the description of Gigadibs as indicative of Blougram's, rather than Gigadibs's, character and situation. Gigadibs is 'converted' by the Bishop, but to pragmatism and materialism, and to the rapid acquisition of wealth in Australia.

'A Few Reminiscences of Robert Browning' by Hiram Corson (1828–1911) is reprinted in *BIS*. A talk on Browning's orthodoxy given by F. Coventry to the London Browning Society appears in *BSN*. In an interesting piece, C. Dahl and J. L. Brewer convincingly analyse 'Saul' in terms of the four stages of mystic vision defined by Neoplatonic/Hermetic tradition (*BIS*).

In *SBC* D. J. De Laura offers an addendum to his treatment of 'Browning the Spasmodic' in *SBC*, 1974, citing an earlier instance (1840) of the application of the term to Browning.

P. Drew offers another view of 'Ivan Ivanovitch' in *BSN*. The tenor of the tale, to condemn Louscha by presenting Ivan as blameless, reflects the central ethical debate of Victorian England—that between the Intuitionist (Ivan) and Utilitarian (Louscha) schools of morality, with Browning as usual on the side of instinctive rather than calculated moral impulse.

In *SBC* J. Dupras considers rite and apology in Book I of *The Ring and the Book* while M. Tuman in the same periodical sets the poem in the context of nineteenth-century historiography; closely analyzing the metaphor of the alloy and gold ring, Tuman argues that it is inadequate to Browning's understanding of historicism in the poem which is factual but beyond the facts.

W. Franke discusses the grotesque mode in 'Halbert and Hob', a dramatic idyll concerning evolution in which the crucial comparison is between the human condition of Halbert and Hob and the last surviving mammoths, with both groups lacking moral and biological adaptability. Franke compares the northern industrial setting of the poem and its vagueness about the period with that residual saga-world of heathen amorality found in *Wuthering Heights* (*BSN*).

In a piece defending the language and design of 'Pippa Passes', M. P. Garrett argues that Browning's patterning of images and 'precise subtle employment of imagery' give the poem its power (*VP*). Claims for the characterization of Pippa are made in *SBC* by L. B. Horne who discusses the nature of her test and the extent of her awareness. 'To see Pippa's day as a test and ... the way in which that test is safely met' is to bring Pippa

into the centre of the play. David F. Goslee attempts to solve the critical
and biographical paradoxes presented in 'Mr Sludge, "The Medium" ' by
using a combination of biography and criticism in *SBC*.
In focusing on the structural function of the imagery of light in *Sordello*, E. S. Guralnick reaches certain conclusions about the poem similar
to those of Michael Yetman below—that Browning, unlike Sordello, learns
to accept the limitations of language and that Sordello emerges paradoxically as both 'friend' and 'saint' (*VP*). M. G. Yetman reads *Sordello* as an
elaborate justification of Browning's rejection of the authority of the
poet's self; *Sordello*, Browning's *Bildungsdichtung*, reflects his struggle for
poetic identity. The poem testifies both to the tenacious hold of Shelley
on Browning, and to Browning's recognition of his need to free himself of
Shelley's influence. Browning's personal reasons, rather than any historical
sources, dictate Sordello's failure to become a poet of humanity. Although
Sordello increasingly resembles the maturing Browning, his failure results
from his congenital inability to accept the unideal conditions of human
endeavour (*VP*). 'Browning's Narrative Art' is Robert Felger's interest in
SBC. Selecting three classes of narrators—the strictly objective, the dramatically imagined onlooker, and Browning's narrative persona—he concentrates
on the last category in *Sordello* and *Red Cotton Night-Cap Country*.
    R. Hannaford suggests that Grace Melbury and Giles Winterborne
re-enact the story of 'The Statue and the Bust' in *The Woodlanders*; a
reference to the poem in Chapter 46 highlights Grace's new decisiveness
so that the concluding reconciliation with Fitzpiers seems sound (*SBC*).
Also in *SBC* W. V. Harris attempts to broaden the perspective against
which we view satire in 'Caliban upon Setebos' in 'Browning's Caliban,
Plato's Cosmogony, and Bentham on Natural Religion'.
    Drawing a fruitful analogy between Wagner's use of the *Leitmotif* and
Browning's technique, M. D. Hawthorne argues that imagery in *Paracelsus*
integrates form, character portrayal, and theme; initially simple imagery of
nature and decay develops into complex image clusters (*BIS*). M. A. Hicks
speculates on the nature of the unarticulated denouement of *The Inn
Album*, lines 3054–69 in Section VIII (*SBC*). A letter of 1881 from
Robert Buchanan to Furnivall which treats the literary persecution of
himself and Browning is published for the first time in *SBC* by J. Jerrigan.
Also in *SBC* J. Knight notes a possible influence of William Hazlitt's
discussion of Rembrandt's realism on Fra Lippo Lippi's, and J. Loucks
traces the theoretical basis of stanzas vi–ix of 'A Toccata of Galuppi's' to
John Relfe's *Lucidus Ordo*, a book on music theory.
    In *BIS* J. Maynard dutifully describes the specifics of Browning's
evangelical heritage with its emphasis on the Gospel, the mission, and
Christian living. York Street chapel, George Clayton, its educated and
gentlemanly minister, and some of the Brownings' religious books also
figure in the article.
    J. K. McComb ponders the dramatic situation of Childe Roland—is
Roland speaking the poem after death? how reliable is his narration?
Arguing that the horror and pain of inescapable memory is an important
theme, McComb sees the poem—the final image of Roland as a disembodied
voice—as the climax of a pattern of increasingly painful memories (*ELH*).
And in *PLL* A. Shapiro notes that *King Lear* provides an 'ironic framework'

for 'Childe Roland'; Browning's speaker both contrasts with and resembles Edgar, specifically in connexion with the theme of the artist and 'seeing'. But ultimately Childe Roland, unlike Edgar, undergoes no transformation and growth. The 'lover of trees' in 'De Gustibus' is identified by J. McNally as Alfred Domett, Browning's friend who emigrated to New Zealand (*SBC*). M. K. Mishler interprets the central conflict in 'Karshish' as one of religion rather than rational scepticism and irrational Christianity. Analyzing the tension between the physician's Egyptian beliefs and the new religion reveals it as unifying factor in the poem (*ELN*). In 'Ryunosuke Akutagawa and Browning Study in Japan' in *SBC* Yoshihiko Mukoyama discusses the influence of *The Ring and the Book* on Akutagawa, author of a story 'In the Woods' (1921) which is the basis of *Rashamon*.

In an absorbing article on 'The Proofs of Browning's *Men and Women*' in *SBC* W. S. Peterson notes De Vane's uncharacteristic vagueness on these poems and sets out to examine proofs in the Huntington Library which reveal that the poems in *Men and Women* were 'shaped and reshaped by a discerning critical intellect', with, for example, the line 'Love is best!' originating as 'This is best!'. Peterson, who is the editor of *BIS*, also compiles its annotated bibliography of works about Robert and Elizabeth in 1973.

Browning's career to 1841 is L. Poston's subject in *BIS*. Arguing that the poet's preoccupation with time in *Paracelsus, Strafford, Sordello,* and *Pippa Passes* relates closely to Browning's search for an appropriate form, Poston suggests that Shelley's poetry of 'facet-flashes' was the source of Browning's principle of poetic form.

Having corroborated in detail the conclusion of J. S. Lindsay (*SP*: 39) that the landscape in 'By the Fireside' is Colle de Colma, and not a gorge near Bagni di Lucca as Mrs. Orr suggests, D. Robertson shows discrepancies between the actual scene and the poem's, and concludes that Browning used the setting to veil a poem based on intense personal experience (*BSN*).

Correspondence between the Carlyles and the Brownings and their correspondence with others provide the basis for C. R. Sanders's two-part exploration (*BJR* 1974 and 1975) of the considerable impact of Carlyle (who believed for example that Victorian poets would do better to write prose) on the Brownings' work. While ungainly, the piece is backed with aperçus, among them Sanders's suggestion that 'How it Strikes a Contemporary' is an alternative portrait of Carlyle to set beside the later criticism in the Mandeville of *Parleyings*.

Resisting the common readings of 'Clive' and rethinking the theme of heroism and the role of the speaker, M. Siegchrist suggests that Clive finally faces his inadequacies and that he is correct in his belief that suicide is a shabby escape (*SBC*). He has not the courage to remain alive and to endure calumny. The poem is both a dramatic idyll and a dramatic monologue.

W. Slinn reads *Fifine at the Fair* as dominated by the speaker's vigour and subjective to a degree unusual in Browning's work: Don Juan turns his experience into a form of pageant to determine the reality of a fleeting existence. The act of transformation takes precedence for him but he is niggled by the question of the degree of reality the imaginings attain, a problem which is allied with the degree of reality of his own existence. Slinn's analysis is very close and detailed (*ELH*). In *BSN* M. R. Sullivan argues that one of Browning's lyrics, 'A Woman's Last Word', achieves a psychological revelation involving irony and complexity which rivals some of the more famous dramatic monologues. Apparently generous compromise is simultaneously ignoble surrender, and the poem struggles between the need for assertion and the lure of submission. Ultimately this feminine consciousness collaborates actively in its own destruction in a way unlike the last duchess or Pompilia; here Browning condemns the co-operation of the wife as well as the tyranny of the husband. In *BIS* the same critic reads the eight plays befoe 1855 as studies in moral philosophy and as a prologue to *Men and Women*. The irony of the egoist who loses his selfhood by preferring inhuman perfection to human fallibility is a recurring theme in the plays, six of which are discussed in some detail. Readers familiar with the process of moral degeneration in the plays experience more intensely the tension between sympathy and judgment in the poems of *Men and Women*.

A reference to Plato's theology in the *Timaeus* in 'Caliban upon Setebos' is used by R. W. Witt in *VP* to substantiate the view of Caliban as a satirical portrait of a man over-reliant on reason. An account of Browning's burial reprinted from the memorial edition of the *Pall Mall Gazette* in 1889 appears in *BIS*.

Patrick Scott's attractive edition of *Amours de Voyage*[34] has much to recommend it. Beside a newly edited text, it includes full explanatory and textual notes which record substantive variants in the 1858 and 1862 editions, and a selection of the variants in the earlier manuscripts, some of which are published for the first time. The history of the text is described in a thoughtful introduction. Scott stresses the poetic quality of the poem as a whole, as an alternative to the common suggestion that its sense of actuality stems from its colloquial qualities. Arguing that the humane classicism of the elegiacs makes Claude's disillusion with his earlier enthusiasms tolerable, Scott believes that the poem shows that a scepticism concerning particular things need not lead to general scepticism.

In *N&Q* P. G. Scott identifies *Solutio Sophismatum*, the source of one of the epigraphs to *Amours de Voyage*, as an appendix to the standard undergraduate text on logical method at Oxford, Henry Aldrich's *Artis Logicae Compendium*, or *Rudimenta* (1691). Through detailed comparison of 'The Love Song of J. Alfred Prufrock' and *Amours de Voyage* J. R. Locke concludes that Eliot's debt to Clough is greater than has ye been recognized (*WHR*). In a short note J. P. McGrail gracefully reveal three image motifs—marriage, water, and trees, in Clough's *Bothie* (*VP*) A common source of dancing metaphors in Clough's 'Why should I say see the things I see not' (1849) and Newman's *Loss and Gain* (1848) i the 1842 *British Critic* is revealed by P. McGrane in *N&Q*. He conclude that we can thus see Clough's poem as partly a reply to the kind of argu ments found in *Loss and Gain*.

The extraordinary life and more ordinary work of Olive Custanc

[34] *Amours de Voyage*, by A. H. Clough, ed. Patrick Scott. Victorian Texts I. St Lucia, Queensland: U. of Queensland P., 1974. pp. 82 + 39. $6. pb $3.

(1874–1944) is rescued from oblivion in Brocard Sewell's essay,[35] to which is appended some of her poetry. An aristocrat, she became at sixteen privy to the circle of Beardsley, John Gray, and John Lane, published in *The Yellow Book*, the *Savoy*, and the *Academy*, and in 1897 Lane published the first of her four books, *Opals*. Fantasies of disaster evident in the poetry were realised when she eloped with Lord Alfred Douglas in 1902. Olive Custance published nothing after 1911 and separated from Douglas in 1913. For students of the decadents the life seems as informative as the work.

E. G. Atkinson publishes two letters unrecorded in J. B. Townsend's biography of John Davidson from the poet to Quiller-Couch, and both (dated 1900) pertain to Davidson's contribution to *The Oxford Book of English Verse* (*N&Q*).

In a discussion of Edward Fitzgerald's revisions G. D. Browne (*PBSA*) bears out what is evident from the first four English editions of *The Rubaiyat*—that he was a most conscientious artist, but that textual 'instability' results, in which variants make like claims on authority. Specific related problems are raised through a close consideration of the three editions of Fitzgerald's *Collected Works*.

In *The Contrary View*[25] G. Grigson considers John Gray's 'single masterpiece' 'The Flying Fish', one of the good modern poems of our century, while in the *Journal of the Eighteen Nineties Society* J. McCormack interprets John Gray's life and work between 1890 and 1892 as 'the usurpation of . . . life by a fiction'; allegedly having been Wilde's model for Dorian Gray, John Gray is actually called 'Dorian' by Wilde and his circle. This is a riveting account of Wilde's notion of nature imitating art. In *PQ* S. J. Leach publishes a poem about love (1828 or 1829?) by Arthur Hallam found among the Houghton Papers in Trinity College, Cambridge.

In a genuinely illuminating lecture[36] Peter Levi compares the language and quality of the poetry and prose of Clare and Hardy. Both were countrymen but Hardy's poetry is influenced and enhanced by the consciousness of realities attained in the practice of the novels. Common qualities of their work, including the force and dignity of country language, their extreme sadness, a tendency to neologisms and technical language, result in poetic language that is 'alive and vast', inward, and accurate.

Tom Paulin, a poet, approaches Hardy's poems through stress on his sight, with an accompanying insistence on a humanist rather than deadening positivism[37]. Set against some issues of contemporary poetry, Paulin's Hardy is also remarkably implicated in the development of Victorian poetry as described in *The Finer Optic* by Carol Christ. In a chapter on the nature of Hardy's perception Paulin demonstrates that Hardy remains ambivalent, presenting the lessons of time and experience visually and empirically rather than conceptually, while simultaneously alluding to the

[35] *Olive Custance: Her Life and Work*, by Brocard Sewell. Makers of the Nineties. The Eighteen-Nineties. pp. 37. £1.60.
[36] *John Clare and Thomas Hardy*, by Peter Levi. The John Coffin Memorial Lecture. U. of London, Athlone P. pp. 19. 65p.
[37] *Thomas Hardy: The Poetry of Perception*, by Tom Paulin. Macmillan. pp. x + 225. £7.95.

possibility of a world beyond. Hardy's taste and talent for fact in the poems, and the forms of silhouette, outline, and eidetic images which memory takes, emerge out of well-selected close readings. Only when Hardy frees himself from the 'temporal mechanism' does poetry composed of a series of images transcend its sources, and move into a visionary symbolist dimension, as in 'During Wind and Rain', 'Old Furniture', and other poems in *Moments of Vision*.

Hardy is one of the few Victorian poets who escape G. Grigson's censure in *The Contrary View*, but only at the expense of the novels: 'What I insist on is the amateurism of Hardy as a novelist' and his professionalism as a poet. The essay is otherwise perceptive, even rich, but ultimately Grigson reluctantly admits his distaste for Hardy's celebration of satisfactions only by reiterating their absence. *The Dynasts*, though an impersonal epic drama, is central in L. Jones's detailed and heavily footnoted analysis in *ELH* of the personal, idiosyncratic quality of Hardy's work. Jones finds that his conceptual model of the nature of Hardy's vision closely resembles Hardy's own in the Overworld of *The Dynasts*. In the second section, the idiosyncrasy of Hardy's characters is found in his disregard for manners and his exclusive interest in the most basic passions and drives. Hardy's omniscient narration and style are similarly analysed.

D. Taylor views the rigidity of Hardy's poetry not as poetically limiting, but as part of a deliberate dramatization of development of the patterns of experience from birth to adolescence and vulnerability to the jar of new life (*ELH*). Exploring the imagery of the patterns, Taylor notes that the clarity of the patterns increases with their obsolescence. The piece is suggestive and rich in examples. In *THY* Trevor Johnson makes accessible Edward Thomas's contemporary comments on Hardy's poetry from *In Pursuit of Spring*, 1914, and *A Literary Pilgrim in England*, 1917. To these Johnson adds remarks on Edward Thomas and on his treatment of Hardy's work.

In her casebook on Hopkins's poetry[38] Margaret Bottrall publishes extracts from the poet's own notebooks and letters as well as criticism and correspondence about him. This selection in no way duplicates that of G. H. Hartman in the American Twentieth-Century Views volume (1966); it includes essays by W. Empson, H. Read, Eliot, H. House, C. Devlin, and more modern studies by G. Grigson, E. Schneider, E. Jennings, D. McChesney, P. Wolfe, and J. Sutherland. The brisk introductory review of Hopkins's editions and reputation is uncommonly good. It usefully reveals why Hopkins was so slow in gaining recognition, and the editor notes that the kind of close literary analysis to which his poems are subject today did not exist in connexion with English literature until the twenties. The bibliography is annotated and there is an index.

In an informed essay[39] on the making of 'Spelt from Sibyl's Leaves'

---

[38] *Gerard Manley Hopkins. Poems*, ed. by Margaret Bottrall. Macmillan. pp 256. £3.95. pb £1.75.
[39] 'The Making of a Hopkins Sonnet: "Spelt from Sibyl's Leaves" ', by Norman H. Mackenzie in *A Festschrift for Edgar Ronald Seary*, ed. by A. A. MacDonald, P. A. O'Flaherty, and G. M. Story. Memorial U. of Newfoundland pp. 151–169.

Norman H. Mackenzie uses a largely unpublished Dublin note-book ('a rough scribbling book' which contains drafts of the poem), correspondence, journal entries and poems to describe the poem's growth and Hopkins's state of mind in the winter of 1884–5 when he was Professor of Greek and Latin at UC Dublin. Mackenzie's close reading of the drafts of the poem in the notebook and elsewhere is revealing. Hopkins's professional concern with classical literature is borne out in the poem's debts to Virgil, Plato, and Aeschylus; in a last section its predominant mood, one which fails to work through fear and torment to serenity or triumph, is assessed by its changes of intensity and direction.

In *Landscape and Inscape*[40] Peter Milward makes detailed critical comments on sixteen poems or passages from poems with the aid of photographs by Raymond V. Schoder which illuminate their imagery. Among the poems discussed are 'God's Grandeur', 'Pied Beauty', 'The Windhover', 'The May Magnificat', 'Binsey Poplars', 'Spelt from Sibyl's Leaves', and two passages from 'The Wreck of the Deutschland'. This approach is unevenly successful in that some photographs may usefully expand our understanding of the poetry, but other views seem unnecessary, already within readers' experience. The photographs are mostly of good quality, but the critical commentary is sufficiently serious and learned to take only a small part of its impetus from them. Both of the authors are Jesuits and perhaps this as much as the photographs contributes to the insights of this volume.

In *TSLL* K. Beyette identifies Christian grace and human time as the structural principles that characteristically engender the imagery of Hopkins. Using the poet's analysis of grace in his sermons, Beyette indicates the type of grace Hopkins seeks in the poem primarily through an exegesis of 'As Kingfishers catch fire' and 'To R.B.', but the piece is full and wide-ranging as well. An unobserved reason for the musical quality of the last two lines of 'Binsey Poplars' is suggested by J. D. Cartwright in *Expl*: they echo childhood chants such as 'A tisket, a tasket' or 'It's raining, it's pouring'.

J. J. Driscoll makes 'one more attempt' to illuminate stanza 33 of *The Wreck of the Deutschland* (*VP*) which he views as the climax of the poem, Hopkins's effort to express the depth of his thinking about the mystery of moral evil.

J. Ebbe argues, in a close study of 'Felix Randal', that the complex fabric of one poem by Hopkins can reveal much of Hopkins in microcosm (*VP*).

G. F. Freije brings the Jesuit theory of grace to bear on 'To flash from the flame to the flame then tower from the grace to the grace', the third stanza of the same poem. The poet's union of the simple and the complex is characteristic of his language and thought (*ELN*). J. L. Parini contends in *FMLS* that the structure of St. Ignatius's *Spiritual Exercises* underlies the poem, and governs the sequence of thought and imagery at its deepest level.

[40] *Landscape and Inscape*, by Peter Milward. Photography by Raymond V. Schoder. Elek. pp. 126 + 44 pp. of plates. £6.

All My Eyes See[41] is a publication printed in conjunction with an exhibition on Hopkins's visual world mounted by the Sunderland Arts Centre; accordingly it contains over 250 illustrations, many unpublished, including the first published comprehensive visual documentation of the drawings in Hopkins's four sketchbooks.

Three essays closely dependent on photographs concerning 'Portraits of Hopkins' (Bevis Hillier), 'The Places Hopkins Knew', and 'The People Hopkins Knew' (both by the editor), and a compilation of others' impressions of Hopkins (Norman White) are biographical.

Three solid articles on Hopkins and visual art follow, 'The Context of Hopkins' Drawings' and 'Hopkins as Art Critic', both by Norman White, and 'Hopkins's Drawings' by Jerome Bump, and the bulk of Hopkins's drawing (1862–1889) is reproduced. Tom Dunne contributes a shorter piece on the critical reception of Hopkins's publications. While this volume shares a visual approach to Hopkins with *Landscape and Inscape*, it distinguishes itself from the latter by its visual tact, and perhaps because it does not imply identity of the physical world and the imaginative expression.

G. Grigson, in *The Contrary View*,[25] resists the idea that religion is the 'primary interest' of the best poems or the man. He notes that Hopkins likened himself to Whitman, and speculates that Hopkins 'at risk' without the Jesuits would have been a 'greater, more voluminous poet altogether', if flawed.

In a piece on 'grammaticality' and the poetry of Hopkins in *Lang&S*, A. H. Stewart attempts to apply Yngve's linguistic theory of surface structure independent of deep structure to explain the qualities of Hopkins's style which, she finds, characteristically fails to conserve depth of language.

In a steadily informative piece in *NLR*, A. Thomas traces a source of 'The Windhover' to the pub sign of the 'Hawk and Buckle' in Denbigh, linking the language of falconry in the poem with the heraldic emblem of the House of York from which the nineteenth-century sign derived. He goes on to connect the poem with a reading of a play by C. W. Barraud, one of Hopkins's colleagues at St. Beuno's College, an article in *Once a Week* in 1863 on falconry, the work of the Jesuit poet and martyr, Robert Southwell, Pater's essay on 'Aesthetic Poetry', and Quarles's skilled use of the language of falconry. Thomas also contemplates a pseudonym, Arthur Flash de Weyunhoe, which Hopkins used as an undergraduate in a playful letter to his father (*N&Q*). Carefully and closely examining the overthought of the terrible sonnets, particularly their grammar, M. H. Villarubia reveals an interaction of Ignatius's affective and elective wills which results in subtle psychic anguish for Hopkins (*Renascence*).

The Hopkins Research Bulletin publishes three letters of biographical interest, edited by Graham Storey, from Hopkins to W. A. Comyn Macfarlane (all from 1866) which do not appear in C. A. Abbott's edition of Hopkins's *Further Letters*. A list supplementary to the principal list of 'Books Hopkins Had Access to' in *HRB*, No. 5, also appears. R. L. Starkey publishes with commentary Hopkins's borrowings from the Library

[41] *All My Eyes See—The Visual World of Gerard Manley Hopkins*, ed. by R. K. R. Thornton. Sunderland: Geolfrith P. pp. 148. £3.50 + 50p postage, $12.

Register of Highgate School from March 1860 to November 1862, a time in which 'A Vision of the Mermaid' may have been germinating. The *Bulletin* also contains a bibliography of studies on Hopkins in 1973 compiled by R. Seelhammer and A. Thomas. Reviewing Housman's life and personality as exhibited in his letters, G. Grigson in *The Contrary View* regards the poems as 'a bleeding miracle'.

Wilhelm Gauger's study of motifs of change in Kipling's prose works[42] argues against the classification of these motifs within the framework of any philosophical system and against their interpretation in Freudian terms. The author puts forward an alternative theory which regards them as products of a dynamic process within Kipling's subconscious documenting his progress towards self-realization. (H.C.C.)

In 'Coming to Terms with Kipling' (*UTQ*) P. Hinchcliffe alleges that the author's multiple discontinuous contradictions do not obliterate each other but act as a creative paradox which sometimes results in heightened intensity. Examining notions of history in *Puck of Pook's Hill* and *Rewards and Fairies*, Hinchliffe reveals underlying ironies and potential lines of development stunted or grotesquely displaced by the war. M. E. Karim publishes 'Alnaschar' in *ELN*, an uncollected poem by Kipling which appeared in 1886 in the *Civil and Military Gazette* of Lahore. In *RS* J. V. Grangle scrutinizes the poetry (1880-1905) and anti-imperialism of Sir Wilfrid Lawson, an MP and a contemporary of Kipling. Supporting peace and temperance, Lawson's poetry is primarily that of a moralist and a politician.

J. T. Bratcher examines the occasional and periodical first publication of the poems of Frederick Locker (*PBSA*).

Selected poems by Theo. Marzials,[43] poet, singer, and composer of popular ballads, are edited and introduced by John M. Munro. His poetry is aesthetic in its concern with manner, and Munro notes its affinities with the work of English Parnassians, and its debts to Gautier and Rossetti. But Marzials's poems for all that are never far removed from burlesque.

Rossetti's revised opinion of the poetry of Théophile Marzials is the subject of a letter (1880) published in *N&Q* by John Munro. As a result of unfavourable criticism of *The Gallery of Pigeons* in 1873 (with which Rossetti concurred at the time), Marzials virtually abandoned poetry.

In his new life of William Morris,[44] Jack Lindsay undertakes to provide the strengths of both E. F. Thompson's focus on politics in his 1955 life and P. Henderson's elaboration of Mackail in 1967. On two points Lindsay seems to falter: his tendentious account of Morris's childhood is interleaved with quotations from Morris's works to substantiate the belief that in certain childhood experiences originated central later images and structures; heavy-handed references to childhood persist. But the sympathy and understanding that Lindsay brings to Morris's multiple achievements are impressive. Morris's life involved close relationships with a large number of people, and with these Lindsay is similarly adept, with perhaps the

---

[42] Wilhelm Gauger, *Wandlungsmotive in Rudyard Kiplings Prosawerk*. Munich: Fink Verlag. pp. 262. n.p.
[43] *Selected Poems of Theo Marzials*, ed. by John M. Munro. Beirut: American U. of Beirut, 1974. pp. x + 136. n.p.
[44] *William Morris*, by Jack Lindsay. Constable. pp. xii + 432. £7.50.

exception of Jane, daughter of an Oxford groom, who suffered from 'an almost total lack of education and *the sordid milieu of her upbringing*' (my italics). Less forgiveable is the shocking obscurity of the form of the notes, and the crowding of the bibliography.

In 'Unpublished Lyrics of William Morris' (*YES*), K. L. Goodwin unearths 'Guileful Love', 'Summer Night' and a version of 'Lonely Love and Loveless Death' from a calligraphic illuminated manuscript, 'A Book of Verse', and eight other lyrics from the May Morris Bequest in the British Library; and she presents a classified list of all the unpublished poems and fragments in this collection excluding fragments omitted from larger works. She concludes her illuminating commentary with the suggestion that on the evidence of the poems Morris's passion was rejected by his wife and Georgina Burne-Jones, and that he was forced to confine it to his verse.

In three short pieces on Morris's life and design, poetry, and Icelandic journals in *The Contrary View*,[25] G. Grigson makes a detailed claim for Morris's greatness, with the poems leading us to its essence. While welcoming Yeats's celebration of this 'happiness', Grigson reveals the complementary sadness in 'Shameful Death' and 'The Pilgrims of Hope'.

Morris's debt to Browning and the personality of Guenevere are two perspectives from which R. L. Stallman examines 'The Defence of Guenevere' and 'King Arthur's Tomb' in *SEL*. Guenevere's progress is that of a steadfastness of love rather than a realization of sin. The poems are a single drama with the characters the centre of interest and the archetypal and ritual patterns the stage 'blocking' through which the characters move.

Victorian Poetry devotes a double number (Autumn–Winter) edited by W. E. Fredeman to William Morris. It treats the prose, designs, correspondence, and 'book arts' as well as the poetry and contains illustrations. In his introduction Fredeman considers whether Morris's 'polymathic complexity' explains the relative neglect of Morris. While noting the telling disparity between Morris's practice and theoretical intolerance of the artist in *News from Nowhere*, Fredeman compares Morris's virtuosity with Whitman's.

In 'William Morris and the Uses of the Past' H. Spratt convincingly views the early work as 'a series of experiments . . . to discover why men are driven to overcome their remoteness from history through the imaginative recreation or ritual re-enactment' of fable. Using John Patrick's identification of the (three) poems indebted to Froissart in *The Defence of Guenevere* sequence, D. F. Sadoff explores their 'Exotic Murders: Structural and Rhetorical Irony'. These 'non-escapist moral tales in medieval dress' treat 'the complexities of desire and the world's ironical obstruction of fulfilment'.

The three major articles stress Morris's positive use of the past for purposes of exploration rather than escape from the present. Two quests for a terrestial Eden and for perfect love, the Paradise within, determine the structural design of *The Earthly Paradise*, in which ten tales illustrate joyful love and ten more powerful tales its loss; in 'The Earthly Paradise: Lost' by C. G. Silver, Morris's later prose fictions are also defended from the charge of escapism: his evocative not explicit aesthetic ensures their effectiveness as 'idealist reforming art'.

In a lively article D. R. Balch tackles 'Guenevere's Fidelity to Arthur'

By treating 'The Defence' and 'King Arthur's Tomb' as complementary, he shows her motivation to be more complex than self-preservation: her actions are self-destructive as well, and she is more faithful to Arthur than generally allowed. That Christian asceticism must within the Arthurian legend overcome Launcelot and the sensuous life may be one reason why Morris did not use Arthurian material in a major way.

Accepting the self-confessed escapism of *The Earthly Paradise*, E. Strode interestingly compares the Morris of its crisis—the 'September' to 'November' sections—with Keats's alienation from reality in 'Sleep and Poetry' and 'The Fall of Hyperion', and briefly with Tennyson's in 'The Palace of Art'.

K. B. Valentine correlates Morris's use of 'Motifs from Nature' in the design work and prose romances between 1876 and 1896, to demonstrate that the work of this period 'is all of a piece'. 'The Story of Dorothea', Morris's unpublished tale of the Christian martyr originally composed for *The Earthly Paradise*, is described and assessed by K. L. Godwin. Deeming it as good as several published poems in *The Earthly Paradise*, Godwin relates Morris's theme to Burne-Jones's cartoon and water-colour, and to Swinburne's verse in *Poems and Ballads*.

Morris's unfinished first novel, 'Landscape and Sentiment', is considered afresh by J. Kocmanova, and tentatively related to Meredith's *Ordeal* and *Rhoda Fleming*, the immediate predecessors to the modern novel. R. L. Harris examines an illuminating correspondence between Morris and Eirikur Magnusson, the Icelander who became Sub-Librarian at Cambridge and through whom Morris learned Icelandic.

Two fascinating essays, by A. R. Life on 'Illustration and Morris' "Ideal Book" ' and J. R. Dunlop on 'Morris and the Book Arts Before the Kelmscott Press' treat Morris's spirited contributions of architectural theories of illustration and type-face to book design. Lastly, the reciprocity of the relationship between Morris and the South Kensington Museum is stressed by B. Morris, and J. Lindsay and W. E. Fredeman conclude with their edition of D. G. Rossetti's skit, 'The Death of Topsy'.

I. R. Hark sets out to consider Newman's *The Dream of Gerontius* as 'mind' rather than 'soul' in *Renascence*: the poetic structure informs doctrine with psychological fidelity and mind leads back to soul.

In *L&P* E. Golub fruitfully brings out latent meaning in Christina Rossetti's 'Goblin Market'. Parallels between the scolding that D. G. Rossetti gave Warrington Taylor whose neglected wife had left, the theme of Rossetti's painting *La Pia de' Tolomei* (1868) which commemorates a wife imprisoned by her husband, and Rossetti's relationship with Jane Morris, another neglected woman, are drawn by J. LeBourgeois in *N&Q*.

The poetry of D. G. Rossetti figures importantly in Richard L. Stein's *The Ritual of Interpretation: The Fine Arts as Literature in Ruskin, Rossetti and Pater* (Harvard U.P.) which was not available for review. Also unavailable was W. E. Fredeman's edition of *The P.R.B. Journal* which comprises annotations and the entire *Journal*, only half of which W. M. Rossetti included in his *Preraphaelite Diaries and Letters* in 1900.

John D. Jump's selection of Tennyson's poetry[45] demonstrates the

---

[45] *Tennyson: 'In Memoriam', 'Maud' and Other Poems*, ed. by John D. Jump. Everyman's University Library. Dent. pp. xxi + 237. £1.95. pb 95p.

possibilities of this series at its best—judicious selection, reliable text, annotation, and bibliography, a rich, concise introduction in notable prose, line references, and an index to the *In Memoriam* poems. These combine to make it a recommendable student edition.

In a book on Tennyson's major poems,[46] James R. Kincaid directs attention to the poet's comic mode as an alternative to what Kincaid calls his ironic mode which is characterized by balanced but unreconciled opposites. In chapters spanning Tennyson's long career Kincaid traces a semicircular pattern in which increasingly ironic statement typifies the volumes between 1830 and 1842, various comic strategies *The Princess, In Memoriam*, and *Maud*, and irony the late poems, '*Idylls of the King* surely (being) the major ironic work of art of the century'. Kincaid's categories and readings are quite elaborate, and vary in success. Kincaid's generic perspective is consistently interesting without providing basic new insights. An extensive bibliography, a long appendix on the minor poems, and an index supplement the text.

In *N&Q* J. Adler shows that Tennyson's use of the Miltonic phrase 'subtle beast' in lines 10 and 58 of *Guinevere* grammatically resembles Hallam's use of the same phrase in *Oration on the Influence of Italian works of the Imagination on the Same Class of Compositions in England* (1831) rather than Milton's.

S. C. Allen suggests that a possible source for the weaving image in 'The Lady of Shallott' is a fragment by Sappho found in Hephaestion's *Enchiridion* and marked in Tennyson's copy of *Poetae Lyrici Graeci* (*TRB*), while J. S. Hagen, in *AN&Q*, suggests that the Lady leaves her loom because art is discredited by the discrepancy between the reality of Lancelot and his reflection in the river, both of which flash into her 'crystal mirror'. A source for Guenevere's shudder (lines 55–6) in Francis Grose's *A Provincial Glossary* is mooted by J. M. Bray in *TRB*.

K. J. Fielding brings to light Tennyson's refusal of the position of Lord Rector of the University of Edinburgh in 1868 when Carlyle finished his stint. The spirit of the nominations and elections is revealed through publication of a contemporary parody, reports of meetings, and a broadsheet (*TRB*).

E. Fontana identifies a reference to the summer solstice, the 'boundless day', in *In Memoriam*, XCV, 64 in *Expl*, a point missed by both Ricks and Bradley. Sir Charles Tennyson reports on a revealing talk concerning the spiritual life that the composer Joachim had with Tennyson sometime between 1889 and 1892. In the interview, the poet expresses his belief in material existence in the future life and comments on 'Are God and Nature then at strife', section 55 of *In Memoriam* (*TRB*).

The late S. Gliserman examines connexions between context and literary text, early Victorian science writers and *In Memoriam* being her specific case, in an effort to determine the 'structure of feeling' common to the society and its art (*VS*). Tennyson's response to the writings of William Paley, P. M. Roger, W. Whewell, and Charles Lyell—a theologian a physician, a physical scientist, and a geologist—comprises the first section of the article, which is concluded in the following number with a reading

[46] *Tennyson's Major Poems: The Comic and Ironic Patterns*, by James R. Kincaid New Haven: Yale U.P. pp. xi + 234. $15.

of *In Memoriam* as in part an incorporation of Tennyson's response to these writings. The dual interest in critical theory and practical criticism, and the patience of the scrutiny of both the scientific writing and the poem make this fine article useful to readers of *In Memoriam*. Piecemeal construction of a 'relative chronology' of thirteen stages in Tennyson's composition of 'Balin and Balan' (1885) is D. F. Goslee's detective method of probing Tennyson's narrative technique and this 'underrated' idyll (*HLQ*).

G. Grigson in *The Contrary View*[25] stresses Tennyson's kinship with Poe in a carping and mincing estimate which hardly acknowledges the achievements of *In Memoriam*; Grigson's Tennyson is a poet of mood whose faculty of word and measure needed educating, a poet to whom a selection of gems would do justice.

In *Costerus* J. S. Hagen examines evidence of Tennyson's break with Romanticism in the form of his revisions of 'Audley Court' in the page proofs of the 1842 *Poems*. These, which are not included in Ricks, bear out findings of recent research which suggest that Tennyson in revisions aimed at artistic improvement rather than placating his critics. The five successive versions here from manuscript (in Ricks) to third edition (also in Ricks) show movement from ornament to plainness, description to narration, and satiety to simple calm and contentment.

Describing Tennyson's three visits to the valley of the Cauteretz in the Pyrenees—in 1830, 1861, and 1874, J. C. Hixon notes the poems composed or conceived there—'Oenone', 'All along the valley, stream that flashest white', and *Queen Mary* (*TRB*).

In a detailed and substantial piece on 'Tennyson's Melody' in *GR*, J. Hollander traces Tennyson's aptitude for handling both the emblematic music of mythology and romance, and the imaginatively authentic but figurative music of natural sound from the Juvenilia through *In Memoriam*, *Maud*, and the *Idylls*. Characteristically, Tennyson underscores sound with vision, and image with sound.

In *VN* J. Kolb quotes from three unpublished letters of Hallam to Emily Tennyson to amend Rader by showing that Tennyson's first meeting with Rosa Baring did not occur before the autumn of 1832.

As an antidote to psychological criticism H. Kozicki traces the components of Tennyson's philosophy of history from his naïve faith in providential history, through his unhappiness in the early thirties when the transcendent, the heroic, and society tend towards disintegration, to the more optimistic late thirties when divinity is integrated with the historical process, cycles yield (re)birth, and heroes redeem (*ELH*).

In *Criticism* the same author tellingly argues that the Victorian debate on the relation of past and present is reflected in the medieval ideal of *The Princess*, in which the medieval past and the Victorian present are apprehended through a fusion of one with the other, in that archetypal marriage at the core of the feudal paradigm of the Great House in the frame. The past is both mocked and mourned. The handling of time, memory and art in *The Princess* is related to a mutability theme by C. B. Stevenson in *VP*. The songs and the child references, on the aesthetic and human levels respectively, are keys to Tennyson's exploration of ways of escaping from Time.

In a resonant thoughtful piece in *DR*, R. S. Librach stresses the optimism of the *Idylls*; Tennyson's notion of the poet as an evocator of mythical archetypes and his use of aspects of romance 'alter profoundly the direction of his philosophical theme'. Lack of conflict between the wheels of nature and fortune results in a final affirmation rather than either tragic failure of idealism or tragic conflict of mortal will against an inimical natural order.

T. L. Meyers (*TRB*) locates the source for Mary E. Phillips's report of Tennyson's wish to see the grave of Edgar Allan Poe. In the same periodical J. C. Miller suggests that a fragmentary poem in couplets by Tennyson, 'Napoleon's Retreat from Moscow', is an unfinished entry for the Chancellor's Medal competition at Cambridge in 1828. This reveals Tennyson's rejection of the heroic couplet for 'Timbuctoo', his winning entry of 1829, as an effort to learn from his earlier mistake.

In *CQ* W. Nash reveals structural similarities between the 'Morte d' Arthur' and its frame, 'The Epic', and the alternation of 'round rhetoric' and 'flat conversation' in the English idylls which Tennyson was composing in 1837/8 when he added 'The Epic' to 'Morte'. The degree of inter-dependence of the parts and the resulting meaning emerge from Nash's full and close reading.

In *VP* L. G. Whitbread fills in the background and comments on certain allusions in Tennyson's late occasional poem 'In the Garden at Swainston'.

I. Claphane writes a short obituary of Sir Frances Meynell (1891-1975), Francis Thompson's godchild, and founder of the Nonesuch Press, in the *Journal* of the Eighteen Nineties Society.

Francis Thompson, James Thomson, and Swinburne figure in 'Four Ways of Making Fudge' in *The Contrary View*[25] by G. Grigson, for whom all three fudge poetry, and lamentably attract readers through their confusion of life and art.

'Blake Among Victorians' is the subject of a double number of *BN* (1974). Ian Fletcher edits four lectures on Blake by the poet John Todhunter (1839-1916), delivered in Dublin in 1872-74, which are of considerable interest as examples of Victorian literary criticism. They testify to the continuing influence of Blake on young poets (cf Swinburne and Rossetti), provide good examples of Victorian practical criticism, and attempt to define 'modern' as Arnold does in 1857, as well as contribute to the Victorian debate about Blake initiated by Gilchrist in 1863. Two poems of Todhunter's, 'Lost' and 'Found', and a section of a preface which are indebted to Blake, are unearthed by Michael J. Tolley.

The critical reception in the periodicals of both Gilchrist's *Life* (1863) and Swinburne's *A Critical Essay* (1868) is recorded and assessed by Suzanne R. Hoover and Morton D. Paley respectively, and to students of criticism and the periodicals these pieces are highly recommended. One review of Gilchrist in the *London Quarterly Review* by James Smetham (1821-1889) was actully incorporated in the 1880 (Second) edition of Gilchrist, and Frances A. Carey examines and reproduces some of Smetham's personal marginal illustrations for Gilchrist which exemplify his work, which Rossetti compared to the pictures of Blake and Palmer. This issue of *BN* ends with an interesting unfinished dialogue between Blake and Wordsworth in heaven, written by M. K. Macmillan sometime before April 1889.

In *N&Q* W. Baker centres his discussion round a long unpublished letter

(12 March 1881) from Swinburne to Herbert Spencer concerning Spencer's praise of the poet's pamphlet 'Notes of an English Republican on the Muscovite Crusade' and his (unsuccessful) appeal to Swinburne for political support in another pamphlet on Britain's imperial atrocities.

J. Forbes shows that two flagellation poems by 'Eroneusis' published in a monthly periodical, the *Pearl*, in 1879 and 1880 are by Swinburne (*N&Q*). The publication of these poems helps date Swinburne's flagellation writings, and reveals *The Whippingham Papers* not to be an isolated phenomen; it is even possible that these poems are part of a larger cycle of *Whippingham Papers*.

(b) Drama

The Road to the Stage; or The Performer's Preceptor (1827), apparently the first guide to the stage, is described, assessed, and recommended as a valuable source of information by Michael R. Booth in *NCTR*. It is also interesting and amusing reading for all theatre-goers.

J. A. Davies notes the influence exerted by Charles Lamb on John Forster, by Lamb's writings and by Forster's memory of his friend. Lamb, an object of Forster's hero-worship, contributed to Forster's indignation at the lack of respect accorded to authors, and stimulated his interest in Landor. But more importantly Lamb's ideas seem to dominate Forster's writings on Shakespeare. By publishing parallel texts from Lamb's and Forster's reviews of contemporary productions, Davies reveals the degree of indebtedness 'What emerges is a clear relationship between Forster and romantic criticism.' While Forster's championship of Lamb's ideal encouraged Macready in his return to the original texts, some of Macready's ideas can be seen to have influenced Forster (*RES*).

The efforts of J. T. Grein and George Moore to produce new continental drama of high literary value between 1891 and 1898 in the Independent Theatre Society is J. McDonald's subject in *ThRI*, a continuation in a new series of *ThR*, now published by O.U.P. *Ghosts* and *The Wild Duck* were first produced in English by the Independent Theatre Society, and Brandes's *The Visit*, *A Doll's House*, and Zola's *Thérèse Raquin*, were among the productions resulting from a policy 'aiming to be free from the fetters of convention'. The Society's small troubles with the censor, and the opportunities given to actresses by plays treating the women's social position, are also described in this mildly interesting piece.

The extent to which Victorian music-hall songs reflected or created the politics of its popular audience is explored by L. Senelick in *VS*. Because neither the audience nor the managers or composers were purely or even mostly working-class, the music-hall songs mirrored popular politics far less than the earlier broadside, but their influence in creating public opinion was greater. Consistently anti-liberal and pro-conservative, music-hall songs did not hesitate to affront the largely working-class Liberal vote. And Senelick argues that the music hall may have redirected the self-regarding energies of the working man to imperialism.

In *TN* G. Speaight discusses and reproduces for the first time a water-colour drawing (c. 1859) of the circus in Vauxhall Gardens which 'indicates the pleasant, intimate character' of the building.

Reginald Allan's catalogue, *Sir Arthur Sullivan, Composer and Person-*

age,[47] is so full and copiously annotated and illustrated that it functions autonomously independently of the centenary exhibition and the Gilbert and Sullivan collection at the Morgan Library from which it stemmed. Excerpts from many letters spanning the four decades of Sullivan's creative maturity (1860–1900), plates of Gilbert's manuscript of *The Pirates of Penzance*, programmes, and posters combine to make this an informative volume

Hesketh Pearson's biography of Gilbert and Sullivan (1935), which is reissued[48] with a new introduction by Malcolm Muggeridge, is considerably less scholarly, even anecdotal, but it provides an alternative view of Sullivan, whom Pearson dislikes; of Sullivan's desire to link his name with Tennyson's through setting to music *Songs of the Wrens* Pearson writes 'Sullivan persisted grimly; so grimly indeed that Tennyson . . . offered the composer five hundred pounds to drop the scheme' whereas Gilbert escapes with the following: 'In brief, Gilbert was a strong, full-blooded, impatient and irreverent Englishman, which accounts for some of the vindictiveness and callousness in the *Bab Ballads*.' Much of the material on Gilbert relates to the periodicals and the world of *The Victorian Popular Ballad*.

J. W. Stedman investigates W. S. Gilbert's career as an adaptor of French farces under the name Latour Tomline, his own name being reserved for proto-problem plays. One of these farces, a curtain-raiser called *The Blue·Legged Lady*, had never before been regarded as his work; Stedman prints it from the (only) licence copy and uses it to show Gilbert's spontaneous impromptu skill (*NCTR*).

In *EA*, E. W. F. Tomlin argues that an undated letter from W. C. Macready to George Sand was written in the spring of 1856 when Macready may have been in Paris with Dickens, rather than in November 1853, and that it concerns a performance of her version of *As You Like It* rather than *Mauprat*.

Charles Kean's reputation is disinterred by M. G. Wilson from the biased reviews of Dickens and John Forster, friends under the influence of Kean's rival Charles Macready. Kean successfully pitted the provincial against the London press, but he had greater problems weathering reviews by critic/playwrights such as Jerrold and G. M. Lewes, whose plays Kean was involved in refusing or producing (*VPN*).

Macdonald and Jane's have reissued Hesketh Pearson's enjoyable and informative biography of Wilde,[49] with a new introduction by Peter Quennell. Published in 1946, and in a revised edition in 1954, this biography seems to have made full use of the oral and written sources available at the time, but to champion Wilde. Although Pearson is unwilling to acknowledge Wilde's guilt at the trials his book will remain standard until Ellmann's life appears. Much of Pearson's material, and especially Appendix A on 'Wilde, Douglas, and Ross' is pertinent to Sewell's pamphlet on Olive Custance.

[47] *Sir Arthur Sullivan*, by Reginald Allen in collaboration with Gale R. D'Luhy. New York: Pierpont Morgan Library. pp.xxviii + 215. n.p.
[48] *Gilbert and Sullivan*, by Hesketh Pearson. Macdonald and Jane's. pp. 319. £3.95.
[49] *The Life of Oscar Wilde*, by Hesketh Pearson. Macdonald and Jane's. pp. xvi + 399. £4.95.

4. Nineteenth-Century Prose Fiction

(a) General

'Will you hear the story of Magdalen—in modern times?' John R. Reed provides numerous examples of *Victorian Conventions,*[1] literary and social. He does not attempt to be exhaustive yet his range stretches from character types to deathbeds and inheritance, from the orphan and gipsies to madness. He is careful to distinguish varieties of treatment, ironic strategies, and angles of incidence with real life. Certain conventions— disguise, memory, and the occult—clearly involve profounder considerations of identity, cultural change, and the human condition. A general thesis that the conventions 'reveal a growing dissatisfaction' during the century is more contentious, but undoubtedly backed by much more evidence than usual.

Such matters as the 'combination of scientific theory, ethnocentrism and imaginative writing which lay behind Victorian collective representations of mankind' are Brian V. Street's concern in *The Savage in Literature.*[2] Popular fiction of the period 1858–1920, though it can be up to fifty years out of date, undoubtedly shows the influence of science. The ideas of Darwin, who said he would as soon be descended from a 'heroic little monkey' as from a superstitious savage, inform *The Water Babies,* for instance. This complex is all studied from a modern standpoint, though Street notes that this is perhaps as relative as its Victorian precursors: Haggard's detailed analysis of 'primitive' social institutions may be remarkable, *but* his theoretical framework came from academic contemporaries. There are many valuable points made—the way in which 'kinship' became as vital an interest as 'despotism', the myths of progress giving place to myths of function, and so on. More particularly, Nina Auerbach studies 'Incarnations of the Orphan' (*ELN*) in the novel. Jane Eyre, Becky Sharp, Heathcliff show how 'the strange cunning power of the orphan is yoked to forces of social evolution', but Pip and Lucy Snowe lack the earlier power and magic. James M. Keech writes on 'The Survival of the Gothic Response' (*SNNTS*, 1974) in the Brontës, Dickens, et al.

'*The Historical Novel and Popular Politics in Nineteenth Century England*[3] is less comprehensive than its title suggests', writes Nicholas Rance. This is so. His introduction skates through a number of topics. Then, after a swift survey of mid-century history and historical novels from a progressive angle, he writes on novels like *A Tale of Two Cities, Felix Holt,* and *Vittoria* in more depth, but sometimes too superficially. (If Elizabeth Gaskell 'flicked through the *Annual Registers*' when writing *Sylvia's Lovers,* Dr. Rance must have flicked through her letter on the subject.) His characteristic leap is from the primary text to sages like Ruskin or modern historians like E. P. Thompson. Students with similar interests would do well to read Alistair M. Duckworth's lucid and sympathetic review essay, 'Raymond Williams and Literary History' (*PLL*).

[1] *Victorian Conventions,* by John R. Reed. Ohio U.P. pp. xiii + 561. $15.
[2] *The Savage in Literature: Representations of 'Primitive' Society in English Fiction 1858-1920,* by Brian V. Street. Routledge & Kegan Paul. pp. xii + 207. £5.75.
[3] *The Historical Novel and Popular Politics in Nineteenth-Century England,* by Nicholas Rance. Vision (Critical Studies, ed. Michael Egan). pp. 176. £3.25.

It is helpful to have a professional turn his attention to philosophical influences on George Eliot, but in *Philosophy and the Novel*[4] Peter Jones goes further: he illuminates the theory of knowledge presupposed by types of egoism, concepts and roles of imagination, and psychological determinants. If, for instance, 'exiles feed on hopes', those who 'feed on hope are exiles--from the actual world'. After examining other European fiction, Jones gives his own theory of interpretation. He discriminates neatly between creative and merely subjective responses. He often achieves a welcome, taut formulation of his views: 'Intelligibility is separable from assent, and both are separable from truth'. András Horn contributes a technical article on 'The Concept of "Mimesis" in George Lukács' to *BJA*, 1974. In *SSF* Sally Mitchell writes on 'Implications of Realism: Four Stories from *The London Journal*', by J. P. H., about 'the fallen woman' in mid-century.

'The new theory of dreaming is more sensitive to the full range of what is dreamt, in what order, and in what form', writes Albert D. Hutter in 'Dreams, Transformations, and Literature: the Implications of Detective Fiction' (*VS*); 'we should be talking about latent *structure*, not latent content'. His survey of modern psychoanalytic developments is accompanied by a very full analysis of Wilkie Collins's *Moonstone* and earlier, reductionist accounts of such fiction (where the butler turned out to be another Oedipus, he jokes). Lee Sterrenburg's 'Psychoanalysis and the Iconography of Revolution' (*VS*) deals with the analogies between cannibalism and revolution. As in the previous essay there is a reversal: Hutter's infantile-to-adult becomes Sterrenburg's personal-to-political.

Regressive romances like *Wuthering Heights* and *The Master of Ballantrae* figure largely in a valuable survey by Patrick Brantlinger, 'Romances, Novels, and Psychoanalysis' (*Criticism*). He claims, one notes, that the quality of both literary forms depends 'largely on the truth and subtlety of the rational understanding which their authors bring to them.' *HSL* contains a short review article by Richard W. Noland on Bernard J. Paris's *A Psychological Approach to Fiction: Studies in Thackeray, Stendhal, George Eliot, Dostoevsky, and Conrad* (Indiana U.P., 1974). I have not seen C. N. Manlove's *Modern Fantasy*,[5] which contains studies of Charles Kingsley and George Macdonald.

(b) Individual Novelists

We begin with a close, empirical study of five Scott novels. Lars Hartveit's *Dream within a Dream*[6] uses *The Heart of Midlothian*, *Waverley*, *Guy Mannering*, and *Old Mortality* to display central themes (society, the heroic, law, and religion); then *Redgauntlet* illustrates how they coalesce into the overriding theme of illusion and reality. Hartveit makes much of

---

[4] *Philosophy and the Novel: Philosophical Aspects of 'Middlemarch', 'Anna Karenina', 'The Brothers Karamazov', 'A la recherche du temps perdu' and of the methods of criticism*, by Peter Jones. Oxford: Clarendon P. pp. viii + 216. £4.25. pb £1.75.

[5] *Modern Fantasy: Five Studies*, by C. N. Manlove. Cambridge U.P. pp. viii + 308. £6.50.

[6] *Dream within a Dream: a Thematic Approach to Scott's Vision of Fictional Reality*, by Lars Hartveit. Bergen, Oslo, Tromsö: Universitets forlaget; New York: Humanities P., 1974. Norwegian Studies in English 18. $17.50.

antitheses between, say, a heroic past when rights were won by the private sword and the unheroic present when law maintains social order. Loyalty may be a common virtue, but individuals suffer from conflicting loyalties. Reality itself seems contradictory, and this 'is inherent both in point of view and the overall pattern of antithetic themes.' In 'The Commerical Motif of the Waverley Novels' (*ELH*), Lawrence Poston III also finds contradictions. He shows that although his early writings anticipate Carlyle's 'invectives against the cash nexus', the novels are ambivalent about commercial forces. *Rob Roy* and *The Fortunes of Nigel* are given special stress in this detailed study.

Claire Lamont surveys 'The Poetry of the Early Waverley Novels' (*PBA*), showing Scott's excellence as folk poet, ballad singer and impersonal lyricist in his fiction. Frank McCombie writes on 'Scott, *Hamlet*, and *The Bride of Lammermoor*' (*EIC*), basing his criticism on a study of the manuscript and a comparison with Shakespeare's play as interpreted by J. P. Kemble.

Douglas Bush's *Jane Austen*[7] is a modest companion for the general reader, admirably judged for the purpose. Perhaps some of his comparisons with our own 'age of undisciplined sensibility and defective ethical reason' are not argued fully enough, but the criticism usually ranges from the adequate to the felicitous, such as the comment on Marianne's acceptance of Colonel Brandon: it 'requires the unwilling suspension of disbelief that accompanies a happy ending'. *EA* summarizes Pierre Gonbert, *Jane Austen, Etude psychologique* (Cæn thesis).

Barbara Hardy's *A Reading of Jane Austen*[8] is directed to first-hand analysis of the six major novels, bringing out Jane Austen's treatment of the feelings and the passions, social groups, properties, and possessions. Narrative method is a major interest. In particular Professor Hardy contends that the novel became 'a new and flexible medium in which the individual and society could be revealed together'; Jane Austen quietly, unselfconsciously, created the modern novel. One might regret that the full range of Austen criticism is not drawn upon, but the demonstrations are as usual just and deft. Of course, Austen criticism is growing apace. No less than nineteen new items are brought together in John Halperin's *Bicentenary Essays*,[9] which also contains a full though selective bibliography of modern works. John Halperin, R. A. Brower, S. M. Tave, and J. A. Hodge deal with backgrounds; Katrin Ristkok Burlin, Everett Zimmerman, R. B. Heilman, Karl Kroeber, R. F. Brissenden, K. L. Moler, Barbara Hardy, John Halperin, Joseph Wiesenfarth, and A. Walton Litz treat individual novels; Mary Lascelles, Marvin Mudrick, Donald Greene, Alistair M. Duckworth, and Andrew Wright write on more general topics. B. C. Southam has brought out a facsimile of the manuscript first draft of *Sanditon*,[10] and this unfinished novel has now been completed by an

---

[7] *Jane Austen*, by Douglas Bush. Macmillan (Masters of World Literature). pp. xv + 205. £5.95.
[8] *A Reading of Jane Austen*, by Barbara Hardy. Peter Owen. pp. 192. £4.75.
[9] *Jane Austen: Bicentenary Essays*, ed. by John Halperin. Cambridge U.P. pp. x + 334. £6.75. pb £2.50.
[10] *Sanditon: an Unfinished Novel*, by Jane Austen. Facsimile, ed. by B. C. Southam. O.U.P. pp. xviii + 120. £5.50.

anonymous lady.[11] A brief 'apology' gives an account of the problems involved.

Amongst articles, the December number of *NCF* gathers essays on Jane Austen by distinguished critics: Donald Greene, Martin Price, Valerie Shaw, Francis R. Hart, George Levine, Ruth apRoberts, Walter E. Anderson, K. K. Collins, Mark Kinkead-Weekes, and Andrew Wright. The collection begins with a burlesque ballad from Jane Austen's autograph. Eric Rothstein suggests in 'The Lessons of *Northanger Abbey*' (*UTQ*, 1974) that its strengths are under-estimated; it has a 'controlled restlessness of narrative modes' that is both eighteenth-century and modern. Grete Ek's 'Mistaken Conduct and Proper "Feeling": a Study of *Pride and Prejudice*'[12] is a sensible assessment of the positive values that exist beneath the visible conflicts and antitheses. Marian E. Fowler considers 'The Courtesy-book Heroine of *Mansfield Park*' (*UTQ*, 1974) in the context of its Evangelical age. Joel C. Weinsheimer writes 'In Praise of Mr. Woodhouse: Duty and Desire in *Emma*' (*ArielE*), because Emma's father embodies polar values, order and stability; and in 'The Closure of *Emma*' (*SEL*), John Hagan reassesses the proposal scene and some following chapters to stress the way Jane Austen avoids allegory or fable. Carole Borger's 'The Rake and the Reader in Jane Austen's Novels' (*SEL*) deals with 'deceptive portrayals of her rake figures', which test the moral acuteness of readers as well as the heroines.

A nineteenth-century author who despised the lengthy three-volume format, had read Machiavelli, and mastered the genre of imaginary autobiography (though he liked to base his fiction on cynically observed fact) is more than likely to appeal today. John Galt's *The Member*,[13] now efficiently edited by Ian A. Gordon, has not been reprinted since its first appearance in 1832, the 'first political novel in English', directed at Parliament and the mechanism of government in the years before the first Reform Bill laid its axe 'to the root of the British Oak'. Norma Leigh Rudinsky produces 'A Second Original of Peacock's Menippean Caricature Asterias in *Nightmare Abbey*: Sir John Sinclair, Bart.' (*ES*). Cf. *N&Q* (Feb.), where P. D. de Montfort is cited. *HSL* has two articles that demonstrate Freudian psychological approaches in action: 'Frankenstein's Dream: the Child as Father of the Monster', by Gerhard Joseph, and 'The Monster was a Lady: on the Psychology of Mary Shelley's *Frankenstein*', by Gordon D. Hirsch. Richard J. Dunn considers 'Narrative Distance in *Frankenstein*' (*SNNTS*, 1974).

R. C. Churchill presents 'a mini-anthology as well as a bibliography' of Dickensian Criticism 1836–1975.[14] It contains sections on general criticism, criticism of single works, aspects of Dickens (development, characters, childhood, etc.), and critical comparisons with a number of authors. *The*

---

[11] *Sanditon*, by Jane Austen and Another Lady. Peter Davies. pp. v + 329. £3.50.
[12] Offprint from *Fair Forms: Essays in English Literature from Spenser to Jane Austen*, ed. by Maren-Sofie Røstvig. Cambridge: D. S. Brewer.
[13] *The Member: an Autobiography*, by John Galt, ed. by Ian A. Gordon. Scottish Academic P. (Association for Scottish Literary Studies no. 5). pp. xiii + 128. £2.50.
[14] *A Bibliography of Dickensian Criticism 1836–1975*, by R. C. Churchill. Macmillan (Garland Reference Library of the Humanities Vol. 12). pp. xiv + 314. £15

Dickensian contains so many notes and articles that I am forced to select just a few: Robin Gilmour's 'Memory in *David Copperfield*', Sylvia Manning's 'Dickens, January, and May', Harvey Peter Sucksmith's 'The Melodramatic Villain in *Little Dorrit*', Kathleen Woodward's 'Passivity and Passion in *Little Dorrit*', and Paul Schlicke's 'Bumble and the Poor Law Satire of *Oliver Twist*'.

NCF has Samuel M. Sipe's 'The Intentional World of Dickens's Fiction', which tackles efficiently the problems raised by his various metaphors of transformation, and James E. Marlow's 'Memory, Romance, and the Expressive Symbol in Dickens', which uses Hazlitt's 'precious link that connects together the finer essence of our past and future being' to illuminate an important aspect of Dickens's art. Amongst other general articles Patricia Marks writes briefly on 'O. Henry and Dickens' (*ELN*, 1974) and E. W. F. Tomlin on 'Dickens, Macready and George Sand: a Note' (*EA*). Michael Steig contributes 'A Chapter of Noses: George Cruikshank's Psychonography of the Nose' to *Criticism*. In *SNNTS*, 1974, G. W. Kennedy notes the variety of 'Dickens's Endings', Harry P. Marten compares 'The Visual Imaginations of Dickens and Hogarth: Structure and Scene', and Barry Westburg writes on ' "His Allegorical Way of Expressing It": Civil War and Psychic Conflict in *Oliver Twist* and *A Child's History*'.

As usual there are a number of essays on individual novels. Thomas Jackson Rice writes on 'The End of Dickens's Apprenticeship: Variable Focus in *Barnaby Rudge*' (*NCF*), praising the coherence and ingenuity he is able to find. Branwen Bailey Pratt discusses 'Dickens and Freedom: Young Bailey in *Martin Chuzzlewit*' (*NCF*) and concludes that this descendant of Sam Weller is 'a comic emanation of the life-force' Dickens could never deny. In 'The Broken Glass: Vision and Comprehension in *Bleak House*' (*NCF*), Ian Ousby shows the many Todgers-eye views available. Only Inspector Bucket can manage the 'confused and variegated spectacle of the city'. Dorothy Parker has a note on 'Allegory and the Extension of Mr. Bucket's Forefinger' (*ELN*, 1974), a tag gesture that develops precise allegorical significance at one point but which varies in significance otherwise. In 'The Case of Mr. Jaggers' (*EIC*), A. F. Dilnot makes a case for him.

Angus Easson is careful not to claim too much for 'John Chivery and the Wounded Strephon: a Pastoral Element in *Little Dorrit*' (*DUJ*), but shows successfully how pastoral terms are used to reduce Chivery's 'emotional seriousness (though not his sincerity)' as a suitor for Amy. William Burgan also writes well on 'Little Dorrit in Italy' (*NCF*) with reference to Dickens's earlier travel accounts and the impact of a radically different culture. He notes the 'emotional rhythm of wonder and disenchantment that belong to the total conception of the novel'. Jennifer Gribble treats 'Depth and Surface in *Our Mutual Friend*' (*EIC*), focusing on identity and behaviour problems, especially in Eugene Wrayburn and the Lammles. Lawrence J. Dessner attempts in '*Great Expectations*: the Tragic Comedy of John Wemmick' (*ArielE*), to show that he is 'the novel's most deeply imagined victim'. Elliot L. Gilbert takes Dickens as primarily 'a metaphysical novelist' in 'The Ceremony of Innocence: *A Christmas Carol*' (*PMLA*); Scrooge becomes the master of time and his true self is able to emerge.

Peter L. Shillingsburg's contributors to a supplementary volume of

Costerus[15] engage in fundamental research on Thackeray. Robert A. Colby and John Sutherland provide a preliminary census of his manuscripts, Gerald C. Sorensen discusses the problems of a definitive edition, Joan Stevens and Patricia R. Sweeney investigate his illustrations; Jane Millgate studies 'History *Versus* Fiction: Thackeray's Response to Macaulay', Anthony Burton his collaboration with other artists, Edgar F. Harden 'The Growth of *The Virginians* as a Serial Novel', and so on. This year also sees several general essays. The Victorian cult of the oriental is exemplified by Rida Hawari's detailed study of 'Thackeray's Oriental Reading' (*RLC*, 1974). In 'Thackeray and Marriage' (*EIC*) Laurence Lerner notes the many complications: Thackeray is as sentimental as cynical, the *mariage de convenance* is not simply condemned, etc. In a final section, Lerner distinguishes between personal, literary, and social forces. K. C. Phillipps demonstrates the witty aspects of 'Thackeray's Proper Names' (*NM*, 1974), some of which are not too obvious—e.g., Becky Sharp's descent from the Entrechats of Gascony. Dennis Douglas deals with 'Thackeray and the Uses of History' (*YES*), showing that his historical learning was not impeccable. Douglas also analyses his views of historical fiction, its manners, and morality.

Robin Ann Sheets suggests in 'Art and Artistry in Vanity Fair' (*ELH*) that the role of the novelist as historian and moralist collapses. In 'Narrative Ambivalence and Comic Form' (*TSL*), Bruce K. Martin argues for a 'Not proven' verdict: Becky Sharp's guilt is raised but never finally resolved. John K. Mathison's essay on 'The German Sections of *Vanity Fair*'[16] is now reprinted in his memory with several other pieces by him (on the Immortality Ode, Hopkins's poetic theory, *Northanger Abbey*, and *Wuthering Heights*). David Parker suggests that 'Thackeray's *Barry Lyndon*' (*ArielE*) was a failure because its author could not 'satisfy both art and ethics' in the form he adopted from rogue literature. Elaine Scarry's study of *Henry Esmond*[17] has not been seen (rev. K. J. Fielding, *YES*, 1977). Robert E. Lougy writes on 'Vision and Satire: the Warped Looking Glass in *Vanity Fair*' (*PMLA*), claiming that the novel changed and grew away from simple satire toward a strained version of pastoral.

R. W. Stewart's *Disraeli's Novels Reviewed*[18] provides a large selection of comments on them from 1826, when *Vivian Grey* was criticised in the *New Monthly Magazine*, to 1968. Donald Sultana uses unpublished material in his monograph[19] on Disraeli's Eastern journey in 1830–31. He makes a

[15] *Costerus: Essays in English and American Lang. and Lit.*, N.S., v.II. *Thackeray*, ed. Peter L. Shillingsburg. Amsterdam: Rodopi N.V.; Columbia S.C.: J. Faust. pp. 359. pb Hfl 60, $25.

[16] *The German Sections of 'Vanity Fair' and Other Studies*, by John K. Mathison, ed. by Richard L. Hillier. Laramie, Wyoming: Department of English, U. of Wyoming. pp. xiii + 86. pb, n.p.

[17] *Literary Monographs, Volume 7: Thackeray, Hawthorne and Melville, and Dreiser*, ed. by Eric Rothstein and Joseph Anthony Wittreich Jr. Madison, Wisconsin and London: U. of Wisconsin P. pp. viii + 164. $13.75.

[18] *Disraeli's Novels Reviewed, 1826-1968*, ed. by R. W. Stewart. Metuchen, N.J.: Scarecrow P. pp. 291. $10.

[19] *Benjamin Disraeli in Spain and Malta: a Monograph*, by Donald Sultana. Salzburg Studies in English Literature: Romantic Reassessment 51, ed. by James Hogg U. Salzburg. pp. xvi + 101. pb.

point of relating details to Disraeli's novels and elucidates many obscure allusions. This is a careful piece of work, designed to supplement standard works. I do not think *Disraeli's Reminiscences*,[20] edited by Helen M. and Marvin Swartz, will be as useful. Disraeli wrote them in the 1860s and they are now printed from the manuscript with a brief introduction. No real attempt is made to annotate, on the grounds that the scholar will not need nor the general reader want such help. It is a pity, too, that they do not follow up their interesting comment that Disraeli wrote down these stories to put the past into 'the perspective from which he wanted it to be viewed'. Such criticism is much more developed in Sultana's monograph. His view that Disraeli's later novels were subordinate to politics finds support in an article, 'The Treatment of Rural Distress in Disraeli's *Sybil*' (*YES*). Here Martin Fido stresses the way in which Disraeli subdued its importance for political reasons. The description of Marney, though fairly drawn from Blue Books, 'is easily admired and soon forgotten'.

Terry Eagleton's *Myths of Power*[21] is a relatively short book. The four novels of Charlotte and *Wuthering Heights* receive a chapter apiece, and there is one chapter on the two novels of Anne. Two other sections are more general, 'Categorical structure', 'epiphenomenon', 'over-determination', etc. prove the justice of the sub-title, 'A Marxist Study of the Brontës'. A major claim is that *Wuthering Heights* mediates the ambiguities of the Brontë girls' social position more successfully than Charlotte's works. I have not been able to see F. B. Pinion's *A Brontë Companion* (Macmillan).

BST prints for the first time Charlotte Brontë's sarcastic reply to E. Rigby's hostile review of *Jane Eyre*; it also includes Rachel Trickett's '*Wuthering Heights*: the Story of a Haunting' in a material world (a poetic vision deliberately fitted to 'the context of verisimilitude'), Ruth H. Blackburn's study of '*Thornycroft Hall*: a Rebuttal to *Jane Eyre*' by Emma Jane Warboise, Brett Harrison's 'The Real "Miss Temple" ' (Ann Evans), and a number of other items. Thomas A. Langford discusses 'Prophetic Imagination and the Unity of *Jane Eyre*' (*SNNTS*, 1974).

Emily Brontë's work is treated in Walter L. Reed's *Meditations on the Hero: a Study of the Romantic Hero in Nineteenth-Century Fiction* (Yale U P, 1974), which I have not seen. *EA* reviews Jean-Pierre Petit, *L 'Œuvre d'Emily Brontë: la vision et les thèmes* (Clermont-Ferrand thesis). Jacqueline Viswanathan compares 'Point of View and Unreliability in *Wuthering Heights*, *Under Western Eyes* and *Doktor Faustus*' (*OL*, 1974): all three novels create a world deeply torn asunder' and the reader cannot reject any one side completely, she concludes. Jacques Blondel investigates Imagery in *Wuthering Heights*' (*DUJ*), along lines suggested by theorists like Mark Schorer and G. Bachelard (cp. *YW* 50.319). In *English* John Beversluis re examines the metaphysical relationship of Catherine to Heathcliff. His 'Love and Self-knowledge: a Study of *Wuthering Heights*' underlines the merely dramatic and contingent aspects of the 'I am Heathcliff' passage. Peter D. Grudin discusses '*Wuthering Heights*: the Question

[20] *Disraeli's Reminiscences*, ed. by Helen M. Swartz and Marvin Swartz. Hamish Hamilton. pp. xxv + 166. £5.95.
[21] *Myths of Power: a Marxist Study of the Brontës*, by Terry Eagleton. Macmillan. p. ix + 148. £6.95.

of Unquiet Slumbers' (*SNNTS*, 1974).

In '*Griffith Gaunt*: Paradox of Victorian Melodrama', Arthur Pollard argues strongly in favour of a neglected novelist, Charles Reade, 'direct, simple, sometimes even crude, but also sharp, powerful, and at his best impressively memorable.' Another minor novelist, Charles Kingsley, is written about in an undemanding, readable way by Brenda Colloms.[22] Hayden W. Ward writes on '*Treasure Island* and the Appeal of Boys' Adventure Fiction' for *SNNTS*, 1974.

W. A. Craik undertakes a strictly limited task in *Elizabeth Gaskell and the English Provincial Novel*,[23] to compare five major works of fiction by Mrs. Gaskell with a selection of works by the Brontës, Trollope (especially), George Eliot and Hardy—all of whom, she claims, did not take London or the London audience as a norm. At the level of literary technique Mrs. Craik makes many sensitive, illuminating points, but this is all. It is truly remarkable that she can ignore the existing state of Gaskell criticism, though Mrs. Gaskell herself set something of a precedent in her preface to the first edition of *Mary Barton* when she naïvely disclaimed any concern with that dismal Victorian science of Political Economy. Coral Lansbury's concerns in *Elizabeth Gaskell: the Novel of Social Crisis*[24] are succinctly indicated in her preface: social change and class struggles, women and the family, and psychological realism. These themes are traced in the novels (and also in *The Life of Charlotte Brontë*) but remain, I think disconnected and arbitrarily introduced. The discussions can be sharply unusual: 'Cranford brims over with life and humour, while the sun cities of California and Florida creak with a grotesque vitality that is more terrifying than death'. Some are less plausible, however, and will not command ready assent.

The benefits of reading Elizabeth Gaskell are very obvious in John Lucas's side of ' "Engels, Manchester and the Working Class": a Discussion' (*VS*) with Standish Meacham. His quotations from *North and South* clearly prove certain deficiencies in Engels's knowledge of Manchester; more examples could be found. Meacham concentrates on the psychoanalytical aspects of Stephen Marcus's book (*YW* 55.382), smartly dismissed by Lucas. In 'The Writer as Reader in *Mary Barton*' (*DUJ*, 1974), Michael D. Wheeler examines Elizabeth Gaskell's imaginative response to poems by Caroline Bowles and Caroline Norton and to Elizabeth Stone's *The Young Milliner* (1843). He concentrates on the way in which she develops borrowed material. Harvey Peter Sucksmith writes succinctly on the probable connexion between '*Mary Barton* and William Mudford's *The Iron Shroud*' (*NCF*). A. J. Shelston makes it very clear that '*Ruth*: Mrs. Gaskell's Neglected Novel' (*BJRL*) is seriously flawed, but he also shows that it can survive reductive analysis. In particular, the Ruth-Bellingham relationship is more powerfully imagined than her moral thesis can really allow.

[22] *Charles Kingsley: the Lion of Eversley*, by Brenda Colloms. Constable; New York: Barnes & Noble. pp. 400. £5.
[23] *Elizabeth Gaskell and the English Provincial Novel*, by W. A. Craik. Methuen pp. xii + 277. £6.25. pb £2.90.
[24] *Elizabeth Gaskell: the Novel of Social Crisis*, by Coral Lansbury. Paul Elek (Novelists and Their World Series, ed. G. Hough). pp. 230. £5.95.

In 'Trollope, Balzac, and the Reappearing Character' (*EIC*), Stephen Wall notes that his habit of living with his characters gave him an instinctive bias towards reappearance, though it was hardly 'as organic a principle' as it was with Balzac. He 'proceeds empirically', without Balzac's 'glittering expository eye' for the laws of social life. Mary Hamer's 'Number-length and its Significance in the Novels of Trollope' (*YES*) contends that he often wrote novels in serial form as a mere discipline and that its significance is more than just numerical. Andrew Wright's 'Anthony Trollope as a Reader' (in *Two English Novelists*, W. A. Clark Memorial Library Papers, Los Angeles) contains some unusual and fascinating material. Wright contends that for Trollope both reading and writing were means of making the world be discovered in his youth more endurable. Patrick Waddington documents 'Turgenev and Trollope: Brief Crossings of Paths' (*AUMLA*, 1974). G. M. Harvey writes on 'Trollope's Serial Craft in *The Claverings*' (*WascanaR*). In 'Bulwer-Lytton and the Rhetorical Design of Trollope's *Orley Farm*' (*ArielE*), G. M. Harvey maintains that the novel owes a great deal to Bulwer's theorizing. Analysis shows 'its multiple perspectives of sympathy and irony'.

William Baker's *George Eliot and Judaism*[25] documents the origin and development of her Jewish interests as they appear in her creative work. His source study is apparently exhaustive: newspapers, annotated copies, Pforzheimer notebooks, Josephus, Spinoza, Heine, etc. are all considered. In later chapters Baker analyses the fiction with meticulous care, giving full reference to scholarly research. *Daniel Deronda* especially is placed in its extended historical, literary, and biographical context. See also Hans Mayer, *Aussenseiter* (Frankfurt: Suhrkamp). Barbara Smalley's *George Eliot and Flaubert*[26] is meticulous, and slightly repetitious too. Her thesis is that Eliot and Flaubert are 'pioneers of modern narrative emphases' as novelists of the inner life; both had a disturbed awareness of instability and counterpointed 'inner vision and discordant outer reality in a distinctive manner'; for both the 'drama of incommunicability' was a fresh and urgent theme. Such similarities (and the even more important differences) are worked out in detail, with Henry James being used as a frequent touchstone.

NCF contains ' "Sympathetic Criticism": George Eliot's Response to Contemporary Reviewing', by James D. Benson, and 'George Eliot's Projected Napoleonic War Novel: an Unnoted Reading List', by William Baker. Baker suggests that law reform, military developments, Irish religious freedom, and depressed populations would have been some of the issues treated. William Baker also contributes ' "A Problematical Thinker" to a "Sagacious Philosopher": Some Unpublished George Henry Lewes–Herbert Spencer Correspondence' to *ES*: and in *ELN* publishes a letter from J. W. Cross to Spencer describing George Eliot's unexpected death the night before. Alain Jumeau surveys 'Les romans de George Eliot: genèse d'une tradition critique' for *EA*.

[25] *George Eliot and Judaism*, by William Baker. Salzburg Studies in English Literature: Romantic Reassessment 45. U. Salzburg. pp. iii + 270.
[26] *George Eliot and Flaubert: Pioneers of the Modern Novel*, by Barbara Smalley. Athens: Ohio U.P., 1974. pp. ix + 240. $10.

In 'The Structure of Realisms in *Adam Bede*' (*NCF*), Ian Adam provides a very clear analysis and demonstration of their natures and coherence. Nina Auerbach's 'The Power of Hunger: Demonism and Maggie Tulliver' (*NCF*) takes a new line in finding both Gothic and Paterian intensity in *The Mill on the Floss*; it is well supported. In 'Preachers and the Schemes of Nature in *Adam Bede*' (*NCF*), Christopher Herbert outlines its dialectical method, the way in which Dinah Morris and Mr Irwine embody a division in George Eliot with regard to Nature. Critics of *Middlemarch* continue to provide us with a truly liberal education: in *NCF* Robert A. Greenberg recovers the contexts and explains the relevance of 'Plexuses and Ganglia: Scientific Allusion in *Middlemarch*'. Also, U. C. Knoepflmacher contributes '*Middlemarch*: an Avuncular View', in which Arthur Brooke and other kin are shown to stand for a society without purposeful vision despite its revival of avuncular stereotypes. K. M. Newton extends the search for 'Historical Prototypes in *Middlemarch*' (*ES*) to historical figures, especially Dorothea Schlegel, who ardently left her first husband for a penniless literary man and extreme aesthete who later devoted himself to journalism and politics. Feminine pragmatists turn romantic men into activists. Anthony G. Bradley writes usefully on 'Family as Pastoral: the Garths in *Middlemarch*' (*ArielE*), finding them inadequate as a moral standard. Linda Bamber discovers 'Self-defeating Politics in *Felix Holt*' (*VS*), and Constance Marie Fulmer discusses 'Contrasting Pairs of Heroines in George Eliot's Fiction' (*SNNTS*, 1974).

A facsimile of G. H. Lewes's *Ranthorpe* (1847)[27] is published with a long introduction by Barbara Smalley. It is 'a strangely schizoid work of fiction that combines romance and psychological realism, melodrama and minute analysis', admired by both Poe and Charlotte Brontë. Lewes's awkward attempts to treat the dangers of rôle-playing with psychological realism are compared in detail with George Eliot's more assured treatment of Rosamond Vincy and Gwendolen Harleth, though there is admittedly no proof that Marian Evans ever read *Ranthorpe*. In *E&S*, A. Norman Jeffares recommends the underestimated *Lord Kilgobbin* (1872), Charles Lever's coldly analytical 'portrayal of a country torn with unrest'.

Adam John Bisanz carefully discusses 'Samuel Butler: a Literary Venture into Atheism and Beyond' (*OL*, 1974) against 'pragmatism' from Voltaire and Gibbon to William James. Hans-Peter Breuer's 'Samuel Butler and George Frederick Handel' (*DR*) is a very clear analysis of Butler's preference for the 'direct, transparent, effortless' music of Handel in contrast to the riotous harmony and modulation of his own time. In 'Butler's Metaphorical Man' (*AUMLA*, 1974), R. A. Copland contends that 'his evolutionary thought was largely an exercise of the sympathetic imagination' and his writing full of serious conceits. F. M. Turner's *Between Science and Religion: the Reactions to Scientific Naturalism in late Victorian England* (Yale U.P., 1974) includes a study of Samuel Butler. John Lucas briefly introduces W. H. Mallock's *The New Republic*,[28] a

---

[27] *Ranthorpe*, by George Henry Lewes, ed. by Barbara Smalley. Athens: Ohio U.P., 1974. pp. lvii + viii + 369. $12.
[28] *The New Republic: Culture, Faith and Philosophy in an English Country House*, by W. H. Mallock, intro. by John Lucas. Leicester U.P. (The Victorian Library). pp. 47 + 368 + 32. £4.80.

facsimile of the 1879 edition. He discusses the possible originals of Mallock's characters. Edmund Miller writes on 'Lewis Carroll's Genealogical Oversight in *The Tangled Tale*' (*ELN*, 1974). *NCF* reviews a book I missed last year: Kathleen Blake, *Play, Games, and Sport: the Literary Works of Lewis Carroll* (Ithaca: Cornell U.P., 1974).

Lennart A. Björk brings out the first volume (in two parts: text, notes) of Hardy's *Literary Notes*.[29] A second volume, with analytical index, is to come. This will be a definitive edition of notes that 'cover all but the first few years of his career as a novelist' and appear to be a special selection of the many passages that Hardy transcribed from books, etc. Introduction, apparatus, etc. are meticulous. Björk provides compact summaries of Hardy's reading and in particular he identifies Hardy's reading of imaginative literature, notably foreign. (Cf. the more aesthetic notebook of 1867 printed in an appendix). Timothy O'Sullivan's well illustrated biography of Hardy[30] has a pleasantly straightforward text, though a final note mentions that R. Gittings's *Young Thomas Hardy* (Heinemann) appeared whilst the more popular book was in the press.

Students have much to be grateful for this year. A very useful Casebook[31] on Hardy's later novels is prepared and introduced by R. P. Draper. He stresses the value of critical disagreement and qualification yet ensures that beginners will not be lost in a fog as a result. Hardy novels are appearing in a new paperback edition.[32] The two examples seen have excellent introductions, critical comments on Hardy's revisions, explanatory notes, and other material of value to the student. Other editors of individual volumes are John Bayley, Robert Gittings, Ian Gregor, and J. Hillis Miller. It seems a series well worth possessing. Laurence Lerner's short study of *The Mayor of Casterbridge*[33] is notable for its clear, efficient, and discriminating criticism. Professor Lerner also illuminates several literary contexts, which include Shakespearian models as well as R. Jefferies's *Amaryllis at the Fair* and Zola's *La terre*.

Linda C. Dowling writes interestingly on 'Pursuing Antithesis: Lionel Johnson on Hardy' (*ELN*). Lawrence Jones carefully defines and documents the nature of 'Thomas Hardy's "Idiosyncratic Mode of Regard"' (*ELH*), strongly personal, multiple, and shifting in its perspectives. Its implications for our study of his characterization, action, techniques, and development are outlined. Carole Gerson compiles 'Canada's Response to Hardy: a Look at Nineteenth-Century Literary Attitudes' for *DR*. Leslie H. Palmer discusses the increasing importance of 'The Ironic Word

---

[29] *The Literary Notes of Thomas Hardy*, ed. by Lennart A. Björk, vol. 1. Göteborg: Acta U. Gothoburgensis (Studies in English 29), 1974. pp. xl + xviii + 479. Skr 97.75.

[30] *Thomas Hardy: an Illustrated Biography*, by Timothy O'Sullivan. Macmillan. pp. 192. £6.50.

[31] *Hardy, the Tragic Novels: The Return of the Native, The Mayor of Casterbridge, Tess of the d'Urbervilles, Jude the Obscure*, a Casebook ed. by R. P. Draper. Macmillan. pp. 256. £3.75. pb £1.75.

[32] The New Wessex Edition, gen. ed. by P. N. Furbank. *The Woodlanders*, by Thomas Hardy; intro. by David Lodge. Macmillan, 1974. pp. 416. pb 75p. *A Laodicean*, by Thomas Hardy; intro. by Barbara Hardy, notes by Ernest Hardy. Macmillan. pp. 459. pb 75p.

[33] *Thomas Hardy's The Mayor of Casterbridge: Tragedy or Social History?*, by Laurence Lerner. Sussex U.P. (Text and Context series). pp. 110. £2.50. pb £1.50.

in Hardy's Novels' (*TSL*). In ' "Past Things Retold"': a Study of *Under the Greenwood Tree* and *The Trumpet-Major*' (*DUJ*), Peter Collister looks at two of Hardy's lesser novels, important as 'a real means of escape' from the tragic complexities of life. Mary Jacobus studies 'Sue the Obscure' (*EIC*), setting Sue's theories beside Mill's in *On Liberty* but also noticing her 'split between belief and instinctive behaviour'. If Jude shows the gap between real and ideal, Hardy 'probes the relationship between character and ideas' in a tremendously suggestive way through Sue's obscurity. Peter Morton's '*Tess*: a Neo-Darwinian Reading' (*SoRA*, 1974) is the subject of a critical exchange in the current issue: J. R. Ebbatson seeks to modify what he considers too deterministic an interpretation. Tobey C. Herzog describes 'The Grand [Triangular] Design of Hardy's Major Novels' (*SNNTS*, 1974). Hardy, it would seem, is still attracting a good deal of attention.

Robert S. Baker writes on '*The Ordeal of Richard Feverel*: a Psychological Approach' (*SNNTS*, 1974); its structure, he claims, is inseparable from the development of Richard. In 'Richard Feverel and the Fictional Lineage of Desire' (*ELH*), Christopher Morris concentrates on the way in which language, the mediator or even creator of man's wishes, '*inevitably* dislocates man', who acts on 'fictions presumed to be real'. In 'Portraits of Ladies' (*TSL*), Anna S. Parrill praises Meredith's characterization of Clare Middleton and compares it with Henry James's *Portrait of a Lady*.

Michael Collie's bibliography of Gissing[34] lists all the books published in his lifetime and the first appearances of posthumous works. He has attempted to establish the best texts, since 'reissues have invariably been of the unrevised texts'. Even the photographic reprints by the Harvester Press and by AMS are not in his opinion satisfactory. Collie does not include serial publications or private printings. The introduction outlines Gissing's domestic life and his relations with publishers—he was blatantly exploited, Collie claims. Apart from this, a good deal of information about manuscripts, publication, etc. is given in the notes. Writings about Gissing between 1880 and 1970 have been carefully abstracted by Joseph J. Wolff,[35] who also provides a brief introduction. Adrian Poole's *Gissing in Context* (Macmillan) has not been available. In *Neophilologus* is W. van Mannen's 'George Gissing, Escapist', a general appreciation of his life and works.

'He was a new kind of artist, a new kind of thinker', writes Jack Lindsay enthusiastically in his biography of Morris,[36] 'and despite his roots in Ruskin his sole fellow was Marx.' Even Marx, we are told, lacked Morris's practical and positive approach, whilst Engels suffered from a remote authoritarianism and lack of deep culture that prevented him from understanding Morris's distinctive contributions to Marxist thought. The life itself is read as a patterned development, in particular from childhood

---

[34] *George Gissing: a Bibliography*, by Michael Collie. Dawson; U. of Toronto P. pp. xiv + 129. £7.50.

[35] *George Gissing: an Annotated Bibliography of Writings About Him*, compiled and ed. by Joseph J. Wolff. De Kalb, Ill.: Northern Ill. U.P., 1974. (*ELT* Annotated Secondary Bibliography Series). pp. x + 293. $17.50.

[36] *William Morris: his Life and Work*, by Jack Lindsay. Constable. pp. xi + 432. £7.50.

dreams of an earthly paradise to their 'fully socialised' forms in Morris's last works. This is a clear, detailed, and definite biography, written with particular values and assumptions about 'reality', 'the laws inside all art-activity', etc. In '*News from Nowhere*: Morris's Socialist Anti-Novel' (*VS*), Patrick Brantlinger rather lengthily underlines its obvious differences from ordinary Victorian novels. He takes issue with Lionel Trilling's article, 'Aggression and Utopia, a Note on *News from Nowhere*' (in the 1973 *Psychoanalytic Quarterly*), claiming that Morris's art reflects the decline of liberal individualism and that his thinking anticipates Marcuse on 'surplus repression'.

EA summarizes J. Ben Guigui, *Israel Zangwill, penseur et écrivain, 1864–1926* (Toulouse thesis). Daniel Farson's popular biography of Bram Stoker[37] contains some new biographical information and includes a brief section on Vampirism in Literature. Farson refers to an American *Annotated Dracula*, by Leonard Wolf, which I have not seen. Nor have Kingsley Amis, *Rudyard Kipling and His World* (Thames & Hudson) and I. S. Saponsink, *R. L. Stevenson* (Twayne, 1974) been available.

5. Selected Prose Writers

(a) General

In *The Rural Tradition*[38] W. J. Keith surveys 'more sustained and artistically successful presentations of rural life' from Izaak Walton on. He begins with an account of conflicts between true and false, realistic and sentimental, etc. There follow separate chapters on a number of rural writers who seem to form a loosely knit tradition. Keith examines such topics as Cobbett's politics, Borrow's artistic subtleties, and the Janus-like aspects of Jefferies (whose 'sun-life' anticipates D. H. Lawrence and Llewelyn Powys) with clarity and ease.

(b) Individual authors

Mary Wollstonecraft's *Vindication of the Rights of Woman*[39] is helpfully annotated by Carol H. Poston. The second London edition of 1792 is the copy-text, with significant variants noted. Sections on Backgrounds and Criticism are relatively slight, but there is a selected bibliography and reference to a checklist in the *Mary Wollstonecraft Newsletter* (now *Women in Literature*) for April 1973.

The first volume of the definitive edition of the letters of Charles and Mary Lamb[40] is extensively annotated. In a full introduction Edwin W.

---

[37] *The Man who wrote 'Dracula': a Biography of Bram Stoker*, by Daniel Farson. Michael Joseph. pp. 240. £4.

[38] *The Rural Tradition: William Cobbett, Gilbert White, and Other Non-Fiction Prose Writers of the English Countryside*, by W. J. Keith. Toronto and Buffalo: U. of Toronto P.; Harvester P. pp. xiii + 310. £5.45.

[39] *A Vindication of the Rights of Woman*, by Mary Wollstonecraft. An Authoritative Text, Backgrounds, Criticism, ed. by Carol H. Poston. New York: Norton Critical Edition. pp. ix + 240. $10. pb $2.95.

[40] *The Letters of Charles and Mary Lamb*, ed. by Edwin W. Marrs Jr Vol. 1: Letters of Charles Lamb 1796–1801. Ithaca and London: Cornell U.P. pp. xcv + 293. £15.

Marrs Jr gives an outline biography up to Mary's death in 1847 and a detailed account of the many previous appearances of the letters, though this edition includes a number of unpublished ones. The contents are various and fascinating. All the letters of 1796 and 1797 are to Coleridge; later letters are to Southey, Thomas Manning, William Godwin, and Wordsworth—positively lecturing him on the wonders and joys of *urban* life! Such a clue could hardly have been missed by Fred V. Randel, whose book on *The World of Elia*[41] is a resolutely up-to-date reappraisal. The letter is quoted in the first chapter, where Lamb is seen as an urban, ironic writer who managed to convert his exceptional personal difficulties into 'a cultural paradigm' of the Romantic era. In subsequent chapters Randel discusses Lamb's essays. References to time, space, eating, drinking and playing are subjected to structural analysis, frequent comparisons made with contemporary Romantic poets and essayists back to Montaigne.

Stanley Jones identifies 'Hazlitt's Mysterious Friend Bell: a Businessman Amateur of Letters' (*EA*). Colin J. Horne supplies a useful note, 'Hazlitt on Swift' (*EIC*). Harold Love describes 'An Early Version of Margaret Hazlitt's Journal' (*AUMLA*; v. *YW* 49.262).

In 'The Anapestic Triad: a Structural Paradigm in De Quincey's Imaginative Prose' (*EA*), Michael E. Holstein investigates critical infrastructures, ranging from intentions made explicit to the unconscious pattern of two parallel elements followed by a more important one, a means of transcendence. Memory and reflexion lead to vision. John W. Bilsland places central episodes of 'De Quincey's Opium Experiences' (*DR*) in the context of his life.

Ian Campbell provides a useful short biography and literary study of Carlyle[42] based upon the latest scholarship, to which he himself has contributed. He is often refreshingly definite: Carlyle's spiritual rebirth, for example, is attributed to a selective recalling of his father's powerful influence rather than to his reading of German philosophers. Campbell handles standard material with some skill and assesses previous work on Carlyle. A special chapter is devoted to the principal ideas and their development. In ' "Swim or Drown"': Carlyle's World of Shipwrecks, Castaways, and Stranded Voyagers' (*SEL*), George P. Landow investigates Carlyle's extensive use of an image of major crisis, itself treated more generally by Landow in *RLC*, 1972. In 'Victorian Scientific Naturalism and Carlyle' (*VS*), Frank M. Turner shows how he eased the transition from religious to secular views of life despite his anti-rationalism. Agnosticism, the work ethic, moral aspirations, even a kind of anima mundi were all part of Carlyle's legacy.

Sidney Coulling's *Matthew Arnold and His Critics*[43] (rev. J. Holloway, *TLS*, 8 Aug.) is undoubtedly useful. Arnold is placed firmly in his many contexts. Coulling carefully summarizes Arnold's arguments, quotes aptly

---

[41] *The World of Elia: Charles Lamb's Essayistic Romanticism*, by Fred V. Randel. Port Washington, New York; London: Kennikat P.; Bailey Bros & Swinfen. pp. xii + 170. £10. $9.95.
[42] *Thomas Carlyle*, by Ian Campbell. Hamish Hamilton, 1974. pp. xiv + 210. £4.25.
[43] *Matthew Arnold and His Critics: a Study of Arnold's Controversies*, by Sidney Coulling. Athens: Ohio U.P., 1974. pp. xiv + 351. $10.

from his private letters, and gives the replies of opponents like F. W. Newman; James Spedding on translating Homer is followed by a précis of H. A. J. Munro's answer, and so on to Ichabod Wright! The value of Arnold as a controversialist is variable. In one place Coulling finds him 'at least partially disingenuous', but ultimately he is thought to be consistent enough and, 'to use his own favourite term, the most adequate of all the Victorians.' Joseph O. Baylen writes on 'Arnold, R. R. W. Lingen and Gladstone: an Episode in the Career of Matthew Arnold (1883)' (*EA*). In 'Wordsworth, Pater and the "Anima Mundi": towards a Critique of Romanticism' (*Criticism*), Sharon Bassett analyses the value of Wordsworth's wise passiveness for the later critic and historian of art. Eric Glasgow's *Walter Pater and Greece*[44] is a slight, general essay. Van Akin Burd contributes 'A Week at Winnington: Two New Ruskin Letters of 1864' (*ELN*, 1974).

[44] *Walter Pater and Greece*, by Eric Glasgow. In *Salzburg Studies in English Literature: Romantic Reassessment* 47, ed. James Hogg. U. Salzburg. pp. ii + 108. $12.50. pb.

XIV

The Twentieth Century

MAUREEN MORAN, SUSAN PAINTER and
JAMES REDMOND

The chapter has the following sections: 1. The Novel, by Maureen Moran;
2. Verse by Susan Painter; 3. Drama, by James Redmond.

1. The Novel

This year has been an important one for students of Joyce, D. H.
Lawrence and Orwell and one can also detect an increasing critical interest
in the work of women novelists such as Margaret Drabble and Doris
Lessing. Some excellent general studies contribute to our understanding of
the modern novel, and there are interesting examinations of the little
magazines.

(a) *General studies*
        In *Fable's End: Completeness and Closure in Rhetorical Fiction*[1] David
H. Richter attempts to establish the relationship of theme, argument, and
conclusion in a particular literary genre. He defines rhetorical novels as
those which seek 'the inculcation of some doctrine or sentiment concerning the world external to the fiction', and sets out to trace the ways in
which such fiction has developed with specific attention to the means by
which various authors supply a sense of ending. Distinguishing between the
notion of a simple closing and that of a satisfying and significant completion of the thesis of the work, Richter views the eighteenth-century
rhetorical novel (*Rasselas* and *Candide*) as limited in emotional intensity.
More interesting, however, are Richter's conclusions concerning the
development of new techniques of characterization in the modern novel.
He presents a strong case for viewing *The Lord of the Flies* as an important
attempt to allow the reader to *experience* ending and thus feel the significance of the fable itself. Camus's use of the same representational techniques
to convey an unusual philosophic stance is clearly documented, as is
Pynchon's failure to present a coherent thesis with emotional conviction in
his complex novel *V*. The study concludes with an eloquent defence of
Heller's *Catch-22* as the peak to which rhetorical fiction is tending.
Richter's general conclusions are less satisfying than the individual analyses.
There is an appendix on Bellow's *Herzog*.

[1] *Fable's End: Completeness and Closure in Rhetorical Fiction*, by David H.
Richter. Chicago and London: U. of Chicago P. 1974. pp. x + 214. £9.

Daniel J. Schneider's *Symbolism: The Manichean Vision*[2] is an examination of the work of Conrad, James, Woolf, and Wallace Stevens with emphasis on each author's development of a symbolic scheme. Schneider argues that symbolism arose initially out of man's attempt to unify mind with a hostile, indifferent natural order; a Manichean hypothesis for existence slowly evolved to account for the essential ambiguities of life. It is through symbolic patterns that these polarities are portrayed and may in fact be synthesized. Connexions viewed as impossible in reality are clarified and projected in symbolism; the artist is thus able 'to integrate his materials without distorting reality—doing violence to its complexity.' When Schneider analyzes particular authors to show how symbolic patterns reveal a 'total vision of life', he examines a limited number of representative works and demonstrates how symbols attain meaning. He is particularly interesting on Conrad and Woolf. Wallace Stevens also struggles to resolve the 'war between mind and fact.' Schneider concentrates heavily on the obscurity of Stevens's symbols and provides a 'catalogue' designed to demonstrate the logical thought underlying the symbolic patterns.

A more vital and wide-ranging study is Colin Wilson's *The Craft of the Novel*.[3] For Wilson the creative urge behind writing a novel is 'the writer's attempt to create a clear *self-image*', and it is this which he explores. After a brief consideration of the history of the novel, Wilson engages in an unusual discussion of the parallels between Saki and D. H. Lawrence. It is not Wilson's purpose to provide a totally disinterested examination of a number of modern novelists. Instead, he wishes to suggest the directions in which the modern novel should be moving. Fiction ought to treat a system of values and should be directed towards teaching man about his own complex world; in this way, it contributes to the production of a 'wide-angle consciousness' for both artist and reader. The novelist proclaims not simply what he is but what he is becoming and provides the broad spectrum of experience necessary to help man perceive his own potential and freedom. It would not be difficult to accuse Wilson of writing his own propaganda; his dismissal of Joyce seems idiosyncratic. But his assessment of the egotistical thrust in twentieth-century fiction as a whole raises many interesting questions. Experimental novels do not maintain the essential tension-release-tension cycle and as a result proclaim no true or stimulating 'vision of existence.' Wilson surveys a number of modern writers including John Braine, Kingsley Amis, Faulkner, Nabokov and Beckett, and emphasizes at all times the need for direction. The discussion of modern fantasy is particularly lively. If the novel does not return to the universal, if it fails to show man what he might become, then it is doomed to extinction.

Two short studies deal in part with a number of modern novels. William Righter's *Myth and Literature*[4] touches on Joyce's use of myth as an ordering and controlling device in *Ulysses*, and, less predictably, uses *To*

---

[2] *Symbolism: The Manichean Vision*, by Daniel J. Schneider. Lincoln. Nebraska: U. of Nebraska P. pp. xii + 235. $10.95.
[3] *The Craft of the Novel* by Colin Wilson. Gollancz. pp. 256. £5.
[4] *Myth and Literature*, by William Righter. Concepts of Literature Series. Routledge. pp. viii + 132. £3.50.

the Lighthouse for an investigation of the ways in which mythological associations are used to develop character. Arguing that it is often ineffective to explain a particular psychological state by reference to a more general abstract quality inherent in a myth, he shows that the myth is both simplified and dissociated from its cultural context. Myth is really a more imaginative analysis of the human condition than such a one-to-one 'translation' would seem to allow. Lawrence's *Plumed Serpent* is an instance of a more useful search for a new myth.

In *The Anatomy of the Novel*,[5] Marjorie Boulton provides a useful overview for the novice. Aside from touching on such considerations as those of plot, character, point of view, and verisimilitude, Miss Boulton also provides succinct analyses of *Hard Times, Silas Marner, The Europeans, Anna of the Five Towns*, and *The Secret Agent*. This is a most elementary introduction, but its clarity and precision together with suggestions for further reading make it a valuable one.

Using Roman Jakobson's distinction between metaphor and metonymy in expression, David Lodge attempts to define modernist English fiction (*CritQ*). In the course of an examination of Joyce, Woolf, and Lawrence as well as Gertrude Stein and Hemingway, he finds that the modernist novel states that 'nothing is simply one thing' and thus that metaphor with its two-directional possibilities is the controlling mode of expression. A similar premise is used by Brian Wicker for a fascinating 'interdisciplinary study'[6] of the rhetoric of fiction. On the one hand, narrative consists of a linear story-line or plot; on the other, it has a vertical depth which relates the fictional to the real world, the teller to his tale, and the events to an underlying 'metaphysical' meaning. Part I of this study is theoretical. Like Lodge, Wicker emphasizes the importance of metaphor in fiction. He also discusses its place in religion, and considers the implications of the banishment of nature in modern fiction. Part II is devoted to an application of these observations. Lawrence and Joyce are both depicted as attempting to cope with the 'unseen presences' in life, and both turn to metaphor in an attempt to resolve their difficulties. However, the gradual disappearance of the narrative voice in the works of Waugh and Beckett points up the disintegration of the relationship between the teller and his tale and also the disappearance of the vertical dimension in fiction. Two possible solutions for the loss of underlying metaphoric meanings are discovered in the works of Mailer and Robbe-Grillet. Whichever path is taken, Wicker feels confident that two great streams of modern narrative fiction may be traced. The one stems from Lawrence who emphasizes the vertical dimension by means of his morally responsible narrator. The other is the horizontal tradition of Joyce whose impersonal narrator distrusts the over-emphasis on immaterial and timeless values.

English contains an amusing article by Cedric Watts on a hitherto unidentified' genre of fiction that of the 'Janiform' novels. Gazing in opposite directions simultaneously, novels such as *Pincher Martin, Brighton*

---

[5] *The Anatomy of the Novel*, by Marjorie Boulton. Routledge & Kegan Paul. pp. x + 189. £3.50.
[6] *The Story-Shaped World: Fiction and Metaphysics: Some Variations on a Theme*, by Brian Wicker U. of London: Athlone P. pp. x + 230. £6.

Rock, and *Heart of Darkness* seem to insist on a moral position which is centrally 'paradoxical or self-contradictory'.

The most thorough investigation of modern women novelists is Sydney Janet Kaplan's *Feminine Consciousness in the Modern British Novel*.[7] The study is a detailed analysis of the ways in which Dorothy M. Richardson, May Sinclair, Virginia Woolf, Rosamond Lehmann, and Doris Lessing organize or structure the consciousnesses of women in their work. Emphasis is placed on the experimental techniques gradually developed, but Miss Kaplan also attempts to account for differences in the over-all view of women. For this reason certain areas of the feminine consciousness are constantly assessed in the works of the various writers: sexuality, women's relationship to nature, the social role of women, and most significantly the ways in which women order their perceptions, think, and ultimately create aesthetically. No startling conclusions are reached; however, Miss Kaplan usefully documents certain inconsistencies in the approach of women themselves. New trends in the feminine search for self and reality are also noted. A new gender is proclaimed, and Virginia Woolf's androgynous consciousness is a case in point.

Lesbian Images[8] is intended to probe images of lesbian women in literature, but Jane Rule is more to the point when she says it is 'a statement of my own attitudes towards lesbian experience as measured against the images made by other women writers in their work and/or lives.' She touches briefly on a number of writers including Radclyffe Hall, Gertrude Stein, Vita Sackville-West, Ivy Compton-Burnett, Elizabeth Bowen, Violette Leduc, Anaïs Nin, Elizabeth Jane Howard, and Louise King. There is little analytical comment; very often plot summary suffices, and the author's tendency to 'type' her subjects does little to further either literary or psychological understanding.

Rosalind Miles's examination of *The Fiction of Sex*[9] is also lacking in rigorous analysis but provides a general overview of the basic themes and techniques of twentieth-century women writers such as Dorothy Richardson, Vita Sackville-West, Virginia Woolf, and Katherine Mansfield. The lure of romance, the threat of neo-pornography, and the New Women are considered. Miss Miles criticizes writers of her sex for a failure to move beyond domestic issues or personal exploration, and she concludes, should women novelists continue in this, they will perpetuate the stereotypes which already exist.

Other general studies include several thematic explorations of twentieth-century fiction. F. A. Lea considers modern prophets who expose the fallacy of the pursuit of happiness as the greatest goal in *Voices in the Wilderness*.[10] This difficult book contains chapters on Blake, Wordsworth, and Carlyle, as well as examinations of the work of Conrad, Lawrence, John Middleton Murry, and Arthur Koestler. Lawrence is seen as a campaigner against both the Christian ethic of loving self-sacrifice which often leads to

[7] *Feminine Consciousness in the Modern British Novel*, by Sydney Janet Kaplan. London: U. of Illinois P. pp. 182. £6.
[8] *Lesbian Images*, by Jane Rule. Peter Davies. pp. x + 246. £3.90.
[9] *The Fiction of Sex*, by Rosalind Miles. Vision Press. 1974. pp. 208. £3.40.
[10] *Voices in the Wilderness: From Poetry to Prophecy in Britain*, by F. A. Lea. Bentham P. pp. viii + 238. £3, pb £2.

destruction and hatred and the modern tendency towards introspection and self-analysis. Lea perceptively argues that Lawrence's ' "phallic consciousness" ' is often a straightforward war against the spiritual rather than an invitation to restore the whole man. Middleton Murry's romantic commitment to ' "the heart's affection" ' is assessed in terms of Murry's relationship with Lawrence. As is typical of Lea's approach, Murry's theory is compared to his practice to show that he did develop away from narcissistic tendencies. Finally, Lea makes a spirited attempt to restore Koestler's reputation as a prophetic figure. He likens the approach to Marxism in *Darkness at Noon* to the Romantic battle with Materialism, and praises Koestler as one who experienced what he wrote. Yet Lea is forced to conclude that *Darkness at Noon* offers no prescription but rather a 'palliative' in its 'counsel of despair.'

C. N. Manlove's *Modern Fantasy*[11] provides a useful starting place for the student of this increasingly important genre. Manlove's intention is to be comprehensive. Chapters are devoted to Charles Kingsley, George MacDonald, C. S. Lewis, Tolkien, and Peake. In all cases Manlove discovers that the writers are faced with a basic dilemma. They must somehow reconcile the vast gulf between the fantasy worlds they create and the reality they know exists. What is most revealing about this study is Manlove's own harsh critical appraisal of the writers whom he studies. In his opinion, no writer successfully creates mythic depth in his novels of fantasy, with the exception of Peake and, at times, MacDonald. Tolkien comes in for particular scorn. Even Peake's work suffers from an inherent weakness caused by the initial isolation of the fantasy world which Titus inhabits. Not one writer seems to handle successfully the blend of real and supernatural. Self-consciousness and author-manipulation remain glaring flaws, and Manlove offers no hope that these will be expunged in future.

Brian Street's examination[12] of the representations of Asian and African alien people in later nineteenth-century and twentieth-century literature is primarily anthropological in orientation. The works of Rider Haggard, R.-M. Ballantyne, Kipling, Buchan, Forster, Conan Doyle, and Edgar Rice Burroughs are cited in defence of Street's contention that 'popular literature used the classification and the hierarchy of nineteenth-century science as a framework for presenting fictional accounts of primitive peoples.'

There have also been some fascinating memoirs, letters, and biographies this year. The selected letters of J. R. Ackerley[13] not only reveal a complex personality and a lover of careful, finished workmanship but also cast light on Ackerley's relationships with Forster, Strachey, Stephen Spender, Sacheverell Sitwell, Clive Bell, Wyndham Lewis, Herbert Read, and many others. Neville Braybrooke has also included several useful appendices: cut

[11] *Modern Fantasy: Five Studies*, by C. N. Manlove. Cambridge U.P. pp. viii + 308. £6.50.
[12] *The Savage in Literature: Representations of 'Primitive' Society in English Fiction 1858-1920*, by Brian V. Street. International Library of Anthropology Series. Routledge & Kegan Paul. pp. xii + 207. £5.75.
[13] *The Letters of J. R. Ackerley*, ed. by Neville Braybrooke. Duckworth. pp. xxxvi + 354. £12.50.

passages from *Hindoo Holiday* and *We Think the World of You*, and the script of a radio broadcast entitled 'Forster and *The Listener*'. Ronald W. Clark's *Life of Bertrand Russell*[14] makes use of much previously unpublished material to provide a vision of the man and more than a glimpse of an era and intellectual circle. This absorbing biography casts light on Russell's relationship with Lady Ottoline Morrell and also indicates the extent of the philosopher's association with Joseph Conrad, D. H. Lawrence, Katherine Mansfield, Vivien Eliot, Siegfried Sassoon, Lytton Strachey, and Aldous Huxley. *Closing Times*[15] is Dan Davin's account of his friendships with Julian Maclaren-Ross, W. R. Rodgers, Louis MacNeice, Enid Starkie, Joyce Cary, Dylan Thomas, and Itzik Manger. Chatty and filled with gossip, each chapter relates incidents which capture a particular personality. In *New Review* (1974) B. Bergonzi attacks the current cult of Bloomsbury as simple fascination with modern pastoral myth. Finally, Graham Greene edits the memoirs of 'Dottoressa' Moor of Capri,[16] the Bohemian and eccentric friend of Axel Munthe, Norman Douglas, the Compton Mackenzies, and Greene himself. Neither Helen Corke's autobiography *In Our Infancy* (Cambridge U.P.) nor Brian Dobbs's *Dear Diary* (Elm Tree Books/Hamish Hamilton) has been made available for review.

In a series of articles in *New Review* (1974–1975) Ian Hamilton provides succinct histories of *The Little Review*, *New Verse*, *Poetry*, and *Horizon*, and Ronald Hayman considers *The Calendar of Modern Letters* which set the critical scene for *Scrutiny*. Dougald McMillan's *transition, 1927-38*[17] chronicles the rise and fall of an American little magazine published in Paris. It was essentially a pioneering work, dedicated to experimentation and innovation, particularly of a verbal nature, and sought work which presented the subconscious in an unmediated way. Under the editorship of Eugene Jolas, a sympathetic hearing was accorded such writers as Kafka, Joyce, and dadaists like Hugo Ball, as well as Gertrude Stein, Dylan Thomas, and Samuel Beckett. McMillan scrutinizes *transition's* philosophy, provides an extended account of Joyce's struggle to publish *Finnegans Wake* and its appearance in *transition* as 'Work in Progress', and clarifies a few obscurities in the novel. The book concludes with two appendices: a reproduction of the title pages of *transition*, and Jolas's own homage to Joyce and *Finnegans Wake*.

The remaining general studies are of a more popular nature. Brian Ash[18] writes about the social implications of so-called serious science fiction stories. He provides a history of science fiction; there is much plot summary and Ash's conclusions are rather predictable. Mason Harris offers the first two in a series directed towards a theory of science fiction in

[14] *Life of Bertrand Russell*, by Ronald W. Clark. Jonathan Cape and Weidenfeld. pp. 766. £6.95.
[15] *Closing Times*, by Dan Davin. Oxford U.P. pp. xxii + 190. £4.95.
[16] *An Impossible Woman: The Memories of Dottoressa Moor of Capri*, ed. by Graham Greene Bodley Head. pp. 205. £3.
[17] *transition, 1927-38: The History of a Literary Era*, by Dougald McMillan. Calder and Boyars. pp. viii + 303. £8.50.
[18] *Faces of the Future—The Lessons of Science Fiction*, by Brian Ash. Paul Elek/Pemberton Publishing. pp. vi + 213. £3.95.

WCR. He hopes to show that science fiction has more in common with the realistic tradition of fiction than with fantasy. Detailed analysis is offered of H. G. Wells's 'The Time Machine' as well as *The Island of Dr. Moreau*. An examination of *Moreau* provides ample proof of its complexity, and a good case is made for viewing Wells as the source of a divided tradition of science fiction. Brian Aldiss writes in *New Review* of the illustrations which traditionally accompany science fiction stories, and traces the constant shift between innovation and cliché.

The heroines of women's magazine romance from the eighteenth century to the present day are surveyed by Mirabel Cecil in *Heroines in Love*.[19] Most of the stories are simply variations on a theme; infidelity, nostalgia for the past, and thwarted love are constant concerns of this fiction in any given period. However, Miss Cecil also documents changes of approach. While the subject-matter is undeniably thin, Miss Cecil has provided a useful history of a certain type of escapist literature. Each chapter consists of a review of the magazine romance of a particular historical period as well as a representative extract. Amusing contemporary illustrations accompany the text.

In *The Dangerous Edge*,[20] Gavin Lambert presents a serious account of literature which centres on the criminal world of violence, obsession, and fear. The authors he treats—Wilkie Collins, Conan Doyle, Chesterton, Buchan, Ambler, Graham Greene, Simenon, Chandler, and Hitchcock—are artists who pursue the mystery of the criminal mind in an attempt to isolate and analyze those undercurrents and tensions within the self which force an individual to escape from society by killing his conscience and leading an anonymous life. 'Suspense, betrayal and pursuit', the life-forces of melodrama, are germane to this type of novel. The examinations of individual authors do not quite live up to the introduction, but Lambert clearly isolates the main concern and theme of each writer. H. R. F. Keating's *Murder Must Appetize*[21] is a slim-volume, nostalgic survey of the Golden Age of detective fiction which produced Dorothy Sayers, Nicholas Blake, E. C. R. Lorac, Anthony Gilbert, Ngaio Marsh, and Agatha Christie, complete with a biographical author guide.

Miscellaneous studies also include David Cecil's anthology[22] of random passages which he has found stimulating and pleasurable. Brief notes accompany the extracts. James Sutherland edits *The Oxford Book of Literary Anecdotes*.[23] Few of the twentieth-century stories are particularly obscure; Virginia Woolf is represented, for example, with one quotation from Quentin Bell's biography. Joyce, Bennett, Conan Doyle, Wyndham Lewis, Lawrence, and Ford Madox Ford are all represented, but for the most part, little new revealing light is shed on personalities or beliefs. A paperback edition of Raymond Williams's 1970 volume on *The English*

[19] *Heroines in Love*, by Mirabel Cecil. Michael Joseph. 1974. pp. 237. £4.50.
[20] *The Dangerous Edge*, by Gavin Lambert. Barrie & Jenkins. pp. xvi + 272. £4.50.
[21] *Murder Must Appetize*, by H. R. F. Keating. Lemon Tree P. pp. 63. £2.
[22] *Library Looking-Glass: A Personal Anthology*, by David Cecil. Constable. pp. xii + 299. £5.50.
[23] *The Oxford Book of Literary Anecdotes*, ed. by James Sutherland. Clarendon P. Oxford U.P. pp. x + 382. £4.25.

Novel from Dickens to Lawrence[24] has appeared, as has *The Bodley Head Book of Longer Short Stories: 1900-1974.*[25] James Michie provides a brief introduction on the nature of the longer short story in the latter as well as an enthusiastic appreciation of the twelve stories by Conrad, Joyce, Huxley, D. H. Lawrence, George Moore, and Graham Greene among others. As noted last year, publishers are increasingly reluctant to send books for review. Among general studies not available for notice this year are: Paul Fussell's *The Great War and Modern Memory* (Oxford U.P.), Christopher Gillie's *Movements in English Literature, 1900-1940* (Cambridge U.P.), Barbara Hardy's *Tellers and Listeners: The Narrative Imagination* (U. of London, Athlone P.) Lawrence L. Langer's *The Holocaust and the Literary Imagination* (Yale U.P.), Hena Maes-Jelinek's *Commonwealth Literature and the Modern World* (Marcel Didier, Brussels), Jeffrey Meyers's *Painting and the Novel* (Manchester U.P.), and S. P. Rosenbaum's *The Bloomsbury Group* (Croom Helm).

(b) *Authors*

Francis M. Sibley writes in *SHR* on 'Tragedy in the Novels of Chinua Achebe.' Characters are committed to a moral vision derived from the very concept of tragedy it delineates. In *Crit*, Beatrice Stegeman investigates the courtroom scene in T. M. Aluko's *Kinsman and Foreman* and finds it an emblem of those opposing forces central to the novel—truth and reality, land and society, written and unwritten law. In the same issue, Geoffrey J. Finch considers the tragic cycle of events and 'existential aloneness' in the work of Elechi Amadi.

An interview with Kingsley Amis by Dale Salwak is recorded in *ConL*. Michael Anthony's *The Year in San Fernando* is explored in a short essay by Anthony Luengo in *ArielE*. The value of the novel lies not in surface action but in Francis's evolution to maturity. David Savage takes exception to Margaret Atwood's *Survival* in *DR* and investigates the theme of the acceptance of responsibility in Canadian fiction.

Nigel Balchin is profiled by Clive James in *New Review* (1974). James finds him a writer of importance for he 'helped create the audience which read Amis in the Fifties,' despite the lack of true humour in his work. Nick Perry and Roy Wilkie examine 'J. G. Ballard and the New Science Fiction' in *Question 9*. Ballard's work is significant in its new emphasis on the study of the individual mind in a surrealistic setting. But Ballard's belief that the external world is real only insofar as it illustrates inner experience is unsound.

A new series of notable short stories has appeared this year. Alan Cattell edits the Pegasus Library Series selection of H. E. Bates.[26] The stories are intended to show Bates's development of the form over forty years, and the volume concludes with elementary questions on each story, designed

[24] *The English Novel from Dickens to Lawrence*, by Raymond Williams. Paladin: Granada Publishing. pp. 159. 60p.
[25] *The Bodley Head Book of Longer Short Stories: 1900-74*, ed. by James Michie. Bodley Head. 1974. pp. 473. £3.50.
[26] *H. E. Bates*, ed. by Alan Cattell. Pegasus Library Series. Harrap Books. pp. 192. £1.30.

to spark classroom discussion. There is also a brief biography of Bates, simplified criticism of the stories, and suggestions for further reading.

In *MFS* Eric Park explores Beckett's use of music in *Murphy* and *Watt*. Music in songs is used 'as the substance of metaphor, as an aid to characterization or plot development, or in the arrangement of patterns of language'. The themes of time and personal identity in *How It Is* are treated in Eric P. Levy's study in *Renascence*. He concludes that Beckett attains an 'exquisite balance between despair and endurance'. 'The Patterns of Negativity in Beckett's Prose' is Wolfgang Iser's subject in *GaR*. Beckett's relentlessly negative prose encourages us to experience the unknowable. While he suggests infinite possibilities, he also provides no frame of reference for choosing amongst them. Life is an indeterminate and undefinable entanglement.

J. G. Riewald has edited an informative collection of essays on Max Beerbohm.[27] In addition to Riewald's introduction, there are twenty essays, two newly published, chosen to illustrate the growth of an analytical and critical approach to Beerbohm. The volume begins with John Rothenstein's introduction to Beerbohm's own *Poet's Corner*. Like the essays by Guy Boas and Louis Kronenberger, Rothenstein's work is a fairly straightforward appreciation of Beerbohm as an artist of caricature. Harold Nicolson and F. W. Dupee examine *Zuleika Dobson*, and Edmund Wilson attempts 'An Analysis of Max Beerbohm'. The editor traces the influence of Oscar Wilde on Beerbohm, while irony and deception in his works are explored by David Stevenson. Memoirs and biographical studies are supplied by Evelyn Waugh, Sir Sydney Roberts, S. N. Behrman, and Edmund Wilson. Beerbohm's critical work as a whole is assessed by Derek Stanford; Roy Huss, on the other hand, focuses on the theatre criticism which he finds close to impressionism. Katherine Lyon Mix investigates Beerbohm's attitude to Shaw, and his poetry and parodies are considered by John Updike and John Felstiner respectively. There are also more general studies and overviews by W. H. Auden, Bruce R. McElderry Jr. and David Cecil, as well as a chronology of important dates and a select bibliography. In *N&Q* Ira Grushow speculates on Beerbohm's projected work, *The Mirror of the Past*, and a character in it. *Max and Will: Beerbohm and William Rothenstein, Their Friendship and Letters. 1893–1945*, edited by Mary Lago and Karl Beckson (John Murray) has not been seen.

After Margaret Drabble's important biography of Arnold Bennett last year, Bennett criticism seems rather sparse. Kenneth Young has provided a short monograph on Bennett.[28] Young draws attention to some major characteristics of Bennett's fiction, such as discord between the sexes and Bennett's crafty technique which, with its slow-moving accumulation of details, creates an impression of verisimilitude. Bennett's ability to remain detached from his characters while penetrating their psychological make-up is also highlighted. Although this volume provides no new insights, it is valuable as a clear and concise introduction.

[27] *The Surprise of Excellence: Modern Essays on Max Beerbohm*, ed. by J. G. Riewald. Hamden, Connecticut: Shoe String P./Archon Books. 1974. pp. xiv + 265.
[28] *Arnold Bennett*, by Kenneth Young. Writers and Their Work Series. Longman. pp. 54. 20p.

Students of Elizabeth Bowen will be pleased to note the posthumous publication of her last book, *Pictures and Conversations*.[29] It contains a few chapters of an unfinished autobiography, the beginning of a new novel (*The Move-In*), her nativity play, and an essay on Proust's Bergotte, as well as her 'Notes on Writing a Novel'. The book is prefaced by a thoughtful and appreciative discussion of Bowen's work by Spencer Curtis Brown.

The Australian novelist Martin Boyd's Langton novels are the subject of an article by Brian McFarlane in *Southerly*. Boyd's work is found to be weakest when it attempts to wrestle with difficult metaphysical problems; his strength lies in his 'sensuous exactness'.

David Daniell's *The Interpreter's House*[30] is a commendably thorough and serious examination of John Buchan's work, with attention not only to the adventure tales but to the historical novels, biographies, and poems as well. Yet even such a thoughtful critical analysis as Daniell makes reveals a certain sameness in Buchan's concerns and techniques. Certainly, many successful writers have pursued the 'tensions between romance and realism' which Daniell discovers in Buchan's writings; but there is little evidence in this study of a writer who constantly develops his craft and deepens his perception or vision of life in any significant or striking way. What is most interesting is Daniell's claim for Buchan's 'literary use of word patterns'.

Dan Davin presents his recollections of Joyce Cary in *Encounter* which are virtually the same as those in *Closing Times*, noted earlier. In *E&S* Helen Gardner reassesses her original impression of Cary's work, and she notes with approval Cary's overriding concern with the private faith of the individual.

John Sullivan has drawn up a catalogue for a centenary exhibition in honour of G. K. Chesterton.[31] Although this is by no means exhaustive, it is a useful listing of first editions, original drawings and illustrations as well as notebooks, manuscripts and typescripts. In *LMag*, G. Almansi probes the eroticism of Leonard Cohen's novels, and finds that the Canadian is most successful when 'he closes both eyes to reality and explores devious and surrealistic ways of describing the world of sex'. Nonetheless, there is a dichotomy in Cohen's work between sex as a 'dirty' game and love as a 'clean' relationship.

The third edition of Douglas Hewitt's *Conrad: A Reassessment*[32] has appeared. First published in 1952, the book is a straightforward explication of Conrad's major novels and short stories. The new edition contains a new preface and a revised conclusion in which Hewitt reiterates his basic premise that Conrad is not 'a systematic metaphysical thinker'. In *Out of My System*,[33] Frederick Crews scrutinizes Conrad's *Heart of Darkness* in

[29] *Pictures and Conversations*, by Elizabeth Bowen. Allen Lane. pp. xlii + 194. £4.50.
[30] *The Interpreter's House: A Critical Assessment of the Work of John Buchan*, by David Daniell. Nelson. pp. xxii + 226. £3.95.
[31] *G. K. Chesterton 1874-1974: An Exhibition of Books, Manuscripts, Drawings and Other Material Relating to G. K. Chesterton*, compiled by John Sullivan. National Book League. pp. 27. £1.
[32] *Conrad: A Reassessment*, by Douglas Hewitt. Third ed. Bodley Head. pp. xvi + 42. £2.50.
[33] *Out of My System: Psychoanalysis, Ideology, and Critical Method*, by Frederick Crews. New York: Oxford U.P. pp. 214. £5.50.

an effort to show how psychoanalysis can be used as a tool. This is a difficult book to assess. A collection of essays, reviews, and lectures ranging from thoughts on student politics to considerations of post-Freudians and the New Left in American society, it is centred loosely on 'psycholiterary' investigation with emphasis on Freud. Crews's principal interest in fiction is in the neurotic temperaments it seems to disclose; and his psychological observations on the artistic personalities he considers are not very original, albeit lively. He reduces *Heart of Darkness* to a series of images related to the traumatic remembrance of a primal sexual scene, nothing more. Five of Conrad's tales collected for the Pegasus Library Series by Esmor Jones[34] are followed by elementary classroom questions as well as a biography of Conrad and suggestions for further study.

Despite the scarcity of book-length studies on Conrad, there has been some excellent periodical work. In the first issue of *Conradiana*, Frank B. Evans discusses 'The Nautical Metaphor in "The Secret Sharer" '. He finds the nautical manoeuvre of the ship a clue to the interior experience of the captain and a key to his relationship with Legatt. Douglas A. Hughes examines 'Il Conde' to discover the true nature of the Count's peculiar adventure. A close study of the suggestive details found in the story shows that the Count is a homosexual, fabricating 'to preserve his reputation'. By analyzing the short stories in *A Set of Six*, Addison C. Bross demonstrates Conrad's concern with the nature of individual belief and the way in which it gives meaning to our motives. While it is clear that Conrad hates self-delusion which can create a nightmare world, he also has 'respect for human belief's uncanny power to impose upon reality a subjective meaning often unwarranted by objective evidence'. Christof Wegelin reflects on the character of Captain MacWhirr in 'Typhoon'. He is typical of Conrad's 'absurd hero', a man who has little, if any, imagination but an impressive fortitude; in this respect he is an excellent illustration of Conrad's interest in the 'multiplicity of truth' and the importance of every aspect of the universe. 'The Secret Sharer' is probed for comic elements by Dinshaw M. Burjorjee who also assesses the effectiveness of the 'comic counterpoint'. The vacillation between idealism and commercial practicality in 'A Smile of Fortune' is investigated by William Lafferty. Uncertain of his own moral principles the captain hopes to attain the best of both worlds by living in one and desiring the other. Barbara H. Solomon looks at Conrad's method of shaping and framing his narrative material, by comparing 'The Inn of the Two Witches' to Wilkie Collins's treatment of the same incident in 'A Terribly Strange Bed.' This is a useful article which draws some interesting conclusions about Conrad's ability as a psychological narrator. Finally, Theo Steinmann investigates the Count's homosexuality in 'Il Conde' and finds, like Douglas Hughes, that it is revealed only in the most ambiguous and indirect fashion.

Critical articles in the second issue include a complex analysis of Conrad's ethical views on evolution by Stanley Renner: the struggle between self-assertion and self-restraint is frequently depicted in Conrad's treatment of colonization and life on deserted islands. *Heart of Darkness*

---

[34] *Joseph Conrad*, ed. by Esmor Jones. Pegasus Library Series. Harrap. pp. 200 n.p.

is the subject of a number of perceptive studies. Lee M. Whitehead finds that Marlow serves a function much like that Nietzsche attributes to the Greek tragic chorus in *The Birth of Tragedy*. C. T. Watts concentrates on the manager's plot against Kurtz as indicative of Conrad's attitude to the evolutionary process; European civilization is nothing more than a 'hypocritical and perverse sophistication of savagery.' V. J. Emmett Jr. compares Carlyle and Conrad in a study of Kurtz as the 'charismatic villain' appealing to the greed and lust of the Id. Betsy C. Yarrison explores the significance of the many literary allusions in the novel which seem to point to the notion of a 'heroic pilgrimage'. David M. Martin considers Kurtz as an embodiment of two different Satanic traditions, and Richard P. Sugg writes perceptively of 'The Triadic Structure of *Heart of Darkness*.' Reason, passion and imagination gradually synthesize in Marlow and enable him to re-evaluate the body-mind dualism which seems pervasive in this life. Joan Baum urges readers to bear in mind the real exploitation of the Congo by so-called benevolent nations while reading *Heart of Darkness*. In this way, the 'vicious statements of fiction may take on a darker meaning'. Captain Whalley in 'The End of the Tether' demonstrates the impossibility of arresting flux and the process of ageing for Daniel R. Schwarz. Donald W. Rude and David Leon Higdon provide their continuing supplement to Conrad bibliographical studies. (A further checklist compiled by the same authors also appears in the third issue of *Conradiana*.)

Thomas C. Moser opens the third number with an essay on the relationship between Conrad, Ford Madox Ford, and the sources of *Chance*, that most Fordian of Conrad's novels. Peter D. O'Connor draws attention to patterns of imagery in *Almayer's Folly* to determine the function of Nina. Richard C. Stevenson discusses the significance of Stein's famous prescription of 'how to be' in *Lord Jim*. Emphasis is placed on the mysterious paradoxical nature of Stein's words, for in this way they best illuminate Jim's own ambiguous death. Jackson Heimer reflects on 'Betrayal in *The Secret Agent*.' Gloria L. Young writes of the indifferent chance which seems to rule the universe in 'The End of the Tether' and 'Freya of the Seven Isles.' She argues that both Captain Whalley and Jasper have a false view of the sea and fail to perceive the shadow of existential absurdity which overwhelms them. The fourth in a series of articles on Conrad and Shakespeare by Adam Gillon concentrates primarily on *Victory*, and finds that the dramatic, symbolic, and ironic elements of that novel suggest parallels with *The Tempest, Hamlet, King Lear, Macbeth*, and *Othello*.

William W. Bonney also investigates *Victory* in *JNT*, though with emphasis on the disparate narrative modes of the novel which confirm its thematic content; the detachment of the human narrators parallels the message of the disastrous events: ' "he who forms a tie is lost" '. Even Davidson who ends the novel shifts from involvement to detachment. In *Mosaic*, Ian Watt traces the background sources and composition of *Almayer's Folly*, as well as the reception of the novel and the French tradition which influenced Conrad. This is a valuable study, particularly because Watt uses *Almayer's Folly* to demonstrate many of the technical problems which dogged Conrad's path. Russell King adopts a different approach in his comparison of the novel to Lenormand's *Le Simoun* in *RLC*. Conrad shows considerable skill in integrating characters, plot, and background, while Lenormand concentrates primarily on setting as a useful symbol of unconscious forces. *Heart of Darkness* is the subject of three additional articles. In *SSF* Jack Helder writes convincingly of the importance of the 'informative Russian harlequin'. By relating this character to the theatrical tradition of the fool, one can best determine his symbolic and thematic function as an emblem of the struggle between chaos and order, folly and wisdom. William N. Rogers II argues in *ELN* that the opening account by the unnamed narrator establishes the imagery and tonality of the work, especially with reference to the dominoes image. The parallels between *Don Quixote* and *Heart of Darkness* are outlined by Gustavo Pérez Firmat in *CLS*.

The same comparative approach is adopted with rather more point by Elsa Nettels in *ELT* where she notes the similarities between *The Ambassadors* and *Lord Jim*. While the two novelists operate from different underlying principles, human consciousness and action are the main values which inform their work. In *TSLL* Kenneth R. Lincoln reports on 'Conrad's Mystic Humour' which is of a black and mocking kind that 'counsels the reader to resist suffering for the world's blunders'. Joyce Carol Oates in *Novel* attempts to show that the essential tragic vision of *Nostromo* is one which denigrates all human values, even that of 'motiveless destructive evil'. The characters are constantly torn in two directions, encouraged to maintain a sense of community yet warned of establishing any serious bonds and commitments. *A Personal Record* comes under scrutiny by J. M. Kertzer in *UTQ* when he asserts that the work is especially useful as an imaginative treatment of personal experience. J. R. Kehler supplies a note in *ELN* on the epigraph from Chaucer's 'Franklin's Tale' in 'The Rescue', and H. M. Daleski in *CritQ* discusses the problem of self-possession in 'The Secret Sharer'. In *DQR* J. Bakker agrees with Ian Watt and C. B. Cox that 'The Shadow-Line' is more than a simple story of moral maturing. The change from youth to maturity is really symbolic of the struggle of being over non-being.

A monograph by David Rees on Rhys Davies[35] contains a short biographical account as well as indications of the major themes and narrative techniques to be found in the novels and stories. This is a most basic introduction and contains much plot summary. Nevertheless, there is some useful material, particularly the interesting chapter on Davies's own attitude to novel writing, his background, and the influences which he feels have shaped his perception. Hesketh Pearson's study of Arthur Conan Doyle first published in 1943 and reissued in 1974 (White Lion) has not been seen.

Valerie Grosvenor Myer has provided a stimulating treatment of the theme of English puritanism in the work of Margaret Drabble.[36] It is refreshing to find a critic who sees beyond the overtly 'feminist' concerns of Drabble's fictions to discover characters propelled on a search for salvation and faced with complex moral decisions: the heroines are torn between

[35] *Rhys Davies*, by David Rees. Writers of Wales Series. Cardiff: U. of Wales P pp. 74. £1.
[36] *Margaret Drabble: Puritanism and Permissiveness*, by Valerie Grosvenor Myer Vision P. 1974. pp. 200. £3.40.

a desire to follow their own generous instincts and a tendency to adhere to the 'moralistic puritan conscience' they possess. Love is viewed as the solution to inflexible puritanism, and also as the source of any wholeness and beauty. The artistic success of the novels is dependent on this moral tension and its resolution.

Marion Vlastos Libby also challenges feminist readings of *The Needle's Eye* in *ConL* where she explains the importance of fate in the novel. In *DQR* Monica Lauritzen Mannheimer explores the same novel with a view to outlining the search for identity by Rose and to some extent Simon. She finds the 'compulsive need for self-negation' inherent in both characters and concludes that the novel is pessimistic in its suggestion that self-realization is remote. Margaret Drabble defends the novel against these charges in reply in the same issue. She concedes that the novel shows no everlasting, romantic happiness, but she feels that the portrayal of a low-key happiness is more realistic and helps her to examine the 'possibility of living, today, without faith, a religious life'.

S. Nagarajan considers 'The Anglo-Indian Novels of Sara Jeannette Duncan' in the *Journal of the University of Poona*. Sara Duncan is admittedly a minor novelist, but deserves praise for capturing the 'feel' of a particular milieu.

Suzanne Henig edits her 1973 interview with Lawrence Durrell in *VWQ*, and Walter G. Creed studies *The Alexandria Quartet* in *EA* in an attempt to account for Darley's shift from a belief in 'impersonal' truth to a total reliance on the subjective response to experience.

Several articles have appeared this year on Ford Madox Ford's *The Good Soldier*. In *Mosaic*, Thomas C. Moser considers the possibility that the vividness in the novel might in fact be due to a biographical slant. The 'Dedicatory Letter' is examined by Lawrence Thornton in *MFS* who believes that it sheds light on the important theme of suffering. The relationship of form and meaning in the novel is delineated in *ELT* by H. Wayne Schow. He finds that the formlessness of the narrative *is* the content, mirroring Dowell's own lack of moral direction. William P. Peirce writes on the 'Epistemological Style of Ford's *The Good Soldier*' in *Lang&S*. There is also an account by Max Webb in *SoR* on Ford and the Baton Rouge Writers' Conference. Ford sponsored literary internationalism to prevent provincialism.

The most important Forster publication seen this year has been John Colmer's study[37] of Forster as an 'ironic moralist' in a transition period. Colmer looks at Forster in terms of his intellectual and literary background and environment. Forster wrote still cognizant of the Victorian tradition, and much of the depth and tension of his work stems from the conflict between individual aspirations and the restrictions of an inflexible Victorian social morality. Colmer investigates the influence of Romanticism on Forster's art form, and places him somewhere between the Edwardians and Georgian symbolists. There follows a careful analysis of Forster's work, clearly demonstrating the novelist's concern with serious psychological analysis as well as with the future of English society. Some useful

---

[37] *E. M. Forster: The Personal Voice*, by John Colmer. Routledge & Kegan Paul. pp. xii + 243. £5.95.

comparisons are made between manuscript and published versions of the novels. *Arctic Summer, Maurice*, and the homosexual short stories are treated as examples of Forster's skilful use of literary conventions to treat taboo subjects. There is a fine account of Forster's sojourns in India and Forster is also assessed as a critic, biographer, essayist, lecturer, and broadcaster. Colmer concludes that Forster, is suspicious of the state's attempts to organize people into good citizens through conformity'. By sympathy and detachment Forster successfully conveys a sense of 'moral realism' by showing the contradictions in our moral life and urging the connexions of our social and unconscious selves.

Bonnie Blumenthal Finkelstein approaches what should be an interesting subject—Forster's women characters [38] She discusses Forster's six novels and argues that in each an alienated individual (either a woman or a homosexual) struggles to maintain his or her distinctive nature and avoid stereotypes of convention. 'Only connect' is the theme of every novel, whether it applies to sexual contraries within or between individuals or to social relationships between the sexes. However, her point of view is somewhat limited, and Dr. Finkelstein analyzes the novels in a perfunctory way. Oliver Stallybrass's edition of Forster's *The Life To Come and Other Stories* (1972) has appeared in paperback.[39]

In *TQ* James R. Baker examines Forster's work to show the development of his insight into European civilization and his analysis of Western man. He notes that Forster was not naive about the 'disintegration of the humanistic ideal'. In *Mosaic*, Paul B. Armstrong considers *Howards End* in terms of the existential philosophy of the Swiss psychoanalyst Ludwig Biswanger, and in *ELT* J. R. Ebbatson usefully concentrates on the Schlegel sisters and the theme of illegitimacy in order to show that George Meredith and Mark Rutherford may well have influenced Forster. In *SNNTS* Sena Jeter Naslund argues that *A Passage to India* supports Forster's contention in *Aspects of the Novel* that 'fantasy prepares the reader for prophecy'. She demonstrates how Forster's call for a loving spiritual realm is offset by his modulations 'from objective descriptions to fanciful ones'. In *Critical Inquiry*, Martin Price writes on characterization in the novel, noting tensions derived from the conflict between the public mask and 'the deeper impersonal self'. Individuals who escape from 'social responsibility' do so either by 'despair or obliviousness'. Finally, Richard S. Cammarota applies sonata form to the novel in *ELT*. This musical pattern illuminates the internal design of the novel and reveals the repetition, development, and synthesis of key themes. The following have not been available for notice: the Abinger edition of *Where Angels Fear to Tread*, edited by Oliver Stallybrass (Edward Arnold), and E. M. Forster's *Letters to Donald Windham* (Bertram Rota).

Lorna Sage interviews John Fowles in *New Review* (1974). In *LMag* a review article on *The Ebony Tower* allows John Mellors to re-examine Fowles's work as a whole. In *ConL* Roberta Rubenstein discusses irony in

---

[38] *Forster's Women: Eternal Differences*, by Bonnie Blumenthal Finkelstein. New York and London: Columbia U.P. pp. xiv + 184. $9.90.
[39] *The Life to Come and Other Stories*, ed. by Oliver Stallybrass. Penguin. pp. 282. 60p.

The Magus, and finds that the author's failure to provide a 'consistent focus' for his reader undermines his work aesthetically and philosophically. In *ArielE* Jeanne Delabere-Garant discusses a recurrent character type in the early novels of Janet Frame. A new introduction to William Golding[40] has been produced by Stephen Medcalf. It includes succinct thematic analyses of the 1934 *Poems*, as well as the novels and novellas. A short commentary on the radio play, *Break My Heart*, concentrates primarily on the script. Medcalf concludes with a rather idiosyncratic comparison of Golding with post-Puritan New England writers. Danielle Escudié more usefully compares Golding with Angus Wilson in her impressive study of alienation in modern English novelists.[41] Man is a stranger to himself, and in a broader sense, men are strangers to each other. Golding's heroes look inward to find a predatory nature beneath the gloss of civilization; they turn for consolation to what is primarily Christian morality. Wilson's tentative solution lies in the direction of liberal humanism. This is a difficult but rewarding study. The extensive bibliography is also useful. Bob Dixon in *Question 8* writes scathingly on Golding's falsification of 'anthropological fact'. More pertinent is John Robinson's examination of Pincher Martin's imagination and its 'will-to-power' in *RMS*. Virginia Tiger's study of William Golding (Calder and Boyars) was not available.

Sam Adams's monograph on Geraint Goodwin[42] contains some biographical information and brief discussions of various novels and stories, and a great deal of plot summary. Adams glances in the direction of recurrent emphases and technical strengths, such as description and characterization.

There is a review essay on Nadine Gordimer by Christopher Hope in *LMag*. Bruce Bassoff has written a perceptive study of the novels of Henry Green, called *Toward Loving*.[43] Green's place in twentieth-century literature lies 'away from the role of the cultural ombudsman and in the area of epiphany represented by Joyce's *Dubliners* and Woolt's *To the Lighthouse*'. Most of the analysis treats Green's use of syntactic and discursive figures. These poetic devices enable him to investigate the nature of humanity without engaging in philosophical exposition. Bassoff pays tribute to the rich and complex handling of social and erotic themes in *Loving*. The appendix includes plot summaries of Green's novels.

Leopoldo Duran finds in *ContempR* that Graham Greene's *The Hint of an Explanation* reveals man's wretchedness before God. In *ArielE* Theo Q. Dombrowski analyzes 'techniques of intensity' in Greene's novels. An unusual style contributes to our impressions that the world is violent and confusing, despite the fact that our actions have 'transcendent significance'. In *Question 9*, Peter Faulkner compares *The Honorary Consul* to Wilson's

[40] *William Golding*, by Stephen Medcalf. Writers and Their Work Series. Longman. pp. 43. 20p.
[41] *Deux Aspects de l'Aliénation dans le Roman Anglais Contemporain, 1945-65: Angus Wilson et William Golding*, by Danielle Escudié. Paris: Didier. pp. 554. 130F.
[42] *Geraint Goodwin*, by Sam Adams. Writers of Wales Series. Cardiff: U. of Wales P. pp. 114. £1.
[43] *Toward Loving: The Poetics of the Novel and the Practice of Henry Green*, by Bruce Bassoff. London: U. of South Carolina P. pp. xii + 180.

As If By Magic and finds that both works contain evidence of 'humanistic attitudes', Wilson's explicitly and Greene's paradoxically. Michael B. Wiilmott writes in *English* of the childhood world in L. P. Hartley's *The Go-Between, The Shrimp and the Anemone*, and *The Brickfield*. Hartley is best when treating childhood 'in a bygone setting' and when he mixes realism and symbolism.

The Short Stories of Frank Harris,[44] a selection of fifteen stories written between 1894 and 1924, include some vivid American western tales, stories of passion and maudlin sentiment, and religious fictions about Christ and His disciples. Some of the stories are quite dynamic, but it is difficult to be persuaded by Gertz's observations on Harris as a possible influence on Joyce and Lawrence. Linda Morgan Bain's biography of Harris[45] is a curious book. No documentation for the 'facts' is supplied, and it is difficult to feel that a case is made for viewing Harris as more than a scoundrel and pornographer. Philippa Pullar's *Frank Harris* (Hamish Hamilton) was not available for detailed examination.

Lily Zähner's *Demon and Saint in the Novels of Aldous Huxley*[46] is an examination of the novels and the historical studies with particular attention to two human tendencies presented therein: the movement 'to fulfilment in God' and 'the trend towards evil'. In simple analyses of Huxley's works, Miss Zähner argues that synthesis is all-important to him. 'It is the *individual* mystic with his *individual* action or judicious inaction that may ultimately save the way'. It is only with mystical religion that the whole man is called into action. In *RMS* Donald Watt considers two stories by Huxley ('Good and Old-Fashioned' and 'Under Compulsion') which are not found in the Eschelback and Shober Bibliography. 'Science and Conscience in Huxley's *Brave New World*' is Peter Firchow's interesting search for Huxley's scientific sources in an effort to demonstrate why Huxley and his contemporaries distrusted science (*ConL*). Charlotte Legates's analysis of the importance of Brueghel to Huxley in *WHR* identifies possible technical influences of the painter. *Aldous Huxley*, edited by Robert E. Kuehn for the Twentieth Century Views series (Prentice-Hall) was not available; nor was Donald Watt's *Aldous Huxley: The Critical Heritage* (Routledge & Kegan Paul).

There is a profile of Christopher Isherwood in *New Review* by Brian Finney, and in *ConL* Alan Wilde writes on Isherwood's narrators. He detects a relationship between 'the equivocal treatment of the self' and 'the decade's characteristic attitude toward language' as a means of describing surface details rather than of probing underlying meaning. John Holloway compares 'Narrative Structure and Text Structure' in *A Meeting by the River* and Muriel Spark's *The Prime of Miss Jean Brodie*. Techniques are plotted in charts and diagrams to show how narrative is a set of 'runs of events' (*Critical Inquiry*).

[44] *The Short Stories of Frank Harris: A Selection*, ed. by Elmer Gertz. Carbondale and Edwardsville: Southern Illinois U.P. pp. xvi + 299. $8.95.
[45] *Evergreen Adventurer: The Real Frank Harris*, by Linda Morgan Bain. Research Publishing. pp. 121. £2.
[46] *Demon and Saint in the Novels of Aldous Huxley*, by Lily Zähner. Swiss Studies in English. Berne: A. Francke. pp. 201. sFr. 25.

Twenty short stories by W. W. Jacobs have been collected and edited by Hugh Greene.[47] In a brief introduction, Jacobs is praised as the 'best humorous writer of our time' together with P. G. Wodehouse and George Birmingham. D. R. M. Wilkinson comments in *DQR* on the mythic treatment of race relationships in Dan Jacobson's *The Trap* and *A Dance in the Sun*. Ruth Marie Faurot's volume on Jerome K. Jerome (Twayne) has not been seen. In the *New Review*, Yolanta May interviews Ruth Prawer Jhabvala.

Of prime importance to Joyce studies this year is Richard Ellmann's edition of the *Selected Letters of James Joyce*,[48] compiled from the three volumes of Joyce letters already in existence. This new selection includes ten letters not previously published and restores unpublished passages to others, especially in letters to Harriet Weaver. But it is Joyce's personality which the letters particularly illumine: his confidence in himself as an artist, his great devotion to his family, his 'socialism' and his waning support for Sinn Fein ideals. There are also frequent instances of his adoption of a variety of masks. Joyce's letters to Nora Barnacle alone make this selection worthwhile. Also welcome is the *Topographical Guide to James Joyce's 'Ulysses'*,[49] prepared by Clive Hart and Leo Knuth, which consists of two separate booklets. Volume I provides a background to the topography of Dublin, a detailed outline of the movements of characters, and an explanation of the maps which comprise Volume II. Hart and Knuth hope their work will clarify 'Joyce's pattern of relationships'. Arthur Power recalls his conversations with Joyce in a slim volume edited by Clive Hart[50] and interesting primarily for what it reveals of Joyce behind the mask. There is some useful material on Joyce's knowledge of Russian prose, a few revealing remarks on *Ulysses* (notably on Bloom's relationship with Gerty MacDowell), observations on the daily habits and interests of Joyce, as well as records of Joyce's opinion on many of his contemporaries. What emerges is an imaginative soul torn between the conflicting claims of romanticism and realism. Kenneth Grose writes on Joyce[51] for the non-scholar in a simplified treatment of the basic elements of style and theme in, for example, *Ulysses*, with detailed analyses of each chapter and attention to Homeric parallels, techniques and symbols. The chapter on *Finnegans Wake* purports simply to indicate a few of the many layers of meaning; but Grose's approach in this case seems designed to discourage all but the 'intrepid' from reading the novel.

JJQ begins with a special double issue on textual studies. William H. Quillian opens the number with a full transcription of Joyce's manuscripts for his 1912 *Hamlet* Lectures. There is a brief introductory essay by

[47] *Selected Short Stories of W. W. Jacobs*, ed. by Hugh Greene. Bodley Head. pp. 238. £2.75.
[48] *Selected Letters of James Joyce*, ed. by Richard Ellmann. Faber and Faber. pp. xxxii + 440. £12.50, pb £6.50.
[49] *A Topographical Guide to James Joyce's 'Ulysses'*, by Clive Hart and Leo Knuth 2 vols. Colchester. Essex: U. of Essex: Wake Newsletter P. pp. 73 + 18 maps. £4.
[50] *Conversations with James Joyce*, by Arthur Power, ed. by Clive Hart. Millington. 1974 pp. 111. £3.
[51] *James Joyce*, by Kenneth Grose. Literature in Perspective Series. Evans Bros. pp. 150. £1.50.

Quillian together with annotative comments throughout the transcription. The manuscripts themselves show the state of Joyce's aesthetic development in 1912; there is much emphasis on fact and on the physical reality of the play. Myron Schwartzman traces the development of an early draft of the 'Cyclops' episode of *Ulysses*. He argues in a brief essay that the V.A.8 Copybook shows us Joyce the technician as opposed to Joyce the artist. Joyce wanted us to see Bloom 'objectively' so as to understand the limits of his toleration of hatred and prejudice. A transcription of the draft accompanies the article. Michael Groden writes independently on the same subject, and stresses the importance of this episode for *Ulysses* stylistically. There is an encyclopaedic completeness here which influenced other sequences. Alan M. Cohn supplies a supplemental James Joyce checklist for 1972.

The Spring number begins with a report on a five-day seminar on Joyce at the University of Hawaii in 1974. Robert Adams Day examines a single sentence from the 'Proteus' episode of *Ulysses* which in its images of water, birds, parents, and children forms a web of association in Joyce's work. M. David Bell considers 'the model farm at Kinnereth' in *Ulysses*, and speculates on sources for Joyce's 'Zion theme'. Marguerite Harkness writes on the 'Circe' episode as a key to symbols and characters in the novel. Nathan Halper thinks it unlikely that Michael Bodkin (Michael Furey of 'The Dead') is buried in Oughterard as Richard Ellmann suggests. The significance of Stephen's composition of his villanelle in *Portrait* is suggested by Charles Rossman. Stephen yearns to escape to an abstract heaven, not seeing that it is his earthly experience which will stimulate his art. In an interesting comparison of Wittgenstein and Joyce, David A. White notes that Wittgenstein's philosophical considerations on language help us to understand Joyce's own linguistic development from language ordered by logic to language controlled by language games. Brief notes include: Nathan Halper on Yva Fernandez's translation of 'Clay', James Penny Smith on an early American Joyce enthusiast, Julian B. Kaye on 'Joyce's Use of the Word Pervert', Martin Bidney on Russian references in *Finnegans Wake*, and comments on *Ulysses* by Joseph Cotter, James Penny Smith, Ioanna Ioannidou, Richard M. Kain, and Philip J. West.

The fourth issue begins with Bonnie K. Scott's article on John Eglinton, his relationship with Joyce, and his appearance in the 'Scylla and Charybdis' episode of *Ulysses*. Richard M. Kain supplies an unpublished letter from Joyce to Eglinton. Eileen Kennedy uses textual analysis to examine Fr. Flynn in 'The Sisters'. David J. Leigh turns to Joyce's *Portrait* to show that Joyce's attitude to the artist is revealed in a number of passages by linguistic ambiguities which demonstrate the limitations of Stephen's own Thomistic aesthetic theories. Fritz Senn notes an effective technique used by Joyce in *Ulysses*—that of metastasis or sudden transitions from one subject to another. The importance of Bloom's daughter in *Ulysses* as a 'reflection of Molly and Bloom united' is suggested by Tilly Eggers. Shari Benstock's difficult article on the library scene in *Ulysses* centers on the gnomonic method and figures in Joyce's work. It is a method which 'stresses not the process of creation but the nature of what has been created'. Craig Carver pursues the links between Hermes's talisman, Bloom's potato, and impotence in *Ulysses*, and Christopher Lauer comments on Joyce's love of games and the game motif in *Wake, Ulysses,* and *Portrait*. Other brief notes are by Alan Jutzi on the John Hinsdale Thompson Collection of Joyce material at Huntington library, Victory Pomeranz on a term in 'An Encounter', and Michael Harry Belchner on sources for a reference in *Portrait*. Miscellaneous material on *Ulysses* is presented briefly by Fritz Senn, Peter Alderson Smith, Stuart Hirschberg, and Patrick White.

In *SSF* Joan Zlotnick comments on the similarities between Joyce's 'The Sisters' and Sherwood Anderson's 'The Philosopher'. She makes a case for the influence of Joyce's story on Anderson's tale. Also in *SSF* is a useful compendium of money references in *Dubliners* by Jane Somerville. Money becomes an emblem in the book for a loss of vitality and meaning. Joseph M. Garrison Jr. also writes on *Dubliners* in *Novel*. He traces the development of a narrator who comes ultimately to be 'free of the bias of his own perception of things'.

Useful material on *Finnegans Wake* includes M. L. Troy's accumulation of 'Some Ancient Egyptian Themes Initiated on the First Page of *Finnegans Wake*' in *SN*. This connexion with ancient myths gives a sense of timelessness to the novel. In *IUR* Lorraine Weir inquires into the topology and history of Phoenix Park in order to assess its use as a structuring device in *Wake*. Louis O Mink comments on the complex verbal success of the novel in *SHR*. Form, not truth, is the prime consideration; all levels of meaning are of equal value. Thus, the book expresses 'what it feels like to live'.

The use of the riddle in *Ulysses* is one of a number of useful articles on that novel. Patrick A. McCarthy claims in *TSLL* that riddle helps Joyce to probe 'problems of identity, to reflect those aspects of relationships that the characters cannot approach more directly, and to symbolize the elusive, relative nature of all knowledge', in addition to supporting the quest theme. Suzette A. Henke writes on 'Joyce's Bloom: Beyond Sexual Possessiveness' in *American Imago*. She feels that both Bloom and Molly are liberated in their marriage from 'sexual obsession' by their own sexual failings or indiscretions. Michael Groden in *TCL* discusses the influence of *Ulysses* on Faulkner's *The Sound and the Fury*, primarily from a technical point of view. Giorgio Melchiori tries to pinpoint the time and place when Stephen Dedalus and Bloom are rejected. He argues in *E&S* that the crucial episode is 'The Wandering Rocks' in *Ulysses*. John MacNicholas treats Joyce's use of Wagner in *Exiles* in *CompD*, Dolores Palomo finds similarities between Chaucer and Joyce in methods of narration, language, and thematic concerns in *Mosaic*, and Arnold Goldman writes of the International Joyce Symposium in Paris in *Encounter*.

A great many works on Joyce appeared but were not made available for examination: James S. Atherton's *Finnegans Wake: The Books at the Wake* has been reissued (Paul P. Appel), Zack Bowen has written *Musical Allusions in the Works of James Joyce* (Gill and Macmillan), and Thomas E. Connolly prepared *The Personal Library of James Joyce: a Descriptive Bibliography* (Norwood, 1974). Other works not seen include Leo Daly's *James Joyce and the Mullingar Connection* (Dolmen P.), Stan Gebler Davies's *James Joyce: A Portrait of the Artist* (Davis-Poynter), Rigby Graham's *'James Joyce's Tower,' Sandycove* (Brewhouse P.), a reissue of Clive Hart's *Concordance to Finnegans Wake* (Paul P. Appel), the new

Faber and Faber paperback *Finnegans Wake*, Mark Shechner's *Joyce in Nighttown* (U. of California Press), William York Tindall's *The Joyce Country* (Wildwood House), and Geoffrey Keane Whitelock's *Cricket in the Writings of James Joyce* (the author). *A Wake Newsletter* was also not available for detailed review.

Leona Gom looks at the first person narrative technique of Margaret Laurence in *DR*, while in *WCR* she demonstrates the importance of external and internal geography in the works of Margaret Laurence.

The most dynamic work on Lawrence this year has been Philip Callow's *Son and Lover: The Young Lawrence.*[52] Callow sets out to describe Lawrence's development up to 1919. The book is not a critical biography or even a psychological deterministic study. Rather, it draws on recently published material as well as more familiar biographical material to reveal the essential paradoxes inherent in Lawrence and his work. Relying on his own techniques as a novelist, Callow tellingly exposes the background of Lawrence's day-to-day existence, although one might wish to emphasize that heavy reliance on *Sons and Lovers* for the reconstruction of actual events in Lawrence's past is dangerous. Several contentious issues are raised, such as Lawrence's possible bisexuality. A limited edition of Martha Gordon Crotch's *Memories of Frieda Lawrence*[53] which consists of four chapters from the author's unpublished memoirs, treats her friendship with Frieda in Venice shortly after the death of Lawrence. The details of the battle over Lawrence's estate are interesting. In *D. H. Lawrence on Education*[54] the editors argue that Lawrence's statements on education are 'inseparable from his arguments about life and society'. The first section includes an 'Autobiographical Sketch' in which Lawrence challenges traditional views on 'knowing' and 'education'. Passages from *Women in Love* and *The Rainbow* are extracted, as well as some early short stories, to show Lawrence's growing emphasis on the individual (pupil and teacher) as a creature whose singular essence should be allowed to develop. The writings from Lawrence's last years indeed reveal a more humane and flexible approach. The editors conclude that the key to Lawrence's philosophy of education is 'the connection he makes between the deepest personal awareness and growth, and a more general awareness, including learning about the natural world and its many forms of life'.

In the first number of *DHLR* L. Michael Ross examines the two versions of Lawrence's 'Sun' and finds the less well known 'Black Sun' version superior. Leslie M. Thompson considers possible sources for Lawrence's 'The Man Who Died', and Keith Cushman traces the development of 'The Shadow in the Rose Garden' through three versions. Rewriting, he argues, was a creative business for Lawrence. Keith Sagar considers 'The Genesis of "Bavarian Gentians" ', and Paul Delany compares the rainbow images in the works of Lawrence and Forster in the hopes of finding a possible

[52] *Son and Lover: The Young Lawrence*, by Philip Callow, Bodley Head. pp. 316 £6.
[53] *Memories of Frieda Lawrence*, by Martha Gordon Crotch. Edinburgh: Tragara P. Limited ed. pp. 37.
[54] *D. H. Lawrence on Education*, ed. by Joy and Raymond Williams. Penguin 1973. pp. 242. £1.

influence on Lawrence. Langdon Elsbree draws together a number of amusing essays by Joanne Trautmann, Sanford Pinsker, William R. Lowery, and James Cox for a forum 'On the Teaching of D. H. Lawrence'. Emile Delavenay surveys recent biographical works on Lawrence and Frieda von Richthofen with emphasis on the *facts*. There is a useful 1974 checklist of Lawrence scholarship compiled by Richard D. Beards, as well as some additions by Dennis Jackson to the 1973 bibliography on masters and honors theses on Lawrence. The number concludes with James C. Cowan's detailed review of the transcription of a 1952 panel discussion on Lawrence at UCLA in addition to the usual notes, reviews, and checklist of research in progress.

The second issue opens with Michael Squires's essay on 'Scenic Construction and Rhetorical Signals in Hardy and Lawrence', drawing attention to similarities of 'both fictional technique and philosophic vision'. Chaman Nahal notices the use of colour in Lawrence's early and later poetry. Lawrence's early verse is also the subject of Evelyn Shakir's examination of his distrust of art as dangerous artifice and his guilt over ' "unmanning" fantasies'. Keith Cushman views 1912-1915 as the crucial creative point for Lawrence. The final revision of *The Prussian Officer and Other Stories* and its many echoes in *The Rainbow* can be seen in philosophical content as 'part of the same great artistic moment'. Charles L. Ross traces the genesis of *Women in Love* as a record of Lawrentian energy, Evelyn J. Hinz responds to four papers delivered at the Lawrence seminar at the 1974 MLA convention, and current books on Lawrence are reviewed in Kingsley Widmer's 'Lawrence as Abnormal Novelist'. There are bibliographical notes and additions by Toshitaka Shirai who lists Japanese theses on Lawrence (1968-1975), and Dennis Jackson who adds more doctoral dissertations to the *DHLR* lists for 1970 and 1972. Harry T. Moore responds to Delavenay's review essay in the preceding issue.

'D. H. Lawrence and Women' is the theme for the third issue. Half the number is occupied by Charles Rossman who finds that Lawrence's attitude to women is liberal despite its occasional reactionary appearance. The overlapping ideas of Lawrence and Schopenhauer on sex and love are charted by Eleanor H. Green. Virginia Hyde considers the importance of Will Brangwen's capacity for vision in *The Rainbow* and *Women in Love*, while the courtship and marriage of Tom Brangwen and Lydia Lensky is viewed as an example of Lawrence's concept of love by Lucia Henning Heldt. There is also an exchange between Brian Finney and Michael L. Ross concerning Ross's earlier article this year on the various versions of 'Sun'.

John Worthen writing in *RMS* takes issue with Professor George Zytaruk's 1973 claim that Jessie Chambers, not her sister May, wrote memoirs of Lawrence in the third volume of Nehls's *Composite Biography*. Professor Zytaruk supplies a spirited answer to Worthen's attack. There is a valuable article by Lydia Blanchard on Lawrence's sympathetic attitude to vital women trapped by society in *MFS*. F. von Broembsen's discussion in *WHR* of 'Mythic Identification and Spatial Inscendence' is a difficult study of mythic polarities in the novels. The governing power in the world seems to depend for Lawrence on an 'impersonal cosmic-spiritual force', and this mythical note removes Lawrence's work from our world based on self-recognition. In *Novel* Taylor Stoehr considers 'mentalized sex' in Lawrence's work. He finds that the great distruster of consciousness cultivates our unconscious selves by an apparent appeal to conscious reason and sympathy. Consciousness can never be totally obliterated; whenever Lawrence realizes this 'the heart goes out of the fiction'.

Tamara Alinei analyzes the repetitive character and situation patterns of *Sons and Lovers* in *DQR*, while in *MFS* Michael Squires centres his discussion of 'the scene of recurrence' on *The Rainbow*. Darlene H. Unrue also considers *The Rainbow* as well as *Women in Love* in *DR* when she writes on 'Lawrence's Vision of Evil'. Art as a lie in *St. Mawr* is Michael Ragussis's subject (*PLL*); we must discriminate between Lou's 'faith and her credulity' if we are to understand her. *St. Mawr* is also treated by M. Scholtes in *DQR* as an example of Lawrence's belief in the 1920's as both an end and a transition for society. In *ConL*, Shirley Rose reflects on 'Physical Trauma in D. H. Lawrence's Short Fiction'. 'Tickets, Please' is viewed both as a disguised Dionysian myth by E. Kegel-Brinkgreve in *DQR*, and as an instance of Lawrence's use of setting as symbol by P. Michel-Michot in *RLV*.

In *TSLL* Del Ivan Janik investigates the unifying theme of death and re-birth in the *Last Poems*, and in *ConL* Mark Spilka compares the works of Lawrence and Doris Lessing with regard to themes, values, and techniques. Some useful books not available for notice are: Leloy Garcia and James Karabatsos's *Concordance to the Short Fiction of D. H. Lawrence* (U. of Nebraska P.), Brian John's *Supreme Fictions* (McGill-Queen's U.P.), Harry T. Moore's *The Priest of Love* (Heinemann), and Michael Squires's *The Pastoral Novel: Studies in George Eliot, Thomas Hardy, and D. H. Lawrence* (U.P. of Virginia).

In *TQ* Keith N. Hull suggests that the original seven chapters which opened *The Seven Pillars of Wisdom* are the keys to the book and T. E. Lawrence.

Annis Pratt and L. S. Dembo have collected nine essays on Doris Lessing from *ConL*[55] by John C. Carey, Evelyn Hinz, John Teunissen, Ellen Morgan, Michele Wender Zak, Dagmar Barnouw, Lynn Sukenik, Sydney Janet Kaplan, Douglass Bolling, and Nancy Shields Hardin. Also included are Florence Howe's 1966 'Conversation with Doris Lessing', a selective checklist, and an introduction by Annis Pratt. C. J. Driver conducts an interview with Doris Lessing in *New Review* (1974). *The Summer Before the Dark* is examined by Barbara F. Lefcowitz in *Crit* in an attempt to account for the seemingly pessimistic end. Kate's imaginative self is seen as the key. In *SNNTS* Marjorie J. Lightfoot analyzes *The Golden Note-book* in terms of the notion of 'breakthrough' to explain both the characters and the technique of this complex novel. Abstraction defeated by actual experience is the underlying theme in Doris Lessing's mature fiction according to Robert S. Ryf in *MFS*.

Matthew Corrigan observes in *Boundary 2* that Malcolm Lowry's own 'predilection for self-realization' stifled his limited 'sense of characteriza-tion'. Roger Leslie Hyman claims in *QQ* that Hugh MacLennan's fiction

[55] *Doris Lessing: Critical Studies*, ed. by Annis Pratt and L. S. Dembo. Madison Wisconsin: U. of Wisconsin P. pp. xii + 172. £3.

presents 'structured analyses of his country's character and identity', and in *ArielE* Sister Catherine Kelly analyzes the structure of *Two Solitudes* when considering the novel as a symbol of Canada.

Two collections of Katherine Mansfield's stories have appeared. In a sensitive introduction to the New Zealand stories,[56] Ian A. Gordon acknowledges that these stories treat New Zealand as a new Arcadia, but he also demonstrates how the techniques and themes manifested in these tales 'sustain the underlying unity of her work'. Anthony Adams and Esmor Jones draw on four volumes for their anthology[57] which includes questions for study, a short biography, and discussion of Mansfield's attitude to her fiction. T. O. Beachcroft argues in *English* (1974) that an idyll by Theocritus might well have influenced Mansfield's mix of narrative and 'interior mime' in her stories.

Robin Maugham's biography of Frederic and Somerset Maugham (1966) is now in paperback.[58] Barry Cameron records 'A Conversation with John Metcalf' in *QQ*, and D. A. N. Jones has a profile of Brian Moore in *New Review*.

In *ELT* Eileen Kennedy considers the extent to which Turgenev's *Sportsman's Sketches* influenced George Moore's *The Untilled Field*. In the same number Francis L. Nye maintains that Moore altered the story of Heloïse and Abélard to fit the romantic version of their love in Pater's *Renaissance*. Nye also draws attention to Moore's dependence on Charles de Remusat's accounts of the lovers. Colin Middleton Murry's *One Hand Clapping* (Gollancz) was not provided for review.

Iris Murdoch is the subject of several interesting essays this year. In *MQ* Zohreh Tawakuli Sullivan considers the importance of fantasy and demonic psychological magic in *The Flight from the Enchanter*, Ben Obumselu explores the extent of Murdoch's indebtedness to existentialism in *ELH*, and Patricia Stubbs compares Iris Murdoch and Muriel Spark in *English* with particular attention to their notions of fiction.

In *CQ* R. A. D. Grant attributes L. H. Myers's critical unpopularity to his attack on liberal humanism. *V. S. Naipaul: A Critical Introduction* (Macmillan) by Landeg White was not seen, but in *English* (1974) Margaret Shenfield compares Naipaul's *A House for Mr. Biswas* to Wells's *The History of Mr. Polly*. She finds the former's ironic vision and interest in the problems of humanity the more satisfying.

A monograph on P. H. Newby by George Sutherland Fraser[59] serves as a basic introduction since it stresses over-all themes in the novels and offers some of Newby's own comments on his work. The effective mixture of tragedy and farce in the Anglo-Egyptian novels goes far to making these Newby's greatest artistic achievement. E. C. Bufkin's study[60] concentrates

[56] *Undiscovered Country: the New Zealand Stories of Katherine Mansfield*, ed. by Ian A. Gordon. Longman. pp. xxii + 370. £4.75.
[57] *Katherine Mansfield*, ed. by Anthony Adams and Esmor Jones. Pegasus Library Series. Harrap. pp. 160.
[58] *Somerset and all the Maughams*, by Robin Maugham. Penguin. pp. 320. 75p.
[59] *P. H. Newby*, by George Sutherland Fraser. Writers and Their Work Series. Longman. 1974. pp. 34. 40p.
[60] *P. H. Newby*, by E. C. Bufkin. English Authors Series. Boston: Twayne. pp. 144. $6.95.

more fully on structure and techniques. Bufkin identifies archetypal patterns of separation, quest, crisis, and return which emphasize Newby's concern with spiritual and imaginative renewal. Yet he is not so naive as to suggest they are a permanent solution to the problems of humanity. Bufkin reveals limitations in Newby's technique, but he supports his claim that Newby is an important contemporary novelist comparing him with James and Conrad.

Anne Clissmann's critical introduction to Flann O'Brien[61] is the first full-length analysis of O'Brien's work. One cannot but feel the author's acknowledged ignorance of Gaelic in the limitations of her comments on O'Brien's style and linguistic development. Nevertheless much material here is valuable and, if Miss Clissmann's very detailed analyses sometimes seem unimaginative, she certainly provides ample evidence of the cruel mixture of 'mockery, arrogance and humility' so characteristic of O'Brien. Lorna Sage offers an over-view of O'Brien in *New Review* (1974).

In *A Reader's Guide to George Orwell*[62] Jeffrey Meyers sees the writings as an attempt to come to terms with personal experience, as a progression from guilt to compassion to a sense of responsibility for men. Meyers is particularly good on the way in which Orwell's themes have influenced his style. He traces the development from the early novels to *1984*, noting that until Orwell finds his own personal means of expression which combines reporting techniques and 'personal narrative' his novels demonstrate a lack of imaginative creation and a circular structure and pattern without advance or hope. *1984* is an excellent example of Orwell's refined technique. There is a useful chapter on Orwell criticism, and a bibliography. *The Road to Miniluv: George Orwell, the State and God* by Christopher Small[63] is similar in approach to Meyers's, though more uneven. Small asserts that the vision expressed in *1984* results from Orwell's subjective perception of the external world and personal experience as well as an objective adjudication of facts. Thus, he probes Orwell's personal past by examining the early works. Orwell is viewed as torn between love of surface (beauty, nature) and the impulse to explore the horrors below. While *Animal Farm* is a more objective 'expression of despair', *1984* is a plunge back into subjectivity and the journey beneath the surface. Believing *1984* to be the 'product of personal neurosis', Small investigates the defiance and submission bred in Orwell's childhood, with its repressed homosexuality and failure to find an outlet for a strong religious impulse. Small also looks at possible influences on the futuristic novel, including Zamyatin's *We* and Jack London's *The Iron Heel.*

In *The Road to 1984*[64] William Steinhoff argues that the novel's main themes stem largely from Orwell's reading and his environment. Starting with Utopian fiction and the influence of political writers such as James

[61] *Flann O'Brien: A Critical Introduction*, by Anne Clissmann. Dublin: Gill and Macmillan; New York: Barnes & Noble. pp. xiv + 370. £9.50.
[62] *A Reader's Guide to George Orwell*, by Jeffrey Meyers. Thames and Hudson pp. 192. £3.50, pb £1.95.
[63] *The Road to Miniluv: George Orwell, the State and God*, by Christopher Small Gollancz. pp. 220. £4.80.
[64] *The Road to 1984*, by William Steinhoff. Weidenfeld & Nicolson. pp. x + 288 £5.

Burnham, Steinhoff evokes Orwell's milieu, including the problems of faith, pacifism, and the press in that period. Orwell's main theme is that of 'a hidden or overt rebellion against a way of life accepted by most but intolerable to the protagonists'. *1984* is seen as a warning against the 'perversions to which a centralized economy is liable' as well as a criticism of totalitarianism. Steinhoff concludes that Orwell's work marks a different approach to Utopia. 'The hedonistic utopia was finished as an ideal' and Orwell successfully helped to modify 'people's expectations of the future'.

Bernd-Peter Lange studies the relationship in Orwell's novels between literary form and political content.[65] The author concentrates on Orwell's technique which enabled him 'to make political writing into an art' rather than on the novels' political content on which so much West German criticism has concentrated. The discussion centres on *The Road to Wigan Pier* and on *1984* which are offered as examples of political purpose and ideological bias shaping the literary forms of reportage and 'antiutopia' respectively. [H.C.C.]

The Spring number of *MFS* is devoted to Orwell. Martin Green notes that life at Eton did not stimulate Orwell in his search for maturity. John V. Knapp claims that 'purple passages' in *Burmese Days* seem to partake of the allegorical nature of *Animal Farm*, while Orwell's concept of a retreating movement in modern history comes under scrutiny by Richard I. Smyer who sees it in *A Clergyman's Daughter* 'in the form of Mrs. Creevy's harsh authoritarianism and Dorothy's descent into a condition of radically diminished consciousness for the purpose of regaining a past at once timeless and free of sexual tensions'. Nicholas Guild analyzes the import of Gordon Comstock's marriage and submission to the world of money in *Keep the Aspidistra Flying*. Robert J. Van Dellen finds that *Coming Up for Air* shows the need for a new order to replace the old dehumanizing system, but the same novel for Jeffrey Meyers serves as the thematic midpoint between the books on poverty and the later political works. Melvyn New examines Orwell's anti-semitic attitudes and James Connors claims that *1984* was not the result of the influence of Zamyatin's *We* but is developed from Orwell's own ideas about totalitarianism. There is a selected Orwell checklist compiled by Jeffrey Meyers.

In *ELN* D. Rankin attempts to clarify the intention behind *1984* by examining Orwell's own comments on the novel. Several interesting sidelights emerge from Alex Zwerdling's study of the development of Orwell's socialist faith in *New Review* (1974). All the works show an odd combination of conservative and radical tendencies. Yet, even when Orwell accepts that his ideals might never be realized he does not give way to total pessimism in *1984*. Zwerdling views this futuristic novel as a study of how the democratic state can avoid totalitarianism or uproot this evil once it is established. Significantly, only the latter process is an impossible task in Orwell's eyes. Jeffrey Meyers's *George Orwell: The Critical Heritage* (Routledge & Kegan Paul) was not seen.

Hilary Spurling introduces the beautifully produced *Drawings of Mervyn*

---

[65] *Literarische Form und politische Tendenz bei George Orwell*, Bernd-Peter Lange. Braunschweiger Anglistische Arbeiten. Technische Universitat Braunschweig. pp. 152.

Peake[66] taken from Maeve Gilmore's collection. These drawings range from sketches of children and animals through caricatures, portraits, and book illustrations, to surrealist drawings of monsters and incubi. Most striking is Peake's disconcerting ability to capture physical essence and personality in a few well-chosen lines. *Mervyn Peake: Writings and Drawings* by Maeve Gilmore and Shelagh Johnson (Academy Editions) was not available for notice.

In *New Review* (1974) Alan Brownjohn presents a profile of Anthony Powell, and in the 1975 volume James Tucker offers a who's who of characters in *A Dance to the Music of Time.*

The *Autobiography* of John Cowper Powys is treated by David A. Cook in *MP* as a study in self-analysis. Powys reaches out to 'archetypes of a cosmic experience once shared by all matter'. He learns to accept and value sexual instincts as strengtheners of the creative impulse. Powys's *Letters: 1937-1954* (U. of Wales P.) was not made available. An anthology of the best stories of T. F. Powys, *God's Eyes a-Twinkle*[67] (1947), has been reissued with a preface by Charles Prentice suggesting the mythical significance of the tales. T. F. Powys's 1931 parable of Death's visit to a small village[68] has also reappeared. J. B. Priestly's *Outcries and Asides* (Heinemann) and *Particular Pleasures* (Heinemann) have not been seen.

John Mellors reviews the work of V. S. Pritchett in *LMag.* The second volume of Kathleen Raine's autobiography[69] contains intimate glimpses of Virginia Woolf, Malcolm Lowry, and Graham Greene, and gives considerable insight into her own development of a personal poetic vision up to the end of the Second World War.

Cecil Woolf has edited a number of stories, poems and letters by the notorious Frederick Rolfe.[70] *The Armed Hands* contains sixteen uncollected stories, book reviews, and miscellaneous writings by 'Baron Corvo'. Rolfe's argumentative disposition, his love of obscure information, and his own homosexual proclivities are all revealed by the choice and handling of subjects. *The Collected Poems,* almost half of which are published for the first time, with illustrations designed by Rolfe himself, are primarily of 'archaeological' interest as they are for the most part awkward and technically limited. In letters published in full for the first time Rolfe describes in vivid detail his homosexual activities and his pecuniary hardship in Venice.

Janet Hitchman admits that her biography of Dorothy L. Sayers[71] is

[66] *The Drawings of Mervyn Peake.* introd. by Hilary Spurling. Davis-Poynter. 1974. pp. 113. £8.
[67] *God's Eyes a-Twinkle,* by T. F. Powys, preface by Charles Prentice. Bath: Cedric Chivers. 1974. pp. xvi + 454. £3.80.
[68] *Unclay,* by T. F. Powys. Bath: Cedric Chivers. 1974. pp. 343. £2.60.
[69] *The Land Unknown,* by Kathleen Raine. Hamish Hamilton. pp. 207. £4.50.
[70] *The Armed Hands and Other Stories and Pieces,* by Frederick Rolfe, ed. by Cecil Woolf. Cecil and Amelia Woolf. 1974. pp. 137. £2.50. *Collected Poems,* by Frederick Rolfe, ed. by Cecil Woolf. Cecil and Amelia Woolf. 1974. pp. 79. £2.10. *The Venice Letters,* by Frederick Rolfe, ed. by Cecil Woolf. Cecil and Amelia Woolf. 1974. pp. 80. £2.10.
[71] *Such a Strange Lady: An Introduction to Dorothy L. Sayers (1893-1957),* by Janet Hitchman. New English Library. pp. 203. £2.95.

not the scholarly definitive biography but rather an introduction to a 'strange' woman whose real self remains difficult to discern. The book contains an account of the development of Sayers's artistic skills, though there is little in the way of critical analysis. Miss Hitchman indulges in bizarre asides to her readers, and the author's breezy slang is often ludicrous and embarrassing. Future biographers will be greatly indebted to Miss Hitchman, but future work there must indeed be.

Alan Sillitoe's selected essays and lectures from 1960 to the present have been collected in *Mountains and Caverns*.[72] The volume includes a long autobiographical piece, shorter essays on his early reading, appreciations of Arnold Bennett, Robert Tressell's *The Ragged Trousered Philanthropist*, and some miscellaneous studies on the poor, hatred, and the Olympic Games. In *SSF* Norma Phillips considers Sillitoe's use of Joyce's 'Counterparts' as a shaping device for characters, theme, and structure in 'The Match'.

C. P. Snow's narrative method in the 'Strangers and Brothers' sequence is investigated by P. J. Widdowson in *RMS*. The basic flaw in Snow's fiction is his failure to allow the novel itself to comment by means of its own organic life; this failure is related to Snow's critical theory and rejection 'of the novel of "sensibility" and "experiment" '. In *ArielE* R. T. Robertson observes a change in the 'New Zealand tradition of dream narrative' when he considers 'The Nightmare of Kiwi Joe: C. K. Stead's Double Novel'. In *Southerly* John B. Beston writes of literary allusions in Randolph Stow's *To the Islands* and L. T. Hergenhan argues that the world of that novel is not simply one of dream symbolism, without any relation to the real world. Jesse F. McCartney reports in *ELT* on 'The Frank Arthur Swinnerton Collection' at the University of Arkansas which includes correspondence from Wells, Conrad, and Maugham.

Ean Cochrane Macinnes Begg's short pamphlet, '*The Lord of the Rings and The Signs of the Times*'[73] is more concerned with what imaginative literature tells us about our own age than with any critical assessment of the work. Marion Perret has an interesting article in *ArielE* on the significance of hand imagery in *The Lord of the Rings*. *Amon Hen*, the bulletin of the Tolkien Society of Great Britain, was not available, nor was Alec Waugh's *A Year to Remember: A Reminiscence of 1931* (W. H. Allen).

Dudley Carew, a contemporary of Evelyn Waugh at Lancing, has written a tribute to him.[74] The reminiscences of their time at Lancing and their friendship throughout the 1920's are based on diaries, memories and some of Evelyn Waugh's own material.

In the *Evelyn Waugh Newsletter*, Jeffrey M. Heath writes on 'The Year's Work in Waugh Studies'. Robert Murray Davis reprints two letters to *The Times* which might possibly be by Waugh, and Winnifred M. Bogaards supplies errata and addenda to the Whitston Waugh Checklist.

[72] *Mountains and Caverns*, by Alan Sillitoe. W. H. Allen. pp. 160. £2.95.
[73] *The "Lord of the Rings" and The Signs of the Times*, by Ean C. M. Begg. London: Guild of Pastoral Psychology. pp. 23.
[74] *A Fragment of Friendship: A Memory of Evelyn Waugh When Young*, by Dudley Carew. Everest Books. 1974. pp. 96. £1.75.

Calvin W. Lane offers 'Evelyn Waugh's Radio and Television Broadcasts, 1938–1964', while Francis S. Heck investigates themes of Proust and Gide in *Brideshead*. Jeffrey Heath considers the basic dilemma of self-evasion and absurdity in *A Handful of Dust*. J. W. Scheideman treats the significance of Miss Vavasour in the *Sword of Honour* trilogy, and Hans Otto Thieme provides a supplementary checklist of Waugh criticism. Richard Gill offers additional proof from Waugh himself that no houses served as models for Hetton and Brideshead. Winnifred Bogaards again supplements the Whitston Waugh Checklist. The satire of 'journalese' is considered by D. Paul Farr in his *ConnR* essay on style in *Scoop*. In *ES* Jeffrey M. Heath argues that 'To the extent that *Brideshead* is still regularly misread, one must concede that Waugh is at fault. . .' Waugh's use of irony to resolve the contradictions between ethical standards and external reality is investigated by Marston LaFrance writing in *DR* on *Sword of Honour*. *Evelyn Waugh* by Christopher Sykes (Collins) was not seen.

Stephen Gill's *Scientific Romances of H. G. Wells*[75] is divided into four sections: literary and social background together with biographies of Wells and his predecessors; analyses of the short stories and novels; evaluations of Wells; and a chronology and bibliography. Despite such a comprehensive structure this is a disappointingly superficial study. Plot summary and heavy uncritical reliance on other critics are characteristic. Even 'romance' is dismissed in several brief pages.

Three useful articles on Wells appear in *ELT*. Richard Hauer Costa studies Wells's dialogue novels and compares *Mr. Britling* with James's *The Ambassadors* in an attempt to show that Wells did not abandon his responsibilities as novelist, but tried always to maintain 'fictive plausibility'. William J. Scheick analyzes *Apropos of Dolores* by the application of Spengler's views on culture and civilization. The novel, usually viewed as insignificant, emerges as Wells's version of a new art form. Finally, Max A. Webb considers the place of *Tono-Bungay* in the 'foundling' novel tradition. *The Wellsian* was not available.

Alan Lawson has produced a thorough annotated bibliography of Patrick White[76], encompassing all his works and all references to him and his work. In *Southerly*, three writers consider various aspects of White's fiction: Anthony J. Hassall looks at the theme of loneliness in *The Cockatoos*, while Veronica Brady argues that Laura should be seen as the central character of *Voss*; *Riders in the Chariot* takes on new spiritual depths when one considers the allusions to Jewish mysticism which are pointed out by Susan Moore, and in *LiNQ* Rodolfo Delmonte shows that the search for values in a shifting world which is the underlying theme of the novel contributes to its religiousness and ambiguity for no absolute answer is supplied. Also in *LiNQ* Hedwig Rohde argues that White is developing an Australian tradition of fiction which is not simply an English off-shoot.

Robert C. Holder examines the position of the artist as prophet in the

[75] *Scientific Romances of H. G. Wells: A Critical Study*, by Stephen Gill. Cornwall, Ont., Canada: Vesta Publications. pp. 155. £4.50.
[76] *Patrick White*, by Alan Lawson. Australian Bibliographies Series. Melbourne and London: Oxford U.P. 1974. pp. xii + 131. £2.95.

fiction of Charles Williams in *Renascence*. Williams's artists differ from many creators pictured in modern fiction. For Williams, the artist is a spokesman for a 'broadly Christian doctrine'. Jonathan Raban has a profile of Angus Wilson in *New Review* (1974). David Jasen's portrait of P. G. Wodehouse[77] purports to be a definitive biography. The work is thorough but rather pedestrian, and such sweeping statements as 'P. G. Wodehouse is the funniest writer in the world' suggest a certain lack of rigorous analysis and evaluation. Jasen emerges as an enthusiastic and uncritical admirer. However, the serious student of Wodehouse's comic methods will find raw material that may prove stimulating. In the *ContempR* there is a brief tribute to Wodehouse by R. C. Churchill. In *N&Q* Robert A. Hall Jr. considers the reasons for changes in the ending of *Leave it to Psmith*.

Jeremy Hawthorn's examination of alienation in *Mrs. Dalloway*[78] is at times obscured by references to works of only peripheral bearing on the subject. His analysis centres on the paradoxical nature of Clarissa. The city experience which forms the setting of the novel serves as a useful symbol of alienation, while the party represents a possible solution in the form of escape. Nevertheless, the only true solution lies in communal giving. Hawthorn also looks at the class attitudes which limit the effectiveness of the projected solution for he disapproves of Virginia Woolf's disinterest in making contact with the classes outside of Clarissa's realm. A catalogue of the books from the library of Virginia and Leonard Woolf has been compiled[79]. This collection forms a sizeable part of the Monks House library and that of the Victoria Square house. Many typographical errors and a haphazard arrangement make the book difficult to use, but the volumes described, coming as they do from the libraries of Leslie Stephen and Clive Bell among others, are interesting; and it is of course useful to know the works to which the Woolfs most certainly had access.

Klaus Schwank contributes to the discussion on Woolf's use of symbols with a difficult but rewarding study of *Jakob's Room, Mrs Dalloway*, and *To the Lighthouse*[80]. The very large number of thematic symbols employed (as e.g. the leaf-tree-forest group) is considered against the context of Woolf's concept of reality and of the 'patterns' of reality fashioned by the literary imagination.

The *Virginia Woolf Quarterly* has once again returned to circulation. Articles on the Woolfs in I, iv include Germaine Brée's examination of similarities between Gide's Vaneau milieu and the 1922 Bloomsbury group. Leland Fetzer reminds us of the collaboration of Leonard Woolf, Lawrence and Koteliansky on the English translation of Bunin's 'The Gentleman

---

[77] *P. G. Wodehouse: Portrait of a Master*, by David Jasen. Garnstone P. pp. xxii + 294. £5.25.
[78] *Virginia Woolf's Mrs. Dalloway: A Study in Alienation*, by Jeremy Hawthorn. Text and Context Series. Chatto & Windus (for Sussex U.P.). pp. 111. £2.50, pb. £1.
[79] *Catalogue of Books from the Library of Virginia & Leonard Woolf*. Brighton: Holleyman & Treacher. pp. 366.
[80] *Bildstruktur und Romanstruktur bei Virginia Woolf*, Klaus Schwank. Anglistische Forschungen Heft 107. Carl Winter Verlag, Heidelberg. pp. 204.

from San Francisco'. Roger Fry's Omega Workshops are discussed by Pamela Fry Diamand, and Stephen D. Fox writes on the implications of the 'hidden protagonist' in 'An Unwritten Novel'. The novel makes sense when we see the narrator as a main character. David H. Flood considers Leonard Woolf's *The Village in the Jungle* as a masterpiece in its symbolic portrayal of modern man alienated from nature and exploiting his fellow creatures. There are also book reviews on Graham Greene, Nigel Nicolson's *Portrait of a Marriage* and Marc Alyn's study of Lawrence Durrell.

In Volume Two Doris L. Eder writes on Eliot as a model for Louis in *The Waves*. There is a facsimile reproduction of Virginia Woolf's will, and Suzette Henke analyzes the characters of Mrs. Ramsay and Lily Briscoe to show that understanding and artistic vision depend on our openness to daily experience. Both characters are lovers in their own way. Virginia R. Hyman disagrees with critics who see Mr. Ramsay as Leslie Stephen. Rather, Stephen pervades the entire novel and in this we might see Virginia Woolf's own imaginative reconciliation with him. There is also a bibliography of the Hogarth Press compiled by Suzanne Henig and book reviews on twentieth-century fiction.

In *ConL* Marilyn R. Farwell writes intelligently on androgyny, and decides that Virginia Woolf opts most often for its traditional meaning of fusion. In *UTQ* Susan M. Kenney discusses *Between the Acts* to illuminate the basic conflicts in Woolf's life and to understand her suicide as an 'affirmation of her own integrity'. In *The Waves*, only the artist can provide an alternative to the rigidity of the novel structure and of the universe, according to Mary Steussy Shanahan in *MLQ*. Only the artist controls the waves and is borne along by them. In *Criticism* Sharon L. Proudfit investigates the ambivalent attitude to women in *The Years*, and Grace Radin offers an examination of the original holograph draft of the novel in *MR* to account for the shift from experimentation in the first version to a more compressed work without the ideological content. In *Mosaic*, Ellen Hawkes Rogat notes that Virginia Woolf's non-fiction work 'still shapes the way we think about the creativity of women'. Gillian Workman traces the development of Leonard Woolf's attitudes to imperialism in *ArielE*. Robin Majumdar and Allen McLaurin's *Virginia Woolf: The Critical Heritage* (Routledge & Kegan Paul) was not made available.

Cara Ackerman considers 'Yeats' Revisions of the Hanrahan Stories, 1897 and 1904' in *TSLL* and argues that the changes show a developing sense of symbol.

2. Verse

It is encouraging to find that Hugh Kenner's *The Pound Era*[1] is now in paperback. The age of Ezra Pound, T. S. Eliot, James Joyce, and Wyndham Lewis is scrutinized with the pellucid intelligence that we always appreciate from this critic. The intellectual preoccupations, the movements in poetry, the influences from the East, are recorded in a style which

---

[1] *The Pound Era: The Age of Ezra Pound, T. S. Eliot, James Joyce and Wyndham Lewis*, by Hugh Kenner. Faber. pp. xiv + 606. £2.50.

combines brilliant critical insight with fascinating details of human interest. This masterly volume is highly recommended. Alex Preminger, Frank J. Warnke, and O. B. Hardison, Jr., edit the enlarged edition of the *Princeton Encyclopedia of Poetry and Poetics*[2]. A supplement of some 75,000 words is appended to the original edition of 1965. We are now able to consult essays by specialists on structuralism, projective verse, and Swahili poetry among many other useful additions. This invaluable reference work deals with the history of poetry, techniques of poetry, poetics and criticism, and the relationship of poetry to other fields of interest. A comprehensive guide is provided by this volume both for the scholar and the general reader.

Jonathan Culler's *Structuralist Poetics: Structuralism, Linguistics and the Study of Literature*[3] is 'an account of structuralism based. . .on possible relationships between literary and linguistic studies'. The several ways in which structuralists have applied linguistic models to the study of literature are established and analysed according to their success or failure. The use of linguistics 'as a model which suggests how a poetics should be organized' is examined. The notion of 'literary competence' is postulated as that which enables us to interpret literary works, 'an implicit understanding of the operations of literary discourse which tells one what to look for'. The conventions for writing literature are looked at, as is the reader's ability to 'naturalize', 'to make literature into a communication, to reduce its strangeness'. There follows an examination of how structuralists have approached or would approach the lyric and the novel. Finally, Culler replies to the theorists associated with the review *Tel Quel*; he anticipates their attack on his view of structuralism and defends his standpoint. It is concluded that 'Structuralism has succeeded in unmasking many signs; its task must now be to organize itself more coherently so as to explain how these signs work'. This is a fascinating account of an intricate mode of literary criticism. See also *New Review*, where F. W. Bateson questions 'Is Your Structuralism Really Necessary?'

J. B. Harmer's *Victory in Limbo*[4] is a comprehensive history of the Imagist movement in Britain and America from its beginnings in 1908 to the last of Amy Lowell's anthologies in 1917. The development of Imagism is discussed with close reference to poems by Richard Aldington, Joseph Campbell, Padraic Colum, Hilda Doolittle, John Gould Fletcher, F. S. Flint, Ford Madox Ford, T. E. Hulme, D. H. Lawrence, Amy Lowell, Ezra Pound, and Edward Storer. The intricacies of those poetic theories surrounding, opposing, and subsumed in Imagism are fully stated. The technique of Imagism is seen to have influenced modern British and American poets such as Keith Douglas, Jim Morrison, Kenneth Rexroth, and Edward Dorn. The difficulties of Dr. Harmer's subject are revealed in his conclusion: 'Any attempt to sum up the Imagist aesthetic leaves one floundering in a quagmire'.

[2] *Princeton Encyclopedia of Poetry and Poetics*, ed. by Alex Preminger, Frank J. Warnke, and O. B. Hardison, Jr. Macmillan. pp. xxiv + 992. £12, pb £4.95.
[3] *Structuralist Poetics: Structuralism, Linguistics and the Study of Literature*, by Jonathan Culler. Routledge & Kegan Paul. pp. xi + 301. £5.50, pb £2.75.
[4] *Victory in Limbo: Imagism 1908-1917*, by J. B. Harmer. Martin Secker & Warburg. pp. 238. £6.

A. T. Tolley's *The Poetry of the Thirties*[5] surveys the poets of that decade. An historical approach offers a clear picture of the ideological climate of the period; it is stressed that 'for the first time, there existed a generation of writers who had grown up under the influence of the great makers of twentieth-century literature and thought—under the influence of Proust, Eliot, Joyce, Lawrence and Freud'. C. Day Lewis, W. H. Auden, Louis MacNeice, Stephen Spender, Rex Warner, Norman Cameron, and John Betjeman were at Oxford in the latter half of the nineteen-twenties; for these poets as for the Cambridge group of the same period—William Empson, Ronald Bottrall, Julian Bell, John Lehmann, and James Reeves—the importance of Eliot as a poet and a critic was enormous. The problems of writing political poetry, and the importance of periodicals—especially Geoffrey Grigson's *New Verse*—at this time are emphasized. The significance is examined of the poetry of David Gascoyne, John Pudney, George Barker, Dylan Thomas, John Cornford, Philip O'Connor, Kathleen Raine, and Vernon Watkins. The verse drama of Auden and Isherwood, the light verse of William Plomer, and the proletarian poetry of Idris Davies and Julius Lipton are placed in context. The impact of the Spanish Civil War is assessed. The new poets of the later thirties, including Roy Fuller and Francis Scarfe, are looked at. In a concluding chapter it is noted that 'The most striking common quality of the poetry that gives the immediate feeling that it could have been produced at no other time...is a capacity to give the quality of English life and to elucidate the English experience of the decade'. Moreover, despite the importance of Eliot and his generation in shaping the sensibility of the decade it is seen that, apart from their preoccupation with imagery, the thirties' poets did not follow the revolutionary example: they generally used traditional forms and wrote 'poems *about* things'. An individuality of experience flavours thirties' poetry; however, there is no 'unified vision of experience'.

Terence Brown's *Northern Voices: Poets from Ulster*[6] studies some Northern Ireland poets in the context of their common background of 'cultural, social and emotional complexity'. The author is not concerned to point to a poetic tradition in Ulster; rather he attempts to shed light on the work of individuals. The historical background is established, and assessments are made of the following twentieth-century poets: John Hewitt, Louis MacNeice, W. R. Rodgers, Robert Greacen, Roy McFadden, Padraic Fiacc, John Montague, Seamus Heaney, James Simmons, Derek Mahon, Michael Longley, and Patrick Kavanagh.

John Ryan's *Remembering How We Stood*[7] is a collection of reminiscences concerning literary Dublin and Dubliners of the decade 1945–1955. The book is divided into two sections, the first of which deals with Dublin and establishes a context for the following discussion of the author's literary acquaintances; included are anecdotes about Brendan Behan, Patrick Kavanagh, Brian O'Nolan (Flann O'Brien) and Padraic Colum.

[5] *The Poetry of the Thirties*, by A. T. Tolley. Victor Gollancz. pp. 445. £6.50.
[6] *Northern Voices: Poets from Ulster*, by Terence Brown. Gill and Macmillan. pp. 248. £9.25.
[7] *Remembering How We Stood: Bohemian Dublin at the Mid-Century*, by John Ryan. Gill and Macmillan. pp. xiv + 168. £3.25.

Orage as Critic[8] brings together a collection of A. R. Orage's literary criticism. The majority of the passages are chosen from the column 'Readers and Writers' which appeared in *The New Age* from 1913 to 1921. The extracts are arranged thematically. We are introduced to Orage's criticism by a selection of his writing on the theory and method of discussing literature; other sections examine culture and society, the nature of literature and criticism, literary genres and the media, Victorian and Edwardian literature, modern literature, the English language, and style. Extracts from writings on Georgian poetry, Vorticism, Ezra Pound, T. E. Hulme, and T. S. Eliot will be of particular interest. A short bibliography is provided.

The Black Rainbow[9], edited by Peter Abbs, is a collection of essays on the contemporary breakdown of culture. Together with papers on the modern novel, language, music, architecture, and philosophy, are included two essays on poetry. Ian Robinson's 'Paper Tygers or, the Circus Animals' Desertion in the New Pop Poetry' is a hostile discussion of three anthologies: *Love, Love, Love, Children of Albion, Poetry of the Underground in Britain*, and *The Mersey Sound*. He concludes: 'If the Children of Albion do succeed in abolishing the critical petty fogs and imposing themselves comfortably as the radiant new dawn, if they succeed in becoming contemporary English literature (though the term will presumably fall into disuse) that will be the end of our poetry past and present'. David Holbrook's 'Ted Hughes's "Crow" and the Language for Non-Being' discovers Crow to be 'the embodiment of egoistic nihilism' and points to the 'deepest objection to *Crow*. . .that as a depressing picture of existence as victimization it merely twists even stronger chains round the sensibility—so that any attempt to find and exert the dynamics of love, meaning, responsibility and freedom seems futile. One simply opts for egoistical survival'.

Graham Martin and P. N. Furbank edit a volume of 'Critical Essays and Documents' for the Open University Press[10]. The collection brings together critical appreciations of individual poets and statements exploring more general topics crucial to twentieth-century poetry. The anthology was assembled for a specific Open University course; however, its wider value is clear. The editors stress that one of their purposes 'was to give an idea of the many different kinds of writing that go by the name of "literary criticism" '. The general section contains writings by W. K. Wimsatt, J. Middleton Murry, Ernest Fenollosa, Ezra Pound, F. R. Leavis, Hugh Kenner, T. S. Eliot, W. B. Yeats, William Empson, T. E. Hulme, E. D. Hirsch, Graham Hough, Yvor Winters, I. A. Richards, Jon Silkin, C. Day Lewis, W. H. Auden, R. Ellmann, C. Fiedelson, Donald Davie, Philip Hobsbaum, Alan Bold, and Ian Hamilton. Among these are such landmarks in literary criticism as T. S. Eliot's 'Tradition and the Individual Talent' and W. B. Yeat's 'The Symbolism of Poetry'. The poets given individual attention include W. B. Yeats, W. H. Auden, Dylan Thomas, T. S. Eliot,

[8] *Orage as Critic*, ed. by Wallace Martin. The Routledge Critics Series. Routledge & Kegan Paul. pp. 218. £5.95.
[9] *The Black Rainbow: Essays on the present breakdown of culture*, ed. by Peter Abbs. Heinemann. pp. 247. £3.80.
[10] *Twentieth Century Poetry: Critical Essays and Documents*, ed. by Graham Martin and P. N. Furbank. Open University P. pp. xiv + 450.

Hugh MacDiarmid, Philip Larkin, and Ted Hughes. Denis Donoghue's 'T. S. Eliot's *Quartets*, a new reading', George Orwell and Hugh Kenner on Yeats, and Empson on Dylan Thomas are to be found in this section. D. J. Brindley's *My Poetry is Life*[11] is an examination of teenage poetry writing. The author has 'tried to approach the teaching of poetry writing from the viewpoint of the adolescent: first by seeking to understand him as a person rather than as a child; then by finding out what he is really thinking and what is of most importance to him so that he may write meaningfully; and finally by outlining a method of work which, while concentrating on essentials of good writing, allows free play to the creative imagination'. Poems by teenagers, and teaching aids are included; practical problems are faced, teaching programmes are suggested, and themes for writing are listed. This is a textbook useful more for the teacher than the scholar.

Laurence Lerner's *An Introduction to English Poetry*[12] concentrates on fifteen poems from the Middle Ages to the present in order to illustrate 'the main kinds and styles of English poetry'. Essays on two twentieth-century poems are included: Wallace Stevens's 'To an Old Philosopher in Rome' and W. H. Auden's 'City Without Walls'. In the conclusion the author discusses the possibility of a general pattern for poetry interpretation. In his own essays he has included 'both an intrinsic and an extrinsic discussion for every poem', he has introduced relevant poems for comparison with that under discussion, he has identified the genre, discussed the form, and he has finally attempted an evaluation. A reading list is appended.

Robin Skelton's *The Poet's Calling*[13] is a sensitive account of the difficult situation of the poet. Firsthand experience is drawn upon for the most part; the wisdom of other poets backs up personal deductions and observations. The poet's life as a child and the vision of the Muse are examined. The poet as priest and as craftsman are confronted; we are shown examples of the worksheets of Kingsley Amis, James K. Baxter, Anne Sexton, and Robert Francis. It is demonstrated that the poet needs a considerable amount of scholarship. The experiences that trigger off poetic creation are delved into with reference to poems by William Jay Smith, John Wain, Barbara Howes, Richard Eberhardt, and Tony Connor. Some modern poetic techniques are investigated. The question of the twentieth-century poet's authority is raised and examined with reference to the development of Yeats's career. The conflict between the poet's need to create and his need to support himself is stressed.

Volumes three and four of Joseph Campbell's *The Masks of God* have now been published in England. *Occidental Mythology*[14] and *Creative Mythology*[15] follow *Primitive Mythology* and *Oriental Mythology* to com-

[11] *My Poetry is Life*, by D. J. Brindley. Ilfracombe, Devon: Arthur H. Stockwell. pp. 209. £2.

[12] *An Introduction to English Poetry*, by Laurence Lerner. Edward Arnold. pp. x + 230. £5, pb £1.95.

[13] *The Poet's Calling*, ed. by Robin Skelton. Heinemann and New York: Barnes & Noble. pp. x + 214. £1.50.

[14] *The Masks of God*, Volume III: *Occidental Mythology*, by Joseph Campbell Souvenir P. and New York: The Viking P. pp. 752. £4.50, pb £2.25.

[15] *The Masks of God*, Volume IV: *Creative Mythology*, by Joseph Campbell. Souvenir P. and New York: The Viking P. pp. xvii + 730. £4, pb £2.

plete a fascinating series. *Occidental Mythology* traces the evolution of the key Western myths. *Creative Mythology* examines the post-medieval situation where the orthodox tradition is disintegrating and the non-theological revelations of creative individuals can communicate with the 'value and force of living myth'. This volume will be especially helpful for those interested in T. S. Eliot.

The St. James Press has published the first set of five volumes in the Poetry Reprint Series.[16] They include Robert Graves's *Over the Brazier*, H. D.'s *Sea Garden*, Wallace Stevens's *Harmonium*, John Betjeman's *Mount Zion*, and Conrad Aiken's *Earth Triumphant*.

Cora Kaplan's *Salt and Bitter and Good: Three Centuries of English and American Women Poets*[17] is a beautifully presented anthology of selected poetry by English and American women who are no longer living. The poems are chosen to illustrate 'what it has meant over some 300 years, to be a woman and a poet'. A valuable introduction and interesting biographical notes about each writer stress the importance of the articulation in verse of women's experience; the twentieth-century poets represented—Hilda Doolittle, Marianne Moore, Edna St. Vincent Millay, Vita Sackville-West, Dorothy Parker, Louise Bogan, Stevie Smith, and Sylvia Plath—are seen as part of a tradition of women's poetry.

W. H. Auden's wide-ranging collection of essays, *The Dyer's Hand*[18], first published in England in 1963, has been reissued. This volume contains general essays on poetry, music, opera, reading, writing and criticism, as well as papers on specific writers and topics: for example, on Kafka, *Othello*, D. H. Lawrence, Robert Frost, and Marianne Moore. In *ConL* Lucy S. McDiarmid and John McDiarmid examine 'Artifice and Self-Consciousness in Auden's "The Sea and the Mirror" '. An intricate analysis shows that 'There is a progressive self-consciousness in the styles of the three main sections that works in tandem with the growing sense of artificiality ...Like the three inner sections as a whole, each lyric follows the pattern of a movement from art to life to some absolute which makes art and life both look insubstantial'. It is concluded that 'Auden is grappling not with Shakespeare but with the idea of the artist's "unique importance" '.

Margaret L. Stapleton has compiled a bibliography of the work of Sir John Betjeman[19] which aims to be 'as complete as possible a listing of published works in English by and about him'. Ralph J. Mills, Jr., points out Betjeman's most important themes in 'John Betjeman's Poetry: An Appreciation' which introduces the bibliography.

Robert Brainard Pearsall's study[20] details Rupert Brooke's life and work with the intention of stating a clear separation between the two.

[16] Poetry Reprint Series, Set One. St. James Press and New York: St. Martin's P. £10.
[17] *Salt and Bitter and Good: Three Centuries of English and American Women Poets*, by Cora Kaplan. London and New York: Paddington P. and Toronto: Random House of Canada. pp. 304. £4.95.
[18] *The Dyer's Hand and other essays*, by W. H. Auden. Faber. pp. xii + 527. £2.25.
[19] *Sir John Betjeman: A Bibliography of Writings by and about him*, by Margaret L. Stapleton, with an essay by Ralph J. Mills, Jr. Metuchen, N.J.: The Scarecrow P. pp. v + 143. $6.
[20] *Rupert Brooke: The Man and Poet*, by Robert Rainard Pearsall. Amsterdam: Rodopi N. V. pp. 174.

Chapters on the climate of Brooke's Rugby and King's College, Cambridge, are for this reason dealt with separately from accounts of his literary activities at school and at University. However, the two categories inevitably overlap at crucial points. An analytical survey of the development of the poetry is made throughout, and the author ends his examination by considering Brooke's status as a minor poet. He observes that 'The final myth about Brooke was. . .the myth of his extinction'.

There is a Brian Coffey Special Issue in *IUR* with a bibliographical note and introductory essay by James Mays.

In 'The Proper Words' (*IUR*) Hugh Shields considers Padraic Colum's 'She moved through the fair' in an interesting discussion of the relationship between literary pastiche of folk song and folk culture, a relationship which has been recurringly interesting for the past two centuries.

William M. Chace's *The Political Identities of Ezra Pound and T. S. Eliot*[21] has been unavailable for notice: see, however, Bernard Crick's critical review (*TLS*: May 30). Stephen Spender's excellent introductory volume for the 'Fontana Modern Masters' series[22] traces the development of Eliot's canon. The major poems, plays, and criticism are analyzed with reference to Eliot's ritualistic attitude. We are directed to the conclusion that 'after "Little Gidding" Eliot stopped writing out of the centre of his ritualistic sensibility and wrote out of the periphery of conscience'. The progression in Eliot is seen to be from concern for the subjective to the realms of politics, education, and culture. This introduction to Eliot is enhanced by reproductions of paintings by Piero della Francesca, Giovanni Bellini, Francis Bacon, and Turner, which serve to emphasize Eliot's visual imagination.

Elisabeth W. Schneider's *T. S. Eliot: The Pattern in the Carpet*[23] aims to perceive in the poetry 'something of the continuity persisting beneath development and change'. Eliot's search for a style is discussed with reference to W. E. Henley, John Davidson, Arthur Symons, Ernest Dowson, the French Symbolists, and the Imagist Movement. It is demonstrated that 'Prufrock' introduces the theme of subjective change that recurs throughout the canon. There follows a detailed examination of 'Gerontion', *The Waste Land*, 'The Hollow Men', 'Ash Wednesday', the Ariel poems, 'Coriolan' and *Four Quartets*, with close attention to their thematic continuity.

Alexander Sackton has compiled a bibliography of *The T. S. Eliot Collection of The University of Texas at Austin*[24] This volume is well-illustrated, and it includes descriptions of his syllabuses, leaflets and broadsides, musical settings and recordings, the manuscripts of his literary works, of his notes, the manuscripts of poems, essays and notes on Eliot, and the musical settings, and iconography of his work as well as more standard material. The compiler details the complex dovetailing of this

[21] *The Political Identities of Ezra Pound and T. S. Eliot*, by William M. Chase. Stanford U.P. and O.U.P. pp. 238. £5.25.
[22] *Eliot*, by Stephen Spender. Fontana. pp. vii + 251. 80p.
[23] *T. S. Eliot: The Pattern in the Carpet*, by Elisabeth W. Schneider. U. of California P. pp. ix + 226.
[24] *The T. S. Eliot Collection of the University of Texas at Austin*, compiled by Alexander Sackton. The Humanities Research Center. The U. of Texas at Austin. pp. 407. $18.95.

edition with Gallup's revised edition of *T. S. Eliot: A Bibliography* (1969). Harold L. Weatherby's *The Keen Delight: The Christian Poet in the Modern World*[25] will be useful to readers of Eliot's poetry in its demonstration that 'The modern shift of emphasis from reason to experience [in interpretation of faith] imposes a sharp limitation on the scale of Catholic theology and poetry...Newman, Hopkins, and Eliot tend either to leave the creation out of account, to treat it as an obstacle to the knowledge of God, or to regard it as a medium of God's felt presence rather than of knowledge...Newman, Hopkins, and Eliot...are inclined to substitute intimations of immortality for a true science of the holy'. The author analyzes *Four Quartets* in this context, discovering that 'Eliot's imagery gives us what he never gave in prose statement—evidence that he understood the nature of mystical wisdom'. In conclusion, with reference to Jacques Maritain and Etienne Gilson, the author examines the problem of writing religious poetry in a secular age.

The Family Reunion is examined in Patrick Roberts's *The Psychology of Tragic Drama*[26], which elucidates some ancient and modern tragedies with a psychoanalytical approach. In a section on plays dealing with the Orestes myth, the author finds that in Eliot's play the themes of 'man's neurotic fear of woman, woman's frightening tenacity, the bitterness of family tensions' are expressed more adequately than the religious theme. An illuminating comparison with *Hamlet* is drawn. It is concluded that Eliot's 'avowedly religious aims in *The Family Reunion*, and his curious ambivalence towards psychology, seem to direct our attention elsewhere, but the play gains abundant life from a compulsive presentation of Oresteian guilt that seems to admit a Freudian influence in the very act of turning its back on it'.

The T. S. Eliot Newsletter has now been re-named *The T. S. Eliot Review*: it is to be published twice a year from York University, Toronto, and includes notes, short papers, and reviews. In *DR* Louis K. MacKendrick comments on 'T. S. Eliot and the *Egoist*: The Critical Preparation'. While Eliot was Assistant Editor for the *Egoist*, he contributed a number of critical reviews as well as two formal articles, 'In Memory of Henry James' and 'Tradition and the Individual Talent'. The magazine acted as 'a testing-ground for his maturing literary theories', and, 'by the time that the *Egoist* ceased publication his interests perceptibly came together, and one central result is "Tradition and the Individual Talent" '.

James S. Whitlark discovers 'More Borrowings by T. S. Eliot from "The Light of Asia" ' (*N&Q*). The wheel-motif is common to Sir Edwin Arnold's 'The Light of Asia' and Eliot's *Murder in the Cathedral*, 'Burnt Norton', and a draft of 'The Fire Sermon'. Eliot's Simeon in 'A Song for Simeon' owes a debt to Arnold's Asita. In *RES* V. J. E. Cowley discovers 'A Source for T. S. Eliot's "Objective Correlative" ' in a sermon by Newman.

Joyce Hamilton Rochat writes on 'T. S. Eliot's "Companion" Poems: Eternal Question, Temporal Response' (*ContempR*). 'Prufrock' and

[25] *The Keen Delight: The Christian Poet in the Modern World*, by Harold L. Weatherby. Athens: The U. of Georgia P. pp. 167. $7.50.
[26] *The Psychology of Tragic Drama*, by Patrick Roberts. Routledge & Kegan Paul. pp. 234. £5.95.

'Gerontion' are companion poems in that 'the questions that Prufrock poses for himself are answered by Gerontion. Where Prufrock sees the human condition obscurely, Gerontion sees it in stark relief'. Stephen Kirk's 'The Structural Weakness of T. S. Eliot's *The Waste Land*' (*YES*) explores the demands made on the reader of a poem which 'has no thread, logical, discursive, or narrative'. It is claimed that the fragmentary structure of *The Waste Land* works against the reader's search for unity of content: '*The Waste Land* has no unity: it is several poems. The fact that they are read as a unit is fortuitous, depending on typographical collocation alone'. In *CritQ* there are two interesting pieces: Barbara Everett in 'Eliot In and Out of *The Waste Land*' writes on Wagnerism among other influences on the poem, and in 'The Obstetrics of *The Waste Land*' Gareth Reeves argues that Eliot's 'Impersonal theory of Poetry' was 'a deliberate attempt by an author possessed with a highly subjective imagination to hide the fact that he was not capable of treating in poetry his personal experience head-on'.

Christopher Ricks's 'A Note on "Little Gidding" ' (*EIC*) examines in relation to the poem two pieces of Eliot's criticism which were published in French and have not been translated into English: 'Note sur Mallarmé et Poe' (*Nouvelle Revue Francaise* 1st November 1926) and Eliot's talk 'Charybde et Scylla' (given 25th March 1952, published in *Annales du Centre Universitaire Méditerranéen*). These interesting commentaries are used by Ricks to show that 'Eliot's own aftersight and foresight about 'Little Gidding' are witnessed in two pieces of his criticism which seem, surprisingly, not to have become part of the critical ambience of the poem'.

James Hogg writes on *James Elroy Flecker's 'Hassan': A Near Master-Piece?*[27] The evolution of the play, the London production in 1923, and subsequent productions are examined. The author concludes that the play is 'very rich in texture' and that 'it has scarcely received the detailed critical attention it deserves'.

Stanley M. Wiersma considers 'Christopher Fry's Definition of the Complete Pacifist in "The Dark is Light Enough" ' (*ArielE*). The play is compared with the earlier *A Sleep of Prisoners*: 'Though the literary form of the two pieces is very different, the intellectual content is much the same: violence as self-assertion, violence as loyalty to the state, violence as loyalty to God, and, finally, violence to be endured but not to be inflicted'. It is concluded that '*Sleep* communicates the idea of the ascent to God through the creatures, *Dark* the experience'.

James S. Mehoke's *Robert Graves: Peace-Weaver*[28] is a study of the Myth as a religious and social force. The author assumes 'that religion implies ultimate justice in the Cosmos, that the war experience had robbed Graves of this religious assurance, and that his new sense of confidence emanates from a Myth which restores his lost sense of justice'. It is suggested that the Myth is Graves's 'vehicle for a return to religion without civil

[27]*James Elroy Flecker's 'Hassan': A Near Master-Piece?*, by James Hogg. Poetic Drama and Poetic Theory Series, vol. 26. Salzburg Studies in English Literature. pp. 121.
[28]*Robert Graves: Peace-Weaver*, by James S. Mehoke. The Hague and Paris: Mouton. pp. 167.

war'. Graves's prose and poetry, and attitudes of other critics are examined in relation to the Myth, and it is concluded that 'if Graves fails to convince us that final solutions will be reached by way of goddess-worship, he gives us insight into a profoundly religious experience'.

Keith Sagar's The Art of Ted Hughes[29] is the first full-length study of the poetry. It is claimed that Hughes must be regarded as a poet of major status, one whose work is profoundly visionary in quality. We are offered detailed analyses of The Hawk in the Rain, Lupercal, Wodwo, Crow and Prometheus on His Crag. Although Hughes is not attempting to formulate a philosophy, the later work in particular draws on 'the roots and sources of the myths and legends in the depths of the human psyche' to create richness. A long and detailed bibliography is a valuable appendix to this stimulating volume.

Jeremy Hooker's short study[30] emphasizes that David Jones's work embodies the archetypal pattern of initiation as a unifying structural principle. He illustrates this with reference to In Parenthesis, The Anathemata, and the poems included in the collection The Sleeping Lord and other fragments. The labyrinth is shown to recur both as an important symbol and a shaping pattern.

Alan Brownjohn's pamphlet in the WTW series[31] examines Philip Larkin's life and the development of his poetry, his prose fiction, and jazz journalism. High Windows is seen to be Larkin's most important volume; it brings together the earlier themes and motifs and reveals 'an ever more confident and resonant use both of verse forms and of that immensely varied and flexible language that he has made his own'. A select bibliography is appended. Hermann Peschmann's 'Philip Larkin: Laureate of the Common Man' (English) assesses the poet's accomplishment from The North Ship to High Windows; it is suggested that Larkin 'is...the most important English poet of his generation'. In 'The Other Larkin' (CritQ) J. R. Watson writes appreciatively deciding that 'one of Larkin's greatest strengths as a poet is his position as homo religiosus, with an intuitive awareness of the tenuous sacred in the midst of the profane'.

Chaman Nahal examines 'The Colour Ambience in Lawrence's Early and Later Poetry' (DHLR). With reference to Look! We have Come Through! and Last Poems the use made by Lawrence of colours is detailed. 'The basic colours employed by Lawrence in his poetry are three: red, green, and black. . . . The most intense poetic effect is created by Lawrence when indicating a contrast amongst the shades so offered.' Evelyn Shakir writes on ' "Secret Sin": Lawrence's Early Verse' (DHLR). Lawrence's ambivalent attitude to writing poetry is examined: 'According to Lawrence, writing poetry is the attempt not only to know but also to heal oneself. . . But the guilty discoveries made in the process are sufficient to create considerable anxiety'. Analysis of individual poems shows that 'Lawrence's earliest poems make abundantly clear the powerful desires and fears that will continue to provide the emotional impetus behind his later verse, and

[29] The Art of Ted Hughes, by Keith Sagar. C.U.P. pp. 213. £5.90. $16.95.
[30] David Jones: An Explanatory Study of the Writings, by Jeremy Hooker. Enitharmon P. 22 Huntingdon Rd., London N.2. 9DU. pp. 68. £2.55, pb £1.65.
[31] Philip Larkin, by Alan Brownjohn. Longman for the British Council. pp. 32.

which, in the years that follow, he will explore with increasing frankness and self-awareness'.

Terence Brown's study: *Louis MacNeice: Sceptical Vision*[32] argues that 'the central determining factor in MacNeice's poetry and thought, far from being a decent, liberal, but rather commonplace agnosticism, was a tense awareness of fundamental questions, rooted in philosophical scepticism'. A biographical introduction describes MacNeice as an 'Anglo-Irish exile', whose early apprehension of the tension of opposites was to become pervasive in his life and work. It is established that, although MacNeice is attracted to Romantic themes and imagery, this tendency is counteracted by a cynical realism. Criticism of the modern age recurs, often expressed in the theme of the alienated self, and the world is seen as inescapable through romantic daydream. Nevertheless MacNeice expresses a 'sceptic's faith': 'life in all its variety is valuable because it is the opposite of stasis and death'. The technical aspects of the poetry, including imagery, allegory, and poetic form, are examined in detail to illustrate MacNeice's view of the world. A. J. Minnis's 'Louis MacNeice: The Pattern and the Poem' (*YES*) claims that 'MacNeice is a philosophical poet, a modern "Metaphysical", and has certain urges towards a kind of secular mysticism'. The themes of time and 'fusion', and the images of the Quest predominate. Individual poems are analyzed, including 'Snow', 'Plurality', 'Western Landscape', 'Meeting Point', and 'Trilogy for X', to show 'three fundamental aspects of his pattern, namely "pluralism", "mystic monism" and "historicism"'.

Dominic Hibberd's *WTW* pamphlet[33] stresses that for Wilfred Owen 'the war brought the fulfilment of a poetic destiny that had been taking shape all his life'. Owen originally used pararhyme in lyric poetry; he then adopted the technique for his war poems. Owen is seen to be primarily an elegist: 'his major poems are laments for the dead rather than exposures of the horror of war'. This succinct introduction to Owen's life and poetry provides the reader with a bibliography and with a valuable list of the probable dates of composition of the poems, the latter reflecting Dr. Hibberd's particular area of research. Hilda D. Spear's ' "I Too Saw God"; The Religious Allusions in Wilfred Owen's Poetry' (*English*) concentrates on the section of Owen's *Collected Poems* called by C. Day Lewis 'War Poems', to show 'how Owen adapted the Christian myth to the circumstances of twentieth-century warfare'.

Derek Parker edits *Sacheverell Sitwell: A Symposium*[34]. Among the contributors are Cyril Connolly, C. P. Snow, Raymond Mortimer, Kenneth Clark, Thornton Wilder, Susan Hill, and Hugh MacDiarmid. The tributes include reminiscences about Sacheverell Sitwell's life and brief surveys of his work. John Smith's 'Shall These Bones Live?' examines the development of the poetry and concludes that 'Agamemnon's Tomb' 'must surely be seen, in the long run, as one of the finest poems of some length written

    [32] *Louis MacNeice: Sceptical Vision*, by Terence Brown. Gill and Macmillan, and New York: Barnes and Noble. pp. 215. £4.95.
    [33] *Wilfred Owen*, by Dominic Hibberd. Longman for the British Council. pp. 44.
    [34] *Sacheverell Sitwell: A Symposium*, ed. by Derek Parker. Bertram Rota. pp. xiv + 94. £5.

in English in our time'. Humphrey Searle writes on 'Sacheverell Sitwell's Books on Music'. The volume ends with Hugh MacDiarmid's poetic tribute: 'The Goal of all the Arts'.

Constantine Fitzgibbon's *The Life of Dylan Thomas*[35] is now an Aldine paperback. We are offered an intelligent, lucid, and flowing account unmarred by excessive rhapsody; this well-researched volume is very welcome in its new edition. Andrew Sinclair's *Dylan Thomas: Poet of his People*[36] is a lavishly illustrated biography that leads us sympathetically through the poet's life by demonstrating that Thomas 'was born to a divided bardic tradition, a bi-lingual speech, a split-minded people, a provincial bias; only his home was safe, first with his parents, finally with Caitlin, the womb with a view.' Three sets of answers by Thomas at different stages in his career concerning his attitude to poetry, 'Dylan on Dylan', offer the reader an insight into the development of the poet's opinions, providing a useful critical apparatus. In 'Image as Structure: Dylan Thomas and Poetic Meaning' (*CritQ*) Alan Young offers an analysis of 'I, in my intricate image' raising the question of Thomas's relationship with the theory and practice of surrealist verse.

In *ArielE* Michael Kirkham writes on 'Edward Thomas's Other Self'. 'The Other' 'offers itself, more than any other single poem, as a key to Thomas's poetic world'; the poem is analyzed to show Edward Thomas's personal sense of loss of 'the capacity for firmly based, lastingly satisfying relationships and the sort of social group where such relationships could be formed'. Thomas's two selves are revealed: both the solitary and the individual with a need for social fulfilment make up the poet's nature. In *CritQ* Michael Edwards's 'The Poetry of Hardy and Edward Thomas' offers a detailed and perceptive analysis of the two poets' contrasting use of landscape and of inanimate nature, defending Thomas from the complaint that his work is 'impersonal': 'the "sympathy" felt *is* impersonal but not indifferent, dispassionate but not lacking in compassion'.

John P. Frayne and Colton Johnson have collected and edited the second volume of *Uncollected Prose by W. B. Yeats*[37]. This welcome book contains reviews, articles, and other miscellaneous prose from 1897 to 1939. Whereas Volume One covered a ten-year span in Yeats's life and brought together many items dealing with the founding of the Irish literary movement the second volume covers over forty years and presents several issues. The editors explain: 'as Yeats grew older, more famous and surer of the uses of his prose, there was less and less which he did not intend from the outset for publication or, if it appeared, initially in the periodicals, which he did not reprint himself'. Although the editors have attempted to bring together 'every piece of prose published in Yeats's lifetime which he acknowledged or which can reasonably be attributed to him and which is not currently in print', some writings have been impossible

---

[35] *The Life of Dylan Thomas*, by Constantine Fitzgibbon. Aldine Paperback. pp. ix + 422. £2.25.

[36] *Dylan Thomas: Poet of his People*, by Andrew Sinclair. Michael Joseph. pp. 240. £6.25.

[37] *Uncollected Prose by W. B. Yeats*, Volume Two, ed. by John P. Frayne and Colton Johnson. Macmillan. pp. 543. £20.

to locate. Yeats's prefaces to books by others and writings lacking firm evidence of authorship have also been excluded. Articles on the Irish National Theatre form the major part of this substantial volume. There are also fourteen pieces which describe the Celtic Revival and link it with the symbolist movement, six articles on folklore and nine on the Hugh Lane bequest. An index is provided for Volumes One and Two. This collection will be much appreciated by Yeats scholars; the notes and introductions are especially helpful, and the volume is illustrated by well-chosen photographs some of which have been hitherto unpublished.

A. Norman Jeffares and A. S. Knowland have written *A Commentary on the Collected Plays of W. B. Yeats*[38]. Detailed annotation is supplied for each of the plays including Yeats's notes to various editions, his comments in letters and critical and autobiographical writings, and quotations from his poems which elucidate the plays' meaning. Details of the plays' versions, casts, and performances are given, obscure references are explained, Irish expressions are clarified, and the work of critics and scholars is referred to where appropriate. This is an indispensable reference work for readers of the plays.

The *Yeats Studies Series* aims to supply important Yeats material which has so far remained unpublished, and to do so in a critical context. The first volume of the series, *Yeats and the Theatre*[39], is edited by Robert O'Driscoll and Lorna Reynolds. Micheál Macliammóir writes on 'How Yeats Influenced My Life In The Theatre'; James W. Flannery and Karen Dorn contribute papers on Yeats's association with Gordon Craig; Douglas N. Archibald examines '*The Words Upon the Window-pane* and Yeats's Encounter with Jonathan Swift'; David Fitzpatrick looks at 'W. B. Yeats in Seanad Éireann'. Richard Taylor compares *At the Hawk's Well* with its Japanese source, a Nō play entitled *Yōrō*, the translated text of which is published for the first time. Robert O'Driscoll examines 'Yeats on Personality: Three Unpublished Lectures'. David R. Clark and James B. McGuire present two typescripts of Yeats's versions of *Sophocles' King Oedipus* and *Sophocles' Oedipus at Colonus*. Joseph Ronsley introduces 'Yeats's Lecture Notes for "Friends of My Youth" '. The editors append 'Suggested Guidelines for Catalogue of Yeats Manuscripts'. Phillip Marcus catalogues the Yeats manuscripts in the Olin Library of Cornell University. Colin Smythe writes 'A Note on Some of Yeats's Revisions for *The Land of Heart's Desire*'.

The excellent Dolmen Press series, New Yeats Papers, has not before been given notice in these pages. The first in the series, by William M. Murphy, deals with *The Yeats Family and the Pollexfens of Sligo*[40]. It is illustrated with drawings by John Butler Yeats, many of which have been hitherto unpublished. A genealogy of the Pollexfens and Yeatses is included. Kathleen Raine's *Yeats, the Tarot and the Golden Dawn*[41] was the

[38] *A Commentary on the Collected Plays of W. B. Yeats*, by A. Norman Jeffares and A. S. Knowland. Macmillan. pp. xxvi + 313. £10.
[39] *Yeats and the Theatre*, ed. by Robert O'Driscoll and Lorna Reynolds. Macmillan. pp. xiii + 288. £10.
[40] New Yeats Papers I: *The Yeats Family and the Pollexfens of Sligo*, by William M. Murphy. Dolmen P. and O.U.P. 1971. pp. 88. £1.25.
[41] New *Yeats*, Papers II: *Yeats, The Tarot and The Golden Dawn*, by Kathleen Raine. Dolmen P. and O.U.P. 1972. pp. 78. £2.75.

second comprehensive and well-illustrated study of the series. New Yeats Papers III[42] publishes Yeats's contribution to the report of the committee established by the Irish Government in 1926 to consider the designing of an Irish coinage. Other pieces on the consideration of the Irish coinage set a context for Yeats's, and the volume is amply illustrated with photographs of the designs which underwent scrutiny. New Yeats Papers IV[43], by Richard J. Finneran, examines the development of Yeats's prose fiction. It is illustrated with photographs of bindings and drawings which decorated various editions of the prose works. James White's *John Butler Yeats and the Irish Renaissance*[44] is the fifth in the series; the author examines Yeats's father as a portrait painter, and includes many reproductions. Appended is a checklist of all of John Butler Yeats's paintings and drawings in public collections. In George Mills Harper's *'Go Back to Where You Belong': Yeats's Return from Exile*[45] Yeats's preoccupation with the image of the exile is discussed. Liam Miller writes at length on the history of *The Dun Emer Press, Later the Cuala Press*[46]. Kathleen Raine's *Death-in-Life and Life-in-Death: 'Cuchulain Comforted' and 'News for the Delphic Oracle'*[47] examines Yeats's preoccupation with the nature of immortality and the philosophy in these poems. Robert O'Driscoll writes on *Symbolism and Some Implications of the Symbolic Approach: W. B. Yeats During the Eighteen-Nineties*[48]. He explores especially 'the primary levels of meaning in works which have to this point in time received little critical attention': *The Celtic Twilight, The Secret Rose, Stories of Red Hanrahan, Rosa Alchemica, The Tables of the Law, The Adoration of the Magi, The Wind Among the Reeds, Where There is Nothing* and *The Unicorn from the Stars*. George Mills Harper's *The Mingling of Heaven and Earth: Yeats's Theory of Theatre*[49], establishes that Yeats had developed 'a coherent and comprehensive' aesthetic of the theatre. Stanley Sultan's *Yeats at His Last*[50] is concerned with the importance of the volume *Last Poems and Two Plays* (Cuala P. 1939) which orders the poems differently from the standard editions. Edward O'Shea investigates *Yeats as Editor*[51], looking at the Irish editions of 1888 to 1906, Yeats's work as editor of the

---

[42] New Yeats Papers III: *W. B. Yeats and The Designing of Ireland's Coinage*, ed. by Brian Cleeve. Dolmen P. and O.U.P. 1972. pp. 75. £1.25.

[43] New Yeats Papers IV: *The Prose Fiction of W. B. Yeats: the Search for 'Those Simple Forms'*, by Richard J. Finneran. Dolmen P. and O.U.P. 1973. pp. 42. £1.25.

[44] New Yeats Papers V: *John Butler Yeats and the Irish Renaissance*, by James White. Dolmen P. and O.U.P. 1972. pp. 72. £1.50.

[45] New Yeats Papers VI: *'Go Back to Where You Belong': Yeats's Return from Exile*, by George Mills Harper. Dolmen P. and O.U.P. 1973. pp. 43. £1.25.

[46] New Yeats Papers VII: *The Dun Emer Press, Later the Cuala Press*, by Liam Miller. Dolmen P. and O.U.P. 1973. pp. 131. £2.50.

[47] New Yeats Papers VIII: *Death-in-Life and Life-in-Death: 'Cuchulain Comforted' and 'News For the Delphic Oracle'*, by Kathleen Raine. Dolmen P. and O.U.P. 1974. pp. 63. £2.75.

[48] New Yeats Papers IX: *Symbolism and Some Implications of the Symbolic Approach: W. B. Yeats During the Eighteen-Nineties*, by Robert O'Driscoll. Dolmen P. and O.U.P. pp. 84. £2.90.

[49] New Yeats Papers X: *The Mingling of Heaven and Earth: Yeats's Theory of Theatre*, by George Mills Harper. Dolman P. and O.U.P. pp. 48. £1.85.

[50] New Yeats Papers XI: *Yeats at his Last*, by Stanley Sultan. Dolmen P. and O.U.P. pp. 48. £1.85.

[51] New Yeats Papers XII: *Yeats as Editor*, by Edward O'Shea. Dolmen P. and O.U.P. pp. 80. £2.40.

Dun Emer and the Cuala Press, and his *The Oxford Book of Modern Verse*. Morton Irving Seiden's *William Butler Yeats: The Poet as a Mythmaker 1865 -1939*[52], first published in 1962 by Michigan State U.P., is reprinted. The author concentrates on the importance of Yeats's attempt to create a personal religion; the poems based on the faith expressed in *A Vision* are 'the fragments of a great myth'. As well as attempting to delineate the relation between *A Vision* and Yeats's other writings, the author tries 'to distinguish in *A Vision* between objective and metaphorical statements, fact and error, private opinion and dispassionate wisdom, and explicit and implicit levels of meaning'. Seiden first leads us through Yeats's quest for a faith by looking closely at the sources and analogues of *A Vision*, by analyzing the early works as stages in its growth, by examining its first and revised versions, and finally by evaluating the myth. In the second half of the book the author uses *A Vision* as 'a kind of prose gloss' to Yeats's later poems and plays.

Edward Malins has written *A Preface to Yeats*[53]. This excellent handbook offers the reader information on this historical and literary background, including biographical summaries, the history of Ireland as it relates to Yeats the poet's reading, and *A Vision*. There is a critical survey of some of Yeats's poems. A particularly good feature of the study is a clearly presented reference section which gives details of Yeats's family, friends, and acquaintances, and which provides a gazetteer of places with Yeatsian associations as well as a list of places referred to in the poems— Yeats's most frequently used symbols are tabulated, with their origins, connexions and attributes. The derivations and pronunciations of certain Irish place names are included. Further reading is recommended. This is an admirable introduction to the complexities of Yeats.

Dudley Young's stimulating volume[54] presents Yeats as a symbolist mage: 'His arts derive from European Romanticism, the occult, alchemy and *symbolisme*, and he needs neither a thriving society nor the consent of a large and faithful congregation in order to practise. Indeed quite the reverse: his magic prospers when his society is dissolving, and its complexity is such that it could never edify more than a small elect.' Individual poems are examined with illuminating analysis. We are helped to see Yeats's connexion with past poetic tradition (Mallarmé) and with contemporary literature (Samuel Beckett).

David Lenson's *Achilles' Choice: Examples of Modern Tragedy*[55] contains a chapter on Yeats's idea of tragedy. It is stressed that Yeats's version of 'the tragic dialectic'—'an intrusion of one order upon another, incompatible one'—developed throughout his career. Firstly, *The Countess Cathleen, The Land of Heart's Desire*, and *The Unicorn from the Stars* are examined. It is then shown that Yeats's concept of tragedy changed after the writing of *A Vision*: 'Suddenly order and disorder are no longer

[52] *William Butler Yeats: The Poet as a Mythmaker*, by Morton Irving Seiden. New York: Cooper Square Publishers. pp. 397. $12.50.
[53] *A Preface to Yeats*, by Edward Malins. Longman. pp. xii + 212. £2.
[54] *Out of Ireland: The Poetry of W. B. Yeats*, by Dudley Young. Carcanet P pp. 169. £3.50.
[55] *Achilles' Choice: Examples of Modern Tragedy*, by David Lenson. Princeton N.J.: Princton U.P. pp. ix + 178. £5.95.

personal or national issues. If they are to be significant, they must partake directly of the Absolute, rechristened Spiritus Mundi'. In 'The Gyres' and 'Lapis Lazuli', 'Yeats' notion of tragedy becomes clear and explicit.' The author asks 'whether a cyclic idea of time and history does not destroy the possibility of genuine tragedy', and concludes that 'What keeps Yeats within the tragic scope is that things do not return in particular, but rather in general'.

David C. Nimmo's 'W. B. Yeats and W. J. Turner' (*ES*) observes that the poems by Turner which appear in Yeats's *The Oxford Book of Modern Verse: 1892-1935* have been tampered with: for example, there are 'stanzas missing without any indication of their omission'. 'The Seven Days of the Sun' has been 'radically changed from the original order', and by omitting one particular line in this poem Yeats was 'cutting out the line which did not appeal to him philosophically'. He was thus 'able to render the ideas in Turner's poem close to those in his own poem, "The Tower" '.

Rosemary Puglia Ritvo writes on '*A Vision* B: The Plotinian Metaphysical Basis' (*RES*). Her thesis is that 'In spite of its strange terminology and its apparent confusions and contradictions, *A Vision* B is a remarkably consistent work which reveals that the poet had carefully studied Plotinus in an effort to understand the "revelations" of the Instructors'. This is elaborated in a detailed study of the similarities between Yeats's System and Plotinus's philosophy. In Krishna Rayan's 'Yeats and the "Little and Intense" Poem' (*EIC*) several of the short poems are analyzed in order to demonstrate that 'If the rhetoric of micro-suggestions came to Yeats readily and frequently, it must be because he found from his own practice that of all forms the slight poem could most easily be at the same time both cohesive with a single image or idea supplying its structure and uncontrived like a swift look or a chance word.'

James D. Boulger considers 'Moral and Structural Aspects in W. B. Yeats's Supernatural Songs' (*Renascence*). The poems mark a return to the world of *A Vision*, presenting difficulties for the Christian critic. An examination of the poems takes the author to the conclusion that 'Yeats's way was not the Christian way, but he was serious and to be taken seriously in this phase of his poetry'.

Antony Coleman's 'A Calendar for the Production and Reception of *Cathleen Ni Houlihan*, (*MD*) traces the evolution of the play from January 1902 to August 1904. The production details, the stage directions, Yeats's various comments on the play, and the reviews of it are examined with the help of generous quotations. The question of Lady Gregory's part in the play is discussed: in Yeats's dedication of the play to Lady Gregory he was 'acknowledging the certain obligation he owed Lady Gregory for instruction in the vocabulary and rhythms of country speech. . .To urge a more substantial obligation in *Cathleen Ni Houlihan* is to misread the language of courteous gratitude'. In an afterword it is suggested that the play was influenced by *Little Eyolf*. It is concluded that 'Yeats had annexed the dynamic energies of politics to his art; despite his later reservations and qualifications he cannot have been unaware that he too had assisted at the birth of "a terrible beauty" '.

In 'Singular Voices: Monologue and Monodrama in the Plays of W. B. Yeats' (*MD*) Andrew Parkin examines the general qualities of the stage monologue and monodrama. He proceeds to describe Yeats's use of monologue in *The Land of Heart's Desire, Where There is Nothing,The Shadowy Waters, On Baile's Strand, The Resurrection, The Only Jealousy of Emer*, and *The Death of Cuchulain*. The use of monodrama is examined in *The Dreaming of the Bones* and *Calvary*; in *The Only Jealousy of Emer* and *The Words Upon the Window-Pane* we find 'the use of monodrama within the larger framework of a different dramatic form'. In *Purgatory* there is 'neither total monologue nor total monodrama, but a most effective variation which haunts the border country between monologue and dialogue, drama and monodrama'. It is concluded that Yeats 'develcped a mastery of dramatic structures compressed and subtle enough to give extraordinary intellectual and emotional weight to the one-act play'.

3. Drama
Useful bibliographical information is offered in the specialist journals and in separate volumes. 'Modern Drama Studies: An Annual Bibliography' (*MD*) records work on British drama in its European and world context. Irish drama is covered in the context of Anglo-Irish literature in the bibliographical lists in the *Irish University Review*. Karl-Heinz Stoll's *The New British Drama: A Bibliography with Particular Reference to Arden, Bond, Osborne, Pinter, Wesker* is published from Bern by Lang. In *English Drama (excluding Shakespeare): Select Bibliographical Guides*[1] twentieth-century drama is covered in sections contributed by Margery M. Morgan, Ann Saddlemyer, Allardyce Nicoll, and John Russell Brown. *The Drama Scholars' Index to Plays and Filmscripts*[2], compiled by Gordon Samples is a selective bibliography of plays to be found in anthologies, series, and periodicals. International drama is covered in this unique supplement to the bibliographical works in the field.

Pitman's new series The Theatre Today is well started with two interesting volumes. Peter Ansorge's *Disrupting the Spectacle*[3] surveys experimental and fringe theatre in Britain between 1968 and 1973. Special attention is paid to Howard Brenton, David Hare, Snoo Wilson, Nancy Mekler, Pip Simmons, Charles Marowitz, Inter-action, the Welfare State, Max Stafford-Clark, John McGrath, Trevor Griffiths, and David Edgar. Garry O'Connor's *French Theatre Today*[4] has a chapter on Beckett in the course of surveying the main playwrights and directors at work in France. Both volumes have useful lists of plays.

The Irish Theatre Series continues with its fifth and sixth volumes. In his study of Denis Johnston[5], Harold Ferrar argues persuasively for the importance of his contribution to the Irish stage and the analysis of Johnston's plays leads to a convincing conclusion: 'All of his work is a testament to Johnston's commitment—to historical and moral realism

[1] *English Drama (excluding Shakespeare): Select Bibliographical Guides*, ed. by Stanley Wells. O.U.P. pp. ix + 303. £4.25, pb £1.75.
[2] *The Drama Scholars' Index to Plays and Filmscripts*, by Gordon Samples. Metuchen N.J.: Scarecrow P., Inc. (1974) pp. xii + 464. $12.50.
[3] *Disrupting the Spectacle*, by Peter Ansorge. Pitman. pp. 87. £2.50, pb £1.25.
[4] *French Theatre Today*, by Garry O'Connor. Pitman. pp. 118. £3.50, pb £1.95.
[5] *Denis Johnston's Irish Theatre*, by Harold Ferrar. Dolmen P. pp. 144, pb £1.75.

(though his dramaturgy may urge this realism through radical stylization) and to a joyous philosophy of hope and unsentimental pity earned by fearless confrontation of fact'. The sixth volume of the Irish Theatre Series is the first volume of *The Modern Irish Drama: a documentary history*[6], which will be put together in an unspecified number of volumes by Robert Hogan and James Kilroy: the documentation is detailed and well presented so that letters, articles, memoirs, and contemporary newspaper reviews give a comprehensive and at times exciting account of the private and public tensions involved in the initiation of literary drama in Dublin. Hugh Hunt's lecture *The Theatre and Nationalism in Ireland* is published as a pamphlet by the University College of Swansea.

Some interesting general studies are to be noticed. In *The English Morality Play*[7] Robert Potter begins and ends his long intricate narrative in the twentieth century. The book's prologue discusses William Poel's production of *Everyman* in 1901, and the final chapter discusses modern religious and 'morality' plays, with special reference to Shaw, Yeats, Hofmannsthal, Eliot, and Brecht. In *Movements in English Literature 1900-1940*[8] Christopher Gillie offers a twenty-page discussion of plays by Shaw (*The Doctor's Dilemma*), Yeats (*Purgatory*), Synge (*The Playboy*), O'Casey (*Juno and the Paycock*), and Eliot (*The Family Reunion*).

In *Six dramatists in search of a language*[9] Andrew Kennedy offers a theoretical discussion of linguistic problems which modern dramatists must confront, as well as detailed and perceptive analyses of some plays by Shaw, Eliot, Beckett, Pinter, Osborne, and Arden. In *English Comedy*[10] Allan Rodway has chapters on the 'Origin and Nature of Comedy', on 'Critical Terminology', and on 'Comedy and English Society'. He discusses a very wide range of novels, poems, and plays, with special emphasis on Shaw and Stoppard among the twentieth-century dramatists. Equally interesting and equally wide ranging is J. L. Styan's *Drama, Stage and Audience*[11] where the chapter headings indicate the wide scope of a volume where the questions are large and general but the discussion firmly tied to specific examples: 'Communication in drama', 'Dramatic signals', 'Genre and style', 'Conditions of performance', 'Acting and role-playing', 'Non-illusory theatre', and 'Audience'. In *ThQ* there is much of general interest in the regular features under the heading 'Production Casebook' there are detailed accounts of drama in performance; Howard Brenton and John McGrath are subjects in the series of substantial articles based on interviews. Kenneth Tynan's *A View of the English Stage, 1944-63* is published by Davis-Poynter. Herman J. Weiand edits *Insight IV*, published from Frankfurt by Hirschgraben: the volume discusses more than thirty

[6] *The Irish Literary Theatre, 1899-1901*, by Robert Hogan and James Kilroy. Dolmen P. pp. 164 £4.90.
[7] *The English Morality Play*, by Robert Potter. Routledge & Kegan Paul. pp. ix + 286. £6.95
[8] *Movements in English Literature*, 1900-1940, by Christopher Gillie. C.U.P. pp. vii + 207. £4.25.
[9] *Six dramatists in search of a language*, by Andrew Kennedy. C.U.P. pp. xiv + 271. £5.
[10] *English Comedy*, by Allan Rodway. Chatto & Windus. pp. x + 288. £4.50.
[11] *Drama, Stage and Audience*, by J. L. Styan. C.U.P. pp. viii + 256. £5.

modern plays—including work by Arden, Orton, Osborne, Pinter, Stoppard, Synge, and Wesker. In *Soviet Literature* Valentina Ryapolova considers 'Britain: Problems of Political Drama'. Useful reviews of current productions appear in *Drama* and John Weightman contributes to *Encounter* with his distinctive intelligence and vigour. John Russell Taylor's *Directors and Directions*[12] surveys the work of distinguished film makers of the nineteen-seventies. There are informed and interesting chapters on Claude Chabrol, Pier Paolo Pasolini, Lindsay Anderson, Stanley Kubrick, Andy Warhol and Paul Morrissey, Satyajit Ray, Miklós Jancsó, and Dušan Makavejev.

In 'Individual and Society in the Early Plays of John Arden' (*MD*) Paul W. Day discusses the structures and themes of *Waters of Babylon*. *Live Like Pigs*, and *Serjeant Musgrave's Dance*, and in *ETJ* Robert Skloot has 'Spreading the Word: The Meaning of Musgrave's Logic'. Stanley Kauffmann's 'A Life in the Theatre' (*Horizon*) traces the career of Harley Granville-Barker, emphasizing the importance of his work with G. B. Shaw.

Beckett the Shape Changer[13] brings together essays by John Chalker, Harry Cockerham, Martin Dodsworth, Brian Finney, Barbara Hardy, Charles Peak, Victor Sage, and Katharine Worth. Beckett's fiction, radio plays, and *Film* are discussed as well as his work for the stage; there are select lists of Beckett's works and of critical studies. Ruby Cohn's *Samuel Beckett: A Collection of Criticism* (N.Y.: McGraw-Hill) has not been inspected, nor has James Eliopoulos's *Samuel Beckett's Dramatic Language* (*The Hague: Mouton*) or Meinhard Winkgens's *Das Zeitproblem in Samuel Becketts Dramen* (Bern: Lang). In 'Beckett Directs *Godot*' (*ThQ*) Walter D. Asmus, who assisted Beckett with his production at the Schiller Theater, gives a very interesting account of their rehearsals; and in the same number Alan Schneider discusses more than twenty years' collaboration in his ' "Any Way You Like, Alan": Working with Beckett'. There are three essays on Beckett in *MD*. In 'Beckett's *Play*: The Circular Line of Existence' Shoshana Avigal discusses Beckett's ironical rejection of 'the linear concept of existence'; in 'Being and Perception' Vincent J. Murphy discusses *Film* with special reference to Beckett's study of Proust; and in 'Dada, Surrealism, and the Genesis of *Not I*' Enoch Brater decides that 'In *Not I* Beckett has found it possible to reconcile his metaphysical dilemma and his histrionic inclinations'. Enoch Brater also writes on 'The "Absurd" Actor in the Theatre of Samuel Beckett' (*ETJ*), and on 'Brecht's Alienated Actor in Beckett's Theatre' (*CompD*). Frederick Busi notes some 'Joycean Echoes in *Waiting for Godot*' (*RS*), and in *Hispania* (1974) the same critic has '*Waiting for Godot*: A Modern *Don Quixote*?' Martin Esslin, who worked intimately with Beckett on the B.B.C. productions, writes interestingly on 'Samuel Beckett and the Art of Broadcasting' (*Encounter*).

In '*An Giall* and *The Hostage* Compared' (*MD*) Richard Wall contrasts Brendan Behan's 'restrained' tragi-comedy in Irish with the English adaptation where the jocularity is in 'rather bad taste'; Paul M. Levitt offers

---

[12] *Directors and Directions: Cinema for the Seventies*, by John Russell Taylor Eyre Methuen. pp. 327. £5.

[13] *Beckett the Shape Changer*, ed. by Katharine Worth. Routledge & Kegan Paul pp. 227. £4.95.

'Hostages to History: Title as Dramatic Metaphor in *The Hostage*' (*NS*). In 'A Myth for All Seasons: Thomas More' (*ColQ*) Michael Anderegg compares Robert Bolt's play and the film version. In 'The Aggressive "Theatrum Mundi"' of Edward Bond' (*MD*), Adolf K. H. Barth reads *The Narrow Road to the Deep North*, although it is subtitled 'A Comedy', as a play in some ways related to 'the European tradition of tragic and religious drama'. In 'Edward Bond: Violence and Poetry (*Drama*) John Peter writes mainly on *Bingo*. In *RLV* Leo Truchlar has *'Lear* oder die Pornographie der Gewalt'. Horst Oppel and Sandra Christen's *Edward Bond's 'Lear' and Shakespeare's 'King Lear'* was published in 1974 (Wiesbaden: Steiner). In 'Joyce contra Wagner' (*CompD*) John MacNicholas points to some Wagnerian echoes in James Joyce's play *Exiles*. In *ConL* Michael A. Cohen writes on 'Politics vs. Drama' in Conor Cruise O'Brien's *Murderous Angels*.

The first volume of the projected three volumes of Sean O'Casey's letters, edited by David Krause and covering the years 1910 to 1941, is the most important work to be noticed in this section[14]. As a record of O'Casey's development and of his complex relationships with his contemporaries in Dublin and London, the letters make an indispensable companion for the autobiographies and a necessary commentary on the writing and reception of the plays. David Krause's editorial work is admirable. We must also welcome the new twice-yearly *Sean O'Casey Review* which publishes essays and notes on O'Casey's life, work, and milieu. In *Eire* Ronald Ayling's 'To Bring Harmony' traces some recurrent patterns in O'Casey's plays, and Lawrence J. Dessner writes on 'Art and Anger in the *Autobiographies*'. In *CLQ* Patrick R Murphy offers 'Sean O'Casey and the Avant-garde'; Werner Besier's *Der junge Sean O'Casey* (Bern: Lang) was published in 1974.

The most substantial study of Pinter is the chapter 'Pinter: The Roots of the Relationship' in Patrick Roberts's wide-ranging study *The Psychology of Tragic Drama*[15] in the series Ideas and Forms in Literature. In the first part of the study, headed 'The Exploration of the Primitive', the Pinter chapter concentrates on *The Birthday Party*, *The Caretaker*, and *The Homecoming*, seeking through detailed analysis to 'show the truth and cogency with which Pinter explores primitive levels of relationship, while at the same time achieving "this recognizable reality of the absurdity of what we do and how we behave and how we speak" that makes his work accessible to a relatively wide audience. In this blend of the two levels of experience he writes in the finest tradition of poetic drama'. Whether expressing his admiration for Pinter or his reservations, Patrick Roberts is cogent and persuasive.

Errol Durbach writes on 'The Caretaker: Text and Subtext' in *English Studies in Africa*; and Horst Groene in *LWU* considers 'The Caretaker—Interpretationsprobleme bei Pinter'. Rüdiger Imhof in *Anglia* has 'Forschungsberichte und Bibliographien zu Harold Pinter'. The same writer has compiled *Pinter: a Bibliography* (a *Theatre Quarterly* publication for the

[14] *The Letters of Sean O'Casey*, Volume I: 1910–1941, ed. by David Krause. Cassell. pp. xxx + 972. £12.50.
[15] *The Psychology of Tragic Drama*, by Patrick Roberts. Routledge & Kegan Paul. pp. 234. £5.95.

British Theatre Institute) and in *NS* offers 'Harold Pinters *revue sketches als Schullektüre der gymnasialen Oberstufe (Sekundarstufe 11)*'. In *QJS* Robert Skloot in 'Putting out the Light' considers the staging of *Old Times*, and in 'Rehearsal as Critical Method' (*MD*) Lawrence I. Eilenberg refers to his experience of rehearsals at Cornell in his analysis of *Old Times*. Peter Shaffer has an article in *Vogue* (February) discussing the ritual effects in his play *Equus*. John Russell Taylor wrote the pamphlet on Peter Shaffer published by Longman for the British Council (1974). Hesketh Pearson's biography *Bernard Shaw*[16] is reissued. The first version appeared in 1942 and the complete version in 1961 [*YW*.42.260]. Shaw did much to help Pearson, supplying hundreds of anecdotes, and contributing passages with his own hand. An informed and engaging study; it is good that the book is kept in print. *Who's Who in Shaw*[17] is the seventh in a series which already included volumes devoted to Chaucer, Shakespeare, Jane Austen and the Brontës, Dickens, and Hardy. The list of characters is complete and Phyllis Hartnoll offers the appropriate information with her usual economy and efficiency.

The specialist journals devoted to Shaw, *The Shavian*, *The Independent Shavian*, and *The Shaw Review* continue: the last named is the most substantial and it offers a very detailed 'continuing checklist of Shaviana', which notices reprints of Shaw's works as well as critical studies, reviews, dissertations, and recordings.

In 'Biblical Myth Shavianized' (*MD*) Susan C. Stone contrasts Shaw's use of Biblical myths in *Back to Methuselah* and *The Simpleton of the Unexpected Isles*. In 'Exploiting Art: The Pictures in Bernard Shaw's Plays (*MD*) Stanley Weintraub considers Shaw's use of specific paintings and popular genres. In 'G. B. "Owlglass" Shaw' (*N&Q*) Norbert Greiner gives an account of Shaw's election in his last year as 'Honorary Citizen of the Town of Moelln'.

In 'Shaw's Heaven and Hell' (*Contemporary Review*) Raymond S. Nelson writes on *Man and Superman*, and in *N&Q* Virginia E. De Moss suggests that an account of an eighteenth-century production of Rousseau's opera *Pygmalion* is 'The Probable Source of Eliza Doolittle's Plumed Hat'. In 'The Epilogue One More Time: Shaw and the Tragedy of Waste' (*WHR*) Pat M. Esslinger-Carr writes on *St Joan*: in the series Salzburg Studies in English Literature, Erwin Stürzl and James Hogg supply a record of *The Stage History of G. B. Shaw's 'St Joan'*; and William Searle offers the comparative study *The Saint and the Skeptics: Joan of Arc in the Work of Mark Twain, Anatole France, and Bernard Shaw* (Detroit: Wayne State U.P.). In 'Exile and the Kingdom: The Incipient Absurdity of Milton and Shaw' (*Mosaic*) Joseph Frank compares *Heartbreak House* and *Samson Agonistes*. Karl-Heinz Schoeps's study *Bertolt Brecht und Bernard Shaw* (Bonn: Bouvier) was published in 1974. Daniel Dervin's *Bernard Shaw: A Psychological Study* is published by Bucknell U.P., Lewisburg, and Josephine Johnson's *Florence Farr: Bernard Shaw's 'New Woman'* by Smythe, Gerrards Cross.

A few pieces on Tom Stoppard's plays are offered. In *ETJ* Helene

---

[16] *Bernard Shaw*, by Hesketh Pearson. MacDonald and Jane's. pp. 520. £4.95.
[17] *Who's Who in Shaw*, by Phyllis Hartnoll. Hamish Hamilton. pp. 247. £2.75.

Keyssar-Franke considers 'The Strategy of *Rosenkrantz and Guildenstern are Dead*', and Gillan Farish writes on the same play in 'Into the Looking-Glass Bowl: An Instant of Grateful Terror' (*UWR*). In *The Use of English* David Self offers 'On the Edge of Reality: Some Thoughts on the Studying of Tom Stoppard', and in *ZAA* Leonard Goldstein has 'A Note on Tom Stoppard's *After Magritte*'. Nicholas Grene's critical study of Synge's plays[18] is well informed both about the dramatic and literary contexts and about the Irish localities that were so important an influence on Synge's work. The six plays are considered in turn with perception and sympathy. Synge's stature is fairly estimated and the nature of his talent well defined. In ways very different from those of Wilde, or Shaw, or Beckett, Synge's comedies are very funny: 'his sense of humour is certainly not a gay or light hearted one. At his funniest he is deeply disturbing, showing us an absurdity which cuts into our most basic beliefs in what is normal. He can pursue a comic image wherever it may take him, even to the edge of tragedy. Yet his humour, satirical and black as it often is, can be distinguished from that of twentieth-century writers who followed him by an ultimate balance and sanity in his comic attitude. Synge's is not a neurotic vision, if by that we mean a view of the world plainly distorted by the obsessions of the individual artistic personality',

E. H. Mikhail's bibliography of Synge[19] usefully brings together information about books, articles, recordings, reviews, and such unpublished material as theatre programmes and dissertations. As Robin Skelton notes in his Foreword to the volume, the bibliographical list indicates the curious range of critical reactions to Synge: 'He has been viewed as primarily a satirist, as essentially a romantic, as a thoroughgoing realist, and as the most subtle of symbolists'. That there are 2,500 entries indicates the quantity as well as the range of critical response to Synge's work.

In the *Irish University Review* Malcolm Kelsall in 'Synge in Aran' argues forcefully that far from being, as Synge claimed, 'a direct account of my life on the islands...inventing nothing, and changing nothing that is essential', *The Aran Islands* 'is in the main an artistic creation written, like many romantic works of art, to reveal the *Weltanschauung* of its author'. Malcolm Kelsall also edits *The Playboy of the Western Word* (Benn), supplying an introduction. In *CLQ* Paul M. Levitt considers 'The Two Act Structure of *The Playboy of the Western World*', and William J. Free 'Structural Dynamics in *Riders to the Sea*'.

In 'Peter Terson's Vale of Evesham' (*MD*) Gillette Elvgren discusses Terson's plays with affection and admiration, the final comparison being with Chekhov. In *Criticism* Cynthia Davis considers 'The Voices of *Under Milk Wood*', and Anthony M. Aylwin offers *Notes on Arnold Wesker's Roots*', in a pamphlet published by Methuen. In 'Arnold Wesker's Centre Fortytwo: a Cultural Revolution Betrayed' (*ThQ*) Frank Coppieters offers a substantial, detailed account of the movement's beginnings, early progress, and subsequent demise.

[18] *Synge: A Critical Study of the Plays*, by Nicholas Grene. MacMillan. pp. xii + 202. £7.95.
[19] *J. M. Synge: A Bibliography of Criticism*, by E. H. Mikhail. Macmillan. pp. xiii - 214. £7.50.

From two distinguished teachers come volumes which sum up many years of experience and which ought to find a place in every collection of books on drama. Cicely Berry's *Your Voice and How to Use it Successfully*[20] and *Voice and the Actor*[21] cover the theory of voice production, and offer many exercises and much expert guidance. Litz Pisk in *The Actor and His Body*[22] reveals the wisdom and perception which made her one of our greatest teachers of movement. Each of these three volumes is well-illustrated.

In *Everymania*[23] Norman MacDermott offers an account of the Hampstead Everyman Theatre from 1920 when he founded it to 1926 when it went into bankruptcy. G. B. Shaw's 'The Present Predicament of the Theatre', a speech delivered in Hampstead in 1919, serves as an introduction, and there are detailed lists of productions and cast lists. In *The Gaiety Years*[24] Alan Hyman gives a lively and enthusiastic account of The Gaiety Theatre up to 1915 with reference to the years of burlesque, but also to Irving, Tree, Ellen Terry, Mrs. Patrick Campbell, Gilbert and Sullivan, Wilde, Pinero, and Shaw—with an amusing account of the 1914 production of *Pygmalion*. Richard Findlater's biography of *Lilian Baylis*[25] does justice to a lady and an era of theatrical history which crucially influenced twentieth-century English theatre, opera, and ballet: necessary reading as well as a delight.

[20] *Your Voice and How to Use it Successfully*, by Cicely Berry. Harrap. pp. 160. £2.80.
[21] *Voice and the Actor*, by Cicely Berry. Harrap. pp. 141. £3.50.
[22] *The Actor and His Body*, by Litz Pisk. Harrap. pp. 95. £4. Limp, £2.50.
[23] *Everymania*, by Norman MacDermott. Society for Theatre Research. pp. viii + 136. £2.
[24] *The Gaiety Years*, by Alan Hyman. Cassell. pp. xi + 230. £3.75.
[25] *Lilian Baylis: The Lady of the Old Vic*, by Richard Findlater. Allen Lane pp. 320. £6.

XV

American Literature to 1900

MARY JARRETT

Bibliographies of current articles are published quarterly in *AL* and annually in the summer supplement of *AQ*. *American Literary Scholarship*[1] summarizes work on individual authors, genres, and periods. This volume includes for the first time a section in which French, Italian, German, Scandinavian, and Japanese critics review the year's European and Japanese criticism of American literature. The survey for 1974[2] was published in 1976. David K. Kirby's *American Fiction to 1900*[3] is an extremely useful bibliographical guide. A very specialized bibliography is *American Diaries in Manuscript, 1580-1954*[4] by William Matthews. *American Studies Abroad*[5] sounds helpful, but is disappointing. The essays on 'American Studies in Europe' by Marcus Cunliffe and 'American Studies in Britain' by J. E. Morpurgo in particular are so vague and generalized that it is hard to see what use they are intended to be.

As usual, there are several books this year on the shadowy borderline between history and literature. An example is *The Many Voices of Boston: A Historical Anthology 1630-1975*[6], which presents a wide ranging series of comments on Boston, prefaced by a number of clear and concise historical introductions. The first section, 'The Founders', which spans the years 1630 to 1689, is especially useful as background for Hawthorne's *Scarlet Letter*. Emory Elliott's *Power and the Pulpit in Puritan New England*[7], which contains a discussion of the themes and language of the Puritan sermon in the seventeenth century, is unfortunately somewhat limited by its opaque language. Two articles shed light on the language of Cotton Mather: Carol Gay's 'The Fettered Tongue: A Study of the Speech Defect of Cotton Mather' (*AL*) and Gustaaf Van Cromphout's 'Cotton Mather as

---

[1] *American Literary Scholarship: An Annual: 1973*, ed. by James Woodress. Durham, N.C.: Duke U.P. pp. xvi + 490.

[2] *American Literary Scholarship: An Annual: 1974*, ed. by James Woodress. Durham, N.C.: Duke U.P. 1976. pp. xii + 492.

[3] *American Fiction to 1900: A Guide to Information Sources*, by David K. Kirby. Detroit: Gale Research. pp. xvii + 296.

[4] *American Diaries in Manuscript, 1580-1954: A Descriptive Bibliography*, by William Matthews. Athens: U. of Georgia P. 1974. pp. xvi + 176.

[5] *American Studies Abroad*, ed. by Robert H. Walker. Contributions in American Studies. Westport, Conn., and London: Greenwood P. pp. xi + 160.

[6] *The Many Voices of Boston: A Historical Anthology 1630-1975*, ed. by Howard Mumford Jones and Bessie Zaban Jones. Boston and Toronto: Atlantic Monthly P., Little Brown. pp. xv + 448.

[7] *Power and the Pulpit in Puritan New England*, by Emory Elliott. Princeton U.P. pp. xi + 240.

Plutarchan Biographer' (*AL*), and Mason I. Lowance Jr.'s *Increase Mather*[8] has a very competent chapter on 'The Shaping of the Puritan Sermon', with a telling use of quotation.

The United States: A Companion to American Studies[9], edited by Dennis Welland is a collection of essays offering a variety of kinds of background material: it includes an admirably clear chapter by Douglas Grant, 'The Emergence of an American Literature', in essence a survey from Edward Taylor to Mark Twain. Edward Taylor's poetry is treated comprehensively in William J. Scheick's *The Will and the Word*[10], a competent interpretation of 'the best poetry to emerge from seventeenth-century New England culture' in relation to New England Puritan orthodoxy. Scheick admits that Taylor's *Preparatory Meditations*, written over a span of forty-three years (1682–1725), have a remarkably static quality; he concludes that since there is, generally speaking, no development, divergence, or progress in the thought or artistry of Taylor's verse, 'We are moved less by any display of poetic pyrotechnics than by Taylor's unequivocal commitment to his inward quest for love, conversion, identity — for Being, eternal life'.

Harold P. Simonson's *Jonathan Edwards: Theologian of the Heart*[11] is equally illuminating on the connexions between poetry and religious belief, particularly in his chapter, 'Religious Language', which includes accounts of the 'Limitations of Language', of 'Language as "Occassional" Cause', and of 'The Sermon'. *Jonathan Edwards: His Life and Influence*[12] basically comprises two short papers on Edwards: 'Imagery and Analysis: Jonathan Edwards on Revivals of Religion' by Conrad Cherry, and 'The Brazen Trumpet: Jonathan Edwards's Conception of the Sermon' by Wilson H. Kimnach. The remainder of this slender volume is made up of a brief 'Symposium' and Charles Angoff's rather trite 'Introductory Remarks'.

The difficulties inherent in the study of early American Literature are indicated in the opening sentence of Edward H. Cohen's introduction to his *Ebenezer Cooke: The Sot-Weed Canon*[13]: 'The literature of the American colonial period has suffered at the hands of the scholar because he has traditionally evaluated it as philosophy, theology, social or political or cultural history — but seldom as literature'. Cohen strives to rectify this by placing Cooke in the small literary coterie of Maryland poets that emerged in the seventeen-twenties, but at the same time showing how Cooke managed to achieve a distinctive personal identity, and to transcend a mere

[8] *Increase Mather*, by Mason I. Lowance Jr. TUSAS. New York: Twayne, 1974. pp. 185.
[9] *The United States: A Companion to American Studies*, ed. by Dennis Welland. Methuen. 1974. pp. 528 with 6 illustrations.
[10] *The Will and the Word: The Poetry of Edward Taylor*, by William J. Scheick. Athens: U. of Georgia P. 1974. pp. xvi + 181.
[11] *Jonathan Edwards: Theologian of the Heart*, by Harold P. Simonson. Grand Rapids, Michigan: William B. Eerdmans. 1974. pp. 174.
[12] *Jonathan Edwards: His Life and Influence*, ed. by Charles Angoff. Leverton Lecture Series. Rutherford, Madison, Teaneck, and London: Fairleigh Dickinson U.P. pp. 65.
[13] *Ebenezer Cooke: The Sot-Weed Canon*, by Edward H. Cohen. Athens: U. of Georgia P. pp. x + 125.

imitation of Augustan modes, an aspect examined in Robert D. Arner's article 'Ebenezer Cooke's *Sotweed Redivius*: Satire in the Horation Mode' (*MissQ*). Cohen's study is the first book-length account of Ebenezer Cooke's life and poetry. He covers the full range of Cooke's writing, but his most valuable chapter is the first, a detailed analysis of Cooke's best and best-known work, *The Sot-Weed Factor* (1708), which is at the same time an analysis of Cooke's comedy.

William K. Bottorff in his introduction to *My Mind and Its Thoughts*[14] by Sarah Wentworth Morton (1759–1846) places her firmly in the Christian meditative tradition of New England, and points out that her work resembles in form and sentiment the 'Contemplations' and 'Meditations' of Anne Bradstreet. Sarah Wentworth Morton's *Thoughts* are no more than mildly interesting, but they deserve to be reprinted for their historical interest. Also of historical interest are the *Early Vermont Broadsides*[15] presented by John Duffy. Beautifully reproduced, they range in date from 1777 to 1821, and have an excellent critical introduction by Mason I. Lowance Jr.

The material in Lewis Leary's *Soundings: Some Early American Writers*[16] has almost all been published before, but it is well worth the gathering together in one volume at last. A number of the essays in this important collection are on relatively little-known writers: 'Nathaniel Tucker: Expatriate Patriot'; 'Samuel Low: New York's First Poet'; 'Royall Tyler: First Gentleman of the American Theatre'; 'Charles Crawford: A Forgotten Poet of Early Philadelphia'; 'Joseph Brown Ladd of Charleston'; 'Hugh Henry Brackenridges's *Modern Chivalry*'; 'John Blair Linn 1777–1805'; 'The Education of William Dunlap'; 'Thomas Branagan: Republican Rhetoric and Romanticism in America'; and 'The Literary Opinions of Joseph Dennie'. Leary also writes on Benjamin Franklin, whose *'Sayings of Poor Richard'*[17] has recently been edited by Paul Leicester Ford: in 'Benjamin Franklin and the Requirements of Literature' Leary speaks of the 'Ventriloquist' function of much of the humour. In 'Philip Freneau: A Reassessment' Leary concludes that although Freneau wrote much bad poetry, had little or no direct influence on American literature, and had only one effective theme (that of sorrow for the frail duration of mortality), he nevertheless wrote a few brief lyrics of outstanding worth. He has this year edited two facsimile volumes of Freneau, *The 'Poems' (1786) and 'Miscellaneous Works' (1788) of Philip Freneau*[18], and *The Writings in*

---

[14] *My Mind and Its Thoughts, in Sketches, Fragments, and Essays*, by Sarah Wentworth Morton, with introd. by William K. Bottorff. New York: Scholars' Facsimiles and Reprints. pp. 295.

[15] *Early Vermont Broadsides*, ed. by John Duffy, with introd. by Mason I. Lowance Jr. Hanover, N.H.: U.P. of New England, pp. xx + 51 with 26 illustrations.

[16] *Soundings: Some Early American Writers*, by Lewis Leary. Athens: U. of Georgia P. pp. x + 332.

[17] *'The Sayings of Poor Richard'*: The Prefaces, Proverbs, and Poems of Benjamin Franklin Originally Printed in Poor Richard's Almanacs for 1733-1758, ed. by Paul Leicester Ford. New York: Burt Franklin Reprints. 1974. pp. 288.

[18] *The 'Poems' (1786) and 'Miscellaneous Works' (1788) of Philip Freneau*, ed. by Lewis Leary, with memoir by Evert A. Duyckinck. New York: Scholars' Facsimiles and Reprints. pp. 407 + 429.

Prose and Verse of Hezekiah Salem[19]. In the latter volume all the 'works' of Freneau's invented character Hezekiah Salem are collected together for the first time. Leary points out in his introduction that Freneau, like Cooper, Irving, James, and other New Yorkers, 'found the psalm-singing sons of New England ridiculous, the perfect butts for often imperfect ridicule', and he suggests that the Connecticut-born Salem's literary descendants include Cooper's David Gamut and Irving's Ichabod Crane.

Soundings includes an essay on 'James Fenimore Cooper's Lover's Quarrel with America', in which Leary concentrates on *Home as Found* (1838), and one on 'Washington Irving: An End and a New Beginning'. Here Leary assesses Irving's achievement as essentially the successful stretching of a small talent, but at the same time sees him as ushering in the American Renaissance. Charles Neider, in his introduction to the *Complete Tales*[20], an edition using the 1895 Autograph Edition of Irving's works, is far less dispassionate and analytical. Neider gives a brief biography of Irving, and a pleasant, unassuming summary of the stories, but critical comment is largely restricted to such ejaculations as 'How he can write!'

The texts of 'Rip Van Winkle' and 'The Legend of Sleepy Hollow',[21] based on Irving's revised edition of 1848, have been reissued by Sleepy Hollow Restorations, in a large print suitable for children, and with twelve handsome illustrations, coloured by Fritz Kredel, but designed and etched by Felix O. C. Darley, of whose work Irving himself enthusiastically approved. Handsomely illustrated too is the (abridged) *Life of George Washington*[22], which Irving published in five volumes from 1855 to 1859 and regarded as the 'crowning effort' of his literary career. The *Life* is biased as history, as Richard B. Morris shows in his introduction, but it contains some vivid glimpses, like that of the veteran Herkimer, wounded in the fighting of 1776, who 'died like a philosopher and a Christian, smoking his pipe and reading his Bible to the last'.

Harold T. McCarthy's *The Expatriate Perspective*[23], besides discussing twentieth-century writers, deals with Cooper, Hawthorne, Melville, and Twain, but his treatment is not especially original. He writes best on the rather well-worn topics of Cooper's savagely satirical reaction to a greatly changed America on his return from Europe, and of Hawthorne's measuring of man's individual significance against the history of Rome.

Louise K. Barnett, in her study *The Ignoble Savage: American Literary*

[19] *The Writings in Prose and Verse of Hezekiah Salem Late of New England To Which is Added an Account of His Last Yankee Venture*, by Philip Freneau, ed. by Lewis Leary. New York: Scholars' Facsimiles & Reprints. pp. 87.
[20] *The Complete Tales of Washington Irving*, ed. by Charles Neider. New York: Doubleday. pp. xxxvii + 798.
[21] *Rip Van Winkle & The Legend of Sleepy Hollow*, by Washington Irving, with introd. by Haskell Springer. Tarrytown, N.Y.: Sleepy Hollow Restorations. 1974. pp. 128 with 12 illustrations.
[22] *Life of George Washington, by Washington Irving*, ed. and abridged by Jess Stein with introd. by Richard B. Morris. Tarrytown, N.Y.: Sleepy Hollow Restorations. pp. xxi + 721 with 30 illustrations.
[23] *The Expatriate Perspective: American Novelists and the Idea of America*, by Harold T. McCarthy. Rutherford, Madison, and Teaneck: Fairleigh Dickinson U.P. 1974. pp. 244. See *YW* 55. 529–30.

Racism, 1790-1890[24], also writes best on Cooper and Hawthorne. But in Cooper's case she is guilty of twisting the text to fit her argument. She claims that in American literature a certain restraint and decorum marks the conflicts between white men, as opposed to the conflicts between white men and Indians, and she uses as an example the understanding between the French and the English in *The Last of the Mohicans*: 'In contrast to this deference, the Indian allies of the French treacherously attack the English. But this is quite alien to the spirit of Cooper's account of the massacre, in which it is Montcalm, the French commander, who, far more than the Indians, is stigmatized as acting treacherously. This does not mean that Cooper has a high opinion of Indian morality: Lewis Smith writes accurately, if unoriginally, on Cooper's limited sympathies with the Indian in 'History and Race in the Leatherstocking Tales' (*Hiroshima Studies in English Language and Literature*). In her section on 'The Subversive Periphery of the Frontier Romance', Louise K. Barnett writes particularly well about Hawthorne, and she also pays some attention to Melville's literary treatment of the Polynesians, but her book concentrates almost wholly on the Indian, and she says nothing at all about the literary treatment of the Negro.

Black literature is still receiving much critical attention. Roger Whitlow offers a simple and factual but skimpy survey in *Black American Literature: A Critical History*[25]. His critical analysis tends to be on the level of: 'The sense of elation is found in such lines as, "I'm so glad, so glad, I'm so glad, so glad,/Glad I got religion, so glad"'. In *The Way of the New World*[26] Addison Gayle Jr. examines the development of the black novel. He deprecates the fact that early black writers attempted to create a literature patterned on that of the whites, and that 'The courageous men and women who set examples for Blacks yet unborn, by stealing away from slavery, murdering masters and overseers, and committing untold acts of rebellion against the slave system, find little recognition in their poems and novels'. Gayle concentrates on William Wells Brown, Frank Webb, Martin Delany, Paul Laurence Dunbar, and Charles Waddell Chesnutt. He writes of *Clotel, or the President's Daughter* (1853), the first novel written by a black man of American descent, that she 'is no less a romantic image than that concocted by the imagination of Mrs. Stowe', whereas he congratulates Martin Delany's *Blake; or the Huts of America* (1859) on being the most telling attack on Mrs. Stowe's 'caricature' of Uncle Tom. Gayle also speaks very highly of Frank Webb's novel *The Garies and Their Friends* (1857): 'In terms of structure, character development, and theme, it is the finest production by a black writer between 1853 and 1900, the publication date of Charles Chesnutt's *The House*

[24] *The Ignoble Savage: American Literary Racism, 1790-1890*, by Louise K. Barnett. Contributions in American Studies. Westport, Conn., and London: Greenwood P. pp. xii + 220.

[25] *Black American Literature: A Critical History*, by Roger Whitlow. Totowa, N.J.: Littlefield, Adams. 1974. pp. x + 287.

[26] *The Way of the New World: The Black Novel in America*, by Addison Gayle Jr. New York: Doubleday. pp. xx + 339.

398   AMERICAN LITERATURE TO 1900

Behind the Cedars. Paul Laurence Dunbar, however, although assessed as a major black novelist, Gayle accuses of having 'identified with whites emotionally, intellectually, and spiritually' and having all too often 'sanctioned their evaluation of Blacks'.

Robert Bone in *Down Home*[27] deals with the development of the black short story, which he treats as 'a child of mixed ancestry', deriving from two different cultural heritages, one Euro-American, literary, and cosmopolitan, and the other African-derived, oral, and rooted in the folk community. Bone early on in his study, however, abandons the black folk-tale as an important influence; he identifies three primary sources of the imaginative power of the black short story: the black American's deep attachment to the Protestant tradition, and especially to the Bible, his deep affection for the rural South, and his deep anxiety about his future role in American society. In the sections of his book which are concerned with the nineteenth century, Bone writes particularly well on the 'local-colour school' of the eighteen-eighties and eighteen-nineties. He discusses, for example, the way in which 'Like all local colorists, Dunbar and Chesnutt were torn between an urge toward realism and the constraints of a romantic form'. Bone takes a view similar to Addison Gayle's in his critical diagnosis of Dunbar: that he limited his art, as Chesnutt did not, by his adherence to a pastoral romanticism.

Black Poetry in America[28] aims at correcting what Blyden Jackson sees as the condescending and mistaken view that early black literature has little intrinsic value. As he puts it: 'Because concern for the black American experience among the general public is of such recent date, the assumption is too often made that what was written in the past is of importance only as a prologue to the black literature which is being written now: that it is only now that black American literature has come of age, so to speak, and that almost everything written before possibly the 1960s may be dismissed as preparatory work'. Jackson's own essay is devoted solely to twentieth-century work, whereas Louis D. Rubin Jr.'s essay examines 'The Search for a Language, 1746–1923'. Rubin writes, for example, of the dilemma of the black poet who, like Dunbar, felt that he was forced into using the dialect form, and who, in any case, had only the unsatisfactory and uncongenial alternative of the ornate literary language of the day, 'with its reliance upon abstractions and its bloodless idealism'.

Most of the writers who have contributed to *A Singer in the Dawn*[29], a collection of essays on Dunbar, have dealt, at least glancingly, with this dilemma of language. Jay Martin, in his 'Foreword: Paul Laurence Dunbar: Biography Through Letters', sees Dunbar as being 'thrust toward genteel society and the pressures to satisfy its various demands'. Saunders Redding, in 'Portrait Against Background', Dickson D. Bruce Jr. in 'On Dunbar's

[27] *Down Home: A History of Afro-American Short Fiction from Its Beginnings to the End of the Harlem Renaissance*, by Robert Bone. New Perspectives on Black America. New York: G.P. Putnam's Sons. pp. xxii + 328.
[28] *Black Poetry in America: Two Essays in Historical Interpretation*, by Blyden Jackson and Louis D. Rubin Jr. Baton Rouge: Louisiana State U.P., 1974, pp. xiv + 119.
[29] *A Singer in the Dawn: Reinterpretations of Paul Laurence Dunbar*, ed. by Jay Martin. New York: Dodd, Mead. pp. 255.

"Jingles in a Broken Tongue": Dunbar's Dialect Poetry and the Afro-American Folk Tradition', and Myron Simon in 'Dunbar and Dialect Poetry' all speak of the pitfalls and limitations inherent in Dunbar's use of the dialect form. It is accordingly the more striking that Darwin T. Turner, in 'Paul Laurence Dunbar: The Poet and the Myths', which is easily the best and the most truly critical of all the essays, states categorically that: 'Dunbar's standard-English verse is talented but not exceptional. His unique contribution to American literature is his dialect poetry'. Turner also makes the following points, all, as he feels, contrary to popular belief: that more than most English or American poets of his time, Dunbar depended on a quantitative metre and perfected a rhythmical phrasing; that images of blood and chains appear in more than ten per cent of his poems—'scarcely. . .what one would expect from a gay child of nature'; that Dunbar was not a pastoral poet; that most of his poems are not written in dialect but in 'the most elegant nineteenth-century English which he could manage'; that he used not only Negro dialect, but created a dialect suggesting the speech of white residents of Kentucky, Ohio, and Indiana; and that, finally, 'he was an educated, conscious creator of rhythmic songs, of likable people, and desirable retreats from a materialistic, urbanized age'. Other essays in the collection are Gossie H. Hudson on 'The Crowded Years: Paul Laurence Dunbar in History', Arna Bontemps on 'The Relevance of Paul Laurence Dunbar', and a trite 'Afterword' by Nikki Giovanni. James A. Emanuel writes on 'Racial Fire in the Poetry of Paul Laurence Dunbar', concluding that there is not much racial fire, but enough. To the section on the fiction, Addison Gayle Jr. has contributed a study of the novels. Kenny J. Williams offers a very good account of 'The Masking of the Novelist', and Bert Bender writes on 'The Lyrical Short Fiction of Dunbar and Chesnutt', concluding that both Dunbar and Chesnutt struggled against the mechanical formula fiction which prevailed during the time they were writing, but that Dunbar did so through lyricism and Chesnutt through irony.

Stephen Butterfield writes clearly and perceptively of *Black Autobiography in America*[30]. What makes this work particularly useful is his consistent attempt to place such autobiography in the context of better known literature. He writes, for example, that 'The identity of the slave narrator grows around his desire for freedom. . .In the literature of the master culture, specifically in the stories of Edgar Allan Poe, characters are given a precise individuality through their class, lineage, address life-style, or set of tastes. . .The opposite is true of the slave narrator. Again and again we discover in the first few pages of his account that he begins with nothing: he is uncertain of his exact age, he has no name of his own or his name changes whenever he is sold, he cannot trace his family much further back than his mother, and he is punished whenever he shows the slightest aspiration to become more than a piece of property. . .Poe, Melville, Gogol, Conrad, and many others have explored the Symbolism of the mask, but here it is real; the Symbol is contained in the reality rather than the other way around. If the mask slips, the author does not

[30] *Black Autobiography in America*, by Stephen Butterfield. Amherst: U. of Massachusetts P. 1974. pp. viii + 303. See *YW* 55. 512–13.

suffer an existential crisis, but arrest, capture, whipping, and possibly death. The influence of the split identity experience continues far beyond this period, offering a partial explanation for the predilection toward irony and satire in black writing'. Butterfield writes, too, of specific influences on the language of the slave narrative: those of sermons, the Bible, abolitionist journalism and oratory, and the prose style inherited from eighteenth-century England. He is illuminating on the religious mysticism which the confrontation with the wilderness inspires alike in the writer of the slave narrative and the writer of the Puritan autobiography, and he finds a 'terrible parallel' between the two forms of literature.

Several of the essays in *Emerson: Prophecy, Metamorphosis, and Influence*[31], a collection edited by David Levin, touch on the autobiographical element in his work. Sacvan Bercovitch, in 'Emerson the Prophet: Romanticism, Puritanism, and Auto-American-Biography', comes to the conclusion that Emerson 'carried the Puritan errand to new heights of eloquence and vision, in a Romantic assertion of the self that fused autobiography and history in the evolving spiritual biography of America'. Maurice Gonnaud writes on 'Emerson and the Imperial Self: A European Critique', Harold Bloom on 'The Freshness of Transformation: Emerson's Dialectics of Influence', and Daniel B. Shea, making analogies between Emerson and Saul Bellow, on 'Emerson and the American Metamorphosis'.

James M. Cox, in 'R. W. Emerson: The Circles of the Eye', and Albert Gelpi, in 'Emerson: The Paradox of Organic Form', both discuss Emerson's famous statement, 'I become a transparent eyeball'. Phyllis Cole in an excellent essay on 'Emerson, England, and Fate' compares Emerson's reactions to England with those of some of his American contemporaries, notably Melville.

Hyatt H. Waggoner's study of *Emerson as Poet*[32] opens with a review of 'A Century of Critical Agreements and Disagreements'. Waggoner goes on to survey Emerson's poems, and what he terms 'The Poetry of the Prose', but his final judgement is harsh enough: 'Community, friendship, love, grief, tragedy—these are all effectively absent from or effectively distorted in Emerson's vision, and together they encompass no insignificant slice of human experience'. The personal coldness which Waggoner suggests here also suggests itself in the case of Thoreau, notably in a rather chilly essay on 'Love' on *Early Essays and Miscellanies*[33]. This is a collection of fifty-three early pieces, dating from 1828 to 1852. It includes a major essay on Sir Walter Raleigh not published during Thoreau's lifetime, and a fragmentary college piece never published before. All but one of the *Early Essays* were written at Harvard, and *The Dial* published several of the *Miscellanies*. The collection covers a wide range of subjects, and is a useful addition to Thoreau scholarship, but it must be admitted that it

[31] *Emerson: Prophecy, Metamorphosis, and Influence*, ed. by David Levin. Selected papers from the English Institute. New York and London: Columbia U.P. pp. vii + 181.
[32] *Emerson as Poet*, by Hyatt H. Waggoner. Princeton U.P. 1974. pp. xiii + 211.
[33] *Early Essays and Miscellanies*, by Henry D. Thoreau, ed. by Joseph J. Moldenhauer and Edwin Moser, with Alexander C. Kern. Princeton U.P. pp. 430 with 5 illustrations.

does not make compulsive reading. Thoreau's *Maine Woods*[34], published in an authoritative edition by Princeton University Press in 1972, has been reissued illustrated by the work of Herbert W. Gleason, one of the great American landscape photographers of the early twentieth century.

Individual and Community: Variations on a Theme in American Fiction[35] is a distinguished collection of essays which includes studies of Charles Brockden Brown and Hawthorne. (Louis D. Rubin Jr.'s essay on Twain appears in another collection published this year, and is discussed later in this chapter.) J. V. Ridgely's 'The Empty World of *Wieland*' exhibits the Brockden Brown critic's usual pessimistic propensity for plot-summary. But Ridgely argues convincingly that *Wieland* illustrates, among other things, Brown's perceptions about the spiritual state of America.

Edgar A. Dryden, in 'The Limits of Romance: A Reading of *The Marble Faun*', writes cogently on the functions of Rome, art, and ruins in Hawthorne's work, and he is especially good on the carnival near the end of the story. Dryden feels that to Hawthorne 'The games of childhood have become the sign of the exiled adult'. Roy Harvey Pearce, in 'Day-Dream and Fact: The Import of *The Blithedale Romance*', also discusses the significance of the childhood world for Hawthorne. Pearce makes the chronological connexion between *The Blithedale Romance* and *A Wonder-Book (1851)* and *Tanglewood Tales (1853)* in order to emphasize the fact that *The Blithedale Romance* was written at a time 'when Hawthorne was most deeply concerned to demonstrate that Arcadianism was quite properly a stage in the development of the child's life'. Pearce persuasively asserts that Blithedale's Arcadian world is essentially, and inappropriately, a child's world, to which Hawthorne shows that all concerned 'willy-nilly regress in their desperate attempt to find a place where what they take to be their gifts and commitments can be realized'. James H. Justus offers a fine analysis of 'Hawthorne's Coverdale: Character and Art in *The Blithedale Romance (AL)*.

'*Remember the Ladies?: New Perspectives on Women in American History*[36] includes an essay on Anne Hutchinson by Carol V. R. George which constitutes a useful background for *The Scarlet Letter*. Two recent instalments[37] in the indispensable Centenary Edition of Hawthorne's work have each an excellent 'Historical Commentary' by J. Donald Crowley, 'Textual Commentary' by F. B. Fredson Bowers, and 'Bibliographical Information' by John Manning. This edition is essential for anyone making a serious study of Hawthorne.

Harry C. West (*NCF*) suggests that Hawthorne found much of his material for 'The Artist of the Beautiful' in Isaac D'Israeli's *Curiosities of*

---

[34] *The Illustrated Maine Woods*, by Henry D. Thoreau, ed. by Joseph J. Moldenhauer. Princeton U.P. 1974. pp. xxiii + 347 with 48 illustrations.

[35] *Individual and Community: Variations on a Theme in American Fiction*, ed. by Kenneth H. Baldwin and David K. Kirby, Durham, N.C.: Duke U.P. pp. xvii + 222.

[36] '*Remember the Ladies*': *New Perspectives on Women in American History: Essays in Honor of Nelson Manfred Blake*, ed. by Carol V. R. George. Syracuse U.P. pp xvi + 201.

[37] *Twice-Told Tales* and *Mosses from an Old Manse*, by Nathaniel Hawthorne. (Centenary Edition of the Works of Nathaniel Hawthorne, ed. by William Charvat, Roy Harvey Pearce, and Claude M. Simpson, Vol. IX and Vol. X) Ohio State U.P., 1974. pp. 637 + 664.

Literature, Roger P. Wallins (*SSF*) discusses the relationship between Robin and the narrator in 'My Kinsman, Major Molineux', and Max L. Autrey writes thoughtfully on 'Flower Imagery in Hawthorne's Posthumous Narratives' (*SNNTS*).

Artful Thunder: Versions of the Romantic Tradition in American Literature[38], another of this year's illuminating collections of essays, contains a comparison by Edward Stone of Aeschylus's House of Atreus with Hawthorne's 'House of Pyncheon' in *Seven Gables*. Sydney J. Krause writes, with the usual prudent plot-telling, on 'Romanticism in *Wieland*: Brown and the Reconciliation of Opposites'. There is a study of '*Walden*: Yoga and Creation' by David Hoch, an essay on Emily Dickinson by Thomas M. Davis, and a rather woolly comparison between Emerson and Howard Nemerov by Gloria Young. There are five Melville essays: one on a linguistic joke in *Mardi* by Donald J. Yannella, one on Melville's attitude to 'geniality' by Marjorie Dew, and three perceptive contributions to *Moby-Dick* studies by Harrison Hayford, Sanford E. Marovitz, and Wilson Heflin. Hayford and Marovitz both examine the connexions between the characters of Ahab and Ishmael, and Heflin proposes five real-life incidents of the whale-fishery in 1842 and 1843 as sources for 'The Town-Ho's Story' of Steelkilt and Radney.

In addition, there are two essays on Poe. Nathalia Wright suggests that Roderick Usher appears both more complex and more credible if he is viewed specifically as an artist, and Eric Mottram writes brilliantly on 'Poe's Pym and and the American Social Imagination'.

Penguin has issued a new edition of *Arthur Gordon Pym*[39], based on the text of the first American edition, and including in the Appendix not only suggestions about *Pym*'s influence on *Moby-Dick*, but also Jules Verne's sequel to *Pym*, *Le Sphinx des Glaces*. There is a valuable, straightforward introduction by Harold Beaver, putting *Pym* in its historical context. Paul Zweig's *The Adventurer*[40] has a chapter on 'The New Mythology of Adventure: Edgar Allan Poe', in which Zweig writes of Poe's exploitation of fear in the Gothic manner, and then concludes that 'The novelistic incoherence of *Pym* conceals a powerful symmetry. Pym's voyage toward the south is doubled by his voyage into terror'. Burton R. Pollin (*SIR*) writes about the influence of Fouque's Undine on Poe, particularly in 'The Fall of the House of Usher', and Robert Coskren (*SSF*) discusses the disintegration of the self in 'William Wilson'.

Walter L. Reed's *Meditations on the Hero: A Study of the Romantic Hero in Nineteenth-Century Fiction*[41] has a little in 'Prolegomenon: The Romantic Hero and the Dialectical Form' on Hawthorne's narrative mode,

---

[38] *Artful Thunder: Versions of the Romantic Tradition in American Literature in Honor of Howard P. Vincent*, ed. by Robert J. DeMott and Sanford E. Marovitz. Kent, Ohio: Kent State U.P. pp. xv + 312.

[39] *The Narrative of Arthur Gordon Pym of Nantucket*, by Edgar Allan Poe. ed. by Harold Beaver. Penguin. pp. 311.

[40] *The Adventurer*, by Paul Zweig. J. M. Dent. 1974. pp. x + 275 with 18 illustrations.

[41] *Meditations on the Hero: A Study of the Romantic Hero in Nineteenth-Century Fiction*, by Walter L. Reed. New Haven and London: Yale U.P. 1974. pp. x + 207.

but it is relevant to this chapter chiefly for its discussion of Melville's depiction of Ahab and Ishmael in *Moby-Dick*. Ahab absorbs most of Gerard M. Sweeney's attention in *Melville's Use of Classical Mythology*[42]. Sweeney claims that his study is necessary because there has hitherto been a failure to identify precisely what aspect of a mythic character Melville might be using at any given moment. This ignores the fact that Melville himself was not over-precise about this.

James Barbour writes on '*The Composition of Moby-Dick*' (*AL*), and Stephen C. Ausband in 'The Whale and the Machine: An Approach to *Moby-Dick*' (*AL*) argues that Ahab has various classical analogies, 'And he is, unquestionably, a machine. Melville associates him consistently and convincingly with mills, trains, generators, and the fires of industry'.

The argument of *That Lonely Game: Melville, 'Mardi', and the Almanac*[43] is a very elaborate one, based on Melville's supposed use of astrological patterns. Maxine Moore significantly expresses her admiration for Viola Sachs's equally dubious and unhelpful Cabalistic numerological approach to *Moby-Dick*[44]. *That Lonely Game* contains in its first chapter a convincing enough suggestion that Melville was 'irked by British incredulity regarding the intellectual potential of the American common man', and that as a result he composed a work which he considered to be extraordinarily original. In a later chapter Maxine Moore convincingly shows that *Mardi* shares many characteristics with the traditional masque: Melville's work is like *The Faerie Queene*, *The Divine Comedy*, and *Comus* in that it 'progresses from one symbol-laden tableau to another and displays the stellar and planetary mythology, the pageantry of holiday and season, and the involvement of current affairs, in turn and simultaneously'. But it is unlike them in that it is the work of a trickster who demands that his work be laboriously decoded with the help of the almanac. Hennig Cohen, in his polite but highly sceptical foreword, makes evident his disquiet that any Melville novel should be treated as a code to be broken; furthermore, he points out that Maxine Moore has not properly coped with *Mardi*'s history of composition. To accept her theories it would be necessary to credit Melville not only with astrological expertise, but with a gift of prophecy.

R. Bruce Bickley argues far more convincingly in *The Method of Melville's Short Fiction*[45]. His thesis is that Melville's art of ironic portraiture reaches its peak in his short stories. The two best elements in Bickley's study are his discussions of the influence of Irving and Hawthorne on Melville's short fiction and the development of Melville's narrative persona. Bickley, however, makes White-Jacket's wearing of his white jacket altogether too conscious and deliberate.

Merton M. Sealts Jr. has usefully gathered together *The Early Lives of*

---

[42] *Melville's Use of Classical Mythology*, by Gerard M. Sweeney. Melville Studies in American Culture. Amsterdam: Rodopi. pp. 169.

[43] *That Lonely Game: Melville, 'Mardi', and the Almanac*, by Maxine Moore, with foreword by Hennig Cohen. U. of Missouri Studies. Columbia: U. of Missouri P. pp. xxv + 281 with 83 illustrations.

[44] *La Contre-Bible de Melville: 'Moby-Dick' dechiffré*, by Viola Sachs. Paris and La Haye: Mouton. pp. 122.

[45] *The Method of Melville's Short Fiction*, by R. Bruce Bickley Jr. Durham, N.C.: Duke U.P. pp. xv + 142.

Melville[46] in a volume which illustrates both the genesis and transmission of critical ideas about Melville, and the evolution and development of the major biographical essays about him. Sealts opens well with a reference to Book XVII of *Pierre*, in which Melville offers a satirical treatment of 'Young America in Literature'—in the same year as the first biographical sketch of himself. The contemporary documents which Sealts uses include short articles on Melville from four contemporary reference works published between 1852 and 1890, six retrospective essays of 1891–1892, and reminiscences of Melville by his wife and two of his granddaughters.

Thomas L. McHaney offers an admirable discussion of the relationship between '*The Confidence-Man* and Satan's Disguises in *Paradise Lost*' (*NCF*), and Christopher W. Sten gives an excellent interpretation of 'Vere's Use of the "Forms": Means and Ends in *Billy Budd*' (*AL*), asserting of Captain Vere's decision to execute Billy that, 'Like all great literature, *Billy Budd* ends not so much with an answer and an ideological stand as with a question and a challenge to remake the world in a more benevolent image'. Milton R. Stern also examines the central role of Captain Vere, but specifically in relation to changing trends in Melville criticism, in his introduction to the fine new Bobbs-Merrill edition of *Billy Budd*[47]. This edition follows the Hayford and Sealts text in most of its corrections, but does in some cases make consistency and grammatical corrections secondary to what Melville actually wrote; it contains full and detailed accounts of the novel's composition, text, and history.

Edward S. Grejda in *The Common Continent of Men*[48] moves doggedly through the Melville canon arguing for Melville's liberal views on race. He is forced to make a number of grudging admissions: 'Herman Melville in *Typee* raises no overt cry for racial equality, utters no abolitionist proclamations'; 'race is not a major concern in *Redburn*'; 'Since *Pierre* contains only white characters, it is only peripheral to a study devoted to nonwhite figures'. He is forced, too, to argue rather obliquely that, for example, 'Ethan Allen, though white, embodies characteristics which Melville frequently attributes to his nonwhite characters. Like them, he has been exasperated into savagery, in this case by a people supposedly enlightened', or that 'Old Pierre Glendinning, John Paul Jones, Ethan Allen—heroes, patriots, warriors—all are cast in the mold of Melville's dark-skinned savages'.

In his long and pedestrian study *The Image of the Jew in American Literature*[49], Louis Harap takes a rather sterner view of American literary attitudes to the Jewish race. He makes a gloomily comprehensive socio-

---

[46] *The Early Lives of Melville: Nineteenth-Century Biographical Sketches and Their Authors*, by Merton M. Sealts Jr. Madison: U. of Wisconsin P. 1974. pp. xiii + 280 with 31 illustrations.

[47] *Billy Budd, Sailor: An Inside Narrative*, by Herman Melville, ed. by Milton R. Stern. Indianapolis: Bobbs-Merrill. pp. lx + 184 with 16 illustrations.

[48] *The Common Continent of Men: Racial Equality in the Writings of Herman Melville* by Edward S. Grejda. Port Washington, N.Y., and London: Kennikat P. 1974. pp. 165.

[49] *The Image of the Jew In American Literature from Early Republic to Mass Immigration*, by Louis Harap. Philadelphia: Jewish Publication Society of America. 1974. pp. xiii + 596.

logical and literary survey of prose, fiction, and drama from early republic to mass immigration, and concludes, for example, that the Fireside Poets— Bryant, Whittier, Longfellow, Holmes, Lowell—'showed no particular grasp of Jewish issues'. The Fireside Poets appear to be currently enjoying only a tepid defence from their critics. John B. Pickard in his introduction to his definitive edition of *The Letters of John Greenleaf Whittier*[50] freely admits that 'As a letter writer Whittier did not lavish time and care in drafts and redrafts in an attempt to unfold his inner being as did Emily Dickinson, nor did he express a profound sense of the poet's craft and dedication to the beautiful as did John Keats'. The letters, in other words, are almost unmitigatedly dull. There are occasional real glimpses of Whittier's personality, such as his comment on Hawthorne's death: 'And so Hawthorne is at rest—the rest he could not find here. God—the All-Merciful—has removed him from the shadows of time—wherein he seemed to walk himself like a shadow— to the clear sunlight of Eternity'. But these are all too rare. Although the volumes contain very useful biographical notes, the letters themselves are quite remarkably unrevealing.

Pickard's rather defeatist note is echoed in Eleanor M. Tilton's introduction to the new Cambridge Edition of Oliver Wendell Holmes[51]. She records of Holmes that: 'During all the years he taught at the Harvard Medical School, he was assigned the one o'clock lecture hour because he could keep the hungry and the weary alert'. But as far as his poetry is concerned, she ends weakly: 'It cannot be said that Holmes was no poet; it has to be said that he was so many other things as well'.

There is a depressive edge, too, to the equivalent introduction by George Monteiro to the new Cambridge Edition of Longfellow[52]. Monteiro finds it only 'tenable to argue. . .that Longfellow's poetry. . .is nevertheless valuable on its own terms', and he is tentative about the possibility of readers being tolerant of Longfellow's moral mission. The Cambridge Edition of Holmes adds a hundred and forty-four poems to those collected in the editions of 1891 and 1895. The text of the Longfellow volume is that of the original Cambridge Edition of 1893, prepared by Horace D. Scudder. In each case the bulk of the introduction is biographical.

By contrast, the new Penguin edition of Whitman[53] contains scarcely any introduction at all, although there is a table of dates in Whitman's life. This edition contains all of Whitman's known work, apart from manuscript fragments left at his death. The principal text is that of the 1891–1892 'death-bed' edition of *Leaves of Grass*, but earlier versions of many of the poems are included in the notes.

[50] *The Letters of John Greenleaf Whittier*, ed. by John B. Pickard, Cambridge, Mass., and London: Belknap P., Harvard. U.P. 3 vols. Vol. 1, pp. xxxv + 684 with 8 illustrations. Vol. 2, pp. x + 482 with 7 illustrations. Vol. 3, pp. xi + 735 with 8 illustrations.
[51] *The Poetical Works of Oliver Wendell Holmes*, ed. by Eleanor M. Tilton. Cambridge Edition. Boston: Houghton Mifflin. pp. xxv + 457.
[52] *The Poetical Works of Henry Wadsworth Longfellow*, with introd. by George Monteiro. Cambridge Edition. Boston: Houghton Mifflin. pp. xxvii + 689.
[53] *The Complete Poems*, by Walt Whitman, ed. by Francis Murphy. Penguin English Poets. Penguin. pp. 892.

Stephen A. Black's *Whitman's Journeys into Chaos: A Psychoanalytic Study of the Poetic Process*[54] is more straightforward than its title suggests. Black investigates Whitman's poetic processes as they developed between 1855 and 1865, and he uses 'chaos', unexceptionably enough, to stand for Whitman's unconscious, so that the 'journeys into chaos' are the poems. He chooses the 1855–1865 time-span because he feels that nearly all of Whitman's important poetry belongs here, although the fact that we are so accustomed to knowing Whitman through the 1891–1892 *Leaves of Grass* may tend to obscure this for us. Black asserts that after 1865 O'Connor's title of 'Good Gray Poet' fitted 'like a comfortable cloak beneath which Whitman concealed his aging body and exhausted soul'. Although he is far from original in his view that Whitman was not overtly and actively homosexual, but chiefly autoerotic, Black interestingly substantiates his view that the poems usually end with Whitman's conflicts unresolved and his anxieties little relieved. Nor does Black follow former psychological interpreters of Whitman in seeing the poems as records of past events, but prefers to regard the poems' composition as the crucial psychological activity of Whitman's life. He is particularly illuminating in his discussion of Whitman's early fiction: he sees its artistic failure as arising from Whitman's employment of stock situations and devices of characterization, upon which his own unconscious attitudes and assumptions then intruded.

In the course of his study, Stephen A. Black observes of Whitman's mother that: 'There were problems with her husband and anxieties about money; her first son died of syphilis in an insane asylum; the marital difficulties of her second daughter, a near-psychotic, demanded constant attention; her third son, an alcoholic, married a prostitute and died at thirty-six; her last son, an epileptic, was deformed and retarded'. Yet Jerome M. Loving in his edition of the *Civil War Letters of George Washington Whitman*[55] assures us that 'the Whitman family was in many ways representative in nineteenth-century America'. Loving, however, does argue persuasively for 'the diverse and yet ordinary nature of Walt Whitman's family' and for this family's effect on his poetry—and specifically for the influence of his brother's letters and diary, terse and inarticulate as they are, on Whitman's Civil War poetry; Whitman read his brother's war diary in December 1864 and recorded in his own diary that, 'It is merely a skeleton of dates, voyages, places camped in or marched through, battles fought, etc'. but '. . .It does not need calling in play the imagination to see that in such a record as this lies folded a perfect poem of the war'. And John Burroughs, as Perry D. Burroughs reminds us in his useful and concise study of this important early Whitman critic[56], wrote of the effect of the war on Whitman that: 'His whole character culminates here'. The *Civil War Letters*, in short, are a valuable contribution to Whitman scholarship.

Russell A. Hunt writes with pleasing clarity on 'Whitman's Poetics and

[54] *Whitman's Journeys into Chaos: A Psychoanalytic Study of the Poetic Process*, by Stephen A. Black. Princeton U.P. pp. xv + 255.

[55] *Civil War Letters of George Washington Whitman*, ed. by Jerome M. Loving, with foreword by Gay Wilson Allen. Durham, N.C.: Duke U.P. pp. xvi + 173 with 7 illustrations.

[56] *John Burroughs*, by Perry D. Burroughs. TUSAS. New York: Twayne. 1974. pp [xi] + 146.

the Unity of "Calamus" ' (*AL*), arguing against the phallic significance of the calamus plant, a clarity which is unfortunately not emulated by John Snyder in *The Dear Love of Man: Tragic and Lyric Communion in Walt Whitman*[57]. His title is taken from Whitman's line in 'The Base of All Metaphysics': 'The dear love of man for his comrade, the attraction of friend to friend', and, as invariably when he quotes Whitman directly, one is struck by the contrast between Whitman's poetic clarity and Snyder's critical obscurity: Snyder makes heavy weather of precisely those philosophical distinctions which Whitman cuts through in his poetry. He is at his best when he concentrates on discussion of Whitman's imagery—for instance, his imagery of eyesight and the voice.

Harold Bloom in *A Map of Misreading*[58] writes in general terms of Emerson's influence on American poets, and then proceeds to an examination of one poem each by Whitman, Emily Dickinson, and Wallace Stevens as 'representative post-Emersonian poems'. Whitman's 'As I Ebb'd with the Ocean of Life' is used as evidence for Bloom's claim that 'Whitman is at once the greatest and the most repressed of American poets'. But Emily Dickinson's 'Because I could not stop for Death' is used less skilfully, and Bloom makes the Emerson connexion far less clear.

Robert Weisbuch offers some perceptive analyses of individual poems in his study of *Emily Dickinson's Poetry*[59]. He suggests, too, that Emily Dickinson's lack of concern for current political issues and urgent social questions stems from her 'own brand of fatigue', that is, her distaste for sermons and law-giving. But Weisbuch's work is spoilt by, for example, his rigid plan of following what he calls 'the course of a Dickinsonian death' to examine Emily Dickinson's emotions at each stage—an ill-conceived notion, which appears to spring from his resentment of the absence of clear shifts in style and thought during her poetic career: 'She thus robs the critic of one of his most valuable tools, the tracing of a chronological development'. Weisbuch's work is also spoilt by a needlessly aggressive attitude towards other critics. He speaks of 'the widely held assumption that Dickinson is impossibly obscure'. Whose assumption?

L. Edwin Folsom writes of winter as a primary source of Emily Dickinson's realism in ' "The Souls That Snow": Winter in the Poetry of Emily Dickinson' (*AL*). Laura Benét's *The Mystery of Emily Dickinson*[60] is a very slight biographical account, presumably intended for juveniles.

Two writers for juveniles are honoured in *Behind a Mask*[61] and *Waiting for the Party*[62]. Madeleine Stern has selected four of Louisa May Alcott's stories to support the argument that 'Her own anger at an unjust world she transformed into the anger of her heroines, who made of it a powerful

[57] *The Dear Love of Man: Tragic and Lyric Communion in Walt Whitman*, by John Snyder. The Hague and Paris: Mouton. pp. 260.
[58] *A Map of Misreading*, by Harold Bloom, New York: O.U.P. pp. 206.
[59] *Emily Dickinson's Poetry*, by Robert Weisbuch. Chicago and London: Chicago U.P. pp xv + 202.
[60] *The Mystery of Emily Dickinson*, by Laura Benét, New York: Dodd, Mead. 1974. pp. xii + 112 with 24 illustrations.
[61] *Behind a Mask: The Unknown Thrillers of Louisa May Alcott*, ed. by Madeleine Stern. New York: William Morrow. pp. xxxiii + 277.
[62] *Waiting for the Party: The Life of Frances Hodgson Burnett 1849-1924*, by Ann Thwaite. Secker & Warburg. 1974. pp. xii + 274. 28 illustrations.

weapon with which to challenge fate'. Ann Thwaite, too, concentrates on
the aggressive heroine in her biography of Frances Hodgson Burnett, and
draws attention to the fact that the aggressive heroine of Hawthorne's
Blithedale Romance is called Zenobia Fauntleroy, which may have influenced Frances Hodgson Burnett's choice of surname for her most
famous hero.

Ernest Earnest in *The American Eve in Fact and Fiction, 1775-1914*[63]
uses diaries, memoirs, and biographies to show that the fictional representation of women in American fiction was far less aggressive than the reality.
The title of the book is misleading in inviting comparison with R. W. B.
Lewis's *The American Adam* (1955), for here 'Eve' means no more than
'Woman'. Henry James and William Dean Howells are the novelists most
extensively discussed, but there is a wide range of reference.

The Dispossessed Garden[64] by Lewis P. Simpson similarly stresses the
divergence between literature and reality—in this case between the idyllic
pastoral image of the South and the slaveholding reality. Simpson shows
how the vision of Virginia as a paradise, in contrast to a wilderness, first
appears in developed form in Robert Beverley's *The History and Present
State of Virginia* (1705), which blends the delights of the natural garden
and the plantation garden, and finds a memorable symbol in the summer
house of Colonel William Byrd I,—a symbol which foreshadows the evocation in literary imagining of a pastoral plantation situated in a timeless
'Old South'. Simpson claims too that Jefferson's vision of the yeoman
farmer in *Notes on Virginia* represents 'not only a pastoral purification of
European influences but of the influence of slavery'. He goes on to write
of John Pendleton Kennedy's novel *Swallow Barn* (1831) and to point its
connexion with the work of Poe: 'If the image of Usher' somber and
dreary garden, dominated by a melancholy mansion beside a "black and
lurid tarn", is a Gothic inversion of the harmony of the standard English
pastoral domain, it can as easily be an inversion of John Pendleton
Kennedy's Swallow Barn'. He writes also of the way Mrs. Stowe in *Uncle
Tom's Cabin* transforms Simon Legree's plantation garden into a horrifying
symbol of modernity, and of the mask of 'comical-pastoral' adopted by
William Gilmore Simms in his reply to *Uncle Tom's Cabin*, his novel
Woodcraft (1852). This is a well written and important study.

*William Elliott Shoots a Bear: Essays on the Southern Literary Imagina-
tion*[65] by Louis D. Rubin comprises a collection of essays written over a
period of ten years and all directed towards the same question, of why
southern writers write like southern writers. The title essay is about one of
the earliest and best known books about indoor life in the South, William
Elliott's *Carolina Sports by Land and Water* (1846), and the way Elliott's
artistry was limited by his consciousness of the social implications of
slavery. The other nineteenth-century essays are 'Uncle Remus and the

---

[63] *The American Eve in Fact and Fiction, 1775-1914*, by Ernest Earnest, Urbana,
Chicago, and London: U. of Illinois P. 1974. pp. 280.
[64] *The Dispossessed Garden: Pastoral and History in Southern Literature*, by
Lewis P. Simpson. Mercer U. Lamar Memorial Lectures. Athens: U. of Georgia P.
pp. x + 109.
[65] *William Elliott Shoots a Bear: Essays on the Southern Literary Imagination*, by
Louis D. Rubin Jr. Baton Rouge: Louisiana State U.P. pp. xii + 279.

Ubiquitous Rabbit' (see *YW* 55. 488), 'The Passion of Sidney Lanier', and 'Politics and the Novel: George W. Cable and the Genteel Tradition', in which Rubin argues that Cable's *John March, Sotherner* (1895) is a novel in which 'A banal, wearisome romantic love plot is joined with the most searching, realistic, honest depiction of southern society during the late nineteenth century ever penned'. Finally, there is ' "The Begum of Bengal' ': Mark Twain and the South', in which Rubin brilliantly examines the concept of status in Mark Twain's life and work: 'It was, in short, splendid to be a Virginian and an aristocrat—if you had no conscience to plague you for your sins'. Rubin points to the literary tradition of Twain's day which was based on the humour implicit in the confrontation of gentlemanly refinement and breeding with the shrewdness and realism of the new American. He notes that Twain, chastizing the South's reliance on rhetorical embellishment, is chastizing an aspect of himself. He reveals how *A Connecticut Yankee* envisions feudal England in terms of the South. In short, he show how strongly Twain's art remained marked by his Southern experience throughout his life, and he concludes perceptively that: 'Had Samuel Clemens been born in the Deep South and had things worked out there in the same way, the literary result might well have been the equivalent of the Quentin Compson of *The Sound and the Fury*, holding desper ately to concepts of Southern honor in a world of Snopeses and change, and finding a resolution only in tragedy. But this was the border South, and he was Sam Clemens of Missouri, who perceived the absurdity equally with the pathos'.

The conclusion of Arthur G. Pettit's *Mark Twain and the South*[66] also makes an analogy between Twain and Quentin Compson. Pettit says, 'To take seriously Mark Twain's last writings about the South is to realize that for this Southerner there would be no Canaan, no new Jerusalem, no catharsis of the white conscience, no final purging of white guilt, and no notion that black and white might ever live in equality and brotherhood. With this message Mark Twain ended his career as commentator on the South and the black race. Like Faulkner's Quentin Compson he cursed the South and in doing so decried a part of himself, and remained a Southerner to the end'. During the course of this fascinating and instructive study, Pettit makes particularly good use of Twain's unfinished manuscripts. He is also very illuminating on George Washington Cable's influence on Twain, especially in his 'self-censorship', on the development of Twain's attitude to racialist jokes, and on the role of Roxana in *Pudd'nhead Wilson*. James W. Gargano writes on *'Pudd'nhead Wilson*: Mark Twain as Genial Satan' (*SAQ*) to counter Fiedler's view of Twain as a 'bitter social historian'. Tom H. Towers, in ' "I Never Thought We Might Want to Come Back": Strategies of Transcendence in *Tom Sawyer*' (*MFS*), adopts an exactly opposite line of argument: that Twain is really much grimmer than he seems. He argues, for example, that, since in the anatomy book scene Becky makes it clear that she expects to be punished, not so much for tearing the page as for sexual curiousity, 'When Tom takes Becky's whipping, they are bound together in criminality and secret sexual

[66] *Mark Twain and the South*, by Arthur G. Pettit. Lexington: U.P. of Kentucky, 1974. pp. x + 224.

knowledge'. Similarly, the cave sequence is a Romantic quest which ends in unexpected terror and loneliness. *In Tom Sawyer*, just as in *Huckleberry Finn*, freedom and community, or love, are revealed as incompatible, and both books reveal the profound despair of Twain's artistic vision usually identified in later works like *Pudd'nhead Wilson* or *The Mysterious Stranger*. Coleman O. Parsons (*MissQ*) gives an interesting account of Twain's 1896 South African tour, and Helen L. Harris examines prejudice towards Indians in 'Mark Twain's Response to the Native American' (*AL*). Twain's burlesques are the most entertaining element in the otherwise rather pedestrian account of *Setting in the American Short Story of Local Color 1865-1900*[67] by Robert D. Rhode, and there are a few pertinent remarks about Twain in J. Golden Taylor's 'The Western Short Story' and Max Westbrook's 'The Practical Spirit: Sacrality and the American West', both in *Western Writing*[68], edited by Gerald W. Haslam, otherwise of little interest. *The Western Story: Fact, Fiction, and Myth*[69], edited by Philip Durham and Everett L. Jones, is an anthology obviously intended as a school text. A very serious omission is that, although there are notes on the contributors, each item is not dated. But there is a stimulating introduction, much better than Jenni Calder's *There Must be a Lone Ranger*[70] at 'examining the particular potency of a myth that continually outwits history', which is the latter study's professed aim. Jenni Calder deals mainly with films, and makes no attempt at literary criticism when she does discuss books, but she offers a little useful background material from the eighteen-seventies and eighteen-eighties.

Clayton L. Eichelberger has written a helpful *Guide to Critical Reviews of United States Fiction, 1870-1910*[71], and Drewey Wayne Gunn has compiled a bibliography of *Mexico in American and British Letters*[72], and has now in addition written a literary study of *American and British Writers in Mexico, 1556-1973*[73]. It is rather a plodding book, and contains little of interest on pre-twentieth century literature, but it does include a brief discussion of Stephen Crane's tales set in Mexico.

The most important essay in *American Literary Naturalism: A Reassessment*[74], edited by Yoshinobu Hakutani and Lewis Fried, is Thomas A. Gullason's perceptive 'Stephen Crane: in Nature's Bosom', which distin-

[67] *Setting in the American Short Story of Local Color 1865-1900*, by Robert D. Rhode. Studies in American Literature. The Hague and Paris: Mouton. pp. 189.
[68] *Western Writing*, ed. by Gerald W. Haslam. Albuquerque: U. of New Mexico P. 1974. pp. 156.
[69] *The Western Story: Fact, Fiction, and Myth*, ed. by Philip Durham and Everett L. Jones. New York, Chicago, San Francisco, and Atlanta: Harcourt Brace Jovanovich. pp. ix + 369.
[70] *There Must be a Lone Ranger*, by Jenni Calder. Hamish Hamilton. 1974. pp. xiii + 241 with 14 illustrations.
[71] *A Guide to Critical Reviews of United States Fiction, 1870-1910*, by Clayton L. Eichelberger. Metuchen, N.J.: Scarecrow. 1974. pp. 351.
[72] *Mexico in American and British Letters: A Bibliography of Fiction and Travel Books, Citing Original Editions*, by Drewey Wayne Gunn. Metuchen, N.J.: Scarecrow. 1974. pp. vii + 157.
[73] *American and British Writers in Mexico, 1556-1973*, by Drewey Wayne Gunn. Austin and London: U. of Texas P. 1974. pp. xii + 301.
[74] *American Literary Naturalism: A Reassessment*, ed. by Yoshinobu Hakutani and Lewis Fried. Heidelberg: Carl Winter Universitatsverlag. pp. v + 207.

guishes Crane's work from that of the 'typical naturalist'. The other nineteenth-century essays, all shrewd and valuable in their way, are 'Edgar Watson Howe, Our First Naturalist' by Sydney J. Krause, 'Naturalism and Robert Herrick: A Test Case' by Charles Child Walcutt, and 'Dreiser; "Extreme and Bloody Individualism" ' by Philip L. Gerber.

Similarly, the most important nineteenth-century section of Peter Aichinger's *The American Soldier in Fiction, 1880-1963*[75], not surprisingly, is that on *The Red Badge of Courage*, which Aichinger finds 'academic' in quality compared with the stories of Ambrose Bierce. *The Red Badge of Courage* has now been issued as part of the University of Virginia's edition of Crane's works[76]. This volume establishes the text of the novel for the first time by using it as its copy-text the Barrett-Virginia manuscript which was the basis for the lost typescript that served as printer's copy for the first edition. There is a full textual commentary, and an introduction by J. C. Levenson giving the novel's historical background, an accout of its growth and of the influences upon it, especially that of Tolstoy's *Sebastopol*, and a critical estimate of its place in Crane's work.

The University of Virginia edition of Crane's *Poems and Literary Remains* has been used as the text for Andrew Crosland's *Concordance to the Complete Poetry of Stephen Crane*[77], whereas Herman Baron's *Concordance to the Poems of Stephen Crane*[78], is geared to *The Poems of Stephen Crane: A Critical Edition*, edited by Joseph Katz.

Forest Caroll Edwards writes acutely of 'Decorum: Its Genesis and Function in Stephen Crane' (*TQ*). Frank Bergon in *Stephen Crane's Artistry*[79] examines Crane's prose style, his imaginative gift, his sense of story, and his choice of a suitable subject. Bergon devotes considerable effort to an analysis of *Maggie*, and to a large extent his effort is repaid, but his conclusion, an attempt to define 'The Limits of Crane's Artistry', is a failure, descending into mere critical jargon.

Kenneth Graham's *Henry James: The Drama of Fulfilment*[80] is written consciously in reaction to other critics. Graham attempts, with a fair degree of success, to look with a new freshness at the fiction, in reaction to the increasing 'sophistication' of current James criticism. He dicusses seven works: *Madame de Mauves, Daisy Miller, Roderick Hudson, The Aspern Papers, The Tragic Muse, The Spoils of Poynton*, and *The Wings of the Dove*. The best sections of the book are his lively analysis of *Madame de Mauves* and his spirited defence of *The Tragic Muse*.

[75] *The American Soldier in Fiction, 1880-1963: A History of Attitudes toward Warfare and the Military Establishment.* by Peter Aichinger. Ames: Iowa State U.P. pp. xxv + 143.
[76] *The Red Badge of Courage*, by Stephen Crane, ed. by Fredson Bowers, with introd. by J. C. Levenson. U. of Virginia Edition of *The Works of Stephen Crane*, Vol II. Charlottesville: U.P. of Virginia. pp. xcii + 420 with 9 illustrations.
[77] *A Concordance to the Complete Poetry of Stephen Crane*, by Andrew T. Crosland, with foreword by T. H. Howard-Hill. Detroit: Gale Research. pp. xx + 189.
[78] *A Concordance to the Poems of Stephen Crane*, by Herman Baron, ed. by Joseph Katz. Boston: G. K. Hall. 1974. pp. xv + 311.
[79] *Stephen Crane's Artistry*, by Frank Bergon. New York and London: Columbia U.P. pp. xi + 174.
[80] *Henry James: The Drama of Fulfilment: An Approach to the Novels*, by Kenneth Graham. Oxford: Clarendon P. pp. xvi + 234.

William T. Stafford offers *A Name, Title, and Place Index to the Critical Writings of Henry James*[81]. Annette Niemtzow in 'Marriage and the New Woman in *The Portrait of a Lady*' (*AL*) writes on James's father's views on divorce, and suggests that 'new woman led James on a new path to modernism'. Ronald Wallace examines Jamesian comedy in his intelligent study of *Henry James and the Comic Form*[82], which includes a discussion of *The Blithedale Romance* as a possible source for the 'germ' of *The Sacred Fount*, a study of *The Bostonians* as the opposition of two kinds of egotists, and an examination of five novels (*The American, The Europeans, The Tragic Muse, The Awkward Age*, and *The Portrait of a Lady*) as they follow the conventional mythic pattern of comedy. The most interesting part of the study, however, is his extended illustration of what James is doing in *The Spoils of Poynton*: 'In a sense, James is parodying his own previous romance comedies but, more importantly, he is parodying the whole convention of romance comedy'.

Reading Henry James[83] by Louis Auchincloss is another lively and helpful critical study, splendidly illustrated by Beerbohm cartoons of James. Auchincloss impatiently dismisses 'the passionate concern of American scholars with the question of James's attitude toward his native land', holding that basically James simply did not have an attitude until he was sixty. He examines James's failure to make his characters reveal themselves in dialogue, with its consequence: his failure as a playwright. He traces the development of James's attitudes toward sex, and he muses on *The Turn of the Screw*, concluding that James himself never decided on any one interpretation of the ghosts.

Granville H. Jones, in *Henry James's Psychology of Experience*[84], writes better on *The Turn of the Screw* than on any other work. His division of the book into 'Children and Adolescents', 'Young Adults', and 'The Middle-Aged and the Elderly', is not very inspiring, and much of his time is taken up with what are in effect plot summaries, and with unexceptionable, but farily naive interpretations. But he writes well of the way that in *The Turn of the Screw* James inverts the moral and social order to explore the relationship between children and adults.

E. A. Sheppard devotes a whole book to *Henry James and 'The Turn of the Screw'*[85]. It is too long, and dwells with too much patient care (for ninety-five pages) on '*The Turn of the Screw* and the Society for Psychical Research', but he writes extremely well on, for example, the connexions between James's story and *Jane Eyre*, on Henriette Deluzy as a suggested model for the governess, and, most beguiling suggestion of all, on George Bernard Shaw as the model for Peter Quint.

[81] *A Name, Title, and Place Index to the Critical Writings of Henry James*, by William T. Stafford. Englewood, Colorado: Microcards Editions. pp. 270.
[82] *Henry James and the Comic Form*, by Ronald Wallace. Ann Arbor: U. of Michigan P. pp 202.
[83] *Reading Henry James*, by Louis Auchincloss. Minneapolis: U. of Minnesota P. pp. 181 with 12 illustrations
[84] *Henry James's Psychology of Experience: Innocence, Responsibility, and Renunciation in the Fiction of Henry James*, by Granville H. Jones. The Hague and Paris: Mouton. pp. xiv + 310.
[85] *Henry James and 'The Turn of the Screw'*, by E. A. Sheppard. Auckland and London: Auckland U.P. and O.U.P. 1974. pp. xii + 292 with 21 illustrations.

XVI

American Literature:
The Twentieth Century

EDWARD GALLAFENT and DAVID JARRETT

The chapter is divided as follows: 1. General; 2. Poetry; 3. The Novel;
4. Drama. Parts 1 and 3 are by Edward Gallafent, and Parts 2 and 4 by
David Jarrett.

1. General

American Literature Since 1900[1], Volume Nine of the Sphere Books
History of Literature in the English Language, attempts to cover all
American writing to the present day. In part this collection of essays seems
aimed at undergraduates, and some of the essays are successful under-
graduate guides to particular areas, such as Malcolm Bradbury and David
Corker on the origins of Modernism, Dennis Welland on American fiction
between the wars, David Morse on American Theatre in the age of O'Neill,
Aleksandar Nejgebauer on poetry 1945–60 (see below, Section 2), and
Ursula Brumm on Faulkner. Other guides have to cut a path through
worlds usually felt to be much more confusing to the student. Marshall
Van Deusen makes a lucid job of this for movements in Literary Criticism,
and Eric Mottram's essay 'Sixties American Poetry, Poetics and Poetic
Movements', even though it turns into something of a bibliography for the
use of such students as have access to a very good library, at least presents
this as an area worth exploring. It is a pity that in praising this area he has
simultaneously to deny the value of others; the necessity of damning
Lowell in order to praise Olson still needs to be proved.

Generally the book is not attempting a comparative exercise; the only
article on English and American Literature, 'American Poetry and the
English Language, 1900–1945', by Geoffrey Moore, is far below the
standard of the others. In 'this attempted re-assessment of Twentieth
Century American Verse' the terms of the re-assessment sadly lack definition. The inadequate standard of 'memorability', used in several crucial
places in the essay, is never expanded or defended; Moore attacks contemporary verse by setting up the questionable figures of 'younger readers'
who 'have no ear for memorability of diction', being rather 'impatient to
"know what the poem means" '. Altogether the dismissals in the essay are
finally just assertions, which cannot be allowed to pass unchallenged when
they involve figures where the arguments for importance are substantial

[1] *American Literature Since 1900*, ed. by Marcus Cunliffe. Sphere Books. pp. 419.
£1.30.

(see below, Section 2).

The other area of weakness is contemporary prose. There is a satisfactory contribution on minority group writers from Arnold Goldman, but the other article on post-war prose, Leslie Fiedler's, concentrates on the question of the adequacy of traditional criticism, and is not intended as a guide to the new novelists. Marcus Cunliffe's list in his preface, of novelists who have 'seemed extraordinarily relevant...only to be supplanted' is a remarkable one, including as it does figures to whom the book gives substantial attention such as Baldwin and Bellow, and others who are scarcely mentioned again such as Burroughs and Vonnegut, or, extraordinarily, never mentioned again, Thomas Pynchon. Another omission which Cunliffe attempts in vain to remedy in his essay 'Literature and Society' is that of the influence of film on American literature. The select bibliographies are fairly satisfactory, although there are a few serious omissions; Hugh Kenner's seminal The Pound Era is not listed, and the Hemingway bibliography lists Young's Ernest Hemingway (1952) rather than his complete revision Ernest Hemingway: A Reconsideration (1966).

Hugh Kenner's A Homemade World[2] is in many respects the obverse of his earlier The Pound Era. While the earlier book looks at both a period of history and a poetic seen as forged around a single figure, here the concentration is on a number of diverse figures whose work has less contact with Europe and more with the provincial in America, America as a homemade world, composed of the overlapping constructions, built according to homemade rules, of Fitzgerald, Hemingway, Faulkner, Marianne Moore, Wallace Stevens, and William Carlos Williams. Obviously in such a book there will be problems of coherence, but one of its strengths is that Kenner avoids trying to suggest that coherence exists where it does not. The 'homemade' is not turned into a quality which we are asked either simply to admire or reject. There is still the problem of Kenner's own attitude in particular cases, which seems unclear, but momentary confusion is obviously preferable to forcing these figures to fit a thesis (see below, Section 2).

Of the poets one of the major successes of the book is the treatment of Williams, where the most substantial area of potential overlap with The Pound Era is given new energy by being made part of a wider discussion centered on Wallace Stevens. The excellent comparison of their aesthetics has only one oddity, the conclusion that Williams's writing on poetry has had 'no effect whatever'. Perhaps at least Ginsberg, a figure not mentioned by Kenner in this book, would deny this. The other figure which Kenner treats with complete assurance is Marianne Moore whose homemade quality is felt as being synonymous with the honesty that Kenner feels 'Modern American writing is about'.

Of the novelists there is a valuable mapping of the importance of figures such as Pater, Wilde, and Mallarmé to the work of Faulkner and Hemingway, but further than this Kenner's relation to these writers, and particularly Faulkner, is difficult to understand. Faulkner is obviously

[2] A Homemade World: The American Modernist Writers, by Hugh Kenner. New York: Alfred Knopf. pp. xviii + 221 + ix. $8.95.

approachable in terms of the homemade, but here this seems to become synonymous with 'jerry-built' for Kenner, although he never quite says so. Overall, the least satisfactory figure is that of Fitzgerald. The introduction via the Horatio Alger books is a bold juxtaposition, but some of the commentaries on *The Great Gatsby* are eccentricities that are not given the required support.

Thomas LeClair writing on black humour (*Crit.*) argues that the fact and awareness of death are central to this area of comedy, and he looks at this in detail in Updike's *The Centaur*, Bellow's *Mr. Sammler's Planet*, and a number of other novels in lesser detail. Trying to cover a great deal of ground rather too rapidly, he goes on to ask what effect black humour has had on fictional technique, and how it is related to death in American culture.

American popular culture is the subject of *Superculture: American Popular Culture and Europe*[3] which attempts to define this area and explore its influence in Europe. The attempts at definitions are the most interesting part of the book. The three opening essays, by C. W. E. Bigsby, Leslie Fiedler, and Marshall McLuhan, vary widely in approach from the historical in Bigsby to the highly impressionistic in McLuhan, and each is lively in its different way. The rest of the book is devoted to essays sketching particular areas of culture. Bigsby points out in his preface that these essays must be limited in scope if they are to be of any value, and some writers provide successful introductions to their fields, particularly Bryan Wilson on religion and Paul Oliver on jazz. Some others, such as David Crystal on language, Michael Watts on pop music, and Martin Esslin on television, work nearly as well, while the approach of others seems oddly quirky. Peter Masson's piece on advertising is devoted largely to the histories of advertising agencies in Europe and the United States, and Thomas Elsasser on film is concerned with the history of French film criticism. The weakest area is, perhaps suggestively, the essays on literature. Neither Jens Peter Becker (detective fiction), Gerard Cordesse (science fiction), nor Roger Lewis (comics) can find a happy place to start, and the confusion of aim between setting out the history of a facet of popular culture and commenting on its nature is very acute here. The other main fault of the book would seem to be an editorial one. Despite the division of the book into essays discussing general and specific fields, the worst of the latter are spoilt by callow generalizations. It is of no value, after reading Fiedler and McLuhan, to be told by Peter Masson that America is a 'relatively young society, based on the pioneering spirit of its early settlers', or by Magnus Pyke that uniformity is 'a feature of the current technological age', and the whole of Cordesse's essay is seriously at fault in this respect.

Ivan Doig's *The Streets We Have Come Down*[4], an anthology subtitled 'Literature of the City', attempts to bring out the beauty and terror of 'the American cityscape'. The emphasis of the anthology is strongly towards

[3] *Superculture: American Popular Culture and Europe*, ed. by C. W. E. Bigsby. Paul Elek. pp. xiii + 225. £4.95.
[4] *The Streets We Have Come Down: Literature of the City*, ed. by Ivan Doig. New Jersey: Hayden Books. pp. 214.

sociologists and anthropologists, particularly when it moves from description to analysis. The literary contributions to the description of the city made by Joan Didion, Don Marquis, James Tate, Thomas Wolfe, and James Baldwin, seem to have more to do with beauty than terror, even when menace is their subject, as it is Baldwin's and Didion's. The delicate reproduction of mood here seems to have little to do with the breakdown talked about in the best articles, such as the extract from Alvin Toffler's *Future Shock* and Tom Wolfe's account of his time with the anthropologist Edward T. Hall. It is a pity the anthology chooses so clearly to ignore those areas of writing in which the literature of the city has experimented most excitingly; an extract from the work of, say, Burroughs or Ginsberg, would have had more to do with Toffler's proposition that 'The city's principal product is not rags, words, or money. It is novelty'.

Southern Literary Study: Problems and Possibilities[5] is a record of a conference of Southern scholars held at the University of North Carolina in 1972. The book reprints four papers. Louis Rubin's 'Southern Literature and Southern Society' concentrates mainly on problems rather than possibilities, making the point, repeated by other scholars, that there is not one South but many Souths, and arguing that scholars have been 'too literal, too unimaginative and too often uncritical' in dealing with this material. Richard Beale Davis's 'Early Southern Literature' begins with a bibliographical essay on the work done in this field up to 1972, and suggests some areas of research which may be fruitful. Arlin Turner's 'Dim Pages in Literary History', on the post civil-war South, again concentrates on the problem of defining the South and goes on to outline some research areas. These essays are all useful, but by far the most rewarding piece in the book is Lewis Simpson's 'The South's Reaction to Modernism', in which he discusses Allen Tate's picture of the South as struggling between modernism and traditionalism in the light of the recent view of the South as 'a slave society structured by class' put forward by the historian Eugene Genovese. Simpson sees Tate as having 'fostered the legend of a traditonalism rooted in Europe' and as having by this obscured the view of the Old South as the 'peculiar institution'. The essay ends by relating this to ideas of community in both black and white contexts.

The rest of the book is made up of five transcripts of panel discussions on areas of Southern scholarship: Colonial, nineteenth-century and twentieth-century literature, 'The Continuity of Southern Literary History', and 'Thematic Problems in Southern Literature'. These are mainly concerned with possibilities for future research and the book concludes with an editors' note and appendix listing the topics. It is difficult to know whether, in the light of future developments in the subject, the marshalling function which constitutes the bulk of this book will seem to have been necessary. Certainly it emerges from the book that the conference was a good idea, but perhaps, Simpson's essay apart, it was not entirely a good idea to make a book out of it.

William T. Going, in the introductory chapter to his *Essays on Alabama*

[5] *Southern Literary Study: Problems and Possibilities*, ed. by Louis Rubin and C. Hugh Holman. Chapel Hill: U. of North Carolina P. pp. xiii + 235.

Literature[6] states that his essays are 'not intended as a history of the literature of the state', and acknowledges that 'there has never been a major literary figure who has either lived in or consistently written about the state'. The essays are a number of short pieces on minor figures, such as Harper Lee and Shirley Ann Grau, or figures of interest only in terms of literary history, such as Samuel Minturn Peck. Also there are pieces on native Alabamians famous in terms which have nothing to do with the state, such as Zelda Fitzgerald and Sara Mencken, and outsiders looking in at Alabama, such as Lillian Hellman and Philip Henry Gosse. Some of these figures are more and some less interesting, but Going never makes a convincing case for any substantial part of that interest residing in anything specific to Alabama, and the impression that the book's perspective is a random one, throwing no new light on anything, is very strong. Some topics seem contrived, such as the comparison of Stribling's *The Store* and Lee's *To Kill a Mockingbird*, or the extraordinarily trivial note on Grau's *The Keepers of the House*. The book does include two essays on William March, and the first of these, on March's uncollected stories, is of some interest, although the attempt to talk about 'March's Alabama' in the second essay is vitiated by Going's own admission that March's Reedyville functions as an 'Everytown'. In all the book seems too eclectic, an undertaking with no substance to its raison d'etre.

The title of the collection of Allen Tate's work, *Memoirs and Opinions 1926-1974*,[7] is slightly deceptive, since the book deals with memoirs stretching back to well before World War I, although the bulk of the 'Opinions' are essays written in the last ten years. In his preface Tate explains that the section entitled 'Memoirs' arises out of an attempt to write an 'entire book of memories'. He wrote only 'A Lost Traveller's Dream' which might have begun such a book and deals with Tate's childhood and family, and 'Miss Toklas' American Cake' which of course deals with the Paris of the Twenties. As it stands, the rest of the section is made up of reprintings of pieces on other contemporaries, the Fugitives, Sylvia Beach, John Peale Bishop, St. John Perse, Ransom, Faulkner, and T. S. Eliot. Reading the two new pieces it is possible to see something of why they were so difficult to write and led nowhere. Tate's attitude is not a nostaliga for the Twenties and Thirties of his own past, but a yearning for an older world, lost almost as he perceived it. Under the heading of 'Opinions' Tate has reprinted uncollected essays of the last decade including work on Frost as Metaphysical Poet, Poe's Poetry, Valery, *Sanctuary*, and Translation. He has also chosen to rescue two much older pieces, his essay on Hart Crane's *White Buildings* (1926) and 'The Fallacy of Humanism' (1929), here retitled 'Humanism and Naturalism'. James H. Justus (*SoR*) writes on restlessness in the South, beginning with images of the South in Fitzgerald, and going on, after a rather too familiar sketch of the Southern Agrarians, to look at restlessness in Twain, Wolfe, Faulkner, and others. It

[6] *Essays on Alabama Literature*, by William T. Going. Studies in the Humanities No. 4. University, Alabama: U. of Alabama P. pp. 176. $6.75.
[7] *Memoirs and Opinions 1926-1974*, by Allen Tate. Chicago: Swallow P. pp. xi + 225. $8.95.

is a useful contrast to the view of the South promulgated by Tate, although the detail of some of Justus's examples is questionable.

Makers of American Thought[8] collects seven of the University of Minnesota Pamphlets on American Writers published during the last fifteen years. The collection opens with Louis Auchincloss's essay on Henry Adams and Gay Wilson Allen's on William James, and Ralph Ross, in his introduction, presents Adams and James as representative of two contrasting directions in American thought. It does seem, however, that the other essays dissipate this contrast as much as they reinforce it, and Ross uses the introduction only as a way of mentioning the other figures included very briefly: H. L. Mencken by Philip Wagner, Van Wyck Brooks by William Wasserstrom, and Kenneth Burke by Merle E. Brown. Ross says disappointingly little about the reasons behind the inclusion of Reinhold Niebuhr (by Nathan A. Scott), and indeed the book must be viewed almost entirely as seven reprinted essays rather than any continuing argument. The one exception to this is possibly Sherman Paul's essay on Randolph Bourne which does stress Bourne's connexions with William James. The book includes brief bibliographies of the seven writers.

2. Poetry

The United States: A Companion to American Studies[1], edited by Dennis Welland, and *American Literature since 1900*[2], edited by Marcus Cunliffe, are comparable volumes in that they seem to be directed towards the general student; and in each there is an essay on twentieth-century poetry by Geoffrey Moore. In *The United States* his chapter is 'Fiction and Poetry since 1918', which covers a good deal of ground without rendering its subject tedious or obscure. Yet such surveys have their dangers. For example, it is noticeable that, although Pound and Eliot are represented as the great 'instigators' of modern American poetry, they are not dealt with in any detail. Perhaps it is assumed that their poetry is too well known, but this book is primarily an introduction, and Wallace Stevens's 'Sunday Morning', well enough known too, is explicated in considerable detail for a chapter of this length. The account of American poetry gets sketchier as it progresses, moving very swiftly through the 'forties, 'fifties, and 'sixties, and occasionally Moore makes interesting observations which cry out for further resolution before confronting the reader. For example, this question is left dangling after some remarks on the Whitman tradition in American poetry: 'And what are Eliot's *Four Quartets* and Stevens's *Notes Toward a Supreme Fiction* but songs of their respective selves, each as quietly American, in its own way, as Whitman's was brashly so?' Sentences, too, like 'But we must not forget, in speaking

[8] *Makers of American Thought*, ed. by Ralph Ross. Minneapolis: U. of Minnesota P. pp. 301.

[1] *The United States: A Companion to American Studies*, ed. by Dennis Welland. Methuen, 1974. pp. 528; 6 illustrations.
[2] *American Literature since 1900*, ed. by Marcus Cunliffe. History of Literature in the English Language. Barrie & Jenkins/Sphere Books. pp. 419.

of the early period in modern American poetry, to mention some other names which are also very important' reveal the problems inherent in surveys of this kind. However, Moore's tone is disarmingly familiar and his approach reassuringly common-sensical—as when he comments after his passage on Crane's *The Bridge*: 'Ho-hum. At least Eliot could say "No! I am not Prince Hamlet, nor was meant to be"—although that was before the less obtrusively pretentious, but equally American high seriousness of *The Waste Land*, with its notes and its symbolism and its air of speaking *ex cathedra*. There is something in the cultural atmosphere which has made Americans try the big thing'. He is similarly level-headed, and not unkind, in his adverse judgements on Archibald MacLeish and Carl Sandburg, and even in the case of Charles Olson he allows that his critical study of *Moby-Dick* is 'superb' before dismissing 'the pretentious Maximus poems' as 'only a sort of Poundian pastiche'. One senses that Moore is not entirely sympathetic to the 'homemade' quality of American poetry celebrated with irony, affection, and sometimes wonder, in Hugh Kenner's book discussed below.

Moore's essay in *American Literature since 1900*, 'American Poetry and the English Language, 1900–1945', provides an instructive comparison and contrast of English and American poets of the period. A comparison of A. E. Housman and Edwin Arlington Robinson, for example, reveals the distinctive amateurish and honestly homely quality of the American, features, Moore reminds us, of American poetry from the seventeenth century on. 'Lowell confesses; Larkin professes' is his neat formulation of the difference between two contemporaries: ' "Come off it," says Larkin: "I am serious," says Lowell'. As in his other essay Moore quotes the six-principle manifesto of Imagism, here going on to say that he does not believe that 'Imagism as such. . .ever produced great poetry'. He quotes two of Pound's best known imagist poems and concludes, 'These are offered as poems, but poems they are not'. It is questionable whether such distinctions are relevant with material like this. As for that now almost apotheosized poem of William Carlos Williams, 'The Red Wheelbarrow', Moore calls it one of Williams' 'notorious experiments in Imagism', says that it leaves 'something to be désired', and leaves it at that. Moore concludes, generally, that the American poet is drawn to 'artificiality', 'high seriousness', and 'unhumorous dedication'; that, unlike the English poet, he is a preacher and experimenter; that he displays an 'interminable restless casting about for self-identification'.

This last perception is echoed in the next essay in *American Literature since 1900*, 'Poetry 1945–1960: Self versus Culture' by Aleksandar Nejgebauer, composed of sections on Richard Wilbur, Randall Jarrell, John Berryman, Karl J. Shapiro, Theodore Roethke, and Robert Lowell, all poets responding to the 'post-war existentialist nausea in Western Europe'. But, says Nejgebauer, 'the Existential open was not a sudden void in place of age-old tradition but a return to the only true American tradition— starting from Paumanok again, towards a new Frontier, in a quest for new identity'. Although the title of the essay sets its cut-off date at 1960 a number of volumes published after that date are considered, including, for example, Berryman's *Short Poems* (1967), Roethke's *The Far Field* (1964), and Lowell's *Notebook 1967–1968* (1969). Nejgebauer writes as if he too were perched on this last date wondering what might happen next: 'Whatever new turn Lowell's poetry may take, it will hardly be away from his commitment to the European tradition on which the bourgeois main culture in the United States is based. . . .' Lowell, of course, has published a number of important volumes between 1969 and 1975, but they are not taken into account here, nor in Eric Mottram's chapter, 'Sixties American Poetry, Poetics and Poetic Movements', in which the most recent Lowell volume mentioned is *Near the Ocean* (1967).

Mottram's essay is dense, energetic, and exciting. Its sense of commitment to and involvement in the American scene with which it deals is in marked contrast to Geoffrey Moore's detached view. Mottram seems impatient with Lowell, whose *Life Studies* he calls 'an exercise in secularized New England exhibitions of conscience', and a 'tourism of the ego', whereas he devotes much space to the sympathetic presentation of Charles Olson's work and the influence of his ideas. He documents redefinitions of poetry from Olson, Creeley, Duncan, and later waves of Black Mountain writers, through the Beats, to Richard Goldstein's *The Poetry of Rock* and the consideration of the lyrics of Tuli Kupferberg, Tim Hardin, the Doors, and Bob Dylan; and he includes a section on black poets of the sixties, concentrating particularly on Leroi Jones and the impressive veteran, M. B. Tolson, poet laureate of Liberia. This chapter does not quote poetry and comment upon it; but there is a sense of urgency about it which should send its readers out to find the poetry itself.

Donald Barlow Stauffer's *A Short History of American Poetry*[3] is a competent survey from the beginnings to contemporary poetry, and he manages to be properly critical as well as inclusive. The University of Minnesota Press has gathered together seven of its previously published pamphlets on modern American poets and included them in one volume[4] with an introduction by Denis Donoghue. Grover Smith writes on Archibald MacLeish; Ralph J. Mills Jr. on Richard Eberhart and on Theodore Roethke; M. L. Rosenthal on Randall Jarrell; William J. Martz on John Berryman; Jay Martin on Robert Lowell; and Peter Meinke on Howard Nemerov. The volume has been interestingly reviewed (*TLS*) by Thomas Byrom, who questions the value of these poets' preoccupation with their own suffering.

Ralph J. Mills Jr., the author of two of the pamphlets, accepts the definition of his criticism as romantic and personalist, and offers himself, in his *Cry of the Human: Essays on Contemporary American Poetry*[5], not as a scholar or a theorist but as an 'enthusiast-commentator who wishes to bring to attention some contemporary poets and their poems'. The title of his book is taken from a poem by David Ignatow, one of the poets on whom he concentrates in this study. The others are Theodore Roethke, Galway Kinnell, Donald Hall, and Philip Levine. 'Creation's Very Self: On

[3] *A Short History of American Poetry*, by Donald Barlow Stauffer. New York: E. P. Dutton, 1974. pp. xvii + 459.
[4] *Seven American Poets from MacLeish to Nemerov: An Introduction*, ed. by Denis Donoghue. Minneapolis: U. of Minnesota P. pp. 329.
[5] *Cry of the Human: Essays on Contemporary American Poetry*, by Ralph J. Mills Jr., with foreword by Richard Eberhart. Urbana, Chicago, and London: U. of Illinois P. pp. xvi + 275.

the Personal Element in Recent American Poetry', the first essay of this volume uses Yeats's 'pregnant phrase' 'both to distinguish certain of the pronounced personal qualities evident among contemporary poets of the last three decades or so, and to provide a partial–but only partial–survey of the very different kinds of writers and writings involved'. This is an attractive book because it seeks to display the poetry, not the critic, who remains so unassuming and modest that he can be convincing in even quite extravagant claims, such as he makes for Philip Levine's poetry, which, 'praiseworthy at the start, has developed by momentous strides in the past decade. His new poems make it impossible for him to be ignored or put aside. He stands out as one of the most solid and independent poets of his generation–one of the best poets, I think, anywhere at work in the language'. In his essay on Theodore Roethke, Mills develops his longstanding interest in Roethke's treatment of the evolution of the self, this time through a reading of the 'North American Sequence' and 'Sequence, Sometimes Metaphysical' of The Far Field, Roethke's last book. The third essay, 'Earth Hard: David Ignatow's Poetry', is, perhaps, the best, making particularly apt use of quotation, and showing well the way in which Ignatow 'answers' Whitman's optimistic view of America; it is possible, however, that Mills pays too little attention to the humorous element in Ignatow's poetry. 'A Reading of Galway Kinnell' sounds a stronger note of adverse criticism, in dealing with Kinnell's occasional pretentiousness and his preoccupation with physical suffering. Nevertheless, when Mills considers Kinnell's long ambitious poem 'The Avenue Bearing the Initial of Christ into the New World', he puts it in the exalted company of Leaves of Grass, The Bridge, Paterson, and 'something' of The Waste Land and The Cantos. In 'Donald Hall's Poetry', Mills uses Hall's own comments on his poetry, together with judiciously chosen quotations, to trace the patterns of Hall's imagery.

Like Mills, Roy P. Basler, in The Muse and the Librarian[6], is concerned to champion some of his favourite poets—Carl Sandburg, Lee Anderson, Oscar Williams, and M. B. Tolson, for example. But, as one who has been arranging readings and similar activities at the Library of Congress for many years, he is interested in the politics of poetry as well as in the poets. He provides fascinating glimpses of great poetry festivals upstaged by the Cuban Missile Crisis, of controversies over literary awards and the relation of poets to government, and of Frost's cannily engineered assault on Washington, the President, and the nation. Basler reveals astonishing statistics, such as that Merrill Moore published over two thousand sonnets in his lifetime and that there are a further sixty thousand filed away in the Library of Congress, which means that Moore wrote, on average, five sonnets a day for thirty years—surely a statistic to rival that which so horrifies David Harsent in 'Metre Merchant' (TLS), where he computes that Rod McKuen's poetry currently sells to the tune of five thousand copies a day. Basler's style and stance can be infuriating as well as engaging, as when he boasts: 'Since Walt Whitman, only a few major American writers (maybe two at most) demonstrate to my satisfaction that they

[6] The Muse and the Librarian, by Roy P. Basler. Contributions in American Studies. Westport, Conn., and London: Greenwood P., 1974. pp. 207.

truly believe in poetry', or: 'I have never been entirely sure what "surrealistic" means'. He is consistently, consciously lowbrow, and continues Williams's war against Eliot and academic poetry; and his attacks can be heavy and personal, like that which he launches against James Dickey, whose 'ridicule' of some of Lee Anderson's work he characterizes as 'an ex-night-figher pilot's unspent fury after more than a hundred missions guarding bombers unloading bombs on Orientals more than a decade before'. In his last chapter, an essay on erotic poetry, Basler turns quickly from his subject, by a transition not altogether natural, to poetry involving excremental unpleasantness, as if there were no recent poetry that combined frankness with tenderness in treating the erotic. Further, after complaining about metaphors and similes being used as a substitute for direct literary criticism, he indulges himself in some of the most extravagant similes I have ever encountered: '. . .reading [Merrill] Moore's poetry is like reading a sort of Parnassian *Readers' Digest*, wholly rather than partly written to order, by a remarkable stable of Heliconian hacks assembled for the purpose of getting out a Twentieth Century Issue that will preserve for all time the essence of *It*, triple distilled occasionally, but always at least once, through the editorial worm which turns sensations and ideas in rough draft into acceptable copy, not always at the recommended temperature, but refined sufficiently to provide an effective stimulant'. Basler's book is buoyant with such energy; its relevant chapters are: 'The Muse and the Librarian'; 'Yankee Vergil—Robert Frost in Washington'; 'Your Friend the Poet—Carl Sandburg'; 'Proteus as Apollo: The Poetry of Merrill Moore'; 'The Poet as Composer—Lee Anderson'; 'A Letter to Ali Baba' (on Oscar Williams); 'The Heart of Blackness: M. B. Tolson's Poetry'; and 'The Taste of it: Observations on Current Erotic Poetry'.

Chapters concerning poetry in Hugh Kenner's admirable *A Homemade World: The American Modernist Writers*[7] are 'So Here it is at Last' (on Pound and Amy Lowell; also general); 'Something to Say' (on Williams and Stevens); 'Disliking It' (on Marianne Moore); and 'Classroom Accuracies' (on the Objectivists, Zukofsky in particular, and on Olson). There is also a lively and wide-ranging introduction which gives an account of the principal writers of American modernism and which explains, very briefly, why Kenner has chosen not to consider Lowell, Frost, Crane, and Cummings. He opens with a reference to James Joyce, to whose vision of his craft he cleverly links the world of American modernism: Joyce's *A Portrait of the Artist as a Young Man*, celebrating the artificer Dedalus, a new saint 'whose miracles were explicable', was begun in 1904, 'the year after two Americans, sons of a bishop of the Church of the United Brethren in Christ, had flown on manmade wings at Kitty Hawk. . . .Their Dedalian deed on the North Carolina shore may be accounted the First American input into the great imaginative enterprise, on which artists were to collaborate for half a century'. Kenner sees American modernist art as sharing a 'homemade' quality with the mechanics of the Wright brothers, and he stresses the fact that modernists through Pound and Williams to Oppen

[7] *A Homemade World: The American Modernist Writers*, by Hugh Kenner. New York: Alfred A. Knopf. pp. xviii + 221.

and Zukofsky are bound together by a doctrine of perception that has affected all modern poetry.

Kenner's first chapter sets the scene for this American 'renaissance' spiritedly and sometimes satirically. His irony is used effectively when he writes of Amy Lowell, or of Horace Liveright, who saw to the publication of *The Waste Land, Personae, The Enormous Room, The Bridge, An American Tragedy*, and O'Neill's plays, but whose 'most visible energies' went into such projects as arranging a nudist camp safari for all the literary editors in New York to promote a book on nudism, or cashing in on the dirty bits in Petronius. Liveright made a commercial success out of the popularization of Freud and Trotsky, and 'it had been the absence of any market for his Pick-Quick toilet paper that inspired him to join Alfred Boni in founding the Modern Library'. Kenner points out that Liveright's career tells us more about publishing in his time than does that of Maxwell Perkins, an editor who had a strong belief in the talents of his authors, among whom were Fitzgerald and Hemingway. Among Kenner's conclusions about 'homemade' American modernism are '. . .it is characteristic of American genius that the casual eye does not easily distinguish it from charlatanry', and 'Purity of intention lies at the center of American achievement', so that Poe and Pound, for example, are redeemed because they believed 'with purity of heart' in what they did, 'whereas Miss Lowell settled for getting by, with whatever show of expertise would suffice to placate the natives'. Kenner feels, too, that American Literature is 'tricky' for the critic, because the American writer tends to invent the criteria by which he is to be understood. None of these conclusions is strikingly original, and Kenner's chapter on Williams and Stevens chooses some familiar texts for analysis, including 'The Red Wheelbarrow', 'The Man with the Blue Guitar', 'Sunday Morning', and 'Thirteen Ways of Looking at a Blackbird', but it is probably a mark of the quality of this book that it can afford to take such risks. Kenner acknowledges Williams's 'naive realism, through which any philosopher would promptly drive a Mack truck', but which still liberated him 'from anxieties he hadn't patience for', and he explains that Williams was writing 'homemade' philosophy in which 'he floundered as grievously explaining the Imagination in the 1920's as he did explaining his other discovery, the Variable Foot, in the 1950's'. Similarly, Kenner, while deeply appreciative of Stevens's achievement, can present him with realistic irony: 'Every agnostic supposes he is the first, and Stevens talked as though his theme were the agnostic's plight. . . Stevens took the dissolution of Christianity inculcated in Reading, Pa., for the summons to a new humanism, a life's work'. But his praise for the often cranky or naive American homemade realism can be correspondingly high, as in his assessment of Marianne Moore's work: 'She resembles Columbus, whose mind was on something other than opening new worlds, and [who] died supposing he had shown how to sail to China. For the language flattened, the language *exhibited*, the language staunchly condensing information while frisking in enjoyment of its release from the obligation to do no more than inform: these are the elements of a twentieth-century American poetic, a pivotal discovery of our age. And it seems to have been Marianne Moore's discovery'. In his chapter on the Objectivists, whose 'sometime allies Stevens and Williams had been', Kenner writes well on the importance of the University classrooms in American life and letters. He does not pretend that classrooms produce poets, but he happily avoids the anti-academic bias of Basler's book, and, surprisingly enough in the present climate, hardly even deprecates the New Criticism. J. B. Harmer's excellent *Victory in Limbo: A History of Imagism 1908-1917*[8] inevitably confirms the view encountered in Kenner of Amy Lowell trailing behind Pound in Imagist theory, as it also confirms T. S. Eliot's high opinion of H. D.'s translations of Euripides. Harmer, in his first chapter, places Imagism in its context as a reaction to the spirit that was making a 'dying art' of poetry in Edwardian England. He also considers some of the sources, English, American, and French, of the movement, and when looking at the poetry itself is able (thanks to the nature of the Imagist poem) to quote widely. Though mainly concerned with the relatively short period of 'official' Imagist movements, Harmer also traces the influence of Imagism on such Black Mountain disciples as Ed Dorn and such rock poets as Jim Morrison.

Anyone who writes about Williams's 'The Little Red Wheelbarrow' is in danger of being accused of insensitivity to poetry. Dickran Tashjian does refer to Williams's most widely known poem in *Skyscraper Primitives: Dada and the American Avant-Garde, 1910-1925*[9], and, though he has an interesting story to chronicle, his chapters on poetry are not wholly satisfactory as literary criticism. What is revealing is the context in which they are placed, so that we can look at Crane and Cummings in relation to magazines like the *Aesthete, Broom, Secession*, and *The Little Review*, and their editors and writers. The path of Dada's influence upon Crane's use of technology appears tortuous indeed; the ideas of T. E. Hulme or the Futurists on the machine seem closer to Crane. Nor does Tashjian ever fully explain what is implied in Williams's statement: 'I didn't originate Dadaism, but I had it in my soul to write it'. In fact, Tashjian writes too much on Williams and not enough on Williams's relation to Dada. There are a number of well-chosen illustrations, including a reproduction of Charles Demuth's *I Saw the Figure Five in Gold*, based on Williams's 'The Great Figure', which is discussed in the text. Cummings is shown to have benefitted from Dada in his typographical experiments and 'his other anti-art attitudes', although as he matured he 'had little need of Dada'. Directly relevant are the chapters on Williams, Hart Crane, and Cummings, and there are also separate chapters on important Dada and neo-Dada magazines.

'Well, well, another young one wanting me to make a poet out of him with nothing to work on', said Ezra Pound when Robert McAlmon was first introduced to him. McAlmon never amounted to much as a poet, though Pound later spoke highly of him after he had virtually given up literature and taken to selling trusses in his brother's El Paso store. He was associated with many of the leading American writers of the 'twenties, and published Williams's *Spring and All*, as well as works by Hemingway and

[8] *Victory in Limbo: A History of Imagism 1908-1917*, by J. B. Harmer. Secker & Warburg. pp. xvii + 238.
[9] *Skyscraper Primitives: Dada and the American Avant-Garde, 1910-1925*, by Dickran Tashjian. Middletown, Conn.: Wesleyan U.P. pp. 283 and 64 illustrated plates.

Gertrude Stein. Sanford J. Smoller's *Adrift Among Geniuses: Robert McAlmon Writer and Publisher of the Twenties*[10] gives a picture of McAlmon, his times, and his associates, and it is perhaps invidious to ask whether we read it solely for the second and third of these three aspects. Smoller certainly believes that McAlmon (more a prose-writer than a poet) has been undervalued as a writer, and puts much of the blame on the influential demands of the New Criticism.

Another work focussing on the 'twenties and containing some relevant material is Edmund Wilson's posthumous *The Twenties: From Notebooks and Diaries of the Period*[11], which provides fascinating and often amusing glimpses of, for example, Edna St. Vincent Millay and E. E. Cummings.

Alan D. Perlis in 'Science, Mysticism and Contemporary Poetry' (*WHR*) notes that whereas I. A. Richards had assumed that science and poetry are 'fundamentally different occupations', science observing and poetry speculating, modern psychology helps the modern poet to close the gap. Perlis writes of Jung, Yeats, and the collective unconscious, and quotes Galway Kinnell, whose *Book of Nightmares* 'probes beneath the surface forms of our behaviour to the universal norms within', and A. R. Ammons, as a poet scientifically close and faithful in his observations and recordings.

The *South Dakota Review* furnishes a symposium on 'The Writer's Sense of Place', including interviews with such poets as Gary Snyder, Richard Eberhart, and W. D. Snodgrass, and commentaries and essays by, for example, Robert Bly and Richard Wilbur.

Black poets writing between 1910 and 1940 are presented in a new anthology[12], divided rather uneasily into a number of overlapping sections. As the editors, Arthur P. Davis and Michael W. Peplow, concede: 'A protest poem could equally as well appear in the Race Pride section; a Race Pride selection might just as easily appear in Africa, About the Folk, or Nigger Heaven'. Nevertheless, the editors offer in their introduction a clear historical explanation for 'The New Negro Renaissance', and also provide useful supporting material for each section, together with a chronology, biographies, and a bibliography. The anthology is therefore a welcome one, for as Davis and Peplow rightly claim: 'An interesting period in itself, the Renaissance is truly fascinating when examined as the seedbed of modern black literature'. The poets of another anthology, *The Forerunners: Black Poets in America*[13], are similarly seen, as the anthology's title suggests, as 'the literary godparents of today's black poets'. The book is a selection of poems read at a festival of black poets held at Howard University, co-produced by the book's editor, Woodie King Jr.; it has a perceptive introduction by Addison Gayle Jr. Both anthologies are likely to prove more valuable to the student than Bernard

[10] *Adrift Among Geniuses: Robert McAlmon, Writer and Publisher of the Twenties*, by Sanford J. Smoller. University Park and London: Penn. State U.P. pp. 389 and 23 illustrations.
[11] *The Twenties: From Notebooks and Diaries of the Period*, by Edmund Wilson, ed. by Leon Edel, New York: Farrar, Straus and Giroux. pp. 557 and 9 illustrations.
[12] *The New Negro Renaissance: An Anthology*, ed. by Arthur P. Davis and Michael W. Peplow. New York: Holt, Rinehart and Winston. pp. xxxi + 538.
[13] *The Forerunners: Black Poets in America*, ed. by Woodie King Jnr., with introd. by Addison Gayle Jr. and preface by Dudley Randall. Washington, D.C.: Howard U.P. pp. xxix + 127.

W. Bell's short study, *The Folk Roots of Contemporary Afro-American Poetry*[14], which suffers from a lack of clear definition of his terms. Bell himself points out that all the contemporary poems he examines are in a literary tradition, but asserts vaguely that 'they nevertheless pulsate with the vibrancy and fluidity of folk art'.

Haskell House have issued a reprint of Mark Van Doren's study of Edwin Arlington Robinson[15], but although the book purports to be about the man and his career, there is not much here on either. The book is really an appreciation of the poetry. Robinson's long poems make him, in Van Doren's opinion, a major poet, whereas the still famous shorter poems had established him as 'a great minor poet'.

Frank Lentricchia, in *Robert Frost: Modern Poetics and the Landscapes of Self*[16], rejecting what is implied in J. Hillis Miller's exclusion of Frost from *Poets of Reality*, presents him as a subtle and sophisticated modernist. Frost, he says, combines in his poetry the Kantian notion, dear to romantics, that mental acts constitute the world of experience, with a tough-minded realism which derives from William James's pragmatism: Lentricchia initiates this line of argument by quoting and analyzing Frost's 'All Revelation'. Much of Lentricchia's study concentrates on Frost's concern with the relationship between interior and exterior landscapes. Part One, 'Landscapes of Self', examines the 'recurrent symbols' of Frost's poetic landscapes, while Part Two, 'Landscapes of Modern Poetics', explores the aesthetic and philosophical dimensions of Frost's poems within the more inclusive context of post-Kantian literary theory. Lentricchia writes particularly well on the reverberating symbolic features of Frost's landscapes: the dark trees, which are a synecdoche for the immensity of external reality, the brook, suggestive of Emersonian romanticism, and the house, a metaphor of self, which can be a sanctuary or a hell, in a world which 'makes hiding an urgent psychic necessity'.

Donald J. Greiner's *Robert Frost: The Poet and His Critics*[17] is also a valuable contribution to Frost studies. Its clear organization will make it particularly useful. It has a chapter on letters, biographies, and memoirs, a chapter on criticism 1913–1925, and a chapter on hostile Frost criticism, besides discussions of Frost's literary heritage, particularly his relation to Wordsworth, Emerson, and Thoreau, of his nature poetry, and of Frost's own pronouncements on the art of poetry.

There is a slightly regretful air about John T. Flanagan's *Edgar Lee Masters: The Spoon River Poet and his Critics*[18], which has to conclude 'At the moment Masters' poetical fame seems to be in heavy eclipse'. There is no collected edition of his poems, and his work as dramatist,

[14] *The Folk Roots of Contemporary Afro-American Poetry*, by Bernard W. Bell. Broadside Critics Series, ed. by James A. Emanuel. Detroit, Michigan: Broadside P., 1974. pp. 80.
[15] *Edwin Arlington Robinson: the Man and his Career*, by Mark Van Doren New York: Haskell House. pp. 93.
[16] *Robert Frost: Modern Poetics and the Landscapes of Self*, by Frank Lentricchia. Durham, N.C.: Duke U.P. pp. xiii + 200.
[17] *Robert Frost: The Poet and his Critics*, by Donald J. Greiner. Chicago: American Library Association, 1974. pp. xv + 330.
[18] *Edgar Lee Masters: The Spoon River Poet and his Critics*, by John T. Flanagan. Metuchen, N.J.: Scarecrow P. 1974. pp. viii + 175.

historian, biographer, and novelist has never received much attention—certainly hardly any flattering attention. It is surprising to find that Flanagan's is 'the first book-length analysis of Masters', since it is not so much a critical analysis of Masters's works as an account of critical responses to them, 1898–1942, prefaced by a short account of his life. After each chapter the books and reviews cited are listed in the order in which they are treated in that chapter. Naturally the chapter on *The Spoon River Anthology* is the longest and contains the post positive reactions to Masters. Thereafter we learn that later collections were not regarded as an advance on the *Anthology*, that faults became increasingly evident, that the *Domesday Book* appeared flat and unselective, that Masters's novels 'have left no great impression on the critics and historians of American fiction', although some were modestly praised in their time, and that his biographies of Lincoln and Twain were criticized as cranky and bad-tempered, if challenging, and that of Whitman as repetitive and undocumented.

Although Hugh Kenner can confidently claim that 'not even American Literature any longer contains Amy Lowell', this year has seen the publication of two books about her. One, Jean Gould's *Amy: The World of Amy Lowell and the Imagist Movement*[19], is a biography, the other, Glenn Richard Ruihley's *The Thorn of a Rose: Amy Lowell Reconsidered*[20], mediates uncertainly between criticism and biography. Ruihley regrets that Amy Lowell's poetry 'has sunk to the status of a footnote to her career', but when he remarks that a poem might appear inferior 'in the setting of scholarly analysis', although not of her life, he does little to help. On the basis of these two books, it is doubtful whether the situation deserves to be remedied. Both tend to be sentimental rather than critical: thus Ruihley's page and a half relating to 'Patterns', of which less than a page is on the poem itself, begins, 'When Amy Lowell died suddenly one May afternoon while great shocks of lilac bloom punctuated the contours of her estate, her niece, hastily summoned, bared the mystery of the vault in Miss Lowell's great, high-ceilinged library'. Such reverential sentimentality is, in fact, more characteristic of Jean Gould's biography; and though Gould's title contains a reference to the Imagist movement, it is Ruihley who writes interestingly on Imagism. Gould disposes of it extremely quickly and conventionally, whereas Ruihley, through reference to Zen consciousness and to Pound's preface to *A Quinzaine for this Yule* (1909), comments upon and tries to account for the mystical and ephiphanic qualities of much Imagist poetry.

Jean Gould's biography is hard going not just because of its sentimentality, but also because of its clichés. But Amy Lowell does remain good material for stories, as she has always been: she even made headlines in the *New York Tribune* because of her liking for cigars. Gould also gives an account of the friendship between Amy Lowell and D. H. Lawrence, missing, I think, the irony in Lawrence's assurance to Amy that she herself was 'bigger' than her poetry. Amy Lowell's is a distressing story of deprivation and of a minor talent structuring an elaborately ritualistic and deliberately unconventional poet's life. This is not the book to persuade anyone that Amy Lowell's poetry is better than one might have thought— and a footnote reading 'From Amy Lowell's famous poem "Lilacs" ' has a hollow ring. Gould may give us a picture of 'Amy Lowell, from left to right' (as the joke about her photograph has it), but it is a picture which lacks depth.

Donald Davie's introduction to *Pound*[21], which includes a chronology and bibliography, uses biography effectively, as when he contrasts Pound's and Eliot's relationships with England. Davie is, too, often ingenious in his suggestions, as when he uses Allen Upward's discussion of 'Babu English' to claim that Pound's eccentric vocabulary in *Homage to Sextus Propertius* represents a particularly subtle attack on imperialism. He almost regrets that *Hugh Selwyn Mauberley* is such an accomplished poem, for 'it looks as if it will figure in Pound's *Oeuvre* like Gray's "Elegy" in the poetry of Gray, as a relatively early piece which unsympathetic readers can use as a stick with which to beat later work that the poet set more store by'.

Davie stresses that Pound was impressed by Hardy, although they never met, and he includes a chapter on 'Rhythms in the Cantos' demonstrating Pound's fine ear. He seriously overestimates Pound's scholarly expertise, however, comparing Yeats and Pound in a manner unfavourable and unfair to the former. Eugene Paul Nassar's *The Cantos of Ezra Pound: The Lyric Mode*[22] is a more persuasive study. Nassar's aim is to give 'a coherent overview and a detailed analysis of the lyrical passages in *The Cantos*. "Lyrical" is used in the broad sense, to encompass passages in Pound that dramatize aesthetic or psychic experience, using the language of symbol and myth, accompanied often, though not always, by an elevation of diction and melody'. Wherever the significance of Pound's patterning of his work eludes him, Nassar is charitable or respectful, hesitating 'to label anything in Pound as uncontrolled rant or ramble'; it is to his credit that he clearly admits to his failure to unravel certain passages. In addition, he does offer many valuable interpretations: for example, of the significance of the city of Wagadu to a passage in *The Pisan Cantos*. The book is divided into sections on the various cantos; although there are some repetitions, these are deliberate, for Nassar anticipates that his work will be consulted for reference as well as read straight through by some students. In a review (*RES*) of William M. Chace's *The Political Identities of Ezra Pound and T. S. Eliot*[23], Bernard Bergonzi remarks that Chace, 'like other American Liberals. . .seems to find the fascist Pound a more sympathetic figure than the conservative Eliot'. Louis Simpson's *Three on the Tower: The Lives and Works of Ezra Pound, T. S. Eliot and William Carlos Williams*[24], though it does not spare Pound the fascist and anti-semite,

[21] *Pound*, by Donald Davie. Fontana Modern Masters. Fontana/Collins. pp. 125.
[22] *The Cantos of Ezra Pound: The Lyric Mode*, by Eugene Paul Nassar. Baltimore and London: Johns Hopkins U.P. pp. xi + 164.
[23] *The Political Identities of Ezra Pound and T. S. Eliot* by William M. Chace. Stanford U.P.; London: O.U.P. 1974. pp. xviii + 238.
[24] *Three on the Tower: The Lives and Works of Ezra Pound, T. S. Eliot and William Carlos Williams*, by Louis A. M. Simpson. New York: William Morrow. pp. 373.

gives a good idea of why this should be. Simpson does not bring much in the way of new facts about Pound's life, nor is he offering a radically fresh approach to the poetry, and his short-sentence style can become grating. But his last section on Pound, telling of his caging and his horrifying isoltion, is masterly and deeply moving. Neither Eliot, successful and honoured, nor Williams, tickled at receiving in his last years the adulation of hundreds of cheering Wellesley girls, can engage our sympathies so much. Simpson goes into the lives of his subjects only in so far as they are directly relevant to the poetry, so he does not concern himself with, for example, Pound's life with his wife and Olga Rudge in Rapallo. (In this context it is strange that, in the section on Eliot, he simply gives a Jungian analysis of 'Marina' and does not relate it at all to Eliot's life.) Imagism is sensibly represented by Simpson as much more than 'physical poetry', being, he says, 'rather mysterious'. He argues that the two parts of *Hugh Selwyn Mauberley* do not hang together, and, countering the view of a critic like Hugh Kenner on the value of external reference in poetry, he says frankly, 'There are stretches of the *Cantos* that consist of little more than references. They must have been easy to string together—they are impossible to read with pleasure and therefore they teach us nothing'. Despite all the length and complexity of the *Cantos*, Pound, says Simpson, 'is still an Imagist, and the poets of the nineties are with him on this voyage'.

The view that the *Cantos* differ from Pound's early imagistic poetry because Imagism could render only the static, not dynamic, is contradicted by Suzanne Juhasz in her *Metaphor and the Poetry of Williams, Pound, and Stevens*[25]. 'Patterns of metaphor', she observes, 'create a nondiscursive method by which to link and develop images into a complex, long work'. She points out that not only is the Chinese ideogram, which Pound encountered through Fenollosa, a metaphor, but that Pound's images are all metaphors too, 'because an image is a verbal equation for an emotional and intellectual complex in an instant of time'. At times Juhasz can be rather elementary in her explications, and her lists of words can grow self-defeatingly too long. But she writes interestingly on metaphor as a structuring agent in the *Cantos*, particularly in her discussion of Pound's use of compound words. On the other hand, Joseph N. Riddel in 'Pound and the Decentered Image' (*GR*), acknowledges, as Pound had done, the failure to make the *Cantos* finally cohere, and he writes eloquently about their 'rag-bag' form.

Charles Olson and Ezra Pound: An Encounter at St. Elizabeth's[26] is a remarkable book. It is edited from a collection of Olson's papers which he labelled 'Pound case', and among which are Olson's poems about Pound, excerpts from *The Pisan Cantos*, correspondence from Pound, Olson's recollections of meetings with Pound, and often troubled records of Olson's feelings about the 'Pound case'. As Catherine Seelye, the editor, tells us, it is more an 'Olson book' than a 'Pound book', but there are a number of striking and frightening pictures of Pound—'this swearing, swift, slashing creature'—who both fascinates and repels Olson.

[25] *Metaphor and the Poetry of Williams, Pound, and Stevens*, by Suzanne Juhasz. Lewisberg: Bucknell U.P. 1974. pp. 292.
[26] *Charles Olson and Ezra Pound: An Encounter at St. Elizabeth's*, ed. by Catherine Seelye. New York: Crossman. pp. xxvi + 147.

Cummings has not been particularly well served by Bethany K. Dumas in E. E. Cummings: A Remembrance of Miracles[27], which has chapters on 'Life and Times', 'Early Poetry', 'The Poetry', 'The Prose', 'The Drama', 'An Appraisal'. The style is poor and the insights pedestrian.

MR reminds us that Cummings was a fairly accomplished draughtsman —he called himself 'an author of pictures, a draftsman of words'—by reproducing eighteen of his forty-six pencil, ink, and brush drawings which make up the Dial Collection of the Art Museum in Worcester, Mass. Dagmar Reutlinger (MR) explains how the collection was assembled, and offers some technical comments on the style of drawing. Robert Tucker (MR) provides an essay in which he reminds himself of the qualities of Cummings's poems, and concludes that the drawings 'complement nicely the most effective and memorable' of them.

The poetry of Wallace Stevens is treated in the works by Hugh Kenner and Suzanne Juhasz cited above. Juhasz is less full and less good on Stevens than on Williams; she concentrates on Notes toward a Supreme Fiction, which 'is built upon a pattern of metaphors placed in apposition to literal, abstract statements. The metaphors function to embody the abstract statements that they modify'. Susan B. Weston in 'The Artist as Guitarist: Stevens and Picasso' (Criticism) suggests that it was not so much the Armory Show of 1913 nor the Picasso Retrospective Exhibition in Hartford, Conn., in 1934 that explains the Cubist aesthetic of The Man with the Blue Guitar as the 1935 issue of Cahiers d'Art—'usually relegated to a scholarly footnote'. She directs attention to the way in which one article in particular, 'Picasso Poète' by Breton, affected Stevens: 'Breton's article, more than Picasso's guitars, provides a remarkable parallel with Stevens' use of the guitar'. Adelyn Doughty (TSLL) gives a technical analysis of the sound structures in 'Farewell to Florida'.

Paul L. Mariani's William Carlos Williams: The Poet and his Critics[28] is another volume of a useful series, serving as a bibliography, as an account of developments in writing about Williams since 1910, and, to some extent, as an overview of 'the nature and quality of American criticism in the act of listening to [one of] its artists'. After an Introduction it is divided thus: 'Williams's Initial "Impact": 1910–1930'; 'Holding Action: 1930–1945'; 'Putting Paterson on the Map: 1946–1961'; 'Floodtime: The Response to Williams: 1946–1963'; 'The Critical Current. Towards Canonization: 1963–1973'. References cited are listed by author at the end of the chapter. Mariani still feels embattled when he writes about Williams, because it was not till the nineteen-sixties that 'respectable critical analysis of his real achievement' began, and because so few critics take Williams 'seriously' as anything except a poet. So he bristles, in a way rather reminiscent of Williams, when he counters Charles Tomlinson's claim that Williams was 'taken seriously' by British readers in the mid-sixties: 'Williams does not seem to have made any serious impact on the shape of modern British poetry. And English critics still get their backs up when-

[27] E. E. Cummings: A Remembrance of Miracles, by Bethany K. Dumas. Vision P. 1974. pp. 157.
[28] William Carlos Williams: The Poet and his Critics, by Paul L. Mariani. Chicago: American Library Association. pp. 271.

ever they think Williams is being thrust upon them'. 'Serious' is a word
that recurs, and generally it is synonymous with 'approving'. Mariani's
survey is 'comprehensive', though he points out that he has eschewed some
commentaries on the grounds that they are irresponsible. He has also
written interestingly elsewhere (*TCL*) on Williams's late poems.
Rod Townley's *The Early Poetry of William Carlos Williams*[29] considers
the poetry up to and including *Spring and All*. Its chapters are: 'Early
Years, 1900-1909'; 'Transition Years, 1910-1917'; '*Kora in Hell: Improvi-
zations*'; '*Sour Grapes*'; '*Spring and All*'. This study could well be used as a
preparation for a reading of later and longer works, though Townley
observes that 'readers without a vested interest in the matter may find that
these longer works tend, for the most part, to break apart in their hands'.
His main theme concerns the two voices of Williams, a duality implicit in
the poet's very name with its dark, romantic Carlos lurking between 'the
two bland Williams' and in the alter ego he chose for himself in a number
of works, 'Evan Dionysus Evans'. Townley stresses the importance of the
secret and lost early notebooks of Williams, containing, apparently, out-
pourings of Whitmanesque free verse written at the same time that he was
writing bad, derivative, and acceptable Keatsian verse. He accepts James E.
Breslin's view of Williams's early repression, and suggests that the notorious
Poems of 1909 may have been intended as an end rather than a beginning.
Good use is made of the theme of the two voices in the section on *Kora in
Hell*; Townley sees no overall structure in the book except in the central
metaphor of the dance which, 'unlike a march. . .is not going anywhere',
and in the alternation of the 'chthonian' voice and the 'italic tone', which
are analogous to the Whitman and Keats voices of the early Williams, to
the passionate Carlos and the genteel son of a cultured Englishman. *Sour
Grapes*, says Townley, demonstrates Williams's 'continuing imagist orientation long after the movement had waned in Europe', and the two voices
are still in evidence here. First and revised versions of 'The Great Figure'
are compared to illustrate the risks involved in Williams's technique, which
Townley likens to the Zen art of drawing in ink on rice paper. His view of
Spring and All confirms Breslin's observation that the volume presents 'a
continuous process of surrender and assertion—the way to renewed individuality', and Townley sets it in the context of the modernist movement
generally, where artists, like Gris, Le Corbusier, and Stravinsky, became
'scientists of technique'. 'The work of art', he says, sounding like Hugh
Kenner in *A Homemade World*, 'was something to set going, to get off the
ground like a Wright brothers' plane'.
    Suzanne Juhasz, in *Metaphor and the Poetry of Williams, Pound, and
Stevens*, gives much attention to Williams, at the expense of Pound and
Stevens. She devotes two chapters exclusively to Williams, examining the
function of metaphor in some short poems, in 'Asphodel, That Greeny
Flower', and in *Paterson*. She also provides appendices listing all the metaphors of these last two poems. 'Asphodel' demonstrates how a long poem
may be organized and unified through the use of metaphors built around
one figure, in this case the flower. And *Paterson* is constructed on a pattern

[29] *The Early Poetry of William Carlos Williams*, by Rod Townley. Ithaca and
London: Cornell U.P. pp. 203.

of metaphors referring to 'a branch and a bud (Book 1); the flight of grass-hoppers (Book 2); the beautiful thing and a burning bottle (Book 3); Madame Curie and the radiant gist (Book 4); and the Unicorn and the Virgin (Book 5)'. Of course there have been many who have recognized the importance of metaphor to Williams since J. Hillis Miller asserted that there was 'no basis for metaphor' in the world of his poetry, but this does not devalue Juhasz's analysis. Margaret L. Bollard, concentrating on the 'interlace' pattern, has also written on elements that serve a unifying purpose in *Paterson (TCL)*.

Joseph N. Riddel's *The Inverted Bell: Modernism and the Counter-poetics of William Carlos Williams*[30] is likely to appeal more to students of critical theory generally than to those interested primarily in Williams's poetry. It is a book in which words you might have thought perfectly normal are enclosed estrangingly in inverted commas, are italicized, or split by a dash, so that we have 'ex-ists' instead of 'exists'. But Riddel does eventually come to consider *Paterson*, and I should say that others (*ALS* 1974) have found the 'Structuralist or Post-Structuralist' techniques of this study particularly exciting.

'Who Buried H. D.?' asks Susan Friedman (*CE*). And it is remarkable how little of H. D.'s considerable and varied output is generally known, though short early poems like 'Oread' and 'Heat' continue to be anthologized. Friedman claims that H. D. has been neglected because 'She was a woman, she wrote about women, and all the ever-questioning, artistic, intellectual heroes of her epic poetry and novels were women'. She takes issue with Joseph N. Riddel and Norman N. Holland for assuming that H. D.'s poetry was a product of her unresolved penis envy.

Ann Cheney says that her study of Edna St. Vincent Millay[31] is a 'psychological biography, hoping to catch the nuances of her essence'. It certainly isn't a psychological biography, her analysis of 'Renascence' and account of Millay's lesbianism notwithstanding. The Village itself is evoked in simplistic generalizations, and references to 'Fauvianists' and 'Marcel Duchamps' do not inspire confidence.

Two Hart Crane books from 1974 but not previously mentioned in *YW* are *Letters of Hart Crane and His Family*[32], edited by Thomas S. W. Lewis, and Margaret D. Uroff's *Hart Crane: The Patterns of his Poetry*[33]. Lewis's handsome and painstaking edition of the correspondence, superseding Brom Weber's *The Letters of Hart Crane* (1965), gives us the letters that passed between Hart (or Harold, as he always remained to his father) Crane, his father, his mother, and his grandmother, and Lewis supplies linking paragraphs which fill out the relevant details of their lives. The letters show Crane torn between his avidly demanding mother, Grace, and his rather bemused father, Clarence, who wanted a steady conventional

[30] *The Inverted Bell: Modernism and the Counterpoetics of William Carlos Williams*, by Joseph N. Riddell. Baton Rouge: Louisiana State U.P. 1974. pp. xxxv + 308.
[31] *Millay in Greenwich Village*, by Anne Cheney. University, Alabama: U. of Alabama P. pp. 160.
[32] *Letters of Hart Crane and His Family*, ed. by Thomas S. W. Lewis. New York and London: Columbia U.P. 1974. pp. xxiv + 675.
[33] *Hart Crane: The Patterns of his Poetry*, by Margaret D. Uroff. Urbana, Chicago, and London: U. of Illinois P. 1974. pp. 236.

success for his son. Margaret D. Uroff resists the biographical approach to Crane, who has fascinated many, as tortured souls often do; she focuses her attention firmly on the poetry—so firmly, in fact, that it is sometimes difficult to judge the quality of the poetry whose intricate weavings of patterns she examines. She argues that in *The Bridge* Crane 'continued to expand and explore. . .the imaginative concerns that interested him from the beginning', and she tries to repair the damage done by too great a separation of Crane's lyric and epic poetry. Chapters are devoted to those recurrent patterns that, says Uroff, give coherence to his work: 'The Poet as Violator', 'The Poet as Possessor', 'The World in Flight', 'The World in Stasis', 'The Impulse to Mastery'. The *Expl* gives two notes on Crane this year.

A 'poor-minded exile from the forests of Grimm' is how Robert Lowell described Randall Jarrell, and it is with this image that Helen Hagenbüchle begins her study of Jarrell, *The Black Goddess: A Study of the Archetypal Feminine in the Poetry of Randall Jarrell*[34]. She notes some of the previously-remarked tensions evident in Jarrell's poetry, between consciousness and unconsciousness and between intuition and intellect, for example, and emphasizes the high value that Jarrell placed on ambiguity: Jarrell's predilection for the phrase 'and yet', for suggestive hyphens, and for dots trailing off at the end of thoughts or poems, all demonstrate his dislike of fixity. But what Hagenbüchle concentrates on is the image of the mother in Jarrell's work, showing that a child's loss of confidence in the mother is used by him 'as a metaphor for man's helpless despair', and that the most powerful of his archetypal symbols is the Great Mother, who figures in his work in all the expected Jungian guises.

Theodore Roethke seems to attract critics whose deep feeling for his poetry manifests itself in a celebratory quality in their writing. Ralph J. Mills has been mentioned above, and Rosemary Sullivan, in her study of Roethke's poetry[35], tells us that if she has 'one overriding intention. . .it is to celebrate the poetry'. Her book gives a balanced view of Roethke's work, however, arguing for its unity and sense of development, which, she says, confirm its claim to major status. She stresses the importance of Jung and Maud Bodkin to an understanding of the poetry, early and late. After modestly asserting that her themes are 'those which must preoccupy all studies of Roethke', she summarizes some of them: 'his sensitivity to the subliminal, irrational world of nature; his relationship to his dead father, who occupies the center of his work. . .; his attempts to explore other modes of consciousness which carried him to the edge of psychic disaster. . .; his interest in mysticism. . . his debts. . .; to the poetic ancestors from whom he learned his craft; and the calm joyousness which rests at the core of his work'. Anthony Libby, in 'Roethke, Water Father' (*AL* 1974) shows Roethke to be a dominant influence on recent American 'mystical or oracular poets'.

[34] *The Black Goddess: A Study of the Archetypal Feminine in the Poetry of Randall Jarrell*, by Helen Hagenbüchle. Swiss Studies in English. Bern and Zurich: A. Francke Verlag. pp. 187.
[35] *Theodore Roethke: The Garden Master*, by Rosemary Sullivan. Seattle and London: U. of Washington P. pp. 220.

Robert Lowell's achievement is weighed by Helen Vendler in 'The Difficult Grandeur of Robert Lowell: A Consideration of "Our Greatest Contemporary Poet" ' (*AM*), which is well-written, having some fine, evocative phrases. Vendler gives an admiring but unsparing review of Lowell, taking into account the 1973 publication of *History, For Lizzie and Harriet*, and *The Dolphin*, which swept aside the idea that his powers were declining. These volumes, she says, 'with their tenderness toward the earth and its offerings, contain the first legitimate continuance of Shakespeare's sonnets since Keats'. She sees Lowell not as a disappointed idealist, but as a 'philosophical nihilist', and defends him from the charge that he lives as a poet by a kind of 'cannibalism'. Stephen Yenser's study of Lowell's poetry[36] includes good analyses of individual poems (though he misinterprets 'Hawthorne') which are genuinely critical, and his judgements are sometimes quite severe. He considers the range of Lowell's poetry and is careful to trace similarities from volume to volume, but whether this achieves the intended illustration of the continuity of the poetry is open to question. George McFadden's ' "Life Studies"—Robert Lowell's Comic Breakthrough' (*PMLA*) represents the 'Life Studies' poems as Lowell's use of Freudian myths of maturation in which the parents are subjected to 'comic degradation' so that the poet can be renewed. This renewal is reflected in the new, open style of the poetry, says McFadden.

J. D. McClatchy's essay on W. D. Snodgrass (*MR*) is an appreciation of the verse which is the successor to the severe homely lyrics of Hardy and Frost. It examines Snodgrass's work through the influences on it—including Rimbaud, Lowell, Jarrell, Ransom, and Roethke—and is centred on *Heart's Needle*, to which Lowell's *Life Studies* owes a debt, and *After Experience*. We are given fairly close readings of individual poems, and McClatchy is also concerned to classify groupings and sequences of poems. The later volume, he says, shows a modification of the confessional mode of *Heart's Needle*, as 'awareness' grows into 'understanding'.

Poems by John Berryman ('World's Fair'), Sylvia Plath ('The Couriers'), and Galway Kinnell ('The Bear') are treated in *Expl.*

3. The Novel

James Woodress's *American Fiction, 1900–1950: A Guide to Information Sources*[1] opens with some thirty pages of general bibliography covering the period, and recognizing the novel, the short story, and interviews with authors as separate categories. The bulk of the work is forty-four bibliographical essays on those writers whom Woodress sees, in 1973, as being the most significant, a number which is large enough to take in most of the writers for whose inclusion a clear argument could be floated. The essays are generally accurate and helpful, even where they have to be very highly selective; one minor fault is that while they generally direct a

---

[36] *Circle to Circle: The Poetry of Robert Lowell*, by Stephen Yenser. Berkeley, Los Angeles, and London: U. of California P. pp. xii + 370.

[1] *American Fiction, 1900–1950: A Guide to Information Sources*, ed. by James Woodress. Detroit: Gale Research Company. pp. xxii + 260.

student to the best book length studies of a writer, in dealing with publish-ed collections of essays Woodress is less helpful in making distinctions between the qualities of the various volumes often consulted by students. Among the less obvious authors included are Pearl Buck, Walter Van Tilburg Clark, Floyd Dell, Vardis Fisher, Jesse Stuart, B. Traven, and Owen Wister.

William Peden's *The American Short Story 1940-1975*[2] is a revised and expanded version of his *The American Short Story* (1964). It is a discursive survey of short stories written in the period and it contains an appendix giving basic bibliographical information on 'One Hundred-Plus Notable or Representative American Short Story Writers'. The bulk of the book, considered as a critical text, is valueless; crucial theoretical questions suggested by the title are never really raised, and a huge number of stories by a huge number of writers is talked about in 190 pages, with a critical vocabulary that is almost never more than vaguely impressionistic. Ob-viously the major theoretical question is how we should approach the short stories of so many writers whose work is in greater or lesser part in another form; Peden deals at length with Updike, Tennessee Williams, Bernard Malamud, and James Baldwin, among others, without any sub-stantial reference to their other work. It might be said that the set task or the available space makes this a necessity, but the problem is not even seriously acknowledged. What is true of individual figures is also true of areas of contemporary American literature; it is not possible, as Peden does, to write on the short stories of Jewish or Negro writers without at least raising the question of whether those stories do constitute an entity of a more than totally artificial kind, whether there is such a thing as the Negro short story, and if so what it is that has made this form appropriate in this cultural context. Peden is also inconsistent; an issue ignored with regard to Williams and Updike is used to dismiss, by implication, Robert Creeley, Peden saying that his 'poetry. . .seems to me far more important than his short fiction'.

The discussions of individual writers, of which the book is mostly composed, are along the following lines. We are told that one author, Joyce Carol Oates, 'can do beautiful small things with her left hand that many more experienced writers very often cannot do with both hands', or that three of Salinger's stories are 'alive with an intense sensitivity to the nuances of human experience', that his minor stories are 'peopled with brilliantly portrayed characters', and that his dialogue is 'at its best superb'. This is regrettably typical. The weight of all this uninformative praise is leaden. This, together with the book's failure concerning the short story as a genre, and the problems concerning social and economic conditions and their relationship to literary form make the book's contribution to English studies negligible.

In complete contrast *Enemy Salvoes: Selected Literary Criticism by Wyndham Lewis*[3] is a welcome collection, hopefully tantalizing enough to

---

[2] *The American Short Story: Continuity and Change 1940-1975*, by William Peden. Boston: Houghton Mifflin. pp. vi + 215. $7.95.
[3] *Enemy Salvoes: Selected Literary Criticism by Wyndham Lewis*, ed. by C. J. Fox. Vision P. pp. 272. £4.95.

be effective in its avowed purpose, 'the republication in full of key Lewis books long out of print'. Here nothing is reprinted in its entirety, all the material having been edited by C. J. Fox, who offers highlights from some of Lewis's most celebrated criticism in anything from two pages (on Cervantes) to seventeen (on Orwell). Fox supplies a brief but adequate contextual introduction to each piece, and also footnotes mainly referring the reader to his sources. There are four pieces on general topics, but the main bulk of the book is made up of Lewis's writings on his contemporaries, including James, Stein, Anderson, Hemingway, Faulkner, and Pound, and on figures important to Lewis and his times such as Cervantes and 'The Russians'. The final eight pieces are subtitled 'Writers and Politics' by Fox, but this only stresses a consistent concern in the whole of the book as clear in the essays on D. H. Lawrence and Hemingway as it is in those on Flaubert, André Malraux, Camus, and Sartre. The general introduction by C. H. Sisson is disappointing, being neither long nor detailed enough to place Lewis in the context of his age, admittedly a formidable task. Sisson looks at Lewis's criticism and compares its neglect to the canonization of Eliot's critical writings, but the essay does not raise the vital question of how their relative critical reputations have depended upon the estimates made of their respective creative work. Another large omission is D. H. Lawrence, whose critical work would seem to present itself naturally for comparison and who is scarcely mentioned in the essay.

Another useful publication of material from this period is Edward Wagenknecht's edition of James Branch Cabell's letters.[4] Wagenknecht's selection centres around Cabell's letters to his editors and those men of letters who were enthusiastic supporters of his work, such as Burton Rascoe and Hugh Walpole. Of correspondence with other novelists there is strikingly little apart from that which charts his friendship with Ellen Glasgow and a few letters to Sinclair Lewis and Marjorie Kinnan Rawlings. Cabell emerges as entirely apart from the mainstream of contemporary writing, almost as if he were unaware that it existed; apart from what is indicated in a couple of minor notes to Scott Fitzgerald about *The Beautiful and Damned* included here, he seems to have read almost nobody except Sinclair Lewis. to whom he confessed 'I don't know any of my contemporaries, as reading-matter', an attitude to which he seems to have adhered most of his life, so the book is of relatively little interest outside its own immediate field.

Percy Lubbock's sketch of Edith Wharton, published in 1947, was entitled *A Portrait of Edith Wharton*. The reader's main misgiving, encountering R. W. B. Lewis's very substantial and scholarly new biography of Wharton[5], might be that just this element of portraiture would be lost. The reasons are clear; Wharton's life was so long, her literary relations so complex, stretching, as Lewis comments, from Longfellow to Moravia, her social worlds, from her New York girlhood in the 1860s and 70s to her final years in her two French homes in the 1920s and 30s, so various. More than this, her energies as a hostess, to the great and the unknown, were so

[4] *The Letters of James Branch Cabell*, ed. by Edward Wagenknecht. Norman: U. of Oklahoma P. pp. xvii + 277. $15.
[5] *Edith Wharton: A Biography*, by R. W. B. Lewis. Constable. pp. xiv + 592. £6.50.

unflagging that she might easily disappear under a mountain of biographical annotation of her minor guests, or become a footnote to the stories of the more decidedly famous. It is Lewis's achievement that he does not try to make Wharton a clearer or simpler figure by excluding any of this material, but lets her portrait emerge out of this density of context. The great achievement of the biography is the sense that Lewis doesn't feel any need to make Edith Wharton into a resonant figure; she is that already, and his role is brilliantly to order the material, knowing when and how to pause and view them in depth.

A particular social world was often linked with one or more individuals in Edith Wharton's life. Thus in the opening of the book Lewis spends some time characterizing the world of her childhood and her complex familial and social ties, and through this comes some way to explaining her unlikely marriage to Teddy Wharton. Teddy Wharton, so clearly unable to meet his wife on so many levels, remains one of the enigmas of the book, but Lewis presents what evidence there is and never steps beyond careful speculation as to the nature of the incompatibility. The same relation between milieu and individual is fascinatingly portrayed dealing with Wharton's intense sexual awakening through her relationship with the American journalist Morton Fullerton. Here again there is an abundance of material to work with, and Lewis controls it finely, using Wharton's private diary as the main source of his narrative, but giving us also supporting literary material, the poem 'Terminus' which is included in his text, and the extraordinary erotic fragment 'Beatrice Palmato', printed as an appendix to the book. This makes for absorbing reading, but the less immediately gripping areas of Edith Wharton's life, such as her role as hostess, also have their interest. Lewis builds up, in his accounts of Wharton's circles, a sense of an ongoing world of friends; over the length of the book, figures such as Henry James, Bernard Berenson, Kenneth Clark, or Walter Berry emerge as being loyal over great stretches of time. Part of the force of Lewis's portrait lies in his assembling a view of Wharton seen through so many brilliant eyes. Lewis is thorough and informative on Wharton's stormy relationships with her various publishers, and interesting on the way her financial needs, particularly in later years, may have influenced the kind of work she wrote. It is largely from these perspectives that Lewis views the fiction; a lucid account of Wharton's writing career is maintained in the biography, but the concentration is distinctly on the writer rather than the work. This is perhaps related to clear concentration on the literal rather than the psychological, an interest in 'the flesh and blood woman' rather than the 'far psychological fields' suggested by the fiction, and, as Lewis admits himself in his discussion of *Italian Villas and their Gardens*, by some of the biographical detail also.

Also writing on Wharton is Curtis Dahl (*MFS*) who demonstrates how the opening verses of Chapter Seven of 'Ecclesiastes' are the source, not only of the title of *The House of Mirth*, but also of much of the rest of the book. Dahl argues that the whole of Wharton's text puns on this chapter, constituting an 'ambiguous sermon' on it. Elizabeth Ammons (*AL*) sees misinterpretations of *The Reef* as having arisen from an over-simple understanding of its 'fairty-tale complexion', and suggests that Wharton argues that the fantasy of deliverance by a Prince Charming is not a dream of freedom for women, but a celebration of the male-dominated status-quo.

Malcolm Cowley, writing on Conrad Aiken (*SoR*), stresses his strong concern for his privacy as an individual, and attributes in part the public neglect of his work to this. In this timely article Cowley also looks at the movement towards New England Transcendentalism in Aiken's late work. Although James McLintock's *White Logic: Jack London's Short Stories*[6] is a survey of all nineteen volumes, McLintock avoids making any very high claims for more than a very small number of the stories, and concentrates on the major impulses behind particular groups. He discusses the early books (1898–1902) in terms of the influence of Kipling and other magazine writing at the turn of the century, and goes on to relate London's work to the contemporary debate between realism and romance, seeing him as a thinker influenced by the Social Darwinism of Herbert Spencer and Ernst Haeckel. His main claims for London's artistry are in his discussions of the Malemute kid series and the Alaskan stories (1898–1908) where he stresses London as a precursor of later twentieth-century American writing in his concern with violence and death, his final pessimism, and his sense of the limits of rationality. McLintock recognizes that this is not a novel view of London, but it is useful to see it reflected in the short stories rather than his other work. The later chapters deal with London's decline as a short story writer (1906–11); McLintock discusses the socialist stories and the south sea stories, and connects their intellectual basis with the Alaskan volumes, and then covers the last books, London's 'stack of hack', of which little can be usefully said. The book concludes with an interesting chapter on London's stories of 1916, demonstrating their reliance on his reading of Jung, and in particular Jung's definition of the libido. In all, the book is an adequate study, leaving the reader with the feeling that little more remains to be said about this mass of material.

In *The Quixotic Vision of Sinclair Lewis*[7], Martin Light views the conflict of realism and romance in Lewis's work as an expression of Quixotism. Light, who defines Quixotism as 'an affliction that begins under the influence of readings in romantic literature and continues as a protagonist, thus inspired, ventures forth into a world he both finds and makes', attempts to explore this in both life and works, but even in this short study, too much seems to be made of far too little. The first two chapters, dealing with Lewis's life and his early reading, are not without interest, but here much more work needs to be done to establish the whole context which those figures set up, of which Quixotism is only a very small part. Making the connexion with Dickens, for example, it is neither illuminating, nor, clearly, adequate to say only that 'We should note that Pickwick, primary among Dickens's characters, is a quixote'.

The main body of the book is a series of short essays on Lewis's major works. Here the crucial problem is that the thesis is only at the centre of the discussion for brief moments. It works for *Main Street*, although too little is made of the relationship to *Madame Bovary*, and for *Elmer Gantry*

[6] *White Logic: Jack London's Short Stories*, by James I. McLintock. Grand Rapids, Michigan: Wolf House Books. pp. xii + 206. $10.
[7] *The Quixotic Vision of Sinclair Lewis*, by Martin Light. West Lafayette, Indiana: Purdue U.P. pp. xiii + 162. $6.50.

where Frank Shallard seems to fit it well, but for most of the other books it is marginal or of no relevance at all. Hence the other chapters, 'The Apprentice Fiction', *Babbitt, Arrowsmith*, and 'The Later Fiction's are of little interest in terms of Quixotism, and of no great novelty as a general survey of Lewis's work. The thinness of the material is perhaps indicated by the decay of the main definition; by Chapter Four the quixote has become simply 'a creature of fancy', and in the conclusion of the book, Light suggests only that 'some element of fancy invariably remains throughout Lewis's work'.

Another thesis is Mona Pers's *Willa Cather's Children*[8], which sets out to be a 'critical study which attempts to establish the overall importance of children in her writings'. Pers describes three functions of children, as a way of characterizing adult figures, as symbols of love and hope, and as 'point of view characters', but it is not in fact along these lines that the three parts of the book are organized. One of the main flaws of this very disappointing study is that its organizational principle is loose and highly questionable. In Part One Pers looks at the 'extent and nature of this interest', Part Two discusses the 'recovery' of Cather's 'childhood self', and Part Three the consequences of her 'child-centred attitude'; in all three parts Pers looks at Cather's life and how it 'influenced' or 'affected' her works. The book moves far too loosely between works and life, as if the obviousness of the connexion in Cather's case made that connexion somehow simple. Very often parallels between work and life are presented as if they were explanations of a critical nature, but the problem remains that the book offers nothing beyond the general establishment of the 'importance' of children to Cather. The sections on childlessness and on male child protagonists are potentially more interesting than many, but the book is also weakened by lack of understanding of general technical issues in the novel, and of wider cultural attitudes.

A vastly more interesting work is *The Art of Willa Cather*[9] which springs out of an international seminar held at the University of Nebraska in 1973. The book contains general reassessments by Eudora Welty, Marcus Cunliffe, and Donald Sutherland, a piece on Cather and European Tradition by James Woodress, and views of her from French, Japanese, and Italian perspectives by Michel Gervaud, Hiroko Sato, and Aldo Celli. Cather's technique is dealt with in an essay by James E. Miller, and all these essays are followed by brief transcripts of audience discussions, excepting those by Welty and Cunliffe. In Part Two, 'Recollections', Alfred A. Knopf remembers Cather, and Leon Edel talks about Cather's intimate friend Edith Lewis.

Cather studies are also forwarded by the publication of JoAnna Lathrop's *Willa Cather: A Checklist of her Published Writing*[10], which records all printings and reprintings, apart from collectors' limited editions, of Cather's work in the United States. The list is in chronological order of

[8] *Willa Cather's Children*, by Mona Pers. Studia Anglistica Upsaliensia No. 22. Uppsala. pp. 124.
[9] *The Art of Willa Cather*, ed. by Bernice Slote and Virginia Faulkner. Lincoln: U. of Nebraska P. 1974. pp. xii + 267. pb $3.45.
[10] *Willa Cather: A Checklist of her Published Writing*, by JoAnna Lathrop. Lincoln: U. of Nebraska P. pp. xiii + 118.

first publication, including, of course, her extensive work as a journalist, and a short appendix on her student writing. James Woodress's vital biography, *Willa Cather: Her Life and Art*[11], originally published in 1970, has also been reprinted as a paperback.

Other work on minor figures includes an interesting essay by Michael Baumann (*MLQ*) on the enigmatic figure of B. Traven, suggesting that detailed study of Traven's language may well be a good starting-point for unravelling some of the biographical problems. While it is firmly established that Traven originally wrote everything in German, his German prose is full of anglicisms, and Baumann examines these and suggests various possible explanations and their biographical implications. He also looks at the work Traven re-wrote in his inadequate English, and finally discusses how this might contribute to further study of different editions of the books and to 'placing' him in the context of the whole of American literature.

In the context of an issue of *TCL* devoted to Surrealism, William Wasserstrom writes on the various schools of thought and movements in the arts which influenced Gertrude Stein, attempting to assess their relative importance.

The most substantial contribution to Hemingway studies is the collection of essays on the short stories edited by Jackson J. Benson[12]. It is subdivided in a way which might lead the reader to expect more than locally interesting analyses of particular stories, into Groupings, Technique, Interpretations, and an Overview. The book sadly disappoints any such expectations, though in every section there are essays which help to clarify particular texts. In the 'Groupings' category there is little exploration of the significance of the Spanish or African settings of the stories discussed in Carlos Baker's and Martin Light's articles, although these analyze the texts interestingly. Other contributions here are less successful; Clinton S. Burhans on *In Our Time* approaches the problem of unity through the character of Nick Adams, but seems to be evading the issue when he says of the protagonists of 'Soldier's Home' and 'A Very Short Story' that they are figures who 'could be Nick Adams without any substantial or significant change'. Hemingway chose not to name these figures as Nick Adams, and this is what needs examining. Again, Philip Young's essay on the Nick Adams stories gets no further than playing the dangerous game of identifying the characters with their Oak Park originals and finally offers no explanation for why Hemingway might have treated Nick as he did. The technical question of the appropriateness of the short story form is not raised.

The section on Story Technique promises to be more interesting, and does contain some suggestive information in articles by Charles A. Fenton on 'The Revision of "Chapter Three" from *In Our Time*' and by Carl Ficken on 'Point of View in the Nick Adams Stories'. But several of the essays fail to explain how technical points might modify our response;

[11] *Willa Cather: Her Life and Art*, by James Woodress. Lincoln: U. of Nebraska P. pp. 288. pb $3.50.
[12] *The Short Stories of Ernest Hemingway*, ed. by Jackson J. Benson. Durham: Duke U.P. pp. xv + 375.

rather we are given assertions that the stories are now more interesting from Sheldon Grebstein on 'Mother of a Queen' and Julian Smith on 'In Another Country'. The 'Interpretations' section, the longest in the collection, contains some of the best work. Joseph DeFalco's psychological approach to the initiation in 'Indian Camp', and 'The Doctor and the Doctor's Wife', Earl Rovit on dignity in 'In Another Country', Richard Hovey, again psychological, on 'Now I Lay Me', Marian Montgomery on 'The Gambler, The Nun and The Radio', Horst Kruse on 'The End of Something', and Gennaro Santangelo on 'The Snows of Kilimanjaro' are all valuable readings. There are clear and interesting essays from Julian Smith on 'A Canary for One', and Warren Bennett on 'A Clean, Well-Lighted Place'. Elsewhere the material is more familiar as in Brooks and Warren's exemplary analysis of *The Killers* reprinted from *Understanding Fiction*. Other essays seem more like notes, and in some cases, quibbles; Peter L. Hays on 'Hemingway and the Fisher King', Anselm Atkins on 'After the Storm', and John V. Hagopian on symmetry in 'Cat in the Rain' all seem to be making fair but very minor comment. The weakest of the essays in this section is Virgil Hutton's 'The Short Happy Life of Macomber', where, in his anxiousness to correct the usual interpretation of the story as favourable to Wilson, Hutton attempts the unlikely feat of blackening him totally.

In one particular respect, that of comparing Hemingway to other writers, the book is strikingly weak. Ray B. West on Faulkner and Hemingway does no more than demonstrate that both writers are major contributors to the form, Frank O'Connor's flippant and ill-argued piece on Hemingway and Joyce is one of the worst in the book, and Benson's own comparison of Hemingway with Kafka is also scarcely adequate. The book concludes with a comprehensive checklist of criticism on the stories.

A much slighter work is William F. Nolan's short account of Hemingway's last years, *Last Days of the Lion*[13]. Originally written in 1964 and republished here with minor revisions, it is an impressionistic account using Hemingway's bodily deterioration as its central metaphor, and seeing Hemingway's suicide as the logical outcome of his beliefs, 'the law of safari'. Also included in the volume is a poem by Nolan on Hemingway, 'Now Never There', and a critical checklist of the biographical work, quite useful in so far as it does not scruple to damn the worthless or opportunistic.

An important aid to Hemingway studies is Audre Hanneman's very substantial supplement to her 1967 bibliography of Hemingway[14]. This covers the period 1966–1973, including the publication of *Islands in the Stream* and *The Nick Adams Stories* and the republication of *By-Line: Ernest Hemingway*. The section listing reviews includes interesting excerpts, reflecting the changing response to Hemingway during these years. The divisions and coverage of this supplement follows that of the 1967 volume, being extremely thorough and comprehensive.

There is an interesting chapter on Hemingway in John McCormick's

[13] *Hemingway: Last Days of the Lion*, by William F. Nolan. Santa Barbara: Capra Press. 1974. pp. 38. pb $2.50.
[14] *Supplement to Ernest Hemingway: A Comprehensive Bibliography*, by Audre Hanneman. Princeton: Princeton U.P. pp. xii + 393. £11.70.

Fiction as Knowledge[15], comparing him with Montherlant, looking at both writers in relation to the Romantic movement, but seeing Hemingway as 'outside or beyond history' as compared to Montherlant. McCormick supports this by a comparison of *A Farewell to Arms* with *Le Songe*. The twentieth anniversary issue of *MFS* reprints Warren Beck's 1955 article on 'The Short Happy Life of Francis Macomber', and in an addendum to it Beck discusses the subsequent attack made on his critical method by Mark Spilka, and defends his reading of the story and his understanding of it as an 'autonomous work'.

Less interesting is Clinton Burhans's comparison of Hemingway and Vonnegut (*MFS*) which yields little beyond the obvious vast dissimilarity between these two writers. Burhans sees the dissimilarity as illuminating 'the course of thought and art over the past century', but the thesis proves too vast for the article.

The new concordance to F. Scott Fitzgerald's *The Great Gatsby*[16] is the first computerized concordance to be published for an American novel, and it covers all the words in Fitzgerald's text. The method of presentation is that of 'Key Word in Context', locating in context every word in the novel excepting about 170 common terms, such as 'I', 'is', and 'have', for which location but not context is given. There are complete word frequency lists, in alphabetical and numerical order. The text used is that of the 1925 first printing of the novel, as emended by Matthew Bruccoli in his *Apparatus for a Definitive Edition of 'The Great Gatsby'*, and the concordance appears to have been extensively and carefully proof-read. As long as mere numerical frequency of use is not used too crudely, the book will serve as a valuable aid to discussion of Fitzgerald's style and language.

A Faulkner Miscellany[17] is a revision of the summer 1973 issue of *MissQ*. It is mainly concerned with work on Faulkner's early and unpublished texts and includes articles by Noel Polk on the play '*Marionettes*', Thomas McHaney on *Elmer*, and Keen Butterworth on the manuscripts and typescripts of Faulkner's poetry. A number of other short pieces on unpublished material add to our knowledge of *The Town, Intruder in the Dust*, and the New Orleans Sketches. Of the other material published here for the first time, the most important is a new version of Faulkner's 1933 introduction to *The Sound and the Fury* differing substantially from the version published in *SoR* in 1972.

The chapter on Faulkner in John McCormick's *Fiction as Knowledge*[15] relates him to Broch and Musil and discusses the place of history in his work, while acknowledging that what is mainly crucial here is Faulkner's Southernness. While not a vitally informative piece, it is good to see Faulkner treated in the company of major twentieth-century European writers. In the same vein Michael Groden (*TCL*) writes successfully on similarities of technique between *Ulysses* and *The Sound and the Fury* but

[15] *Fiction as Knowledge: The Modern Post-Romantic Novel*, by John McCormick. New Brunswick, New Jersey: Rutgers U.P. pp. 184. $9.
[16] *A Concordance to F. Scott Fitzgerald's 'The Great Gatsby'*, compiled by Andrew T. Crosland. Detroit: Gale Research Company. pp. xvi + 425. $35.
[17] *A Faulkner Miscellany*, ed. by James Meriwether. Jackson: U.P. of Mississippi. 1974. pp. x + 166. $8.50.

specific reliance by Faulkner on Joyce, while admittedly probable, remains unproved. While generally handling the texts well, Groden does not entirely avoid the pitfall of taking obvious similarities to be significant and there is no very clear sense of what if any similarities are unique to these two texts. Other interesting explications of Faulkner are given by H. R. Stoneback (*MFS*) who argues persuasively that 'Pantaloon in Black' is based, both in emotional tone and situational content, on a blues song, and Joel Grossman (*AL*) who traces the source of the phrase used in *Knight's Gambit* and *Sanctuary*, 'less oft is peace'. There is a substantial article by Stephen M. Ross (*TSLL*) on the mixing of past and present tense narratives in *As I Lay Dying*. Ross demonstrates the careful craft of the Tull sections, showing how the tense chosen reflects Tull's proximity to the Bundrens, and argues cogently for the psychological consistency of the tenses given to Darl, and effectively refutes R. W. Franklin's charges (*MFS*, 1967) that the novel was hastily put together.

George Lensing (*SoR*) rightly stresses the family as central metaphor in *Absalom, Absalom!*, although he includes Quentin and Shreve in a figure of 'the expanded family' without exactly explaining what qualities bind them together into such a unit. Brent Harold (*AL*) sees in Faulkner a critique of 'the languages of over-conceptualization, intellectual detachment, and domination'. In the course of this article he makes some interesting points about *The Sound and the Fury*, although his view of the central place of the Nobel Prize speech in our understanding of Faulkner seems dubious. Also James G. Watson (*MFS*) discusses the rather doubtful and elusive figure of the prophet in Faulkner's fiction, and Victor Sandburg (*MFS*) applies Eliot's definition of the 'objective correlative' to Faulkner's work.

William White in his *Nathanael West: A Comprehensive Bibliography*[18] refers to his first bibliography published in 1958, and comments on the growth of interest in West. The bulk of this interest is in the form of articles, individual and collected, and White includes sections on theses and chapters and material in more general works. The writing of West himself is thoroughly documented, though White takes the books title by title in all languages, which makes interest in West abroad more difficult to assess. There are useful sections on West's films and his two unpublished plays, and a section on reviews which might have benefited from some short quotations, considering that the interest of the book falls so clearly on West's changing reputation. The appendix of uncollected writings which takes up the last third of the book includes juvenilia and versions of parts of *Miss Lonelyhearts* and one piece from *The Day of the Locust* published in periodicals. Two of the extracts from *Miss Lonelyhearts* are particularly interesting in being written from a first person point of view.

One of the most prolific writers of this period is Steinbeck; the 800 pages in the collection *Steinbeck: A Life in Letters*[19] edited by Elaine Steinbeck and Robert Wallsten represent only a small proportion of those

[18] *Nathanael West: A Comprehensive Bibliography*, by William White. The Serif Series Bibliographies and Checklists No. 32. Kent State U.P. pp. xi + 209. $8.
[19] *Steinbeck: A Life in Letters*, ed. by Elaine Steinbeck and Robert Wallsten. Heinemann. pp. xv + 906. £8.

known to exist. Printed here are a large number of letters to his literary agent Elizabeth Otis and his editor Pascal Covici, which will clearly be of value in exploring his literary work. A few letters reflecting his friendship with the biologist Ed Ricketts show how Steinbeck attempted to apply Ricketts's ideas to his view of society. Apart from this, the selection concentrates very much on Steinbeck's personal and familial life, as well as letters to F. D. Roosevelt and Lyndon Johnson. As its title implies, the book is a kind of biographical narrative, with a running commentary from the editors interspersed among the letters. Some of this commentary is helpful, although occasionally it is absurdly intrusive, interrupting the text of a letter in order to inject information more properly appropriate to a footnote. Basic biographical information is provided in tabular form at the beginning of each chapter, but, despite the editors' claim at the end of their introduction, the life of Steinbeck remains to be written.

Writing on Steinbeck, Linda Pratt (*SoR*) looks at the way his work moves away from history towards myth after he became concerned with the migrant situation. She compares his work to James Agee's *Let Us Now Praise Famous Men*, and sees Steinbeck as sharing American values, Agee as opposed to them.

The best work in the collection *The Achievement of William Styron*[20] edited by Robert K. Morris and Irving Malin, seems to spring out of the debate concerning Styron's relationship to Southern literature. One excellent essay here is by Louis Rubin, who argues, in 'Notes on a Southern Writer in our Time', that *Lie Down in Darkness* was originally accepted as being a Southern novel in the tradition of Faulkner, but that in fact 'the historical dimension is almost entirely absent in the novel'. Rubin discusses the relationship between Styron and Faulkner, and concludes that Styron is joined to older Southern writers by his assumption 'that a community role is desirable'. Also persuasive is George Core's essay '*The Confessions of Nat Turner* and the Burden of the Past', which discusses the technique of this novel and puts it in the context of the historical novel. The other vital essay in the collection is Seymour Gross and Eileen Bender's refutation of the attacks made by black critics in 'History, Politics, and Literature: The Myth of Nat Turner'. The essay is a close examination of Thomas Gray's *The Confessions of Nat Turner* (1831) and Styron's other sources. It emerges, particularly convincingly in some of the concluding examples, such as the figure of Etheldred Brantley, that the accusation levelled against Styron, that he 'is guilty of distorting the facts of history is itself not supported by the facts'. There are a number of other useful essays; John Lyons writes on the language of *Lie Down in Darkness*, and Jan Gordon looks again at Styron's Southernness in the context of the same novel. Irving Malin writes on symbolic structures in *The Long March*, and Robert Morris on *In the Clap Shack*. The least successful essays are those of Robert Phillips, who argues in 'Mask and Symbol in *Set This House on Fire*' that the novel 'purposefully lacks sequence and order', and Norman Kelvin's 'The Divided Self: William Styron's fiction from *Lie Down in Darkness* to *the Confessions of Nat Turner*. Kelvin attemts to explore his not un-

[20] *The Achievement of William Styron*, ed. by Robert K. Morris and Irving Malin. Athens: U. of Georgia P. pp. 280. $12.

THE TWENTIETH CENTURY 445

interesting thesis that Styron's work is full of 'flawed romanticism' over the whole range of the work, but there is insufficient space here to develop it. The book also includes a good interview with Styron in which he offers commentary suggestive of lines for further research and a bibliography by Jackson R. Bryer.

There are a number of articles on Southern writers. Rose Burwell (*Crit*) explicates the Jungian figure of Elena Howe in Joyce Carol Oates's *Do With Me What You Will*, discussing her progress through the novel in terms of Jungian 'individuation', and William Stuckley (*Crit*) explores the three marriages in Eudora Welty's *The Optimist's Daughter*, and argues that they are vehicles for larger insights, particularly insights into social class distinctions in the novel. M. Wynn Thomas (*AL*) reads Katherine Anne Porter's 'Noon Wine' as being an exploration of the nature of 'direction' in human life, seeing the order of the story as the reader's gradual mastery of 'the fine confusion of people's talk'. Robert Miller (*SoR*) looks at religious consciousness in the fiction of Flannery O'Connor and sees her as distinctly part of a protestant tradition; particularly he concentrates on her interest in the experience of grace. Ann Pearson (*Crit*) argues, but not entirely convincingly, that the apparent lack of 'overall purpose' in Shirley Ann Grau's fiction is mistaken, and that the closeness but indifference of nature is its focal point.

Stanley T. Gutman's *Mankind in Barbary: The Individual and Society in the Novels of Norman Mailer*[21] comments that in all of the novels men are 'strangers in their society', and he explores the forces that inform this idea. He begins by looking at power and endurance in *The Naked and the Dead*, and goes on to treat *Barbary Shore* and *The Deer Park* as explorations of differing kinds of political failure. In a lucid essay on 'The White Negro' he places Mailer's essay in its intellectual context and raises the question, pursued for the rest of the study in analyses of *Why Are We in Vietnam?*, *An American Dream*, and *The Armies of the Night*, of whether Mailer confuses 'personal salvation' and 'social redemption'. Most of the studies are helpful and stimulating, those on the latter two books particularly so. Technical considerations, and particularly narrative stance clearly play a large part in Gutman's response to the texts; the weaknesses he finds in this respect in *The Deer Park* and *Why Are We in Vietnam?* seem to have resulted in less interesting chapters. Gutman concludes with a twofold explanation of Mailer's present position, offering the idea that the American scene is no longer vital enough to sustain his talents, and also that Mailer's egotism may be finally fatal, 'ultimately reduction of the world to the self appears as a reduction of the world'.

Laura Adams's interview with Mailer (*PR*) touches on *An American Dream*, Mailer's journalism, and his plans for a 'novel large in scope'. The war between God and the Devil is here too, as he continues his exploration of that subject. Adams has also written a bibliography of Mailer[22] listing

[21] *Mankind in Barbary: The Individual and Society in the Novels of Norman Mailer*, by Stanley T. Gutman. Hanover, New Hampshire: U.P. of New England. pp. xi + 226.

[22] *Norman Mailer: A Comprehensive Bibliography*, by Laura Adams. Scarecrow Author Bibliographies No. 20. Metuchen, New Jersey: Scarecrow Press. 1974. pp. xix + 130. $6.

all work by and on him up to 1973. It does not include foreign editions and criticism not in English, and some anthology entries. As both Adams and Robert Lucid, in his introductory essay, make clear, the Mailer storage vault is crammed with matter, and this book cannot be regarded as a comprehensive guide to unpublished material, although there is a section on such unpublished work as is 'finished in some sense and therefore theoretically publishable'.

Joyce Markle, in her *Fighters and Lovers: Theme in the Novels of John Updike*[23] makes a thorough case for the coherence of Updike's world. She is mainly concerned to stress the links made between sexuality and death; she also suggests that Updike sees Christianity 'being reabsorbed by the pagan religions which preceded and surrounded it', and explores both Christian and Mythic imagery in the novels. The argument is approached by treating each of the novels individually in chronological order of composition. The chapter on *Rabbit, Run*, which reveals Updike's patterns of geometrical imagery, and that on *Couples*, which places it in the context of the earlier novels, are most illuminating. The least satisfactory part is the discussion of *Bech: A Book*; Markle opposes it to the other works by defining it as 'comic' rather than 'serious', but these terms are not subtle enough, as Markle seems to feel. The end of the book, almost as an afterthought, offers a few paragraphs on comedy in the other novels, but here there is clearly much more work to be done, and the conclusion is disappointing, offering no pointers as to the direction of Updike's work.

The question of comedy in Updike is taken up by Joyce Carol Oates (*MFS*), who sees his novels as comedies dealing with events that have 'failed to justify themselves as tragedy'. She relates this to religious feeling in some of his characters, and compares his work to that of Flannery O'Connor. Michael Olivas's bibliography of Updike[24] includes all work by him and an annotated bibliography of criticism published between 1967 and 1973.

An issue of *Salmagundi* devoted to Saul Bellow opens with an interview concerned with contemporary culture and his attitude to Freud. John Bayley writes on *Mr. Sammler's Planet*, putting it in the context of its ancestry in the European novel, and setting it against the 'modern', with its stress on the 'authentic'. Bayley argues that the novel succeeds by being 'partial and incomplete', and avoiding the danger of any single consciousness brooding over it. Robert Boyers writes on nature and social reality in the same novel, and discusses our ambiguous response to Sammler, particularly in the scene of the fight between Eisen and the pick-pocket. Ben Belitt offers a highly impressionistic piece on 'depth' in Bellow's fiction, and Harold Kaplan writes on the 'transcendence downward' of Herzog and Sammler.

Another collection on Bellow[25] is edited by Earl Rovit, who argues that the critical status of Bellow's work is now clearly established; he has

[23] *Fighters and Lovers: Theme in the Novels of John Updike*, by Joyce B. Markle. New York: New York U.P. 1973. pp. 205.

[24] *An Annotated Bibliography of John Updike Criticism 1967-1973, and a Checklist of his Works*, by Michael A. Olivas. New York: Garland Publishing. pp. x + 91. $13.

[25] *Saul Bellow: A Collection of Critical Essays*, ed. by Earl Rovit. Twentieth Century Views Series. Englewood Cliffs, New Jersey: Prentice-Hall. pp. viii + 176. £1.55.

tried to balance well-known with new material. Reprinted in the collection
are essays by Gordon Lloyd Harper, Denis Donoghue (on *Dangling Man*),
John J. Clayton (on *The Victim*), Richard Poirier (on *Herzog*), Ruth Wise,
and Marcus Klein. The most interesting piece is by Irving Malin on Bellow's
play *The Last Analysis*, which discusses the problem of finding a critical
approach, and sees Bummidge as both comedian and analyst. Malin links
the play firmly with the other works through the concern with birth and
death, and 'a sense of play, of mirror images, of secret fun'. Also valuable
are Richard Pearce's essay on Henderson and Herzog in the context of
Bellow's relationship to the traditional novel, and Ben Siegel on *Mr.
Sammler's Planet* in which he establishes the complexity of Bellow's connexion with Sammler. Rovit's own essay on Mailer and Bellow as 'secret
sharers' suggests that the opposition between the two is a contemporary
response which might appear limited in the future. The most disappointing
essay is Victoria Sullivan's 'The Battle of the Sexes in Three Bellow
Novels', a reductive piece defining Bellow's heroines as only 'a classic
bith' or 'a certified ball-breaker', hardly deepening the reader's understanding of this interesting area of Bellow's writing. Also writing on Bellow,
Steven Axelrod (*AL*) argues that while Bellow's Henderson is explicitly
non-Jewish, he is implicitly Jewish and defines himself in Jewish terms,
particularly at the end of the novel.

The same series's volume on Malamud[26] contains ten essays and an
interview with the author by the editors, Leslie and Joyce Field. The
introduction is a sensible summary of Malamud's work, but the interview
itself is uninteresting, a 'mail interview' in which Malamud gives nothing
away. The essay by Same Bluefarb 'The Syncretism of Bernard Malamud'
makes little use of a number of parallels drawn between Malamud's work
and that of James, Dostoyevsky, Hawthorne, and a number of other
sources and traditions. There are two useful new essays; Richard Astro's
'In the Heart of the Valley: Bernard Malamud's *A New Life*' gives the biographical background to the novel and argues that Malamud tried to stay
too close to his experience at Oregon State and put too much trivial detail
into the novel. The essay concludes that the 'academic novel' may be
'vulgar literary fun' and unsuitable for Malamud's purposes. Leslie Field's
'Portrait of the Artist as *Schlemiel*' tries to define *schlemiel* and place the
term in Jewish American literary culture, and goes on to apply this to
Pictures of Fidelman. The collection also reprints essays by Sheldon
Norman Grebstein, Sanford Pinsker, Cynthia Ozick, Renee Winegarten,
John Alexander Allen, Gerald Hoag, and William Freedman, and includes
a chronology of dates and a selected bibliography.

Sanford Pinsker's weak *The Comedy that 'Hoits'*[27] covers all of Philip
Roth's fiction from *Goodbye, Columbus* to *My Life as Man*. A great deal
of space is taken up with explicating the various novels in terms of plot,
rather than critical assertions, and Pinsker has the irritating and obfuscating
habit of putting quotation marks around terms which clearly require

[26] *Bernard Malamud: A Collection of Critical Essays*, ed. by Leslie and Joyce
Field. Twentieth Century Views Series. Englewood Cliffs, New Jersey: Prentice-Hall.
pp. x + 179.
[27] *The Comedy that 'Hoits': An Essay on the Fiction of Philip Roth*, by Sanford
Pinsker. Columbia: U. of Missouri P. pp. 121. $5.

further definition but don't get it here; hence we are told that *Portnoy's Complaint* exhausts the possibilities a 'thicker' novel would exploit, or that *'The Breast*. . .is more "exercise" than novel. . .its very "symbolism" . . .overwhelms more mundane, but essential elements like "story" ' '. There seem to be glimpses in the book of an attitude which finds Roth and his context deeply repugnant; the assertion that *The Breast* and *Our Gang* were the product of a 'shoddy cultural moment', the pejorative connotations which the word 'experiment' has in some chapters, and the unsupported sneer at Vonnegut in the chapter on *The Great American Novel*, all point this way. Pinsker claims to admire Roth, while disliking, as it appears from this book, a very substantial portion of his work.

A collection of pieces on Nabokov[28], described as 'A Book of Things', is as varied as its title suggests. There are a number of useful pieces carrying on the systematic annotation of Nabokov's texts, such as Kevin Pilon's chronology of *Pale Fire*, Carl Proffer's glossary of allusions to Russian literature in *Ada*, and, couched in the form of critical articles, Anna Maria Salehar on Fyodor's creativity in *The Gift*, Anthony Olcott's satisfying study of *The Real Life of Sebastian Knight*, William W. Rowe on bedrooms, numbers, fire, Lewis Carroll, and squirrels in *Pnin*, and Alden Sprowles's annotation of Kinbote's commentary to *Pale Fire*, in support of his argument that Kinbote is insane. Other worthwhile critical articles include Stephen Suagee's insistence on humour in reading *Despair*, Larry Gregg's irritatingly self-conscious and tricky piece on *Eugene Onegin*, stressing the importance of the whole of Nabokov's five volumes, and two articles on the relationship between Pnin and Nabokov by Paul Grams and William Carroll, who also writes on the story 'Signs and Symbols'. Ludmila Foster does useful scholarly work in her survey of Nabokov in Russian emigré criticism, and P. M. Bitsilli's 1936 review of *Invitation to a Beheading* and *The Eye* is translated and reprinted. D. Barton Johnson contributes two highly technical articles, an examination of 'phonoaesthetic systems' in the English and Russian texts of the closing poem of *The Gift*, and an exploration of synaesthesia and polychromatism in Nabokov's work, particularly *Speak, Memory*. One of the most interesting essays in the collection is William Rowe's 'The Honesty of Nabokovian Deception', in which he demonstrates that the reader of Nabokov is often deceived by his preconceptions rather than by literally false information. Another substantial piece is Alfred Appel's long and well-illustrated article on the Lolitas of the movies, which appears in a slightly different form in his *Nabokov's Dark Cinema*.

Also on Nabokov, Mathew Winston (*TCL*) writes on the dangers, as exemplified by Humbert Humbert in *Lolita*, of seeing other people as fictional characters and treating them accordingly. Elizabeth Prioleau (*TCL*), also writing on *Lolita*, traces the influence of *Through the Looking Glass*. Dabney Stuart (*MLQ*), writing on *Speak, Memory* argues that the book should properly be regarded as fiction, and demonstrates that this is a point of view encouraged by Nabokov, although he does not support this by comparing it with the acknowledged fiction; nothing very substantial emerges from the article, which seems to be something of a quibbling with terms.

One of the most disappointing books on modern novelists is John Kuehl's *John Hawkes and the Craft of Conflict*[29]. Kuehl claims that the book treats 'the relationship between Hawkes's central theme and his craft', and that the work prior to 1960 is 'exclusively death-oriented' but in the later work 'Eros exists alongside Thanatos'. He chooses not to examine texts individually, but areas such as landscape, myth and ritual, and time, in all of the work. Apart from a great deal of annotation, the critical language used is either clotted or unhelpful, such as when he says, of the Osiris and Fisher King myths in *The Beetle Leg*, that their use 'conveys landscape/setting, tone, characterization, action, and meaning concurrently'. The book closes with an interview with Hawkes by the author; it is sad that some of Hawkes's tentativeness expressed here with regard to annotating recurrent symbol and reference in his novels has not influenced Kuehl who ignores Hawkes's comment that names have 'no special intended meaning or significance'.

The issue of *TCL* concentrating on the work of Thomas Pynchon, offers a fine essay by Richard Poirier, discussing Pynchon's audience in the context of his vastness of intellectual range of reference. He concludes that Pynchon is a 'great novelist of betrayal', and that his vision is not 'one of cultural deprivation, but rather of cultural inundation'. Scott Sanders looks at paranoia and anomie in his work, and finally questions whether it is not finally solipsistic, presenting a particular social condition as if it were universal, and reifying technology. William Vesterman discusses and analyzes a number of poems and songs in the novels, W. T. Lhamon looks at the idea of pentecost in *V*, which he describes as 'entropy with value added', and Lance Ozier explicates some of the mathematical imagery, particularly the double integral, in *Gravity's Rainbow*. There is also an annotated bibliography on selected articles of Pynchon criticism.

Another important article on Pynchon is by Neil Schmitz (*PR*) relating his work to that of D. Barnes in *Nightwood* and J. Hawkes in *The Cannibal*, but distinguishing Pynchon by his 'loathing for the continuity of the obscene in history'. Concentrating on *Gravity's Rainbow* he sees its final struggle as being only between modes of death, between the Bourgeois and the Heroic, and the ethic of the book finally as 'the ethic of the desperado, not the ethic of the survivor'. Mathew Winston (*TCL*) offers a basic biographical sketch of Pynchon, better than nothing although vastly limited by this author's complete secretiveness.

Michael Goodman's annotated bibliography of William Burroughs[30] is the first basic bibliographical tool to all of his work, including the letters held at Columbia and the Grove Press Collection of Burroughs material as well as critical articles. The bibliography is largely limited to work written in English.

There are a number of other notable articles on modern novelists.

[29] *John Hawkes and the Craft of Conflict*, by John Kuehl. New Brunswick, New Jersey: Rutgers U.P. pp. xii + 195. $10.
[30] *William S. Burroughs: An Annotated Bibliography of his Works and Criticism*, by Michael B. Goodman. New York: Garland Publishing. pp. 96. $13.

Christopher Morris (*Crit*) interestingly brings the vocabulary and ideas of the French structuralist Jacques Lacan to bear on John Barth's *Lost in the Funhouse*, and James F. Walter (*TCL*) places *Giles Goat-Boy* in a tradition of literature which has as its primary theme 'interior division and illness caused by a division between human faculties which naturally complement each other'. On Kesey, Robert Forrey (*MFS*) argues the case against *One Flew Over the Cuckoo's Nest*, seeing it as conservative and sexist. On Dickey, Paul Italia (*MFS*) writes on the pervasive presence of sexuality in *Deliverance*, demonstrates the sexual implications of the hunt, and explores the relationship between Ed Gentry and his 'double', the hillbilly he kills. An interview with Dickey by David Arnett (*ConL*) concentrates on *Deliverance* and its relationship to some of the poems.

An issue of *Critique* partly devoted to Barthelme begins with a series of fragments from his writing, which is followed by attempts to say something helpful by Larry McCaffery and Betty Flowers, although the task seems almost hopeless. Tom Whalen, writing on 'The Party', simply ends by asking the same questions as Barthelme asks in the text: 'Is this a successful party?' 'Is this the best we can do?' Jerome Klinkowitz contributes a checklist of work by and on Barthelme from 1957 to 1974; at least we can still do this.

An interesting article on Vonnegut is by Wayne McGinnis (*Crit*), who discusses the cyclical nature of *Slaughterhouse Five*, noting that not only the content but the form of the novel, being without climaxes, is circular. Peter Koenig (*ConL*) writing on Gaddis, defends *The Recognitions* as a major work, following the lead of Tony Tanner, and gives a sketch of the history of the book's failure to claim critical attention. He stresses the parodic aspects of the work, with some help from notes made available to him by the author.

There are a number of interesting articles promoting little known writers. Albert Carter (*Crit*) traces the common patterns of game-playing ending in nemesis in the first three of Thomas McGuane's novels, seeing him as increasingly successful, particularly in *Ninety-Two in the Shade*. Douglas Bolling (*Crit*) makes a case for Ralph Wurlitzer, and particularly his third novel, *Quake*, following up his 1973 article on the two earlier books, and locating *Quake* in the context of the work of Pynchon and Barth. Ruth Laney (*SoR*) interviews David Madden, partly on *Bijou*, partly on the importance of his being a Southerner, and partly on his novel in progress. Scott Sanders's interview with Stanley Elkin, and an article by Thomas LeClair (both *ConL*), suggest that Elkin's heroes are distortions of the ordinary rather than exotic products.

Two unusual areas of the work of more well-known writers are represented in John Hammond's essay on the prose of the poet Robert Creeley (*Crit*), arguing that the stories are about the sexual imaginations of the characters and that Creeley has little interest in their public worlds, and Frank Shelton's (*Crit*) attempt to rescue from obscurity Robert Coover's second novel, *The Universal Baseball Association Inc.*, stressing its 'balanced perspective'.

Timely articles on two Black novelists are Howard Faulkner's (*MFS*) on William Melvin Kelley, demonstrating his use of traditions and sources in white literature, and Jerry Bryant's (*Crit*) on John A. Williams, concentrating on *Sissie* and *The Man who Cried I Am*, and arguing that the main political contention of that novel is 'that the black who discovers and reveals the truth is a dead man'.

Ray Bradbury is an extremely difficult figure to categorize, and William Nolan's *The Ray Bradbury Companion*[31] is a checklist of his contributions to all the many media in which he has worked, and a chronology of his life and career. The checklist is a comprehensive one, although it lays no claim to being a formal bibliography, and Nolan does not include any information on reprints or foreign language editions. The book is sumptuously produced and profusely illustrated, including a 'photolog' of Bradbury's life and a large number of facsimiles of his writings. It also contains a checklist of work on Bradbury, and a short introductory essay by the writer.

Finally, at the ragged edge of the novel in this century comes the figure of the private eye, whose course from Pinkerton to Dirty Harry is charted in William Ruehlmann's *Saint with a Gun*[32]. Part of his study is devoted to the origins of detective fiction in Europe and America, looking at Vidocq, Poe, and Conan Doyle among others, and making a distinction between the detective as aesthete (Dupin) and the detective as working man (Marlowe). Ruehlmann writes interestingly and subtly on the most substantial of the American figures, Chandler and Hammett, being particularly careful in his analysis of Hammett's attitude to Sam Spade in *The Maltese Falcon*. He goes on to record the shift from professional ethics in the heroes of these writers to private ones in Spillane's Mike Hammer, and looks briefly at the work of Ross McDonald and Brett Halliday. Ruehlmann gives disappointingly little concentrated attention to some obviously suggestive areas, such as the private eye's attitudes to women and homosexuals, obviously so important to the genre. His closing chapter looks at some recent killers in fiction and fact, such as Charles Manson, but the discussion here cannot be truly adequate without more space given to the influence of film and television, and the heart of the book remains with Philip Marlowe and the Continental Op.

4. Drama

Dennis Welland, the editor of *The United States: A Companion to American Studies*[1], has contributed the chapter on drama. In the section 'Drama in America: O'Neill, Miller, and Tennessee Williams' he deals with *Long Day's Journey into Night*, *The Glass Menagerie*, and *A Streetcar Named Desire*, and concentrates on *Death of a Salesman*. 'Albee and After' looks at *The Zoo Story*, *Who's Afraid of Virginia Woolf?* and *A Delicate Balance*, and then at James Baldwin's *Blues for Mister Charlie*, Leroi Jones's *Dutchman*, and Robert Lowell's *The Old Glory*. On drama since 1964

[31] *The Ray Bradbury Companion*, by William F. Nolan. Detroit: Gale Research. Company. pp. xiii + 339. $28.50.
[32] *Saint with a Gun: The Unlawful American Private Eye*, by William Ruehlmann. New York: New York U.P. 1974. pp. xvi + 155.

[1] *The United States: A Companion to American Studies*, ed. by Dennis Welland. Methuen. 1974. pp. 528; maps.

there are one and a half pages of generalized comment. The chapter's perspective is markedly English, especially when Welland remarks that America has produced no high artificial comedy like that of Congreve, Sheridan, Wilde, and Shaw; this is true, but it would be useful if he were to say something too about the work of a successful writer of comedies in America such as Neil Simon.

More dramatists and plays are considered in David Morse's shorter 'American Theatre: The Age of O'Neill' in *American Literature since 1900*[2]. After briefly referring to Bronson Howard and Clyde Fitch, Morse surveys O'Neill's work from *The Dreamy Kid* to *Mourning Becomes Electra*. Before coming on to the late plays, he writes on some of the significant drama of the 'twenties and 'thirties; he conveys particularly well the sense of excitement and involvement in expressionist drama, in vaudeville-style experiments, and the New Playwrights Theatre, which paved the way for theatre with an 'authentic' socialist conscience, after the Great Crash, drawing in, for example, the Group Theatre and the Marxist Theatre Union. However, Morse does not neglect the often depressing commercial vulgarity of the life of the drama in America, pointing out that despite the achievement of O'Neill, Rice, Odets, Green, Hellman, and others, 'it would be idle to pretend that this serious drama was more than marginalia in the pages of the commercial theatre. The impression made on Americans by the Provincetown Players seems small enough if it is measured against the Ziegfeld Follies or *Abie's Irish Rose....*'

Because Morse's chapter was written in 1971, it includes no reference to Louis Scheaffer's fine biography of O'Neill, the second volume of which appeared in 1973[3].

Morse notes that 'The originality of O'Neill's early work has often been exaggerated. The main tradition of the American theatre, in the hands of David Belasco and James A. Herne had been melodrama modified by more naturalistic styles of acting and production and it was this that O'Neill continued...'. David Belasco has been well served by Lise-Lone Marker's *David Belasco: Naturalism in the American Theatre*[4], which, incidentally, tells how James O'Neill played the part of Christ in a spectacular Passion Play produced by Belasco, and utilizing a real flock of sheep and a hundred mothers with babies to represent the Massacre of the Innocents.

Marker has examined Belasco's prompt-books, and concludes that, for example, he gradually moved away from ' "athletic" expression of scenic emotion' to a simpler style of acting. She distinguishes four styles in Belasco's theatre: what he himself called 'costume plays of manners and customs', like *Madame Butterfly* and *Sweet Kitty Bellairs*; the American frontier drama, like *The Girl of the Golden West*; social dramas, like *The Easiest Way*; and his last style, his Shakespearean manner, represented by one production only, of *The Merchant of Venice*. Marker shows in her book how Belasco's attention to accuracy of detail and atmosphere

[2] *American Literature since 1900*, ed. by Marcus Cunliffe. History of Literature in the English Language. Barrie & Jenkins/Sphere Books. pp. 419.
[3] *O'Neill: Son and Artist*, by Louis Sheaffer. Boston and Toronto: Little, Brown, 1973. pp. xviii + 750 with 71 illustrations.
[4] *David Belasco: Naturalism in the American Theatre*, by Lise-Lone Marker. Princeton U.P. pp. xiv + 248 with 16 illustrations.

amounted to obsession: one of his preparations for the $65,000 production of *Sweet Kitty Bellairs* was to despatch an agent to Bath 'to buy all the principal properties'. Among the excellent photographs in this book are several of *Sweet Kitty Bellairs*: a play typical of Belasco's method in that he paid far more attention to style of presentation than to the literary quality of the text.

O'Neill's knowledge of nineteenth-century literature and his interest in American cultural evolution are emphasized by Lowell A. Fiet (*FTJ*). Fiet's focus is *A Touch of the Poet*, intended as the fifth play in an eleven-play cycle, *A Tale of Possessors, Self-dispossessed*, on the theme of the roots of American experience. He shows that O'Neill's play recalls such earlier dramas as James Steele MacKaye's *Hazel Kirke* (1880) and James A. Herne's *Shore Acres* (1892), although the optimism of their conclusions is not possible for the more modern O'Neill. Arthur H. Nethercot, in 'Madness in the Plays of Eugene O'Neill' (*MD*), opens by recalling Louis Scheaffer's remark in *O'Neill: Son and Playwright* (1968) that no biographer had dealt with O'Neill's 'preoccupation with insanity' which figures in 'five or six plays'. Five or six? Madness, according to Nethercot, 'actually throbs—sometimes powerfully and sometimes almost undetectably—in forty-two of the forty-five printed plays'. And he proceeds to catalogue all the varieties of insanity until one is reminded of Nabokov's parody of torrid 'realism'—' "He acts crazy. We all act crazy, I guess. I guess God acts crazy". Nethercot has also written on *More Stately Mansions* (*ETJ*), where he makes the same point about Scheaffer's understatement of the madness theme in O'Neill's plays.

That the anarchist Emma Goldman was the inspiration for O'Neill's 'offstage character of Rosa Parritt and for the betrayer co-plot of *The Iceman Cometh*' is the contention of Winifred L. Frazer in *E. G. and E. G. O.: Emma Goldman and 'The Iceman Cometh'*[5]. It is worked out in some detail, although Frazer's observation that during O'Neill's 'schooldays he was frequently in Manhattan near her (Emma Goldman's) base of operations' is not one of her stronger points. Edmund Wilson[6] gives an amusing account of meeting O'Neill, and also provides a negative assessment of his work—'he depends too much upon hatred'.

Another O'Neil is the subject of an article by Maureen A. Shea (*TS*), who tells of the 'power and passion' of the Tragedy Queen Nance O'Neil whose career, beginning in the 1890s, continued successfully into the 1930s. Shea concludes: 'That her projections of grand passion could survive until 1935 is testimony to romanticism's magnetic hold on the "modern" twentieth century'.

Irving Wardle's essay on 'American Theatre since 1945' in *American Literature since 1900* is not exclusively concerned with literary texts. He responds perceptively to the problems of Broadway, the development of 'Off-Broadway', and even of 'Off-Off-Broadway'. Wardle intends not to

[5] *E. G. and E. G. O.: Emma Goldman and 'The Iceman Cometh'*, by Winifred L. Frazer. U. of Florida Humanities Monograph. Gainesville: U.P. of Florida. 1974. pp. 105.
[6] *The Twenties: From Notebooks and Diaries of the Period*, by Edmund Wilson, ed. by Leon Edel, New York: Farrar, Straus & Giroux. pp. xv + 557 with 9 illustrations.

give a 'comprehensive account of American theatre since the war', but to stress 'points of new growth'. 'As a result', he says, 'there is more about lofts than about the Lincoln Centre'. Tennessee Williams and Arthur Miller are treated interestingly together; for example '. . .in a curious way, each suggests a character that the other might have created. Just as the marriage of Miller the intellectual to Marilyn Monroe might have furnished Williams with a plot, so Williams' solitary, fugitive life illustrates Miller's preoccupation with those (like the hero of *Focus*) who barricade themselves from the world'. Wardle explains the high quality of naturalistic acting that contributed to the success of Miller and Williams by tracing the American adoption of psychological realism encouraged by Stanislavsky. The Moscow Art Theatre gave rise to the Group Theatre in America, teaching Stanislavsky's System which became the Method, the postwar 'lingua franca' of American acting, associated with Lee Strasberg. The Method ultimately failed, Wardle observes, because it came to betray Stanislavsky's aim of creating ensembles and began to create stars instead.

In telling how only Albee and Simon 'among serious dramatists' have succeeded on Broadway since Williams and Miller, Wardle does not, as would be all too easy, denigrate Simon, but says generously that he is doing something 'to uphold the good name of the commercial theatre'. Of Albee he says that, although his Absurdist tag is justified, his most obvious forerunner is O'Neill. There is a section on Joseph Papp's 'anachronistically heroic position in the postwar American scene', followed by a view of the tribal Living Theatre of Julian Beck and Judith Malina, and their heirs in Joseph Chaikin's Open Theatre. The Becks are treated respectfully here, but they come in for a virulent attack by Ronnie Davis in 'The Radical Right in the American Theatre' (*TQ*). Davis also savages Joseph Chaikin and Richard Schechrer, but he says that it is the Becks that 'are the most dangerous and obnoxious, for they suffer in the cause of, and bring out the worst elements of, the metaphysical religiosity in the American white middle class'. In watching the naturalistically portrayed torture and brutality of *The Brig*, Davis claims, 'attention finally focusses on the actors—not on the conditions'.

The self-consciously avant-garde drama of E. E. Cummings has a chapter devoted to it in Bethany K. Dumas' book on the poet[7], in which we are told of the first performance of *Him* and the inevitable and perhaps sought-for adverse reactions to it; there is in addition a fairly full account of the bizarre plot of *Santa Claus*. Dumas's chapter has already achieved a certain notoriety for containing the sentence: 'And the message is couched in that very traditional form, blank verse, which has long and generally been accepted as that best adapted to dramatic verse in English'.

Eric Bentley's criticism of Arthur Miller—that he cannot make up his mind whether to be social or psychological—is the starting point for Orm Overland's 'The Action and Its Significance: Arthur Miller's struggle with dramatic form' (*MD*). He shows how Miller, despite his distrust of realistic drama as a 'usable medium', is still drawn to realism. To illustrate this he draws attention to his two centres of interest in *All My Sons*. Barry Gross

---

[7] *E. E. Cummings: A Remembrance of Miracles*, by Bethany K. Dumas. Vision P. 1974. pp. 157.

treats this play as a failure (*MD*) because the realistic mode of the play, particularly in the case of Chris Keller, 'is not adequate to the social relation Miller requires the play to represent'. Lawrence D. Lowenthal's 'Arthur Miller's *Incident at Vichy*: A Sartrean Interpretation' (*MD*) suggests that *Incident at Vichy* 'is an explicit dramatic rendition of Sartre's treatise', *Reflexions sur la Question Juive.*

'Maybe I am a machine, a typist,' ponders Tennessee Williams in his *Memoirs*[8]. 'A compulsive typist and a compulsive writer. But that's my life, and what is in these memoirs is mostly the barest periphery of that which is my intense life, for my intense life is my work'. So, in these conversational, disjointed, but intriguing recollections, Williams tells us, for example, more about the friend in whose Harvard room he finished *The Glass Menagerie* than he does about the play itself. But to read of his life with Miss Edwina, his oppressive mother, and Miss Rose, the tragic sister going mad and knowing it, is like reading a resumé of a drama by Williams. And the sequel is fittingly extravagant and painful—Miss Rose, old, institutionalized, lobotomized, snatching cigarettes from visitors whenever she can. Anecdotes of encounters with the famous, including Faulkner, Dylan Thomas, Carson McCullers, Sartre and Simone de Beauvoir abound among the trivia.

Richard Coe, in 'Beyond Absurdity: Albee's Awareness of Audience in *Tiny Alice*' (*MD*), asserts that true absurdist drama is inaccessible to a conventional audience, and argues that in *Tiny Alice* Albee has been able, through his 'parabolic realism', 'to portray the major absurdist themes on the story level, without surrendering audience identification with the protagonist, and even to suggest a direction for other dramatists intent on absurdist themes'.

In 'The Rise and Fall of the New Woman in American Drama' (*ETJ*) Debora S. Kolb tells how, between the eighteen-nineties and early nineteen-twenties, movements for women's rights at first agitated for better educational opportunities, and later began to stress the economic potential of women. Feminism, she feels, reached a peak around 1920—and then degenerated into femininity. These social developments were reflected in the drama of the forty-year span which Kolb covers. The dramatists she mentions include James Herne, Rachel Crothers, Augustus Thomas, Jesse Lynch Williams, and George Kelly. Kolb observes that none of these authors was simplistic on the subject of the New Woman, and that the quality of many of the plays is high.

Earl G. Schreiber writes on *Everyman* and von Hofmannsthal's *Jedermann* and their adaptations in America (*CD*), including the intriguing *Everyman and Roach* with its Death Machines and Discotheques.

Donal L. Loeffler's *An Analysis of the Treatment of the Homosexual Character in Dramas Produced in the New York Theatre from 1950 to 1968*[9] has not undergone the transformations we expect when a disserta-

[8] *Memoirs*, by Tennessee Williams. Doubleday: New York, pp. 264 with 144 illustrations.
[9] *An Analysis of the Treatment of the Homosexual Character in Dramas Produced in the New York Theatre from 1950 to 1968*, by Donal L. Loeffler. New York: Arno P. pp. 201.

tion becomes a book. There is an untidy variety of typefaces, for example, and chapters begin and end with the same laborious 'This chapter shows. . .', 'This chapter has shown. . .' formulae throughout. Loeffler concludes that homosexuality is now presented with more accuracy on stage, that homosexuality is now treated as 'a pronounced awareness of the additive relations of cultural and environmental conditions', that it is no longer used simply to shock, nor is it regarded as necessarily tragic or farcical. *CE* devoted an issue to the subject of 'The Homosexual Imagination', containing articles like 'Giving a Gay Course' and 'Towards a Gay Criticism'; we need some better set books than Loeffler's.

Index I. Critics

Index II. Authors and Subjects Treated